W9-AXB-653

WILLIAM LANGLAND lived from *c.* 1330 to *c.* 1387. He was born near Malvern, in Worcestershire, and educated for a career in the Church, but appears to have married and never proceeded beyond minor orders. Little is known about his life apart from what can be learnt from the work on which he spent the years from 1360 or earlier to the time of his death, earning his living as a psalter-clerk in London, mainly, and possibly returning to the West Country in his last years. His great alliterative poem *Piers Plowman* exists in three versions, A, B and C (though recently a fourth version, called 'Z', has been claimed as his work, a version earlier than A). Of these only the B-text is extant in a completed form. It was this that was published in 1550 and has generally been regarded as the finest of the three as poetry.

Piers Plowman stands at the centre of medieval English Literature along with Chaucer's *Canterbury Tales,* which in many ways it complements. It is unique in its impassioned concern for social justice, religious integrity and personal 'truth'; but its message inspires rather than compromises its poetic art, which is more varied and flexible than that of any other of the Alliterative Makers.

AUBREY VINCENT CARLYLE SCHMIDT, Fellow and Tutor in English at Balliol College, Oxford, read English at Oxford, where he won the Violet Vaughan Morgan, Charles Oldham and Shelley-Mills Prizes. He was Senior Scholar of Merton, Andrew Bradley Research Fellow of Balliol and, after a year as lecturer at University College, Dublin, Fellow of Exeter College, Oxford. His published work ranges from Langland and Chaucer to T.S. Eliot and Geoffrey Hill. He is co-editor of the medieval scholarly journal, *Medium Aevum.*

WILLIAM LANGLAND

The Vision of
Piers Plowman

A Critical Edition of the B-Text based on
Trinity College Cambridge MS B. 15. 17 with
selected variant readings, an Introduction,
glosses, and a Textual and Literary
Commentary

by

A. V. C. Schmidt

Fellow of Balliol College, Oxford

J. M. Dent & Sons Ltd
London
Charles E. Tuttle Co., Inc.
Rutland, Vermont
EVERYMAN'S LIBRARY

© Introduction, commentary, notes and editing
David Campbell Publishers Ltd, 1978
© Appendix, David Campbell Publishers Ltd,
1984
© Glossary, David Campbell Publishers Ltd,
1987
All rights reserved

Made in Great Britain by
Guernsey Press Co. Ltd, Guernsey, C.I. for
J. M. Dent & Sons Ltd
91 Clapham High Street, London SW4 7TA
and
Charles E. Tuttle Co., Inc.
28 South Main Street
Rutland, Vermont
05701, U.S.A.

This edition first published in Everyman's
Library in 1978
Reprinted with revisions and corrections, 1982
and 1984
New edition, 1987
Reprinted 1989
Reissued 1991

This book if bound as a paperback is
subject to the condition that it may
not be issued on loan or otherwise
except in its original binding

British Library Cataloguing in Publication Data
Langland, William
The vision of Piers Plowman.—(Everyman's
university library).
I. Title   II. Vision of Piers Plowman
III. Schmidt, Aubrey Vincent Carlyle.
IV. Series
821´.1   PR2010

ISBN 0 460 87094 7

Everyman's Library
Reg. U.S. Patent Office

Contents

For Judith

'Conseille me, Kynde,' quod I, 'what craft be best to lerne?'
'Lerne to love,' quod Kynde, 'and leef alle othere.'

Acknowledgments

I wish to thank the Master and Fellows of Trinity College, Cambridge, for permission to publish their B-text of *Piers Plowman*, MS B. 15. 17. I am also grateful to the following for permission to print variant readings from *Piers Plowman* manuscripts belonging to them or in their care: the Bodleian Library, Oxford; the Syndics of Cambridge University Library; the Board of the British Library; the President and Fellows of Corpus Christi College, Oxford; the Provost and Fellows of Oriel College, Oxford; the Principal and Fellows of Newnham College, Cambridge; and the Trustees of the Huntington Library, California.

In the course of preparing this edition, I have incurred many obligations to colleagues and friends. I particularly wish to thank Professor John Burrow for reading part of the text and textual commentary and Mr Edward Wilson for doing the same and also for reading the literary commentary. Their learning and care have greatly helped me, and I only wish that time had allowed me to press their good will still further; I know they would have saved me from many errors and inadequacies. I am also grateful to Mr Vincent Quinn, Librarian of Balliol College, for many kindnesses without which my task would have been slower and much more tedious. I also wish to thank Dr Derek Brewer, Master of Emmanuel College, for his help and hospitality while I was working on *Piers Plowman* manuscripts in Cambridge. I am indebted to my mother-in-law Mrs Yvonne Jackson for typing the Index and Bibliography.

Part of the work on this edition was done during a period of sabbatical leave, and I am grateful to Oxford University for a term's leave from lecturing and to Balliol College for two terms' leave from teaching and administration. I also wish to thank my pupils for their tolerant forbearance, after my sabbatical leave had ended, of what may occasionally have seemed to them an obsessive interest in research. Having produced this book for their successors, I am especially conscious of how much I owe to them and to their predecessors over the last ten years.

Any editor of *Piers Plowman* will be aware of how much he owes to previous workers in this field. I apologize to all scholars whose work I have drawn on without apparent acknowledgment. I hope they will make as free with my work as I have with theirs. Among the debts I am most deeply conscious of, I wish to mention what I owe to Skeat's edition, especially its inexhaustibly erudite and interesting notes. Among the work of living scholars, I am especially indebted to the edition of the Prologue and Passus I-VII in the Clarendon Series by Professor Bennett, with its wealth of fresh first-hand historical and literary scholarship; and to the great Athlone Press edition of the B-text by Professors Kane and Donaldson, which has been a guide, inspiration and challenge throughout, and which must rank as one of the most important contributions to literary scholarship in our time. To recover Langland's text and to elucidate its meaning for students and the general reader is a rewarding, but also a daunting, task. Without the work of the scholars I have named, I could not have attempted let alone completed an edition such as this, and it is my hope that they in particular will find something in it to interest them.

My final acknowledgment is to my wife. In many ways, this is her book as much as mine. Not only did she compile the Index, prepare the Bibliography and analyse the variants, she helped in dozens of ways, domestic, secretarial and scholarly, to enable me to get on with this book day in and day out without distraction. It would be impossible to dedicate it to anyone else.

A. V. C. S.

Second Edition

For this Second Edition I have made no major changes but have added an indexical glossary as a supplement to the marginal glosses and footnote translations. It attempts to be fairly comprehensive, but reasons of space have prevented any effort at complete exhaustiveness. I wish to acknowledge many hours of invaluable assistance from my wife in the preparation of the Glossary.

A substantial step forward in the study of Langland's language has been made by Prof. M.L. Samuels, 'Langland's Dialect', *Medium Ævum* LIV (1985), 232–47.

Oxford, 1987

A.V.C.S.

Introduction

I THE VERSIONS OF *PIERS PLOWMAN*

Piers Plowman exists in three versions which have been known, ever since Skeat named them over a century ago, as the A, B and C texts. Like Skeat and most students of the poem, I believe these to represent three successive states of a single work by one man. The first version, A, consists of a Prologue and twelve passus, just over 2500 lines, and is unfinished.[1] But in some MSS we find an 'A' text supplemented or 'completed' by a text of another version. Thus Trinity College, Cambridge MS R 3.14 (T) completes from C after A Passus XI, while British Museum MS Harley 3954 is a B-text *up to* about Passus V 127 and *thereafter* an A-text. B is a complete revision of A which adds eight passus and some 4000 lines. Three B-MSS, the closely related British Museum Additional 10574, Cotton Caligula A XI, and the Bodleian MS 814 (BmCotBo), are B-texts from Passus III to the end, but have a C beginning (Prologue to II 131) followed by an A text of II 90-212. The C version is a further revision of B with much re-arrangement, new material and minute verbal alteration. It has a Prologue and twenty-two passus, though in many MSS, including the one Skeat printed, the Prologue is taken as Passus I and the total number of passus becomes twenty-three. The last two passus, corresponding to B XIX and XX, are possibly unrevised. Whether or not C is the poet's final word, critics and readers generally have agreed that the B-text is on the whole the most enjoyable version of the three, though the other two have distinctive merits which make them worth reading.

It is the B-text of *Piers Plowman* which was printed by Robert Crowley in 1550, though Crowley knew of the existence of other manuscripts and possibly other versions of the poem. It was thus in the B version that the poem was known to and influenced English poets such as Spenser, Marlowe and possibly Shakespeare, until in 1813 Thomas Whitaker printed a C-text. In 1824 Richard Price discovered the existence of the earliest version when editing Thomas Warton's *History of English Poetry*, and a manuscript of this was published by Skeat in 1867. In 1842 a B-text based on an early MS, Trinity College, Cambridge B. 15. 17 (the basis of the present edition) was published by Thomas Wright, with useful notes, and in 1869 Skeat printed Bodleian Laud Misc 581, an even better MS of the B-text, supplemented with readings from other MSS. In 1873 Skeat went on to print the C-text, regrettably from·the same corrupt MS, Phillips 8231, which Whitaker had used. In addition to his many valuable observations on the text, Skeat provided a massive body of notes containing lexical, historical and interpretative comment which has remained the basis of modern study and· appreciation of *Piers Plowman* and much of which has not been superseded.

It is in Skeat's editions for the Early English Text Society, his two-volume

xi

Oxford 'Parallel-Text' edition, and his school edition of the Prologue and Passus I-VII that the poem has become familiar to modern readers. But the progress of textual scholarship during this century has rendered Skeat's texts obsolete. His A and C texts were based on highly corrupt manuscripts, while his B-text, though based on the best extant MSS, contains the errors that were present in the common original or archetype of all the B-MSS. In 1960, nearly a century after Skeat's A-text was made known, there appeared the first volume of the Athlone Press edition of *Piers Plowman*, edited by George Kane. Much valuable work had been done in the interim by, in particular, R. W. Chambers and J. G. Grattan,[2] but Kane's book started afresh with a revaluation of the manuscript evidence and the problems of textual transmission. Its impact upon not only *Piers Plowman* studies but medieval literary scholarship as a whole was dramatic. Kane successfully showed the extent to which scribal corruption, unconscious or conscious, obstructed the recovery of the original by the traditional editorial method of recension and compelled the editor to consider the use of reconstruction and conjecture when he knew the archetypal text to have been corrupted by the same processes that had corrupted its descendants, the actual MSS and their group ancestors.

The methods pioneered by Kane were applied in a radical and extended fashion in the edition of the B-text by Kane and E. T. Donaldson published in 1975. Both works are intended for scholars and are difficult of access and use to the specialist student, let alone the general reader. Nonetheless, their influence on subsequent editions is bound to be deep and far-reaching. The basic arguments of Kane and Donaldson can only be accepted or refuted, they cannot be by-passed. There is no way of going back to Skeat and no point in reproducing his texts as the original work of the poet or anything approaching it. A summary of the processes of reasoning that lie behind my editorial decisions will be found in the Textual Commentary at the end of this book. I do not claim to have solved all major problems left unsolved by previous editors; but I hope I have not overlooked any. This edition is intended for the widest possible use, and I have attempted to supply what has long been needed, a modern text and concise literary and historical commentary to serve as a basis for study and criticism.

II AUTHORSHIP, AUDIENCE AND DATE

Piers Plowman has a serious claim to be the greatest English poem of the Middle Ages. It was certainly one of the most popular. Over fifty manuscripts of the three versions survive, compared with over eighty of Chaucer's *Canterbury Tales* and sixteen of his *Troilus and Criseyde*, and some forty of Gower's *Confessio Amantis*. Crowley prefaced his 1550 printing of the poem with an enthusiastic introduction, and he met a receptive audience: the work was reprinted twice in the same year and then again by Owen Rogers in 1561. In these editions *Piers Plowman* was as accessible to the Elizabethan reader as the works of Chaucer. But even in its own day the poem must have made a powerful impact, as is attested by the well-known letter of the insurrectionary leader John Ball to the peasants of Essex. This is dated 1381 and so may allude to the B-text (see below), with its powerful dramatization of a conflict between the peasant hero Piers and a contemptuous priest in Passus VII:

> '. . . stondeth togidre in Godes name, and biddeth Peres Ploughman
> go to his werk . . . And do wel and bettre, and fleth synne . . .'[3]

The quarrel between Piers and the priest is removed from the C-text, and it is tempting to speculate that the author wished to dissociate himself from the atrocities, including the murder of churchmen, which occurred during the Peasants' Revolt of that year. It may indeed have been dangerous to be known as the author of a work the name of whose hero was used as a slogan by dangerous revolutionary preachers, no matter what the real intentions of the writer himself. This may be one reason why virtually nothing is known about the poet except what can be deduced from the text itself. The official documents which give a quality of historical solidity to Chaucer and Gower do not exist.

The internal and external evidence for the authorship of *Piers Plowman* has been authoritatively studied and evaluated by Professor Kane.[4] His conclusion is that the poem in all its versions is the work of William Langland, as Skeat believed. Such is the statement of one of the oldest and fullest ascriptions, that of the Trinity College, Dublin MS of the C-text, and since it is the strongest piece of external evidence, I reproduce it here. It is written in a very early fifteenth-century hand on folio 89b of TCD MS D.4.1:

> Memorandum quod Stacy de Rokayle pater willielmi de Langlond qui stacius fuit generosus & morabatur in Schiptoun vnder whicwode tenens domini le Spenser in comitatu Oxoniensi qui predictus willielmus fecit librum qui vocatur Perys ploughman.[5]

> It is worth recording that Stacy de Rokayle was the father of William de Langlond; this Stacy was of gentle birth and lived in Shipton-under-Wych-wood, a tenant of the Lord Spenser in the county of Oxfordshire. The aforesaid William made the book which is called *Piers Plowman*.

The authority of this ascription has been convincingly defended by Professor Kane. It is confirmed by the statement of the poem's narrator in Passus XV 152 of the B-text:

> 'I have lyved in londe,' quod I, 'my name is Longe Wille.'

Professor Kane has shown (ch. IV) that it was the convention in French and English dream vision poems for the author to incorporate his 'signature' in the text, sometimes in an oblique fashion. B XV 152 both confirms the Christian name given in the Dublin ascription and also, if *Longe, londe* is an anagrammatic signature, the surname. The word *Longe* performs at least one other function, to note a feature of the poet known, presumably, to his immediate audience, his height, a 'fact' confirmed by the 'autobiographical' passage in the C-text (VI 23–4 in Skeat's edition: 'Ich am . . . to long, leyf me, lowe for to stoupe').

Apart from the bare fact of his name, there is no very early and reliable evidence of an external kind about Langland. Our knowledge of him must be gathered from his own direct statements in the three versions of his poem or deduced from such matters as his knowledge of the Bible, the law and religious and other writings. Here the assumptions we start with will inevitably influence our conclusions. I assume, on the strength of Professor Kane's arguments from literary history,[6] that the portrait Langland gives of himself is generally true in its external particulars, though it is not scrupulously autobiographical and there is considerable room for poetic distortion in the interests of ironic or didactic purposes. Thus, since the conditions of medieval publication presuppose that the first audience of a manuscript work had personal knowledge of the author, such characteristics of Langland as his height, his being married and his having a daughter, like the plumpness and bookishness of Chaucer in his poems, may be taken as authentic, as 'facts'. A number of other statements about himself belong roughly to this category: that he was given an education, that he sang psalms for a living and that he lived in London but had lived in the country, specifically in the Malvern region. A passage from the C-text, here quoted from the Huntington MS, gives the flavour of the poet's self-revelations:

'When I yong was, many yer hennes,	
My fader and my frendes fonde me to scole,	*provided; university*
Tyl I wyste witterly what Holy Writ menede,	
And what is best for the body, as the Bok telleth,	
And sykerest for the soule, by so I wole contenue.	*surest; persevere*
And fond I nere, in fayth, seth my frendes deyede,	*never; since*
Lyf that me lykede but in this longe clothes.	
And yf I be labour sholde lyven and lyflode deserven,	*by; livelihood*
The laboure that I lerned beste, therwith lyven I sholde:	
In eadem vocatione in qua vocati estis manete	
[Let every man abide in the same calling in which he	
was called (1 Cor 7: 20)].	
And so I leve yn London and uppe lond bothe.	*in the country*
The lomes that I labore with and lyflode deserve	*tools; win (by)*
Ys Paternoster and my prymer, *Placebo* and *Dirige*,	*prayers (for the dead)*
And my sauter som tyme and my sevene psalmes.	
This I segge for here soules of suche as me helpeth,	*say*
And tho that fynden me my fode vouchen saf, I trowe,	
To be welcome when I come, otherwhile in a monthe,	*make (me) welcome*
Now with hym, now with here—on this wise I begge	
Withoute bagge or botel but my wombe one	*stomach only*
(C VI 35–52).	

In this passage the poet is defending himself against Reason's objections to his way of life, and claims that as an educated man he is not obliged to perform manual labour to earn a living; clerks like himself, he argues, moreover, should only receive the tonsure

                    yf he come were
Of frankeleynes and fre men, and of folke ywedded   (C VI 64).

This plainly seems to imply that the speaker could meet these criteria himself, and *frankeleynes* is a vernacular equivalent of *generosus* in the Dublin ascription. The phrase *folke ywedded* would seem to rule out Langland's illegitimacy (countenanced by Salter and Pearsall in their note to this passage); it was not the case at this time that a man automatically took his father's surname.

We do not know when Langland was born, since the various references to the Dreamer's age, e.g. in XI 47, are hard to interpret exactly. As for the date of his death, the only evidence we have is the statement of John But in a MS of the A-text (Rawlinson Poetry 137), which also contains a clear reference

xiv

to the other versions of the poem. I quote from Kane's edition of the A-text, lines XII 99–105:

> Wille þurgh inwit [wiste] wel þe soþe,
> Þat þis speche was spedelich, and sped him wel faste,   *profitable*
> And wrouȝthe þat here is wryten and oþer werkes boþe
> Of peres þe plowman and mechel puple also.
> And whan þis werk was wrouȝt, ere wille myȝte aspie,
> Deþ delt him a dent and drof him to þe erþe   *blow*
> And is closed vnder clom, crist haue his soule.   *'buried'*

This implies perhaps that Langland died suddenly, but also that he had completed his work. If the John But who names himself in the line immediately following is the man identified by Edith Rickert[7] as having died in 1387, Langland's death would fall some time between then and the probable date of the C-text, about 1385. Since the poet describes himself as already old in the B-text (XX 186ff), we could safely conjecture that he was at least fifty in 1379, the date of completion of B. This would give his probable dates as 1330–1386, but a substantial margin of error must be allowed for.

The historical Langland is, if we ignore the internal evidence of the poem, little more than a name, and nothing is known of his descendants, if any survived him. But it is highly probable that he had patrons, though he does not speak of financial support from them in the 'autobiographical passage'. The number of extant copies of his poem in all its versions testifies to strong interest in his work, and while no manuscript dates from his lifetime, the textual evidence indicates that one or more copies of the A and B texts were made by scribes and used by the poet. Kane and Donaldson have demonstrated (pp. 98–127) that Langland used a scribal copy of the B text when revising to C. The copying of so long a work would have been an expensive undertaking. None of the surviving manuscripts are *de luxe* copies like the Ellesmere *Canterbury Tales* or the Corpus Christi, Cambridge *Troilus*, but many are executed and rubricated by skilled professional scribes and their careful if modest presentation is in keeping with what we know of the early owners of these and other (lost) manuscripts. As Professor Burrow has shown from a study of the wills of people who bequeathed *Piers Plowman* MSS,[8] these owners were, in the first instance, clerics, though some were educated laymen who were not courtiers, let alone magnates, but presumably had an interest in Langland's religious theme. The original dialect of *Piers Plowman* was not such as to render it inaccessible to a *Southren man* (see Chaucer's *Parson's Prologue* I, 42) as a work like *Sir Gawain and the Green Knight* might have been. Its form might have been associated with the North and West of the country (see next section) but educated London readers would have experienced little difficulty in its language and style, and *Piers Plowman* has every appearance of being, like Gower's *Confessio Amantis*, 'A bok for Engelondes sake' (*CA* Prol 24). When Robert Crowley printed it, he drew attention to the age of the poem's language, not the strangeness of its dialect: 'The Englishe is according to the time it was written in . . . ,' and he recommended the work not for its antiquarian appeal but for the direct relevance of its message to the serious religious concerns of contemporary readers: 'Loke not vpon this boke therfore, to talke of wonders paste or to come, but to amende thyne owne misse, which thou shalt fynd here most charitably rebuked' (printed in Skeat, vol II, pp. xxxiii*f*). The glosses and notes of modern editions are primarily means of enabling the text to release its original power.

The date of *Piers Plowman* has already been touched upon in connection with Langland's life. The A-text cannot be earlier than 1362, since A V 14 refers to a memorable south-western wind on a Saturday evening which is independently recorded by a chronicler as occurring on 15 January 1362 (a Saturday). Professor Bennett has argued from other allusions for a date between 1367–70 for A.[9] We do not know if Langland worked continuously on his poem, but a reference to the mayoralty of John Chichester in B XIII 268–70 places the B-text securely after 1370. The Parliament of Rats and Mice in the Prologue alludes to the Good Parliament of 1376, and in Passus XIX, as Professor Bennett has shown convincingly,[10] there are allusions to the warfare between the rival popes that broke out in April 1379 after the Great Schism of the previous year. This lets us date the writing of B between about 1377 and 1379. The C-text is harder to date from internal evidence. Its reference to the unpopularity of King Richard in IV 208–10 of his edition made Skeat elect for a date about 1393; but it is clear that this passage, which speaks of 'customes of covetyse the comune to distruye' and of 'Unsyttynge suffraunce', fits very well with conditions in 1384–5, when Richard and his court 'were giving rise to widespread anxiety'.[11] This is also the date to which the two pieces of external evidence point. One is an allusion to a C-text passage in *The Testament of Love* by Thomas Usk, written perhaps a year before his death by execution in 1388. The other is the reference to Langland's death by John But, mentioned above, which, if he is the But who died in 1387, indicates a date for C around 1385–6. By this date, Chaucer had completed *Troilus and Criseyde* and was about to begin work on the *General Prologue*. This is the first of his writings to show the possible influence of Langland, and it is not over-fanciful to recognize in his portrait of the ideal ploughman a tasteful tribute to his (?recently deceased) contemporary:

> A *trewe* swynkere and a good was he,
> Lyvynge in pees and *parfit charitee* (*GP* 531–2).

The italicized words would readily suggest to his audience the qualities of Langland's Piers and perhaps even help to remove misgivings aroused by John Ball's use of Piers as a symbol of peasant militancy.

If the generally accepted dates of the three versions are correct, it would seem reasonable to conclude that Langland spent the last twenty-five years of his life, the years of his maturity, engaged in a single enterprise, the construction of a poem which in depth, intensity and richness of organization challenges comparison with works of the order of *Paradise Lost* and *The Divine Comedy*. We have no mention of any 'earlier and other creation' by Langland; but it is hard to credit that the A-text, an assured if undeveloped literary work, was his very first effort at writing a poem.†

III THE LITERARY TRADITION OF *PIERS PLOWMAN*

In all three texts Langland employed the dream-vision form which was the common property of medieval English poets, whether they wrote accentual-syllabic or alliterative verse and whether they lived in London or Cheshire.

Langland also used the verse form that he must have learnt in his youth in Worcestershire, the home of the one named alliterative poet apart from himself, Layamon, author of the *Brut*. The works of the Alliterative Revival have recently received a comprehensive survey from Thorlac Turville-Petre in his book of that title, and Professors Salter and Hussey have previously considered the question of Langland's debt to earlier alliterative poems.[12] It emerges that Langland owes very little to the few he can be shown to have known, notably *Wynnere and Wastoure* (1352–3) and, less surely, *The Parlement of the Thre Ages* (? late C14th), whilst several alliterative poets of the late fourteenth and early fifteenth century were deeply indebted to *Piers Plowman*. *The Crowned King*, *Pierce the Ploughmans Crede*, *Mum and the Sothsegger* and *Death and Liffe*[13] may all be classed as written by followers, if not disciples of Langland. It is not possible here to examine in any detail the many points of contact between Langland and such poets as the author of the *Parlement*, whose line describing Elde—

He was ballede and blynde, and alle babirlippede. (158)

is either derived from or the source of Langland's describing Envy—

He was bitelbrowed and baberlipped, with two blered eighen (V 188).

(The Langland line as quoted is reconstructed from the A and C texts; in the B-archetype it read as two lines divided before *with*, the second line being completed with the phrase *as a blynd hagge*, which the present text rejects as scribal. In its archetypal form the line is even closer to that from the *Parlement*, a fact which may point to indebtedness on the *Parlement*-poet's part rather than Langland's: the lines seem too close to have coincided simply through shared use of formula-like phrases.)

In attempting to isolate the important differences between *Piers Plowman* and other alliterative poems, I do not choose the learned, Latinate qualities of Langland's writing (which, after all, are heavily concentrated in some passages and sections and totally lacking in others). Although Langland's Latin expressions, when embedded in the structure of a verse-line, can give an individual and sometimes intense colouring to his poetry (as in Passus XVIII, discussed below), they seem to me accidental rather than essential elements of his style taken as a whole. The features I select, though negative, are pervasive. One is the absence of the ornamental diction inherited from Old English poetry; the other, related to the first, is the lack of interest in description for its own sake, whether of clothing, scenery or architecture. (The second at least of these qualities *is* found even in Langland's followers.) Langland did not lack visual imagination, as I shall argue in discussing his imagery in section VI; but his was not a pictorial poetry. In this he is closer to Shakespeare than to Spenser or the Chaucer of the *Knight's Tale* and the *General Prologue*. The second feature can be briefly illustrated by comparing the description, excellent in itself, of a beautiful natural scene in fragment 'M' of *Mum and the Sothsegger*, lines 889ff, with the passage of *Piers Plowman* which clearly inspired it, Will's vision of nature in *PP* XI 319ff.

The author of *Mum*, with a lively relish for particulars, describes

The breris with thaire beries bent over the wayes
As honysoucles hongyng uppon eche half,

Chesteynes and chiries that children desiren
Were loigged undre leves ful lusty to seen (899–90).

Langland *can* match the tactile immediacy of *bent* and *loigged*, as in his pungent evocation of greedy clerics:

Thei ben *acombred* with coveitise, thei konne noght *out crepe*,
So harde hath avarice *yhasped* hem togideres (I 196–7).

It is not clear in these lines whether we are to visualize a snail in its shell or a man locked in a chest, or both, or neither. It is doubtful whether we are meant to visualize at all. The images here are essentially half-realized, because they function as part of an imaginative metaphor, rich in suggestion. And the metaphor subserves an intellectual and moral purpose. In a similar way Langland, in describing nature, eschews the seductive decorative possibilities afforded by the alliterative medium. His sweeping, generalized vision of nature moves swiftly from 'the sonne and the see and the sond' to 'briddes and beestes' and 'Wilde wormes', through 'Man and his make', to arrive, with characteristic emphasis, at the social, moral and religious realities which for him were ultimates and inescapable:

Povertee and plentee, bothe pees and werre,
Blisse and bale—bothe I seigh at ones,
And how men token Mede and Mercy refused (XI 331–3).

Langland's emotional world is of immense circumference. Its poles are the all-too-human ridiculous of XX 195–8:

For the lyme that she loved me fore, and leef was to feele—
On nyghtes, namely, whan we naked weere—
I ne myghte in no manere maken it at hir wille,
So Elde and heo hadden it forbeten

with its rueful-ironic, bitter-sweet and mock-pathetic tones, to the religious sublime of XVIII 57–61, with its real pathos, tragic depth and stark grandeur:

'*Consummatum est*,' quod Crist, and comsede for to swoune,
Pitousliche and pale as a prison that dieith;
The lord of lif and of light tho leide hise eighen togideres.
The day for drede withdrough and derk bicam the sonne.
The wal waggede and cleef, and al the world quaved.

Langland's genius here expresses itself in a complex holding-together of the multitudinous associations clustering around this supreme moment. The understatement of *swoune*, the recalling of the 'poor naked wretches' for whom the Lord of Life and Light dies and with whom he is identified in his utter desertion, these are set against the spectacle of a fearful personified day and an upheaval of creation in which man-made *wal* and God-made *world* are drawn together, through the alliterative binding, to bring home the immensity and the closeness of the event, on which the salvation of each individual soul and all humankind utterly depends. It is astonishing poetry, whether considered integrally or in the minutiae of such details as the strange, haunting phrase *leide hise eighen togideres*, which comes with infinite gentleness after the majestic extended half-line preceding it. Such density cannot be paralleled in the works of the other alliterative poets, the author of *Sir*

Gawain and *Pearl* included. Imaginative power of this order can scarcely be equalled after the Old English *Dream of the Rood* and before Shakespeare's tragedies.

Langland was a poet of the capital, not, in spite of his origins, a provincial writer; yet he did not use the form of verse inherited from France by the leading writers of his day, the court poets Chaucer and Gower, and handled almost as fluently by anonymous redactors of romance such as the contributors to the Auchinleck manuscript. In using alliterative long lines, he achieved two things: he broadened and deepened the main stream of English poetry by handling more than adequately material of major significance left untouched by both Chaucer and Gower, and, by doing so, brought a form otherwise restricted to the provinces of England into the central literary tradition, where it remained stubbornly while the rest of alliterative poetry languished forgotten or unknown.

This achievement has not, perhaps, secured recognition even in our time. The more immediately appealing quality of the *Gawain-Pearl* poet, who is possibly the most accomplished virtuoso amongst the alliterative poets, has tended to conceal from students and non-specialists as a whole—and perhaps also from specialists—the less obviously attractive but, I believe, profounder virtues of Langland's work considered not as preaching or versified theology but quite simply as poetry. Langland does not have Chaucer's variety of form and mood, but he has a perhaps greater emotional range, encompassing not only comedy, both coarse and sophisticated, but also religious sublimity, which finds expression characteristically in daring metaphor and wordplay. Langland was in the alliterative tradition but not of it. He rejected many of the sensuous beauties of the form in order to open up its hidden potential and make possible a wide range of tones and inflexions in his exploration of the experience of common humanity. His poem stands at the centre of medieval English literature with the work of Chaucer. Hopkins, perhaps because he failed to find the surface richness he sought in his own poetry, was moved to dismiss *Piers Plowman* as 'not worth reading'.[14] T. S. Eliot, however, who had alluded to Chaucer's *General Prologue* in the opening of *The Waste Land*, paid an appropriate tribute to Langland in the opening of his last great poem, *Little Gidding*, which recalls both the opening of Langland's *Prologue* and his ecstatic lines on the Holy Ghost in Passus XVII:

> Midwinter spring is its own season
> Sempiternal though sodden towards sundown,
> Suspended in time, between pole and tropic.

In doing so he showed an unerring sense of the nature of poetic tradition.

IV THE STRUCTURE OF *PIERS PLOWMAN*

Probably few critics today would agree with C. S. Lewis that Langland is 'confused and monotonous, and hardly makes his poetry into a poem.'[15] Some of the best criticism of recent years, such as that of Burrow and Frank,[16] has brought out the poem's structural coherence, both as a whole and at the level of individual visions. If confusions still exist, some are of the critics' making, and one even goes back to Skeat. This is the unhappy practice of seeing *Piers Plowman* as made up of a *Visio* (Prologue and Passus I–VII) and a *Vita* (Passus VIII–XX). There is no authority in the B-MSS for this division, though many A-MSS speak of a 'Visio de Petro Plowman' and a 'Vita de Dowel, Dobet & Dobest secundum Wyt & Reson'. Skeat, analysing the B-text, saw the *Vita* as 'altogether a new poem' though 'intended . . . to be the sequel and completion of the former portion' (II, li). If this *was* true of Langland's aim in A (which is doubtful), there is no sign that it was true when he wrote B. The theme of Dowel is introduced by Holy Church as early as Passus I 128–33 and is memorably affirmed in Truth's pardon to Piers in VII 110–14. Passus VIII, in which Will sets out 'for to seke Dowel' does not begin 'a new poem', but presupposes what has gone before and develops material latent in the first seven passus. Both the plan of the poem as a whole and the many verbal anticipations and echoes indicate that the B-text was conceived as a unified work of art. It has great complexity, admittedly, but there are three structural principles which help us to grasp its no less impressive unity.

The first of these is the protagonist's quest. Will is commonly called 'the Dreamer'; but some 230 lines are devoted to waking episodes. Some of these, like the long passage opening Passus XX and those between VII and VIII help to impart a sense of Will's life advancing, with setbacks, from youth to age, from lust for knowledge to love and spiritual understanding. There is real progression. Will first seeks 'wondres' (Prol 4); he proceeds to seek Dowel (VIII 2); after his visions of Patience and Charity he grows 'wery of the world' (XVIII 4). Whilst at his final awakening it is not he but Conscience who sets out as a pilgrim (XX 381), it has become clear that Will has advanced from identification with the folk of the field (V 61) and later with their representative, the Active Man Haukyn, to a real if implied identification with Conscience, who sets out to 'walken as wide as the world lasteth', as Will in the Prologue 'wente wide in this world'. The quest 'wondres to here' has become one 'to seken Piers the Plowman' (XX 383).

In addition to their narrative function in forwarding Will's 'pilgrimage', the waking episodes introduce the themes of the succeeding and reflect upon the significance of the preceding dream visions. The longest one, between the second and third visions, indicates a major advance and a new vista opening out before Will. His dream experience has made him 'to studie / Of that I seigh slepyng' (VII 144–5) and left him 'pencif in herte' for Piers Plowman (a phrase suggesting love-melancholy). A recipient so far, he becomes an active seeker. But in the continuation of the waking section that begins VIII he does not seek Piers, but asks all he meets who and where Dowel is, has an unsatisfactory encounter with two Friars Minor who think they know, and resumes the lonely wandering of the Prologue before having his third dream. The waking episodes strengthen our sense of Will as a real man, no 'dreamer' retreating from life into visions, but a vexed individual striving to translate the truth of visions into the practice of daily living. The nameless dreamer in *Pearl* is rapt from his body to 'gon in Godes grace / In aventure ther mervayles meven' (63–4), and after being wakened through his own rash impulse to 'hente' more than is his 'by right' (1195–6), must continue living without further visions, though not without the comfort of what he *has* seen. His unique experience answers a particular 'wo' (56), just as a dream brings the narrator of Chaucer's *Book of the Duchess* relief for a 'sicknesse' (36) and that of *The Parliament of Fowls* light upon 'a certeyn thing' he has sought 'to lerne' (20). Langland's dreams are part of a whole life: Will's response to each helps to shape and precipitate the one that follows, just as each dream works to change his life.

The interplay between sleep and waking gives dramatic urgency to the dreams themselves, which are the second main structural principle in the poem. They are eight in number (ten if we count the inner dreams of Visions 3 (3a) and 5 (5a) as numbers 4 and 6). Vision 1 occupies Passus I–IV; Vision 2 Passus V–VII; Vision 3 VIII–XII, enclosing the first inner dream (3a) at XI 4–404; Vision 4 occupies XIII–XIV. Vision 5 extends from XV to XVII and encloses the second inner dream (5a) at XVI 20–167, while Visions 6, 7 and 8 each occupy one Passus (XVIII, XIX, XX). Division into vision and passus ('step') appears in the text and is authentic. Some manuscripts additionally head the seven passus VIII–XIV 'Dowel', the four XV–XVIII 'Dobet' and the last two, XIX–XX, 'Dobest', which correspond respectively to Visions 3–4, 5–6 and 7–8. These divisions may go back to authorial rubrics and certainly point up recognizable concentrations of interest in character and theme: Dowel on Will and Haukyn, learning and patience; Dobet on Piers and Christ, and charity; Dobest on the Holy Ghost and the Church, and grace. But they mislead as much as help if they imply an exclusive interest in Dowel, Dobet *or* Dobest in each passus-group. The three are considered together, even if the full meaning of Dobest cannot be brought out until Christ's victory over death and triumphant rule are explained by Conscience to Will in terms of 'conquest'. Certainly it would be incorrect to equate Charity (shown in XVII–XVIII as the highest virtue, potent where Faith and Hope fail) with Dobet rather than Dobest on the mere grounds that the Tree of Charity and the Samaritan, exemplar of Charity, happen to appear in the section headed 'Dobet'. Though less dubious than the term *Vita*, these headings must be treated with caution when analysing the poem.

That the last six visions commence with a new beginning is signalized by the deliberate echoes in Passus VIII of the Prologue's *somer seson*, which advances during Will's search for Dowel. But as I have said, Passus VIII follows straight on from the concerns expressed in Passus VII, and if a major division is sought it cannot easily be found between what some critics distinguish as *Visio* and *Vita*. Such a division, arguably, *does* exist between the first four and the last four visions (Prol–XIV, XV–XX). A key to this division is the character Haukyn, whose appearance in XIII–XIV has long been seen as linking the supposed *Visio* and *Vita*. But even more than he *connects* separate sections (let alone poems), Haukyn *concludes* a sequence of visions which may be described as 'carnal' rather than 'ghostly'. Haukyn's tears at the end of XIV are properly religious tears. They do not flow from fear of damnation like Will's at V 61 or Robert the Robber's at V 463, but from an awareness, however rudimentary, of having betrayed God's love, which won the grace of 'cristendom' for men at the cost of Christ's death:

'Allas,' quod Haukyn the Actif Man tho, 'that after my cristendom
I ne hadde be deed and dolven for Dowelis sake!' (XIV 320–1).

In the next passus (XV) Will, after hearing Anima's description of the Tree of

Charity, 'swoons' at the name of Piers and experiences the most mystical of his visions, a symbolic disclosure of the activation, to redeem man, of the same divine love Haukyn had wept at betraying.

Piers dominates the inner dream of XVI and saves Will from the error of men like the *Pearl*-dreamer who try to 'more hente / Then moghte by ryght upon hem clyven' (1195). Piers states that the tree is mysterious beyond man's grasp:

> 'the Trinite it meneth'—
> And egreliche he loked on me, and therfore I spared
> To asken hym any moore therof . . . (XVI 62–5).

And because Will has by now learnt 'patience', the virtue whose inner essence is humility, he does not 'ask any more' but *refrains* from re-enacting Adam's sin, concupiscence for the fruit of the tree of knowledge, the desire (stemming from pride) to 'be as gods, knowing good and evil' (Gen 3:5). Will wants to taste not knowledge but charity, not to 'know' but to 'know how to love'. His humility saves him; though he wakes from the inner dream at 167, he goes on to receive a series of revelations which climax in the vision of Christ's victory over hell and death, and on seeing this he applies to himself the utterance of the privileged apostle Paul (I Cor 12: 4): 'I heard secret words which it is not granted to man to utter' (XVIII 396a). By *not* 'asking' Will has received.

The second inner dream, which leads to the disclosure of secret truths, is precipitated by Will's violent access of *pure joye* (XVI 18) at Piers' name. The *first* inner dream also comes after a powerful surge of emotion, but contrasts sharply with the second, since the emotion is not love but 'wo and wrathe' at Scripture's rebuke of him for lacking self-knowledge (XI 5). Though 'ravysshed' into a vision of Middle Earth and of Nature, he is spiritually unprepared to understand it; and though 'fet forth by ensaumples to knowe, / Thorugh ech a creature, Kynde my creatour to lovye' (XI 324–5), he cannot respond to the revelation of God in creation. He therefore fails to grasp Reason's profound affirmation about God, that 'al he wrought was *wel ydo*' (XI 394), which bases Dowel (later shown as the charity of Christ, the 'new creation') in God's *initial* act of love, his creation of the world. Will awakens blushing with shame and says, much like the dreamer in *Pearl*—

> Wo was me thanne
> That I in metels ne myghte moore have yknowen (XI 404–5).

The crucial change in Will is to abandon lust to know for humility before God's purposes, and he achieves this through his experiences in XIII with Patience, a crucial figure in the poem, whose name links him with the suffering God who has the right to take vengeance but refrains, shows mercy and even dies for his enemies. As Reason says, preparing Will for his trying encounter with the gluttonous doctor of divinity: 'Who suffreth moore than God? . . . no gome, as I leeve' (XI 378). To learn this truth properly is for Will to begin to be *symple of herte* 'humble', and humility, 'patience', as he discovers, is 'the pure tree' on which 'groweth the fruyt Charite' (XVI 8–9).

Much of *Piers Plowman*'s later visions elaborates I Corinthians 8:2–3: 'And if any man think that he knoweth any thing, he hath not yet known as he ought to know. But if any man love God, the same is known by him.' To be

'known by God' (= acknowledged, loved) is to 'know even as I am known'
(1 Cor 13:12), and the way to that knowing is through charity, which 'is not
puffed up', though 'knowledge puffeth up' (8:1), but 'is patient, is kind'
(13:4). When Will asks Kynde in XX 'what craft be best to lerne?' the answer
he gets is 'Lerne to love' (207–8). The nature of this 'craft' Will learns in the
four visions he has after learning patience. They could even be called 'love-
dreams' (see XVI 20 (*C*), which may use the phrase). In them Will receives
what St Paul calls 'spiritum sapientiae et revelationis, in agnitione eius . . .
illuminatos oculos cordis', 'a spirit of wisdom and of revelation, in the know-
ledge of [Jesus Christ] . . . the eyes of [the] heart enlightened' (Eph 1:17–18).

Will's development through his dreams and waking vicissitudes gives the
poem linear progression—this in spite of its being a *dialogus* (as the colophon
of the Trinity MS has it), tense with almost dialectical alternation of attitudes.
But *Piers Plowman* shares with other fourteenth century poems a principle of
circularity. Fitt II of *Sir Gawain* opens by contrasting nature's annual self-
renewal with man's linear progress from cradle to grave. Its hero's own
experience, however, is to meet at the end of his quest for the Green Knight
not the expected death, but an unexpected new birth into self-knowledge. He
discovers both that perfection is not attained once for all in this life but can
be lost, that loss entails sin, shame and guilt, and also that failure can be
redeemed, perfection re-won—and lost again. The *Pearl*-dreamer tries to cross
the river and break out of the inexorable quotidian cycle of recurrence of a
life grown empty without his Pearl, but his impulse is not to God's *paye*
'good pleasure' and he wakes abruptly into that life; yet he is left with the
consolation the vision brought, and, in the daily recurrence of the liturgy of
the eucharist, which gives shape and meaning to historical time, finds a
figurative foreshadowing of the heavenly Jerusalem which also comforts him
in his 'longeyng hevy' (1180), until the time of release. Langland uses a
circular principle, but because his poem consists of several visions not just
one, he has space to develop it into a principle of *recapitulation*.

Piers Plowman traces the development not only of an individual but of a
whole society, the historical community of Christians. It begins with things as
they are: an individual who is a 'doted daffe' (I 140), forgetful of the truth
necessary for salvation, which Holy Church repeats to him like a mnemonic
formula for a child:

Whan alle tresors arn tried, Truthe is the beste (I 134–5, 206–7).

That the individual will can grow in appreciation of this profoundly simple
and profoundly difficult affirmation makes for progression and linearity; and
the same is true of the community. In Passus V Will and the folk repent; but
Will becomes a 'doted daffe' in succumbing to Fortune's false promises in
XI, while the field of folk, who collectively in V and in XIV through Haukyn
experience the 'sharp salve' of Shrift, fall in XX to the friar who 'gloseth
there he shryveth' and 'clene foryeten to crye and to wepe.' Langland gives
many exemplars of heroic holiness—the hermit and martyr saints, and,
supremely, Christ. But he places in the foreground an image of common
humanity, Will himself and his double Haukyn, man immersed *in* the fleshly
world *of* which he is not, cyclically washing his 'cote of cristendome' yet
unable to 'kepen it clene an houre' (XIV 12). Against Haukyn's 'So hard it

is . . . to lyve and to do synne. Synne seweth us evere . . .' (XIV 322–3), a cry just this side of despair, all that can be set is hope in God's grace, which his faith assures the dreamer will not fail a man of good will, however heavy his burden of sin:

> The goode wil of a wight was nevere bought to the fulle:
> For ther nys no tresour therto to a trewe wille (XIII 192–3).

It is a *trewe wille* that in the end will find the *tresor Truthe*.

The faith on which hope builds is faith in the reality of the Incarnation, grasped in all its implications for man the sinner, the 'kynde of Kryst' that 'comfort kenned' to the *Pearl*-dreamer when his 'wreched wylle in wo ay wraghte' (55–6). The chief implication is that if God became man, men can become like God. The reality of this implication is exemplified in the saints (hence the deep preoccupation of medieval people with veneration of the saints). Langland also exemplifies it in his rich and strange creation Piers. Piers begins as the servant of Truth (as Sir Gawain is the devotee and exemplar of perfection); yet he can succumb to gluttony (V 255) and after receiving pardon resolves to abandon 'bely joye' for 'preieres and penaunce' (VII 119–20). It is this Piers who in XIX 262–3 is made Grace's 'prowor and plowman . . . for to tilie truthe'. His spiritual ploughing in XIX recapitulates his earthly ploughing in VI, but also grows out of it. Grace builds on nature. Because Piers in his earthly role could 'travaille as Truthe wolde' and his 'teme dryve' (VI 139, 134), and in spite of his aching belly in VI turn to God, he receives in XIX spiritual 'greynes—cardynales vertues', including Temperance, so that 'sholde nevere mete ne meschief make hym to swelle' (285). And as Piers' earthly ploughing was menaced by wasters, so in XIX his effort under Grace 'to tilie truthe / And the lond of bileve, the lawe of Holy Chirche' (335–6) is menaced by the Deadly Sins under Pride:

> greven he thynketh
> Conscience and alle Cristene and Cardinale Vertues . . . (338–9).

And as the sins of the folk of the field were repented with bitter tears, so in the early church

> . . . wellede water for wikkede werkes,
> Egreliche ernynge out of mennes eighen (XIX 380–1).

But Langland was no nostalgic idealist. *Ecclesia semper reformanda est* because the individuals who compose the Church are always prone to sin. This constant awareness on the poet's part accounts for the sombre tone of *Piers Plowman*: the grotesque humanness of the sins in Passus V is absent from the devilish crew who assault Unitee in Passus XX. Yet Langland never loses hope, because his vision of Piers, man's hope of responding to grace and becoming like God, never deserts him.

I have examined here only one example of the principle of recapitulation in the poem; most of the others are noted in the Commentary as they occur. I have been discussing the main design of *Piers Plowman*; but what is true of the whole is true of the parts, down to the smallest unit, as a detailed analysis of the Prologue would demonstrate. There is not space in this section for such an analysis, but in the next, where I look at the poem's themes, I shall inevitably be also considering the structure of the individual visions which present the themes. The lay-out of the entire work may be determined by a type of narrative progression, the growth of the dreamer's soul; but the plan of the dream-visions themselves is determined by immediate thematic concerns—Meed, the Deadly Sins, Patience, Charity—and to these I now turn.

V THE POEM'S THEMES

Vision One has three movements but one theme: the true purpose of and value in life. The Prologue's *vision* sets individual and field of folk against the stark alternatives of heaven and damnation (tower and dungeon). Christians at *all* times risk becoming immersed in the world; Langland sees obsession with wealth as the special problem of *his* day, when the Christian church itself was becoming engrossed in temporal possessions. The Rat Fable does not disrupt the vision of society, since its concern is not merely topical politics but the perennial issue of power in society and the need for a central authority to maintain social order. Passus I is *explanation*. Holy Church answers Will's six urgent questions about the purpose of life and criticizes men for pursuing worldly treasure (meed) instead of spiritual (truth). Truth is a way of life as well as the object of man's search; 'tho that *werche wel* ... And enden ... in truthe ... shul wende to hevene, / Ther Treuthe is in Trinitee ...' (130–3). Thus HC introduces 'Dowel' in summarizing the demands of God's law. After 'things seen' (vision) and 'things said' (explanation) we have 'things done' (action). Passus II–IV are a dramatic trial-at-law. Holy Church is guardian of the true treasure; now we see put to the test the claims of her antitype Lady Meed, the false treasure men seek. The power and allure of money are symbolized by a woman in scarlet and gold radiating the pride of life and the lust of the flesh. Her trial ends with a (provisional) victory of Reason and Conscience over Meed in the high councils of national life.

Vision Two considers the condition of the people as a whole. As Burrow has shown,[17] its action has four stages: sermon, confession, pilgrimage and pardon. A sustained personification-allegory like Vision One, it also has detailed realistic description of ordinary life in the confessions and the ploughing of the half-acre. Though it opens with Will's repentance in response to Reason's sermon, its central figure is not the Dreamer but the Ploughman. Piers enters when the folk are trying to make satisfaction by following Reason's injunction, 'Seketh Seynt Truthe' (V 57). A model son of the Church whose 'coveitise' (52) is not Meed but Truth, he demonstrates in action how to 'werche wel' so as to 'wende to heven'. For such action he obtains Truth's pardon, which the church's institutional representative, the priest, cannot recognize as a 'true' pardon. Piers' tearing it, as Frank argues,[18] stands for his rejection of the idea of paper pardons as a substitute for doing well, not disagreement with the words on the pardon, which repeat Holy Church's teaching. The scene illustrates Langland's hatred of all that de-spiritualizes religion and substitutes form for substance, ceremony or procedure for sincerity of heart (which is truth operative in the individual).

The waking interlude after Vision Two leads to a second prologue. Will is to seek Truth in his own way because each Christian must make a personal pilgrimage: a life of sincere obedience to God cannot be lived by proxy and each must 'do well' for himself. Will chooses the intellectual way: he seeks a definition of Dowel. This means consulting the representatives of knowledge and learning. The long *Vision Three* therefore has Will thinking for himself ('meeting Thought'), arriving at Knowledge or Understanding ('Wit'), meeting Study and being sent to Clergie and Scripture. He is vexed by the discrepancy between what the educated know and how they live when he finds that 'clerkes of Holy Kirke that kepen Cristes *tresor*' (471) often have a less sure hold on 'truth' than the simple and unschooled. Voicing his disillusionment with learning he receives a rebuke from Scripture for the wrong spirit of his approach and is plunged into an inner dream in which the pagan emperor Trajan, who was saved from hell for '*lyvyng* in truthe' (161), shows the nature of God's justice. Will questions God's ways in asking why nature is free of the disorder and unreason that afflict man, and Reason's rebuke to the rebuker wakes him into the outer dream. Here Ymaginatif resolves Will's main doubts by showing knowledge of the truth in an intellectual sense to be necessary but not sufficient for salvation: 'lyvyng in truthe' is also essential. He reconciles with the Church's doctrine of the necessity of baptism the salvation of Trajan, who exercised 'trewe truthe' (XII 288) as a 'tresor / To kepe with [his] comune' (XII 293–5).

After this protracted *dialogus*, *Vision Four* moves towards action. Passus XIII has two parts (linked by the imagery of food, material and spiritual) and two memorable characters, the gluttonous Doctor of Divinity and the Active Man. Each is contrasted with Patience, who is neither active nor contemplative in the traditional way, but who is spiritually active because his 'food' is the word and sacrament of God. At Conscience's dinner it becomes clear that *Do*wel cannot be knowledge as such but must be an *active* virtue (charity), the basis of which is a *passive* one (patience). The Active Man balances the learned (but spiritually myopic) friar, as the type of the uneducated layman, whose Christian baptism does not guarantee the well-doing without which salvation cannot be attained. A second necessary sacrament, confession, is the theme of XIV. Haukyn learns that the remedy for sin (of which the root is pride) is humility (the root of charity); this is what Patience means by 'poverty'. Haukyn, as Will's *alter ego*, has advanced the quest from one for Dowel (VIII 13) to one for Charity (XIV 97), to be found 'in poverte ther pacience is' (217). The nature of charity itself, the fruit of the tree of patience, is to be dealt with in the next vision.

The foregoing outline of the thematic structure of the first four visions runs the risk, like all summaries, of over-simplifying a very complex and subtle organization. To counteract this danger, which is unavoidable if one attempts to clarify the themes for a reader unfamiliar with Langland, I offer a more extended analysis of the long *Fifth Vision*, before returning to a more summary mode for the last three. This provides an opportunity also to look back over the earlier visions which, as I argued in section IV, hang together in much the same way as do the last four, starting with Passus XV. The powerful action of the Sixth Vision flows from what is learnt of the nature of Charity in the Fifth, in which Piers returns as a crucial figure. But this vision, which contains the mystical inner dream, opens with a discursive enounter with the character Anima, who recalls the personifications of intellectual faculties in the Third Vision. The difference is that Anima is more specifically the human soul as the theatre in which God's grace operates, rather than the rational mind as such. We leave behind in Vision Four the exemplar of the outer social life, Haukyn, and enter an inner world. Anima attacks Will's special vice, in which he repeats the fault of Adam, 'Coveitise to konne and to knowe science', which leads away from holiness (doing well). He also attacks the institutional church, which, though the divinely ordained means of sacramental grace, can become a source of corruption (because its human agents, the clergy, set a bad example of teaching one thing and doing another and so by their hypocrisy infect the people). The image he uses is of a tree (XV 96–102). Will's problem is not unrelated to this dilemma of a corrupt clergy: if charity is something active, why can it not be experienced in operation in the world?

Anima sets out to answer Will's questions, which keep raising themes dealt with right at the beginning of the poem. Will has resumed the role temporarily taken over by Haukyn in Vision Four, and his question at XV 176 echoes Haukyn's at XIV 101–2: is charity possible for the rich? This recalls his question to Holy Church in Passus I: what is the treasure which saves the soul instead of destroying it? Her answer, 'Truth', Will had been unable to take in more than a cognitive sense, because of his undeveloped spiritual state, and so the whole Third Vision had been spent exploring what could be learnt of Dowel, the way to Truth, by the intellect. Yet Holy Church had pointed out that Truth was a matter of Love, the content of the Old Law given to Moses and the motive of Christ's incarnation, culminating in his death, which established the New. She had used the image of the plant of peace, the heavenly seed coming to eat the soil of human nature and so grow into a potent, penetrating weapon of God's purpose. This image now grows into that of the tree of charity and Christ as the jousting knight. In assuring Will that charity *is* possible to those not literally poor, Anima nonetheless emphasizes the need for detachment from the world. He recapitulates Holy Church's attack on the covetousness of the clergy and extends it further to argue that their obsession with material things has destroyed their power to evangelize: their inferiority to the saints of old is dramatically summed up in their inability to perform miracles, including the miracle of suffering for Christ's sake. The 'red noble' (537) is 'reverenced' (a powerful word, suggesting idol-worship) before the bloodstained rood of Christ. The evil stems from Constantine's endowment of the Church, which allied the spiritual city with the city of this world.

The inner dream of Vision Five is introduced in Passus XVI by Anima's reply to Will's question, What does charity mean? The mention of Piers' name which precipitates it is not the first in this vision: twice before, at XV 199 and 211, Anima had spoken of the depth of Piers' vision and his knowledge of the profound truth that Charity can be 'known' 'Neither thorugh wordes ne werkes, but thorugh wil oone' (210). It is in this sense that the inner vision is a 'love-dream' (see XVI 20): it is the revelation which comes to a will purged by patience, not to an intellect that has taken much thought. The image of the tree of charity thus defies discursive explication; but this is not to say that it is incoherent or contradictory. The fruits have to be actual human beings because the tree grows in man's body, and it is from the actuality of human nature that God develops his great purpose, through the incarnation of his son. But human actuality is *historical*: it is thus a logical step to see the fruits in a historical perspective extending from Adam to Christ. Piers' role in this action is perhaps the hardest to explain, if not actually to comprehend. One way of putting it would be to see XVI 86–8 as a vivid imaginative rendering of human nature taking into itself the divine, of the mystery of the Incarnation being viewed, so to speak, from man's side (since it is impossible to view it from God's). Piers is perhaps more readily under-stood not as the human nature of Christ *per se* so much as that *potential* for becoming human which Christians believe was *actualized* in God's Word 'becoming flesh'. Langland sets out to meditate dramatically on the dogma of the Incarnation just as in XVII he does with the dogma of the Trinity. As the very core of what is distinctive in Christianity, it cries out for interpretation, representation through imagery and action, and Langland's response is the inner vision open to 'wil oone'. Presumably its very nature is such that it can only be 'known' by 'wil oone': discursive analysis cannot get at the heart of what the dogma any more than the vision teaches about God's love for man.

The strange image of the tree itself had lasted for only a short while, as though the mystical experience was too much for Will to bear, and Piers had warded off his clumsy gesture at probing further with the mind. The strange dissolves into the familiar—the story of Christ's passion and death—yet Langland succeeds in his task of revivifying this profound but hackneyed theme with an intensity of personal engagement expressed in his audacious use of the figure of Piers. When the Dreamer wakes from the inner vision the narrative has been stopped at the moment of Jesus' arrest on Holy Thursday. The Dreamer has advanced considerably under Piers' guidance; but he is not yet ready to meet the embodiment of charity, Jesus himself, 'face to face'. He first must be prepared, his rough ways made plain, by becoming acquainted with the workings of God's purpose in the Old Testament, which laid the basis for fulfilment in the New. Hence he must meet Abraham, exemplar of the faith on which charity is built. Abraham's discourse leaves Will conscious of the power of sin and, like Haukyn at the end of Vision Four, weeping religious tears, 'gracious drops'. To grasp the power of God's love he must first grasp the power of the opposition offered by the human will to that love.

With an increasing sense of drama, the Fifth Vision develops towards the climactic disclosures of Passus XVIII. The quest of Hope and Faith for Jesus fuses with that of Will for Piers, whom he had lost at XVI 168; but first the object of both quests is indirectly encountered in the person of the Good Samaritan. It is he who instructs Will that there is no contradiction between faith and love of God and neighbour (through keeping the Commandments) as forms of Dowel: both are complementary and they are perfected by active charity. This it is that heals wounded humanity. The power of sin, which had made Will weep, he vividly brings out by his image of unkindness, supremely manifested in murder, as a quenching of the very light and warmth of God's initiative to man (which we call grace), a piercing of the palm of the Trinity, an attack on God's own nature, which is love, and of which the image is the created human being, our fellow man. The Samaritan describes the very acts which have resulted in the wounding of the traveller whom he rescues. Against the power of evil, whether that of the devil or that of countless human acts of will, only an immense act of divine power, a *maistrie*, will suffice, and it is this that the Crucifixion of Jesus constitutes.

Although the last three visions are short and ostensibly self-contained, each occupying one passus, they form part of a grand action which began in XV with Anima and does not conclude till the last line of the poem. There is none of the variety and contrast which characterized the first four visions; a single concentrated purpose—to give the audience experiential knowledge, *kynde knowyng*, of the nature of charity, God's love, in action—pervades and directs the *Sixth Vision*. It is a story which occurred in time and is recapitulated annually in the Church's liturgy, with a smaller weekly cycle culminating in the Easter of each Sunday. But it is a story with an end—and with it time is to end; until then, there is the cycle of man sinning, repenting, being forgiven, falling again, sustained only by God's promise of ultimate release from sin, a promise concretely embodied in the Eucharist received with especial devotion at Easter. The Sixth Vision is closely linked with the two that follow, and it displays the tightest thematic organization of any section of the poem. Earlier organizing devices had been the trial, the ploughing, the argument, the images of food and clothing, the image of charity as a tree; this triple vision is built around a battle, or rather two battles, a 'joust', which is a victory for the hero although he is seemingly overcome, and a siege, which is a real, if temporary, defeat for the hero's followers.

Throughout the narrative action, links are sustained with the themes of XVI and XVII through the character Faith. A mighty argument as well as an action is being worked out, as the debate of the Four Daughters of God and Christ's debate with Lucifer show. God's purpose is vindicated completely because his act is not pure *maistrie*, a show of superior force, but an assertion of wisdom and truth over the falsity of the devil. Thus Christ's binding of Lucifer with chains is intellectually as well as dramatically satisfying. But the triumph of Christ is not the triumph of the Church in history: that can only come at the end of time. The founding of the Church is God's initiative; but from there on man is an active partner in the work of salvation, and his weaknesses form a part of the enterprise as well as the strength which is divine in origin. In XIX the action of V is recapitulated in reverse: Piers is given the power of pardon *before* he begins to plough his field with spiritual seeds; but in so far as he represents the continuing human witness to Christ, his work is under continual threat from the powers opposed to God: 'Now is Piers to the plow. Pride it aspide . . .' (XIX 337). With the passing of the apostolic age, the defence of Christianity is in the hands of Conscience, who sums up all those who live conscientiously the faith they profess. If they are few, then the Church will be weak. Because grace requires a man's free will to co-operate with it, there can be no triumph of the Church over the world like that of Christ once for all over the power of the devil which assailed him. The holiness of the Church depends on man as well as God.

In the Seventh Vision the focus had been on the Christian community in history. The *Eighth Vision* opens with Will brought firmly back into the picture, and he is never completely lost sight of. We see him afflicted by age and making his choice between the world and the spirit; but the chief protagonist in this vision is Conscience, whose role corresponds closely to that of Piers in Passus VI. As Piers had called on Hunger for help against the wasters, Conscience calls on Kynde to desist from his punishment of sinners with plague. The Dreamer is caught up then in a world intoxicated with the pride of life in its most basic sense—the relief at having survived the Black Death which leads to belief in man's self-sufficiency and also to a new recklessness in the pursuit of worldly enjoyment and a new and total neglect of God. In the onslaught of sin upon those who are seeking, within Unity, to lead a life according to God's will, the sacrament of penance, which had been shown to be vital to the individual Haukyn, is also seen to be indispensable for the health of the community. The hypocrisy of the flattering friar corrupts this sacrament, which depends essentially on the sincerity of the penitent's contrition and on the maintaining of a truthful relationship with God. Now the threat has come from within: the friars are part of the Church. Even Conscience can be deceived, though he cannot be destroyed. He cannot leave Unity, but he must turn aside from the clergy whose standing has been so gravely compromised by their venal attitude to spiritual things. His only resort is the image of human charity in which the creative power of Kynde and the saving power of Grace unite to inspire and sustain the Christian in the darkest moments of history as, in his old age, the Dreamer, when physical power fails and death approaches. This image, Piers, now contains all the accumulated meaning which the developing understanding of Will has given it, and Piers Plowman's name is ringing in his ears as he awakes finally from his long series of visions.

VI LANGLAND'S POETIC ART

I have already touched briefly on the sublime qualities of Langland's poetry in the B-text (section III), qualities which have been appreciated by critics from Warton and Skeat to Lewis. The combination of the grand and the homely has been discussed with especial sensitivity by Nevill Coghill.[19] I wish here to concentrate on four aspects of his art which distinguish Langland from his fellow alliterative writers and his major contemporaries Chaucer and Gower. Three of these ally him more closely with a poet like Shakespeare—his delicately expressive rhythms, his wordplay, and his use of expanded metaphor and thematic imagery. One, his use of Latin words and phrases as part of his English verse, suggests affinities with medieval lyric poetry. I shall examine this first.

Latin quotations, usually not forming part of the English verse, play a major role in forwarding the argument of many passages in *Piers Plowman*. But sometimes Langland integrates the quoted phrases into the structure of the alliterative line. He does not necessarily expect his audience to *identify* the quotation: he often gives the source and the effect is not quite that of an Augustan poet 'quoting' from a classical source to delight his educated readers; but he seems to appeal to several levels of literacy in his audience. Thus Anima, warning Will not to enquire too closely into God's secrets, quotes from Proverbs a caution against eating too much honey and translates it for 'Englisshe men' (XV 55–9), reflecting in this the contemporary practice in sermons of translating Latin Biblical passages for the *lewed* congregation.[20] But when just a few lines later Anima quotes from St Bernard, while he gives his authority, he works the text into his English sentence, incorporating it into the metrical structure and offering no translation:

'*Beatus est*', seith Seint Bernard, '*qui scripturas legit*
Et verba vertit in opera* fulliche to his power' (XV 60–1).

Other examples in XV occur at 212, 215, 268–9 and 286, and their effect is to impart a singular depth and authority to the speaker's statements. The learned tongue was above all the sacred speech of prayer and worship, and something of the lustre of liturgical Latin rubs off on words and phrases not actually from the liturgy.

Langland may have learned this use of Latin to enrich English poetry from the macaronic lyrics, in which Latin phrases forming part of the rhyme scheme give resonance and theological depth to the homely vernacular, as in the well-known Marian song *Of One that is so Fair and Bright*:[21]

> Al the world it wes furlorn
>   thoru *eua peccatrice*
> toforn that ihesu was iborn
>   *ex te genitrice;*
> thorou *aue*, e wende awei,
> the thestri nist ant com the dai
>   *salutis,*
> the welle springet out of the
>   *virtutis.*

Here the first and second Latin phrases are free-standing—adding to the sense, not inseparably bound to the preceding syntax. The last two, directly dependent noun-genitives, operate differently, with an effect of disclosing hidden truths. The images of dawn and spring in the English carry directly to an uneducated reader (Christ as light of the world and living water); but the abstract Latin nouns give intellectual precision, for those who can render them, to the images, making the dawn 'salvation', the water 'goodness and strength', while not actually concealing anything from those who cannot, since the English already contains the sense in image-form. This lyric's nuances suggest private meditative prayer rather than public worship, and the bolder effects of Langland are more closely paralleled in macaronic processional carols such as *Make we joye nowe in this fest*:[22]

> A solis ortus cardine,
> So mythty a lord was none as he,
> For to oure kynde he hath yeve gryth,
> Adam parens quod polluit.

Here the Latin, untranslated, forms part of a narrative-argument, and the carol stands midway between English song and Latin hymn. The evidence that Langland learnt from such hymns is Anima's quotation in XV 387 from one of the most famous, *Pange lingua*, of a text comforting to the uneducated faithful served by negligent priests:

> Ac if thei overhuppe—as I hope noght—oure bileve suffiseth;
> As clerkes in Corpus Christi feeste syngen and reden
> That sola *fides sufficit* to save with lewed peple . . . (XV 385-7).

Langland's macaronic sublime reaches its peak in the Sixth Vision, Passus XVIII being richly veined with Gospel expressions from the readings of Holy Week. It is phrases like those quoted at 46–7, 50 and 57 which must have inspired him with the confidence to execute his interpretative innovations (we forget in the onrush of the poetry how theologically audacious Langıand's equation of Piers with Christ must have seemed to his first audience):

> 'This Jesus of his gentries wol juste in Piers armes,
> In his helm and in his haubergeon—*humana natura*.
> That Crist be noght biknowe here for *consummatus Deus*,
> In Piers paltok the Plowman this prikiere shal ryde;
> For no dynt shal hym dere as *in deitate Patris*' (XVIII 22–6).

The last phrase uses Latin to express an idea too difficult perhaps to translate; the first validates the already familiar chivalric metaphor with a Latin translucent if not quite transparent; while the second points forward to the unforgettable phrase quoted in full at 57—' "*Consummatum est*", quod Crist'—and delicately hints that the summit of divine goodness was reached in God's *kenosis*, his self-emptying to assume the humble human shape of the 'ploughman' clad in 'armour' no sturdier than a *paltok*.

The verse-rhythms of *Piers Plowman* often have the heavy emphasis characteristic of the form; but Langland has a special fondness for alliterating (especially but not exclusively in the second half-line) words of low semantic rank (i.e. not nouns, verbs and main adjectives). This tendency, from one standpoint a technical weakness, appears not in heightened sequences like those discussed but in quiet, undramatic passages, like the great forty-line sentence describing Haukyn in XIII 271–310. Here are six instances where the alliterating stressed syllable in the b-half is a pronoun, indefinite adjective, adverb, prefix and the verb *to be*. The stress-effect of vowel-alliterating lines like 281—'And inobedient to ben undernome of any lif lyvynge'—with its subsidiary consonant stress-patterns of *b* and *l*, is entirely characteristic of Langland, and quite unlike the rest of alliterative poetry. The effect of a line like XIII 260

> 'For er I have breed of mele, ofte moot I swete'

may be compared to that of Shakespeare's late verse, with its skilful counterpointing of speech-stresses against the metrical beat:

> for either thou
> Must as a foreign recreant be led
> With manacles through *our* streets, or else
> Triumphantly tread on thy country's ruin
>
> (*Coriolanus* V iii 113–6).

The last line shows Marlowe's canorous monotone replaced by a plangent but also kinetically imitative line of genuinely dramatic power, while in line 115, even more impressively, the 'little' word *our* is made to enact a sense both physical and rich in poignant ambiguity. It is towards a poetic texture of similar density that Langland, abandoning the typical qualities of the form, moves in his equally dramatic suggesting of the *effort* of Haukyn's work through placing the full stave-weight on the 'little' word *of* in the a-half, with which *ofte* in the b-half chimes emphatically. Another means to this effect of powerful bareness is his throwing the stress *off* the semantically higher and aurally more salient nouns *breed* and *mele* and the verb *moot*, although a perceptible secondary stress-pattern is set up by the *m*-alliteration under the main vowel-alliteration. Lines like this are not uncommon in *Piers Plowman*, and repay close study. They constitute an adventure into uncharted territory comparable to the Jacobean dramatists' movement from Elizabethan lyrical blank verse to a medium close to heightened speech. It is not impossible that Shakespeare learnt something from reading Langland; certainly the alliteration of the last line in the quoted passage is highly suggestive.

Another quality of Langland's poetry that constantly brings Shakespeare to mind is his wordplay. He not only puns more frequently than any English poet before Shakespeare, he uses the pun in a serious, responsible and illuminating way. His word-play may be said to grow out of his metre: the alliterative poet compelled to choose words beginning with the same sound often stumbles into homophony more easily than the writer of rhyming or blank verse. An apparent example of this process is XVIII 86, a line describing the result of Longeus' piercing of Christ's side:

> The blood sprong doun by the spere and unspered the knyghtes eighen.

But more memorable here than the play on *spere* and *unspered* is the bold compressed personification of Christ's healing blood opening Longeus' eyes (locked in blindness and so ignorance of the man he has pierced) which anticipates the image two hundred lines later of Christ's soul as a light unlocking hell to *lightliche bynde* Satan (269):

> A spirit speketh to helle and bit *unspere* the yates (261).

The intellectual excitement of Langland's poetry owes much to our sense that he is *exploring* experience through language. Exploration leads to discovery. We have to read the text with close attention—closer attention than Hopkins seems to have brought to it. Under the often plain surface, all is agitation and life. Another example is Haukyn's account of his slanders:

> 'Avenged me fele tymes other frete myselve withinne
> As a shepsteres shere, ysherewed men and cursed hem' (XIII 329–30).

The two verbs in 330 are near-synonyms; but the homophonic play on *shere* and *sherewed* compels attention to a meaning latent in the following psalm-quotation, which links *malediccione* 'cursing' with *lingua . . . gladius acutus*, though Langland's creation of a kind of metaphysical identity between the sharp instrument and the act of cursing one's fellow men is no more than hinted at by the Latin.

A no less serious and a more complex pun—witty as well as just—occurs in Peace's comment on the flattering friar (aptly called Sire *Penetrans-domos*) who 'was my lordes leche—and my ladies both'. Here he hints at the near-homophone *lecher*, but in the next line develops the 'physician' part of the image more effectively with another pun:

> 'He salved so our wommen til some were with child' (348).

Here the play is on 'heal' and 'greet (sexually)', *salue*, but a still further irony unfolds from the veiled allusion to the Annunciation (perhaps suggested by *my ladies* 347) which resulted in the Virgin Mary's conception of Christ the Saviour. The friar's salutations bring not healing (cf. 373) but 'enchantment' (379), a devilish undoing of the divine works of healing. These examples, chosen not quite at random, are far from exceptional; they point to the constant presence in Langland's poetry of vigorous and witty thought, as well as the piercing intuition and deep feeling which have always been recognized.

These qualities in potent combination characterize Langland's extended image of the Trinity as a blazing torch in Passus XVII. The effect here is one not of intense concentration, however, but of accumulation and extension. It is a mistake to approach this, any more than the preceding image of palm, fist and fingers, as a suasive analogy. Langland's aim seems to be to appeal to common experience in order to make ordinary people *feel* what the working of God's spirit in the soul is like. So he relies on our 'kynde knowyng' of cold and darkness and the season in which more than any other light cheers and fire sustains. From a miniature genre-scene of contemporary life of 'werkmen / That werchen and waken in wyntres nyghtes' (220–1) he moves to an equally homely figure for the Father and Son frozen into immobility by man's sin until the Holy Spirit 'flawmeth as fir' and 'melteth hire myght into mercy' (228–9)

> as men may se in wyntre
> Ysekeles in evesynges thorugh hete of the sonne
> Melte in a mynut while to myst and to watre (229–31).

The development of the image reaches its climax in the description of man's *unkyndenesse* as a wind 'that quencheth, as it were, / The grace of the Holy Goost', a supreme evil exemplified in the murder of the virtuous man, a 'torche' ablaze with divine grace:

> And whoso morthereth a good man, me thynketh, by myn inwit,
> He fordooth the levest light that Oure Lord lovyeth (281–2).

We may think of Othello's

> Put out the light, and then put out the light (V ii 7).

Othello sees Desdemona as the 'cunning'st pattern of excelling nature' and knows not 'where is that Promethean heat / That can thy light relume'. These are 'Renaissance' concepts alien to Langland, whose torch and taper are suggested by domestic reality and the immemorial symbolism of the Christian liturgy; but there is a genuine connaturality of poetic vision between Shakespeare, with his particular choice of situation and word, and Langland, seeing the 'fordoing' of a gracious human person (whether 'with mouth or with hondes', in body or reputation, by slander or murder) as the extinguishing of 'lif and love, the leye of mannes body' (278).

In discussing the structure, thematic development and art of *Piers Plowman* I have been attempting to offer readers familiar with Chaucer and the *Gawain-Pearl* poet suggestions in support of my claim for the work's standing as the greatest of medieval English poems. The scope of Langland's aim—to encompass human experience between the poles of tower and dungeon—is recognized; but he is still criticized for weak construction and prosaic style. I have tried to indicate, however summarily, that he possessed poetic genius adequate to his ambitious conception. I hope to argue this claim in detail in a forthcoming study and demonstrate that in the B-text, the most daring and dynamic of the poem's three versions, he fully achieved his aim.

VII THE TEXTUAL PROBLEMS OF THE B-VERSION

This section is intended to put before the reader certain basic conclusions which have emerged from my editing of the B-text. It is not offered as a summary of all the problems faced by an editor nor as an outline of editorial method; these would require a whole book. Individual problems are discussed, concisely but, I hope, fully, in the textual commentary as they arise.

THE MANUSCRIPTS

The B-version appears whole or in part in 18 MSS and 3 printed editions. Kane and Donaldson (pp. 14–15) reject MSS Huntington Library 114 and Sion College Arc. L. 40 2/E (MS S) as useless for editing; I have accordingly not consulted these. The rest are R (Oxford Bodleian MS Rawlinson Poetry 38, of which four leaves are BM Lansdowne 398, fols 77–80); F (Oxford, Corpus Christi College 201); L (Oxford Bodleian MS Laud Misc. 581, printed by Skeat and Bennett); M (British Museum Additional 35287); H (BM Harley 3954, a B-text only in Prol-V 127; see Ka, pp. 7–8); G (Cambridge University Library MS Gg. 4. 31); Y (Cambridge, Newnham College, Yates-Thompson MS); O (Oxford, Oriel College MS 79); C^2 (Cambridge University Library MS Ll. 4. 14); C (C.U.L. MS Dd. 1. 17); Bm (British Museum MS Additional 10574), Bo (Oxford, Bodley 814), Cot (BM Cotton Caligula A XI) (these three cited jointly as B when agreeing); W (Cambridge, Trinity College MS B. 15. 17, printed by Wright, K-D and in this edition); Hm (Huntington Library MS 128); Cr^1, Cr^2 Cr^3 (Robert Crowley's three prints of 1550, cited as Cr when agreeing).

The MSS are discussed by Skeat (II vi–xxx) and more fully by Kane and Donaldson (pp. 1–15). Sk's brief classification is superseded by K-D's exhaustive account (pp. 16–69), which is fundamental for textual criticism of the poem. The interested reader should consult expecially their table of variational groups on p. 21 and their discussion of the relations between the two families of MSS RF (which I call α) and WHmCrGYOC²CBLMH (which I call β) on pp. 63–9. I accept their argument that there was extensive convergent variation in all stages of transmission and also that each family constitutes a (defective) representative of a homogeneous B-tradition, not an earlier or later stage in the evolution of the poem. The blurring of genetic relations between groups and members of groups through the tendency of scribes to make the same mistake independently, and the bifid stemma produced by the independent descent of α and β from the archetype (Bx) are factors which effectively rule out editing by recension, for it becomes nearly impossible to eliminate from consideration the readings of any group or individual MS. This is the case even before we consider what evidence there is that MSS were corrected or contaminated from either lost B-MSS or the A and C traditions of the poem. Such evidence exists in the case of three and probably five witnesses (FGH, HmB). This makes elimination of F and of groups g and w (see diagram below) impossible, since some of the readings in question are superior on intrinsic grounds to those of the other MSS. The relationship between w, g and LMH is unknown, so no effective stemma can be made below the level of the sub-archetypes α and β. Finally, the retention in LMH of probable β readings by pure descent rules out the elimination of these witnesses in any case. Nevertheless, even if recension is not feasible, it is possible to acquire in the course of examining all the readings a certain understanding of the character and tendencies of particular MSS, even those like F which have a complex history. Some MSS *are* more trustworthy than others, even though this cannot be demonstrated for lack of space. The diagram below represents the lines of vertical transmission so far as these appear secure; lateral transmission is deliberately excluded but is discussed in reference to the individual MSS affected.

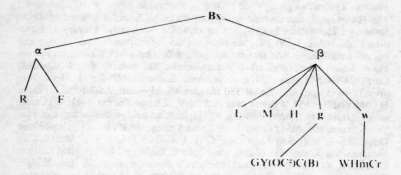

THE ARCHETYPE, SUB-ARCHETYPES AND GROUPS, AND INDIVIDUAL MANUSCRIPTS

The *Archetype* (Bx) is constructed from the sub-archetypes when they agree; from α or β when either appears superior on intrinsic grounds or in the light of secure readings in the A and C traditions; in a few cases from individual MSS where they are judged to preserve α or β either in isolation or against the other witnesses; by reconstruction when neither α nor β can be securely established.

The *Sub-archetypes* are judged by K-D to be of nearly equal value. My analysis shows α to be markedly superior. I adopt into the text some 500 α-readings, of which about 160 are not certain because supported by only one of the two available witnesses. Some 300 of these are supported by C, some 30 by A and some 70 by AC jointly, leaving just over 100 unsupported by the other traditions. By contrast I adopt only some 260 β-readings, of which about 13 are uncertain. Of these about 114 are supported by C, 13 by A and 8 by AC, leaving some 125, about half, unsupported by the other traditions. Both α and β *omit* about the same number of lines from Bx, but the above figures argue for making an α-MS the basis of the text. R appears right in some 140 readings (some 50 sole and 90 supported by other traditions) as against F in some 90 cases (about 70 supported by other traditions, the rest supported by F alone). Unfortunately R is seriously defective in the beginning and end of the poem, while F is a highly sophisticated MS from which α-readings have often to be recovered with difficulty. In default of a good α-MS being discovered, the B-text must be based on a β-MS. The obvious choice is L, the completest and best; but this is inferior to W in spelling and grammar, and since the text requires considerable emendation anyway, the accidentals become of great importance in guiding choice of the base-MS. Neither α nor β, so far as they can be recovered, shows signs of lateral transmission.

The *Groups* are g, w and L, M, H (which have group-status). g is adopted twice, in V 533 (supported by AC) and XIII 348 (supported by C) and twice when supported by one other B-MS, at XII 136 (F, with C) and XIX 15 (Hm, with C). In several other cases constituent members of g (including the sub-group B, Cot, a member of B, and O and C² severally) preserve what seems the correct and may be a group reading (see below), though I suspect either felicitous individual variation or lateral transmission. w nowhere stands as sole support for the text, but cannot be eliminated since its constituents WHmCr all provide what seems the correct (β = Bx) reading (confirmed by A, C or AC). I suspect lateral transmission in the case of *HmCr*, although Hm at XIII 330 may be a happy guess; while *W's* unsupported readings at I 154, XII 194, 195, I take as felicitous variations and those at VI 116, XV 551, XVII 20, XIX 111, supported by C, I take as examples of W varying to coincide with the C tradition. *L* provides the text in four readings (XIX 38, 41; XX 6, 87) where, supported by C, it is likely to stand in pure descent from β, which may even have been its exemplar. So regularly is it the best β witness, with no sign of lateral transmission, that I always correct W from L when β seems right and only turn to another β-MS in a few cases. *M* is less faithful to β than L but preserves by pure descent or possibly intelligent correction at XII 246, XV 73 (unsupported) and VI 119 (with AC), VIII 49 (with A). *H* is a B-text for less than a third of the poem, following B Prol-V 105 with A V 106-XI.

Individual manuscripts provide the text in some 65 cases, too many to specify here, in which support appears from one or both of the other traditions. In 11 cases, including those from W and M specified above, there is no support from A or C; most of the readings seem to me felicitous variations but correction from a B-tradition superior to that of Bx cannot be ruled out entirely. Each of these cases is discussed in the textual commentary, so there is no need to consider them here. But something must now be said about the problem of lateral transmission, which may affect several of the MSS. The two main possibilities are: correction from a superior B-tradition to that of Bx, or contamination from MSS of the A and C versions. I find little evidence for the former and a certain amount for the latter. Memorial contamination in particular is more than likely if the scribes of the B-MSS had also copied MSS of A and C. In some cases, e.g. *H* and *B*, the text includes one of the other versions. Crowley, we know, had examined other *Piers Plowman* MSS and may have adopted A or C readings (six of those in the text are supported by C, two by AC). *Hm* XIII 99 has a hard reading which may well come from C, and this serves to call in question the pure descent of its three other readings supported by AC. K-D believe that *F* (see pp. 165ff.) contains corrections from a superior B-tradition. I find, on the contrary, only two cases where F seems right *in the absence of* R, I 149 and XIX 403 (both unsupported from A or C) and each I take to stand for α. In the cases where F is adopted *in preference to*

R, usually with support from A or C, we need suppose only that R varied from α at this point and F did not. XI 106 is adopted from *G* as the hardest reading, but may be a felicitous correction by the G-scribe; the other 12 readings from G, supported by AC (Prol 182 by C) may be due to contamination from one or both other traditions. If a B-MS such as K-D hypothesize ever existed, it must have been superior by definition to α and β; yet no MS of either sub-archetypal tradition (F or G) shows any knowledge of the lines missing from the other, lines which must have been contained in the hypothetical source. The problem remains, however, after allowing for contamination of B-MSS from the A and C traditions (something which K-D do not consider), of what to do with the readings recognized as superior but also suspected as probably not derived from a B-source. I have adopted them, for reasons given below.

EMENDATION OF THE ARCHETYPE

Emendation of the Archetype is necessitated by the high incidence of corruption caused by the whole range of scribal tendencies to error analysed by Kane in the Introduction to his edition of the A-text and illustrated comprehensively by K-D in their Introduction, ch. III. I find some 750 corrupt readings which I think possible to correct; there are many more which I leave for lack of evidence upon which to emend. In emending I have followed a procedure broadly similar to that of K-D, though as the Textual Commentary shows, I frequently differ from them both in recognition of error and in correction of it. In *discriminating* readings, I frequently agree with them; in *emending*, I follow them in finding the B original preserved in the A or C tradition where strong arguments seem to me forthcoming. In about 160 cases I adopt the jointly attested reading of AC, in about 50 that of A, in about 130 that of C, in preference to Bx. The most persuasive argument for this procedure that I know is the fact that support from A and C in *discriminating* B-readings is so massive and points to the certainty that many A lines were never revised in B and many B lines never revised in C. (In some 250 cases the true B-reading can be discriminated amongst the B-MSS in the light of A, while the same may be done in the light of C in nearly 900 cases).

In a sense all emendation of the archetype, from A, AC, C or the individual B-MSS possibly contaminated from them, is a form of 'reconstruction'; and all reconstruction is a kind of 'conjecture'. Although at their extremes reconstruction (e.g. restoring the order of a b-half line so that it scans) and conjecture (supplying a word needed by the sense) are different activities, I do not distinguish them as sharply as K-D, and so in listing them I have added them together. As well as fourteen emendations from Skeat and one each from Wright and Bennett, I have adopted 260 of Kane and Donaldson's reconstructions and conjectures and added 163 of my own. This is fewer than K-D's total, partly because I sometimes disagree with them that Bx is corrupt and partly because I occasionally refrain from emending for lack of certainty either of corruption or of the worth of any available correction. Since this is a critical edition, I have examined each reading in the light of the evidence, including the AC readings, themselves not always certain; but I have been reluctant to diagnose corruption on grounds of sense, metre, or style *alone*. The metrical criteria I adopt may be gauged from the Appendix on Langland's verse. I have only emended *metri causa* when *none* of the three types of line (*aaax, aaaxy/aaabb, axax*) can be identified, and not always then; I have tried to bear in mind the possibility that Langland occasionally wrote lines less regular than those of the scribe of F, say, and also that his metrical practice changed from **B** to **C** as it seems to have changed from **A** to **B**.

I consider it the editor's duty, nonetheless, to print what he believes the author wrote, and to give reasons for his decision. If my text is nearer to that of Skeat than K-D's, it is not because I have deliberately sought to produce a 'conservative' edition. In coming to different conclusions from Kane and Donaldson I have often used their methods and considered possibilities and approaches first suggested by them. Naturally I believe that my text is nearer to the original than theirs; but in the end it is not the judgment of textual experts which ensures the acceptance of a reading or indeed of a text. There are many more experienced readers of Langland than scholars who have specialized in the analysis of textual problems. It is to their scrutiny that I offer my text and Commentary, and I hope that they will conclude I have done more to restore and illuminate than to damage and obscure the work of the poet they admire.

VIII EDITORIAL PROCEDURE

The text of this edition is based on MS Trinity College, Cambridge B. 15. 17, first printed by Thomas Wright in 1842 and used by Kane and Donaldson as the base of their Athlone Press edition. This MS (W) is the earliest of the B-MSS (about 1400) and although its text is far inferior to that of MS L it has the advantage of a regular spelling and grammatical system close to that of Langland's day. The MS closely resembles the work of the scribe of the Hengwrt and Ellesmere MSS of *The Canterbury Tales*.

TEXT

1 *Spelling*

I have printed the MS as it stands except that

   i All abbreviations are silently expanded

  ii Small spelling errors (a mere handful) and words damaged by cropping of the MS are silently corrected

 iii Obsolete ME letters are given their appropriate modern equivalent: *gh* or *y* for ȝ, *th* for þ

 iv The letters *v* and *j* are printed for MS *u* and *i* when their values are consonantal and *v* as *u* when a vowel; *s* is printed for *z* after *t* (*servaunts*); the name *Ihesu(s)* is printed *Jesu(s)*.

  v Capitalization is editorial, though I have taken note of the MS practice and sometimes followed its guidance

 vi All readings adopted from other MSS of **B** or the **A** and **C** texts are given in the spelling of W without notice.

2 *Punctuation and Paragraphing* are editorial, though I have examined the paragraph-division of W, L and other carefully paragraphed MSS and have often followed them. Other sectional divisions are editorial, and I have not recorded large capitals in the MS.

APPARATUS

1   I record the reading of W whenever the text departs from it, as also changes in lineation. In order to make the text pleasanter to read, I do not mark these, reserving square brackets exclusively for readings adopted from the A and C versions and for reconstructed or conjectural readings. The reader interested in B-readings preferred to W's should therefore consult the apparatus closely throughout.

2   The first entry in the Apparatus, the *lemma*, has the spelling of the MS it comes from. This should cause no difficulty, however, as the forms are nearly always easily identifiable and it has the advantage of giving the reader only authentic forms, so that the question of whether a reading is substantive or accidental cannot be obscured by normalized spelling. When one or more letters of the lemma are *italicized*, this means that MSS specified as supporting the reading except only the MS from which the lemma is taken contain different letters to those italicized. In most instances they are merely accidental variants, but the interested reader who is in doubt should consult the corpus of variants given by Kane and Donaldson. To save space, I frequently *abbreviate* both lemmata and variants, but not where difficulty in identifying the word(s) in the text might arise. I have checked against the originals all lemmata except the few taken from MS Hm, for which I have relied on K-D. *Lemmata from the A-text* come from Kane's text, or from his variants, in the few instances where I depart from his reading. Lemmata and all other readings from the *C-text* come from Huntington Library MS 143 (X), which I have consulted in the facsimile edited by R. W. Chambers. This is the MS used by Salter and Pearsall in their 'York' selections and is the basis of the forthcoming Athlone edition of the C-text. Where I have departed from MS X I have used readings, usually from the Trinity and Ilchester MSS (T and I), which may be identified in the apparatus to Skeat's C-text. Limitations of space prevent exact specification of the C-MS used where I reject X, but the most important cases are noted. I have followed the Passus-numbering to be adopted by the editor of the Athlone text, with 'Prologue' standing for 'Passus I' in Skeat's C-text and 'Passus XXII' for Skeat's 'XXIII', with corresponding adjustment throughout. However, in order to facilitate comparison, I have used Skeat's C-text line-numbering. This is to save the reader time and trouble and to make it possible to continue using the valuable 'Scheme of Contents' tables in Sk vol IV. i.

3   The *Sigla* include the B-MSS specified under 'The Manuscripts', p. xxxv above (*q.v.*), the symbols for the archetypal readings of each version, Ax, Bx and Cx, the group sigla α, β, w and g (on which see section VII of the Intro.) and the symbols A and C, representing the presumed originals of these versions respectively. The query sign is used where any of these is uncertain: thus ?A, C means that a reading is supported by the C version, about which there is no doubt, and by the A version, about which there is doubt.

4   *Other symbols* used in the Apparatus are (i) &r 'all B-MSS other than those (if any) specified elsewhere in the variant-entry', whether immediately after the lemma (e.g. Prol 29 *kairen*) or in later position (e.g. Prol 42); (ii) &c 'and

two or more other B-MSS'—used where extensive individual variation makes determination of group or sub-archetypal readings impossible; (iii). (*C*) 'see the Textual Commentary' for discussion of the reading; (iv) *so* K-D, Sk, etc. 'reading first printed by . . . .' In referring to Kane and Donaldson's edition I frequently give a page reference: if this comes after '*so* K-D' it means that I find their discussion there adequate and generally do not discuss the matter myself; if it comes after '*cf.* K-D' I mean that I differ from them but regard their discussion as persuasive and to be consulted; v) *rec* 'reconstructed by'.

GLOSSES AND TRANSLATIONS

1 The *marginal glosses* of words and phrases are on the generous side, especially towards the beginning of the text, and some words liable to cause difficulty are glossed more than once. The problems of Langland's syntax are dealt with in the footnote-translations, which sometimes become paraphrases. A capital letter is used to signalize the first word in the line. The sign / indicates an alternative rendering. Round brackets enclose words not in the original but needed to fill out the sense. Square brackets enclose elucidation of the meanings of words or phrases that cannot be translated easily and also Biblical and other quotations which Langland has quoted only in part.

2 Many *individual words* receive further discussion in the Commentary and (*C*) after a gloss or translation refers to this. Most (about sixty) are in the Textual and Lexical Commentary, but a few not arising from or bearing on textual problems appear in the Literary and Historical Commentary. Lack of space precludes a complete formal glossarial index, but most problems of meaning have been dealt with, though a number of difficulties of interpretation require the Textual Commentary to be consulted.

COMMENTARY

This is divided into two for ease of reference. The first part is mainly for the specialist and presupposes familiarity with the methods of textual criticism, but is probably not too technical for those interested to enquire into the basis of the edited text. It takes the place of a Textual Introduction and should be easier to use, especially for the beginner. To save space, quotations are usually abbreviated, and the Commentary needs to be used in close conjunction with the text and variants. The second part provides the student with literary and historical information needed to understand the text and a small amount of general interpretative comment. Limits of space have meant keeping documentation to a minimum; for this the longer notes of Skeat and Bennett should be consulted, along with the books and articles referred to by short title. For convenience to the reader I have used easily accessible standard works such as Poole's *Medieval England*, the Oxford English History, the Middle English readers of Sisam and Bennett & Smithers, and a number of secondary works many of which are available in paperback. I have used the Colunga-Turrado edition of the Vulgate Bible (Madrid, 1965) and the Douay-Rheims Version for translations. Psalms are therefore numbered according to the practice of these versions, as are Biblical books (Kings I and II are I and II Sam in A.V.). Full details of works cited and a selection of those consulted are given in the Bibliography unless given in full *ad loc.*

THE INTRODUCTION
This is designed to acquaint the student with basic background information about the poem and its author, to offer an interpretative sketch of the whole work and to give a concise account of the textual problems facing the editor. The sections on Structure, Themes and Poetic Art are kept brief since there is a considerable amount of detailed literary discussion in the Commentary.

ABBREVIATIONS
These are the standard ones, the most frequent being *OED* Oxford English Dictionary; *MED* Middle English Dictionary, ed. H. Kurath and S. M. Kuhn (Ann Arbor, Michigan); *CT The Canterbury Tales*; *P.L. Patrologia Latina*, ed. J. P. Migne; Bn J. A. W. Bennett's edition of B Prol and Passus I–VII; Ka George Kane's edition of the A-text; K-D George Kane and E. Talbot Donaldson's edition of the B-text; Sk W. W. Skeat's Early English Text Society edition of *Piers Plowman*, versions A, B and C, in four parts (SkC= Sk's C-text); S-P E. Salter and D. S. Pearsall's edition of selections from the C-text; Wr Thomas Wright's 1887 edition of the B-text; *SB Breviarium ad Usum Insignis Ecclesiae Sarum*, ed. F. Procter and C. Wordsworth (3 vols., Cambridge, 1879); *ST* the *Summa Theologica* of St Thomas Aquinas (Madrid, 1961); *OBMLV The Oxford Book of Medieval Latin Verse*, ed. F. J. Raby.

Notes

1   For a concise summary of the relations between the three versions, see Kane and Donaldson, *B-version*, pp. 70–3. Passus XII of A is found only in MSS RUJ, of which U breaks off at line 19a and J at line 88, the final nineteen lines appearing only in MS R; see Kane, *PP: the A-version*.
2   Especially important is their article 'The Text of "Piers Plowman" ' (*MLR* 26 (1931) 1–51) and Chambers's facsimile of C-MS Hm 143.
3   Easily accessible in Sisam, *C14th V & P*, pp. 160–1.
4   *PP: The Evidence for Authorship* (1965).
5   Reproduced in pl. 1, *Evidence*.
6   See generally George Kane, *The Autobiographical Fallacy in Chaucer and Langland Studies* (1965).
7   'John But, Messenger and Maker' (*MP* 11 (1913–14), 107–116).
8   'The Audience of *PP*' (*Anglia* 75 (1957), 373–84).
9   'The Date of the A-Text of PP' (*PMLA* 58 (1943), 566–72).
10   'The Date of the B-Text of PP' (*MÆ* 12 (1943), 55–64).
11   McKisack, *The Fourteenth Century* (Oxford, 1959). p. 436.
12   T. Turville-Petre, *The Alliterative Revival* (Brewer, Cambridge, 1977); S. S. Hussey, 'Langland's Reading of Alliterative Poetry' (*MLR* 60 (1965), 163–70); E. Salter, '*PP* and "The Simonie" ' (*Archiv für das Studium der neueren Sprachen und Literaturen* 203 (1967), 241–54).
13   The last two are discussed by A. C. Spearing in *Medieval Dream-Poetry*, pp. 162–70.
14   *The Letters of Gerard Manley Hopkins to Robert Bridges*, ed. C. C Abbot (Oxford, 1935), p. 156.

15 *The Allegory of Love* (Galaxy repr. N.Y. 1958), p. 161.
16 J. A. Burrow, 'The Action of Langland's Second Vision' (*EC* 15 (1965),
247–68, repr. Blanch, *Style*, pp. 209–27); R. W. Frank, *PP and the Scheme of
Salvation* (New Haven, 1957).
17 In his article, 'Action', cited above.
18 Frank, 'Pardon Scene'; Miss Woolf's learned and ingenious argument that the
pardon represents God's bare justice and its tearing the mercy and forgiveness
shown in the Redemption (Woolf, 'Tearing') I find attractive but unconvincing
in context.
19 'God's Wenches and the Light that Spoke (Some notes on Langland's kind of
poetry)', in *English and Medieval Studies presented to J. R. R. Tolkien*, ed. Norman
Davis and C. L. Wrenn (1962), pp. 200–18.
20 On Langland and pulpit rhetoric see A. C. Spearing, 'The Art of Preaching
and *PP*', in his *Criticism and Medieval Poetry* (2nd edn 1972), pp. 107–34, and
G. R. Owst, *Literature and Pulpit in Medieval England* (2nd edn, Blackwell,
Oxford), index *s.v.*
21 No. 17 in Carleton Brown, ed., *English Lyrics of the XIIIth Century* (Oxford,
1932).
22 No. 12 in Richard Greene, ed., *A Selection of English Carols* (Oxford, 1962).

† *Additional Note* (1984)

Since the appearance of the second printing of this book, there has been published
an important contribution to our understanding of *Piers Plowman*, an edition of
the text in MS Bodley 851 by A. G. Rigg and Charlotte Brewer, *Piers Plowman:
the Z Version* (Toronto, Pontifical Institute of Mediaeval Studies, 1983). I am con-
vinced by the argument of the editors that this represents a draft version of the
poem anterior to the A-text. In addition to the arguments from the version's
structural coherence and original lines, the presence in 'Z' of a unique type of
'transitional' alliterative line (see Appendix, p. 360) points to its being authentic
Langland (I discuss this question in a forthcoming study of 'The Authenticity of
the Z-text: an examination of the metrical criteria' *MÆ* LIII (1984)).

Bibliography

The Bibliography includes all books and articles referred to by short title in the Introduction and Commentary and a selection of the main works consulted but not specifically mentioned. The place of publication of books is London unless otherwise specified. (A useful aid to study is A. J. Colaianne: *Piers Plowman. An Annotated Bibliography of Editions and Criticism 1550–1977* (New York/London, 1978).)

Aers, David: *PP and Christian Allegory* (1975).

Alford, John A.: 'Note on *PP* B XVIII 390: "Til Parce It Hote"', *MP* 69 (1972), 323–5.

'Haukyn's Coat: Some Observations on *PP* B XIV 22–27', *MÆ* 43 (1974), 133–38.

'Some Unidentified Quotations in *PP*', *MP* 72 (1975), 390–99.

'The Role of the Quotations in *PP*', *Spec.* 52 (1977), 80–99.

Anderson, M. D.: *History and Imagery in British Churches* (1971).

Arias, L. (ed.): *Tratado sobre La Santisima Trinidad* (Madrid, 1968). [Augustine's *De Trinitate*].

Bennett, H. S.: *Life on the English Manor* (Cambridge, 1937, repr. 1974).

Bennett, J. A. W.: 'The Date of the B-Text of *PP*', *MÆ* 12 (1943), 55–64.

Bennett, J. A. W. and Smithers, G. V.: *Early Middle English Verse and Prose* (Oxford, 1966).

Blanch, Robert J. (ed.): *Style and Symbolism in PP: A Modern Critical Anthology* (Knoxville, 1969).

Bliss, A. J. (ed.): *Sir Orfeo* (Oxford, 2nd edn. 1966).

Bloomfield, M. W.: *The Seven Deadly Sins* (Michigan, 1952).

'*PP* and the Three Grades of Chastity', *Anglia* 76 (1958), 227–53.

PP as a Fourteenth Century Apocalypse (New Brunswick, 1961).

Bradley, Henry: 'Some Cruces in *PP*', *MLR* 5 (1910), 340–2.

Chambers, R. W. (ed.): *PP: The Huntington Library MS (HM 143)* (San Marino, Calif., 1936).

Chroust, A-H.: *Aristotle* (2 vols., 1973).

Cohn, Norman: *The Pursuit of the Millenium* (Paladin, repr. 1972).

Comparetti, D.: *Vergil in the Middle Ages*, tr. E. F. M. Beneche (repr. 1966).

Daly, S. R.: 'Peter Comestor: Master of Histories', *Spec.* 32 (1957) 62–73.

Davis, Norman (ed.): *Non-cycle Plays and Fragments*, EETS, S.S.1(1970).

Davlin, Sr. M. C.: '*Kynde Knowynge* as a Major Theme in *P.P. B*', *RES* n.s. 22 (1971), 1–19.

Donaldson, E. T.: *PP: The C-Text and its Poet* (New Haven and London, 1949).

'The Grammar of Book's Speech in *PP*', *Schlauch Studies*, Warsaw 1966, repr. Blanch, 264–70.

Bibliography

Doob, P. B. R.: *Nebuchadnezzar's Children: Conventions of Madness in M. E. Literature* (New Haven and London, 1974).

Dunning, T. P.: 'Langland and the Salvation of the Heathen', *MÆ* 12 (1943), 45–54.

'The Structure of the B-text of *PP*', *RES* n.s. 7 (1956), 225–37, repr. Blanch.

Evans, J. and Serjeantson, M.: *English Medieval Lapidaries* EETS O.S. 190 (1933).

Frank, R. W.: 'The Pardon Scene in *PP*', *Spec.* 26 (1951), 317–31.

'The Art of Reading Medieval Personification-Allegory', *ELH* 20 (1953), 237–50.

PP and the Scheme of Salvation (New Haven, 1957).

Freud, S. (tr. Strachey): *The Interpretation of Dreams* (1954).

Gaffney, W.: 'The Allegory of the Christ-Knight in *PP*', *PMLA* 46 (1931), 155–68.

Gilchrist, J.: *The Church and Economic Activity in the Middle Ages* (1969).

Goodridge, J. F., trans.: *Piers the Ploughman* (Penguin, 1959, 2nd edn. 1966).

Harwood, Britton J.: 'Clergye and the Action of the Third Vision in *PP*', *MP* 70 (1973), 279–90.

'Liberum Arbitrium in the C-Text', *PQ* 52 (1973), 680–95.

'Imaginative in *PP*', *MÆ* 44 (1975), 249–63.

Harwood, Britton J. and Smith, R. F.: 'Inwit and the Castle of *Caro* in *PP*', *Neuphilologische Mitteilungen* 71 (1970), 48–54.

Hassall, W. O.: *The Holkham Bible Picture Book* (1954).

Hort, G.: *PP and Contemporary Religious Thought* (1938).

Hulme, W. H. (ed.): *The Middle English Harrowing of Hell and Gospel of Nicodemus*, EETS E.S. 100 (1907).

Huppé, B. F.: 'The Date of the B-Text of *PP*', *SP* 38 (1941), 36–44.

' *Petrus, id est, Christus*: Word Play in P.P.' *ELH* 17 (1950), 163–90.

Hussey, S. S.: 'Langland, Hilton and the Three Lives', *RES* n.s. 7 (1956), 132–50.

'Langland's Reading of Alliterative Poetry', *MLR* 60 (1965), 163–70.

(ed.): *PP: Critical Approaches* (1969).

Jenkins, Priscilla: 'Conscience: The Frustration of Allegory', in Hussey, *Approaches*, 125–42.

Jones, H. S. V.: 'Imaginatif in *PP*', *JEGP* 13 (1914), 583–8.

Jusserand, J. J.: *English Wayfaring Life in the Middle Ages* (1899).

Kane, George: *Piers Plowman: The A Version* (1960).

Piers Plowman: The Evidence for Authorship (1965).

Kane, G. and Donaldson, E. T.: *Piers Plowman: The B Version* (1975).

Kaske, R. E. 'Gigas the Giant in *PP*', *JEGP* 56 (1957), 177–85.

'The Speech of "Book" in *PP*', *Anglia* 77 (1959), 117–44.

' "*Ex vi transicionis*" and Its Passage in *PP*', *JEGP* 62 (1963), 32–60, repr. with revisions, in Blanch 228–63.

'Holy Church's Speech and the Structure of *PP*', in B. Rowland, ed.: *Chaucer and M.E.: Studies in honour of R. H. Robbins* (1974).

Kean, P. M.: 'Love, Law and *Lewte* in *PP*', *RES* n.s. 15 (1964), 241–61' repr. in Blanch, 132–55.
'Langland on the Incarnation', *RES* n.s. 16 (1965), 349–63.
'Justice, Kingship and the Good Life in the Second Part of *PP*', in Hussey, *Approaches*, 76–110.

Keen, M.: *The Pelican History of Medieval Europe* (repr. 1975).

Kirk, Rudolf: 'References to the Law in *PP*', *PMLA* 48 (1933), 322–8.

Leff, Gordon: *Medieval Thought: St. Augustine to Ockham* (Pelican, 1958).

Lewis, C. S.: *The Discarded Image* (Cambridge, 1964).

McKisack, May: *The Fourteenth Century, 1307–1399* (Oxford, 1959).

Maguire, S.: 'The Significance of Haukyn, *Activa Vita*, in *PP*', *RES* 25 (1949) 97–109; repr. Blanch, *Style and Symbolism in PP*.

Mâle, Emile: *The Gothic Image*, tr. D. Nussey (Fontana, 1961).

Mann, Jill: *Chaucer and Medieval Estates Satire* (Cambridge, 1973).

Marcett, M. E.: *Uthred de Boldon, Friar William Jordan and PP* (N.Y., 1938).

Middleton, Anne: 'Two Infinities: Grammatical Metaphor in *PP*', ELH 39 (1972), 169–88.

Mitchell, A. G.: 'Lady Meed and the Art of *PP*', Chambers Memorial Lecture 1956, repr. in Blanch, 174–93.

Mustanoja, T. F.: 'The Suggestive Use of Christian Names in M.E. Poetry', in J. Mandel and B. A. Rosenberg (eds.), *Medieval Literature and Folklore Studies: Essays in Honour of Francis Lee Utley* (New Brunswick, N.J., 1970), 51–76.

Offord, M. Y.: *The Parlement of the Thre Ages*, EETS 246 (1959).

Orsten, E. M.: '"Heaven on Earth"—Langland's Vision of Life Within the Cloister' (*American Benedictine Review*, 1970; seen in summary only).

Owen, D. L.: *Piers Plowman: A Comparison with some earlier and contemporary French Allegories* (1912).

Peebles, R. J.: 'The Legend of Longinus in ecclesiastical art and in English Literature', *Bryn Mawr Monographs* 9 (1911).

Poole A. L. (ed.): *Medieval England* (2 vols., Oxford, 1958).

Postan, M. M.: *The Medieval Economy and Society* (Pelican 1972, repr. 1975).

Quirk, R.: 'Langland's Use of *Kind Wit* and *Inwit*', *JEGP* 52 (1953), 182–9.

Raby, F. J. E.: *The Oxford Book of Medieval Latin Verse* (Oxford, 1974).

Rosental, J. T.: *The Purchase of Paradise: Gift-Giving and the Aristocracy, 1307–1485* (1972).

Russell, G. H.: 'The Salvation of the Heathen, The Exploration of a Theme in *PP*', Journal of the Warburg and Courtauld Institutes 29 (1966), 101–16.
'Some Aspects of the Process of Revision in the C-Text of *PP*', in Hussey, *Approaches*, 27–49.

St. Jacques, R.: 'Langland's "Spes" the Spy and the Book of Numbers', *N&Q* n.s. 24 (1978), 483–5.
'Liturgical Associations of Langland's Samaritan', *Traditio* 25 (1969), 217–30.

Salter, E. and Pearsall, D.: *Piers Plowman* [*Selections from the C-Text, with Introduction*], York Medieval Texts (1967).

Schmidt, A. V. C.: 'A Note on the Phrase "Free Wit" in the C-Text of *PP*, XI 51', *N&Q* n.s. 15 (1968), 168–9.

'A Note on Langland's Conception of "Anima" and "Inwit"', *N&Q* n.s. 15 (1968), 363–4.

'Two Notes on *PP*', *N&Q* n.s. 16 (1969), 168–9.

'Langland and Scholastic Philosophy', *MÆ* 38 (1969), 134–56.

Schroeder, Mary C.: '*PP*: The Tearing of the Pardon', *PQ* 49 (1970), 8–18.

Schweitzer, Edward C.: '"Half a Laumpe Lyne in Latyne" and Patience's Riddle in *PP*', *JEGP* 73 (1974), 313–27.

Sisam, K. (ed.): *C 14th Verse and Prose* (Oxford, repr. 1962).

Smalley, Beryl: *English Friars and Antiquity in the Early Fourteenth Century* (Oxford, 1960).

Smith, Ben H.: 'Patience's Riddle: *PP* B XIII', *MLN* 76 (1961), 675–82.

Traditional Imagery of Charity in PP (The Hague, 1966).

Southern, R. W.: *Western Society and the Church in the Middle Ages* (Pelican, 1970).

Spearing, A. C.: *Medieval Dream-Poetry* (Cambridge, 1976).

Stanley, E. G.: 'The B Version of *PP*: A New Edition', *N&Q* n.s. 22 (1976), 435–7.

Strutt, J. (ed. Cox): *The Sports and Pastimes of the People of England* (1903 edn. repr. 1969).

Thomson, J. A. F.: 'Piety and Charity in late medieval London', *Journal of Eccl. Hist.* 16 (1965), 178–95.

Vernet, F.: *Medieval Spirituality* (Eng. edn. 1930).

Webb, J. (ed.): *A Roll of the Household Expenses of Richard de Swinfield, Bishop of Hereford* [*during*] *1298–90* (Camden Society, 1854).

Willard, J.: 'Illustrations of the Origin of *Cy Près*', *Harvard Law Review* 8 (1894–5), 69–92.

Wilson, Edward: *The Gawain-Poet* (Leiden, 1976).

Woolf, Rosemary: 'The Tearing of the Pardon', in Hussey, *Approaches*, 50–75.

Wright, T. (ed.): *The Anglo-Latin Satirical Poets and Epigrammatists of the C 12th*, Rolls Ser. 59 (1872).

The Latin Poems commonly attributed to Walter Mapes (Camden Society, 1841).

Political Poems and Songs relating to English History, Rolls Ser. 14 (2 vols.), 1859.

Yunck, John A.: *The Lineage of Lady Meed: The Development of Medieval Venality Satire* (Notre Dame, Indiana, 1963).

Ziegler, P.: *The Black Death* (Pelican, repr. 1971).

Zupitza, J. (ed.): *The Romance of Guy of Warwick*, EETS E. S. 42 (1883).

Prologue

In a somer seson, whan softe was the sonne,	*mild; sun*
I shoop me into shroudes as I a sheep were,	
In habite as an heremite unholy of werkes,	
Wente wide in this world wondres to here.	*hear*
5 Ac on a May morwenynge on Malverne hilles	*But; morning*
Me bifel a ferly, of Fairye me thoghte.	*marvel*
I was wery forwandred and wente me to reste	
Under a brood bank by a bourne syde;	
And as I lay and lenede and loked on the watres,	*leaned (over)*
10 I slombred into a slepyng, it sweyed so murye.	
Thanne gan I meten a merveillous swevene—	*dream (v. & n.)*
That I was in a wildernesse, wiste I nevere where.	*uninhabited place; knew*
A[c] as I biheeld into the eest an heigh to the sonne,	*east; high*
I seigh a tour on a toft trieliche ymaked,	*knoll; choicely*
15 A deep dale bynethe, a dongeon therinne,	*valley; dungeon*
With depe diches and derke and dredfulle of sighte.	*dark*
A fair feeld ful of folk fond I ther bitwene—	*field; found*
Of alle manere of men, the meene and the riche,	*kinds; humble*
Werchynge and wandrynge as the world asketh.	*Working; requires*
20 Somme putten hem to the plough, pleiden ful selde,	*themselves; seldom*
In settynge and sowynge swonken ful harde,	*planting; toiled*
And wonnen that thise wastours with glotonye destruyeth.	
	obtained that which

2 I dressed myself in garments as if I were a sheep (C).
6 I had a strange and marvellous experience, from the land of Fairy (=of a super-
   natural kind), it seemed (C).
7 I was tired, having wandered astray, and turned aside to rest myself.
10 I fell into a sleep, it (the stream) made so sweet a sound (C).
11 Then I proceeded to dream a wonderful dream.
14 I saw a tower upon a hillock, elegantly built.
20 Some devoted themselves to ploughing, very rarely took a holiday.

Prologue] *Prologus* A–MS R (*so* Sk) (*C*).
2 into] w (?=β) F (?=a), AC; in
   rest exc. B; R *def. to* 125 (*C*).
   shroudes] W&r, ?C; shro*u*bes Cr,
   many C–MSS; a shroude H, A (*C*).
   sheep] schep H, ?A, C (*C*).
7 forwandred] β, ?A; of wandrynge
   Cr, F (?=a) H, some A–MSS
   (*cf. also* C).

8 bourne] CrGH, F (?=a), A;
   bournes W&r (?=β).
10 sweyed] WF&c; sweyued L&c;
   sweuenyd H, *some* A–MSS (*C*).
13 Ac] A (*so* K–D); And W; *om* L&r(*C*).
20 þe] *om* FG, *some* AC–MSS; *cf.* Ka
   p. 433.
22 þese] F (?=a), AC; *om* W&r
   (?=β); *see* K–D *pp*. 154, 165.

And somme putten hem to pride, apparailed hem therafter,

dressed; accordingly

In contenaunce of clothynge comen disgised.
25 In preieres and penaunce putten hem manye,   *prayers*
    Al for the love of Oure Lord lyveden ful streyte   *strictly, ascetically*
    In hope to have heveneriche blisse—
    As ancres and heremites that holden hem in hire selles,   *cells*
    Coveiten noght in contree to cairen aboute
30 For no likerous liflode hire likame to plese.
    And somme chosen chaffare; they cheveden the bettre— *trade; succeeded*
    As it semeth to oure sight that swiche men thryveth;   *prosper*
    And somme murthes to make as mynstralles konne,   *entertain; know how*
    And geten gold with hire glee—[gilt]lees, I leeve.   *singing; believe*
35 Ac japeres and jangeleres, Judas children,   *jesters; chatterers*
    Feynen hem fantasies, and fooles hem maketh—   *Devise; fools*
    And han wit at wille to werken if they wolde.
    That Poul precheth of hem I wol nat preve it here: *St Paul; prove*
    Qui loquitur turpiloquium is Luciferes hyne.   *servant*
40   Bidderes and beggeres faste aboute yede   *Beggars; went*
    [Til] hire bely and hire bagge [were] bredful ycrammed, *belly; brimful*
    Faiteden for hire foode, foughten at the ale. *Begged falsely; ale house*
    In glotonye, God woot, go thei to bedde,   *gluttony; knows*
    And risen with ribaudie, tho Roberdes knaves; *obscenities; vagabonds (C)*
45 Sleep and sory sleuthe seweth hem evere.   *wretched sloth; follow*
    Pilgrymes and palmeres plighten hem togidere *vowed, pledged themselves*
    For to seken Seint Jame and seintes at Rome;   *seek St James (C)*

---

24 Came tricked up in an outward show of (fine) array.
27 In the hope of obtaining the blessed happiness of the kingdom of heaven.
28–30 (Such) as anchorites and hermits who keep to their cells And have no
    desire to go wandering about the land In order to indulge their bodies with
    luxurious living.
36–7 Think up grotesque forms of amusement and turn themselves into buffoons
    Though they possess the free use of their intelligence, should they wish to work.
38–9 That which St Paul preaches concerning them I will not exemplify here—
    (that) 'He who utters foul speech' is the devil's serving-man (C).

24 dis-] L&r, A; de-W.
25 pen.] L&r, A; *pl.* WHmF, *most*
    C-MSS.
27 haue] L&r *exc* F, A; h. after wGH
    (a.] þera. H).
29 Coueiten] AC; And c. Bx; *see*
    K-D *p.* 151.
    kairen] LMGO, F (?=α), ?AC;
    carien W&r (*exc* C), *most*
    AC-MSS.
34 giltlees] A (*sugg.*Wr); synnelees
    W&r (not s. OC²) (*C*).
    leeue] trowe GH, A (*C*).

37 wit] F (?=α) H, AC; hire w.
    W&r (?=β).
    wolde] WH, C; sholde L&r (?=Bx)
39 *Line om* F.
    Qui] L&r, A; But *Qui* W.
41 *Line om* F.
    Til . . . ycr.] AC (b./b. *trsp.* C);
    Wiþ h.b.a.h.b. of breed f.ycr. ?Bx
    (of *om* H; b./b.] L&c, *pl.* W&c).
42 fouȝten] W&r (?=β); & f.
    F (?=α) H, C, *many* A-MSS.
44 risen] W&r, C; r.vp FH, *some*
    A-MSS.

Wenten forth in hire wey with many wise tales,	*way; speeches*
And hadden leve to lyen al hire lif after.	*leave; tell lies; life*
50 I seigh somme that seiden thei hadde ysought seintes:	*saw; said*
To ech a tale that thei tolde hire tonge was tempred to lye	*tongue; tuned*
Moore than to seye sooth, it semed bi hire speche.	*truth*
Heremytes on an heep with hoked staves	*crowd; crooked*
Wenten to Walsyngham—and hire wenches after:	
55 Grete lobies and longe that lothe were to swynke	*lubbers; tall; labour*
Clothed hem in copes to ben knowen from othere,	*Dressed; distinguished*
And shopen hem heremytes hire ese to have.	
	turned themselves into; comfort, ease
I fond there freres, alle the foure ordres,	
Prechynge the peple for profit of [the wombe]:	*belly (cf. Phil 3: 19)*
60 Glosed the gospel as hem good liked;	*Expounded; at will*
For coveitise of copes construwed it as thei wolde.	*greed; interpreted*
Manye of thise maistres mowe clothen hem at likyng	
	Masters; can; as they like
For hire moneie and hire marchaundise marchen togideres.	
	money; merchandise
Sith charite hath ben chapman and chief to shryve lordes *(a)*	*merchant; confess*
65 Manye ferlies han fallen in a fewe yeres.	*strange events*
But Holy Chirche and hii holde bettre togidres	*Unless; they; co-operate*
The mooste meschief on molde is mountynge up faste.	
	greatest misfortune; earth
Ther preched a pardoner as he a preest were:	*as if he were a priest*
Broughte forth a bulle with bisshopes seles,	*bull (C); seals*
70 And seide that hymself myghte assoillen hem alle	*absolve*
Of falshede of fastynge, of avowes ybroken.	*deceit; vows*
Lewed men leved hym wel and liked hise wordes,	*Uneducated; believed*
Comen up knelynge to kissen his bulle.	*Came; on their knees*
He bonched hem with his brevet and blered hire eighen,	*struck; dimmed; eyes*
75 And raughte with his rageman rynges and broches.	*got; bull; brooches*

63 For the money (they obtain) tallies with the wares (they offer in return).
64 Since (those who should stand for) Charity have become sellers of wares and foremost (in wishing) to hear the confessions of noblemen . . .
67 The forces making for a calamitous upheaval are rapidly reaching full strength.
74–5 He struck them with his letter of indulgence and bedimmed their sight And obtained by means of his official document rings and brooches (*sc.* in payment for pardon) (*C*).

48 Wenten] AC (*so* K-D); They w. W&r (T.] & F).
50–4 om F; *50–2 possibly spurious; see* (*C*).
59 þe w.] AC (*so* K-D); her wombys H; hemselue W&r (?=Bx).
62 Maystris] F (?=α) G, A (*so* K-D); *cf.* C; m. Freris LW (m.*sg.* W). mowe] L&r (?=Bx), AC; now W.

64 Siþ] A; For s. *All* B-MSS; Ac s. C; *see* K-D *p.* 86.
67 vp] G, ?A, C (*so* K-D); vp wel C²O; wel W&r (om F).
69 with] L&r, AC; w. many wGH.
72 hym] L&r (hem F), AC; it W.
73 h.b.] F (?=α) H, A (*so* K-D); *pl.* W&r (?=β), C.

3

The Vision of Piers Plowman

—Thus ye gyven youre gold glotons to helpe, *gluttonous rogues*
And leneth it losels that leccherie haunten! *hand it to wretches; indulge in*
Were the bisshop yblessed and worth bothe his eris, *holy; ears*
His seel sholde noght be sent to deceyve the peple. *seal (of authorization)*
80 Ac it is noght by the bisshop that the boy precheth— *fellow, rogue*
For the parisshe preest and the pardoner parten the silver *divide*
That the povere [peple] of the parissche sholde have if they ne were.
poor people
Persons and parisshe preestes pleyned hem to the bisshop
Rectors; vicars; complained
That hire parisshes weren povere sith the pestilence tyme, *poor; since; plague*
85 To have a licence and leve at London to dwelle, *official permission*
And syngen ther for symonie, for silver is swete. *sing (masses) for payment*
Bisshopes and bachelers, bothe maistres and doctours— *b., m., d. of divinity*
That han cure under Crist, and crownynge in tokene
And signe that thei sholden shryven hire parisshens, *parishioners*
90 Prechen and praye for hem, and the povere fede— *feed*
Liggen at Londoun in Lenten and ellis. *Reside; Lent; other times*
Somme serven the King and his silver tellen, *keep account of*
In Cheker and in Chauncelrie chalangen his dettes *make demand for*
Of wardes and of wardemotes, weyves and streyves. *'waifs and strays'*
95 And somme serven as servaunts lordes and ladies,
And in stede of stywardes sitten and demen. *(the) position; judge*
Hire messe and hire matyns and many of hire houres
Mass(es); divine offices
Arn doone undevoutliche; drede is at the laste *are done undevoutly; dread*
Lest Crist in Consistorie acorse ful manye! *(his) Court (C); condemn*
100 I parceyved of the power that Peter hadde to kepe—
comprehended; in his keeping
To bynden and unbynden, as the Book telleth— *Bible (Mt 16: 15)*
How he it lefte with love as Oure Lord highte *commanded (cf. Lk 22: 32)*
Amonges foure vertues, most vertuous of alle vertues, *powerful*

80 It is not in accordance with (the intentions of) the bishop that the rogue preaches (C).
88 Who have the responsibility under Christ and the (clerical) tonsure as a symbol . . .
93–4. In the (courts of) Exchequer and Chancery claim the dues arising to him From guardianship-cases [Bx] and from ward-meetings and from lost property and strayed beasts.
96 And in the position(s) of stewards (in manorial households) sit and pass judgment (in the manor courts) (C).

76 ȝe] AC (*so* K-D); þei β; men F (?=α); þe puple H.
ȝoure] AC; hire Bx; *see* K-D *p.* 79.
helpe] H, AC (*so* K-D); kepe W&r (?=Bx).
77 losels] AC; swiche l. W&r (?=β); þo l. F; *see* K-D, *p.* 80.
þat] L&r (=Bx), AC; as WCr.

82 *Line om* H.
p.peple] AC (*so* K-D); p. poraille YOC²M (?=β); por. WHmLC; p. men F (?=α) (C).
103 most v.] F (?=α), C; (þe) beste W&r (=β).
alle v.] W&r; v. C; hevene F.

4

That cardinals ben called and closynge yates   *gates*
105 There Crist is in kyngdom, to close and to shette,   *Where; shut*
And to opene it to hem and hevene blisse shewe.
   (i.e. those who practise) the vv.
Ac of the Cardinals at court that kaughte of that name   *snatched*
And power presumed in hem a Pope to make   *took for granted*
To han the power that Peter hadde, impugnen I nelle—
   I shan't find fault (with them)
110 For in love and in lettrure the eleccion bilongeth;
   learning; election (of popes)
Forthi I kan and kan naught of court speke moore.   *Therefore*
Thanne kam ther a Kyng: Knyghthod hym ladde;   *came; led*
Might of the communes made hym to regne.   *common people; reign*
And thanne cam Kynde Wit and clerkes he made,   *'Native Intelligence'*
115 For to counseillen the Kyng and the Commune save.   *counsel; protect*
The Kyng and Knyghthod and Clergie bothe   *Learning also*
Casten that the Commune sholde hem [communes] fynde.
   Arranged; food; provide
The Commune contreved of Kynde Wit craftes,   *devised; through; skills*
And for profit of al the peple plowmen ordeyned   *established*
120 To tilie and to travaille as trewe lif asketh.   *till; labour; honest*
The Kyng and the Commune and Kynde Wit the thridde   *third*
Shopen lawe and leaute—ech lif to knowe his owene.
   Created; justice; person
Thanne loked up a lunatik, a leene thyng withalle,   *lean; moreover*
And knelynge to the Kyng clergially he seide,   *learnedly, like a scholar*
125 'Crist kepe thee, sire Kyng, and thi kyngryche,   *protect; kingdom*
And lene thee lede thi lond so leaute thee lovye,   *grant; rule; may love you*
And for thi rightful rulyng be rewarded in hevene!'   *just; (may you) be*
And sithen in the eyr on heigh an aungel of hevene   *thereupon; air on high*
Lowed to speke in Latyn—for lewed men ne koude
   Came down; did not know how to
130 Jangle ne jugge that justifie hem sholde,   *Argue; judge; that (which)*
But suffren and serven—forthi seide the aungel: *therefore*

108–9 *Either (a)* ... to make a pope—(that is), assumed they had the power St Peter possessed *or (b)* to make a pope have [attribute to the papacy] the power &c *(C)*.
117 Brought it about that the common people should (be obliged to) provide sustenance for them (*cf.* 'commons' = 'food').
130–1 Dispute and discriminate (the arguments) which should vindicate them, but (only how to) ... (*or that may be rel.,* s. and s. *indic.*)

105 cr. is] L&r (is *om.* Hm), C; is cr. W.
  in] L&r, C; in his WHmF.
109 þe] F (?=α) H, C; þat W&r (=β)
110 in (2)] WCr²³ FH, C; *om* r.
117 hem communes f.] hire c. f. C;

hemself f. W&r (*trsp.* F); *see* K-D p. 92 (C).
122 lyf] F (?=α); man W&r (?=β) (C).
125 *Here* R *begins.*
126 lene] leve FCr, C.

'"*Sum Rex, sum Princeps*"; *neutrum fortasse deinceps!*
O qui iura regis Christi specialia regis,
Hoc quod agas melius—iustus es, esto pius!
135 *Nudum ius a te vestiri vult pietate.*
Qualia vis metere, talia grana sere:
Si ius nudatur, nudo de iure metatur;
Si seritur pietas, de pietate metas'.
  Thanne greved hym a goliardeis, a gloton of wordes,   *grew angry; buffoon* (C)
140 And to the aungel an heigh answerde after:
'*Dum* "*rex*" *a* "*regere*" *dicatur nomen habere,*
Nomen habet sine re nisi studet iura tenere'.
  Thanne [c]an al the commune crye in vers of Latyn   *proceeded to; verse*
  To the Kynges counseil—construe whoso wolde—   *whoever wishes*
145 '*Precepta Regis sunt nobis vincula legis!*'
  With that ran ther a route of ratons at ones   *troop; rats; once*
  And smale mees myd hem: mo than a thousand   *mice; with; more*
  Comen to a counseil for the commune profit;   *the public good*
  For a cat of a court cam whan hym liked   *came when he pleased*
150 And overleep hem lightliche and laughte hem at his wille,
                               pounced on; easily; seized
  And pleide with hem perillousli and possed aboute.   *played; dashed* (*them*)
  'For doute of diverse dredes we dar noght wel loke!   *fear*
  And if we grucche of his gamen he wol greven us alle—
                         complain; game; injure
  Cracchen us or clawen us and in hise clouches holde,   *Scratch; clutches*
155 That us lotheth the lif er he late us passe.   *is hateful to us; let*
  Mighte we with any wit his wille withstonde,   *ingenious plan; oppose*
  We myghte be lordes olofte and lyven at oure ese'.   *above*
  A raton of renoun, moost renable of tonge,   *eloquent/voluble*
  Seide for a sovereyn [salve] to hem alle,   *perfect remedy for* (C)

132–5 (You say) 'I am King, I am Ruler;' you may perhaps be neither in future.
O you who administer the sublime laws of Christ the King, in order to do better
what you do, as you are just, be godly! Naked law requires to be clothed by you
with a sense of your duty to God. Sow such grain as you wish to reap . . .
136–8 If the law is nakedly administered (*lit.* stripped bare) by you, then let
(judgment) be measured out (to you) according to the letter (*lit.* naked law). If
goodness is sown (by you), may you reap goodness (C).
141–2 Inasmuch as a king has his name from (the fact of) being a ruler [ultimately
the word *rex* is from *regere* 'to rule'], he possesses the name (alone) without the
reality unless he is zealous in maintaining the laws (C).
145 The king's bidding has for us the binding force of law (C).
152 For fear of various perils we (scarcely) even dare peep (out).
155 (To the point where) we hate living—before he (will deign to) let us go.

143 can] gan Bx (C).   150 his] W&r; *om* F, C.
144 *Line om* α.   152 dredes] dedes OC² (C).
148 Comen] And c. *All* B-MSS (C).   159 salue] *conj* K-D *p.* 197; help Bx.
149 court] L&r, C; contree wGMH.   h.a.] α; hymselue β.

160 'I have yseyen segges', quod he, 'in the Cite of Londoun   *seen men; saic*
    Beren beighes ful brighte abouten hire nekkes,   *Wear necklace:*
    And somme colers of crafty work; uncoupled they wenden
                                    collars; skilful; unleashec
    Bothe in wareyne and in waast where hem leve liketh,
                                warren; waste; they pleasl
    And outher while thei arn elliswhere, as I here telle.   *at other time:*
165 Were ther a belle on hire beighe, by Jesus, as me thynketh,   *it seems to ml*
    Men myghte witen wher thei wente and awey renne.   *know; rul*
    And right so', quod that raton, 'reson me sheweth   *teache:*
    To bugge a belle of bras or of bright silver   *buj*
    And knytten it on a coler for oure commune profit   *fastel*
170 And hangen it upon the cattes hals—thanne here we mowen   *neck; can heal*
    Wher he ryt or rest or rometh to pleye;   *Whether; rides; rests; goes fortl*
    And if hym list for to laike, thanne loke we mowen   *he wishes to spor.*
    And peeren in his presence the while hym pleye liketh,   *appeal*
    And if hym wratheth, be war and his wey shonye'.   *he is angry; path; shui*
175   Al the route of ratons to this reson assented;   *line of reasoninģ*
    Ac tho the belle was ybrought and on the beighe hanged   *whel*
    Ther ne was raton in al the route, for al the reaume of France,   *realn*
    That dorste have bounden the belle aboute the cattes nekke,
                            would have darec
    Ne hangen it aboute his hals al Engelond to wynne,   *neck*
180 [Ac] helden hem unhardy and hir counseil feble,   *though.*
    And leten hire laboure lost and al hire longe studie.   *considerec*
     A mous that muche good kouthe, as me tho thoughte,   *had good sensl*
    Strook forth sternely and stood bifore hem alle,   *Went sharply forwarc*
    And to the route of ratons reherced thise wordes: *deliverec*
185 'Though we hadde ykilled the cat, yet sholde ther come another
    To cracchen us and al oure kynde, though we cropen under benches.   *crep.*
    Forthi I counseille al the commune to late the cat worthe,   *let . . . bl*
    And be we nevere so bolde the belle hym to shewe.

180 But believed themselves not bold enough and their plan a poor one.

162 wenden] L&r *exc* FH; wente*n*
   wG.
163 leue] L&r; self wG; best FH.
   lyketh] LRF&c (?=Bx); liked
   WH&c.
165 Ihesus] α; Iesu β.
166 awey r.] hire wey roume C (*so*
   K-D).
167 And] *om* F, C.
170 L&r (?=Bx), C; *line om* wG.
   vpon] L&r; aboute Cr²³ F, C.
171 *Line om* α.
   rometh] Y, C; renneþ WL &
   most (*cf.* 166).

175 þe] α, C (*so* K-D); þis β.
   reson] FH&c, C (*so* K-D); r. þe
   WLR &c.
179 his] α, C; þe cattes β; K-D *p.*
   157.
180 Ac] *sugg.* K-D; But F; Alle W;
   þei H; And L&r.
182 tho] G, C; *om r.*
185 had Iculled] α, C; h. *om* L&r
   (?=β); killen wGHY.
186 cra-] LROYC (?=Bx), C; ca-
   W&r.
188 so] *om* W *only.*

The while he caccheth conynges he coveiteth noght oure caroyne, *rabbits; carcasses*
190 But fedeth hym al with venyson; defame we hym nevere. *feeds; dishonour*
For bettre is a litel los than a long sorwe: *loss; long-lasting*
The maze among us alle, theigh we mysse a sherewe! *dismay; though; villain*
For I herde my sire seyn, is seven yeer ypassed, *father say; ago*
"Ther the cat is a kitoun, the court is ful elenge". *Where; kitten; wretched*
195 That witnesseth Holy Writ, whoso wole it rede— *whoever; read*
Ve terre ubi puer rex est, &c.
For may no renk ther reste have for ratons by nyghte. *man; because of*
For many mennes malt we mees wolde destruye, *mice; destroy*
And also ye route of ratons rende mennes clothes, *tear*
200 Nere the cat of the court that kan you overlepe; *Were it not for; spring on*
For hadde ye rattes youre [raik] ye kouthe noght rule yowselve. *way; could*
'I seye for me', quod the mous, 'I se so muchel after, *foresee such consequences*
Shal nevere the cat ne the kiton by my counseil be greved, *advice; offended*
Ne carpynge of this coler that costed me nevere. *talking; cost*
205 And though it costned me catel, biknowen it I nolde, *wealth; make known*
But suffren as hymself wolde [s]o doon as hym liketh—
Coupled and uncoupled to cacche what thei mowe. *can*
Forthi ech a wis wight I warne—wite wel his owene!' *wise man; know/keep*
(What this metels bymeneth, ye men that ben murye, *dream signifies*
210 Devyne ye—for I ne dar, by deere God in hevene)! *Interpret; dare*
Yet hoved ther an hundred in howves of selk— *coifs; silk*
Sergeants, it semed, that serveden at the Barre, *Barristers-at-law*
Pleteden for penyes and pounded the lawe, *Pleaded; belaboured*
And noght for love of Oure Lord unlose hire lippes ones. *(would) unloose*
215 Thow myghtest bettre meete myst on Malverne Hilles
more easily measure mist
Than get a 'mom' of hire mouth til moneie be shewed! *murmur*
Barons and burgeises and bondemen als *serfs too*

192 (It would be) utter confusion among us all, even though we should be free of (one particular) evil person.
196 Woe to the land where the king is a child (Eccl 10: 16) (C).
205–(6) And even though it [the cat's oppressions] *were* to cost me (some of my) wealth, I would be unwilling to acknowledge it (publicly) But (would rather) let him . . .
208 i.e. mind his own business.
211 Further, there milled about a hundred in coifs of silk.

189–92 *copied after* 197 *All* B-MSS; *not in* C; *re-ordered* K-D *p.* 176.
189 owre] L&r; youre W.
193 is] *om* CrG, C.
200 þe (2)] RF &c, C; þat WL &c.
201 reik] ?C (*sugg.* Bn); wille *All* B-MSS; *see* K-D *p.* 92 (C).
204 Ne] L&r, C; Thoruȝ W.

205 it (1)] αG, C; it hadde β.
206 so] to W&r *exc* H (C).
d. as] W&r; slen þat F.
212 semed] L&r (=Bx), A; bis. w.
213 pownded] F (?=α; poudres R), A (*so* K-D); pountyd H; poundes W&r (=β).

8

I seigh in this assemblee, as ye shul here after;   *gathering*
Baksteres and brewesteres and bochiers manye,   *Bakers; brewers; butchers*
220 Wollen webbesters and weveres of lynnen,   *Wool-weavers; linen*
Taillours and tynkers and tollers in markettes,   *Tailors; toll-collectors*
Masons and mynours and many othere craftes: *miners*
Of alle kynne lybbynge laborers lopen forth somme— *kinds of; living; ran*
As dykeres and delveres that doon hire dedes ille   *ditchers; diggers; work*
225 And dryveth forth the longe day with '*Dieu save Dame Emme!*'   *pass*
Cokes and hire knaves cryden, 'Hote pies, hote!   *Cooks; servants; cried*
Goode gees and grys! Go we dyne, go we!'   *geese; pork; dine*
Taverners until hem tolden the same: *Inn-keepers; unto*
'Whit wyn of Oseye and wyn of Gascoigne,   *Alsace; Gascony*
230 Of the Ryn and of the Rochel, the roost to defie!'
            Rhine; La Rochelle; roast; digest
--Al this I seigh slepyng, and sevene sythes more.   *sleeping; times*

Passus I

What this mountaigne bymeneth and the merke dale   *signifies; dark*
And the feld ful of folk, I shal yow faire shewe.   *clearly*
A lovely lady of leere in lynnen yclothed   *face*
Cam doun from [the] castel and called me faire,   *graciously*
5 And seide, 'Sone, slepestow? Sestow this peple—   *Do you see*
How bisie they ben aboute the maze?   *(their) vain wanderings*
The mooste partie of this peple that passeth on this erthe,
            greatest part, majority
Have thei worship in this world, thei wilne no bettre;   *honour; desire*
Of oother hevene than here holde thei no tale'.   *take no account*
10 I was afered of hire face, theigh she faire weere, *afraid; though; might be*
And seide, 'Mercy, madame, what [may] this [be] to mene?'

225 God save you, mistress Emma! (*C*).
5–6 Son, are you asleep? Do you see these people—how preoccupied they are,
(wandering) about (in) a maze (of worldly concerns)?

231 L&*r*; *line om* WYF.   4 þe] C?A; a Bx (*C*).
   I s.] G, AC; s. I L&*r*.   6 ben] L&*r*, AC; b. alle wG.
                          8 wilne] kepe GH, *most* A-MSS (*so* Ka).
Rubric Passus primus de visione.   11 may . . . to] C, H (to *om* H); is
1 þis] þe C?A.   þis to W&*r*.

'The tour upon the toft', quod she, 'Truthe is therinne,   *hillock*
And wolde that ye wroughte as his word techeth.
For he is fader of feith and formed yow alle
15 Bothe with fel and with face and yaf yow fyve wittes   *skin; gave; senses*
For to worshipe hym therwith while that ye ben here.   *with which to*
And therfore he highte the erthe to helpe yow echone   *commanded; each one*
Of wollene, of lynnen, of liflode at nede   *with the necessities of life*
In mesurable manere to make yow at ese;   *moderate degree*
20 And comaunded of his curteisie in commune three thynges:
                                                generosity; grace; common
Are none nedfulle but tho, and nempne hem I thynke,
                                           necessary; those; name; intend
And rekene hem by reson—reherce thow hem after.
                                              enumerate; in order; declare
'That oon is vesture from chele thee to save,   *clothing; the cold; protect*
And mete at meel for mysese of thiselve,
25 And drynke whan thow driest—ac do noght out of reson, *are dry; in excess*
That thow worthe the wers whan thow werche sholdest.
                                              so that; end up; the w. (for it)
For Lot in hise lifdayes, for likynge of drynke, *love of (the pleasures of) d.*
Dide by hise doughtres that the devel liked: *that which pleased*
Delited hym in drynke as the devel wolde,   *Had his pleasure*
30 And leccherie hym laughte, and lay by hem bothe—   *took to himself*
And al he witte it the wyn, that wikked dede: *blamed entirely on*
*Inebriemus eum vino dormiamusque cum eo, ut
servare possimus de patre nostro semen.*   (Gen 19: 32)
Thorugh wyn and thorugh wommen ther was Loth acombred,   *overcome*
And there gat in glotonie gerles that were cherles.   *begot; children*
Forthi dred delitable drynke and thow shalt do the bettre.
                                           Therefore; respect; delightful
35 Mesure is medicine, though thow muchel yerne. *Moderation; much; long for*
Al is nought good to the goost that the gut asketh,   *spirit*
Ne liflode to the likame that leef is to the soule.
Leve nought thi likame, for a liere hym techeth—   *Believe, trust; liar*
That is the wrecched world, wolde thee bitraye.   *(that) would like to*

24 And food at meal (time), to prevent suffering [*not* 'discomfort' (BnSk)] to
   yourself.
27 For Lot, during the days of his life, (for love of) the pleasures of drink . . .
31*a* (Come), let us make him drunk with wine, and let us lie with him, that we may
   preserve seed of our father (Gen 19: 32).
33 And there begot in (his) drunkenness children of base character.
37 Nor (is everything) that is of value to the soul a benefit to (man's) physical
   nature.

12 vpon] Cr(F), C; on WHmG; vp   36 Al is n.] AC (*so* K-D *p.* 80); It is
   L&r (C).   n. al *All* B-MSS.
23 chele] L; cold W.   37–8 *so* R&c, AC; 37b, 38a *om* WL;
31*a* -briemus R (*so* Vulg.); -briamus   re-ord. Sk.
   W.   37 þe(1)] G, AC (*so* K-D); þi W&r.

40 For the fend and thi flessh folwen togidere,   *devil; pursue*
  And that [shendeth] thi soule; set it in thin herte.   *injures*
  And for thow sholdest ben ywar, I wisse thee the beste.'   *be on guard; advise*
    'A, madame, mercy,' quod I, 'me liketh wel youre wordes.   *thank you*
  Ac the moneie of this molde that men so faste holdeth—   *earth; hold(s)*
45 Telleth me to whom that tresour appendeth.'   *treasure belongs*
    'Go to the Gospel,' quod she, 'that God seide hymselven, *Gospel (words)*
  Tho the poeple hym apposede with a peny in the Temple *When; questioned*
  Wheither thei sholde therwith worshipe the kyng Cesar.
                                    by means of it; Caesar
  And God asked of hem, of whom spak the lettre,   *spoke; inscription*
50 And the ymage ylike that therinne stondeth?   *like(wise); stands*
    ' "Cesares", thei seiden, "we seen it wel echone."   *Caesar's; see*
    ' "*Reddite Cesari*," quod God, "that *Cesari* bifalleth,   *belongs*
  Et que sunt Dei Deo, or ellis ye don ille."   *do evil*
  —For rightfully Reson sholde rule yow alle,   *in proper manner, justly*
55 And Kynde Wit be wardeyn youre welthe to kepe,   *guardian; protect*
  And tutour of youre tresor, and take it yow at nede,   *overseer; give*
  For housbondrie and he holden togidres.'   *thrifty management*
    Thanne I frayned hire faire, for Hym that hire made,
                           asked; courteously; f.t. sake of
  'That dongeon in the dale that dredful is of sighte—
60 What may it bemeene, madame, I yow biseche?'   *signify; beseech*
    'That is the castel of care—whoso comth therinne   *whoever comes*
  May banne that he born was to bodi or to soule!   *curse (the fact)*
  Therinne wonyeth a wight that Wrong is yhote,   *dwells; being; called*
  Fader of falshede—and founded it hymselve.   *falsehood*
65 Adam and Eve he egged to ille,   *incited; evil*
  Counseilled Kaym to killen his brother,   *Cain*
  Judas he japed with Jewen silver,   *deceived; Jews'*
  And sithen on an eller hanged hym after.   *then; elder-tree (C)*
  He is lettere of love and lieth hem alle: *hinderer; lies to/deceives*
70 That trusten on his tresour bitrayed arn sonnest.'   *Those who; soonest*

50 And (asked who) the image that stood within likewise (represented)?
52-3 'Render to Caesar', said God, 'the things that are Caesar's, and to God,
    the things that are God's' (Mt 22: 21).

41 And t.] AC (*so* K-D); This a. t.
  W&r *exc* F (= Bx).
  shendeþ] A (?C), *sugg.* K-D; seeþ
  W (?=β); sueth R (?=α).
  soule] Y, A (*so* K-D); s. and W&r, C.
  sett] G, A?C (*so* K-D); seith W (C).
43 A] F, AC; *so* K-D; *om* W&r.
44 holdeþ] β, A; kepeth α ?C (C).
45 Telleth] R (?=α; Tell ȝee F), AC;
  Tel W&r (=β).
  to w.] F, AC (*so* K-D *p.* 168); to
  w. madame W&r (m.t.w. RH).

49 hem] L&r; hym W.
50 ilyke] L; was lik W.
57 he] H, AC; *so* K-D; heo R (?=he
  a); hij W (=β).
58 hir (2)] L&r, AC; me W.
60 bemeene] F&c, AC (*so* K-D); be
  to m. W.
64 and] W&r; he FHm, A.
68 after] LR, A (*cf.* C); selue W.
70 b. aren] αG, A (*so* K-D); bitrayeþ
  he hem W; b.h. L& *most* (?=β).

11

Thanne hadde I wonder in my wit what womman it weere   *mind; might be*
That swiche wise wordes of Holy Writ shewed,
And halsede hire on the heighe name, er she thennes yede,
                                        adjured; (God's) n.; went
What she were witterly that wissed me so faire.   *certainly; counselled*
75 'Holi Chirche I am,' quod she, 'thow oughtest me to knowe.   *recognize*
I underfeng thee first and the feith taughte.   *received; to you*
Thow broughtest me borwes my biddyng to fulfille,   *pledges*
And to loven me leelly the while thi lif dureth.'   *loyally; lasts*
Thanne I courbed on my knees and cried hire of grace,   *bent; for mercy*
80 And preide hire pitously to preye for my synnes,
And also kenne me kyndely on Crist to bileve,   *teach; properly*
That I myghte werchen His wille that wroghte me to man: *created me a man*
'Teche me to no tresor, but tel me this ilke—   *direct; same* (*thing*)
How I may save my soule, that seint art yholden.'
                                        you who; holy; considered
85 'Whan alle tresors arn tried,' quod she, 'Treuthe is the beste.   *tested*
I do it on *Deus caritas* to deme the sothe;   *appeal to; judge*
It is as dereworthe a drury as deere God hymselven.   *precious; love-gift*
Who is trewe of his tonge and telleth noon oother,   *speaks nought else*
And dooth the werkes therwith and wilneth no man ille,
                                        acts accordingly; intends
90 He is a god by the Gospel, agrounde and olofte,   *according to*
And ylik to Oure Lord, by Seint Lukes wordes.   *(cf. Lk 12: 33)*
The clerkes that knowen this sholde kennen it aboute,   *make known*
For Cristen and uncristen cleymeth it echone.   *(non)Christian; claim*
'Kynges and knyghtes sholde kepen it by reson—
95 Riden and rappen doun in reaumes aboute,   *suppress; realms*
And taken *transgressores* and tyen hem faste   *lawbreakers; bind; securely*
Til treuthe hadde ytermyned hire trespas to the ende.   *decided; offence; finally*
For David in hise dayes dubbed knyghtes,
And dide hem sweren on hir swerd to serven truthe evere.
                                        made; swear; sword(s)
100 And that is the profession apertly that apendeth to knyghtes,
                                        plainly; pertains

74 To tell me exactly who she, who counselled me thus graciously, might be.
81 And also to instruct me in the right and true way of believing in Christ.
86 I ground my affirmation (that this is) truly to be judged (so) on the text *God is love* (1 Jn 4: 8).
90 He is divine, according to the Gospel, (in the estimate of those) on earth (and those) in heaven (*cf.* XVIII 45).

73 halsede] F (?=α; hasked R), AC   91 And] And ek A; And also C.
(*so* K-D); asked β.   92 þis] it H, A.
76 þe] þe thye G.   98–9 *copied after* 103, 100–103 *copied*
77 Thou] CrF, AC (*so* K-D); And W.   *after* 97 *in all* B-MSS; *re-arr.* (*as in*
80 to] RF&c, AC; *om* W&c.   A) K-D *p.* 104.
82 *Line om* α.   100 þe] LR, A; *om* W.
88 Who] For who AC.

And naught to fasten o Friday in fyve score wynter,   *fast one Friday*
But holden with hym and with here that wolden alle truthe,   *support; seek*
And never leve hem for love ne for lacchynge of silver—
                                for the sake of getting
And whoso passe[th] that point is apostata in the ordre.   *exceeds*
105 'But Crist, kyngene kyng, knyghted ten—   *king of kings*
Cherubyn and Seraphyn, swiche sevene and another,   *seven such*
And yaf hem myght in his majestee—the murier hem thoughte—
                 gave; pleasanter; it seemed to
And over his meene meynee made hem archangeles;   *lesser troop(s)*
Taughte hem by the Trinitee treuthe to knowe,
110 To be buxom at his biddyng—he bad hem nought ellis. *obedient; commanded*
  'Lucifer with legions lerned it in hevene,
[And was the lovelokest to loke after Oure Lord {one}]
                 loveliest; behold; alone
Til he brak buxomnesse; his blisse gan he tyne,   *broke obedience; lose*
And fel fro that felawshipe in a fendes liknesse   *fiend's likeness*
115 Into a deep derk helle to dwelle there for evere.
And mo thousandes myd hym than man kouthe nombre *more; with; count*
Lopen out with Lucifer in lothliche forme   *Leapt; loathsome*
For thei leveden upon hym that lyed in this manere: *Because; believed; lied*
Ponam pedem in aquilone, et similis ero Altissimo.
120 And alle that hoped it myghte be so, noon hevene myghte hem holde,
But fellen out in fendes liknesse [ful] nyne dayes togideres,
Til God of his goodnesse [garte the hevene to stekie *made; stick fast*
And gan stable it and stynte] and stonden in quiete. *cause it to rest*
  'Whan thise wikkede wenten out, wonderwise thei fellen—
                 in strange manner
125 Somme in eyr, somme in erthe, somme in helle depe;   *air*
Ac Lucifer lowest lith of hem alle: *lies*

103 And never abandon them out of partiality [*sc.* towards wrongdoers] nor for bribes.
104 And whoever infringes (the duties imposed by) that virtue, is / proves himself an apostate against the Order (of Knighthood).
105–6 ... made ten (orders of) 'knights', Cherubim and Seraphim, seven (orders) like these, and one other (order)—[*sc.* making up ten].
119 I shall set my foot in the north, and I shall be like the Most High (St Augustine, *after* Is. 14: 13–14; *see* Kellogg *art cit*, Bn).

102 wolden alle] W&*r*; aske*þ þe* G, A (*so* K-D).
104 passi*þ*] AC (*so* K-D); passed *All* B-MSS.
  is] Y, AC (*so* K-D); was W.
106 anothre] L, AC; o*þ*ere W.
112 *From* A *sugg.* K-D; *om all* B-MSS.
  to ... one] to loken on after oure lord A-MSS ChTH² (Ka *varr. q.v.*) (*C*).
113 Til] *a*, A (*so* K-D); But for *β*.

118 hym] Lucyfer F (*so* K-D *p.* 173).
121 ful] *not in* B-MSS; *conj* K-D *p.* 199.
122b–123a *rec.* K-D *p.* 188; gan stablisse and stynte/And garte *þe* heuene to stekie W.
124 wonderw.] LR; in w.w. W.
125 eyre] L, AC; *þe* e. W.
  some (2)] G, AC (*so* K-D); and s. W&*r*.
126 lith] LR, AC; l. yet W.

I ʒr pride that he putte out, his peyne hath noon ende.   *displayed; torment*
ʌ nd alle that werchen with wrong wende thei shulle   *must go*
After hir deth day and dwelle with that sherewe;   *evil one*
130 Ac tho that werche wel as Holy Writ telleth,
And enden as I er seide in truthe, that is the beste,   *end; previously*
Mowe be siker that hire soules shul wende to hevene,   *May be certain*
Ther Treuthe is in Trinitee and troneth hem alle.   *enthrones*
Fo·thi I seye, as I seyde er, by sighte of thise textes—
135 Whan alle tresors arn tried, Truthe is the beste.
Lereth it th[u]s lewed men, for lettred it knoweth—
      Teach it to; uneducated; educated (men)
That Treuthe is tresor the trieste on erthe.'   *choicest*
'Yet have I no kynde knowynge,' quod I, 'ye mote kenne me bettre
      natural; must teach
By what craft in my cors it comseth, and where.'   *power; body; arises*
140 'Thow doted daffe!' quod she, 'dulle are thi wittes.   *silly fool*
To litel Latyn thow lernedest, leode, in thi youthe: *Too; man*
Heu michi quia sterilem duxi vitam iuvenilem!
It is a kynde knowynge that kenneth in thyn herte   *instructs (you)*
For to loven thi Lord levere than thiselve,   *more dearly*
No dedly synne to do, deye theigh thow sholdest—   *mortal, serious*
145 This I trowe be truthe; who kan teche thee bettre,   *believe is; if anyone can*
Loke thow suffre hym to seye, and sithen lere it after;   *See; allow; then learn*
For thus witnesseth his word; worche thow therafter.   *act accordingly*
'For Truthe telleth that love is triacle of hevene: *the healing remedy*
May no synne be on hym seene that that spice useth.   *visible*
150 And alle his werkes he wroughte with love as hym liste,   *as he wished*
And lered it Moyses for the leveste thyng and moost lik to hevene,
      taught it (to); dearest
And also the plante of pees, moost precious of vertues: *peace; powers, virtues*
For hevene myghte nat holden it, so was it hevy of hymself,
Til it hadde of the erthe eten his fille.   *eaten (C)*
155 And whan it hadde of this fold flessh and blood taken,   *earth*
Was nevere leef upon lynde lighter therafter,   *leaf; linden tree*
And portatif and persaunt as the point of a nedle,   *portable; piercing; needle*

136 Teach such a lesson to uneducated men, for the educated are familiar with it.
139 By (means of) what power in my body it (*sc.* a direct natural knowledge of
    truth) arises, and in what part of it.
141*a* Alas, what a useless life I led in my youth! (*proverbial*).

130 Ac] L; And W.
136 þus] AC (*so* K-D); this RL; þise
  W.
I 141–II 40 defective in MS R.
142 þat] AC; *so* K-D; quod she þ.
  All B-MSS.
147 L&r (worche] C, A; worcheth L,
  corr. Sk); *line om* wGH.

149 that s. vseþ] F (?=α); þ.v.þ.sp.
  W&r (?=β).
152 plant] Cr, AC (*so* BnK-D);
  plentee W.
153 so was it] F (?=α); it w. so W&r
  (?=β).
154 eten] W; ʒeten L, C (*C*).
  his f.] it selue Cr, C (*C*).

That myghte noon armure it lette ne none heighe walles.

(So) that; armour; stop

' Forthi is love ledere of the Lordes folk of hevene,   *Lord of heaven's*

160 And a meene, as the mair is, [inmiddes] the kyng and the commune;

intermediary; mayor; commons

Right so is love a ledere and the lawe shapeth: *determines*

Upon man for hise mysdedes the mercyment he taxeth.   *fine; imposes*

And for to knowen it kyndely—it comseth by myght,

originates; power (of God)

And in the herte, there is the heed and the heighe welle.

chief fount and source

165 For in kynde knowynge in herte ther [coms]eth a myght—

And that falleth to the Fader that formed us alle,   *pertains, is the work of*

Loked on us with love and leet his sone dye   *Son; die*

Mekely for oure mysdedes, to amenden us alle.   *Meekly, humbly*

And yet wolde he hem no wo that wroughte hym that peyne,   *wished; torment*

170 But mekely with mouthe mercy he bisoughte,   sc. *from God*

To have pite of that peple that peyned hym to dethe.   *on; tortured*

'Here myghtow sen ensample in hymself oone—   *example; alone*

That he was myghtful and meke, and mercy gan graunte   *powerful*

To hem that hengen hym heigh and his herte thirled.   *hung; pierced*

175 ' Forthi I rede yow riche, haveth ruthe of the povere, *counsel; pity on; poor*

Though ye be myghty to mote, beeth meke in youre werkes,

summon to a law-court; be

For the same mesure that ye mete, amys outher ellis,

mete out; wrongly or otherwise

Ye shulle ben weyen therwith whan ye wenden hennes:

weighed; depart from (life)

Eadem mensura qua mensi fueritis remecietur vobis.

For though ye be trewe of youre tonge and treweliche wynne,

honestly earn (profit)

180 And as chaste as a child that in chirche wepeth,

But if ye loven leelly and lene the povere   *Unless; faithfully; give to*

Of swich good as God sent, goodliche parteth,   *sends; liberally share*

Ye ne have na moore merite in Masse ne in houres   *the Divine Office*

165 For in/through the natural knowledge in the heart, there springs (into being) a power . . .

178a For with the same measure that you shall mete withal it shall be measured to you again (Lk 6: 38).

182 Divide kindly with them such possessions as God sends you (*play on* good, *goodliche*).

160 inm.] bitwene BxCx (*C*).
165 in(1)] of Cr, C.
   in(2)] of G, C.
   comsiþ a m.] AC (*so* K-D *p.* 82); begynnyth a m. G; *a* m. b. W&r.
170 he] *om* W *only.*

174 heye] G, AC (*so* K-D); on h. W&r.
176 -y] GCr, AC (*so* K-D); -ful W&r.
177 mes.] F&c, AC; *pl.* W.
182 Of] F (?=a), AC (*so* K-D); *om* W&r.
183 ne(2)] L, AC; nor W.

Than Malkyn of hire maydenhede, that no man desireth.   *virginity*
185 For James the gentile jugged in hise bokes   *noble, good; concluded*
That feith withouten feet is [feblere] than nought,   *work(s); weaker, worth less*
And as deed as a dorenail but if the dedes folwe: *dead; door-nail; deeds*
Fides sine operibus mortua est &c.
    'Forthi chastite withouten charite worth cheyned in helle;   *shall be chained*
It is as lewed as a lampe that no light is inne.   *pointless*
190 Manye chapeleyns arn chaste, ac charite is aweye;   *chaplains; absent*
Are none hardere than hii whan [hii] ben avaunced: *they; promoted*
Unkynde to hire kyn and to alle Cristene,   *Unkind, unnatural*
Chewen hire charite and chiden after moore—   *Consume; complain (for)*
Swich chastite withouten charite worth cheyned in helle.
195 Manye curatours kepen hem clene of hire bodies;   *parish-priests; chaste*
Thei ben acombred with coveitise, thei konne noght out crepe,
        weighed down; creep
So harde hath avarice yhasped hem togideres.   *fastened*
And that is no truthe of the Trinite, but tricherie of helle,
        fidelity; faithlessness
And lernynge to lewed men the latter for to deele.   *a lesson; later; give*
200 For [thise ben wordes] writen in the [Euaungelie]:   *Gospel*
"*Date, et dabitur vobis*—for I deele yow alle.   *give, distribute to*
And that is the lok of love that leteth out my grace,   *lock*
To conforten the carefulle acombred with synne."   *frightened, anxious*
    'Love is leche of lif and next Oure Lord selve,   *physician; closest; himself*
205 And also the graithe gate that goth into hevene.   *direct way*
Forthi I seye as I seide er by sighte of the textes:
Whan alle tresors ben tried, Treuthe is the beste.
    'Now have I told thee what truthe is—that no tresor is bettre—
I may no lenger lenge thee with; now loke thee Oure Lord!'
        longer remain; protect

184 Than (ill-favoured) Molly from her virginity, which no man wants (anyway)
    (*Malkyn* = an ugly, sluttish woman).
187*a* . . . faith without works is dead (Js 2: 26).
199 And (a bad) example to uneducated people to be tardy in giving (alms).
201 Give; and it shall be given to you (Lk 6: 38).

186 *fait*] Y, F (?=α), **AC** (*so* K-D);   196 out c.] F (?=α), ?**AC** (*so* K-D);
þe f. W.   cr.o. H; doon it from hem W.
    feblere . . . n.] **AC** (*so* K-D);   200 For] C², **AC** (*so* K-D); Forþi
wersse þ.n. H; (ri3t) noþyng   W&r.
worth*i* W&r.   þ.ben w.] **AC** (*so* K-D); b. þese
187 *nayle*] GH, **AC** (*so* K-D); tree   w. H; þise w.b. W&r.
W&r.   Euaungelie] **AC** (*so* K-D); gospel
    dedes sg. G.   *All* B-MSS.
191 non] F (?=α) G, **AC** (*so* K-D);   202 that (2)] CrF&c, **AC** (*so* K-D); and
no men W&r.   WL&c.
    herder] G, **AC** (*so* K-D);   206 syght off] GH, **AC** (*so* K-D);
Auarouser W.   *om* W&r.
    hij (2)] A; thei *All* B-MSS.

Passus II

Yet I courbed on my knees and cried hire of grace,   *Still further; bent; favour*
And seide, 'Mercy, madame, for Marie love of hevene,   *love of Mary in*
That bar that blisful barn that boughte us on the Rode—
        bore; blessed child; Cross
Kenne me by som craft to knowe the false.'   *skill; recognize*
5 'Loke upon thi left half, and lo where he stondeth—   *hand; see*
Bothe Fals and Favel, and hire feeres manye!'   *Deceit; their companions*
  I loked on my left half as the Lady me taughte,   *instructed*
And was war of a womman wonderliche yclothed—   *aware; marvellously*
Purfiled with pelure, the pureste on erthe,   *Trimmed; fur; finest*
10 Ycorouned with a coroune, the Kyng hath noon bettre.   *Crown(ed)*
Fetisliche hire fyngres were fretted with gold wyr,   *Gracefully; adorned; wire*
And thereon rede rubies as rede as any gleede,   *red; glowing coal*
And diamaundes of derrest pris and double manere saphires,   *highest value*
Orientals and ewages envenymes to destroye.
15 Hire robe was ful riche, of reed scarlet engreyned,   *fast-dyed*
With ribanes of reed gold and of riche stones.   *bands*
  Hire array me ravysshed, swich richesse saugh I nevere.
I hadde wonder what she was and whos wif she were.   *whose; might be*
'What is this womman,' quod I, 'so worthili atired?'   *nobly dressed*
20 'That is Mede the mayde,' quod she, 'hath noyed me ful ofte,
        (who) has harmed
And ylakked my lemman that Leautee is hoten,   *disparaged; lover; called*
And bilowen h[ym] to lordes that lawes han to kepe.   *told lies about; administer*
In the Popes paleis she is pryvee as myselve,   *palace; intimate*
But soothnesse wolde noght so—for she is a bastard,   *truth(fulness)*
25 For Fals was hire fader that hath a fikel tonge,   *treacherous*
And nevere sooth seide sithen he com to erthe;   *truth; since; came*
And Mede is manered after hym, right as [asketh kynde]:
        takes after; nature requires
Qualis pater, talis filius. Bona arbor bonum fructum facit.

9 (Her dress) embroidered with a trimming of fur, the very choicest in the world.
13–14 . . . sapphires of two kinds—Oriental sapphires and sea-coloured sapphires,
(having the power) to act as antidote to poisons (*C*).
21 And disparaged my beloved, whose name is Loyal Faithfulness.
27a Like father like son (*proverbial*) (*C*); (Every) good tree bringeth forth good
fruit (Mt 7: 17).

Rubric Passus secundus de visione vt
supra.
1 courbed] kneled AC.
5 vpon] on F (?=a) H, A?C.
8 wonders] G, AC (so K-D); worþi-
  W&r.

9 purest on] F (?=a) H, A (so K-D;
  cf. C); fyneste vpon W&r.
22 hym] em K-D (cf. C); hire All
  B-MSS (om F).
27 asketh k.] k. a. All B-MSS.
27a Bona] Cr, C (so Vulg.); Bonus W.

17

'I oughte ben hyere than [heo]—I kam of a bettre.   *higher; she; from*
My fader the grete God is and ground of alle graces,   *source, foundation*
30 Oo God withouten gynnyng, and I his goode doughter,   *One; beginning*
And hath yeven me Mercy to marie with myselve;   *to marry me*
And what man be merciful and leelly me love   *whoever is; faithfully*
Shal be my lord and I his leef in the heighe hevene;   *beloved*
And what man taketh Mede, myn heed dar I legge   *whoever; head; wager*
35 That he shal lese for hire love a lappe of *Caritatis*.   *lose; portion; Charity*
'How construeth David the King of men that [cacch]eth Mede,
          explains; take
And men of this moolde that maynteneth truthe,   *earth; support*
And how ye shul save yourself? The Sauter bereth witnesse: *Psalter*
Domine, quis habitabit in tabernaculo tuo, &c.
40 'And now worth this Mede ymaried to a mansed sherewe,   *shall be; cursed*
To oon Fals Fikel-tonge, a fendes biyete.   *fiend's offspring*
Favel thorugh his faire speche hath this folk enchaunted,   *Deceit; bewitched*
And al is Lieres ledynge that [lady] is thus ywedded.   *(through) L's instigat.*
Tomorwe worth ymaked the maydenes bridale;   *will be; wedding (feast)*
45 And there myghtow witen if thow wilt whiche thei ben alle   *might thou know*
That longen to that lordshipe, the lasse and the moore.
          belong; (Mede's) domain
Knowe hem there if thow kanst, and kepe [thee from hem alle],
          Recognize; guard yourself
And lakke hem noght but lat hem worthe, til Leaute be Justice
          criticize; be; Judge
And have power to punysshe hem—thanne put forth thi reson.   *argument(s)*
50 Now I bikenne thee Crist,' quod she, 'and his clene moder,   *commit (to); pure*
And lat no conscience acombre thee for coveitise of Mede.'   *trouble, oppress*
   Thus lefte me that lady liggynge aslepe,   *lying*
And how Mede was ymaried in metels me thoughte—   *i.e. I dreamed*
That al the riche retenaunce that regneth with the False   *retinue; lords it*
55 Were boden to the bridale on bothe two sides,   *bidden*
Of alle manere of men, the meene and the riche.   *(Consisting) of; poor*
To marien this mayde was many man assembled,
As of knyghtes and of clerkes and oother commune peple,   *clerics*
As sisours and somonours, sherreves and hire clerkes,   *assizers (C); sheriffs*
60 Bedelles and baillifs and brocours of chaffare,   *Beadles (C); brokers of trade*

39 Lord, who shall dwell in thy tabernacle? (Ps 14: 1).
51 And allow no (scruples of) conscience (caused by) any greed for lucre (on your
   part) to weigh you down.
58 . . . and other people not of aristocratic or clerical estate.

28 heo] **AC**; she *All* B-MSS (*C*).   45 And] *om* GH, **A**.
36 caccheþ] *conj* K-D *p.* 195; takeþ W.   47 þe from hem alle] **AC** (*so* K-D);
40 to] F&*c* (? =a) G, C; vnto W.   þow þi tonge W (*C*).
41 *Here* R *resumes*.   57 was; man] L&*r*; *pl.* WF.
43 lady] C (*sugg.* K-D *p.* 92); she *All*
B-MSS.

18

Forgoers and vitaillers and vokettes of the Arches;   *Purveyors; advocates*
I kan noght rekene the route that ran aboute Mede.   *number; throng*
Ac Symonie and Cyvylle and sisours of courtes   *Civil Law*
Were moost pryvee with Mede of any men, me thoughte.   *intimate*
65 Ac Favel was the firste that fette hire out of boure   *fetched; (her) chamber*
And as a brocour broughte hire to be with Fals enjoyned.

    match-maker; united
Whan Symonye and Cyvylle seighe hir bother wille,   *saw; joint, of both*
Thei assented for silver to seye as bothe wolde.   *wished*
Thanne leep Liere forth and seide, 'Lo! here a chartre   *ran; here is*
70 That Gile with his grete othes gaf hem togidere,'—
And preide Cyvylle to see and Symonye to rede it.   *requested*

Thanne Symonye and Cyvylle stonden forth bothe   *stand*
And unfoldeth the feffement that Fals hath ymaked,   *deed of endowment*
And thus bigynnen thise gomes to greden ful heighe: *men; cry aloud*
'*Sciant presentes & futuri, &c.*
75 Witeth and witnesseth, that wonieth upon this erthe, *know; (you) who dwell*
That Mede is ymaried moore for hire goodes
Than for any vertue or fairnesse or any free kynde.   *noble lineage, blood*
Falsnesse is fayn of hire for he woot hire riche;   *desires; knows (to be)*
And Favel with his fikel speche feffeth by this chartre

    deceiving; endows (her)
80 To be Princes in Pride, and poverte to despise,   *Princess*
To bakbite and to bosten and bere fals witnesse,   *slander; boast*
To scorne and to scolde and sclaundre to make,   *rail; slander*
Unbuxome and bolde to breke the ten hestes.   *Disobedient; commandments*
And the erldom of Envye and Wrathe togideres,
85 With the chastilet of cheste and chaterynge out of reson.

    little castle; quarrelling
The countee of Coveitise and alle the costes about—   *Greed; regions*
That is usure and avarice—al I hem graunte   *usury; miserliness*
In bargaynes and in brocages with al the burghe of thefte,

    '*deals*'; *brokerage; borough*
And al the lordshipe of Leccherie in lengthe and in brede—

    domain; breadth
90 As in werkes and in wordes and in waitynges with eighes,   *look(ing)s*
And in wedes and in wisshynges and with ydel thoughtes

    clothes; hopes; idle fantasies
Ther as wil wolde and werkmanshipe fayleth.'   *Where; performance*
Glotonye he gaf hem ek and grete othes togidere,
And al day to drynken at diverse tavernes,

---

61 Those who obtain provisions [esp. for the king's itinerant courts &c], those who
   provide them, and lawyers who practise in the ecclesiastical courts.
74*a* Be it known to all present and to come . . . (*legal formula*).
75 Know (for certain) and be witness, (all you who) live on the earth.

75 þis] *om* GFH, A.   91 wedes] wenes *rec.* K-D *p.* 186 (*C*).
84 wraþe] yre C (*C*).

95 And there to jangle and jape and jugge hir evencristen,
argue; mock; fellow-Christian
And in fastynge dayes to frete er ful tyme were.
eat; fully
And thanne to sitten and soupen til sleep hem assaille,
sup
And breden as burgh swyn, and bedden hem esily, *breed; town pigs; at ease*
Til Sleuthe and sleep sliken hise sydes;
make sleek
100 And thanne wanhope to awaken hym so with no wil to amende,
(experience) despair (at)
For he leveth be lost—this is his laste ende.
believes he is; final state
'And thei to have and to holde, and hire heires after, *heirs in succession*
A dwellynge with the devel, and dampned be for evere,
damned
With alle the appurtinaunces of Purgatorie into the pyne of helle; *torment*
105 Yeldynge for this thyng at one yeres ende
Yielding (up); year's
Hire soules to Sathan, to suffre with hym peynes,
pains
And with hym to wonye with wo while God is in hevene.'
dwell; sorrow
In witnesse of which thyng Wrong was the firste,
And Piers the Pardoner of Paulynes doctrine,
? order of Paulines (C)
110 Bette the Bedel of Bokynghamshire,
Reynald the Reve of Rutland Sokene,
the Soke of Rutland
Munde the Millere—and many mo othere.
more besides
'In the date of the devel this dede I assele
seal
By sighte of Sire Symonie and Cyvyles leeve.'
In the sight of; and by
115 Thanne tened hym Theologie whan he this tale herde,
became angry; speech
And seide to Cyvyle, 'Now sorwe mote thow have—
may you be cursed
Swiche weddynges to werche to wrathe with Truthe!
bring about; with which to
And er this weddynge be wroght, wo thee bitide!
For Mede is muliere, of Amendes engendred;
legitimate; born
120 And God graunted to gyve Mede to truthe,
honesty
And thow hast gyven hire to a gilour—now God gyve thee sorwe! *deceiver*
The text telleth thee noght so, Truthe woot the sothe,
For *Dignus est operarius* his hire to have—
wages
And thow hast fest hire to Fals; fy on thi lawe!
joined; fie upon
125 For al bi lesynges thow lyvest and lecherouse werkes.
lies
Symonye and thiself shenden Holi Chirche,
damage
The notaries and ye noyen the peple.
harm
Ye shul abiggen it bothe, by God that me made!
pay (for it); b. of you
'Wel ye witen, wernardes, but if youre wit faille,
deceivers; unless

95 And there to argue in quarrelsome fashion and talk insultingly and pass judgment on their fellow-Christians.
109 . . . of the order of (Crutched Friars, called) Paulines (Sk; *but cf.* Bn).
123 For the labourer is worthy (of his hire) (Lk 10: 7).

100 hym] L; hem W.
101 his] R (?=α (*cf.* C); þe F); hir W&r (?=β).
105 зeres ende] L&r, A; dayes tyme W.
112 Munde] LR&c, AC; ?Maud W.
113 assele] L; ensele W.
116 to] vnto W *only.*
120 -ted] YF&c, ?AC; -teþ W.
122 þe] RF&c, A (*so* K-D); Thi W.

130 That Fals is feithlees and fikel in hise werkes
    And as a bastarde ybore of Belsabubbes kynne.   *born; the devil's kin*
    And Mede is muliere, a maiden of goode,   *noble ancestry*
    And myghte kisse the Kyng for cosyn and she wolde.   *as a cousin; if she*
    Forthi wercheth by wisdom and by wit also,   *work*
135 And ledeth hire to Londoun, there lawe is yshewed,   *take; where; revealed*
    If any lawe wol loke thei ligge togideres.   *provide that they should lie*
    And though justices juggen hire to be joyned with Fals,   *married to*
    Yet be war of the weddynge—for witty is Truthe,   *wise*
    And Conscience is of his counseil and knoweth yow echone,   *intimate with him*
140 And if he fynde yow in defaute and with the false holde,   *at fault; supporting*
    It shal bisitte youre soules ful soure at the laste.'   *oppress; bitterly*
    Herto assenteth Cyvyle, ac Symonye ne wolde,   *was unwilling*
    Til he hadde silver for his se[el] and [signes] of notaries.   *seal*
    Thanne fette Favel forth floryns ynowe   *fetched; enough*
145 And bad Gile, 'Go gyve gold al aboute,   *bade*
    And namely to the notaries, that hem noon faille;   *especially; lack*
    And feffe Fals-witnesse with floryns ynowe,   *retain*
    For he may Mede amaistrye and maken at my wille.'   *dominate; persuade*
    Tho this gold was ygyve, gret was the thonkyng   *When; thanking*
150 To Fals and to Favel for hire faire yiftes,   *gifts*
    And comen to conforten from care the False,   *(they) came; anxiety*
    And seiden, 'Certes, sire, cessen shul we nevere,   *Rest assured; desist*
    Til Mede be thi wedded wif thorugh wit of us alle;   *(the) ingenuity*
    For we have Mede amaistried with oure murie speche,   *pleasant*
155 That she graunteth to goon with a good wille
    To London, to loken if the lawe wolde   *see whether*
    Juggen yow joyntly in joie for evere.'   *J. (that) you be married*
    Thanne was Falsnesse fayn and Favel as blithe,   *pleased; happy*
    And leten somone alle segges in shires aboute,   *had . . . summoned; people*
160 And bad hem alle be bown, beggers and othere,   *ready; others*
    To wenden with hem to Westmynstre to witnesse this dede.   *act, deed*
    Ac thanne cared thei for caples to carien hem thider;   *wanted horses*
    And Favel fette forth thanne foles ynowe   *foals/fools*
    And sette Mede upon a sherreve shoed al newe,   *all newly shod*
165 And Fals sat on a sisour that softeli trotted,   *gently*
    And Favel on a flaterere fetisly atired.   *elegantly dressed*

135 . . . the (process of) law is made manifest (in the courts).

130 feiþ-] feyt- HC; feynt- A (*so* K-D).

131 as] α (*so* K-D); was β; *om* H.

135 lawe] L&r (þe l. MH); it w.

137 with] LRF&c, A; to W.

138 þe] RFGH, ?AC; *om* W&r.

143 seel] CA (*pl.* K-D); seruice *All* B-MSS.

    sygnes (of)] CA (*so* K-D); also þe W&r *exc* F (C).

145 go] FH&c, AC (*so* K-D); to WL&c. gyue] L&r; gyuen W.

147 fals w.] LR, AC; *pl.* W.

148 he] LRF, AC; þei W&r.

153 wytt] GFH, A (*so* K-D); wittes W&r.

158 -nesse] *om* FHm, A.

160 be] LR, AC; to be W.

163 ynowe] of þe best H, A.

166 fet.] feyntly A (*so* K-D) (C).

Tho hadde notaries none; anoyed thei were	*irritated*
For Symonye and Cyvylle sholde on hire feet gange.	*had to go*
Ac thanne swoor Symonye and Cyvylle bothe	*swore*
170 That somonours sholde be sadeled and serven hem echone.	*saddled*
'And late apparaille thise provisours in palfreyes wise;	*like horses*
Sire Symonye hymself shal sitte upon hir bakkes.	*backs*
Denes and southdenes, drawe yow togideres;	*Deans; sub-deans*
Erchedekenes and officials and alle youre registrers,	
	Archdeacons; presiding officers; registrars
175 Lat sadle hem with silver oure synne to suffre—	*be saddled; permit*
As devoutrye and divorses and derne usurie—	*adultery; divorces; secret*
To bere bisshopes aboute abroad in visitynge.	*abroad*
Paulynes pryvees for pleintes in consistorie	*confidential; pleas*
Shul serven myself that Cyvyle is nempned.	*named*
180 And cartsadle the commissarie—oure cart shal he [drawe],	*(have) harness(ed)*
And fecchen us vitailles at *fornicatores*;	*from fornicators*
And maketh of Lyere a lang cart to leden alle thise othere,	*long*
As fobberes and faitours that on hire feet rennen.'	*tricksters; run*
And thus Fals and Favel fareth forth togideres,	*go*
185 And Mede in the middes and alle thise men after.	*midst*
I have no tome to telle the tail that hem folweth,	*leisure; tail/number*
Of many maner man that on this molde libbeth,	*earth; lives*
Ac Gyle was forgoer and gyed hem alle.	*harbinger; guided*
Sothnesse seigh hem wel, and seide but litel,	*Truth(fulness)*
190 A[c] priked his palfrey and passed hem alle,	
	spurred; (light courier's) horse
And com to the Kynges court and Conscience it tolde,	
And Conscience to the Kyng carped it after.	*related*
'Now, by Cryst!' quod the Kyng, 'and I cacche myghte	*if*
Fals or Favel or any of hise feeris,	*companions*
195 I wolde be wroken of tho wrecches that wercheth so ille,	*avenged on; act so evilly*
And doon hem hange by the hals and alle that hem maynteneth.	
	have them hanged; neck; support
Shal nevere man of this molde meynprise the leeste,	*stand bail (for)*
But right as the lawe loke[th], lat falle on hem alle!'	*determines*
And comaunded a constable that com at the firste,	*straight away*

171 And have these provisors got up like riding-horses.
178 Paulines, secret, confidential agents (when it comes to the conduct) of pleas in the bishop's court (*but cf.* Bn).

176 deuout-] R (?=α; d.d.*trsp.* F) (*so* K-D); Auout- β.
180 drawe] AC (*so* K-D); lede *All* B-MSS.
181 vs] oure AC.
183 fobberes] α; fobbis AC (*so* K-D); freres β.

186 hem folweth] LR, AC; hire folwed W.
187 LR, A (*cf.* C); *line om* W.
190 Ac] But F, AC; And W&r.
191 it] *om* G, AC.
198 lokis] AC (*so* K-D); wol loke *All* B-MSS.

200 To attachen tho tyraunts: 'For any [tresor], I hote, *arrest; in spite of; command*
 Fettreth Falsnesse faste, for any kynnes yiftes, *Fetter; kind of*
 And girdeth of Gyles heed—lat hym go no ferther; *smite off*
 And bringeth Mede to me maugree hem alle! *in spite of*
 And if ye lacche Lyere, lat hym noght ascapen *capture; escape*
205 Er he be put on the pillory, for any preyere, I hote.'
 Drede at the dore stood and the doom herde, *judgment*
 And how the Kyng comaunded constables and sergeaunts
 Falsnesse and his felawship to fettren and to bynden. *crew*
 Thanne Drede wente wyghtliche and warned the False, *with alacrity*
210 And bad hym fle for fere, and hise feeris alle. *fear; cronies*
 Falsnesse for fere thanne fleigh to the freres *fled; friars*
 And Gyle dooth hym to go, agast for to dye. *makes him; terrified*
 Ac marchaunts metten with hym and made hym abyde, *stay*
 And bishetten hym in hire shoppes to shewen hire ware, *shut him (up); display*
215 Apparailed hym as a prentice the peple to serve. *Dressed; apprentice*
 Lightliche Lyere leep awey thennes, *Smartly; ran; from there*
 Lurkynge thorugh lanes, tolugged of manye. *pulled about by*
 He was nowher welcome for his manye tales, *falsehoods*
 Over al yhonted and yhote trusse,
220 Til pardoners hadde pite, and pulled hym into house. *indoors*
 They wesshen hym and wiped hym and wounden hym in cloutes, *washed; patched clothes*
 And senten hym [on Sondayes with seles] to chirches, *(bishops') seals*
 And gaf pardoun for pens poundemele aboute. *pence; by pounds at a time*
 Thanne lourede leches, and lettres thei sente *scowled; physicians*
225 That he sholde wonye with hem watres to loke. *dwell; inspect urine*
 Spycers speken with hym to spien hire ware, *Spice-merchants; scrutinize*
 For he kouthe on hir craft and knew manye gommes. *understood; trade; gums*
 Ac mynstrales and messagers mette with hym ones, *messengers; once*
 And [with]helden hym an half yeer and ellevene dayes. *kept, harboured*
230 Freres with fair speche fetten hym thennes,
 And for knowynge of comeres coped hym as a frere; *recognition*
 Ac he hath leve to lepen out as ofte as hym liketh, *roam abroad*

219 Everywhere hounded down and ordered to pack up (and be off).
223 And (there he) distributed pardon(s) for pennies, (a number of them, to the value of several) pounds at a time.
231 And to prevent his being recognized by callers, dressed him in a friar's robes.

200 To] Go C, ?α (& go F; ?(T/G)oo R).
 tresour] AC (*so* K-D); þyng *All* B-MSS.
202 lat] A (*so* K-D); and l. *All* B-MSS.
203 *After* 207 *in all* B-MSS (*om* Y); here as in AC (*sugg.* K-D).
210 feerys] F, AC (*so* K-D); felawes W&r.

215 prentice] L, AC; apprentice W.
216 thence] GH, AC
 þenne RF (=α); þanne W&r (?=β).
222 on . . . seles] AC (*so* K-D); w.s.o.S. *All* B-MSS.
223 gaf] L&r; yeuen W.
229 with] AC (*so* K-D); *om* all B-MSS.
231 And] *om* AC.

And is welcome whan he wile, and woneth with hem ofte.   *dwells*
  Alle fledden for fere and flowen into hernes;   *flew; corners*
235 Save Mede the mayde na mo dorste abide.   *dared remain*
  Ac trewely to telle, she trembled for fere,
  And ek wepte and wrong whan she was attached.   *wrung (her hands); taken*

Passus III

  Now is Mede the mayde and no mo of hem alle,   *no more*
  With bedeles and baillies brought bifore the Kyng.   *By; tipstaffs; bailliffs*
  The Kyng called a clerk—I kan noght his name—   *know*
  To take Mede the maide and maken hire at ese.
5   'I shal assayen hire myself and soothliche appose   *try; truly question*
  What man of this world that hire were levest.   *would be dearest to her*
  And if she werche bi wit and my wil folwe   *wisdom; follow*
  I wol forgyven hire this gilt, so me God helpe!'   *guilt, fault*
    Curteisly the clerk thanne, as the Kyng highte,   *Courteously; ordered*
10 Took Mede bi the myddel and broghte hire into chambre.
                           waist; private room
  Ac ther was murthe and mynstralcie Mede to plese;   *entertainment; music*
  That wonyeth at Westmynstre worshipeth hire alle.   *(All) those who; honour*
  Gentilliche with joye the justices somme   *Courteously; some of the justices*
  Busked hem to the bour ther the burde dwellede,   *Repaired; lady; was staying*
15 Conforted hyre kyndely by Clergies leve,   *permission*
  And seiden, 'Mourne noght, Mede, ne make thow no sorwe,   *Do not weep*
  For we wol wisse the Kyng and thi wey shape   *advise; prepare a way for you*
  To be wedded at thi wille and wher thee leef liketh   *where you desire*
  For al Consciences cast or craft, as I trowe.'   *purpose; skill; believe*
20   Mildely Mede thanne merciede hem alle   *Humbly; thanked*

236 fere] a, **AC** (*so* K-D); drede β.

Rubric Passus tertius de visione vt supra.
1 *Collation of B begins here.*
2 and] CrG &c, **AC** (*so* K-D); a. with W.
3 y can] BH, **AC** (*so* K-D); kan I W.
6 world] RFB, **AC** (*so* K-D); moolde W.

8 gilt] *pl.* RF (*cf.* C).
10 broȝte] mente F (*C*).
11 Ac] R (?=a), **AC** (*so* K-D); And W.
12 þat] B, **AC** (*so* K-D); They þ. W&r exc F.
  at] RF&c, A (*so* K-D); in W.
15 Conf.] **AC** (*so* K-D); And c. H; To conforten W.

Of hire grete goodnesse—and gaf hem echone *For their*
Coupes of clene gold and coppes of silver, *Bowls; pure; cups*
Rynges with rubies and richesses manye, *rich gifts*
The leeste man of hire meynee a moton of golde. *followers; 'mutton' (coin)*
25   Thanne laughte thei leve thise lordes at Mede. *took; from*
With that comen clerkes to conforten hire the same, *learned men*
And beden hire be blithe—'For we beth thyne owene *bade; are*
For to werche thi wille the while thow myght laste.'
Hendiliche heo thanne bihighte hem the same— *Graciously; she; promised*
30 To loven hem lelly and lordes to make, *loyally*
And in the consistorie at the court do callen hire names.
                         have their names called (C)
'Shal no lewednesse lette the clerke that I lovye, *ignorance; impede*
That he ne worth first avaunced for I am biknowen
             will not be advanced; because; acknowledged
Ther konnynge clerkes shul clokke bihynde.' *learned; limp*
35   Thanne cam ther a confessour coped as a frere; *dressed*
To Mede the mayde [mekeliche he loutede] *bowed humbly*
And seide ful softely, in shrift as it were, *confession(al tones)*
'Theigh lewed men and lered men hadde leyen by thee bothe, *Though; lain*
And Falshede hadde yfolwed thee alle thise fifty wynter, *falsehood; deceit*
40 I shal assoille thee myself for a seem of whete, *absolve; horse-load*
And also be thi bedeman, and bere wel thyn er[ende],
             beadsman; (secret) messages
Amonges knyghtes and clerkes, Conscience to torne.' *turn aside, obstruct*
  Thanne Mede for hire mysdedes to that man kneled, *kneeled (in confession)*
And shrof hire of hire sherewednesse—shamelees, I trowe;
             confessed; wickedness
45 Tolde hym a tale and took hym a noble *gave; noble (coin)*
For to ben hire bedeman and hire brocour als. *go-between too*
  Thanne he assoiled hire soone and sithen he seide, *at once; next*
'We have a wyndow in werchynge, wole stonden us ful hye;
             a-building; cost us a great deal
Woldestow glaze that gable and grave therinne thy name,
             If you would; engrave
50 Sykir sholde thi soule be hevene to have.' *Certain*
  'Wiste I that,' quod the womman, 'I wolde noght spare *If I knew; hold back*
For to be youre frend, frere, and faile yow nevere *(would) fail*
While ye love lordes that lecherie haunten *indulge in*
And lakketh noght ladies that loven wel the same. *criticize*

32 clerke] Cra, C (pl. a); leode β; men
  H.
36 meke. he l.] A?C (*see* K-D *pp.* 105–6);
  he mened þise wordes W.
39 -ede] R (?=a; *om* F) (*so* K-D);
  -nesse W.
41 þin erende] AC (*so* K-D); þin
  erdyn H; þi message W.

46 brocour als] W&r; baud after G,
  A; on hand after H (C).
48 stonde] H, AC (*so* K-D); sitten
  W.
51–62 *Lines om* RF (=a); *see* K-D
  p. 221.
51 the] CrHM (*so* K-D); þat W&r
  (*om* Cot).

55 It is a freletee of flessh—ye fynden it in bokes— *frailty*
    And a cours of kynde, wherof we comen alle. *impulse of nature*
    Who may scape the sclaundre, the scathe is soone amended;
                       escape; slander; harm
    It is synne of the sevene sonnest relessed. *soonest; remitted*
    Have mercy,' quod Mede, 'of men that it haunteth *engage in it*
60 And I shal covere youre kirk, youre cloistre do maken, *roof (vb); have built*
    Wowes do whiten and wyndowes glazen, *Walls; have whitewashed*
    Do peynten and portraye [who paied] for the makynge,
                       Have painted & depicted
    That every segge shall see I am suster of youre house.' *man; a sister (C)*
    Ac God to alle good folk swich gravynge defendeth— *engraving; forbids*
65 To writen in wyndowes of hir wel dedes— *good deeds*
    An aventure pride be peynted there, and pomp of the world;
                     Lest perchance; 'vainglory'
    For God knoweth thi conscience and thi kynde wille,
                     inner intention, real motives
    And thi cost and thi coveitise and who the catel oughte. *owned the money*
    Forthi I lere yow lordes, leveth swiche w[rityng]es— *instruct; give up*
70 To writen in wyndowes of youre wel dedes *good deeds*
    Or to greden after Goddes men whan ye [gyve] doles, *call for; alms*
    On aventure ye have youre hire here and youre hevene als.
                     Lest; reward; too

    Nesciat sinistra quid faciat dextra:
    Lat noght thi left half, late ne rathe, *hand; early*
    Wite what thow werchest with thi right syde— *Know; are doing*
75 For thus bit the Gospel goode men doon hir almesse. *bids; give alms*
    Maires and maceres, that menes ben bitwene
                     Mayors; mace-bearers; intermediaries
    The kyng and the comune to kepe the lawes, *common people*
    To punysshe on pillories and on pynynge stooles *punishment-stools*
    Brewesters and baksters, bochiers and cokes—
                     Brewers; bakers; butchers; cooks
80 For thise are men on this molde that moost harm wercheth *earth; do*
    To the povere peple that parcelmele buggen. *buy piecemeal (sc. retail)*
    For thei poisone the peple pryveliche and ofte, *Because; secretly*

72a Let not thy left hand know what thy right hand doth (Mt 6: 3).
76 Mayors and officers of justice [who bear maces], who (act as) intermediaries
    between . . .

62 who p.] C (*so* K-D); and paie
    W&r (C).
63 Ise] α, AC; seye β.
67 god] R (?=a), C (*so* K-D); crist
    W&r.
69–72 *Lines om* FH.
69 writynges] AC (*sg.* K-D); werkes
    All B-MSS.

71 gyue] A (*so* K-D *p.* 88); dele *All*
    B-MSS.
75 bit] L; by W; bit God in *conj*
    K-D *p.* 199 (*cf.* C) (C).
78 on (2)] FH, AC (*so* K-D); *om*
    W&r.
82 poysoun] LRF&c, A; enp. W.

Thei richen thorugh regratrie and rentes hem biggen
grow rich; retail-trade; buy
With that the povere peple sholde putte in hire wombe. *that which; belly*
85 For toke thei on trewely, thei tymbred nought so heighe,
took (profits); would build
Ne boughte none burgages—be ye ful certeyne! *would buy; tenements*
  Ac Mede the mayde the mair h[eo] bisought[e] *beseeched the mayor*
Of alle swiche selleris silver to take, *From; (retail) merchants*
Or presents withouten pens—as pieces of silver, *(sc. in kind, non-monetary)*
90 Rynges or oother richesse the regratiers to mayntene. *retailers; support*
  'For my love,' quod that lady, 'love hem echone,
And suffre hem to selle somdel ayeins reson.' *at unreasonable prices*
  Salamon the sage a sermon he made *wise; discourse*
For to amenden maires and men that kepen lawes, *administer*
95 And tolde hem this teme that I telle thynke: *theme*
Ignis devorabit tabernacula eorum qui libenter accipiunt munera, &c.
Among thise lettrede leodes this Latyn is to mene *men; means*
That fir shall falle and [for]brenne al to bloo askes
fire; burn up; pale ashes
The houses and the homes of hem that desireth
100 Yiftes or yeresyeves because of hire offices. *annual gifts; office*
  The Kyng fro counseil cam, and called after Mede, *from; for*
And ofsente hire as swithe with sergeaunts manye *sent for; at once*
That broughte hire to boure with blisse and with joye. *the chamber*
  Curteisly the Kyng thanne comsed to telle; *began to speak*
105 To Mede the mayde he melleth thise wordes: *utters*
  'Unwittily, womman, wroght hastow ofte; *Foolishly; hast thou*
Ac worse wroghtest thow nevere than tho thow Fals toke. *did you act; took*
But I forgyve thee that gilt, and graunte thee my grace; *favour*
Hennes to thi deeth day do so na moore! *From henceforth*
110 I have a knyght, Conscience, cam late fro biyonde; *(who) has come lately*
If he wilneth thee to wif, wiltow hym have?' *desires; as a w.; will you*
  'Ye, lord,' quod that lady, 'Lord forbede it ellis! *forbid; otherwise*
But I be holly at youre heste, lat hange me soone!' *Unless; wholly; bidding; at once*
  Thanne was Conscience called to come and appere *appear*
115 Bifore the Kyng and his conseil, as clerkes and othere. *others*

83 They become rich through (the profits they make from) selling by retail, and
  buy themselves (properties from which they obtain) incomes.
85–6 For if they earned their living honestly, they (would be unable to) build such
  tall (imposing) houses Or purchase town-properties [from which to derive rents].
92 And allow them to sell to some extent at unreasonable prices.
96 . . . (and) fire shall devour their tabernacles, who love to take bribes (Job 15: 34).

87 heo bisouȝte] AC (so K-D p. 78);
  haþ bisouȝt W&r exc F.
98 for] AC (so K-D); om All B-MSS.
99 þe] LRF&c, AC; om W.
101 fro] LRF, AC; f. þe W.

103 That] L&r; And W.
107 -test þou] G&r (so K-D); -testow
  WLRYC.
114 þan] H(G), AC (so K-D); And
  þ. W&r.

Knelynge Conscience to the Kyng louted,   *bowed*
To wite what his wille were and what he do sholde.   *know; might be*
   'Woltow wedde this womman,' quod the Kyng, 'if I wole assente?
                                                               Will you
For she is fayn of thi felaweshipe, for to be thi make.'
                                               desirous; company; spouse
120   Quod Conscience to the Kyng, 'Crist it me forbede!
      Er I wedde swich a wif, wo me bitide!
      For she is frele of hire feith, fikel of hire speche,   *weak; deceitful*
      And maketh men mysdo many score tymes.   *do wrong*
      In trust of hire tresor she t[en]eth ful manye: *hurts*
125   Wyves and widewes wantounnesse she techeth,   *unchastity*
      And lereth hem lecherie that loveth hire yiftes.   *teaches; gifts*
      Youre fader she felled thorugh false biheste,   *brought down; promise(s)*
      And hath apoisoned popes and peired Holy Chirche.   *poisoned; damaged*
      Is noght a bettre baude, by Hym that me made,   *bawd*
130   Bitwene hevene and helle, in erthe though men soghte!   *were to search*
      For she is tikel of hire tail, talewis of tonge,   *loose; sex; garrulous*
      As commune as the cartwey to [knaves and to alle]—   *servants*
      To monkes, to mynstrales, to meseles in hegges;   *lepers; hedges*
      Sisours and somonours, swiche men hire preiseth,   *praise*
135   Sherreves of shires were shent if she ne were—   *would be ruined*
      For she dooth men lese hire lond and hire lif bothe.   *makes; lose*
      She leteth passe prisoners and paieth for hem ofte,   *go free; pays*
      And gyveth the gailers gold and grotes togidres   *gaolers; groats*
      To unfettre the Fals—fle where hym liketh;   *to flee; he wishes*
140   And taketh the trewe bi the top and tieth hym faste,   *hair; firmly*
      And hangeth hym for hatrede that harm[e]de nevere.   *hatred; did harm*
         'To be cursed in consistorie she counteth noght a russhe
                                            condemned; 'gives not a bean'
      For she copeth the commissarie and coteth hise clerkes.
                                               provides copes, coats for
      She is assoiled as soone as hireself liketh;   *absolved; pleases*
145   She may neigh as muche do in a monthe ones   *nearly; at one time*
      As youre secret seel in sixe score dayes!   *private; seal* (sc. *royal authority*)
      She is pryvee with the Pope—provisours it knoweth,   *intimate; provisors* (C)
      For Sire Symonie and hirselve seleth hire bulles.   *seal; mandates*
      She blesseth thise bisshopes, theigh thei be lewed;   *though; ignorant*

117 shulde] L&r; wolde W.   ech a knaue þat walkeþ W & most
124 In] G, AC (so K-D); om W&r.   (=Bx).
    she] F, AC (so K-D); om W&r.   140 hym] LR, A; hem W.
    teneþ] AC (so K-D); (bi)trayeþ   141 hym] LR, AC; hem W.
    W&r; dysseyuyt H.   harmede] AC (so K-D); harm diþe
125 -townesse] R; -tounes W.   All B-MSS.
128 apoys.] L; enpois. W.   142 russhe] LRF, AC; bene W.
131 talew. of] R (?=a; & t.w. of F),   145 She] F, AC (so K-D); And W&r.
    C?A (so K-D); and t. of hire W.   147 She] AC (so K-D); For she All
132 þe] GH, AC (so K-D); a W.   B-MSS.
    knaues and to alle] AC (so K-D);

150 Provendreth persones and preestes she maynteneth   *provides (prebends) for*
    To h[old]e lemmans and lotebies alle hire lif daies   *mistresses; concubines*
    And bryngen forth barnes ayein forbode lawes.   *children; laws that forbid*
     'Ther she is wel with the kyng, wo is the reaume—   *in favour with; realm*
    For she is favorable to Fals and defouleth truthe ofte.   *injures the honest*
155 By Jesus! with hire jeweles youre justice she shendeth   *damages*
    And lith ayein the lawe and letteth hym the gate,   *lies; blocks his way*
    That feith may noght have his forth, hire floryns go so thikke.
        course; florins
    She ledeth the lawe as hire list and lovedaies maketh,   *likes; love-days (C)*
    And doth men lese thorugh hire love that lawe myghte wynne—
        makes; that which legal proceedings
160 The maze for a mene man, though he mote evere!   *confusion; litigate*
    Lawe is so lordlich, and looth to maken ende: *reluctant*
    Withouten presents or pens he pleseth wel fewe.   *satisfies very*
     'Barons and burgeises she bryngeth in sorwe,   *burgesses; into trouble*
    And al the comune in care that coveiten lyve in truthe,   *desire to*
165 For clergie and coveitise she coupleth togidres.
    This is the lif of that lady—now Lord yyve hire sorwe,
        (manner of) life; give
    And alle that maynteneth hire men, meschaunce hem bitide!   *misfortune*
    For povere men may have no power to pleyne though thei smerte,
        complain; hurt
    Swich a maister is Mede among men of goode.'   *master; property*
170 Thanne mournede Mede and mened hire to the Kynge   *complained*
    To have space to speke, spede if she myghte.
        opportunity; prosper, succeed
    The Kyng graunted hire grace with a good wille: *leave*
    'Excuse thee if thow kanst; I kan namoore seggen,   *say*
    For Conscience accuseth thee, to congeien thee for evere.'   *dismiss*
175 'Nay, lord,' quod that lady, 'leveth hym the werse   *believe*
    Whan ye witen witterly wher the wrong liggeth.   *certainly; lies*
    Ther that meschief is gret, Mede may helpe.   *mishap, ill luck*
    And thow knowest, Conscience, I kam noght to chide,   *quarrel*
    Ne to deprave thi persone with a proud herte.   *revile; attitude of disdain*
180 Wel thow woost, wernard, but if thow wolt gabbe,   *deceiver; lie*
    Thow hast hanged on myn half ellevene tymes,
        taken my side; eleven (i.e. many)
    And also griped my gold, and gyve it where thee liked.   *clutched; given*
    Whi thow wrathest thee now, wonder me thynketh!   *are angry; strange*

150 she] F (?=heo a; a R), AC (so K-D); om W&r.
151 holde] AC (so K-D); haue All B-MSS.
152 -gen] LR, AC; -geþ W.
155 iustice] H, ?AC (so K-D); pl. W&r.
160 moote] GF, AC (so K-D); m. hire WLR.
162 he] R (?=a; it F), A (so K-D); she W&r, C.
168 pleyne] F&c, A (cf. C), so K-D; p. hem WLR.
179 to] HmH, AC (so K-D); om W&r.
182 and] BGF, AC (so K-D); om W&r.
183 Whi] AC (so K-D); And w. W&r (A.] But F).

Yet I may, as I myghte, menske thee with yiftes   *could; honour*
185 And mayntene thi manhode moore than thow knowest.   *support*
   'Ac thow hast famed me foule bifore the Kyng here;   *foully slandered*
For killed I nevere no kyng, ne counseiled therafter,   *advised accordingly*
Ne dide as thow demest—I do it on the Kynge.   *claim; appeal to*
In Normandie was he noght noyed for my sake—   *vexed, troubled*
190 Ac thow thiself, soothly, shamedest hym ofte: *brought disgrace on*
Crope into a cabane for cold of thi nayles,   *Crept; shelter; to prevent*
Wendest that wynter wolde han ylasted evere,   *Thought; lasted*
And dreddest to be ded for a dym cloude,   *dreaded; dark*
And hyedest homward for hunger of thi wombe.   *hurried; belly*
195 Withouten pite, pilour, povere men thow robbedest   *pity; pillager*
And bere hire bras at thi bak to Caleis to selle,   *bore; Calais*
Ther I lafte with my lord his lif for to save.   *Whereas; remained; protect*
I made his men murye and mournynge lette;   *cheerful; prevented*
I batred hem on the bak and boldede hire hertes,   *slapped; emboldened*
200 And dide hem hoppe for hope to have me at wille.   *made; dance*
Hadde I ben marchal of his men, by Marie of hevene!   *marshal (C)*
I dorste have leyd my lif and no lasse wedde,   *pledged; surety*
He sholde have be lord of that lond in lengthe and in brede,   *breadth*
And also kyng of that kith his kyn for to helpe—   *country; kindred, family*
205 The leeste brol of his blood a barones piere!   *brat; equal*
Cowardly thow, Conscience, conseiledest hym thennes—   *(to go from) thence*
To leven his lordshipe for a litel silver,   *abandon; domain*
That is the richeste reaume that reyn overhoveth.   *realm; rain; hovers over*
   'It bicometh to a kyng that kepeth a reaume   *rules; kingdom*
210 To yeve [men mede] that mekely hym serveth—   *obediently serve*
To aliens and to alle men, to honouren hem with yiftes;   *foreigners*
Mede maketh hym biloved and for a man holden.   *considered a 'real' man*
Emperours and erles and alle manere lordes   *earls*
Thorugh yiftes han yonge men to yerne and to ryde.   *young; run (on errands)*
215 The Pope and alle prelates presents underfongen   *receive*
And medeth men hemselven to mayntene hir lawes,   *reward; administer*
Servaunts for hire servyce, we seeth wel the sothe,   *see; truth*
Taken mede of hir maistres, as thei mowe acorde.   *payment; can agree*
Beggeres for hir biddynge bidden men mede.   *in return for their prayers ask*
220 Mynstrales for hir myrthe mede thei aske.   *entertainment*
The Kyng hath mede of his men to make pees in londe.
    to pay his m.; the country
Men that [kenne clerkes] craven of hem mede.   *teach students; request a fee*
Preestes that prechen the peple to goode   *to good conduct*

210 men m.] C; hise m. m. A (*so*
K-D); mede to men *All* B-MSS (*C*).
214 þorgh3] FR (=α), AC (*so* K-D);
For β.
   3ernen] α, C (*so* K-D); renne
WL&c (=β).
215 alle] LR, C; a. þe W.

217 Seruantz] L, AC; Sergeaunt3 W.
222 kenne c.] AC (*so* K-D); teche
children *All* B-MSS.
   of hem] LRF; after W.
223 *Div. from* 224 *after* Mede *All*
B-MSS; *after* goode A (*so re-div.*
K-D).

Asken mede and massepens and hire mete [also].   *mass-pence; food*
225 Alle kyn crafty men craven mede for hir prentices.
          craftsmen; for (training) appr.
Marchaundise and mede mote nede go togideres: *Trade, business; must needs*
No wight, as I wene, withouten Mede may libbe!'   *suppose; can live*
   Quod the Kyng to Conscience, 'By Crist, as me thynketh,   *it seems to me*
Mede is worthi the maistrie to have!'   *sway, victory*
230   'Nay,' quod Conscience to the Kyng and kneled to the erthe,
'Ther are two manere of medes, my lord, by youre leve.   *kinds of reward*
That oon God of his grace graunteth in his blisse
          The one; goodness, blessedness
To tho that wel werchen while thei ben here.   *those; work; sc. on earth*
The Prophete precheth therof and putte it in the Sauter: *Psalter, psalms*
Domine, quis habitabit in tabernaculo tuo?
235 Lord, who shal wonye in thi wones with thyne holy seintes   *dwelling(s)*
Or resten in thyne holy hilles?—This asketh David.   *David asks this*
And David assoileth it hymself, as the Sauter telleth:
          provides a solution, answer
Qui ingreditur sine macula et operatur iusticiam.
Tho that entren of o colour and of one wille,   *in one; single, undivided*
And han ywroght werkes with right and with reson,   *done works*
240 And he that useth noght the lyf of usurie   *engages in; usury*
And enformeth povere men and pursueth truthe: *instructs; honesty*
Qui pecuniam suam non dedit ad usuram, et
    munera super innocentem &c;
And alle that helpen the innocent and holden with the rightfulle,
          support; just
Withouten mede doth hem good and the truthe helpeth—   *furthers honesty*
Swiche manere men, my lord, shul have this firste mede
245 Of God at a gret nede, whan thei gon hennes.
          From; (a time of) g.n. (sc. death)
  'Ther is another mede mesurelees, that maistres desireth:
          immoderate; lords, rulers
To mayntene mysdoers mede thei take,   *support; evil-doers*
And therof seith the Sauter in a salmes ende—   *psalm's conclusion*
In quorum manibus iniquitates sunt; dextra eorum repleta est
muneribus;
250 And he that gripeth hir gold, so me God helpe,

234*a* Lord, who shall dwell in thy tabernacle? (Ps 14: 1).
237*a* He that walketh without blemish, and worketh justice (Ps 14: 2).
241*a* He that hath not put out his money to usury, nor [taken] bribes against the
    innocent (Ps 25: 10).
249 In whose hands are iniquities: their right hand is filled with gifts (Ps 25: 10).

224 also] **A** (*cf.* bothe C); als K-D; at
  þe meel tyme*s All* B-MSS.
225 crafty] L&*r*, **AC**; craftes WCr.
226 M. & m.] H, C (*cf.* A-MS J);
  Marchaunt3 and M. W&*r*.

229 is] α, **AC** (*so* K-D); is wel β.
231 by] α, A; wiþ β.
235 wiþ] RFH (*so* K-D); and w.
  W&*r*.
243 truþe] β; trewe α.

Shal abien it bittre, or the Book lieth!   *pay for it grievously; Bible*
Preestes and persons that plesynge desireth,   *parsons; pleasure*
That taken mede and moneie for masses that thei syngeth,   *money*
Taken hire mede here as Mathew us techeth: *in this world*
Amen, amen, receperunt mercedem suam.
255 That laborers and lewede [leodes] taken of hire maistres,
                                        That which; people; from
It is no manere mede but a mesurable hire.   *moderate, appropriate wage*
In marchaundise is no mede, I may it wel avowe: *trade, commerce; declare*
It is a permutacion apertly—a penyworth for another.
                                        (act of) exchange; manifestly
'Ac reddestow nevere *Regum*, thow recrayed Mede,
                                        (the Book of) Kings; recreant
260 Whi the vengeaunce fel on Saul and on his children?
God sente to Saul by Samuel the prophete   *sent (word)*
That Agag of Amalec and al his peple after   *as well*
Sholden deye for a dede that doon hadde hire eldres.   *ancestors*
"Forthi," seide Samuel to Saul, "God hymself hoteth thee
                                        Therefore; commands
265 To be buxom at his biddynge, his wil to fulfille.   *obedient; will, wishes*
Weend to Amalec with thyn oost, and what thow fyndest there—sle it:
                                        Go; host; slay, destroy
Burnes and beestes—bren hem to dethe!   *Men; burn*
Widwes and wyves, wommen and children,   *Widows*
Moebles and unmoebles, and al thow myght fynde— *Moveables; immoveables*
270 Bren it, bere it noght awey, be it never so riche;   *carry; valuable*
For mede ne for monee, loke thow destruye it!   *In spite of; be sure to*
Spille it and spare it noght—thow shalt spede the bettre." *Destroy; prosper*
And for he coveited hir catel and the kyng spared,   *because; goods*
Forbar hym and his beestes bothe as the Bible witnesseth *Allowed to live*
275 Otherwise than he was warned of the prophete,   *by*
God seide to Samuel that Saul sholde deye,   *must die*
And al his seed for that synne shenfulliche ende.   *ignominiously*
Swich a meschief Mede made the kyng to have   *misfortune*
That God hated hym for evere and alle his heires after.   *heirs*
280 'The *culorum* of this cas kepe I noght to shewe; *conclusion; care, wish*
On aventure it noyed me, noon ende wol I make,   *Lest it should harm*
For so is this world went with hem that han power   *turned*

254a Amen, I say to you, they have received their reward (Mt 6: 5).
271 Take care (not to fail to) destroy it, for (any) bribe or monetary payment (you may be offered).
280 The full implications of this event I have no wish to spell out (C).

254a *Receperunt*] FH, AC (*so* Sk,   265 To] OC² Hm, AC; *om* W&r.
   Vulg.); *Recipiebant* WLR.   278 þe kyng] A (*so* K-D); Saul the k.
255 lewed] RF; lowe WL.   W&r; k.s. F.
   leodes] men F; folk W&r.   280 shewe] LR, AC; telle W.
264 *Div. from* 265 *after* hoteþ *All*
   B-MSS; *re-div.* K-D.

That whoso seith hem sothest is sonnest yblamed!   *most truly; soonest*
'I, Conscience, knowe this, for Kynde Wit it me taughte—
285 That Reson shal regne and reaumes governe,   *reign; realms*
And right as Agag hadde, happe shul somme: *it shall happen to*
Samuel shal sleen hym and Saul shal be blamed,
And David shal be diademed and daunten hem alle,   *subdue*
And oon Cristene kyng kepen [us] echone.   *rule*
290 Shal na moore Mede be maister as she is nouthe,   *at present*
Ac love and lowenesse and leautee togideres—   *humility; right*
Thise shul ben maistres on moolde [trewe men] to save.   *earth; protect*
And whoso trespaseth ayein truthe or taketh ayein his wille,   *against*
Leaute shal don hym lawe, and no lif ellis.
    Justice; execute the law upon; nobody
295 Shal no sergeant for his service were a silk howve,   *lawyer; coif*
Ne no pelure in his [paviloun] for pledynge at the barre.   *fur; cloak*
'Mede of mysdoeres maketh manye lordes,   *out of criminals*
And over lordes lawes [led]eth the reaumes.   *holds sway over; kingdoms*
Ac kynde love shal come yit and Conscience togideres   *with (him)*
300 And make of lawe a laborer; swich love shal arise
And swich pees among the peple and a parfit truthe
    (state of) perfect uprightness
That Jewes shul wene in hire wit, and wexen wonder glade,   *suppose; grow*
That Moyses or Messie be come into this erthe,   *Moses; the Messias*
And have wonder in hire hertes that men beth so trewe.   *should be; righteous*
305 'Alle that beren baselard, brood swerd or launce,   *dagger; broad*
Ax outher hachet or any wepene ellis,   *or; hatchet*
Shal be demed to the deeth but if he do it smythye
    condemned; have it hammered
Into sikel or to sithe, to shaar or to kultour—   *(plough)share; coulter*
Conflabunt gladios suos in vomeres, &c—
Ech man to pleye with a plow, pykoise or spade,   *(is) to be active; pick-axe*
310 Spynne, or sprede donge, or spille hymself with sleuthe;   *manure; destroy*
Preestes and persons with *Placebo* to hunte,   *psalm(s)*
And dyngen upon David eche day til eve.   *pound away upon*
Huntynge or haukynge if any of hem use,   *hawking; practise*
His boost of his benefice worth bynomen hym after.   *shall be taken away*

---

298 And exercises control of kingdoms over (and above) the king's laws.
308*a* . . . and they shall turn their swords into ploughshares (Is 2: 4).
311–12 . . . to 'hunt' (only) with (the psalm) *I will please* (*the Lord*) [Ps 114: 9] And keep pounding away all day at the psalms in his Psalter . . .
314 His boast in his/that he will obtain a benefice will be stripped away from him as a result (of it).

289 vs] AC (*so* K-D); hem *All* B-MSS *exc* F.
    echone] MCr, AC (*so* K-D); alle W.
292 tr. m.] C (K-D *p.* 92); truthe *All* B-MSS.
296 pauelon] C (panelon K-D *p.* 93);

cloke W&r (C).
298 ledeþ] *conj* K-D *p.* 195; ruleþ *All* B-MSS (C).
301 pees] α, C; a *p.* β.
303 into this] to myddel *conj.* K-D *p.* 199 (C).

315 'Shal neither kyng ne knyght, constable ne meire   *mayor*
    Over[carke] the commune ne to the court sompne,   *over-burden; summon*
    Ne putte hem in panel to doon hem plighte hir truthe;
                                               empanel them as jurors; swear
    But after the dede that is doon oon doom shal rewarde
                                        judgment; ?recompense, apportion
    Mercy or no mercy as Truthe [moste] acorde.   *agree*
320 'Kynges court and commune court, consistorie and chapitle—
                                                    chapter (-court)
    Al shal be but oon court, and oon b[ur]n be justice: *person; judge*
    That worth Trewe-tonge, a tidy man that tened me nevere.
                                          will be; good; grieved
    Batailles shul none be, ne no man bere wepene,   *carry*
    And what smyth that any smytheth be smyte therwith to dethe!
                                               forges; struck

    Non levabit gens contra gentem gladium &c.
325 'And er this fortune falle, fynde men shul the worste,   *befall*
    By sixe sonnes and a ship and half a shef of arwes;   *quiver-ful; arrows*
    And the myddel of a moone shal make the Jewes torne,   *be converted*
    And Sarsynes for that sighte shul synge *Gloria in excelsis &c*—
                                        Saracens, Mahometans
    For Makometh and Mede myshappe shul that tyme;   *shall come to grief*
330 For *Melius est bonum nomen quam divicie multe.*'
    Also wroth as the wynd weex Mede in a while.   *angry; became; moment*
    'I kan no Latyn?' quod she. 'Clerkes wite the sothe!   *know*
    Se what Salomon seith in Sapience bokes:
    That thei that yyven yiftes the victorie wynneth,   *give gifts*
335 And muche worshipe have therwith, as Holy Writ telleth—   *honour; obtain*
    Honorem adquiret qui dat munera, &c.'
    'I leve wel, lady,' quod Conscience, 'that thi Latyn be trewe.   *believe*
    Ac thow art lik a lady that radde a lesson ones,   *read*
    Was *omnia probate*, and that plesed hire herte—
340 For that lyne was no lenger at the leves ende.   *line; page's*
    Hadde she loked that other half and the leef torned,   *examined; leaf*
    She sholde have founden fele wordes folwynge therafter: *several*

324*a* Nation shall not lift up sword against nation (Is 2: 4).
330 A good name is better than great riches (Prov 22: 1).
336 He that maketh presents shall purchase victory and honour . . . (Prov 22: 9).
339 But prove [*sc.* put to the test] all things (I Thess 5: 21).

316 karke] C (*so* K-D, *p.* 93); lede   327 torne] αG, C (*so* K-D); to t. β.
    All B-MSS.   335 muche] LRF, C; moost W.
319 Truthe moste] m. trewþe C; T.   haue] CrHmF (hath Cr²³);
    wole *All* B-MSS (C).   hadde W&r.
321 buyrne] C (*so* K-D); baron W&r   338 þat . . . ones] þ. a l. redde F, C.
    (*om* C).   342 fele] fell G (*so* K-D).
322 That] Bm, C (*so* K-D); Thanne
    W&r (C).

Quod bonum est tenete—Truthe that text made.
And so [mys]ferde ye, madame—ye kouthe na moore fynde   *you went wrong*
345 Tho ye loked on Sapience, sittynge in youre studie.   *When*
This text that ye han told were [tidy] for lordes,   *would be; useful*
Ac yow failed a konnynge clerk that kouthe the leef han torned.
                                  lacked; skilful; could . . . have
And if ye seche Sapience eft, fynde shul ye that folweth,
                                  examine; again; that which
A ful teneful text to hem that taketh mede: *painful*
350 And that is *Animam autem aufert accipientium &c.*
And that is the tail of the text of that tale ye shewed—
                                  end; discourse; quoted
That theigh we wynne worshipe and with mede have victorie,
                                though; obtain honour
The soule that the soude taketh by so muche is bounde.'   *payment*

Passus IV

'Cesseth!' seide the Kyng, 'I suffre yow no lenger.   *Stop; will allow*
Ye shul saughtne, forsothe, and serve me bothe.   *be reconciled*
Kis hire,' quod the Kyng, 'Conscience, I hote!'   *command*
  'Nay, by Crist!' quod Conscience, 'congeye me rather!   *dismiss; sooner*
5 But Reson rede me therto, rather wol I deye.'   *Unless; advise*
  'And I comaunde thee,' quod the Kyng to Conscience thanne,
'Rape thee to ryde, and Reson that thow fecche.   *Make haste; fetch*
Comaunde hym that he come my counseil to here,   *inner thoughts*
For he shal rule my reaume and rede me the beste   *realm; counsel*
10 Of Mede and of mo othere, what man shal hire wedde,   *other matters too*

343 . . . hold fast that which is good (I Thess 5: 21).
350 . . . but he carrieth away the souls of the receivers (Prov 22: 9).

344 mys-] *conj* K-D *p.* 199; *om all*
  B-MSS.
345 loked on] souȝte *conj* K-D.
346 tidy] good *All* B-MSS; trewe
  conj K-D (*C*).
351 þ. tale] F; þat WLR; teme *conj*
  K-D (*C*).
  ȝe] LRF; she W.

Rubric *Passus quartus de visione vt*
  supra.
1 seyde] RF, AC (*so* K-D); seiþ WL.
4 raþer] O (=g) H, AC (*so* K-D); er
  for euere W; f.e. LR.
7 þat] F, AC (*so* K-D); *om* WLR.
10 *In* YCr²³ OC², AC (*so* K-D); *line*
  om W&r.

And acounte with thee, Conscience, so me Crist helpe,   *settle*
How thow lernest the peple, the lered and the lewed!'
          teach; educated, uneduc.
'I am fayn of that foreward,' seide the freke thanne,
          content; agreement; man
And ryt right to Reson and rouneth in his ere,   *rides straight; whispers*
15 And seide hym as the Kyng seide, and sithen took his leve.   *then; leave*
  'I shal arraye me to ryde,' quod Reson, 'reste thee a while,'   *prepare*
And called Caton his knave, curteis of speche,   *servant; courteous*
And also Tomme Trewe-tonge-tel-me-no-tales   *true-tongue; lies*
Ne lesynge-to-laughen-of-for-I-loved-hem-nevere.   *lies; at*
20 'Set my sadel upon Suffre-til-I-se-my-tyme,   *saddle*
And lat warroke hym wel with witty-wordes gerthes.
          have him fastened; girths
Hange on hym the hevy brydel to holde his heed lowe,   *heavy bridle; head*
For he wol make "wehee" twies er he be there.'   *neigh twice; before*
Thanne Conscience on his capul caireth forth faste,   *horse; proceeds*
25 And Reson with hym ryt, rownynge togideres   *rides; whispering*
Whiche maistries Mede maketh on this erthe.   *What displays of (her) power*
  Oon Waryn Wisdom and Witty his fere   *One; companion*
Folwed hem faste, for thei hadde to doone   *Followed; business*
In th'Escheker and in the Chauncerye, to ben descharged of thynges,
          released from legal actions
30 And riden faste for Reson sholde rede hem the beste   *in order that*
For to save hem for silver from shame and from harmes.   *disgrace; trouble*
A[c] Conscience knew hem wel, thei loved coveitise,   *(that) they*
And bad Reson ryde faste and recche of hir neither:
          care about; neither of them
'Ther are wiles in hire wordes, and with Mede thei dwelleth—
35 Ther as wrathe and wranglynge is, ther wynne thei silver;   *Where*
Ac there is love and leautee, thei wol noght come there:
          where there; don't wish to
Contricio et infelicitas in viis eorum &c.
Thei ne gyveth noght of God one goose wynge: *care not for*
Non est timor Dei ante oculos eorum &c.
For thei wolde do moore for a dozeyne chiknes   *dozen chickens*
Than for the love of Oure Lord or alle hise leeve seintes!   *dear*

29 In the (courts of) Exchequer and Chancery, (where they intended) to be released
from various legal liabilities.
36a *and* 37a Destruction and unhappiness [are] in their ways; [and the way of
peace they have not known:] there is no fear of God before their eyes (Ps 13: 3).

15 hym] F, AC (*so* K-D); *om* W&r.
   seide (2)] F, C, *some* A-MSS; bad
   W&r.
21 witty-wordes] wytful A (*so* K-D) (C).
24 on] GH, AC (*so* K-D); vpon W&r.
   kaireþ] LRF, A; carieþ W.
28 hem] LRF, AC; hym W.

32 Ac] AC (*so* K-D); And *All* B-MSS.
36 þere (1)] LR, C (*so* K-D); where
   WF.
   wol] W&r; leete F.
38 *After this another line* Or as manye
   capons or for a seem of Otes *All*
   B-MSS (C).

40 Forthi, Reson, lat hem ride, tho riche by hemselve— *those rich men*
　For Conscience knoweth hem noght, ne Crist, as I trowe.' *reckon*
　　And thanne Reson rood faste the righte heighe gate,
　　　　　　　　　　　　　　　　　on the direct high way
　As Conscience hym kenned, til thei come to the Kynge. *instructed*
　Curteisly the Kyng thanne com ayeins Reson, *to meet*
45 And bitwene hymself and his sone sette hym on benche,
　And wordeden wel wisely a gret while togideres. *they talked*
　　And thanne com Pees into parlement and putte up a bille— *Peace; petition*
　How Wrong ayeins his wille hadde his wif taken, *against*
　And how he ravysshede Rose, Reignaldes loove, *carried off; sweetheart*
50 And Margrete of hir maydenhede maugree hire chekes. *i.e. by force*
　' Bothe my gees and my grys hise gadelynges feccheth;
　　　　　　　　　　　　　　　　　pigs; fellows; take away
　I dar noght for fere of hem fighte ne chide. *fear; complain*
　He borwed of me bayard and broughte hym hom nevere
　　　　　　　　　　　　　　　　　(my) bay horse; home
　Ne no ferthyng therfore, for nought I koude plede. *farthing in compensation*
55 He maynteneth hise men to murthere myne hewen, *murder; servants*
　Forstalleth my feires and fighteth in my chepyng, *Forestalls (C); fairs; market*
　And breketh up my berne dores and bereth awey my whete,
　　　　　　　　　　　　　　　　　down; barn-doors; wheat
　And taketh me but a taille for ten quarters otes. *gives; tally-stick (C)*
　And yet he beteth me therto and lyth by my mayde;
　　　　　　　　　　　　　　　　　further; lies; maid-servant
60 I am noght hardy for hym unnethe to loke!' *bold; because of; scarcely*
　　The Kyng knew he seide sooth, for Conscience hym tolde *truth*
　That Wrong was a wikked luft and wroghte muche sorwe.
　　　　　　　　　　　　　　　　　rascal; mischief; trouble
　Wrong was afered thanne, and Wisdom he soughte *afraid*
　To maken pees with hise pens, and profred hym manye, *pence; proffered*
65 And seide, 'Hadde I love of my lord the Kyng, litel wolde I recche *care*
　Theigh Pees and his power pleyned hym evere!'
　　　　　　　　　　　　　　　　　Though; supporters; complained
　　Tho wan Wisdom and Sire Waryn the Witty, *went*
　For that Wrong hadde ywroght so wikked a dede, *Because*
　And warnede Wrong tho with swich a wis tale— *such prudent words as these*
70 'Whoso wercheth by wille, wrathe maketh ofte. *wilfully; causes, arouses*

54–6 Nor any farthing (in payment) for it, in spite of any pleading of mine. He aids
　and abets his retainers to murder my workmen, makes forced purchases in
　advance (of the goods I intend to sell) at fairs and causes brawls in my market.
60 Because of him, I am scarcely bold enough to show my face!

47 vp] H, AC (*so* K-D); forþ W&r.　　58 otes] FM, AC (*so* K-D); of O.
53 and] αH, AC (*so* K-D); he WL.　　　WLR.
54 nauȝte] LRF, AC; ouȝt W.　　　　　59 beteþ] thretiþ F; manasceþ C.
57 berne dores] OCr &c, AC (*so*　　　67 wan] LR, A; wente W.
　K-D); bernes dore WLR.

I seye it by myself—thow shalt it wel fynde: *concerning*
But if Mede it make, thi meschief is uppe;
                      Unless; make (good); over (cf. Bn. p. 146)
For bothe thi lif and thi lond lyth in his grace.'   *at his disposal*
   Thanne wowede Wrong Wisdom ful yerne   *solicited; eagerly*
75 To maken his pees with his pens, handy dandy payed. *by secret bribery (C).*
Wisdom and Wit thanne wenten togidres,
And token Mede myd hem mercy to wynne.   *took; with; obtain*
   Pees putte forth his heed and his panne blody: *brain-pan, skull*
'Withouten gilt, God woot, gat I this scathe.'   *received; injury*
80   Conscience and the commune knowen wel the sothe,   *know the truth*
Ac Wisdom and Wit were aboute faste   *busily set about*
To overcomen the Kyng with catel, if thei myghte.   *through wealth*
   The Kyng swor by Crist and by his crowne bothe   *too*
That Wrong for hise werkes sholde wo tholie,   *endure suffering*
85 And comaundede a constable to casten hym in irens,
'And lete hym noght thise seven yer seen his feet ones.'   *once*
   'God woot,' quod Wisdom, 'that were noght the beste!   *wouldn't be*
And he amendes mowe make, lat Maynprise hym have   *If; can; Bail*
And be borgh for his bale, and buggen hym boote,
                  surety; evil acts; buy; remedy
90 And so amenden that is mysdo, and everemoore the bettre.'
                  that which; ill-done
   Wit acorded therwith, and seide the same,   *agreed*
'Bettre is that boote bale adoun brynge   *reparation; evil; defeat*
Than bale be ybet, and boote nevere the bettre!'   *beaten, punished*
   Thanne gan Mede to meken hire, and mercy bisoughte,   *act humble*
95 And profrede Pees a present al of pure golde.
'Have this, man, of me,' quod she, 'to amenden thi scathe,
                  from; make good; injury
For I wol wage for Wrong, he wol do so na moore.'   *guarantee*
   Pitously Pees thanne preyde to the Kynge   *Forgivingly*
To have mercy on that man that mysdide hym so ofte.   *wronged; injured*
100 'For he hath waged me wel, as Wisdom hym taughte,   *paid*
And I forgyve hym that gilt with a good wille.
So that the Kyng assente, I kan seye no bettre,   *Provided*

88 If (Wrong) is able to make monetary compensation, let Bail assume responsi-
    bility for him and stand as surety for the wrongs he has done, and purchase a
    remedy for (Peace).
92–3 (It is better) that compensation should extinguish wrong done than that
    wrongs should be punished and still no compensation be forthcoming.

75 his (2)] L&r; *om* WH.
80 wel] F, A (*cf.* C) (*so* K-D); *om*
    W&r.
91 seide] witnessede C (*so* K-D) (*C*).
94 Than] CrH, AC (*so* K-D); And þ.
    W&r.

meken] RF (=α), AC (*so* K-D);
mengen WL&c (?=β).
bisouȝte] BFH&c, AC (*so* K-D);
    she b. WLR.
99 so] *om* MG, A.

For Mede hath maad myne amendes—I may na moore axe.'
compensation; ask

    'Nay', quod the Kyng tho, 'so me Crist helpe! *then*
105 Wrong wendeth noght so awey er I wite more.
    Lope he so lightly, laughen he wolde, *If he ran away; easily*
    And eft the boldere be to bete myne hewen. *next time; servants*
    But Reson have ruthe on hym, he shal reste in my stokkes
Unless; pity; stocks
    As longe as [I] lyve, but lowenesse hym borwe.' *humility; stand bail for*
110   Somme radde Reson tho to have ruthe on that shrewe, *advised; villain*
    And for to counseille the Kyng and Conscience after *as well*
    That Mede moste be maynpernour, Reson thei bisoughte. *might; surety*
    'Reed me noght,' quod Reson, 'no ruthe to have *Advise; mercy*
    Til lordes and ladies loven alle truthe *all love honest living*
115 And haten alle harlotrie, to heren or to mouthen it; *obscenity; utter*
    Til Pernelles purfill be put in hire hucche *trimming; trunk*
    And childrene cherissynge be chastised with yerdes, *spoiling; rods*
    And harlottes holynesse be holden for an hyne;
ribalds'; considered worthless
    Til clerkene coveitise be to clothe the povere and fede,
clerks' avarice be(come)
120 And religiouse romeris *Recordare* in hir cloistres *wandering religious*
    As Seynt Beneyt hem bad, Bernard and Fraunceis; *Benedict; Francis*
    And til prechours prechynge be preved on hemselve; *demonstrated in*
    Til the Kynges counseil be the commune profit; *public good*
    Til bisshopes bayardes ben beggeris chaumbres, *horses; dwellings*
125 Hire haukes and hire houndes help to povere religious;
members of religous orders
    And til Seint James be sought there I shal assigne— *indicate*
    That no man go to Galis but if he go for evere; *Galicia (C)*
    And alle Rome renneres for robberes of biyonde *runners; from abroad*

109 ... unless (his own future) humility should act as a surety for (his good conduct).

117 And children, instead of being over-indulged, be disciplined with beating.

118 *Lit.* valued as a farm-labourer—i.e. very cheaply.

120 And members of religious orders who go travelling about sing the offertory 'Remember, Lord' [*sc.* recall their duties in their cloisters; 'meditate upon the Scriptures' (Alford)].

128 And until no (more) hasty travellers to Rome [carry sterling abroad] for the benefit of foreign thieves.

103 made myn amendes] RF (=a), AC (*so* K-D); m. me a. LY&c (?=β); me a. m. W.
105 er] H (or G), AC (*so* K-D); erst wole WLR&c (?=Bx).
106 Lope] AC (*so* K-D); For lope *All* B-MSS.
109 As] HG, AC (*so* K-D); And þat as W&r.

I lyue] AC (*so* K-D); he lyueþ W&r.
110 Summe] HmH, ?A, C (*so* K-D); Som men W&r (Fele F).
117 chast*y*sed] FHHm, AC (*so* K-D); chastynge WLR&c.
128 of] LR, A; *om* WF.

Bere no silver over see that signe of kyng sheweth—   *sea; stamp*
130 Neither grave ne ungrave, gold neither silver—   *stamped, unstamped*
Upon forfeture of that fee, who fynt hym at Dovere,   *money; if anyone finds*
But if it be marchaunt or his man, or messager with lettres,
    Unless; messenger; warrants
Provysour or preest, or penaunt for hise synnes.   *Provisor; penitent*
'And yet,' quod Reson, 'by the Rode! I shal no ruthe have
    further; Cross; mercy
135 While Mede hath the maistrie in this moot-halle.
    sway; council-chamber, court
Ac I may shewe ensamples as I se outher.   *can; others*
I seye it by myself,' quod he, 'and it so were   *for; if*
That I were kyng with coroune to kepen a reaume,   *charged with ruling*
Sholde nevere Wrong in this world that I wite myghte   *know (about)*
140 Ben unpunysshed in my power, for peril of my soule,   *if I could help it*
Ne gete my grace thorugh giftes, so me God save!   *mercy, indulgence*
Ne for no mede have mercy, but mekenesse it made;   *unless; brought it about*
For "*Nullum malum* the man mette with *inpunitum*   *innocence; unpunished*
And bad *Nullum bonum* be *irremuneratum.*"   *wickedness; unrewarded*
145 Lat thi confessour, sire Kyng, construe this [E]ngl[ys]sed,
    translated into English
And if ye werchen it in werk, I wedde myne eris   *practise; bet*
That Lawe shal ben a laborer and lede afeld donge   *carry afield manure*
And Love shal lede thi lond as the leef liketh.'   *rule; you would desire*
Clerkes that were confessours coupled hem togideres   *joined in pairs*
150 Al to construe this clause, and for the Kynges profit,   *interpret*
Ac noght for confort of the commune, ne for the Kynges soule,   *(the) benefit*
For I seigh Mede in the moot-halle on men of lawe wynke,   *saw*
And thei laughynge lope to hire and lefte Reson manye.   *ran*
Waryn Wisdom wynked upon Mede
155 And seide, 'Madame, I am youre man, what so my mouth jangle;
    whatever; may utter
I falle in floryns,' quod that freke, 'and faile speche ofte.'   *meet with; lose*
Alle rightfulle recorded that Reson truthe tolde.   *just men opined, declared*
[Kynde] Wit acorded therwith and comendede hise wordes,
And the mooste peple in the halle and manye of the grete,   *most of the*
160 And leten Mekenesse a maister and Mede a mansed sherewe.
    thought; cursed rogue
Love leet of hire light, and Leaute yet lasse,   *held in low esteem*
And seide it so heighe that all the halle it herde: *loudly*

131 who] GF, AC (*so* K-D); whoso
W&r.
  hym] L&r, AC; it w.
136 oþer] AC (*so* K-D); ouþerwhile
W&r *exc* H (othere o. R).
141 þoru3] α, AC (*so* K-D); for β.
saue] helpe G, A.
142 made] RFH &c, ?A (*so* K-D);
make WL&c.

145 thy] Cr, AC (*so* K-D); youre
W&r.
  Englyssed] englys H; in englis*s*h
AC (*so* K-D); vnglosed W&r
(vn-]en- C²) (C).
158 Kynde] *conj* K-D (*see p.* 181);
And W&r; I H.
162 seide] seiden W *only*.

'Whoso wilneth hire to wyve, for welthe of hire goodes—   *desires to marry*
But he be knowe for a cokewold, kut of my nose!'   *recognized; cuckold*
165 Mede mornede tho, and made hevy chere,   *looked miserable*
For the mooste commune of that court called hire an hore.   *whore*
Ac a sisour and a somonour sued hire faste,   *followed; firmly*
And a sherreves clerk bisherewed al the route: *cursed; crowd*
'For ofte have I,' quod he, 'holpen yow at the barre,   *helped; in court*
170 And yet yeve ye me nevere the worth of a risshe!'   *value; rush*
    The Kyng callede Conscience and afterward Reson,
And recordede that Reson hadde rightfully shewed;
                          declared; justly expounded
And modiliche upon Mede with myght the Kyng loked,   *wrathfully*
And gan wexe wroth with Lawe, for Mede almoost hadde shent it,
                          angry; destroyed
175 And seide, Thorugh youre lawe, as I leve, I lese manye chetes;
                          escheats; reversions
Mede overmaistreth Lawe and muche truthe letteth.   *overcomes; impedes*
Ac Reson shal rekene with yow, if I regne any while,   *settle; reign*
And deme yow, bi this day, as ye han deserved.   *judge*
Mede shal noght maynprise yow, by the Marie of hevene!   *stand surety for*
180 I wole have leaute in lawe, and lete be al youre jangling,
                          justice; protestation
And as moost folk witnesseth wel, Wrong shal be demed.'
    Quod Conscience to the Kyng, 'But the commune wole assente,   *Unless*
It is ful hard, by myn heed, herto to brynge it,   *to this point*
[And] alle youre lige leodes to lede thus evene.'   *loyal subjects; unswervingly*
185 'By Hym that raughte on the Rood!' quod Reson to the Kynge,
                          stretched; Cross
But if I rule thus youre reaume, rende out my guttes—   *Unless*
If ye bidden buxomnesse be of myn assent.'   *Provided you bid obedience*
'And I assente,' seith the Kyng, 'by Seinte Marie my lady,
Be my Counseil comen of clerkes and of erles.   *As soon as . . . is*
190 Ac redily, Reson, thow shalt noght ride hennes;   *quickly; hence*
For as longe as I lyve, lete thee I nelle.'   *abandon; shall not*
    'I am al redy,' quod Reson, 'to reste with yow evere;
So Conscience be of oure counseil, I kepe no bettre.'   *Provided that; require*
    'And I graunte,' quod the Kyng, 'Goddes forbode he faile!
                          God forbid he should
195 Als longe as oure lyf lasteth, lyve we togideres!'   *lasts; let us live*

163 wyue] R (=a), AC; wif WL.
168 a] also a F (so K-D).
175 ʒowre] L&r, C; om WCr[1].
    chetes] LRF, C; eschetes W.
181 moost] alle RF (=a).
    wel] om RFH&c.
183 to (1)] too W only.

184 And] AC (so K-D); om all B-MSS.
189 Be] LR, A; By W.
    comen] LR, A; commune W.
190 hens] H, AC (so K-D); fro me
    W&r.
194 he f.] R (? =a; þou f. F), A (so
    K-D); it f. L&r; ellis W.

Passus V

The Kyng and hise knyghtes to the kirke wente — *church*
To here matyns of the day and the masse after.
Thanne waked I of my wynkyng and wo was withalle — *sleep; sorrowful*
That I ne hadde slept sadder and yseighen moore. — *more deeply; seen*
5 Ac er I hadde faren a furlong, feyntise me hente, — *faintness; seized*
That I ne myghte ferther a foot for defaute of slepynge. — *further; need, lack*
I sat softely adoun and seide my bileve, — *carefully; Creed*
And so I bablede on my bedes, thei broughte me aslepe. — *as; mumbled; prayers*
　And thanne saugh I muche moore than I bifore tolde— — *described*
10 For I seigh the feld ful of folk that I before of seide,
And how Reson gan arayen hym al the reaume to preche,
　　　　　　　　　　　　　　　　　　prepare himself; realm
And with a cros afore the Kyng comsede thus to techen. — *began*
　He preved that thise pestilences were for pure synne,
　　　　　　　　　　　　　　　demonstrated; purely, solely
And the south-westrene wynd on Saterday at even — *evening*
15 Was pertliche for pride and for no point ellis. — *manifestly; other reason*
Pyries and plum-trees were puffed to the erthe — *Pear-trees*
In ensample, ye segges, ye sholden do the bettre. — *As a sign; men*
Beches and brode okes were blowen to the grounde — *Beeches; broad oaks*
And turned upward here tail in tokenynge of drede — *roots; as a fearful portent*
20 That dedly synne er domesday shal fordoon hem alle. — *doomsday; destroy*
　Of this matere I myghte mamelen ful longe, — *mumble, ramble on*
Ac I shal seye as I saugh, so me God helpe,
How pertly afore the peple prechen gan Reson. — *forthrightly*
　He bad Wastour go werche what he best kouthe — *do; knew how to*
25 And wynnen his wastyng with som maner crafte. — *earn what he spent; skill*
He preide Pernele hir purfil to lete, — *trimmings; put aside*
And kepe it in hire cofre for catel at hire nede. — *chest; money*
　Tomme Stowue he taughte to take two staves
And fecche Felice hom fro wyvene pyne. — *punishment (C)*

13 He showed by arguments that the recent outbreaks of the plague were the direct consequence of (the people's) sin(s) (C).
20 That before the (actual) Day of Judgment (itself), (their) mortal sins shall prove the destruction of all of them (C).
29 And bring (his wife) Felice home [to receive a beating there with the two staves] from the punishment meted out to shrewish wives [the cucking or ducking-stool].

Rubric Passus quintus de visione vt supra.
9 sauȝ I] mette me C (*so* K-D). tolde] LRF, **AC**; of t. W.
10 seide] tolde H, A (*so* K-D).
15 pruyde] α, **AC** (*so* K-D); pure p. β; synne H.
17 ȝe s. ȝe] LR&c (*cf.* A); þat ye s. W.
19 taile] α, **AC** (*so* K-D); pl. β.
23 p.g. resoun] F (*so* K-D); R. (*bi*)gan to preche W&r (C).
26 lete] leue **AC** (*so* K-D).
29 wyuene] α, **AC** (*so* K-D); þe w. β; soph. H.

30 He warnede Watte his wif was to blame   *blameworthy; open to reproach*
For hire heed was worth half marc and his hood noght worth a grote,
        a mark; groat (C).
And bad Bette kutte a bough outher tweye   *or two*
And bete Beton therwith but if she wolde werche.   *Betty; unless; work*
   And thanne he chargede chapmen to chastisen hir children: *merchants*
35 'Late no wynnyng forwanye hem while thei be yonge,   *Let; profit; weaken*
Ne for no poustee of pestilence plese hem noght out of reson.
        power; unreasonably
My sire seide so to me, and so dide my dame,   *father; mother*
That the levere child the moore loore bihoveth;   *dearer; teaching; requires*
And Salamon seide the same, that Sapience made—   *the Wisdom writings*
"*Qui parcit virge odit filium:*
40 Whoso spareth the spryng spilleth hise children."'   *switch; ruins*
   And sithen he preide prelates and preestes togideres,   *then*
' That ye prechen to the peple, preve it yowselve,   *That which; practise*
And dooth it in dede—it shal drawe yow to goode.   *do*
If ye leven as ye leren us, we shul leve yow the bettre.'   *live; teach; believe*
45   And sithen he radde Religion hir rule to holde—   *advised; abide by*
'Lest the Kyng and his Conseil youre comunes apeîre *reduce your provisions*
And be stywards of youre stedes til ye be [stew]ed bettre.'
        places; established
And sithen he counseiled the Kyng his commune to lovye:
        to love his common subjects
'It is thi tresor, if treson ne were, and tryacle at thy nede.'   *treason; remedy*
50   And sithen he preide the Pope have pite on Holy Chirche,
And er he gyve any grace, governe first hymselve.   *(spiritual) favour(s)*
'And ye that han lawes to kepe, lat Truthe be youre coveitise
        administer; desire
Moore than gold outher giftes if ye wol God plese;   *or*

31 Because the (cloth of the) head (dress) she wore was worth half a mark (£½) and
his hood not fourpence (*cf. Chaucer* Gen Prol CT 435–5).
35–6 Do not let your prosperity cause a weakening (of their moral character)
during their childhood, and do not, (to make up) for (the hardship and suffering
caused by) the Plague, pander excessively to their every wish.
39a He that spareth the rod hateth his son (Prov 13: 24).
49 ... were it not for (the possibility of) treason, and (it is) a source of (strength
and) healing when you need (it).

31 worþ (2)] *om* RH&c, *some* A-,
most C-MSS (*so* K-D).
32 And] He F, C (*so* K-D).
34 And þ.] *om* AC (*so* K-D).
35 forwan*y*en hem] RF (?=*a*; hem]
om R), AC (*so* K-D); h. f. β.
39a *After this a spurious line* The
englissh of þis latyn *is* whoso wole
it knowe *All* B-MSS (*not in* C); *see*
K-D p. 193.

41 preyed] L&r (?=β; *cf.* A);
prechede W, *some* A-MSS; preued
R (?=*a*; parled F). *i*
42 it] H, AC (*so* K-D); it on W&r
(=Bx; on CrG).
44 leuen] WC²CH; lyuen L&r (*C*).
47 stewid] AC (*so* K-D); ruled W&r
(*om* F) (*C*).
49 tresore ... were] L&r; trewe
tresor W *only.*

For whoso contrarieth Truthe, He telleth in the Gospel, *acts contrary to*
55 *Amen dico vobis, nescio vos.*
And ye that seke Seynt James and seyntes of Rome, *seek, go to visit*
Seketh Seynt Truthe, for he may save yow alle. *Seek*
Qui cum Patre et Filio—that faire hem bifalle *may it go well with those*
That seweth my sermon'—and thus seyde Reson. *follow*
60 Thanne ran Repentaunce and reherced his teme *repeated; theme*
And gart Wille to wepe water with hise eighen. *made; eyes*
Pernele Proud-herte platte hire to the erthe *threw herself flat*
And lay longe er she loked, and 'Lord, mercy!' cryde, *looked (up)*
And bihighte to Hym that us alle made *promised*
65 She sholde unsowen hir serk and sette there an heyre *shift; hair-shirt (C)*
To affaiten hire flessh that fiers was to synne. *subdue; bold/fierce (C)*
'Shal nevere heigh herte me hente, but holde me lowe

pride; seize; (I shall) hold
And suffre to be mysseyd—and so dide I nevere. *put up with reproach*
But now wole I meke me and mercy biseche *make myself meek; beseech*
70 For al that I have hated in myn herte.'
Thanne Lechour seide 'Allas!' and on Oure Lady cryde, *Lecher; cried*
To maken mercy for hise mysdedes bitwene God and his soule

obtain, bring about
With that he sholde the Saterday seven yer therafter

On condition that; on Saturdays
Drynke but myd the doke and dyne but ones. *only with; duck; once*
75 Envye with hevy herte asked after shrifte *for confession*
And carefully *mea culpa* he comsed to shewe. *sorrowfully; (his sins); began*
He was as pale as a pelet, in the palsy he semed, *(stone) ball*
And clothed in a kaurymaury—I kouthe it nought discryve—

coarse cloth; describe
In kirtel and courtepy, and a knyf by his syde; *under-jacket; short coat*
80 Of a freres frokke were the foresleves. *friar's gown; fore-part of s.*
And as a leek that hadde yleye longe in the sonne, *lain*
So loked he with lene chekes, lourynge foule. *lean; grimacing hideously*
His body was to-bollen for wrathe, that he boot hise lippes, *all swollen; bit*

55 Amen, I say to you, I know you not (Mt 25: 12).
58 Who with the Father and the Son . . . (*formula-ending of a prayer or blessing*).
67 Feelings of pride shall never take possession of me, but I shall humble myself . . .
73–4 (Giving assurance) that on every Saturday for the next seven years he would
   drink nothing but water and eat only one meal a day [i.e. as a penance].
76 And sorrowfully (with the words) 'through my fault' began to reveal (his
   sins) (*C*).

54 *After this a spurious line* That god
   knoweþ hym noȝt ne no Seynt of
   heuene *All* B-MSS (*with varr;
   see* K-D *p.* 193).
61 gart] made FHmH, *all* A-MSS *exc*
   A (*see* Ka), ?C.

67 holde] L&r, AC; h. I wole W.
69 *wil* l] L&r, AC; I wole W.
70 For al] β; For α; Of alle AC (*C*).
   þat] F, AC (*so* K-D); þis W&r.
76 *mea culpa*] his co(u)pe A (*C*).

Passus V

And wryngynge he yede with the fust—to wreke hymself he thoughte
    twisting; fist; avenge
85 With werkes or with wordes whan he seyghe his tyme. *should see his chance*
  Ech a word that he warp was of a neddres tonge; *flung out; an adder's*
  Of chidynge and of chalangynge was his chief liflode, *accusing; sustenance*
  With bakbitynge and bismere and berynge of fals witnesse: *calumny*
  This was al his curteisie where that evere he shewed hym. *wherever; appeared*
90 'I wolde ben yshryve,' quod this sherewe, 'and I for shame dorste.
    confessed; if
  I wolde be gladder, by God! that Gybbe hadde meschaunce *misfortune*
  Than though I hadde this wouke ywonne a weye of Essex chese.
    week; 3 cwt. portion
  I have a neghebore neigh me, I have anoyed hym ofte, *near; troubled*
  And lowen on hym to lordes to doon hym lese his silver,
    told lies against; make; lose
95 And maad his frendes be his foon thorugh my false tonge. *foes*
  His grace and his goode happes greven me ful soore. *success; good luck*
  Bitwene mayne and mayne I make debate ofte, *household; quarrel(s)*
  That bothe lif and lyme is lost thorugh my speche. *limb*
  And whan I mete hym in market that I moost hate, *meet*
100 I hailse hym hendely, as I his frend were; *greet; courteously*
  For he is doughtier than I, I dar do noon oother; *Since; braver; dare*
  Ac hadde I maistrie and myght—God woot my wille! *advantage*
   'And whan I come to the kirk and sholde knele to the Roode
    church; Cross
  And preye for the peple as the preest techeth—
105 For pilgrymes and for palmeres, for al the peple after—
  Thanne I crye on my knees that Crist yyve hem sorwe *give*
  That baren awey my bolle and my broke shete. *carried; bowl; torn*
  Awey fro the auter thanne turne I myne eighen *altar; eyes*
  And biholde how [H]eyne hath a newe cote; *coat*
110 I wisshe thanne it were myn, and al the web after: *all the cloth too*
  And of his lesynge I laughe—that li[ght]eth myn herte; *loss; cheers*
  Ac for his wynnynge I wepe and waille the tyme; *profit; bewail*
  And deme men that thei doon ille, there I do wel werse: *judge; where; much*
  Whoso undernymeth me herof, I hate hym dedly after. *reproves for this*
115 I wolde that ech a wight were my knave, *everybody; servant*
  For whoso hath moore than I, that angreth me soore. *angers, vexes sorely*

84 wryngynge . . . þe] wroþliche he
  wroþ his A (so K-D p. 88; cf. C).
89 L&r (soph. F); line om W.
93 neyȝe] L&r, A; by WH.
95 maad] W&r; also R.
97 mayne a. m.] R (cf. A V 79; so
  K-D); manye a. manye WL&c.
105 and] om FH, A.
107 baren] OC²B; bar L&r; beren
  W.

109 how] L&r, A; om W.
  Heyne] A (so K-D); Eleyne W&r.
  haþ] β, A; h. on a.
111 his] R, A (so K-D); mennes W&r.
  liȝteþ] A (so K-D); likeþ LRF&c
  (C).
112 Ac for his] a, A (for) of Ka, so
  K-D); And for hir β (hir] his Y).
113 And] W&r; I F, A (so K-D).
116 For] And F, A.

And thus I lyve lovelees like a luther dogge   *fierce, vicious*
That al my body bolneth for bitter of my galle.   *swells; bitterness*
I myghte noght ete many yeres as a man oughte,   *eat*
120 For envye and yvel wil is yvel to defie.   *ill-will; hard to digest*
May no sugre ne swete thyng aswage my swellyng,   *assuage, lessen*
Ne no diapenidion dryve it fro myn herte,   *cough-medicine (C)*
Ne neither shrifte ne shame, but whoso shrape my mawe?'
    unless someone scrape; stomach
'Yis, redily!' quod Repentaunce, and radde hym to the beste,
    indeed; counselled
125 'Sorwe for synnes is savacion of soules.'   *salvation*
'I am evere sory,' quod [Envye], 'I am but selde oother, *seldom anything else*
And that maketh me thus megre, for I ne may me venge. *thin; avenge myself*
Amonges burgeises have I be, [bigg]yng at Londoun,   *burgesses; trading*
And gart bakbityng be a brocour to blame mennes ware.
    made; slander; agent; goods
130 Whan he solde and I nought, thanne was I redy   *sold (his goods)*
To lye and to loure on my neghebore and to lakke his chaffare.
    scowl; disparage; trade
I wole amende this if I may, thorugh myght of God Almyghty.'   *can*
  Now awaketh Wrathe, with two white eighen,
And nevelynge with the nose, and his nekke hangyng.   *running at*
135 'I am Wrathe,' quod he, 'I was som tyme a frere,   *friar*
And the coventes gardyner for to graffen impes.   *friary's; graft shoots*
On lymitours and listres lesynges I ymped,   *lectors; grafted*
Til thei beere leves of lowe speche, lordes to plese,   *produced; servile*
And sithen thei blosmede abroad in boure to here shriftes.
    blossomed; bedroom(s)
140 And now is fallen therof a fruyt—that folk han wel levere
    i.e. result; much prefer
Shewen hire shriftes to hem than shryve hem to hir persons.   *parish-priests*
And now persons han parceyved that freres parte with hem,   *are sharing*
Thise possessioners preche and deprave freres;   *beneficed priests; revile*
And freres fyndeth hem in defaute, as folk bereth witnesse,   *find fault (with)*
145 That whan thei preche the peple in many places aboute,
I, Wrathe, walke with hem and wisse hem of my bokes.   *teach (from)*
Thus thei speken of spiritualte, that either despiseth oother,
    spirituality (C); each

123 . . . unless my stomach is scraped (clean of it)?
129 And used slander as a means of disparaging men's merchandise (for my own gain).
136 And the friary gardener, (whose job was) to graft scions on trees.
137 Upon friars-mendicant and preaching friars I grafted mendacity.
141 To make their confessions to the friars than to their own parish-priests.

125 for] CrHmFH, A (*cf.* C; *so* K-D);   128 biggyng] *conj* K-D *p.* 195;
  of W&r.   dwellyng *All* B-MSS.
126 euere s.] α, C; s. β.   147 of] LF&c; of my WR&c.
  enuye] AC (*so* K-D); þat segge
  W&r (he F).

Til thei be bothe beggers and by my spiritualte libben,   *live*
Or ellis al riche and ryden aboute; I, Wrathe, reste nevere
150 That I ne moste folwe this wikked folk, for swich is my grace.   *fortune*
  'I have an aunte to nonne and an abbesse: *nun; abbess*
Hir were levere swowe or swelte than suffre any peyne.
    she would rather faint; die
I have be cook in hir kichene and the covent served   *convent*
Manye monthes with hem, and with monkes bothe.   *too*
155 I was the prioresse potager and other povere ladies, *p.'s stew-maker; ladies'*
And maad hem joutes of janglyng—that Dame Johane was a bastard,
    stews of squabbling
And Dame Clarice a knyghtes doughter—ac a cokewold was hir sire,
    cuckold; father
And Dame Pernele a preestes fyle—Prioresse worth she nevere,
    concubine; will be
For she hadde child in chirie-tyme, al oure Chapitre it wiste!
    cherry-time; knew
160 Of wikkede wordes I Wrathe hire wortes made,   *vegetables*
Til "Thow lixt!" and "Thow lixt!" lopen out at ones *liest; leapt; once*
And either hitte oother under the cheke;
Hadde thei had knyves, by Crist! hir either hadde kild oother.
    each of them; killed
Seint Gregory was a good pope, and hadde a good forwit   *foresight*
165 That no Prioresse were preest—for that he [purveiede]:
    should be; provided/foresaw
Thei hadde thanne ben *infamis* the firste day, thei kan so yvele hele counseil.
    badly hide secrets
  'Among monkes I myghte be, ac manye tyme I shonye, *avoid doing so*
For ther ben manye felle frekes my feeris to aspie— *severe; companions*
Bothe Priour and Suppriour and oure *Pater Abbas*;
    Sub-Prior; Father the Abbot
170 And if I telle any tales, thei taken hem togideres,   *get together*
And doon me faste Frydayes to breed and to watre;   *on b. and water*
And am chalanged in the Chapitrehous as I a child were,   *charged*
And baleised on the bare ers—and no brech bitwene! *beaten; breeches*
Forthi have I no likyng with tho leodes to wonye;   *people; dwell*

151 ... who is both a nun and an Abbess ...
164-6 ... had a sound anticipation (in providing) that no Prioress should be (ordained) a priest: [*or* because he foresaw that (if they had been ordained . . .)] they would then have been of ill-repute from the start, so badly can they conceal secrets (*C*).

149-50 *Thus divided* Cr²³ (*so* K-D, *and cf.* C); *div. after* aboute, folwe *as three lines* WLRF&*c* (*C*).
151 abbesse] α, C; A. boþe β.
152 were] LRF&*c*, C; hadde W.
162 hitte] LR&*c*; hite W.

165 purueiede] *conj* K-D *p.* 197; prouided Cr; ordeyned W&*r* (*C*).
167 shonye] L&*r*; s. it W.
171 breed] þerf b. *conj* K-D *p.* 112. (*C*).
174 likyng] l. leue me *conj* K-D *p.* 93 (*C*).

175 I ete there unthende fissh and feble ale drynke.　　*small; weak*
　　Ac outher while whan wyn cometh, whan I drynke wyn at eve,
　　　　　　　　　　　　　　　　　at other times; evening
　　I have a flux of a foul mouth wel fyve dayes after.　　*discharge; a good*
　　Al the wikkednesse that I woot by any of oure bretheren,　*evil; concerning*
　　I cou[gh]e it in oure cloistre, that al oure covent woot it.'　*cough (up); knows*
180 　'Now repente thee,' quod Repentaunce, 'and reherce thow nevere
　　　　　　　　　　　　　　　　　make public, declare
　　Counseil that thow knowest, by contenaunce ne by speche;
　　　　　　　　　　　　　　　Private matters; expression
　　And drynk nat over delicatly, ne to depe neither,　　*daintily; too deeply*
　　That thi wille by cause therof to wrathe myghte turne.
　　Esto sobrius!' he seide, and assoiled me after,　*Be sober* (I Pet 5: 8); *absolved*
185 And bad me wilne to wepe my wikkednesse to amende.　　*desire*
　　　And thanne cam Coveitise, I kan hym naght discryve—　*not describe*
　　So hungrily and holwe Sire Hervy hym loked.　　*hollowly*
　　He was bitelbrowed and baberlipped, with two blered eighen;　*eyes*
　　And as a letheren purs lolled hise chekes—　　*leather; hung down*
190 Wel sidder than his chyn thei chyveled for elde;　*lower; trembled; old age*
　　And as a bondeman of his bacon his berd was bidraveled;
　　　　　　　　　　　　　labourer; with; covered with grease
　　With an hood on his heed, a lousy hat above,　*lice-infested; on top of it*
　　In a [torn] tabard of twelf wynter age;　　　　　*coat*
　　But if a lous couthe lepe the bettre.　　　*Unless; louse; leap*
195 She sholde noght wa[ndr]e on that Welche, so was it thredbare!
　　　　　　　　　　　　　　　　　Welsh flannel
　　'I have ben coveitous,' quod this caytif, 'I biknowe it here;
　　　　　　　　　　　　　　wretch; acknowledge
　　For som tyme I served Symme-atte-Style,　　*at the Style*
　　And was his prentice yplight his profit to wayte.
　　　　　　　　　　　pledged, contracted; look after

188 He had beetling brows, thick lips and inflamed eyes.

176 whan (2)] LR; and w. C; þanne
　W.
　　wyn] WL&c (? = β); wel RF
　(? = α); late C.
179 cou3e] *corr.* K-D *p.* 90 *after* C
　(cou3the X); couþe W & *most*
　(= Bx).
　　oure (2)] WL&c; the F&c (*om* R);
　?oure/þe C.
181 speche] α, C (*so* K-D); ri3t
　WL&c (? = β).
184 me] hym CrM, C.
186 I can] RFOC², C (*so* K-D); kan
　I W&r.
188 bitelbrowed . . . ei3en] AC (*so*
　K-D); *as two lines div. before* Wiþ
　All B-MSS.

wiþ] AC; also W. W& *most* MSS
　(= Bx).
　　ei3en] AC; e. as a blynd hagge
　All B-MSS.
193 torn] AC (*so* K-D); tawn*y* W&r
　(= Bx).
　　Hereafter an additional line Al
　totorn and baudy and ful of lys
　crepyng *All* B-MSS.
194 if] RF&c, AC (*so* K-D); if þat
　WL&c.
　　lepe] α, AC (*so* K-D); ha*n* lopen
　β (C).
　　welche] LR, AC; welþe W.
195 wandre] AC (*so* K-D); walke α;
　ha*n* walked W & *most* (= β).

First I lerned to lye a leef outher tweyne: *a leaf or two (C)*
200 Wikkedly to weye was my firste lesson.   *Dishonestly; weigh*
To Wy and to Wynchestre I wente to the feyre   *Weyhill (C); fair*
With many manere marchaundise, as my maister me highte.   *ordered*
Ne hadde the grace of gyle ygo amonges my ware,   *luck, favour; guile; goods*
It hadde ben unsold this seven yer, so me God helpe!
205 'Thanne drough I me among drapiers, my Donet to lerne,
               betook; grammar (C)
To drawe the liser along—the lenger it semed;   *selvage (C); (so that) it*
Among the riche rayes I rendred a lesson—   *striped cloths; memorized*
To broche hem with a pak-nedle, and playte hem togideres,
        sew; needle (for sewing) packages; fold(ed)
And putte hem in a press[our] and pyned hem therinne   *press; tortured*
210 Til ten yerdes or twelve tolled out thritten.   *yards; stretched . . . to*
'My wif was a webbe and wollen cloth made;   *weaver*
She spak to spynnesteres to spynnen it oute.   *spinners*
The pound that she paied by peised a quartron moore   *weighed; quarter*
Than myn owene auncer wh[an I] weyed truthe.   *steelyard (C); honestly*
215 'I boughte hire barly—she brew it to selle.   *brewed*
Peny ale and puddyng ale she poured togideres;   *thick ale; at one time*
For laborers and lowe folk, that lay by hymselve.
The beste ale lay in my bour or in my bedchambre,   *inner room (C)*
And whoso bummed therof boughte it therafter—   *tasted; accordingly*
220 A galon for a grote, God woot, no lesse,   *groat*
[Whan] it cam in cuppemele—this craft my wif used!   *by cupfuls; trick*
Rose the Regrater was hir righte name;   *Retailer*
She hath holden hukkerye [this ellevene wynter].   *practised retail trade*
Ac I swere now (so thee Ik!) that synne wol I lete,   *may I prosper; abandon*
225 And nevere wikkedly weye ne wikke chaffare use,   *dishonestly; sharp practice*
But wenden to Walsyngham, and my wif als,   *go (on pilgrimage); too*
And bidde the Roode of Bromholm brynge me out of dette.'
             pray; Cross (C)
'Repentedestow evere?' quod Repentaunce, 'or restitucion madest?'
            Did you ever repent or make r.

217 (The ale intended) for labourers, etc. stood apart by itself.

203 ware] LMRF, **AC**; chaffare W&*r*.
206 liser] lys*t* GF, *var.* AC-MSS;
 see K-D *pp*. 153–4.
208 To broche] Brochide A (*C*).
 pak] bat LRF, *some* C-MSS (*C*).
 playte] plaited LR &*c, many*
 A-MSS; band*e* C (*C*).
209 pressour] **AC** (*so* K-D); presse
 All B-MSS.
 pyned] LRF, ?A; pyne W;
 pynned *most* B-MSS, *some* A-MSS,
 C (*C*).
210 tolled] LMRF, **AC**; hadde t. W&*r*.

212 spynnesteres] *β*; a s. α; þe ss. C.
213 þe] **AC** (*so* K-D); Ac þe WLR
 (? = Bx).
214 w. I] **AC** (*so* K-D); whoso *All*
 B-MSS (*so*] þat F) (*C*).
215 barly] R (? = α), **AC** (*so* K-D
 p. 168*n*); b.malt *β*F.
218 ale] *om* A, *some* C-MSS (*so* K-D);
 of alle R.
221 Whanne] **AC** (*so* K-D *p*. 81);
 And yet *All* B-MSS.
223 (þis) e.w.] **AC** (*so* K-D, *om* þ.);
 al hire lif tyme *All* B-MSS.

'Yis: ones I was yherberwed', quod he, 'with an heep of chapmen;

once; lodged; crowd

230 I roos whan thei were a-reste and riflede hire males!'   *got up; rifled; bags*

'That was no restitucion,' quod Repentaunce, 'but a robberis thefte;

Thow haddest be bettre worthi ben hanged therfore   *for it*

Than for al that that thow hast here shewed!'   *confessed to*

'I wende riflynge were restitucion,' quod he, 'for I lerned nevere rede on boke,   *thought; read*

235 And I kan no Frenssh, in feith, but of the fertheste ende of Northfolk.'

know; Norfolk

' Usedestow evere usurie,' quod Repentaunce, ' in al thi lif tyme?'

Did you practise

'Nay, sothly,' he seide, 'save in my youthe;   *except*

I lerned among Lumbardes a lesson, and of Jewes—   *Lombards; from*

To weye pens with a peis, and pare the hevyeste,   *pence; weight; clip*

240 And lene it for love of the cros, to legge a wed and lese it.

lend; lay; pledge; lose (C)

Swiche dedes I dide write if he his day breke;   *bonds: had written; in case*

I have mo manoirs thorugh rerages than thorugh *Miscretur et commodat.*

arrears

I have lent lordes and ladies my chaffare,   *goods*

And ben hire brocour after, and bought it myselve.   *agent; later/to boot*

245 Eschaunges and chevysaunces—with swich chaffare I dele,. *loans; business; deal*

And lene folk that lese wole a lippe at every noble.   *portion; coin (=£⅓)*

And with Lumbardes lettres I ladde gold to Rome,   *bills of exchange; carried*

And took it by tale here and told hem there lasse.'   *tally; counted; less*

'Lentestow evere lordes for love of hire mayntenaunce?'

support, protection (C)

250 'Ye, I have lent lordes, loved me nevere after,   *(who) loved*

And have ymaad many a knyght bothe mercer and draper *silk-, cloth-dealer*

That payed nevere for his prentishode noght a peire of gloves!'

apprenticeship

'Hastow pite on povere men that [purely] mote nedes borwe?'

absolutely must

'I have as muche pite of povere men as pedlere hath of cattes,   *a pedlar*

255 That wolde kille hem, if he cacche hem myghte, for coveitise of hir skynnes!'

'Artow manlich among thi neghebores of thi mete and drynke?'   *charitable*

'I am holden,' quod he, 'as hende as hounde is in kichene;   *courteous; a dog*

Amonges my neghebores namely swich a name ich have.'

particularly; sc. 'dog'

242 I have (got possession of) more properties through (my debtors' failure to pay what they owed me in time) than through (the gratitude felt by them towards me) for compassionately lending to them in their time of need '[Acceptable is the man that] sheweth mercy and lendeth' (Ps 111: 5).

232 bett*er*] L&r; þe b. W.
238 a l. and of iewes] α (and . . . i.] be herte F), C (*so* K-D); and Iewes a l. β.
242 *comm.*] CrCot; *com.* W&r.
250 lent] L&r, ?C; l. to W.
253 purely m.] *mote* W&r (C).

'Now [but thow repente the rather,' quod Repentaunce, 'God lene thee
nevere]   *unless; sooner; grant*
260 The grace on this grounde thi good wel to bisette, *bestow (in charitable acts)*
Ne thyne heires after thee have joie of that thow wynnest,   *enjoy; earn*
Ne thyne executours wel bisette the silver that thow hem levest;
                                                              properly employ
And that was wonne with wrong, with wikked men be despended.
                                            that (which); by, among; spent
For were I a frere of that hous ther good feith and charite is,
265 I nolde cope us with thi catel, ne oure kirk amende,
                                          provide copes; money; improve
Ne have a peny to my pitaunce, so God [pyne] my soule in helle,
                                                    allowance; torment
For the beste book in oure hous, theigh brent gold were the leves,
                                                    though; burnished
And I wiste witterly thow were swich as thow tellest!   *If I knew for certain*
Servus es alterius, cum fercula pinguia queris;
Pane tuo pocius vescere, liber eris.
'Thow art an unkynde creature—I kan thee noght assoille
                                              unnatural; absolve
270 Til thow make restitucion' quod Repentaunce, 'and rekene with hem alle.
                                          settle up what you owe to
And sithen that Reson rolle it in the Registre of hevene   *(until) after; record*
That thow hast maad ech man good, I may thee noght assoille.   *made; can*
Non dimittitur peccatum donec restituatur ablatum.
For alle that han of thi good, have God my trouthe,
Ben holden at the heighe doom to helpe thee to restitue;
                                                    obliged; make restitution
275 And who so leveth noght this be sooth, loke in the Sauter glose,
                                                              Psalter Gloss
In *Miserere mei, Deus,* wher I mene truthe: *speak of*
Ecce enim veritatem dilexisti, &c.   Ps 50:8

268a Seek costly foods, another's slave you'll be;
        But eat your own plain bread and you'll stay free *(source unknown)*.
272a The sin is not forgiven until the stolen goods are returned *(St Augustine,*
        Epistle 153, *section* 20; Opera, *ed. Migne,* ii. 662).
276, 276a In 'Have mercy on me, O God' (Ps 50:3); 'For, behold, thou hast loved
        truth' *(ib.* vs. 8).

259 Now g. l. þ. neuere quod R.
   bu[t] þ. repente þe raþer W&r, *with
   varr.* (C).
266 so God pyne] s. g. W; so mote
   pyȝghne F; of þyne bi LR&c; for
   pyne of *rec.* K-D *p.* 187.
      soule in helle] s. saue W; s. hele
   LR&c; in helle F (C).
268 *After this an apparently spurious
   line:* Or elles that I kouthe knowe it
   by any kynnes wise YOC²CBCr²³ (C).

268a *cum*] L&r; *dum* W.
270 quod r.] R (?=a; *so* K-D
   p. 168n); *om* βF.
272a *abl.*] LRF&c. C; *obl.* W.
273 han] W&r, C; hath LRM.
274 Ben] W&r, ?C; Is LMR, *some*
   C-MSS.
276a *After this a spurious line* þere
   is no laborere wolde leue with hem
   þat knoweth peres þe plowman RF
   (?=a; *in* F *in place of* 276a).

Shal nevere werkman in this world thryve with that thow wynnest.
Cum sancto sanctus eris: construwe me this on Englissh.'   *interpret*
   Thanne weex that sherewe in wanhope and wolde han hanged hymself
                                        rogue; fell into; despair
280 Ne hadde Repentaunce the rather reconforted hym in this manere:
                                     soon; again comforted
   ' Have mercy in thi mynde, and with thi mouth biseche it,
                                     Think of; beg for
   For [his] mercy is moore than alle hise othere werkes—   *greater*
   Misericordia eius super omnia opera eius, &c—
   And al the wikkednesse in this world that man myghte werche or thynke *do*
   Nis na moore to the mercy of God than in[middes] the see a gleede:
                             (compared) to; glowing ember
   Omnis iniquitas quantum ad misericordiam Dei est
   quasi scintilla in medio maris.
285 Forthi have mercy in thy mynde—and marchaundise, leve it!
                               (desire for) goods, wealth
   For thow hast no good ground to gete thee with a wastel   *a cake (with)*
   But if it were with thi tonge or ellis with thi two hondes.
                               sc. by begging or working
   For the good that thow hast geten bigan al with falshede,
                           wealth; originated; deceit
   And as longe as thow lyvest therwith, thow yeldest noght but borwest.
                                    pay (back)
290 And if thow wite nevere to wh[om] ne wh[ere] to restitue,
                              know; make restitution
   Ber it to the Bisshop, and bid hym of his grace   *Bear; beg*
   Bisette it hymself as best is for thi soule.   *Dispose of*
   For he shal answere for thee at the heighe dome,   *Last Judgment*
   For thee and for many mo that man shal yeve a rekenyng: *give an account*
295 What he lerned yow in Lente, leve thow noon oother,
                            (As to) what; taught; believe
   And what he lente yow of Oure Lordes good, to lette yow fro synne'.
                          sc. grace, forgiveness; keep
     Now bigynneth Gloton for to go to shrifte,
   And kaireth hym to kirkewarde his coupe to shewe.   *goes to church; sin*

---

278 'With the holy thou wilt be holy' (Ps 17: 26; ['. . . and with the perverse thou
    wilt be perverted', *ib.* 27]).
282a His tender mercies [*miserationes* Vulg] are over all his works (Ps 144: 9).
284a Compared to God's mercy all wickedness is like a spark of fire in the midst
    of the sea (*thought ult. from* St Augustine; *see* Bn, Sk *ad loc*).
286 For you have no good claim for trying to obtain even the smallest luxury
    (*see* Bn, p. 171).

282 his] goddes *All* B-MSS (*C*).   290 whom ne where] C (*so* K-D
    alle] manye of F.   p. 90); whiche ne (to) who WLR&c.
282a L&r; *l.* om. wGCBF.   298 kair.] LR&c, C; kari. W.
284 inmiddes] in *All* B-MSS (*C*).

Ac Beton the Brewestere bad hym good morwe   *ale-wife*
300 And asked of hym with that, whiderward he wolde. *which way he was going*
   'To holy chirche,' quod he, 'for to here masse,
   And sithen I wole be shryven, and synne na moore.'   *then*
      'I have good ale, gossib,' quod she, 'Gloton, woltow assaye?' *friend; try*
      'Hastow,' quod he, 'any hote spices?'
305 'I have pepir and pione,' quod she, 'and a pound of garleek, *peony seeds*
   A ferthyngworth of fenel seed for fastynge dayes.'   *farthing's worth*
     Thanne goth Gloton in, and grete othes after.   *oaths*
     Cesse the Souteresse sat on the benche,   *?female shoemaker*
     Watte the Warner and his wif bothe,   *warren-keeper*
310 Tymme the Tynkere and tweyne of his [knav]es,   *lads*
   Hikke the Hakeneyman and Hugh the Nedlere, *horse-hirer; needle-seller*
   Clarice of Cokkeslane and the Clerk of the chirche,   *Cock's Lane*
   Sire Piers of Pridie and Pernele of Flaundres,   *Sir P. the priest*
   Dawe the Dykere, and a dozeyne othere—   *Davy the ditcher*
315 A Ribibour, a Ratoner, a Rakiere of Chepe,

                       fiddler; rat-catcher; scavenger; Cheapside
   A Ropere, a Redyngkyng, and Rose the Dysshere, *?lackey; dish-seller*
   Godefray of Garlekhithe and Griffyn the Walshe,   *Welshman*
   And [of] upholderes an heep, erly by the morwe, *old-clothes men; a number*
   Geve Gloton with glad chere good ale to hanselle.

                     (Who) gave; as a treat/bribe
320   Clement the Cobelere caste of his cloke,   *cloak*
   And at the newe feire nempned it to selle.   *put it up for barter (C)*
   Hikke the Hakeneyman hitte his hood after,   *flung down*
   And bad Bette the Bocher ben on his syde.   *asked; butcher*
   Ther were chapmen ychose this chaffare to preise: *bargain; evaluate*
325 Whoso hadde the hood sholde han amendes of the cloke.

                     compensation (for)
     Tho risen up in rape and rouned togideres, *They; haste; whispered*
   And preised the penyworthes apart by hemselve.

            valued; bargains (?iron.); privately

299 Ac] LR&c; And W.
300 of] LR&c, A; at W.
304 H.] AC, *so* K-D; H. ouȝt in þi
   purs *All* B-MSS (o. *om* F) (*C*).
305 pio*yne*] R (?=α), AC (*so* K-D
   p. 168*n*); *pl.* W&r (greynes B).
306 A] LR, ?AC; And a WF.
308 Souteresse] sowestere B, *some*
   AC-MSS (*so* K-D).
310 knaues] AC (*so* K-D); prentices
   All B-MSS (*C*).
313–14 *In the order of* α (*so* K-D; *cf.*
   C); *transp.* β.

313 Sire] β, C; And s. α.
316 -ere (2)] OHm&c (?=β), AC (*so*
   K-D); -eres WL; -eres douȝter α.
318 And of] ?A (Of Ka, *so* K-D
   p. 84), C; And *All* B-MSS.
321 at] W&r (?=β), A; to R (?=α;
   in F), C.
   feyre] R (?=α, *see* K-D *p.* 168*n*),
   AC; f. he W&r (?=β).
326 Þo] R(?=α; þan F)Bm, AC (*so*
   K-D); Two W&r (?=β).
327 þe] α, A; þise β; þe/þise ?C.

[There were othes an heep, for oon sholde have the werse];

number; was bound to have

Thei kouthe noght by hir conscience acorden in truthe,   *agree*

330 Til Robyn the Ropere arise the[i by]sou[ght]e,   *begged to get up*

And nempned hym for a nounpere, that no debat nere.

umpire; dispute should occur

Hikke the Hostiler hadde the cloke   *ostler*

In covenaunt that Clement sholde the cuppe fille   *On condition*

And have Hikkes hood the Hostiler, and holden hym yserved;

H. the H.'s hood; satisfied

335 And whoso repented rathest shoulde aryse after   *had regrets soonest*

And greten Sire Gloton with a galon ale.   *treat G. to . . .*

There was laughynge and lourynge and 'Lat go the cuppe!'   *scowling*

[Bargaynes and beverages bigonne to arise;]   *Barterings; drinking*

And seten so til evensong, and songen umwhile,   *(they) sat; at times*

340 Til Gloton hadde yglubbed a galon and a gille.   *gulped down; ¼ pint*

His guttes bigonne to gothelen as two gredy sowes;   *rumble; greedy*

He pissed a potel in a Paternoster-while,

And blew his rounde ruwet at his ruggebones ende,   *trumpet; backbone's*

That alle that herde that horn helde hir nose after

345 And wisshed it hadde ben wexed with a wispe of firses!   *wax-polished; furze*

He myghte neither steppe ne stonde er he his staf hadde,

And thanne gan he to go like a glemannes bicche   *walk; minstrel's bitch*

Som tyme aside and som tyme arere, .   *backwards*

As whoso leith lynes for to lacche foweles.   *lays; catch birds*

350 And whan he drough to the dore, thanne dymmed hise eighen;

drew; grew dim

He [thr]umbled on the thresshfold and threw to the erthe.   *jostled; fell*

Clement the Cobelere kaughte hym by the myddel   *caught; waist*

For to liften hym olofte, and leyde hym on his knowes.   *up; knees*

Ac Gloton was a gret cherl and a grym in the liftyng,   *terrible*

355 And koughed up a cawdel in Clementes lappe.   *coughed, vomited; mess*

Is noon so hungry hound in Hertfordshire

Dorste lape of that levynge, so unlovely it smaughte!   *lap up; smelled*

328 There was much swearing, for one or the other (of them) was bound to come off worse (*C*).
331 And nominated him umpire, so that there should be no dispute (*C*).
334 And have Hick the Ostler's hood, and consider himself fairly done by.
338 Bargains were made and drinks (to seal the bargains) bought.
342 He pissed ½ gallon in the time (it takes to say) an 'Our Father' (*C*).
345 . . . polished with a handful of furze (*C*).

328 *From* AC (þere] And þ. C; for . . . werse] whoso it herde A); *om all* B-MSS; *see* K-D *p.* 79 *and* (*C*).
330 arise þ. bys.] C (*so* K-D *p.* 90); a. þe southe R (? = α); aroos by þe Southe β (*C*).
334 þe] YM. AC (*so* K-D); *om* WL.

338 *In* AC (*so* K-D *p.* 79); *line om all* B-MSS.
344 nose] LRF, AC; noses W.
351 þrumblide] AC (*so* K-D); tremb͡led LR; stumbled W&c.
357 leuyng] R (? = α; þerof F), C (*so* K-D); *pl.* W&r. it] RF&c, C (*so* K-D); þei WL&c.

With al the wo of this world, his wif and his wenche   *servant-girl*
Baren hym to his bed and broughte hym therinne;   *Carried*
360 And after al this excesse he had an accidie,   *attack of sloth*
That he sleep Saterday and Sonday, till sonne yede to reste.   *went*
Thanne waked he of his wynkyng and wiped hise eighen;   *slumbers*
The first word that he spak was—'Where is the bolle?'   *bowl*
His wif [and his wit] edwyte[d] hym tho how wikkedly he lyvede,
      reproached

365 And Repentaunce right so rebuked hym that tyme:
'As thow with wordes and werkes hast wroght yvele in thi lyve,   *evil; life*
Shryve thee and be shamed therof, and shewe it with thi mouthe.'
      Confess; reveal
'I, Gloton,' quod the gome, 'gilty me yelde—   *yield, admit myself (to be)*
That I have trespased with my tonge, I kan noght telle how ofte
370 Sworen "Goddes soule and his sydes!" and "So helpe me God and hali-
dome!"   *Sworn; sides, relics*
Ther no nede was nyne hyndred tymes;
And overseyen me at my soper and som tyme at Nones,   *forgot myself*
That I, Gloton, girte it up er I hadde gon a myle,   *vomited*
And yspilt that myghte be spared and spended on som hungry;
375 Over delicatly on f[ee]styng dayes dronken and eten bothe,
      Over-luxuriously
And sat som tyme so long there that I sleep and eet at ones.
      at the same time
For love of tales in tavernes [in]to drynke the moore I dy[v]ed;   *dived (C)*
And hyed to the mete er noon [on] fastyng dayes.'   *hastened; food; before*
'This shewynge shrift,' quod Repentaunce, 'shal be meryt to the.'
      open confession
380 And thanne gan Gloton greete, and gret doel to make   *weep; lament*
For his luther lif that he lyved hadde,   *evil life*
And avowed to faste—'For hunger or for thurste,   *In spite of*
Shal never fyssh on Fryday defyen in my wombe   *digest; stomach*

372 And forgot myself (so far as to over-eat) at my evening-meal and sometimes
at my midday-meal (too) (*C*).
374 And (have) spilt/wasted what could have been left/saved and spent on some
hungry person.

359 to] RF (=α), AC (*so* K-D); hom
to W&r (=β; h.] on Bm).
363 spak] Hm, AC (*so* K-D); war*p*
W&r (*C*).
364 His w. a. h.] C; H. wif WCr¹M,
A; H. wytte LRF&r.
wit] inwit C; *not in* B-MSS (*C*).
edwited] C; wytyd A; gan
edwyte *All* B-MSS (*C*).
how . . . lyuede] of wykkidnesse
& synne A; of his synne C.
368 gome] LR; grom W.

370 and h. s.] R (=α; and s. F), C;
so K-D *p.* 182; *om* β (*C*).
help m. g.] RF, C; g.m.h. L;
m.g.h. W.
and halidome] L&r; *om* W;
almyhty C (*C*).
375 feestyng] fastyng *All* B-MSS;
feeste *rec.* K-D *p.* 182.
377 into] to L&r; and for W (*C*).
dyved] dyne*d* W&r; wente F (*C*).
378 on . . . dayes] whan f. d. were
W&r (were] felle F) (*C*).

Til Abstinence myn aunte have yyve me leeve—   *given; permission*
385 And yet have I hated hire al my lif tyme!'

    Thanne cam Sleuthe al bislabered, with two slymy eighen.   *soiled*
'I moste sitte,' seide the segge, 'or ellis sholde I nappe.   *man; fall asleep*
I may noght stonde ne stoupe ne withoute a stool knele.   *stoop*
Were I brought abedde, but if my tailende it made,   *tail-end; caused*
390 Sholde no ryngynge do me ryse er I were ripe to dyne.'
        i.e. of church-bells; ready
He bigan *Benedicite* with a bolk, and his brest knokked,   *Bless me (C); belch*
Raxed and rored—and rutte at the laste.   *Stretched; snored*
'What, awake, renk!' quod Repentaunce, 'and rape thee to shryfte!'
        man; hurry
    'If I sholde deye bi this day,' quod he, 'me list nought to loke.
395 I kan noght parfitly my Paternoster as the preest it syngeth,
        do not know properly
But I kan rymes of Robyn Hood and Randolf Erl of Chestre,
        know rhymes about
Ac neither of Oure Lord ne of Oure Lady the leeste that evere was maked.
        composed
I have maad avowes fourty, and foryete hem on the morwe;   *vows; forgotten*
I parfournede nevere penaunce as the preest me highte,
        carried out; commanded
400 Ne right sory for my synnes, yet [seye I] was I nevere.
And if I bidde any bedes, but if it be in wrathe,   *say; prayers; unless*
That I telle with my tonge is two myle fro myn herte.   *What I say; miles*
I am ocupied eche day, halyday and oother,
With ydel tales at the ale and outherwhile in chirches;
        idle gossip; other times
405 Goddes peyne and his passion, [pure] selde thenke I on it;
        suffering; very seldom
'I visited nevere feble men ne fettred folk in puttes;   *sick; pits (= prisons)*
I have levere here an harlotrye or a somer game of souters,   *obscene story*
Or lesynges to laughen of and bilye my neghebores,   *tell lies (against)*
Than al that evere Marc made, Mathew, Johan and Lucas.
        wrote (in their gospels)

389-90 If I were put to bed, unless (the needs of) my bowels caused it The ringing (of no church bells) would make me get up until I were ready to eat.
394 Even if I should die (, by) this day, I have no wish (so much as) to open my eyes (C).
400 And I say still further—I was never even genuinely sorry for my sins! (C).
407 I prefer to hear a bawdy tale or a shoemakers' summer game [*a play*? *see* Bn].

392 Raxed] ?C (*so* K-D); And *r. All* B-MSS.
394 day q.h.] α (d. *om* F), ?C; day β.
  me . . . loke] y drede me sore C (*so* K-D) (*C*).
400 seye I] ych seyh [neuere þe tyme] C; soþly F; *om* W&r (*C*).
404 in] L&r, C; at W.

cherches] LY&c, C; *sg.* WRF&c.
405 pure] *conj* K-D *p.* 196 *after* C: ful W&r (*om* G).
406 folk] men HmGM, C.
  puttes] prisoun F, C.
408 lesynges] *sg.* W.
  of] α (*cf.* C; *so* K-D); at β.

410 And vigilies and fastyng dayes—alle thise late I passe,   *vigils; let*
    And ligge abedde in Lenten and my lemman in myne armes˙ *lie with; lover*
    Til matyns and masse be do, and thanne moste to the Freres;
                                                 done; must (go);
    Come I to *Ite, missa est* I holde me yserved.   *i.e. at; satisfied*
    I am noght shryven som tyme, but if siknesse it make,   *unless; cause*
415 Noght twyes in two yer, and thanne [telle I up gesse].   *without thinking*
    'I have be preest and person passynge thritty wynter,   *more than*
    Yet kan I neyther sólve ne synge ne seintes lyves rede, *'sol-fa', sing by note*
    But I kan fynden in a feld or in a furlang an hare   *ten-acre area*
    Bettre than in *Beatus vir* or in *Beati omnes*   *the Psalms*
420 Construe clausemel[e] and kenne it to my parisshens. *clause by clause; teach*
    I kan holde lovedayes and here a reves rekenyng,   *settlement-days*
    Ac in Canoun nor in Decretals I kan noght rede a lyne.   *Canon Law*
    'If I bygge and borwe aught, but if it be ytailed,   *buy; recorded*
    I foryete it as yerne, and yif men me it axe   *quickly; ask for*
425 Sixe sithes or sevene, I forsake it with othes;   *times; deny (the debt)*
    And thus tene I trewe men ten hundred tymes.   *injure; honest*
    And my servaunts som tyme, hir salarie is bihynde: *overdue*
    Ruthe is to here the rekenyng whan we shal rede acountes,   *Pitiful*
    So with wikked wil and wrathe my werkmen I paye! *With such ill-will*
430 'If any man dooth me a bienfait or helpeth me at nede,   *good turn*
    I am unkynde ayeins his curteisie and kan nought understonden it;
                                                 in return for
    For I have and have had somdel haukes maneres—   *somewhat hawklike*
    I am noght lured with love but ther ligge aught under the thombe.
                                                unless; lie; thumb
    The kyndenesse that myn evenecristene kidde me fernyere
                                            showed; in times past
435 Sixty sithes I, Sleuthe, have foryete it siththe   *since*
    In speche and in sparynge of speche; yspilt many a tyme   *failure; wasted*

413 If I turn up at (the priest's words of dismissal), 'Go, Mass is finished', I consider that I have fulfilled my obligations satisfactorily.

419–20 Better than I can interpret the clauses that make up (the psalms) 'Blessed is the man' (Ps 1 *or* Ps 111) and 'Blessed are all they . . .' (Ps 127) and teach (their meaning) to my parishioners (*C*).

423–5 If I am buying (anything), and (to do so) borrow any money, unless it is scored upon a tally-stick (as a record of the loan), I forget it as soon (as I have obtained the sum), and if I am asked (to repay) . . . I deny the existence of the loan with oaths.

436 In what I said and in what I failed to say.

412 moste] *so* K-D *after* y muste F
(*cf. C*); go W&r (=Bx).
414 am] RF&c, C (*so* K-D); nam
WL&c.
415 telle I vp gesse] *conj* K-D *p.* 181
after tel ich nauht þe haluendele C;
vp gesse I shryue *me* W&r.
417 Yet] LR&c, C; And y. WF.

420 clausemele] *so* K-D *after* it
clausemel RF (=β); oon clause wel
WL&c (?=β) (*C*).
424 ʒif] LR; if W.
428 is] L&r, C; it is WB.
431 his] LR&c; om W.
433 þe] β, ?C; om α.
435 siþes] *sg.* R (?=α), ?C.

Bothe flessh and fissh and manye othere vitailles,	*foodstuffs*
Bothe bred and ale, buttre, melk and chese	*milk; cheese*
Forsleuthed in my service til it myghte serve no man.	*Spoilt for lack of use*
440 I [yarn] aboute in youthe, and yaf me naught to lerne	*ran; dedicated*
And evere sitthe have I be beggere [be] my foule sleuthe:	
	through; slothfulness

Heu michi quia sterilem vitam duxi iuvenilem!'

'Repentedestow the noght?' quod Repentaunce—and right with that he	
swowned	*(Sloth) fainted*
Til *Vigilate* the veille fette water at hise eighen	*'Keep-watch Wakeful'*
And flatte it on his face and faste on hym cryde	*dashed; earnestly*
445 And seide, 'Ware thee—for Wanhope wolde thee bitraye.	*Beware; Despair*
"I am sory for my synnes", seye to thiselve,	
And beet thiself on the brest, and bidde Hym of grace,	*beat; ask God for*
For is no gilt here so gret that his goodnesse nys moore.'	
	is not greater (than it)
Thanne sat Sleuthe up and seyned hym swithe,	*crossed himself often*
450 And made avow tofore God for his foule sleuthe:	*before*
'Shal no Sonday be this seven yer, but siknesse it [make],	*unless; cause*
That I ne shal do me er day to the deere chirche	*betake myself*
And here matyns and masse as I a monk were.	
Shal noon ale after mete holde me thennes	*food; keep; from there*
455 Til I have evensong herd—I bihote to the Roode!	*promise*
And yet wole I yelde ayein, [y]if I so muche have,	*further; give back*
Al that I wikkedly wan sithen I wit hadde;	*obtained; reason*
And though my liflode lakke, leten I nelle	*sustenance; give up*
That ech man shal have his er I hennes wende;	*go hence (i.e. die)*
460 And with the residue and the remenaunt, bi the Rode of Chestre,	*Cross*
I shal seken truthe erst er I se Rome!'	*first before*

Roberd the Robbere on *Reddite* loked,	*'Give Back' (C)*
And for ther was noght wher[with], he wepte swithe soore.	
And yet the synfulle sherewe seide to hymselve:	

441a Alas what a fruitless life I have led! (*proverbial*).
443 Till 'Be Watchful' [Mt 26: 41 *or* Mk 13: 37], the wakeful one, obtained water from his eyes . . . (*C*).
462 Render [therefore to all men their dues] (Rom 13: 7).

437 manye] WL&c (? = β); myn R; fele F.
438 Bothe] LR&c, C; Boþ W.
440 yarn] *conj* K-D *p.* 183; ran *All* B-MSS; ȝede C.
441 be] for W&r, C; þorghȝ F (C).
442 Rep.] WHmY, ?C; Repentest R (? = α; ȝee r. F); Repentestow L&r. þe] LRF&c, ?C; *om* W&c.
451 it] me R.

make] AC (*so* K-D); lette W&r; line *om* F.
456 And . . . I] what I nam R (? = α; & w. I have take F). ȝif] A; if *All* B-MSS (*C*).
459 man] RF&c, ?A (*so* K-D); m. ne WL&c.
461 erst] *om* Hm, A; tryst F.
463 wiþ] AC (*so* K-D); of *All* B-MSS.

465 'Crist, that on Calvarie upon the cros deidest,
    Tho Dysmas my brother bisoughte thee of grace,   *At that time; begged*
    And haddest mercy on that man for *Memento* sake;   *you had*
    So rewe on this Rober[d] that *Reddere* ne have,   *pity; means to restore (C)*
    Ne nevere wene to wynne with craft that I knowe;   *expect; earn; skill*
470 But for thi muchel mercy mitigacion I biseche: *great; compassion*
    Dampne me noght at Domesday for that I dide so ille!'
                                          Damn; Judgment Day

    What bifel of this feloun I kan noght faire shewe.   *properly*
    Wel I woot he wepte faste water with hise eighen,
    And knoweliched his [coupe] to Crist yet eftsoones,   *guilt; again*
475 That *Penitencia* his pik he sholde polshe newe   *pikestaff; polish afresh*
    And lepe with hym over lond al his lif tyme,   *go with it*
    For he hadde leyen by *Latro*, Luciferis Aunte.   *Robber(y)*

    And thanne hadde Repentaunce ruthe and redde hem alle to knele.
                                          instructed
    'For I shal biseche for alle synfulle Oure Saveour of grace   *for grace*
480 To amenden us of oure mysdedes and do mercy to us alle.   *have ... on*
    Now God,' quod he, 'that of Thi goodnesse gonne the world make,
                                          made the w.
    And of naught madest aught and man moost lik to thiselve,   *everything*
    And sithen suffredest hym to synne, a siknesse to us alle—   *permitted*
    And al for the beste, as I bileve, whatevere the Book telleth:
                        Bible (C), 'the authorities' (Bn.)

    O felix culpa! O necessarium peccatum Ade!
485 For thorugh that synne thi sone sent was to this erthe
    And bicam man of a maide mankynde to save—
    And madest Thiself with Thi sone us synfulle yliche:
                        through; like us sinful (men)

    Faciamus hominem ad imaginem et similitudinem nostram; Et alibi,
    Qui manet in caritate, in Deo manet, et Deus in eo;

467 ... for (his words to you, 'Lord), remember [me when thou shalt come into
    thy kingdom'] (Lk 23: 42) (*C*).
484*a* O happy fault! O necessary sin of Adam! (Liturgy of Easter Saturday; *see*
    Bn *ad loc*).
487*a* Let us make man to our image and likeness (Gen 1: 26); And elsewhere, he
    that abideth in charity abideth in God, and God in him (I Jn 4: 16) (*C*).

466 the] Hm (*by corr.*), A?C (*so* K-D);
    yow W&r (crist F).
468 Roberd] AC; Robbere *All* B-MSS
    (*C*).
469 knowe] RF (=α)Cr, A (owe Ka)
    C; owe W& *most* (=β) (*C*).
471 Dampne] AC (*so* K-D *p*. 81);
    Ne d. *All* B-MSS (*l.* om F).

473 hyse] FCrG, AC (*so* K-D); boþe
    h. W&r.
474 coupe] AC (*so* K-D *p*. 152); gilt
    β; *l.* om α.
481 gonne m.] LR, C; big. to m. W.
483 hym] α, C (*so* K-D); for β.
487 vs] *so* K-D *p*. 179*n*; and vs *All*
    B-MSS (*C*).

And siththe with Thi selve sone in oure sute deidest
                                              then; through; guise, form
On Good Fryday for mannes sake at ful tyme of the day;   *high noon (C)*
490 Ther Thiself ne Thi sone no sorwe in deeth feledest,   *felt*
But in oure secte was the sorwe, and Thi sone it ladde:
                                           bore (away), led (sc. *mankind*)
Captivam duxit captivitatem.
The sonne for sorwe therof lees sight for a tyme   *became invisible*
Aboute mydday whan moost light is and meel-tyme of seintes—
                                                  meal-time (C)
Feddest tho with Thi fresshe blood oure forefadres in derknesse:
                                              You fed at that time
Populus qui ambulabat in tenebris vidit lucem magnam.
495 And the light that lepe out of Thee, Lucifer it blente,   *leapt; blinded*
And blewe alle Thi blessed into the blisse of Paradys!
    'The thridde day therafter Thow yedest in oure sute: *went; (human) form*
A synful Marie The seigh er Seynte Marie Thi dame,   *saw; mother*
And al to solace synfulle Thow suffredest it so were— *comfort; allowed that*
Non veni vocare iustos set peccatores ad penitenciam.
500   'And al that Marc hath ymaad, Mathew, Johan and Lucas   *set down*
Of Thyne doughtiest dedes was doon in oure armes: *(coat of) arms, form (C)*
Verbum caro factum est et habitavit in nobis.
And by so muche it semeth the sikerer we mowe   *more surely; can*
Bidde and biseche, if it be Thi wille   *Pray*
That art oure fader and oure brother—be merciable to us,   *merciful*
505 And have ruthe on thise ribaudes that repenten hem soore *sinners; earnestly*
That evere thei wrathed Thee in this world, in word, thought or dede!'
                                                            angered

     Thanne hente Hope an horn of *Deus tu conversus vivificabis nos*   *seized*
And blew it with *Beati quorum remisse sunt iniquitates,*

488 And then through the person of your Son himself died in our (human) form.
491*a* [Ascending on high], he led captivity captive (Eph 4: 8) (*C*).
494*a* The people that walked in darkness have seen a great light (Is 9: 2) (*C*).
499*a* I came not to call the just, but sinners to penance (Lk 5: 32) (*C*).
501*a* And the Word was made flesh, and dwelt among us (Jn 1: 14).
507 O God, you will turn and bring us back to life (*from* the Mass, *after* Ps 70: 20)
    (*C*).
508 Blessed are they whose iniquities are forgiven (Ps 31: 1).

488 sute] L&*r* (?=Bx; s.þou F); secte
W (*cf.* C) (*C*).
491 þe] β; þat α.
492 si3te] LRF&*c*; li3t WY&*c*, C (*C*).
    for (2)] LRF&*c*, C; of W.
494 Feddest þo] R (?=α; þo f. þou
    F), C; F. W&*r* (=β).
495 And þe] A. þoru3 þe WLR&*c*;
    The C.
    it bl.] α (bl. F), C; was *b*. β.

497 þeraftur] C (*so* K-D); after *All*
    B-MSS (a. 3it F).
501 -tiest] LMRF, C (*so* K-D); -ty
    W&*r*.
502 it] α, C (*so* K-D); me β.
505 ruþe] β, C; mercy α.
506 dede] CrF&*r*, C; *pl.* WLR.
507 *nos*] RFCrG, C; *om* W&*r*.

That alle Seintes in hevene songen at ones
' *Homines et iumenta salvabis, quemadmodum multiplicasti*
misericordiam tuam, Deus!'

510   A thousand of men tho thrungen togideres,   *thronged*
      Cride upward to Crist and to his clene moder   *Cried; pure*
      To have grace to go [seke Truthe—God leve that they moten!] *grant; might*
      Ac there was wight noon so wys, the wey thider kouthe,   *(who) knew*
      But blustreden forth as beestes over ba[ch]es and hilles, *strayed; valleys*
515 Til late was and longe, that thei a leode mette   *man*
      Apparailled as a paynym in pilgrymes wise. *'outlandishly', like a Saracen*
      He bar a burdoun ybounde with a brood liste   *staff; strip of cloth*
      In a withwynde wise ywounden aboute.   *woodbine-fashion*
      A bolle and a bagge he bar by his syde.   *bowl*
520 An hundred of ampulles on his hat seten,   *phials; sat*
      Signes of Synay and shelles of Galice, *Emblems from Sinai (C)*
      And many a crouch on his cloke, and keyes of Rome, *cross-ornament*
      And the vernicle bifore, for men sholde knowe *vernicle in front; so that*
      And se bi hise signes whom he sought hadde.
525   This folk frayned hym first fro whennes he come. *inquired of*
      'Fram Synay,' he seide, 'and fram [the] Sepulcre.
      In Bethlem and in Babiloyne, I have ben in bothe, *Babylon (C)*
      In Armonye, in Alisaundre, in manye othere places. *Armenia; Alexandria (C)*
      Ye may se by my signes that sitten on myn hatte
530 That I have walked ful wide in weet and in drye   *wet*
      And sought goode Seintes for my soule helthe.'   *soul's*
      'Knowestow aught a corsaint,' [quod thei], 'that men calle Truthe?
                               saint('s shrine)
      Koudestow wissen us the wey wher that wye dwelleth?' *direct; person*
      'Nay, so me God helpe!' seide the gome thanne.   *man*
535 'I seigh nevere palmere with pyk ne with scrippe *pilgrim; pike-staff*
      Asken after hym er now in this place.'
      'Peter!' quod a Plowman, and putte forth his hed,
      'I knowe hym as kyndely as clerc doth hise bokes.
                   naturally, intimately; a scholar
      Conscience and Kynde Wit kenned me to his place *directed*

509a Men and beasts thou wilt preserve, O Lord: How hast thou multiplied thy
     mercy, O God! (Ps 35: 7–8).

512 To . . . go] Grace to god R; To
    graunte swich grace F.
    seke] wiþ hem W&r; *om* F.
    God . . . moten] **AC** (*so* K-D);
    truþe to seke W&r (*C*).
514 baches] **AC** (*so* K-D); balkys F;
    bankes W&r.
526 þe s.] **AC** (*so* K-D); oure lordes s.
    W&r; (þe s. F *trspd. with* Synay).
531 soule] RF&c, **AC** (*so* K-D); *pl.* WL.

532 q. þei] **AC** (*so* K-D *p.* 79); *om*
    All B-MSS.
533 wissen] g, **AC** (*so* K-D); auȝt w.
    WLR&c.
534 helpe] glade *sugg.* K-D *p.* 205n
    after A-MS V.
535 seiȝ] ne s. *conj* K-D *p.* 205n.
536 er] YOC²CB, **AC** (*so* K-D); er til
    W&r (til FM).

540 And diden me suren hym si[ththen] to serven hym for evere,

made me; give my word to

Bothe to sowe and to sette the while I swynke myghte. *plant; toil, labour*

I have ben his folwere al this fourty wynter— *follower*

Bothe ysowen his seed and suwed hise beestes, *followed, tended*

Withinne and withouten waited his profit, *looked to, after*

545 Idyke[d] and id[o]lve, ido that he hoteth. *Ditched; dug; done; orders*

Som tyme I sowe and som tyme I thresshe,

In taillours craft and tynkeris craft, what Truthe kan devyse,

I weve and I wynde and do what Truthe hoteth. *weave; wind (yarn)*

For though I seye it myself, I serve hym to paye; *to (his) satisfaction*

550 I have myn hire of hym wel and outherwhiles moore. *pay; from him*

He is the presteste paiere that povere men knoweth: *promptest paymaster*

He withhalt noon hewe his hire that he ne hath it at even.

withholds from; workman

He is as lowe as a lomb and lovelich of speche. *humble; loving*

And if ye wilneth to wite where that he dwelleth, *desire to know*

555 I [wol] wisse yow [wel right] to his place.' *am willing; direct; straight*

'Ye, leve Piers!' quod thise pilgrimes, and profred hym huyre.

dear; payment

'Nay, by [the peril of] my soule!' quod Piers and gan to swere,

'I nolde fange a ferthyng, for Seint Thomas shryne! *would not accept; by*

Truthe wolde love me the lasse a long tyme after.

560 Ac if ye wilneth to wende wel, this is the wey thider: *journey aright*

Ye moten go thorugh Mekenesse, bothe men and wyves, *must; women*

Til ye come into Conscience, that Crist wite the sothe,

'*that C. may know the truth*' (Bn)

That ye loven Oure Lord God levest of alle thynges, *most dearly, above all*

And thanne youre neghebores next in none wise apeire *no way harm, ill-treat*

565 Otherwise than thow woldest h[ii] wroughte to thiselve. *they did, acted towards*

'And so boweth forth by a brook, "Beth-buxom-of-speche", *proceed; mild*

[Forto] ye fynden a ford, "Youre-fadres-honoureth": *Till; honour*

Honora patrem et matrem &c.

Wadeth in that water and wassheth yow wel there,

And ye shul lepe the lightloker al youre lif tyme. *run; more nimbly*

540 sippen] AC (*so* K-D *p.* 81);
sikerly W&r (sewrly F).
542 fourty] LRFM, AC; fifty W&r.
545 Idyked] A (*so* K-D); & bope
diggid F; I dyke W&r.
idolue] A (*so* K-D); deluyd F;
(I) delue W&r.
ido] A (*so* K-D); I do WLR&c.
he] α, A (*so* K-D); trupe β.
550 of hym] α, AC (*so* Sk); *om* β.
555 wol] AC (*so* K-D); shal *All*
B-MSS.
wel rizt] AC (*so* K-D *p.* 79);
witterly þe wey *All* B-MSS.

556 *After this a line* For to wende
wiþ hem,to truþes dwellyng place
All B-MSS; *rej. as spur.* K-D *p.* 193.
557 þe . . . soule] AC (*so* K-D); my
soule perel R (? = α; *p. om* F); my
soules helþe WL&c.
to] AC (*so* K-D); for to Bx.
559 af.] gMF, AC; þeraf. wLR.
560 ȝe] L&r; yow WCr[1].
565 hii] he W&r; be G; thei C.
567 Forto] AC (*so* K-D *p.* 79); Til
All B-MSS.
568 wasscheth] LR, AC; wasshe W.
þere] L&r, AC; þerInne WF(M).

570 And so shaltow se "Swere-noght-but-if-it-be-for-nede-
And-nameliche-on-ydel-the-name-of-God-Almyghty."   *particularly; in vain*
'Thanne shaltow come by a croft, but come thow noght therinne:
                                      (small) field
The croft hatte " Coveite-noght-mennes-catel-ne-hire-wyves-   *is called*
Ne-noon-of-hire-servaunts-that-noyen-hem-myghte."   *(so as) to trouble*
575 Loke thow breke no bowes there but if it be [thyn] owene.
                               branches; unless they are
'Two stokkes ther stondeth, ac stynte th[ow] noght there: *stumps; pause*
Thei highte "Stele-noght" and "Sle-noght"—strik forth by bothe,
                                 Slay; press on
And leve hem on thi lift half and loke noght therafter,   *left hand side*
And hold wel thyn haliday heighe til even.   *observe properly; holy day(s)*
580 'Thanne shaltow blenche at a bergh, "Bere-no-fals-witnesse";
                                  turn aside; hill
He is frythed in with floryns and othere fees manye: *hedged; payments*
Loke thow plukke no plaunte there, for peril of thi soule.
' Thanne shalt thow see " Seye-sooth-so-it-be-to-doone
In-no-manere-ellis-noght-for-no-mannes-biddyng."
585 'Thanne shaltow come to a court as cler as the sonne.   *castle; bright*
The moot is of Mercy the manoir aboute,   *moat*
And alle the walles ben of Wit to holden Wil oute,   *Wisdom, Understanding*
And kerneled with Cristendom that kynde to save,   *crenellated; (human) nature*
Botrased with "Bileef-so-or-thow-beest-noght-saved."   *Buttressed; Believe*
590 'And alle the houses ben hiled, halles and chambres,   *covered*
With no leed but with love and lowe speche, as bretheren [of o wombe].
                                 lead; gentle; one
The brugge is of "Bidde-wel-the-bet-may-thow-spede;"
                            (draw)bridge; Pray; prosper
Ech piler is of penaunce, of preieres to seyntes;   *pillar*
Of almesdedes are the hokes that the gates hangen on.   *hooks*
595 'Grace hatte the gateward, a good man for sothe;   *porter*
His man hatte "Amende-yow"—many man hym knoweth.
Telleth hym this tokene: "Truthe w[oot] the sothe—   *sign; knows*

579 Observe your holy days properly till the late evening (of them).

573 þe] αG, **AC** (*so* K-D); þat β.
575 þow] R (?=α; *line re-wr.* F) Cot,
   AC (*so* K-D); ye W&r (=β).
   be] be on R (?=α).
   þyn] **AC** (*so* K-D); youre W&r
   exc. F.
576 þou] **AC** (*so* K-D); þe C; ye
   W&r (*om* Cot).
583 shall þou] G, **AC** (*so* K-D); shul
   ye W&r (*line om* F).
584 no (1)] L&r (*line om* F); good W.
588 And . . . wiþ] The kernellis beþ
   AC (*so* K-D).

þat] R (?=α), **AC** (*so* K-D
p. 168*n*); man W&r.
591 of o w.] **A** (*so* K-D); *om All*
   B-MSS (*cf. next line in* C).
592 brugge] L&r; brugg W.
596 many] α, C; for m. β, ?A.
   man] LRFM (=?Bx), **AC**; men
   W&r.
597 trewþe] F, **AC** (*so* K-D); þat t.
   W&r (t. *om* Bm).
   woot] **AC** (*so* K-D); knowith F;
   wite W&r.

I parfourned the penaunce that the preest me enjoyned   *carried out*
And am sory for my synnes and so I shal evere
600 Whan I thynke theron, theigh I were a Pope."
   'Biddeth Amende-yow meke hym til his maister ones   *humbly approach*
To wayven up the wiket that the womman shette   *open; wicket; shut*
Tho Adam and Eve eten apples unrosted:
Per Evam cunctis clausa est et per Mariam virginem iterum
patefacta est;
For he hath the keye and the cliket, though the kyng slepe.   *latch-key*
605 And if Grace graunte thee to go in in this wise
Thow shalt see in thiselve Truthe sitte in thyn herte
In a cheyne of charite, as thow a child were,   *chain*
To suffren hym and segge noght ayein thi sires wille.
                      Suffering; against; father's
   'Ac be war thanne of Wrathe, that wikked sherewe:
610 He hath envye to hym that in thyn herte sitteth,   *enmity towards*
And poketh forth pride to preise thiselven.   *praise*
The boldnesse of thi bienfetes maketh thee blynd thanne   *good deeds*
And [so] worstow dryven out as dew, and the dore closed,   *will you be*
Keyed and cliketted to kepe thee withouten   *outside*
615 Happily an hundred wynter er thow eft entre!   *Perhaps; again*
Thus myghtestow lesen his love, to lete wel by thiselve,   *by thinking well of*
And [gete it again thorugh] grace [ac thorugh no gifte ellis].
   'Ac ther are seven sustren that serven Truthe evere   *sisters*
And arn porters of the posternes that to the place longeth. *side-doors; belong*
620 That oon hatte Abstinence, and Humilite another;   *one is called*
Charite and Chastite ben hise chief maydenes;
Pacience and Pees, muche peple thei helpeth;
Largenesse the lady, she let in ful manye—   *Generosity; lets*
Heo hath holpe a thousand out of the develes punfolde.   *pinfold*
625   'And who is sib to thise sevene, so me God helpe,   *related to*
He is wonderly welcome and faire underfongen.   *marvellously; received*
And but if ye be sibbe to some of thise sevene—
It is ful hard, by myn heed,' quod Piers, 'for any of yow alle

603a Through Eve (the gate of Paradise) was closed to all and through the Virgin
   Mary it was made open once again (*From the* Lauds Antiphon *of the* BVM *said in*
   the Monday of the week within the Octave of Easter to the Vigil of the Ascension
   [Bn, *q.v.*]).

603a *-ctis*] CrR&*c*, C (*so* Sk); *-tis*
   WLF&*c*.
     iterum] α, C (*so* Sk); *om* β.
605 in (2)] LM, AC; *om* W&*r*.
606 sitte] LRF, AC; *om* W.
609 Ac] LR, A; And W.
   þat] AC (*so* K-D); þ. is a W&*r*
   (þ.] he F).
613 so] AC (*so* K-D); þanne W&*r*;
   om OC²F.

617 And . . . ellis] AC (*so* K-D *p*. 80;
   ac] and A); And nevere happily eft
   entre but grace þow haue *All*
   B-MSS.
618 Ac] LR, AC; And W.
623 she] *om* AC.
627 if] if þat R (*om* FCrM).
628 q. P.] *om* FG, AC (*so* K-D).

To geten ingong at any gate but grace be the moore!'   *entrance; unless*
630   'Now, by Crist!' quod a kuttepurs, 'I have no kyn there.'   *cutpurse*
'Ne I', quod an apeward, 'by aught that I knowe.'   *ape-keeper*
    'Wite God,' quod a wafrestere, 'wiste I this for sothe,   *wafer-seller*
Sholde I never ferther a foot for no freres prechyng.'   *(go) further*
    'Yis!' quod Piers the Plowman, and poked hem alle to goode,   *urged*
635   'Mercy is a maiden there, hath myght over hem alle;   *who has power*
And she is sib to alle synfulle, and hire sone also,   *kin(swoman)*
And thorugh the help of hem two—hope thow noon oother—
     expect nothing else
Thow myght gete grace there—so thow go bityme.'   *provided; early*
    'Bi Seint Poul!' quod a pardoner, 'paraventure I be noght knowe there;
     perhaps I shan't be known
640 I wol go fecche my box with my brevettes and a bulle with bisshopes lettres.'
     indulgences
    'By Crist!' quod a commune womman, 'thi compaignie wol I folwe.
     prostitute
Thow shalt seye I am thi suster.' I ne woot where thei bicome.
     where they went

Passus VI

'This were a wikkede wey but whoso hadde a gyde *very difficult; unless one*
That [myghte] folwen us ech a foot'—thus this folk hem mened.
     accompany; complained
    Quod Perkyn the Plowman, 'By Seint Peter of Rome!
I have an half acre to erie by the heighe weye;   *plough; near*
5 Hadde I eryed this half acre and sowen it after,   *sown*
I wolde wende with yow and the wey teche.'
    'This were a long lettyng,' quod a lady in a scleyre;   *delay; veil (C)*

1 This would be a very difficult journey for anyone who did not have a guide.

629 ingonge] LR, **AC**; ingoing W.
631 Ne I] LRF, **AC**; Nor I kan W.
635 hem] LRFMCr, **AC**; *om* W&r.
639 k. þere] β; welcome α.

Rubric Passus sextus de visione vt supra.
2 miȝte] **AC** (*so* K-D); wolde *All* B-MSS.

'What sholde we wommen werche the while?'   *do meanwhile*
'Somme shul sowe the sak,' quod Piers, 'for shedyng of the whete;
                                              to prevent; falling through
10 And ye lovely ladies with youre longe fyngres,
   That ye have silk and sandel to sowe whan tyme is   *(See) that; cendal (C)*
   Chesibles for chapeleyns chirches to honoure.   *Chasubles; priests*
   Wyves and widewes, wolle and flex spynneth: *flax; spin*
   Maketh cloth, I counseille yow, and kenneth so youre doughtres.   *teach*
15 The nedy and the naked, nymeth hede how thei liggeth,   *take*
   And casteth hem clothes, for so comaundeth Truthe.   *make*
   For I shal lenen hem liflode, but if the lond faille,   *provide*
   As longe as I lyve, for the Lordes love of hevene.
                                          for the Lord of heaven's love
   And alle manere of men that by mete and drynke libbeth,   *live*
20 Helpeth hym to werche wightliche that wynneth youre foode.'
                                              those (who . . .); vigorously
   'By Crist!' quod a knyght thoo, 'he kenneth us the beste;   *then; instructs*
   Ac on the teme, trewely, taught was I nevere.   *plough-team, (?theme)*
   Ac kenne me,' quod the knyght, 'and by Crist I wole assaye!'   *try*
   'By Seint Poul!' quod Perkyn, 'Ye profre yow so faire
                                              yourself; graciously
25 That I shal swynke and swete and sowe for us bothe,   *toil*
   And [ek] labour[e] for thi love al my lif tyme,   *for love of you*
   In covenaunt that thow kepe Holy Kirke and myselve   *condition; protect*
   Fro wastours and fro wikked men that this world destruyeth;
   And go hunte hardiliche to hares and foxes,   *boldly after*
30 To bores and to bukkes that breken down myne hegges; *boars; deer; hedges*
   And go affaite thi faucons wilde foweles to kille,   *train; falcons*
   For thei cometh to my croft and croppeth my whete.'   *field*
      Curteisly the knyght thanne co[nseyved] thise wordes: *uttered (C)*
   'By my power, Piers, I plighte thee my trouthe   *pledge; solemn word*
35 To fulfille this forward, though I fighte sholde;   *agreement; have to*
   Als longe as I lyve I shal thee mayntene.'   *support*
      'Ye, and yet a point,' quod Piers, 'I preye yow of moore:
                                              one further matter

15 . . . take heed of the conditions in which they live.

17 *After this an additional line* Flessh and breed boþe to riche and to poore *All* B-MSS; *om* AC; *rej. as spur.* K-D *p.* 193.
19 by] Hm, AC (*so* K-D); with F; þoruȝ W&r.
   m. and d.] þe m. A (*so* K-D *p.* 86); þis molde C, A-MS N.
23 Ac] LR&c, ?A; But WF.
26 ek l.] A (*so* K-D); l. C; oþere labours do W&r (C).
30 bukkes] α (boores F), AC (*so* K-D); brokkes β.
31 go] L&r; so W.
32 þei] F, AC; swiche W&r (?=Bx).
33 conseyuede] A, C-MS M (*so* K-D); comsed *All* B-MSS, *most* C-MSS (C).
34 I] AC (*so* K-D); quod he I *All* B-MSS.
37 yow] W&r, C; þe F, A (C).

Loke ye tene no tenaunt but Truthe wole assente;   *trouble; unless*
And though ye mowe amercy hem, lat mercy be taxour   *fine; assessor*
40 And mekenesse thi maister, maugree Medes chekes.   *in despite of Mede*
And though povere men profre yow presentes and yiftes,
Nyme it noght, an aventure thow mowe it noght deserve;
                                                             take; lest perchance
For thow shalt yelde it ayein at one yeres ende   *give it back*
In a ful perilous place—Purgatorie it hatte.   *is called*
45 And mysbede noght thi bondemen—the bettre may thow spede;
                                                             injure; prosper
Though he be thyn underlyng here, wel may happe in hevene *inferior; happen*
That he worth worthier set and with moore blisse: *will be placed higher*
Amice, ascende superius.   *Friend, go up higher* (Lk 14: 10)
For in charnel at chirche cherles ben yvel to knowe,
                                                             charnel-house; hard; make out
Or a knyght from a knave there—knowe this in thyn herte.   *serving-lad*
50 And that thow be trewe of thi tonge, and tales that thow hatie,   *stories; hate*
But if thei ben of wisdom or of wit, thi werkmen to chaste.

                                                             chastise, correct
Hold with none harlotes ne here noght hir tales,   *associate; vulgar buffoons*
And namely at the mete swiche men eschuwe—   *especially; meals; avoid*
For it ben the develes disours, I do the to understonde.'
                                                             they are; story-tellers; I'd have you
55   'I assente, by Seint Jame,' seide the knyght thanne,   *agree*
'For to werche by thi wordes the while my lif dureth.'   *lasts*
'And I shal apparaille me,' quod Perkyn, 'in pilgrymes wise   *clothe*
And wende with yow I wile til we fynde Truthe.'
[He] caste on [hise] clothes, yclouted and hole,   *patched; whole*
60 [Hise] cokeres and [hise] coffes for cold of [hise] nailes,   *leggings; mittens*
And [heng his] hoper at [his] hals in stede of a scryppe: *seed-basket; neck*

38–40 Take care that you trouble no tenant (of yours) unless you have a just cause for doing so/Truth agrees (to your course of action); And even when you are fully justified in fining them, let mercy assess the amount (you exact) and gentle moderation be your governing principle, in spite of desire for gain.

47–8*a* That he will be seated in a more honourable position and (invested) with greater glory: 'Friend, go up higher' (Lk 14: 10). For in the charnel-house (beneath) the church, (the bones of peasants) are hard to distinguish [*sc.* from those of nobles] (*C*).

51 Unless they contain some moral lesson with which to correct your labourers.
52 Do not patronize tellers of obscene stories . . .

38 ye] W&r, C; þou F, A.
41 yow] W&r, C; þe F, A.
42 þow] a, AC (*so* K-D); ye β.
43 ende] L&r, A; tyme W.
45 may] W&r, C; shalt F, ?A (*so* K-D *p.* 170).
51 þei ben] it be YOC²CB, A.
56 w. þe] W&r (=Bx; w. G); word F, A (*so* K-D *p.* 169).

59 He; hise] AC (*so* K-D *p.* 81); And, my W&r (And] I wil F; my] me my LR).
60 Hise (*all*)] A (*first two* C) (*so* K-D); My *All* B-MSS.
61 heng] AC (*so* K-D); hange W&r (y will h. F).
his (1, 2)] AC (*so* K-D); myn *All* B-MSS.

'A busshel of bred corn brynge me therinne,   *seed-corn*
For I wol sowe it myself, and sithenes wol I wende   *afterwards*
To pilgrymage as palmeres doon, pardon for to have.
                      palmers, Jerusalem pilgrims
65 And whoso helpeth me to erie or sowen here er I wende,   *plough*
Shal have leve, by Oure Lord, to lese here in hervest *glean; harvest-time*
And make hym murie thermyd, maugree whoso bigruccheth it.
                  therewith; complain who will
And alle kynne crafty men that konne lyven in truthe, *craftsmen; know how to*
I shal fynden hem fode that feithfulliche libbeth—   *provide; honestly*
70 Save Jakke the Jogelour and Jonette of the Stuwes, *buffoon; brothel*
And Danyel the Dees-pleyere and Denote the Baude,   *dice-player*
And Frere the Faitour, and folk of his ordre,   *Deceiver*
And Robin the Ribaudour, for hise rusty wordes.   *ribald; foul*
Truthe tolde me ones and bad me telle it forth:
75 *Deleantur de libro vivencium*—I sholde noght dele with hem,
                   have dealings with
For Holy Chirche is hote, of hem no tithe to aske, *bidden; demand*
Quia cum iustis non scribantur.
Thei ben ascaped good aventure—now God hem amende!' *by good luck*
  Dame Werch-whan-tyme-is Piers wif highte;   *was called*
His doughter highte Do-right-so-or-thi-dame-shal-thee-bete; *mother; beat*
80 His sone highte Suffre-thi-Sovereyns-to-haven-hir-wille: *superiors*
Deme-hem-noght-for-if-thow-doost-thow-shalt-it-deere-abugge;
                  Judge; pay for it dearly
Lat-God-yworthe-with-al-for-so-His-word-techeth.   *be*
'For now I am old and hoor and have of myn owene,   *grey*
To penaunce and to pilgrimage I wol passe with thise othere;
85 Forthi I wole er I wende do write my biqueste. *Therefore; have written; will*
In Dei nomine, Amen; I make it myselve. *In the name of God; draw up*
' He shal have my soule that best hath deserved it,
And [defende it fro the fend], for so I bileve,
Til I come to hise acountes as my crede me telleth, *reckoning; Creed*

75, 76a 'Let them be blotted out of the book of the living: and with the just let
   them not be written' (Ps 68: 29).

65 or] L&*r*, AC; and WCr.   aske] R (?=α), AC (*so* K-D); take
  sowen . . . wende] any þyng swynke   βF.
  A; eHes to wedyn C (*cf.* K-D   77 now] LMRF, AC; but OC²; *om*
  p. 108).   W&*r*.
67 hym] RF (=α), AC (*so* K-D); hem   86–8 *as two lines div. after* soule α.
  WL&*c* (=β).   88 defende . . . fend] AC (*so* K-D);
70 Iakke] L&*r*, AC; Jagge W.   fro þe f. it def. W&*r* (it d.] Ikeped
72 þe] *om* FCr, C (*so* K-D).   it R; *transp. & soph.* F).
  his] L&*r*; hire W.   for . . . bil.] β, AC; *om* α.
74 forþ] A (*so* K-D); f. after B;   89 crede] RF&*c*, AC (*so* K-D);
  forthere C; after W&*r*.   Credo WL&*c*.
76 hote] W&*r*, C; holde F, A (*so*   me] W&*r* (=β), A; *om* RF (=α), C.
  K-D *pp.* 155, 168n, 170).

90 To have a relees and a remission—on that rental I leve.
release; record; believe
'The kirke shal have my caroyne, and kepe my bones,   *corpse*
For of my corn and catel he craved the tithe.   *i.e. the parish-priest; asked*
I paide it hym prestly, for peril of my soule;   *promptly*
Forthi is he holden, I hope, to have me in his masse   *obliged; think; include*
95 And mengen me in his memorie amonges alle Cristene. *remember me (by name)*
'My wif shal have of that I wan with truthe, and namoore,
earned honestly
And dele among my doughtres and my deere children;   *divide, apportion*
For though I deye today, my dettes are quyte;   *paid in full*
I bar hom that I borwed er I to bedde yede.   *returned; went*
100 And with the residue and the remenaunt, by the Rode of Lukes!
Rood of Lucca (C)
I wol worshipe therwith Truthe by my lyve,
And ben His pilgrym atte plow for povere mennes sake.   *at the*
My plowpote shal be my pikstaf, and picche atwo the rotes,
plough-pusher; separate
And helpe my cultour to kerve and clense the furwes.'   *cut; furrows*
105   Now is Perkyn and thise pilgrimes to the plow faren.   *gone*
To erie this half-acre holpen hym manye;   *plough; helped*
Dikeres and delveres digged up the balkes; *ridges (?left unploughed; Bn p. 204)*
Therwith was Perkyn apayed and preised hem faste.   *pleased; highly*
Othere werkmen ther were that wroghten ful yerne: *eagerly*
110 Ech man in his manere made hymself to doone,
And somme to plese Perkyn piked up the wedes.   *hoed*
At heigh prime Piers leet the plough stonde,   *(=) 9 a.m.*
To oversen hem hymself; whoso best wroghte,   *oversee; whoever*
He sholde be hired therafter, whan hervest tyme come.   *once again*
115   Thanne seten somme and songen atte nale,   *sat; over drink, at ale*
And holpen ere this half acre with 'How trolly lolly!'
helped plough; idle singing

95 And remember to mention me by name in his commemorative prayer [during the Mass].
103 My plough-pusher shall be my pikestaff and separate the roots.

92 he] LR&c, AC; she W&c.
93 hym] LR&c, ?A; ful W; *om* C.
94 Forþi is he] F. he is FG; He is AC.
95 me] F, AC (*so* K-D); *om* W&r (=Bx).
97 douȝtres] BxCx; frendis A (*so* K-D *p.* 102).
103 pote] α, AC (*so* K-D); foot β.
picche] WLR&c, C, A-MSS ULJ; putte *most* A-MSS (*so* Ka, K-D).
atwo] W&r (?=β), C; at R (?=α; awey F), ?A.

105 þese] R (?=α; þe F), AC; hise W&r (?=β).
108 faste] yernc A (*see* K-D *p.* 108).
109 yerne] faste CM, A.
113 who] B, AC (*so* K-D); and w. W&r *exc* F.
115 þanne] FHm, AC (*so* K-D); And þ. W&r.
116 þis] W, C; his L&r (?=Bx); þe A.

69

'Now, by the peril of my soule!' quod Piers al in pure tene, *sheer anger*
'But ye arise the rather and rape yow to werche, *hasten*
Shal no greyn that here groweth glade yow at nede, *grain (of wheat)*
120 And though ye deye for doel, the devel have that recche!' *pain; should care*
   Tho were faitours afered, and feyned hem blynde;
   impostors; pretended to be
   Somme leide hir legges aliry, as swiche losels konneth, *wastrels know how*
   And made hir [pleynt] to Piers and preide hym of grace:
   complained; to be let off
'For we have no lymes to laboure with, lord, ygraced be ye! *thanked*
125 Ac we preie for yow, Piers, and for youre plowgh bothe,
   That God of his grace youre greyn multiplie
   And yelde yow of youre almesse that ye yyve us here;
   pay you back for; alms, charity
   For we may neither swynke ne swete, swich siknesse us eyleth.' *ails, afflicts*
   'If it be sooth,' quod Piers, 'that ye seyn, I shal it soone aspie. *discover*
130 Ye ben wastours, I woot wel, and Truthe woot the sothe; *the facts*
   And I am his olde hyne and highte hym to warne *loyal servant; bidden*
   Whiche thei were in this world hise werkmen apeired. *(who) harmed*
   Ye wasten that men wynnen with travaille and with tene; *effort and pain*
   Ac Truthe shal teche yow his teme to dryve, *(plough)-team*
135 Or ye shul eten barly breed and of the broke drynke; *brook (=plain water)*
   But if he be blynd or brokelegged or bolted with irens, *shackled in chains*
   He shal ete whete breed and [with myselve drynke]
   Til God of his goodnesse [garisoun] hym sende. *deliverance*
   Ac ye myghte travaille as Truthe wolde and take mete and hyre
   food and wages
140 To kepe kyen in the feld, the corn fro the bestes, *For keeping cows*
   Diken or delven or dyngen upon sheves, *(For threshing) corn*
   Or helpe make morter or bere muk afeld. *spread dung on fields*
   In lecherie and losengerie ye lyven, and in sleuthe, *lying, deceitfulness*
   And al is thorugh suffraunce that vengeaunce yow ne taketh!
   (God's) long-suffering
145 'Ac ancres and heremites that eten but at Nones *'Nones', noon-tide hour*

120 And even though you should die of starvation-pangs, the devil take the man
   who should regret it!
122 Some laid their legs in such a way as to seem maimed, as such rascally vaga-
   bonds know how to (*C*).

119 her] M, AC (*so* K-D); *om* W&r
   (? = Bx).
120 recche] RFHmCr, AC (*so* K-D);
   reccheþ W&r.
123 pleynt] mone *All* B-MSS (*C*).
124 For we] W&r (& seyd we F); we
   G, A (*so* K-D).
   ʒe] L&r (*om* F); þe WHm.
127 of] LR, AC; for W.

128 neiþer] BoBmCr, AC (*so* K-D);
   noʒt W&r (*l.om* Cot).
131 olde] holde A (*so* K-D *pp.* 84–5).
   hiʒte] auʒte A.
137 wiþ . . . d.] d. w. myselue W&r
   exc F (*C*).
138 garisoun] amendement *All*
   B-MSS (*C*).
145 but] LRF&c, C; noʒt b. W&c.

70

And na moore er morwe—myn almesse shul thei have,
And of my catel to cope hem with that han cloistres and chirches.
money; clothe themselves
Ac Robert Renaboute shal [right] noght have of myne,
Ne postles, but thei preche konne and have power of the bisshop:
(wandering) preachers
150 Thei shul have payn and potage and [put] hemself at ese—- *bread; soup*
For it is an unresonable Religion that hath right noght of certein.'
Thanne gan Wastour to wrathen hym and wolde have yfoughte,
grow angry
And to Piers the Plowman he profrede his glove. *(i.e. in challenge)*
A Bretoner, a braggere, abosted Piers als *Breton; boastingly defied; also*
155 And bad hym go pissen with his plowgh, forpynede sherewe!
damned scoundrel (C)
'Wiltow or neltow, we wol have oure wille *Like it or not*
Of thi flour and of thi flesshe—fecche whanne us liketh,
And maken us murye thermyde, maugree thi chekes.'
enjoy ourselves; with it
Thanne Piers the Plowman pleyned hym to the knyghte *complained*
160 To kepen hym as covenaunt was fro cursede sherewes *protect; as agreed*
And fro thise wastours wolveskynnes that maketh the world deere:
wolf-natured destroyers
'For tho wasten and wynnen noght, and that [while ilke] *as long as they do*
Worth nevere plentee among the peple the while my plowgh liggeth.'
lies (idle)
Curteisly the knyght thanne, as his kynde wolde, *nature required*
165 Warnede Wastour and wissed hym bettre: *counselled*
'Or thow shalt abigge by the lawe, by the ordre that I bere!'
pay the penalty; my rank
'I was noght wont to werche,' quod Wastour, 'and now wol I noght
bigynne!'—
And leet light of the lawe, and lasse of the knyghte, *set small store by; less*
And sette Piers at a pese, and his plowgh bothe, *valued; pea*
170 And manaced Piers and his men if thei mette eftsoone. *threatened; again*
'Now, by the peril of my soule!' quod Piers, 'I shal apeire yow alle'— *hurt*
And houped after Hunger, that herde hym at the firste. *shouted; straight away*
'Awreke me of thise wastours,' quod he, 'that this world shendeth!'
Avenge; harm
Hunger in haste thoo hente Wastour by the mawe *then; stomach*

151 For it would not be reasonable to expect members of any religious order to
possess absolutely no source of sure sustenance.

146 er] LR&c; er þe W.
147 my] LMRF; *om* W&r.
cope] LR&c; kepe W&c.
148 riȝt] *conj* K-D *p.* 199 (*cf.* 151
below).
150 put] make *All* B-MSS *exc* F (a
pytauwnce [bysyde]) (C).

152 Thanne] YF&c, AC (*so* K-D);
And þ. WLR&c.
162 while ilke] i.w. W&r (wete wel
for soþe F).
174 mawe] L&r, AC; wombe W.

71

175 And wrong hym so by the wombe that al watrede hise eighen.   *wrung; belly*
    He buffetted the Bretoner aboute the chekes
    That he loked lik a lanterne al his lif after.
    He bette hem so bothe, he brast ner hire guttes;   *beat; nearly burst*
    Ne hadde Piers with a pese loof preyed [hym bileve],   *pease-loaf; leave off*
180 They hadde be dolven bothe—ne deme thow noon oother.
                                                   (dead and) buried
    'Suffre hem lyve,' he seide 'and lat hem ete with hogges,
                                                   Allow them to live
    Or ellis benes and bren ybaken togideres.'   *beans; bran; baked*
    Faitours for fere herof flowen into bernes   *fled; barns*
    And flapten on with flailes fro morwe til even,   *threshed; evening*
185 That hunger was noght hardy on hem for to loke   *(so) bold (as to)*
    For a potful of peses that Piers hadde ymaked.   *Because of*
    An heep of heremytes henten hem spades   *crowd; got hold of*
    And kitten hir copes and courtepies hem maked,   *cut; short coats*
    And wente as werkmen with spades and with shoveles,
190 And dolven and dikeden to dryve awey Hunger.   *dug; ditched*
    Blynde and bedreden were bootned a thousand,   *bed-ridden; cured*
    That seten to begge silver, soone were thei heeled;   *sat; healed*
    For that was bake for Bayard was boote for many hungry;   *i.e. horses; remedy*
    And many a beggere for benes buxum was to swynke,   *willing; toil*
195 And ech a povere man wel apaied to have pesen for his hyre,   *satisfied; pay*
    And what Piers preide hem to do as prest as a sperhauk.
                                                 prompt; sparrow-hawk
    And [Piers was proud therof], and putte hem to werke
    And yaf hem mete as he myghte aforthe and mesurable hyre.
                                            afford; fair, fitting
    Thanne hadde Piers pite, and preide Hunger to wende
200 Hoom into his owene erd and holden hym there [evere]:   *land; remain*
    'For I am wel awroke of wastours thorugh thy myghte.   *avenged upon*
    Ac I preie thee, er thow passe,' quod Piers to Hunger,
    'Of beggeris and of bidderis what best be to doone?
    For I woot wel, be thow went, thei wol werche ful ille;   *once you go*
205 Meschief it maketh thei be so meke nouthe,   *Distress (alone); now*
    And for defaute of hire foode this folk is at my wille.   *lack; obedient to me*

---

175 al watred his eyȝes] R (?=α),
   AC; boþe hise eiȝen w. W&r (b.
   om GCr¹²).
179 hym b.] AC (*so* K-D); hunger to
   cesse *All* B-MSS (to *om* α).
180 boþe] LR&c; *om* W.
182 and] L&r; or W.
   After this a line in all B-MSS:
   Or ellis melk and mene ale þus
   preied Piers for hem (þus . . . h.]
   to meyntene here lyvis F) *rej. as*
   spur. K-D *p.* 193.

185 hardy] αG, AC (*so* K-D); so h. β.
189 wiþ . . . sh.] to wedynge and to
   mowynge C (*so* K-D *p.* 152).
197 P . . . þer.] AC (*so* K-D); þer. w.
   P. p. W& *most* (C).
198 as . . . hyre] and monie as þei
   miȝte *as*serue AC (*so* K-D *p.* 81).
200 into] LR, AC; vnto WCr.
   erd] LR, AC; yerd W.
   þ. euere] AC (*so* K-D); styll þ.
   F; þere W&r (=Bx).

[And] it are my blody bretheren, for God boughte us alle.   *by blood; redeemed*
Truthe taughte me ones to loven hem ech one
And to helpen hem of alle thyng, ay as hem nedeth.   *always*
210 Now wolde I wite of thee, what were the beste,   *know from*
And how I myghte amaistren hem and make hem to werche.'   *govern, control*
    'Here now,' quod Hunger, 'and hoold it for a wisdom:
Bolde beggeris and bigge that mowe hir breed biswynke,   *strong; labour for*
With houndes breed and horse breed hoold up hir hertes—
                                      sustain (their lives)
215 Aba[v]e hem with benes, for bollynge of hir wombe;
                        Confound; to stop; swelling
And if the gomes grucche, bidde hem go swynke,   *complain; toil*
And he shal soupe swetter whan he it hath deserved.   *more pleasantly*
    'Ac if thow fynde any freke that Fortune hath apeired   *person; injured*
Or any manere false men, fonde thow swiche to knowe: *try*
220 Conforte hem with thi catel for Cristes love of hevene;   *possessions*
Love hem and lene hem, for so lawe of [kynde wolde]:   *give to; nature*
Alter alterius onera portate.
And alle manere of men that thow myght aspie   *discover*
That nedy ben [or naked, and nought han to spende,
With mete or with mone lat make hem fare the bettre].   *money*
225 Love hem and lakke hem noght—lat God take the vengeaunce;   *blame*
Theigh thei doon yvele, lat thow God yworthe:
                   Though; be (?settle it; Bn p. 209)
Michi vindictam et ego retribuam.
And if thow wilt be gracious to God, do as the Gospel techeth,   *pleasing*
And bilove thee amonges lowe men—so shaltow lacche grace: *obtain*
Facite vobis amicos de mammona iniquitatis.'

215 Discomfort them with [the food we give animals] beans, to prevent their
    bellies from swelling (with hunger) (*C*).
221*a* Bear ye one another's burdens; [and so you shall fulfil the law of Christ]
    (Gal 6: 2).
226*a* Revenge is mine and I will repay [them in due time] (Deut 32: 35, *quoted in*
    Rom 12: 19, Heb 10: 30).
228-8*a* And make yourself a friend of humble people—that way you will
    obtain God's favour (for yourself): 'Make unto you friends.of the mammon of
    iniquity' [=ill-gotten riches] (Lk 16: 9).

207 And it] AC (*so* K-D); It R; &
    yet they YOC²; Thei W&r.
    for] Y, AC (*so* K-D); quod Piers f.
    W&r (f.] & R; *om* G).
210 Now] AC (*so* K-D); And n. *All*
    B-MSS.
    of þ.] ȝif þou wistest A (*so* K-D);
    ar thow wendest C.
215 Abaue] AC (*so* K-D); Abate *All*
    B-MSS (*C*).
    wombe] LR, ?AC; *pl.* WF.
216 go] β; go and a, *some* AC-MSS.

217 *In* β, AC; *line om* a.
218 Ac] R (?=a), AC (*so* K-D); And β.
220 hem] RY, AC (*so* Sk); hym WL.
221 k.wolde] AC (*so* K-D); god
    techeþ WLR&r *with varr* (=Bx).
223-4 or . . . bettre] A (*so* K-D *p.*
    108); *not in* B-MSS.
223 or . . . spende] and nouȝty help
    hem wiþ þi goodes W&r (=Bx).
226 þow] LR (*so* K-D); *om* W&r.
228 low] LRF; lewed W.
228*a vobis*] L&r, AC; *vos* W.

'I wolde noght greve God,' quod Piers, 'for al the good on grounde!'
wealth on earth
230 Mighte I synnelees do as thow seist?' seide Piers thanne.
'Ye, I bihote thee,' quod Hunger, 'or ellis the Bible lieth. *promise*
Go to Genesis the geaunt, the engendrour of us alle: *giant; procreator*
"*In sudore* and swynk thow shalt thi mete tilie, *food; earn by tilling*
And laboure for thi liflode," and so Oure Lord highte. *living; commanded*
235 And Sapience seith the same—I seigh it in the Bible:
(the) Wisdom (writings); saw
" *Piger pro frigore* no feeld nolde tilie— *till*
And therfore he shal begge and bidde, and no man bete his hunger." *relieve*
'Mathew with mannes face moutheth thise wordes— *utters*
That *servus nequam* hadde a mnam, and for he wolde noght chaffare,
pound; trade
240 He hadde maugree of his maister everemoore after; *the disfavour*
And bynam hym his mnam for he ne wolde werche, *(he) took away from*
And yaf that mnam to hym that ten mnames hadde,
And with that he seide, that Holy Chirche it herde:
"He that hath shal have and helpe there it nedeth; *is necessary*
245 And he that noght hath shal noght have, and no man hym helpe,
And that he weneth wel to have, I wole it hym bireve."
that which he thinks; take from
'Kynde Wit wolde that ech a wight wroghte, *should work*
Or in [te]chynge or in [tell]ynge or travaillynge in preieres— *Either; tilling*
Contemplatif lif or Actif lif, Crist wolde men wroghte.
250 The Sauter seith in the psalme of *Beati omnes*,
The freke that fedeth hymself with his feithful labour, *honest*
He is blessed by the book in body and in soule:
Labores manuum tuarum &c.
'Yet I preie yow,' quod Piers, '*pur charite*, and ye konne *for charity; if*
Any leef of lechecraft, lere it me, my deere; *leaf; medicine; teach*
255 For some of my servaunts and myself bothe
Of al a wike werche noght, so oure wombe aketh.' *For a whole week*

233 'In the sweat [of thy face shalt thou eat bread]' (Gen 3: 19).
236 'Because of the cold, the sluggard [would not plough]' (Prov 20: 4).
239 That 'a wicked servant' had a *mina* [=£1], and because he was unwilling to do business (with it) (*cf.* Lk 19: 12*ff. esp.* 22).
250 'Blessed are all they [that fear the Lord] . . .' (Ps 127: 1).
252a 'For [thou shalt eat] the labours of thy hands . . .' (Ps 127: 2).

236 *pro f.*] *propter frigus* AC (*so Vulg.*).
237 And þ.] *om* A (*so* K-D *p.* 86).
238 -theth] α, A; -þed β (-d *om* C).
239 mnam] *glossed* besaunt WLHmM.
  chaffare] it vsen A (*so* K-D *p.* 86).
248 teching] A (*so* K-D *p.* 89);
  dichyng R (?=a); dikynge W&r.
  telling] A (*so* K-D *p.* 89);
  deluynge *All* B-MSS.

249 men wr.] LR; þei wr. W; we wr.
  F; it als A (*so* K-D *p.* 85).
253 yow] W&r, C; þe F, A.
  pur] FHm&c, AC (*so* K-D); par
  WLR.
  ye] W&r (*and cf.* C); þou F, A
  (*so* K-D *p.* 170).

    'I woot wel,' quod Hunger, 'what siknesse yow eyleth;   *afflicts*
Ye han manged over muche—that maketh yow grone.   *eaten*
Ac I hote thee,' quod Hunger, 'as thow thyn hele wilnest,   *health; desire*
260 That thow drynke no day er thow dyne somwhat.
Ete noght, I hote thee, er hunger thee take   *come upon you*
And sende thee of his sauce to savore with thi lippes;
     please, make food tasty to
And keep som til soper tyme and sitte noght to longe;
Arys up er appetit have eten his fille.
265 Lat noght Sire Surfet sitten at thi borde—   *table*
Love hym noght, for he is lecherous and likerous of tonge,   *dainty*
And after many maner metes his mawe is afyngred.
     kinds of food; very hungry
   'And if thow diete thee thus, I dar legge myn eris   *wager; ears*
That Phisik shal his furred hood for his fode selle,   *the medical profession*
270 And his cloke of Calabre with alle the knappes of golde,
     Calabrian fur; buttons
And be fayn, by my feith, his phisik to lete,   *give up; the practice of p.*
And lerne to laboure with lond [lest] liflode [hym faille].
Ther aren mo [li]eres than leches—Lord hem amende!   *impostors; physicians*
They do men deye thorugh hir drynkes er destynee it wolde.'   *make; potions*
275 'By Seint Poul,' quod Piers, 'thise arn profitable wordes!
For this is a lovely lesson, Lord it thee foryelde!   *reward*
Wend now, Hunger, whan thow wolt, that wel be thow evere.'
   'I bihote God,' quod Hunger, 'hennes ne wole I wende   *promise*
[Er] I have dyned bi this day and ydronke bothe.'
280 'I have no peny,' quod Piers, 'pulettes to bugge,   *pullets; buy*
Neither gees ne grys, but two grene cheses,   *pigs; fresh, unmatured*
A fewe cruddes and creme and [a cake of otes],   *curds*
And two loves of benes and bran ybake for my fauntes.   *loaves; children*
And yet I seye, by my soule, I have no salt bacon   *further still*
285 Ne no cokeney, by Crist, coloppes to maken!   *egg; fried eggs and bacon*

258 þat] B, AC (*so* K-D); and þ. W&*r*
   (=Bx).
264 Arise] LR, A; And rys W.
266 Love] MCot, A (*so* K-D); Leve
   W&*r*.
   lecherous] a lechour A.
267 afyngred] alustyd F; alongid A
   (*so* K-D).
269 his . . . h.] OCrFC²B, A (*so* K-D);
   pl. W&*r*.
272 lest . . . faile] AC (*so* K-D); for
   liflode is swete *All* B-MSS.
273 þer aren] R (?=α; Now are F),
   AC (*so* K-D); For murþereris are
   W&*r* (F. manye lechys ben B).
   mo] α, A (*so* K-D); manye β
   (*om* B).

liзeris þ. l.] A, *so* K-D;
morareres þ. l. R; moraynerys þ. l.
F; leches W&*r* (=β); luþer leches
C (*C*).
276 *Line thus* AC (*so* K-D); *trspd.*
   with 277 *All* B-MSS.
278 I] GBF, AC (*so* K-D); *om* W&*r*.
279 Er] AC (*so* K-D); Til *All* B-MSS
   (*C*).
281 Nether] YHm, AC (*so* K-D);
   Ne n. W&*r*.
282 a . . . otes] C (*so* K-D); an
   hauer cake *All* B- *and most* A-MSS
   (*C*).
285 to] OC², AC (*so* K-D); for to
   WLR.

Ac I have percile and porettes and manye [plaunte coles],
parsley; leeks; greens
And ek a cow and a calf, and a cart mare
To drawe afeld my donge the while the droghte lasteth.
By this liflode we mote lyve til Lammesse tyme,
food, sustenance; Lammas (C)
290 And by that I hope to have hervest in my crofte; *by then; field*
Thanne may I dighte thi dyner as me deere liketh.'
prepare; as I'd really like to
Al the povere peple tho pescoddes fetten; *pea-pods; fetched*
Benes and baken apples thei broghte in hir lappes,
Chibolles and chervelles and ripe chiries manye, *Spring-onions; chervil*
295 And profrede Piers this present to plese with Hunger. *to please Hunger with*
Al Hunger eet in haste and axed after moore. *asked*
Thanne povere folk for fere fedden Hunger yerne; *anxiously*
With grene poret and pesen to poisone hym thei thoghte!
cabbage, greens; peas
By that it neghed neer hervest and newe corn cam to chepyng; *then; market*
300 Thanne was folk fayn, and fedde Hunger with the beste— *pleased*
With good ale, as Gloton taghte—and garte Hunger to slepe. *taught; made*
And tho wolde Wastour noght werche, but wandren aboute,
Ne no beggere ete breed that benes inne were, *containing beans*
But of coket and clermatyn or ellis of clene whete,
breads of fine white flour; other kinds (of fine wheat)
305 Ne noon halfpeny ale in none wise drynke, *in no way*
But of the beste and of the brunneste that [brewesteres] selle. *darkest, strongest*
Laborers that have no land to lyve on but hire handes
Deyned nought to dyne aday nyght-olde wortes; *Deigned; eat; greens*
May no peny ale hem paie, ne no pece of bacoun, *satisfy; piece*
310 But if it be fressh flessh outher fissh fryed outher ybake— *or; baked*
And that *chaud* and *plus chaud*, for chillynge of hir mawe. *to prevent*
And but if he be heighliche hyred, ellis wole he chide— *highly paid; complain*
And that he was werkman wroght wa[ri]e the tyme. *curse*

304 But only loaves made of fine white flour, or at least only out of wheat unmixed [with other grains, beans &c].
308 Would not deign to eat on the morrow last night's greens.
311 And that (to be served) 'hot' and 'piping hot', to prevènt their stomachs catching chill.

286 plante colis] A (*from* A-MSS AMH², *so* K-D *p.* 205*n*); cole plauntes W&r (=β); queynte herbes α (q.] propre F).
289 By] A?C (*so* K-D); And by *All* B-MSS.
290 And by] By Cr, A.
291 Þanne] AC (*so* K-D); And þ. *All* B-MSS.
me] W&r, C?A; þe F, *most* A-MSS (*so* K-D).

298 poisone] peysen *Some* A-MSS (*so* K-D *p.* 88, *and see* Ka *p.* 449) (C).
301 to] HmG&c, AC (*so* K-D); go WLR&c.
306 breusteris] AC (*so* K-D *p.* 81); in *Burgh is* to *All* B-MSS.
313 warie] AC (so K-D); waille W&r (*l. om* YOC²CB).

Ayeins Catons counseil comseth he to jangle: *begins; dispute*
Paupertatis onus paciencer ferre memento.
315 He greveth hym ageyn God and gruccheth ageyn Reson,
                     gets angry; grumbles against
And thanne corseth he the Kyng and al his Counseil after   *curses*
Swiche lawes to loke, laborers to greve.   *For decreeing such . . .; grieve*
Ac whiles Hunger was hir maister, ther wolde noon of hem chide,
Ne stryven ayeins his statut, so sterneliche he loked!   *fiercely, sternly*
320   Ac I warne yow werkmen—wynneth whil ye mowe, *obtain (food); are able*
For Hunger hiderward hasteth hym faste!   *is hastening*
He shal awake [thorugh] water, wastours to chaste, *by means of; chastise (C)*
Er fyve yer be fulfilled swich famyn shal aryse:
Thorugh flodes and thorugh foule wedres, fruytes shul faille—*weather; crops*
325 And so seith Saturne and sent yow to warne: *sends as a warning to you*
Whan ye se the [mo]ne amys and two monkes heddes,   *moon*
And a mayde have the maistrie, and multiplie by eighte,
Thanne shal deeth withdrawe and derthe be justice,   *scarcity; judge*
And Dawe the Dykere deye for hunger—
330 But if God of his goodnesse graunte us a trewe.   *truce*

Passus VII

Treuthe herde telle herof, and to Piers sente   sc. *a message*
To taken his teme and tilien the erthe,
And purchaced hym a pardoun *a pena et a culpa*
                obtained an absolute pardon (C)
For hym and for hise heires for everemoore after;

314a [Since nature created you a naked child], remember to bear patiently the
    burden of poverty (*Distichs of Cato*, I, 21 ed. M. Boas, Amsterdam, 1952) (C).

319 his] *þe* FB.
322 þoruȝ] AC (*so* K-D); wiþ W&r;
   sum F.
323 ȝere] RF&c, AC (*so* Sk); *om*
   WL (C).
325 seiþ] AC (*so* K-D) (*re-arr.* F);
   seide W&r.
   sent] LRCr, AC; sen*t*e W&r.

326 mone] *conj* K-D *p.* 181; sonne
   All B-MSS.
330 if] L&r; *om* WF.

Rubric Passus vii us *de visione vt supra.*
1 sente] OCr&c, AC (*so* K-D); he s.
   WLRF&c.
2 taken] L&r; maken WGCr¹ª.

5 And bad hym holde hym at home and erien hise leyes,   *plough; fallow lands*
  And alle that holpen hym to erye, to sette or to sowe,   *plant*
  Or any [man]er mestier that myghte Piers availe—   *(with) any occupation*
  Pardon with Piers Plowman Truthe hath ygraunted.
  Kynges and knyghtes that kepen Holy Chirche   *protect*
10 And rightfully in remes rulen the peple,   *justly; (their) kingdoms*
  Han pardon thorugh purgatorie to passen ful lightly,   *easily*
  With patriarkes and prophetes in paradis to be felawe.   *companion*
    Bysshopes yblessed, if thei ben as thei sholde   *holy*
  Legistres of bothe lawes, the lewed therwith to preche,
                           Expert in canon, civil law
15 And in as muche as thei mowe amenden alle synfulle,
  Arn peres with the Apostles—this pardon Piers sheweth—   *peers, equals of*
  And at the day of dome at the heighe deys to sitte.   *judgment; daïs*
    Marchaunts in the margyne hadde manye yeres,
                         (an addition) in the margin
  Ac noon *A pena et a culpa* the Pope nolde hem graunte,
                         'no absolute pardon' (C)
20 For thei holde noght hir halidayes as Holy Chirche techeth,
                         observe; holy days
  And for thei swere 'by hir soule' and 'so God moste hem helpe'
  Ayein clene Conscience, hir catel to selle.   *(the dictates of) C.; goods*
    Ac under his secret seel Truthe sente hem a lettre,   *private, personal seal*
  [And bad hem] buggen boldely what hem best liked   *buy*
25 And sithenes selle it ayein and save the wynnyng,   *then; profit*
  And amende mesondieux thermyd and myseise folk helpe;
                         hospitals; sick people
  And wikkede weyes wightly amende,   *bad roads; actively*
  And do boote to brugges that tobroke were;   *repair; broken down*
  Marien maydenes or maken hem nonnes;   *nuns*
30 Povere peple and prisons fynden hem hir foode,   *prisoners; provide*
  And sette scolers to scole or to som othere craftes;   *schoolboys; other trade*
  Releve Religion and renten hem bettre.   *Support; endow*
  'And I shal sende yow myselve Seynt Michel myn angel,   *St Michael*

---

18 ... had remission of many years of temporal punishment [*or, more probably*]/
    of punishment in purgatory after death.
32 Aid religious orders and provide them with a more adequate source of income.

7 maner] AC (*so* K-D *p.* 80); ooþer
  All B-MSS.
16 þis] W&r; þus LMRF; such Cr.
17 to] L&r, A; *om* WCot.
19 noon *A*] β, A; no α, ?C.
  nolde] W&r (?=β), ?AC; wolde R
  (?=α; wyll F) CrGB.
  hem] W&r (?=β; *om* G), AC; h.
  nau3t R (?=α; not F).

24 And b. h.] AC (*so* K-D); That þei
  sholde *All* B-MSS.
  what] B, AC (*so* K-D); þat W&r
  (?=Bx).
  liked] β, ?AC; liketh α, *some*
  A-MSS.
31 oþere] kynnes A (*so* K-D *p.* 88).
33 aungel] FHm (*so* K-D), A?C;
  Archa. W&r (?=Bx).

That no devel shal yow dere ne [in youre deying fere yow],

harm; frighten; dying

35 And witen yow fro wanhope, if ye wol thus werche,   *preserve; despair*

And sende youre soules in saufte to my Seintes in joye.'   *safety*

    Thanne were marchaunts murie—manye wepten for joye

And preiseden Piers the Plowman, that purchaced this bulle.   *obtained*

    Men of lawe leest pardon hadde that pleteden for mede,

pleaded (in court)

40 For the Sauter saveth hem noght, swiche as take yiftes,

And nameliche of innocents that noon yvel ne konneth:

especially from; know

Super innocentem munera non accipies.

Pledours sholde peynen hem to plede for swiche and helpe;

Barristers; take trouble

Princes and prelates sholde paie for hire travaille: *efforts*

A regibus et principibus erit merces eorum.

    Ac many a justice and jurour wolde for Johan do moore

Joan (?=a prostitute), ? John

45 Than *pro Dei pietate*—leve thow noon oother!

for love of God; believe (C)

Ac he that spendeth his speche and speketh for the povere

That is innocent and nedy and no man apeireth,   *injures*

Conforteth hym in that caas, coveit[eth noght hise] yiftes,

gifts, payments from him

And [for Oure Lordes love lawe for hym sheweth]— *exercises his legal skill*

50 Shal no devel at his deeth day deren hym a myte   *harm; in the least*

That he ne worth saaf and his soule, the Sauter bereth witnesse:

But he will be saved

Domine, quis habitabit in tabernaculo tuo?

    Ac to bugge water, ne wynd, ne wit, ne fir the ferthe— *buy; fire; fourth*

Thise foure the Fader of Hevene made to this foold in commune:

earth; common

Thise ben Truthes tresores trewe folk to helpe,   *honest*

41, 41a And particularly from simple people who suspect no guile: '. . . nor take bribes against the innocent . . .' (Ps 14: 5).

43a Their payment shall be from kings and princes.

51a Lord, who shall dwell in thy tabernacle? (Ps 14: 1).

34 in . . . yow] *re-arr. so* K-D *pp.* 113–4, 180; f. y. in y. deying W&r (*with varr.*).

39 *As two lines div. after* hadde RF (=a).

    þat . . . m.] þ. p. f. m. for þat craft is shrewed R; For þey f. m. pletyn moore þan mychil for goddes helpe F (*C*).

48 Conf.] β, A; And c. α; That c. ?C. coueitiþ . . . his] AC (cou.] And c. C; h.] here C) (*so* K-D *p.* 79); wiþouten coueitise *of All* B-MSS.

49 for . . . shewiþ] A (*so* K-D *p.* 88); sh. lawe f. o. lordes l. as he it haþ yˡlerned *All* B-MSS (*C*).

51 and h. s.] *om* G; sykirly A (*so* K-D) (*C*).

55 That nevere shul wex ne wanye withouten God hymselve.　　*wane, diminish*
　　Whan thei drawen on to the deth, and indulgences wolde have,
　　His pardon is ful petit at his partyng hennes　　　　　　*small; hence*
　　That any mede of mene men for hir motyng taketh.　　*poor; legal services*
　　Ye legistres and lawieres, [if I lye witeth Mathew]:　*Matthew knows if . . . (C)*
　　Quodcumque vultis ut faciant vobis homines, facite eis.
60　Alle libbynge laborers that lyven with hir hondes,　　　　　*living*
　　That treweliche taken and treweliche wynnen,　　*obtain (wealth); gain*
　　And lyven in love and in lawe, for hir lowe herte　　　　　*humble*
　　Haveth the same absolucion that sent was to Piers.
　　Beggeres and bidderes beth noght in the bulle
65 But if the suggestion be sooth that shapeth hem to begge:
　　　　　　　　　　　　　　　　　　reason; genuine; causes
　　For he that beggeth or bit, but if he have nede,　　　　*begs; unless*
　　He is fals with the feend and defraudeth the nedy,
　　And also gileth the gyvere ageynes his wille;　　　*cheats; against*
　　For if he wiste he were noght nedy he wolde [that yyve]　　*give (to)*
70 Another that were moore nedy than he—so the nedieste sholde be holpe.
　　　　　　　　　　　　　　　　　　　　　　　　　helped
　　Caton kenneth me thus, and the Clerc of the Stories:
　　　　　　　　　　　　　　　　　　Cato; Peter Comestor (C)
　　Cui des, videto is Catons techyng;
　　And in the Stories he techeth to bistowe thyn almesse:
　　　　　　　　　　　　　　　　　　i.e. the Clerk, Comestor
　　Sit elemosina tua in manu tua donec studes cui des.
　　Ac Gregory was a good man, and bad us gyven alle

55 (Commodities) that shall never come into being or cease to be except through (the power of) God Himself.
59a All things (therefore) whatsoever you would that men should do to you, do you also to them (Mt 7: 12).
72 Take heed whom you give [alms] to (*Cato, Distichs, brev. sent.* 17).
73a Let your alms remain in your hand until you have taken pains to find out who you should give to (*C*).

56 þe d.] OYFR&c (þe *om* R;
　?=Bx), C (*so* K-D); deye WL&c.
57 his] RY&c, AC (*so* K-D); Hir
　WF&c.
　his] R (?=a), C (*so* K-D); hir
　W&r.
59 Ye . . . Mathew] *rec.* K-D *p.* 201;
　as two lines div. after truþe: Ye l.
　and l. holdeþ þis for truþe / That if
　þat I lye M. is to blame *All* B-MSS
　(*with varr.*). *After* 59 *an additional
　line* For he bad me make yow þis
　and þis proverbe me tolde W&r
　(*om* F); *see* K-D *p.* 193 (*C*).
60 wiþ] W&r, C; by F, A.
62 herte] α, A (*so* K-D); *pl.* β.

64 and] MCr, AC (*so* K-D *p.* 154);
　ne W&r.
　beth] HmF, AC (*so* K-D); ne b.
　W&r.
68 also] C², C; ek A; a. he W&r (a.
　om FG).
　gyleth] R (?=a), AC (*so* K-D);
　bigileþ W&r.
69 *Div. from* 70 *after* anoþer *All*
　B-MSS; *re-div.* K-D *pp.* 187–8.
　that y.] ȝyue þ. W&r (þ.] yt FG);
　it gyue YOC²CB (*C*).
70 nedy] nedyer αM.
　þan he] and nauȝtier R; þ. h. & F.
71 of þe] LMRF; of W&r.

75 That asketh for His love that us al leneth: *for love of Him; gives*
  Non eligas cui miserearis, ne forte pretereas illum qui meretur
   accipere; quia incertum est pro quo Deo magis placeas.
  For wite ye nevere who is worthi—ac God woot who hath nede.
  In hym that taketh is the trecherie, if any treson walke—   *deceit*
  For he that yeveth, yeldeth, and yarketh hym to reste, *gives; pays; prepares*
  And he that biddeth, borweth, and bryngeth hymself in dette.
                                  borrows; into debt (i.e. sin)
80 For beggeres borwen everemo, and hir borgh is God Almyghty—   *surety*
  To yelden hem that yeveth hem, and yet usure moore:
                             pay; interest on top of it
  Quare non dedisti pecuniam meam ad mensam, ut
   ego veniens cum usuris exegissem utique illam?
  Forthi biddeth noght, ye beggeres, but if ye have gret nede.   *Therefore*
  For whoso hath to buggen hym breed—the Book bereth witnesse—
                                 (money) to buy
  He hath ynough that hath breed ynough, though he have noght ellis:
  Satis dives est qui non indiget pane.
85 Lat usage be youre solas of seintes lyves redyng;
  The Book banneth beggerie, and blameth hem in this manere: *forbids*
  Iunior fui etenim senui, et non vidi iustum derelictum, nec
   semen eius querens panem.
  For [thei] lyve in no love, ne no lawe holde: *observe*
  [Thei] ne wedde no womman that [thei] with deele, *have intercourse with*
90 But as wilde bestes with 'wehee' worthen uppe and werchen, *mount; go to it*
  And bryngen forth barnes that bastardes men calleth.   *children*
  Or the bak or som boon thei breketh in his youthe,   *Either; bone*

75a Do not choose (for yourself) whom to take mercy upon, for it may be that
   you will pass over someone who deserves to receive (your alms): for it is not
   certain for which (act) you may please God more [*sc.* giving to the deserving or
   the undeserving] (Jerome) (*C*).
78 He who gives renders payment [*sc.* to God for his own sins] and (in doing so)
   procures relief for himself [*sc.* from the punishment otherwise due for these].
81–1a Who will pay their almsgivers with interest [*sc.* for the 'use' of their
   money]: 'And why then didst thou not give my money into the bank, that at my
   coming I might have exacted it with usury [*sc.* interest]?' (Lk 19: 23).
84a He is rich enough, who does not lack bread (Jerome) (*C*).
85 Let the practice of reading saints' lives be your comfort.
87 I have been young, and now am old: and I have not seen the just forsaken, nor
   his seed seeking bread (Ps 36: 25).

75a *misere*-] LRF; *miseri*- W.

81a *veniens*] LRF (*so* Vulg.); *veniam*
  W.
  exegissem . . . illam] & *e. u. i.* F
  (*so* Vulg.); *e.i.&c* Cot; *exigere* W
  (*C*).
82 gret] W&r; *om* gF.
87 *nec*] L&r; *ne* W.
  quer. pan.] FY, C (*so* K-D); *&c* WL.

88 F. þei] CA (F. *om* A; *so* K-D);
  F. ye W&r (ye] beggeres F).
89 þei] AC (*so* K-D *p.* 81); Manye of
  yow W&r (o.y.] man F).
  no] AC (*so* K-D); no3t þe *All*
  B-MSS.
  þei] CA (*so* K-D); he F; ye W&r.
92 þei] α, AC (*so* K-D); he β, (?< hy
  Bx; 3e B).

And goon [and] faiten with hire fauntes for everemoore after.

                                  ·beg falsely; children

Ther is moore mysshapen amonges thise beggeres   *deformed people*

95 Than of alle [othere] manere men that on this moolde walketh.   *earth*

Tho that lyve thus hir lif mowe lothe the tyme

That evere he was man wroght, whan he shal hennes fare.   *made; hence*

Ac olde men and hore that helplees ben of strengthe,   *grey*

And wommen with childe that werche ne mowe,

100 Blynde and bedreden and broken hire membres,   *bed-ridden*

That taken this myschief mekeliche, as mesels and othere, *misfortune; lepers*

Han as pleyn pardon as the Plowman hymselve.   *full*

For love of hir lowe hertes Oure Lord hath hem graunted   *humble*

Hir penaunce and hir Purgatorie upon this [pure] erthe.   *very*

105 ' Piers,' quod a preest thoo, ' thi pardon moste I rede;   *explain*

For I shal construe ech clause and kenne it thee on Englissh.' *explain*

And Piers at his preiere the pardon unfoldeth—   *request*

And I bihynde hem bothe biheld al the bulle.

In two lynes it lay, and noght a le[ttre] moore,

110 And was writen right thus in witnesse of truthe:

Et qui bona egerunt ibunt in vitam eternam;

Qui vero mala, in ignem eternum.

 ' Peter!' quod the preest thoo, ' I kan no pardon fynde

But "Do wel and have wel, and God shal have thi soule,"

And "Do yvel and have yvel, and hope thow noon oother

                                expect nothing else

That after thi deeth day the devel shal have thi soule!"'   *But that*

115   And Piers for pure tene pulled it atweyne   *sheer anger, vexation*

And seide, '*Si ambulavero in medio umbre mortis*

Non timebo mala, quoniam tu mecum es.

110a And those who have done well shall go into eternal life; but those who (have done) evil (will go) into eternal fire (Athanasian Creed, *clause* 40) (C).

116–17 (For) though I should walk in the midst of the shadow of death, I will fear no evils: for thou art with me (Ps 22: 4).

93 And] AC (*so* K-D); A. *sippe* W&r.
and] AC (*so* K-D); þey F; *om*
W&r (? = Bx).
here] RF (? = a) OC², AC (*so* K-D);
youre W&r (? = β).
94 amonges] AC (*so* K-D); peple a.
All B-MSS.
95 alle o.] A (*so* K-D); many o. C;
alle *All* B-MSS.
walkeþ] W&r (reignyn Hm), C;
wandreþ F, A (*so* K-D) (C).
96 þo] R (? = a; For þo F), AC (*so*
K-D); And þei β.
97 he . . . m.] L&r (w.h.m. F), A; þei
were men w.
he (2)] L&r, A; þei WHmCr²³.

101 þis m.] LRM, A; þise mm.
WY&c, C (*cf.* Pr. 25).
104 vpon] AC (*so* K-D); here v. a
(h. is open F); h. on β.
pur] AC (*so* K-D *pp.* 82, 196);
om All B-MSS.
106 shal] a, A (*so* K-D); wol β; can
C.
109 In] G, AC (*so* K-D); And in W;
Al in L&r (& al in F).
lettre] AC (*so* K-D *p.* 81); leef
All B-MSS.
113 & hope] F, AC (*so* K-D); h. *rest*.
114 þat] LMRF, A; And Y; But
W&r (*l. om* Cot); *cf.* C.
115 atw.] assondir A (*so* K-D).

'I shal cessen of my sowyng,' quod Piers, 'and swynke noght so harde,   *leave off; labour*

Ne aboute my bely joye so bisy be na moore;   *pleasure in food*

120 Of preieres and of penaunce my plough shal ben herafter,   *In; consist*

And wepen whan I sholde slepe, though whete breed me faille.   *I lack*

'The prophete his payn eet in penaunce and in sorwe,   *bread*

By that the Sauter seith—so dide othere manye.

That loveth God lelly, his liflode is ful esy: *He who loves; faithfully*

Fuerunt michi lacrime mee panes die ac nocte.

125 'And but if Luc lye, he lereth us by foweles   *teaches; birds*

We sholde noght be to bisy aboute the worldes blisse:

Ne soliciti sitis, he seith in the Gospel

And sheweth us by ensamples us selve to wisse.   *parables; how to conduct*

The foweles in the feld, who fynt hem mete at wynter?   *provides; food*

130 Have thei no gerner to go to, but God fynt hem alle.'   *granary; provides for*

'What!' quod the preest to Perkyn, 'Peter! as me thynketh,

Thow art lettred a litel—who lerned thee on boke?'   *educated; taught to read*

'Abstynence the Abbesse,' quod Piers, 'myn a.b.c. me taughte,

And Conscience cam afterward and kenned me muche moore.'

135 'Were thow a preest, Piers,' quod he, 'thow myghtest preche where thow sholdest

As divinour in divinite, with *Dixit insipiens* to thi teme.'

    expositor; as your theme

'Lewed lorel!' quod Piers, 'litel lokestow on the Bible;   *Ignorant wastrel*

On Salomons sawes selden thow biholdest—   *sayings; seldom; look*

Eice derisores et iurgia cum eis ne crescant &c.'

The preest and Perkyn apposeden either oother—   *disputed with each other*

140 And I thorugh hir wordes awook, and waited aboute,   *looked*

And seigh the sonne in the south sitte that tyme.

Metelees and moneilees on Malverne hulles,   *Without food and money*

Musynge on this metels a my[le] wey ich yede.   *dream; went*

Many tyme this metels hath maked me to studie   *ponder (upon)*

145 Of that I seigh slepynge—if it so be myghte;

And for Piers the Plowman ful pencif in herte,

    (to be) on account of P.; pensive

124a My tears have been my bread day and night (Ps 41: 4).
127 Be not solicitous (for your life, &c) (Mt 6: 25; *also in* Lk 12: 22).
136 The fool hath said [in his heart: There is no God] (Ps 13: 1) (*C*).
138a Cast out the scoffer, and contention shall go with him: and quarrels and
reproaches shall cease (Prov 22: 10).

123 seiþ] vs s. and A (*so* K-D).
134 muche m.] better G, ?A (*so* K-D).
135 pieres] L&r; *om* WCrG.
138a Eice] RFO; *Ecce* WL.
    et . . . cr] *om* R (*C*).
139 app-] LRF, A; opp- W.

140 I . . . aw.] W&r; þ.h.w.y aw. F,
    A?C (*so* K-D); I *om* Y.
143 a myle] AC (*so* K-D); a my R
    (?=a; as y my F); and my WL.
146 And] G, AC (*so* K-D); A. also W&r.
    þe] BC; loue þe A (*so* K-D *p.* 99).

And which a pardon Piers hadde, al the peple to conforte,
　　　　　　　　　　　　　　(to think) what sort of pardon
And how the preest inpugned it with two propre wordes. *impugned; fine (C)*
Ac I have no savour in songewarie, for I se it ofte faille;
　　　　　　　　　　　　　　taste for interpreting dreams
150 Caton and canonistres counseillen us to leve　*canon-lawyers; refrain from*
To sette sadnesse in songewarie—for *sompnia ne cures.*
　　　　　　　　　　　　　　Taking seriously dream-interp.
Ac for the book Bible bereth witnesse　　　　　*However, since*
How Daniel divined the dremes of a kyng　　*interpreted, expounded*
That was Nabugodonosor nempned of clerkes . . . *named N. by scholars (C)*
155 Daniel seide, 'Sire Kyng, thi dremels bitokneth　*dream signifies*
That unkouthe knyghtes shul come thi kyngdom to cleyme;
　　　　　　　　　　　　　strange soldiers; claim
Amonges lower lordes thi lond shal be departed.'　*divided*
And as Daniel divined, in dede it fel after:　*it actually turned out*
The kyng lees his lordshipe, and lower men it hadde.　*lost*
160　And Joseph mette merveillously how the moone and the sonne　*dreamed*
And the ellevene sterres hailsed hym alle.　*stars; did obeisance to*
Thanne Jacob jugged Josephes swevene:　*interpreted; dream*
'*Beau fitz*,' quod his fader, 'for defaute we shullen— *Fair son; lack; famine*
I myself and my sones—seche thee for nede.'　*seek; cf. Gen 37: 9–10.*
165　It bifel as his fader seide, in Pharaoes tyme,
That Joseph was Justice Egipte to loke:　　　*Judge; govern*
It bifel as his fader tolde—hise frendes there hym soughte.　*family*
Al this maketh me on metels to thynke—
And how the preest preved no pardon to Dowel,　*(belonged) to Do Well*
170 And demed that Dowel indulgences passed,　*And (I) judged that D. excelled*
Biennals and triennals and bisshopes lettres,　*Biennial, triennial masses (C)*
And how Dowel at the Day of Dome is digneliche underfongen,
　　　　　　　　　　　　　honourably received
And passeth al the pardon of Seint Petres cherche. *is superior to papal pardons*
Now hath the Pope power pardon to graunte　*the Pope has (C)*
175 The peple, withouten penaunce to passen into [joye];
This is [a leef of] oure bileve, as lettred men us techeth: *part, article; faith*
Quodcumque ligaveris super terram erit ligatum et in celis &c.

151 Take no account of dreams, [for while asleep the human mind sees what it
　hopes and wishes for] (*Distichs of Cato* II, 31).
176*a* [And] whatsoever thou shalt bind upon earth, it shall be bound also in
　heaven . . . (Mt 16: 19) (*C*).

147 al] W&*r*; om FG, C.
153 dremes] L&*r*, ?A (*cf.* C); dreem
　WRHm.
155 dreme*l*s] W&*r*; sweuene A (*so*
　K-D *p.* 89) (*C*).
166 loke] kepe A; saue C (*C*).
168 Al] AC (*so* K-D); And al *All*
　B-MSS.

174 *Thus divided from* 175 F, AC
　(*so* K-D *p.* 169); *div. from* 175 *after*
　peple W&*r* (? = Bx).
175 Ioye] AC (*so* K-D *p.* 80); heuene
　All B-MSS.
176 a leef of] A (*cf.* C; *so* K-D
　p. 89); om *All* B-MSS.

And so I leve leelly (Lord forbede ellis!)   *believe faithfully, loyally*
That pardon and penaunce and preieres doon save
Soules that have synned seven sithes dedly.   *times; mortally*
180 Ac to trust on thise triennals—trewely, me thynketh,
It is noght so siker for the soule, certes, as is Dowel.   *sure, certain*
 Forthi I rede yow renkes that riche ben on this erthe,   *advise; men*
Upon trust of youre tresor triennals to have, *Trusting in your wealth to have*
Be ye never the bolder to breke the ten hestes;   *Commandments*
185 And namely ye maistres, meires and jugges,   *rulers; mayors*
That have the welthe of this world and wise men ben holden, *considered*
To purchace yow pardon and the Popes bulles. *(Do not rely on it) to ...*
At the dredful dome, whan dede shulle arise   *judgment; the dead*
And comen alle bifore Crist acountes to yelde—
190 How thow laddest thi lif here and hise lawes keptest,   *you led*
And how thow didest day by day the doom wole reherce. *judgment; declare*
A pokeful of pardon there, ne provincials lettres,
       Neither a bagful; provincial's
Theigh ye be founde in the fraternite of alle the foure ordres
       'as an associate member' (C)
And have indulgences doublefold—but Dowel yow helpe, *unless D. help you*
195 I sette youre patentes and youre pardon at one pies hele! *value; licences; crust*
 Forthi I counseille alle Cristene to crie God mercy,
And Marie his moder be oure meene bitwene, *(to pray to) M.; intermediary*
That God gyve us grace here, er we go hennes,
Swiche werkes to werche, while we ben here,
200 That after oure deth day, Dowel reherce   *might declare*
At the day of dome, we dide as he highte.   *commanded.*

177 lord] AC (*so* K-D); oure l. FG; lordes WLR.
 forbede] FG, AC (*so* K-D); forbode W&r.
180 on] FG, A (*so* K-D); vp(on) C; to W&r (?=Bx).
181 It] a, AC (*so* K-D); *om* β.
186 and] RFO, AC (*so* K-D); a. for WL.
189 bi-] L&r, AC; to- w; a- G.
193 ye] þow A; we C.
 foure] W&r, A; fyue R (?=a), C.

194 but] aG, AC (*so* K-D); b. if β (*l. om* Cr).
198 h. er] BC; er þat F; er A.
Colophon: Explicit visio willelmi de petro plowman. Et sequitur vita de dowell, Dobett, et Do-beste, secundum wytt & reson C[2], (*so* Sk), AC (*Et s.*] *Eciam incipit* A; *Et ... reson om* C).

Passus VIII

Thus yrobed in russet I romed aboute   *coarse woollen cloth*
Al a somer seson for to seke Dowel,
And frayned ful ofte of folk that I mette   *inquired*
If any wight wiste wher Dowel was at inne,   *dwelling*
5 And what man he myghte be of many man I asked.   *what (sort of)*
   Was nevere wight as I wente that me wisse kouthe   *could direct me*
Where this leode lenged, lasse ne moore—   *man lived; humble or great*
Til it bifel on a Friday two freres I mette,
Maistres of the Menours, men of grete witte.   *Minorites, Friars Minor (C)*
10 I hailsed hem hendely, as I hadde ylerned,   *greeted; courteously*
And preide hem, *pur charite*, er thei passed ferther,   *for charity's sake*
If they knewe any contree or costes [aboute]   *regions*
Where that Dowel dwelleth—'Dooth me to witene;   *Let me know*
For [ye] be men of this moolde that moost wide walken,   *in this world*
15 And knowen contrees and courtes and many kynnes places—
                              kinds of dwellings
Bothe princes paleises and povere mennes cotes,   *cottages*
And Dowel and Do-yvele, wher thei dwelle bothe.'   *Do-ill, evil*
'[Marie!]', quod the Menours, '[amonges us he dwelleth],   *(By) Mary*
And evere hath, as I hope, and evere shal herafter.'
20 '*Contra!*' quod I as a clerc, and comsed to disputen,
                         'I dispute that' (formula)
And seide, 'Soothly, *Sepcies in die cadit iustus.*
Sevene sithes, seith the Book, synneth the rightfulle,   *times; just, righteous*
And whoso synneth,' I seide, '[certes] dooth yvele, as me thynketh,   *surely*
And Dowel and Do-yvele mowe noght dwelle togideres.
25 *Ergo* he nys noght alwey at hoom amonges yow freres: *Therefore*
He is outherwhile elliswhere to wisse the peple.'   *sometimes; guide*
'I shal seye thee, my sone,' seide the frere thanne,

---

21 For a just man shall fall seven times [and shall rise again] . . . (Prov 24: 16).

Rubric Passus viii ᵘˢ *de visione et*
  primus de Dowel (C).
11 *pur*] FO, AC (*so* K-D); par WL;
  for R.
12 aboute] AC (*so* K-D *p.* 80); as þei
  wente β; þer þ.w. α.
14–17 *om* α.
14 ȝe] C (*so* K-D *p.* 152); þei β.
18 Marye] F, A (*so* K-D); Amonges
  vs W&r; sothly C (C).

þe] W&r (?Bx *or* β); þo F; a R.
  amongys . . . dw.] F, A (*so* K-D);
  þat man is dwellynge W&r (= Bx;
  trsp. with q. (þe) m. B).
21 seide s.] LM, C; se. hem s. W&r;
  se. R (? = α; *line om* F).
23 certes] AC (*so* K-D *pp.* 82, 109);
  om All B-MSS (C).
25 at hoom] F, AC (*so* K-D *p.* 169);
  om W&r (= Bx).

'How seven sithes the sadde man synneth on the day.   *virtuous; daily*
By a forbisne,' quod the frere, 'I shal thee faire shewe.

                                                         parable; properly, aptly

30   'Lat brynge a man in a boot amydde a brode watre: *Put; boat; wide*
The wynd and the water and the [waggyng of the boot]   *rocking*
Maketh the man many tyme to falle and to stonde.   *rise again*
For stonde he never so stif, he stumbleth if he meve—

                                          firmly; loses footing; move
Ac yet is he saaf and sound, and so hym bihoveth;   *needs must be*
35 For if he ne arise the rather and raughte to the steere,   *sooner; grasp; helm*
The wynd wolde with the water the boot overthrowe,   *capsize*
And thanne were his lif lost thorugh lachesse of hymselve.

                                      his own fault, negligence
'Right thus it fareth,' quod the frere, 'by folk here on erthe.
The water is likned to the world, that wanyeth and wexeth;

                                         world(ly prosperity)
40 The goodes of this grounde arn lik the grete wawes   *earthly goods; waves*
That as wyndes and wedres walweth aboute;   *storms; toss*
The boot is likned to oure body that brotel is of kynde,   *fragile; nature*
That thorugh the fend and the flessh and the frele worlde

                                    (So) that; changeable (MED 2)
Synneth the sadde man [seven sithes a day].

45   'Ac dedly synne doth he noght, for Dowel hym kepeth,   *mortal; protects*
And that is charite the champion, chief help ayein synne;   *against*
For he strengtheth man to stonde, and steereth mannes soule   *strengthens*
That, though thi body bowe as boot dooth in the watre,

                                    So that; sink, dip, go down
Ay is thi soule saaf but thow thiselve wole   *Always; unless*
50 Folwe thi flessh and the fend after—
Do a deedly synne and drenche so thiselve.   *drown*

28 synneþ . . . day] AC (*so* K-D); s.o.þ.d. tyȝde F; on a d. s. W&r (a] þe LRM).

30 a (3)] LR, AC; þe W&r.

31 waggyng . . . boot] AC (*so* K-D *p.* 82); boot w. *All* B-MSS.

32 tyme] ROC²Cr, AC (*so* K-D); a t. W&r.

38 Ryght] F, A (*so* K-D); And W&r; So C.
   it f.] G, AC (*so* K-D); f. i. F; it falleþ W&r (=Bx).

40 þe] F, AC (*so* K-D *p.* 167); to þe W&r (=Bx).

41 -weth] LM, AC; -keþ W&r (*so* K-D; *but cf.* Ka, *n.*).

43 frele] W&r, C; false F, A (*so* K-D).

44 seuen . . . day] *so* K-D; s.s. on þe d. A; a day s. s. W&r.

45 kepeþ] helpiþ F, A (*so* K-D *p.* 169).

47 man] L&r; men W.

48 þat] a, A (*so* K-D); And β (*om* G). þi] LRF, A; þe W.

49 but] LMR, A; b. if W&r. þou þiseluen wole] M, A (*so* K-D); þi. w. L&r; þow *wole* þiselue WCr.

50 Folwe . . . after] If þou folwe þy fowle fleshȝ & the feend þereafter F; F. þi flesshis wil & þe fend(is) aftir A; *line om* W&r (C).

51 so] *om* g, A. selue] R (? =a), A (*so* K-D *p.* 168n); soule βF.

God wole suffre wel thi sleuthe, if thiself liketh;
For he yaf thee to yeresyyve to yeme wel thiselve— *a New Year's gift; govern*
And that is wit and free will, to every wight a porcion,
intelligence; creature; portion
55 To fleynge foweles, to fisshes and to beestes; *flying, 'birds of the air'*
Ac man hath moost therof, and moost is to blame
But if he werche wel therwith, as Dowel hym techeth.'
 'I have no kynde knowyng,' quod I, 'to conceyve alle thi wordes, *take in*
Ac if I may lyve and loke, I shal go lerne bettre.'
60 'I bikenne thee Crist,' quod he, 'that on the cros deyde.'
commend you to; died
And I seide, 'The same save yow fro myschaunce, *misfortune*
And yyve yow grace on this grounde goode men to worthe!'

And thus I wente widewher, walkyng myn one, *far and wide; on my own*
By a wilde wildernesse, and by a wodes side; *edge of a wood*
65 Blisse of the briddes abide me made, *The joyful sound; birds; stop*
And under a lynde upon a launde lened I a stounde *linden; clearing; time*
To lythe the layes tho lovely foweles made. *listen to; songs; those*
Murthe of hire mouthes made me ther to slepe; *(The) merry sound*
The merveillouseste metels mette me thanne *dream*
70 That ever dremed [dr]ight in [doute], as I wene. *man; perplexity*
 A muche man, as me thoughte, lik to myselve, *tall*
Cam and called me by my kynde name. *right, very own*
 'What art thow?' quod I tho, 'that thow my name knowest?' *then*
 'That thow woost wel,' quod he, 'and no wight bettre.'
75 'Woot I,' [quod I, 'who art thow?'] 'Thought,' seide he thanne.
'I have sued thee this seven yeer; seye thow me no rather?'
followed; saw; earlier
 'Art thow Thought?' quod I, 'thoo thow koudest me wisse *then; inform*
Where that Dowel dwelleth, and do me to knowe.'

52–3 God is quite willing to put up with your back-sliding, if that's the way you
 must have it; For he gave you as a pure gift (the power) to govern yourself
 properly . . .
58–9 I cannot understand by my native wit alone the full import of what you say,
 But if I can [learn by] experience and observation, I shall learn better how to do
 so/learn a better lesson [than you teach].

58 -eyue] L&r, AC; -eyuen W.
 alle þi] R (?=a), C; þy F, A
 (so K-D); a. youre β.
60 q. he] WHmRF, C; om L&r (cf.
 A).
62 good . . . worþe] W&r; good ende to
 make F; in good lif to ende A;
 with g. ende to deye C (C).
65 ab. m. m.] a, AC (so Sk); brouȝte
 me aslepe β (cf. A IX 58b).
70 dremed . . . wene] wyȝght in þis
 world as y wene dremede F.

driȝt] A (so K-D); wiȝt W&r.
doute] A (so K-D); world W&r
 (C).
71 lik] AC (so K-D); and l. W&
 (trsp. with 72 and soph. F).
73 art þow] RF&c, AC (so K-D);
 artow WL&c.
75 quod . . . thow] CA (so K-D); who
 art þou F; what þ. a. W&r.
77 Art þ.] LRF, AC; Artow W.
78 to] AC (so K-D); hym to a; þat
 to β (to om Hm).

'Dowel,' quod he, 'and Dobet and Dobest the thridde   *Do-better; third*
80 Arn thre faire vertues, and ben noght fer to fynde.   *far*
    Whoso is trewe of his tunge and of his two handes,
    And thorugh his labour or thorugh his land his liflode wynneth,
    And is trusty of his tailende, taketh but his owene,   *reckoning*
    And is noght dronkelewe ne dedeynous—Dowel hym folweth.
                                given to drink; arrogant
85 'Dobet dooth right thus, ac he dooth muche moore;
   He is as lowe as a lomb and lovelich of speche,   *humble; pleasing, kind*
    And helpeth alle men after that hem nedeth.   *according to their needs*
    The bagges and the bigirdles, he hath tobroke hem alle
                            purses; destroyed, got rid of
    That the Erl Avarous heeld, and hise heires;
90 And with Mammonaes moneie he hath maad hym frendes,
                            Mammon's (cf. Lk 16: 9)
    And is ronne into Religion, and hath rendred the Bible,
                            the religious life; expounded
    And precheth to the peple Seint Poules wordes—
    Libenter suffertis insipientes cum sitis ipsi sapientes:
    [Ye wise], suffreth the unwise with yow to libbe,   *allow; live*
95 And with glad wille dooth hem good, for so God yow hoteth.   *commands*
   'Dobest is above bothe and bereth a bisshopes cro[c]e,   *crosier*
    Is hoked on that oon ende to halie men fro helle.   *hooked; draw*
    A pik is on that potente, to pulte adown the wikked *spike; point, staff; thrust*
    That waiten any wikkednesse Dowel to tene.   *contrive; injure*
100 And Dowel and Dobet amonges hem ordeyned
    To crowne oon to be kyng to [kepen] hem bothe,   *govern*
    That if Dowel or Dobet dide ayein Dobest,   *(So) that; acted against*
    Thanne shal the kyng come and casten hem in irens,   *irons*
    And but if Dobest bede for hem, thei to be ther for evere.
                            intercede; they (were) to be

91 And has entered the ministry (Sk) / a religious order.
93 [For] you gladly suffer the foolish; whereas yourselves are wise (2 Cor 11: 19).

79 q. h.] F, A (*so* K-D; *cf.* [and
    Dob.] q. h. C); *om* W&r (=Bx).
    thrydde] F, AC (*so* K-D); þr. quod
    he W&r (=Bx).
81 *After this a separate line in* F: &
    meeke in his herte & myȝlde of his
    speche (K-D *p.* 171).
90 And] *a*, AC (*so* K-D); A. þus β.
91 into] LMRF, C; to W&r.
92 to] W&r, C; *om* F, A (*so* K-D
    p. 167).
94 ȝe w.] A (*so* K-D *p.* 89); ȝe
    worldliche w. C; And W&r; he seyþ
    ȝee sholde gladly F.
96 croce] AC; crosse *All* B-MSS (C).
97 on] W&r; at F, A.

98 pulte] L (*cf.* C); pelte R (?=α;
    pytten F); putte W; punge A.
100 ord.] L&r (*l. om* F); han o. w (C).
101 kepen] A (*so* K-D; *cf.* C X 100);
    rulen W&r (?=β); *l. om* F, *run
    together with* 106 R (C).
102 *After this a line* & weryn
    vnbuxum to don his byddyngge &
    bown to do Ille F, A (bown) bold
    A *so* K-D) (C).
103 shal] sholde F, A.
    Irens] W&r; presoun F, A.
    After this a line & pitte hem
    þere in penawnce withoute pite or
    grace F, A.
104 *Line om* α.

105   Thus Dowel and Dobet and Dobest the thridde
    Crowned oon to be kyng to kepen hem alle
    And rule the reme by [rede of hire] wittes,   *kingdom; counsel*
    And ootherwise [ne ellis noght], but as thei thre assented.'
    I thonked Thoght tho that he me [so] taughte.
110 'Ac yet savoreth me noght thi seying, so me Crist helpe!   *appeals to me*
    For more kynde knowynge I coveite to lerne—   *a more direct understanding*
    How Dowel, Dobet and Dobest doon among the peple.'
    'But Wit konne wisse thee.' quod Thoght, 'where tho thre dwelle;
    Ellis [n]oot I noon that kan, that now is alyve.'   *Apart (from him); I know*

115   Thoght and I thus thre daies we yeden   *went (about)*
    Disputyng upon Dowel day after oother—   *each day in succession*
    And er we war were, with Wit gonne we mete.   *aware*
    He was long and lene, lik to noon oother;   *tall; lean*
    Was no pride on his apparaille, ne poverte neither;
120 Sad of his semblaunt and of [a] softe [speche].   *Grave; countenance*
    I dorste meve no matere to maken hym to jangle   *urge; dispute, argue*
    But as I bad Thoght thoo be mene bitwene   *asked; intermediary*
    And pute forth som purpos to preven hise wittes,   *line of argument*
    What was Dowel fro Dobet, and Dobest from hem bothe.
                                   (To distinguish) what ...
125 Thanne Thoght in that tyme seide thise wordes:
    'Wher Dowel and Dobet and Dobest ben in londe   *Where; on earth*
    Here is Wil wolde wite if Wit koude teche;   *Will/Desire*
    And wheither he be man or no man this man fayn wolde aspie,   *discover*
    And werchen as thei thre wolde—this is his entente.'   *act; aim*

108 And not in any other manner else, except insofar as those three should agree.
123–4 And propose some line of discussion with which to put his intellect to the
    test And distinguish between, &c.

106 to . . . alle] & be here conseyl
  wirche F, A (*C*).
107 rede of hire w.] hire þre wittes
  W&r (=Bx); reed of hem alle F,
  A (*C*).
108 opere . . . no.] AC (ne] & Ka);
  noon ooþer wise W&r (in n. BM;
  be n. F).
109 so] AC (*so* K-D); so faire me F;
  þus W&r (=Bx; *om* B).
110 *run together with* 111 *All* B-MSS
  exc. F.
    so . . . helpe] F, AC (Crist] God
  A *so* K-D *p.* 171); *om* W&r.
111 For . . . knowynge] F, AC (F.]
  om A *so* K-D, A *C*).
112 am. þe p.] on þis molde F; o.þ.
  erþe A (*C*).

114 noot] not A-MS V (*so* K-D; *cf.*
  Ka); woot W&r; knowe F (*cf.* C)
  (*C*).
116 vpon] W&r, C; on F, A.
117 war w.] R (?=α; *see* K-D *p.*
  168n), AC; w. war βF.
120 a] AC (*so* K-D); *om All* B-MSS.
  speche] AC (*so* K-D); chere *All*
  B-MSS.
126 Wher] Whether RCr.
  and (1)] FB, AC (*so* K-D); *om*
  W&r (?=Bx).
127 teche] C?A; hym t. G, *some*
  A-MSS (*so* Ka); t. hym W&r
  (=Bx) (*C*).
128 And] *om* F.
  no man] RCB (*so* Sk); noon F;
  man L; womman W&r.
129 þis] L&r; thus WHMCr[1].

Passus IX

'Sire Dowel dwelleth,' quod Wit, 'noght a day hennes   *day('s journey)*
In a castel that Kynde made of foure kynnes thynges. *Nature(=God); kinds of*
Of erthe and eyr is it maad, medled togideres,   *air; mixed*
With wynd and with water wittily enjoyned.   *ingeniously joined together*
5 Kynde hath closed therinne craftily withalle   *skillfully*
A lemman that he loveth lik to hymselve.   *beloved*
Anima she hatte; [to hir hath envye]   *Soul; is called; hostility*
A proud prikere of Fraunce, *Princeps huius mundi,*   *horseman*
And wolde wynne hire awey with wiles and he myghte.   *if*
10 'Ac Kynde knoweth this wel and kepeth hire the bettre,   *guards*
And hath doon hire with Sire Dowel, Duc of thise marches.
      placed; Duke; borderlands
Dobet is hire damyselle, Sire Doweles doughter,   *handmaid*
To serven this lady leelly bothe late and rathe.   *loyally; early*
Dobest is above bothe, a bisshopes peere;   *equal*
15 That he bit moot be do—he [bidd]eth hem alle.
      What he commands; directs (C)
[By his leryng] is lad [that lady *Anima*].   *teaching; guided*
'Ac the Constable of that castel, that kepeth [hem alle],   *looks after*
Is a wis knyght withalle—Sire Inwit he hatte,   *'Conscience' (C); is called*
And hath fyve faire sones by his firste wyve: *wife*
20 Sire Se-wel, and Sey-wel, and Here-wel the hende,   *courteous*
Sire Werch-wel-with-thyn-hand, a wight man of strengthe,   *powerful*
And Sire Godefray Go-wel—grete lordes [alle].
Thise sixe ben set to save this lady *Anima*   *preserve, keep safe*
Til Kynde come or sende to kepen hire hymselve.'
25 'What kynnes thyng is Kynde?' quod I, 'kanstow me telle?'
'Kynde,' quod Wit, 'is creatour of alle kynnes thynges,
Fader and formour of al that evere was maked—   *creator, former*

8 The Prince of this world [= the devil] (Jn 16: 11).

Rubric Passus ix ᵘˢ de visione vt supra
et primus de Dobet

3 and] L&r, AC; a. of WB.

4 wittili] OC², AC (*so* K-D *p.* 154);
witterly W&r.

7 to . . . enuye] AC (*so* K-D *p.* 81);
(ac) en. hir hateþ W&r.

9 and] W&r, C; yf FG, A.

11 hath *do*] LR, AC; dooþ WF.
sire] β, AC; *om* α.
Dewk] FGY, AC; is duc WLR.

15 biddeth] ruleþ *All* B-MSS; boldeþ
conj K-D (*C*).

16 *Order as in* C (*so* K-D *p.* 93); *A.*
þat. l. is l. by h. ler. *All* B-MSS.

17 hem alle] AC (*so* K-D *p.* 80); al
þe wacche *All* B-MSS.

22 gr. l.] β, AC; a g. l. α.
alle] AC (*so* K-D); forsoþe Bx.

23 sixe] F, A (*so* K-D); fyue W&r, C.

24 kepen h. h.] F, AC (*so* K-D);
sauen h. for euere W&r (= Bx; s.]
haue Hm).

27 of . . . maked] of alle þynge on
erthe F (*C*).

91

And that is the grete God that gynnyng hadde nevere,   *beginning*
Lord of lif and of light, of lisse and of peyne.   *delight*
30 Aungeles and alle thyng arn at his wille,
Ac man is hym moost lik of marc and of shape.   *feature*
For thorugh the word that he [warp] woxen forth beestes:
    uttered; were produced
Dixit et facta sunt.
  'A[c] he made man [moost] li[k] to hymself,
And Eve of his ryb bon withouten any mene.
    rib-bone; (human) intermediary
35 For he was synguler hymself and seide *Faciamus*—   *singular, quite alone*
As who seith, "Moore moot herto than my word oone:
My myght moot helpe now with my speche."   *power must*
Right as a lord sholde make lettres, and hym lakked [no] parchemyn,
    Just as if; parchment
Though he [wiste] write never so wel, if he hadde no penne,   *knew how to*
40 The lettre, for al the lordshipe, I leve were nevere ymaked!
    I believe would never be
  'And so it semeth [there he seide, as the Bible telleth,
Faciamus hominem ad imaginem nostram]—
He moste werche with his word and his wit shewe.
And in this manere was man maad thorugh myght of God almyghty,
45 With his word and werkmanshipe and with lif to laste.   *action; lasting life*
And thus God gaf hym a goost, of the godhede of hevene,
    spirit(ual soul); from
And of his grete grace graunted hym blisse—
And that is lif that ay shal laste to al his lynage after.   *descendants*
And that is the castel that Kynde made, *Caro* it hatte,
    '*Flesh*', '*a living human body*'
50 And is as muche to mene as "man with a soule."

32*a* [For] he spoke, and they were made (Ps 148: 5).
35 Let us make (Gen 1: 26 *or* 2: 18) (*C*).
36 As if to say, 'More is needed to (bring) this about than my word alone'.
43 He had to act as well as speak, and manifest (the power of his) mind (in that way).

31 sha*p*e] CrCG (C²), A (*so* K-D); shafte W&*r* (*C*).
32 warp] A (*so* K-D *p.* 89); spak *All* B-MSS.
  After this two spurious ll. and a third & al was maad *þorgh his word as his will wolde* F (*cf.* A) (*C*).
33 Ac he] But he F; Saue [man] *þat* he A; And W&*r* (*C*).
  man] Adam Cr; Ad. (a) m. FHm; *glossed* i. adam LM.
  moost lik] *likkest All* B-MSS; ymage A (*C*).

selue] F, A (*so* K-D); self one W&*r* (= Bx; s. *om* M).
37 now] L&*r*; forþ W.
38 no] *om All* B-MSS (*C*).
39 wiste] *conj* K-D *p.* 201; koude *All* B-MSS.
41–2 þere ... nostram] by hym as þe bible telleþ / There he seide *Dixit* & *facta sunt All* B-MSS (bib.] boke g; he] it CB; god F; seide] s. þis sawe *faciamus ... ymaginem* &c F) (*C*).
46 of (1)] L&*r*; þoruȝ W.

And that he wroghte with werk and with word bothe:
Thorgh myght of the mageste man was ymaked.   *the (divine) majesty*
  'Inwit and alle wittes yclosed ben therinne   *'Mind' (C); senses*
For love of the lady *Anima*, that lif is ynempned.   *named*
55 Over al in mannes body he[o] walketh and wandreth,
Ac in the herte is hir hoom and hir mooste reste.
     'special dwelling place' (C)
Ac Inwit is in the heed, and to the herte he loketh
What *Anima* is leef or looth—he lat hire at his wille;
     pleasing or displeasing to A.; leads
For after the grace of God, the gretteste is Inwit.
60   'Muche wo worth that man that mysruleth his Inwit,   *(will) befall; abuses*
And that ben glotons glubberes—hir God is hir̦e wombe:
     gluttonous gulpers; belly
Quorum deus venter est.
For thei serven Sathan, hir soules shal he have:
That lyven synful lif here, hir soule is lich the devel.   *like*
And alle that lyven good lif are lik to God almyghty:
Qui manet in caritate, in Deo manet &c.
65   'Allas! that drynke shal fordo that God deere boughte,
     destroy; redeemed at such a cost
And dooth God forsaken hem that he shoop to his liknesse:
     makes; created in
Amen dico vobis, nescio vos. Et alibi, Et dimisi eos
secundum desideria eorum.
  'Fooles that fauten Inwit, I fynde that Holy Chirche
     lack; read, find in books
Sholde fynden hem that hem fauteth, and faderlese children,
     provide that which
And widewes that han noght wherwith to wynnen hem hir foode,   *obtain*
70 Madde men and maydenes that helplese were—
Alle thise lakken Inwit, and loore bihoveth.   *teaching*
  'Of this matere I myghte make a long tale   *discourse*
And fynde fele witnesses among the foure doctours,   *many*
And that I lye noght of that I lere thee, Luc bereth witnesse.
     concerning; teach

61a . . . whose god is their belly (Philipp 3: 19).
64a He that abideth in charity abideth in God (I Jn 4: 16).
66a Amen, I say to you, I know you not (Mt 25: 12); And elsewhere, So I let them
  go according to the desires of their heart (Ps 80: 13).
71 All these lack the power to exercise rational control (over their own lives), and
  (so) they require guidance and instruction.

53 ycl.] F (=a; Iclothed R); encl. A;
  cl. β.
55 heo] *so* K-D; she Cr; ʒhe Hm; he
  W&r.
56 Ac] LR, A (but FG); And W.

66 he sh.] β; schope hem a.
68 hem (2)] *om* RCr.
  -teth] RY (*so* Sk); -ted WL.
71 loore] l. hem F (*so* K-D *p.* 173).

75   'Godfader and godmoder that seen hire godchildren
    At myseise and at myschief and mowe hem amende

illness; misfortune, distress

    Shul [pre]ve penaunce in purgatorie, but thei hem helpe.   *experience; unless*
    For moore bilongeth to the litel barn er he the lawe knowe   *is due; child*
    Than nempnynge of a name, and he never the wiser!

(merely) conferring a name

80 Sholde no Cristene creature cryen at the yate   *Would; gate*
    Ne faille payn ne potage, and prelates dide as thei sholden.

lack bread or stew; if

    A Jew wolde noght se a Jew go janglyng for defaute   *crying out; lack*
    For alle the mebles on this moolde, and he amende it myghte.

goods; earth; if

    'Allas that a Cristene creature shal be unkynde til another!   *to*
85 Syn Jewes, that we jugge Judas felawes,   *Since; deem (to be); companions*
    Eyther helpeth oother of that that hym nedeth.   *that which he*
    Whi nel we Cristene of Cristes good [as kynde be]

Why won't; with Christ's goods

    As Jewes, that ben oure loresmen? Shame to us alle!   *teachers*
    The commune for hir unkyndenesse, I drede me, shul abye.

common people; pay

90   'Bisshopes shul be blamed for beggeres sake;
    He is [jugged] wors than Judas that yyveth a japer silver

judged; buffoon (C)

    And biddeth the beggere go, for his broke clothes: *because of; torn*
    Proditor est prelatus cum Iuda qui patrimonium Christi
    minus distribuit; Et alibi, Perniciosus dispensator est
    qui res pauperum Christi inutiliter consumit.
    He dooth noght wel that dooth thus, ne drat noght God almyghty,   *fears*
    Ne loveth noght Salomons sawes, that Sapience taughte:

sayings; holy wisdom

    Inicium sapiencie timor Domini.
95   'That dredeth God, he dooth wel; that dredeth hym for love *He who fears*
    And noght for drede of vengeaunce, dooth therfore the bettre.
    He dooth best that withdraweth hym by daye and by nyghte

refrains constantly (from)

92a A traitor along with Judas is the prelate who falls short in distributing Christ's
    goods; And elsewhere, A ruinous giver is he who uselessly consumes what is due
    to Christ's poor (*acc. to* Sk, *perhaps from* Peter Cantor's *Compendium* (= *Verbum
    Abbreviatum*) chs. 43, 47, *ed. Migne*, P.L. 205, *cols.* 135, 150).
94a The fear of the Lord is the beginning of wisdom (Ecclus 1: 16, Ps 110: 10).

75 fader . . . moder] L&*r*; *pl.* WCr.
77 preve] haue *All* B-MSS (*C*).
86 Ey. ii. o. of] Þat ayther h. o. of
    hem α; Ey. of hem h. o. β.
    hym] LR; hem WF.
87 as . . . be] be as k. *All* B-MSS
    (*C*).

91 jugged . . . than] iu. wiÞ *conj*
    K-D *p.* 196; wors Þan *All* B-MSS (*C*)
94 Ne] L&*r*; He wF.
96 And] A; A. drad hym R (? = α; he
    dredyÞ F) (*C*).
    drede] β; loue α.
    dooÞ Þ.] β; to do α (for t. F).

To spille any speche or any space of tyme: *Wasting (idly)*
Qui offendit in uno, in omnibus est reus.
'[Tyn]ynge of tyme, Truthe woot the sothe,   *Losing*
100 Is moost yhated upon erthe of hem that ben in hevene;   *by*
And siththe to spille speche, that spire is of grace,   *next; shoot, sprout*
And Goddes gleman and a game of hevene.   *minstrel; delight*
Wolde nevere the feithful fader his fithele were untempred,   *fiddle; untuned*
Ne his gleman a gedelyng, a goere to tavernes.   *scoundrel*
105 'To alle trewe tidy men that travaille desiren,   *honest upright; labour*
Oure Lord loveth hem and lent, loude outher stille,   *grants at all times*
Grace to go to hem and ofgon hir liflode: *obtain*
Inquirentes autem Dominum non minuentur omni bono.
'[In this world is Dowel trewe wedded libbynge folk],
For thei mote werche and wynne and the world sustene.   *earn; support*
110 For of hir kynde thei come that Confessours ben nempned,   *stock*
Kynges and knyghtes, kaysers and clerkes,   *emperors; clerics*
Maidenes and martires—out of o man come.   *one*
The wif was maad the w[y]e for to helpe werche,   *man*
And thus was wedlok ywroght with a mene persone— *through; intermediary*
115 First by the fadres wille and the frendes conseille,   *family's advice*
And sithenes by assent of hemself, as thei two myghte acorde;   *agree*
And thus was wedlok ywroght, and God hymself it made;
In erthe the heven is—hymself was the witnesse.   *(it) is; (He) himself*
'Ac fals folk feithlees, theves and lyeres,
120 Wastours and wrecches out of wedlok, I trowe,
Conceyved ben in yvel tyme, as Caym was on Eve.   *Cain (C)*
Of swiche synfulle sherewes the Sauter maketh mynde: *rogues; mention*
Concepit dolorem et peperit iniquitatem.
And alle that come of that Caym come to yvel ende.

98a [And] whosoever [shall keep the whole law, but] offend in one point, is become
   guilty of all (Js 2:10).
100 Is the earthly fault most repugnant to those who are in heaven.
106–8 . . . under all circumstances permits Grace to go to them and (enable them)
   to procure their livelihood: '. . . but they that seek the Lord shall not be deprived
   of any good' [Ps 33:11]. In secular society, Dowel is the life of faithfully married
   people.
122a . . . he [= the sinner] hath conceived sorrow, and brought forth iniquity
   (Ps 7:15).

98a vno] W&r (*cf.* Vulg.); *vno verbo*
   F; *verbo* LR (*C*).
99 Tynynge] *conj* K-D *p.* 195;
   Lesynge *All* B-MSS.
101 spyre] LR; spicerie W.
103 his] L&r; þis W.
108 In . . . folk] Trewe w. l. f. i. þis
   w. is dow. *All* B-MSS (*C*).
111 clerkys] FCotBo (*so* K-D; *cf.* A
   X 137); cherles W&r (*C*).
113 wye] *sugg.* K-D; weyȝ F; weye W&r.

114b–17a *om* a.
118 þe (1)] LY; þere R; here F; and
   in WCr.
   is] L&r; *om* WCr.
   was þe] L&r; bereþ WFCB.
121 yuel] cursed A (*so* K-D) (*C*).
   After this a line in A Aftir þat
   adam & she eten þe appil *printed*
   K-D (*C*).
122a *dolorem* RFHm (*so* Vulg; *so*
   K-D); *in dolore* W&r (*C*).

'For God sente to Seem and seide by an aungel,   *Seth (C)*
125 "Thyn issue in thyn issue, I wol that thei be wedded,
And noght thi kynde with Caymes ycoupled ne yspoused."
   stock; joined in marriage
  'Yet some, ayein the sonde of Oure Saveour of hevene,   *against; bidding*
Caymes kynde and his kynde coupled togideres—
Til God wrathed with hir werkes, and swich a word seide,   *grew angry*
130 "That I makede man, now it me forthynketh: *I am sorry*
Penitet me fecisse hominem."
  'And com to Noe anon and bad hym noght lette: *delay*
"Swithe go shape a ship of shides and of bordes.   *Quickly; planks*
Thyself and thi sones thre and sithen youre wyves,
Busketh yow to that boot and bideth therinne   *Hurry; remain*
135 Til fourty daies be fulfild, that flood have ywasshen
Clene awey the corsed blood that Caym hath ymaked.. *accursed race; produced*
  ' "Beestes that now ben shul banne the tyme   *curse*
That evere that cursed Caym coom on this erthe.   *came*
Alle shul deye for his dedes by dales and hulles,   *hills*
140 And the foweles that fleen forth with othere beestes,   *along with*
Excepte oonliche of ech kynde a couple   *species*
That in thi shyngled ship shul ben ysaved."   *tiled, 'clinker-built'*
  'Here aboughte the barn the belsires giltes,   *paid for; ancestor's sins*
And alle for hir forefadres thei ferden the werse.   *on account of; fared*
145 The Gospel is heragein in o degre, I fynde: *against this; read*
Filius non portabit iniquitatem patris et pater non portabit iniquitatem filii.
Ac I fynde, if the fader be fals and a sherewe,   sc. *by experience; wicked*
That somdel the sone shal have the sires tacches.   *somewhat; (bad) qualities*
Impe on an ellere, and if thyn appul be swete   *Graft; elder-tree (C)*
150 Muchel merveille me thynketh; and moore of a sherewe   *A great wonder*
That bryngeth forth any barn, but if he be the same
And have a savour after the sire—selde sestow oother: *taste like; otherwise*
Numquam colligunt de spinis uvas nec de tribulis ficus.

130*a* [for] it repenteth me that I have made them [*sc.* man] (Gen 6: 7).
145–145*a* The Gospel is against this view in one ?respect/passage, I read: 'the son
  shall not bear the iniquity of the father, and the father shall not bear the iniquity
  of the son' (Ezech 18: 20; 'Gospel': *cf.* Jn 9: 1–3).
152*a* Men never [Do men *Vulg*] gather grapes of thorns, or figs of thistles (?)
  (Mt 7: 16).

124 Seem] W&*r*; seyn F (*cf.* A-MS   139 and] RM, AC (*so* K-D); a. by
  T); Seth *some* A-MSS, C (*C*).   W&*r* (*l.* om F).
127 some] W&*r*; Sem Cr (M).   144 for-] L&*r*; om WCr[1]; sake B.
129 wiþ] OYF, A (*so* K-D); for   145 ag-] LRF; ay- W.
  WLR.   146 *et . . . port.*] *nec pater* a, ?C.
130 now] L&*r*, A; *om* WCB.   *filij*] RFCr, C (*so.*K-D); *f. &c*
134 þere] F, AC (*so* K-D *p.* 169); ye   WL.
  þ. W&*r* (=Bx).   152*a* *coligunt*] F, C (*so* Vulg; *so* K-D);
135 þat] LR, A; þ. þe W; & þe F,   *colligitur* WLR; *colligimus* GY.
  ?C.   *vuas*] L&*r*, C; *vua* w.

'And thus thorugh cursed Caym cam care upon erthe,   *trouble, woe*
And al for thei wroghte wedlokes ayein [the wille of God].
155 Forthi have thei maugre of hir mariages, that marie so hir children.
                                       ill-luck, misfortune
For some, as I se now, sooth for to telle,
For coveitise of catel unkyndely ben wedded.   *wealth; unnaturally*
As careful concepcion cometh of swiche mariages   *sorrowful*
As bifel of the folk that I bifore of tolde.
160 For goode sholde wedde goode, though thei no good hadde;
                           good (men/women); goods
"I am *via et veritas*," seith Crist, "I may avaunce alle."   *advance, prosper*
'It is an uncomly couple, by Crist! as me thynketh— *unbecoming match*
To yeven a yong wenche to an [y]olde feble,   *girl; tired old man (C)*
Or wedden any wodewe for welthe of hir goodes   *widow*
165 That nevere shal barn bere but if it be in armes! *unless it be (by carrying it)*
In jelousie joyelees and janglynge on bedde,   *quarrelling*
Many a peire sithen the pestilence han plight hem togideres. *plague (C); joined*
The fruyt that thei brynge forth arn [manye] foule wordes;
Have thei no children but cheeste and chopp[es] hem bitwene. *fighting; blows*
170 Though thei do hem to Dunmowe, but if the devel helpe *take themselves*
To folwen after the flicche, fecche thei it nevere; *flitch, side (of bacon) (C)*
But thei bothe be forswore, that bacon thei tyne. *Unless; forsworn; lose*
'Forthi I counseille alle Cristene coveite noght be wedded *desire . . . (to)*
For coveitise of catel ne of kynrede riche;   *wealth; kindred*
175 Ac maidenes and maydenes macche yow togideres; *virgins (male and female)*
Wideweres and wodewes, wercheth the same;   *do*
For no londes, but for love, loke ye be wedded,
And thanne gete ye the grace of God, and good ynough to live with.

161 'I am the way, and the truth, [and the life]' (Jn 14: 6).

154 þe . . . God] *rec.* K-D *p.* 194;
  goddes wille *All* B-MSS (*l. om*
  Cr¹).
160 For] L&r (=β), C; Therfore W;
  l. om α.
161 alle] L&r (=β), C; yow a. W;
  l. om α.
163 yolde] *conj* K-D *p.* 205; old *All*
  B/A-MSS (*C*).
165 in] L&r (*om* Y, in two F), A; in
  hir W.
166 *Line om* α, *copied after* 168 β;
  re-arr. K-D *after* AC (*C*).
168 þei] L&r; *om* W.
  manye] AC (*so* K-D); but F; *om*
  W&r.
169 cheeste] β; iangelyng α.

choppes] AC (*so* K-D);
  choppyng LG (?=β); clappyng
  WCr; gaying R; *om* F.
170–2 *om* α; *three spurious lines in*
  their place (see K-D *p.* 224).
170 Thogh] CA (*so* K-D); And þ. β.
172 But] B, AC (*so* K-D); And b.
  W&r (=β).
175 macche] β, A; make R (?=α);
  marye F, C.
176 Wydeweres] R (=α; & w. F),
  A?C (*so* K-D); Wodewes β.
  wydewes] RF (=α) HmCr,
  A?C (*so* K-D); widewers W&r
  (=β).

'And every maner seculer that may noght continue,
layman; persevere (chaste)

180 Wisely go wedde, and ware hym fro synne;   *(let him) guard himself*
For lecherie in likynge is lymeyerd of helle.   *pleasure; lime-rod (C)*
Whiles thow art yong, and thi wepene kene,   *sharp, strong*
Wreke thee with wyvyng, if thow wolt ben excused:
Vent (lit. avenge) yourself

Dum sis vir fortis, ne des tua robora scortis.
Scribitur in portis, meretrix est ianua mortis.
  'Whan ye han wyved, beth war, and wercheth in tyme—
have sex at the right time

185 Noght as Adam and Eve whan Caym was engendred.   *begotten*
For in untyme, trewely, bitwene man and womman   *the wrong time (C)*
Ne sholde no [bedbourde] be: but if thei bothe were clene
intercourse; unless; pure

Of lif and in [love of] soule, and in [lawe also],
That ilke derne dede do no man ne sholde.   *intimate act*
190 Ac if thei leden thus hir lif, it liketh God almyghty,   *pleases*
For he made wedlok first and hymself it seide:
Bonum est ut unusquisque uxorem suam habeat propter fornicacionem.
  'That othergates ben geten, for gedelynges arn holden,
otherwise are conceived

And fals folk, fondlynges, faitours and lieres,   *bastards, rogues*
195 Ungracious to gete good or love of the peple;   *Without grace to*
Wandren and wasten what thei cacche mowe.   *destroy; get hold of*
Ayeins Dowel thei doon yvel and the devel serve,
And after hir deeth day shul dwelle with the same
But God gyve hem grace here himself to amende.   *Unless*

183–3a Find an outlet for your (sexual desires) by marrying, if you wish to avoid guilt: 'While young and strong, give not your strength to whores; "Harlot is Death's Gate" is written on (her) doors' (*tradl.* Leonine vss; *cf.* Prov 7: 27).

192 It is good that for fear of fornication every man have his own wife (I Cor 7: 1–2).

193 Those who are begotten in any other way are considered to be worthless creatures.

179–85 *om* α.
179 seculer] s. man **C** (*so* K-D) (*C*).
180 hym] W&*r*; þe G, **C** (*so* K-D).
182 yong] ʒ. an*d* ʒep **C** (*so* K-D *p.* 208).
187 bedb.] **AC** (*so* K-D); bourde (berde R; liggyn F) *on* bedde *All* B-MSS.
188 Of] R (?=α), **AC** (*so* K-D); Boþe of W&*r* (of] in F).
  in loue of] **C**; loue & A; in F; of W&*r* (?= Bx).

l. also] A (*so* K-D); lele wedlok **C**; parfit charite *All* B-MSS (*C*).
190 Ac] OY (*so* K-D); But GCB; And W&*r*.
191 and] a. þus F (*so* K-D *p.* 173). it] *om* FCr²³ (*so* K-D).
193 þat] **AC** (*so* K-D *p.* 80); And þei þ. *All* B-MSS (þat *om* Cot).
194 And] αB, **C**; And þat ben A; As W&*r* (=β).

```
200   'Dowel, my frend, is to doon as lawe techeth.
      To love thi frend and thi foo—leve me, that is Dobet.
      To yyven and to yemen bothe yonge and olde,                care for
      To helen and to helpen, is Dobest of alle.                 heal
        'And thus Dowel is to drede God, and Dobet to suffre,
205   And so cometh Dobest of bothe, and bryngeth adoun the mody—
                                                     from; the proud one
      And that is wikked wille that many werk shendeth,          harms
      And dryveth awey Dowel thorugh dedliche synnes.'
```

Passus X

```
      Thanne hadde Wit a wif, was hote Dame Studie,          who was called
      That lene was of lere and of liche bothe.             lean; face; body
      She was wonderly wroth that Wit me thus taughte,  extraordinarily angry
      And al starynge Dame Studie sterneliche seide.         glaring; spoke
 5      'Wel artow wis,' quod she to Wit, 'any wisdomes to telle
      To flatereres or to fooles that frenetike ben of wittes!'—  crazed in their wits
      And blamed hym and banned hym and bad hym be stille—    reproached
      'With swiche wise wordes to wissen any sottes!'        counsel; fools
      And seide, 'Noli mittere, man, margery perles  Do not cast pearls (Mt 7: 6)
10    Among hogges that han hawes at wille.           pigs; hawthorn-berries
      Thei doon but dryvele theron—draf were hem levere  hog's-wash; preferable
      Than al the precious perree that in paradis wexeth.      jewels (C)
      I seye it by swiche,' quod she, 'that sheweth by hir werkes   concerning
      That hem were levere lond and lordshipe on erthe,     they would rather
15    Or richesse or rentes and reste at hir wille          income; leisure
      Than alle the sooth sawes that Salamon seide evere.     true sayings
```

201 To love (both) your friend and your foe—believe me, that is Do-better.
11 They do nothing but slobber over them—they would prefer husks / swill.

200–3 *om* α.
200 frend] deere *conj* K-D *pp.* 112,
206.
204 þ. d. is] þ. is d. α.

Rubric Passus x ᵘˢ *de visione et ii* ᵘˢ *de
Dowel.*
2 lere . . . b.] lich & of louȝ chere A
(*so* K-D, *p.* 88).
3 me þus] me so Cr, C; so ?A.
4 seyde] L&r (she s. FG); loked W.

'Wisdom and wit now is noght worth a kerse   *cress*
But if it be carded with coveitise as clotheres kemben hir wolle.

combed; comb; wool
Whoso can contreve deceites and conspire wronges   *contrive (C)*
20 And lede forth a loveday to lette with truthe—   *manage; confound honesty*
That swiche craftes kan to counseil [are] cleped;   *Those who know such arts*
Thei lede lordes with lesynges and bilieth truthe.   *tell lies against*
   'Job the gentile in hise gestes witnesseth   *good; story*
That wikked men, thei welden the welthe of this worlde,   *control*
25 And that thei ben lordes of ech a lond, that out of lawe libbeth:

live lawlessly

*Quare impii vivunt? bene est omnibus qui prevaricantur
et inique agunt?*
   'The Sauter seith the same by swiche that doon ille: *concerning*
Ecce ipsi peccatores habundantes in seculo obtinuerunt divicias.
"Lo!" seith holy lettrure, "whiche lordes beth thise sherewes!"

scripture; what; rogues
Thilke that God moost gyveth, leest good thei deleth,   *Those; distribute*
And moost unkynde to the commune, that moost catel weldeth:

wealth; possess
Que perfecisti destruxerunt; iustus autem &c.
30 'Harlotes for hir harlotrie may have of hir goodes,   *Ribald minstrels*
And japeris and jogelours and jangleris of gestes;   *jesters; tellers; tales*
Ac he that hath Holy Writ ay in his mouthe   *always*
And kan telle of Tobye and of the twelve Apostles   *Tobias*
Or prechen of the penaunce that Pilat wroghte   *suffering; caused*
35 To Jesu the gentile, that Jewes todrowe—   *noble, ?gentle; mutilated*
Litel is he loved that swich a lesson sheweth,
Or daunted or drawe forth—I do it on God hymselve!

flattered; advanced; declare
   'But thoo that feynen hem foolis and with faityng libbeth   *pose as; fraud*
Ayein the lawe of Oure Lord, and lyen on hemselve,   *against; lie about*
40 Spitten and spuen and speke foule wordes,   *spew up*
Drynken and drevelen and do men for to gape,   *slobber; make*
Likne men and lye on hem that leneth hem no yiftes—

Compare (satirically); slander
Thei konne na moore mynstralcie ne musik men to glade

musical entertainment

25a Why then do the wicked live . . .? (Job 21: 7); Why is it well with all them that
   transgress and do wickedly? (Jer 12: 1).
26a Behold these are sinners; and yet abounding in the world they have obtained
   riches (Ps 72: 12).
29a For they have destroyed the things which thou hast made; but what (has) the
   just man (done)? (Ps 10:4).

21 þat; aren] AC (a.] ben A; *so* K-D);   33 þe] L&r, C; *om* WY.
   He þat; is *All* B-MSS (*l. om* F).   34 pilat] LR; P. wikkedly W.
28 moste g.] LYGB; g. m. w; m.   36 loued] l. or lete by A; l. or l.
   good g. OC², ?C; m. greu*eth* RFC.   herfore C (*see* K-D *p.* 79).

Than Munde the Millere of *Multa fecit Deus.*
45 Ne were hir vile harlotrye, have God my trouthe,   *Were it not for*
Sholde nevere kyng ne knyght ne canon of Seint Poules
Yyve hem to hir yeresyyve the value of a grote!   *New Year's gift*
  'Ac murthe and mynstralcie amonges men is nouthe   *entertainment; now*
Lecherie, losengerye and losels tales—   *Debauchery; flattery; wastrels'*
50 Glotonye and grete othes, this [game] they lovyeth.   *amusement*
  'Ac if thei carpen of Crist, thise clerkes and thise lewed,   *talk about*
At mete in hir murthe whan mynstrals beth stille,   *feasts, dinners*
Thanne telleth thei of the Trinite [how two slowe the thridde],   *slew*
And bryngen forth a balled reson, and taken Bernard to witnesse,
        crafty argument (MED *s.v.*)
55 And puten forth a presumpcion to preve the sothe.
        supposition, hypothesis; try
Thus thei dryvele at hir deys the deitee to knowe,   *daïs; the divine nature*
And gnawen God with the gorge whanne hir guttes fullen.
        revile; throat; grow full (C)
  'Ac the carefulle may crie and carpen at the yate,   *distressed; wail, cry out*
Bothe afyngred and afurst, and for chele quake;   *hungry; thirsty; cold*
60 Is non to nyme hym neer his noy to amende,   *approach* (C); *trouble*
But hun[s]en hym as an hound and hoten hym go thennes.   *abuse; order*
Litel loveth he that Lord that lent hym al that blisse,   *grants*
That thus parteth with the povere a parcell whan hym nedeth! *shares; portion*
Ne were mercy in meene men moore than in riche,   *humble*
65 Mendinaunts metelees myghte go to bedde.   *Beggars; without food*
God is muche in the gorge of thise grete maistres,
        throat; '*masters of theology*' (ironic)
Ac amonges meene men his mercy and hise werkes.
And so seith the Sauter—I have seighen it [in *Memento*]:
        '*Remember*' (Ps 131)
Ecce audivimus eam in Effrata; invenimus eam in campis silve.
Clerkes and othere kynnes men carpen of God faste,
70 And have hym muche in hire mouth, ac meene men in herte.   *humble*

44 God has done great things (Ps 39: 6).
67 i.e. but it is among humble people that Christian mercy and Christian acts are
to be found.
68*a* Behold, we have heard of it [*sc.* God's tabernacle] in Ephrata: we have found
it in the fields of the wood (Ps 131: 6) (C).

46 canoun] R (?=a; *soph.* F) Cr, A
  (*so* K-D); Chanon β.
47 value] YGOC² (=Bx), A (*so* K-D);
  worth RF (=a); зifte WL&r.
50 þis g.] þ. glee M; þise arn games
  A (*so* K-D); þ. murþe W&r (C).
53 how . . . þr.] AC (*so* K-D *p.* 81);
  a tale ouþer tweye *All* B-MSS.
55 a pr.] pr. A; *pl.* C.
57 wiþ] BC; in A (*so* K-D) (C).

60 Is] L&r, AC; Is þer WB; þ. ys F.
61 hunsen] A (*so* K-D); hunten wM;
  howlen B; heon on L&r (hoen a).
68 in *Memento*] AC (*so* K-D *p.* 110);
  ofte *All* B-MSS.
69 o. k.] β; o. αG; kete A (*so* K-D);
  knyghtes C (C).
70 here] FG, AC (*so* K-D); þe W&r
  (*om* BM).

'Freres and faitours han founde [up] swiche questions   *thought up*
To plese with proude men syn the pestilence tyme, *With which to please; since*
And prechen at Seint Poules, for pure envye of clerkes,

                               St Paul's Cross; hostility (C)

That folk is noght fermed in the feith, ne free of hire goodes,

                               strengthened; generous

75 Ne sory for hire synnes; so is pride woxen   *grown*
In religion and in al the reme amonges riche and povere

                           religious orders; realm

That preieres have no power thise pestilences to lette.   *prevent, stop*
For God is deef nowadayes and deyneth noght his eres to opene,
That girles for hire giltes he forgrynt hem alle.   *children; sins; destroys*

80 And yet the wrecches of this world is noon ywar by oother,
Ne for drede of the deeth withdrawe noght hir pride, *the Black Death, plague*
Ne beth plentevouse to the povere as pure charite wolde, *bountiful*
But in gaynesse and glotonye forglutten hir good hemselve,

                     extravagance; greedily eat up

And breketh noght to the beggere as the Book techeth: *break (=give) bread*
Frange esurienti panem tuum &c.

85 And the moore he wynneth and welt welthes and richesse *possesses*
And lordeth in ledes and londes, the lasse good he deleth.

                         servants; distributes

'Tobye techeth yow noght so! Taketh hede, ye riche, *The Book of Tobias*
How the book Bible of hym bereth witnesse:
Si tibi sit copia, habundanter tribue; si autem exiguum,
illud impertiri libenter stude.
Whoso hath muche, spende manliche—so meneth Tobye—

                     generously (cf. V 260)

90 And whoso litel weldeth, [loke] hym therafter, *let him behave accordingly*
For we have no lettre of oure lif, how longe it shal dure.

                        written assurance; last

80 No worldly wretch, however, takes warning from (what he sees happening to) another.

83 But greedily consume their property in extravagance (esp. of dress) and luxury.

84*a* Deal thy bread to the hungry (Is 58: 7).

86 And (the more) men and land he is lord of, the less of his goods he gives [*prob.* as alms].

88*a* If thou have much give abundantly: if thou have little, take care even so to bestow willingly a little (Tob 4: 9).

71 vp] AC (*so* K-D *p.* 81); *om All* B-MSS.

77 þis p.] α (*so* K-D; *cf.* C); þe p. (*sg.*) β.

78–9 α, C (*so* K-D); *om* β (*C*).

78 noght . . . op.] h. heres to opne R (?=α); not vs to here F, C (*C*).

79 Þat g.] þe gystys F; And good men C.

    here] oure C (*so* K-D) (*C*).

83 hems.] *om* C (*so* K-D).

86 leedis and l.] B; leedes C (*so* K-D); londes W&r (*C*).

87 techeth y.] α (t. F, C, *so* K-D); tellep y. β.

88*a lib. st.*] α, C (*cf.* Vulg.); *st. lib.* β.

89 meneth] L&r; semeþ B; seiþ WF.

90 loke] rule *All* B-MSS; wisse *conj* K-D *p.* 195 (*C*).

Swiche lessons lordes sholde lovye to here,
And how he myghte moost meynee manliche fynde— *retainers; provide for*
Noght to fare as a fithelere or a frere for to seke festes, *dinner-parties*
95 Homliche at othere mennes houses, and hatien hir owene. *At home; hate, shun*
　'Elenge is the halle, ech day in the wike, *Wretched; week*
Ther the lord ne the lady liketh noght to sitte.
Now hath ech riche a rule—to eten by hymselve *rich person*
In a pryvee parlour for povere mennes sake, *private; so as to avoid*
100 Or in a chambre with a chymenee, and leve the chief halle *fireplace; main*
That was maad for meles, men to eten inne, *meals*
And al to spare to spille that spende shal another. *wholly; avoid wasting*
　'I have yherd heighe men etyng at the table *noble*
Carpen as thei clerkes were of Crist and of hise myghtes, *powers*
105 And leyden fautes upon the fader that formede us alle, *they have laid blame*
And carpen ayein clerkes crabbede wordes: *ill-tempered*
"Why wolde Oure Saveour suffre swich a worm in his blisse,
　　　　　　　　　　　　　　　　　　　　　tolerate; serpent
That bi[w]iled the womman and the [wye] after, *deceived; man*
Thorugh whiche wiles and wordes thei wente to helle,
110 And al hir seed for hir synne the same deeth suffrede?
　'"Here lyeth youre lore," thise lordes gynneth dispute, *teaching*
"Of that ye clerkes us kenneth of Crist by the Gospel:
Filius non portabit iniquitatem patris &c.
Why sholde we that now ben, for the werkes of Adam *exist*
Roten and torende? Reson wolde it nevere! *Rot and be torn apart*
Unusquisque portabit onus suum &c."
115　'Swiche motyves they meve, thise maistres in hir glorie,
　　　　　　　　　　　　　　　　　motions; (vain) glory
And maken men in mysbileve that muse muche on hire wordes.
　　　　　　　　　　　　　　　　　bring men into
Ymaginatif herafterward shal answere to youre purpos. *Imaginative (C)*
　'Austyn to swiche argueres, he telleth hem this teme: *proposition*
Non plus sapere quam oportet.
Wilneth nevere to wite why that God wolde *Desire*

---

93 And how he might hospitably provide (employment) for the largest (possible)
　number of household retainers.
102 And entirely in order to avoid 'letting go to waste' what another [*sc.* his heir]
　shall consume.
111–12 At this point your doctrine goes astray, when it comes to what you learned
　men inform us, on the basis of the Gospel, was the teaching of Christ.
114*a* [For] every one shall bear his own burden (Gal 6: 5).
118*a* . . . not to be more wise than it behoveth to be wise (Rom 12: 3) (C).

102 spille . . . sp.] LR; spende þ.
　spille W.
108 wiled] *conj* K-D *p*. 205 (*see also*
　Ka *p*. 156); giled *All* B-MSS, Ax (C).
　wye] A (*so* K-D); man *All*
　B-MSS (C).

110 deeþ] wo A (C).
112 ʒe] L&r; þe WHmCr¹GCBF.
116 muche] *om* FCr, A.
117 ʒowre] L&r; hir W.
118 he, hem] LRF; *om* W.

120 Suffre Sathan his seed to bigile;   *i.e. Adam's seed*
    Ac bileveth lelly in the loore of Holy Chirche,   *faithfully*
    And preie hym of pardon and penaunce in thi lyve,
    And for his muche mercy to amende yow here.   *great*
    For alle that wilneth to wite the whyes of God almyghty, *'whys', reasons*
125 I wolde his eighe were in his ers and his fynger after
    That evere wilneth to wite why that God wolde
    Suffre Sathan his seed to bigile,
    Or Judas the Jew Jesu bitraye.
    Al was as he wolde—Lord, yworshiped be thow—
130 And al worth as thow wolt whatso we dispute.   *will be; argue about*
    'And tho that useth thise havylons to [a]blende mennes wittes
                               tricks (C); blind
    What is Dowel fro Dobet, now deef mote he worthe, *(As to) what; become*
    Siththe he wilneth to wite whiche thei ben alle.
    But if he lyve in the lif that longeth to Dowel,   *Unless; appertains*
135 I dar ben his bolde borgh that Dobet wole he nevere,   *strong surety*
    Theigh Dobest drawe on hym day after oother.'   *pull him along*
      And whan that Wit was ywar what Dame Studie tolde,
    He bicom so confus he kouthe noght loke,
    And as doumb as a dore nail drough hym aside. *withdrew himself to one side*
140 And for no carpyng I kouthe after, ne knelyng to the grounde,
                         for nothing further I could say
    I myghte gete no greyn of his grete wittes,   *grain, morsel*
    But al laughynge he louted and loked upon Studie   *bowed*
    In signe that I sholde bisechen hire of grace.
    And whan I was war of his wille, to his wif gan I loute, *bow, kneel*
145 And seide, 'Mercy, madame; youre man shal I worthe *Thanks; become*
    As longe as I lyve, bothe late and rathe,   *early*
    For to werche youre wille the while my lif dureth,   *lasts*
    With that ye kenne me kyndely to knowe what is Dowel.' *Provided*
    'For thi mekenesse, man,' quod she, 'and for thi mylde speche,
150 I shal kenne thee to my cosyn that Clergie is hoten. *direct; called*
    He hath wedded a wif withinne thise six monthes,
    Is sib to the sevene arts—Scripture is hir name.   *(Who) is kin to*
    They two, as I hope, after my techyng,

---

122 and (the opportunity to make reparation for sin by) penance ...

124 wh.] GYOM (*so* K-D); weyes W&r.
125 fynger] W&r (*l. om* CB); elbowe F; hele A.
128 þe Jew] α, A (*so* K-D); to þe Iewes β.
129 he w.] α, A (*so* K-D); þow woldest β (wolde L) (C).
130 þow] L&r (euere F); þe W.
131 abl.] bl. *All* B-MSS (C).

132 now] LRF; þat W.
133 alle] α, A (*so* K-D); boþe β.
135 I] F, A (*so* K-D); For I W&r.
139 a d. n.] C²F, A (d. n. & F); deeþ and W&r (= Bx) (C).
    aside] C²F (a.] on F), A (*so* K-D); arere W&r (= Bx) (C).
151 sixe m.] s. wykis F; woukes s. A (*so* K-D).
152 þe] L&r, A; *om* W.
153 techyng] bysekynge C², A.

Shullen wissen thee to Dowel, I dar wel undertake.'
direct; 'confidently affirm'

155 Thanne was I as fayn as fowel of fair morwe,   *pleased; bird; morning*
Gladder than the gleman that gold hath to yifte,   *minstrel; as a gift*
And asked hire the heighe wey where that Clergie dwelte, *direct way to where*
'And tel me som tokene,' quod I, 'for tyme is that I wende.'
'word of introduction' (to Clergie)
    'Aske the heighe wey,' quod she, 'hennes to Suffre-
160 Bothe-wele-and-wo, if that thow wolt lerne;
And ryd forth by richesse, ac rest thow noght therinne,
For if thow couplest thee therwith to Clergie comestow nevere.
associate yourself with it
    'And also the likerouse launde that Lecherie hatte—   *lascivious plain*
Leve hym on thi left half a large myle or moore,   *hand; good*
165 Til thow come to a court, Kepe-wel-thi-tunge-
Fro-lesynges-and-lither-speche-and-likerouse-drynkes.   *lies; evil; delicious*
Thanne shaltow se Sobretee and Sympletee-of-speche, *Soberness; simplicity*
That ech wight be in wille his wit thee to shewe;
And thus shaltow come to Clergie, that kan manye thynges.   *knows*
170   'Seye hym this signe: I sette hym to scole,   •
And that I grete wel his wif, for I wroot hire [the bible],
And sette hire to Sapience and to the Sauter glosed.   *glossed*
Logyk I lerned hire, and [al the Lawe after],
And alle the musons in Musik I made hire to knowe.   *measures (C)*
175   'Plato the poete, I putte hym first to boke;   *to learn (to write)*
Aristotle and othere mo to argue I taughte.
Grammer for girles I garte first write,   *children; had written*
And bette hem with a baleys but if thei wolde lerne.   *beat; birch*
Of alle kynne craftes I contreved tooles—   *invented*
180 Of carpentrie, of kerveres, and compased masons,   *carvers; established*
And lerned hem level and lyne, though I loke dymme.
measuring-line; weak-sighted

168 (So) that (as a result) everyone may be willing to reveal his knowledge (to you).
170 Tell him this (as a) sign (of whom you have come from).
177 I first caused grammar(s) for children to be written.
181 And taught them the use of the builder's level (?T-square) and (plumb) line . . .

154 wel] R (? = a), A (*so* K-D); it W&r (*om* Cr).
155 I] R&r, AC; he WHm.
   as] R (? = α; *om* F) CrGM, A?C; also W&r (? = β).
156 Gl.] AC (*so* K-D *p.* 80); And gl. *All* B-MSS.
163 lik.] longe A (*so* K-D *p.* 88). hatte] β, A; is hote α.
164 hym] LRMHm, A; it W&r.
169 þynges] wyttes ?A (*see* K-D *p.* 86, Ka *p.* 455).

171 þe bible] AC (þe] a C) (*so* K-D); manye bokes *All* B-MSS (m. *om* FM) (C).
172 glosed] BHm, AC (*so* K-D); glose W&r (? = Bx).
173 al . . . after] AC (*so* K-D); þe lawys manye F; m. oþere lawes W&r (C).
174 þe] L&r, AC; *om* W.
175 hym] L&r, AC; *om* W.
177 wr.] L&r, AC; to wr. wM.
180 carp. of] capenteris & FGCr³ (&] of Cr³), A (*so* K-D).

'Ac Theologie hath tened me ten score tymes: *vexed, troubled*
The moore I muse therinne, the myst[lok]er it semeth,   *mistier, obscurer*
And the depper I devyne, the derker me it thynketh.   *deeper; ponder*
185 It is no science, forsothe, for to sotile inne.   *argue subtly*
[If that love nere, that lith therinne, a ful lethi thyng it were];   *empty, vain*
Ac for it let best by love, I love it the bettre,   *sets most value upon*
For there that love is ledere, ne lakked nevere grace.
Loke thow love lelly, if thee liketh Dowel,   *you wish to*
190 For Dobet and Dobest ben of loves k[e]nn[yng].   *discipline*
    'In oother science it seith—I seigh it in Catoun—   *secular philosophy; saw*
Qui simulat verbis, nec corde est fidus amicus,
Tu quoque fac simile; sic ars deluditur arte:
Whoso gloseth as gylours doon, go me to the same,
                                            speaks flatteringly; deceivers; you do
And so shaltow fals folk and feithlees bigile—
This is Catons kennyng to clerkes that he lereth.   *instruction; teaches*
195 Ac Theologie techeth noght so, whoso taketh yeme;   *heed*
He kenneth us the contrarie ayein Catons wordes,   *the opposite of*
For he biddeth us be as bretheren, and bidde for oure enemys,
                                                             bids; pray (C)
And loven hem that lyen on us, and lene hem whan hem nedeth,
                                                             against; give to
And to do good agein yvel—God hymself hoteth: *in return for; commands*
Dum tempus habemus, operemur bonum ad omnes,
maxime autem ad domesticos fidei.
200 'Poul preched the peple, that parfitnesse lovede,   *Paul, (who loved . . .)*
To do good for Goddes love, and gyven men that asked,
And [sovereyn]ly to swiche that suwen oure bileve;   *above all; follow; faith*
And alle that lakketh us or lyeth us, Oure Lord techeth us to lovye,
                                                             disparage; slander

186 If it were not for love, that is contained within it, theology would be a vain
   pursuit.
191a Who simulates in his words, but is no true friend at heart—
     Imitate him yourself—thus art is beguiled by art (Cato, *Distichs* I: 26).
199a [Therefore], whilst we have time, let us work good to all men, but especially
     to those who are of the household of the faith (Gal 6: 10).

183 -loker AC; -ier *All* B-MSS.
186 If . . . were] A ful le*þi þ*yng it were
   if *þ*at loue nere *All* B-MSS, *with*
   varr.; Ne were *þ*e loue *þ*at li*þ*
   *þ*erein a wel lewid *þ*ing it were A
   (*so* K-D) (*C*).
187 let] L&r (is led F), A; lete*þ*
   WM.
188 ne] L&r; *þ*er WG; *om* A (*so*
   K-D).

190 ken.] kynne *All* B-MSS; scole A
   (*so* K-D) (*C*).
191a nec] O&r (*so* Sk), A; *vel* WLR.
199 ag-] FCrG, A (*so* K-D); ay-/a*ʒ*-
   W&r.
202 souereynliche] A (*so* K-D *p.* 89);
   namely *All* B-MSS.
   *þ*at] L&r, A; as WG.
   suwen] *β*, A; schewe*th* αG.
203 vs (2)] L&r (on vs FM); *om* w.

And noght to greven hem that greveth us—God hymself forbad it: *injure*
Michi vindictam et ego retribuam.
205 Forthi loke thow lovye as longe as thow durest,   *live, last*
For is no science under sonne so sovereyn for the soule.   *health-giving*
  'Ac Astronomye is hard thyng, and yvel for to knowe;   *difficult, ?evil*
Geometry and Geomesie is gynful of speche;   *geomancy; treacherous*
Whoso thynketh werche with tho t[hre] thryveth ful late— *meddle; will prosper*
210 For sorcerie is the sovereyn book that to the science bilongeth.
   chief; pertains
  'Yet ar ther fibicches in forceres of fele mennes makynge,
   tricks (C); boxes
Experiments of Alkenamye the peple to deceyve;   *alchemy*
If thow thynke to dowel, deel therwith nevere!
Alle thise sciences I myself sotilede and ordeynede,   *subtly planned*
215 And founded hem formest folk to deceyve.   *first of all*
  'Tel Clergie thise tokenes, and to Scripture after,   *cf. 158*
To counseille thee kyndely to knowe what is Dowel.'

  I seide, 'Graunt mercy, madame,' and mekely hir grette,
And wente wightly my wey withoute moore lettyng—   *quickly; delay*
220 And til I com to Clergie I koude nevere stynte.   *stop*
I grette the goode man as the goode wif me taughte,   *greeted*
And afterwardes the wif, and worshiped hem bothe,   *bowed respectfully to*
And tolde hem the tokenes that me taught were.
Was nevere gome upon this ground, sith God made the worlde,
   man on earth; since
225 Fairer underfongen ne frendloker at ese   *More courteously received*
Than myself, soothly, soone so he wiste   *as soon as*
That I was of Wittes hous and with his wif Dame Studie.
  I seide to hem soothly that sent was I thider
Dowel and Dobet and Dobest to lerne.
230   'It is a commune lyf,' quod Clergie, 'on Holy Chirche to bileve,
   'a way of life common to all'

204a Revenge is mine, and I will repay [them in due time] (Deut 32: 35, *quoted in*
Rom 12: 19).
208 ... full of terms which deceive (those who profess or study them).
218 I said, 'Many thanks, my lady', and humbly took my leave of her.

207 is] α, A (*so* K-D); is an β.
208 is] L&r, A; so w.
209 þre] A (*so* K-D); two W&r (C).
210 þe (2)] LY, ?A; þo WHmRF;
  þat BG (*so* K-D, Ka).
  sci.] L&r, A; *pl.* WF(Hm) (C).
211 forc.; mak.] forellis; wittes A
  (*so* K-D) (C).
216 þise t.] L&r; þis tokene WCr[1].
  to] α (*so* K-D); *om* β.

219 my w.] R (?=α; *l. om* F), AC
  (*so* K-D); awey β.
220 I. k.] W&r; k. y. FHm, A.
221 I] R (?=α), AC (*so* K-D *p.* 168*n*);
  And βF.
  þe g. w.] R (?=α; þe lentel lady
  F), A (*so* K-D); studie β.
222 þe w. and] his w. y F, A (*so* K-D).
224 þe w.] heuene A (*so* K-D) (C).
225 -loker] L&r; -lier WCr.

With alle the articles of the feith that falleth to be knowe: *are proper*
And that is to bileve lelly, bothe lered and lewed,
On the grete God that gynnyng hadde nevere,   *beginning*
And on the soothfast Sone that saved mankynde
235 Fro the dedly deeth and the develes power
Thorugh the help of the Holy Goost, the which goost is of bothe—
                                                      which spirit proceeds from
Thre propre persones, ac noght in plurel nombre,   *individual*
For al is but oon God and ech is God hymselve:
Deus Pater, Deus Filius, Deus Spiritus Sanctus—
God the Fader, God the Sone, God Holy Goost of bothe,
                                                      (proceeding) from
240 Maker of mankynde and of [animal]es bothe.   *too*
      'Austyn the olde herof made bokes,   *St Augustine (C)*
And hymself ordeyned to sadde us in bileve.   *set about; confirm; faith*
Who was his auctour? Alle the foure Evaungelistes;   *authority, source*
And Crist cleped hymself so, the [same] bereth witnesse: *i.e. claimed divinity*
Ego in patre et pater in me est; et qui videt me
videt et patrem meum.
245   'Alle the clerkes under Crist ne koude this assoille,   *unravel, explain*
But thus it bilongeth to bileve to lewed that willen dowel. *uneducated people*
For hadde nevere freke fyn wit the feith to dispute,   *subtle understanding*
Ne man hadde no merite, myghte it ben ypreved:
Fides non habet meritum ubi humana racio prebet experimentum.
      '[Siththen] is Dobet to suffre for thi soules helthe   *Next, after this*
250 Al that the Book bit bi Holi Cherches techyng—   *commands*
And that is, man, bi thy myght, for mercies sake, *according to your strength*
Loke thow werche it in werk that thi word sheweth;   *professes*
Swich as thow semest in sighte be in assay yfounde: *trial*
Appare quod es vel esto quod appares.

244–4a And Christ referred to himself in such terms (*sc.* as divine) . . . 'I am in
   the Father and the Father in me' (Jn 14: 10 *or* 11); '[and] he that seeth me seeth
   the Father also' (Jn 14: 9).
247 No man ever had an intellect so exceilent that he could demonstrate the
   truths of faith by argument (*C*).
248a No merit attaches to believing (only) those things that human reason can
   put to the test of experience (Gregory, *Homilies on the Gospels*, II, 26, in Migne,
   Gr. Op. vol. 2, col. 1197).
253a Seem what you are; be what you seem (Pseudo-Chrysostom, *Homily 45 on
   Matthew, P.G.* 56, 885).

235 þe (2)] L&r; *om* W.
236 goost (2)] *om* F (*so* K-D *p.* 173).
237 propre] R (?=α; *so* Sk, *and see*
   K-D *p.* 168n); *om* βF.
240 animales] beestes *All* B-MSS (*C*).
244 same] Euaungelis*tes* W&r (?=β;
   sg. g); euangelieȝ R (?=α; *sg.* F);
   scripture *conj* K-D *p.* 195 (*C*).

244a L&r; *l. om* w.
   est, videt (1)] *om* a.
246 lewed] men g (*C*).
249 Siththen] Thanne *All* B-MSS; So
   conj K-D *p.* 196 (*C*).
   thi] L&r; þe WHmCr (=w).

And lat no body be by thi beryng bigiled,   *manner, outward; deceived*
255 But be swich in thi soule as thow semest withoute.
  'Thanne is Dobest to be boold to blame the gilty,
Sythenes thow seest thiself as in soule clene;   *Since, inasmuch as*
Ac blame thow nevere body and thow be blameworthy: *if*
Si culpare velis culpabilis esse cavebis;
Dogma tuum sordet cum te tua culpa remordet.
God in the Gospel grymly repreveth   *fiercely rebukes*
260 Alle that lakketh any lif and lakkes han hemselve: *blame; faults*
Quid consideras festucam in oculo fratris tui, trabem in
oculo tuo, &c.
Why mevestow thi mood for a mote in thi brotheres eighe, *do you get angry*
Sithen a beem in thyn owene ablyndeth thiselve?   *beam, plank; blinds*
Eice primo trabem de oculo tuo, &c.
Which letteth thee to loke, lasse outher moore?   *obstructs your vision*
  'I rede ech a blynd bosard do boote to hymselve—
           dim-sighted oaf; heal himself
265 As persons and parissh preestes, that preche sholde and teche *parsons (C)*
Alle maner men to amenden, bi hire myghte.   *according to their power*
This text was told yow to ben war, er ye taughte,
That ye were swiche as ye seyde to salve with othere. *in order to heal others*
For Goddes word wolde noght be lost—for that wercheth evere;
270 If it availled noght the commune, it myghte availle yowselve. *Even though*
  'Ac it semeth now soothly, to [sighte of the worlde],
That Goddes word wercheth no [wi]ght on lered ne on lewed *not at all*
But in swich a manere as Marc meneth in the Gospel: *declares*
Dum cecus ducit cecum, ambo in foveam cadunt.
  'Lewed men may likne yow thus—that the beem lith in youre eighen,
           compare
275 And the festu is fallen, for youre defaute,   *mote; fallen (in the eyes)*

258a If to blame others thou desire / Take care blameworthy not to be. / Thy
  teaching flaunts a foul attire / When thine own vices snap at thee (*Anon*).
260a [And] why seest thou the mote that is in thy brother's eye, and [seest not] the
  beam that is in thy own eye? (Mt 7: 3).
263 *Either* less or more (*advbl.*) or, *more likely*, (the) smaller or (the) greater.
268 That you yourselves were following the ideal you held up to others as the
  means to salvation.
273a [And if] the blind lead the blind, both fall into the pit (Mt 15: 14).

258a esse] L&r (*te es.* F); *esto* WHm. 266 my3te] L&r (*soph.* F); *pl.* WHm.
259 gr.] L&r; greuously wF. 267 war] L&r; ywar W.
260a Quid] L&r; *Qui* WHmCot. 268 seyde] L&r (teche F); seye W.
262a de] L&r (*so* Vulg.); in w. 270 If] Thou3 *conj* K-D *p.* 195.
264 *After this a spurious additional* 271 si3te . . . w.] *rec.* K-D *p.* 194; þe
  line For Abbotes and for Priours   worldes si3te *All* B-MSS.
  and for alle manere prelates *All* 272 no wight] no3t *All* B-MSS (owt
  B-MSS (*see* K-D *p.* 193) (*C*).   F) (*C*).

In alle manere men thorugh mansede preestes.   *cursed, wicked*
The Bible bereth witnesse that alle the [barnes] of Israel   *people*
Bittre aboughte the giltes of two badde preestes,   *Grievously paid for the sins*
Offyn and Fynes—for hir coveitise   *Ophni; Phinees (C)*
280 *Archa Dei* myshapped and Ely brak his nekke.   *The ark of God; Heli*
    ' Forthi, ye correctours, claweth heron, and correcteth first yowselve,
                                 grasp this (moral)
And thanne mowe ye manliche seye, as David made the Sauter:
                                 courageously; wrote (in)
Existimasti inique quod ero tui similis: Arguam te,
et statuam contra faciem tuam.
'And thanne shul burel clerkes ben abasshed to blame yow or to greve,
                                 half-educated; trouble
285 And carpen noght as thei carpe now, and calle yow doumbe houndes—
Canes non valentes latrare—
And drede to wrathe yow in any word, youre werkmanshipe to lette,
                                 actions; impede
And be prester at youre preiere than for a pound of nobles,
                               prompter (to act); request
And al for youre holynesse—have ye this in herte.   *entirely*
    'Amonges rightful religious this rule sholde be holde.
                           worthy members of r. orders
290 Gregorie, the grete clerk and the goode pope,   *scholar*
Of religioun the rule reherseth in his *Morales*   *declares; Moralia (C)*
And seith it in ensample for thei sholde do therafter: *in order that they should*
"Whan fisshes faillen the flood or the fresshe water,   *lack; sea*
Thei deyen for droughte, whan thei drie ligge;   *lie dry*
295 Right so religion ro[i]leth [and] sterveth   *strays about; dies, decays*

280 The ark of God came to grief [i.e. was captured] (I Kg [I Sam] 4, *esp. vss* 11, 18).
281 Therefore you men with authority to correct others, take a firm hold on this (lesson) . . .
283 Thou thoughtest unjustly that I should be like to thee: but I will reprove thee, and set before thy face (Ps 49: 21).
285a [dumb] dogs not able to bark (Is 56: 10).

277 alle] LR; al W.
    barnes] *conj* K-D *p.* 197; folk W&r (*l. om* F).
282 manl.] R (?=α; *cf.* 93; so]ply F; *so* K-D *p.* 148); safly W&r (?=β).
    made] LR; m. in W.
285 and] L&r (to F); ne W.
289–300 α; *lines om* β (C).
290 Gr.] R, AC; Seynt Gr. F.
291 rel. þe r.] R, A; Relygyonys r. he F.
    mor.] R, A; bookis F.
292 it] R, A; *om* F.
    for] R; þat F, A.

293 or] R, A; & F.
294 ligge] RF, ?A (*cf.* C); lenge *some* A-MSS (*so* K-D, Ka).
295 *As two lines div. after* roll. R, *after* troll. F; *re-div.* K-D.
    so] C; so be A; so quod Grigori RF.
    roil-] *so* Sk; it r. A; roll- R; troll- F; rot- C.
    and st.] AC (*so* K-D); St. and stynketh and steleth lordes almesses R (St.] It s. F) (C).

That out of covent and cloistre coveiten to libbe."   *desire*
For if hevene be on this erthe, and ese to any soule,   *peace, tranquillity*
It is in cloistre or in scole, by manye skiles I fynde.

                        arguments, reasons; read, note
For in cloistre cometh no man to chide ne to fighte,
300 But al is buxomnesse there and bokes, to rede and to lerne.

                        obedience, co-operativeness
   'In scole there is scorn but if a clerk wol lerne,   *university*
And gret love and likyng, for ech of hem l[er]eth oother.

                      affection; teaches the other
Ac now is Religion a rydere, a romere by stretes,   *roamer, wanderer about*
A ledere of lovedayes and a lond buggere,   *presider at; land-purchaser*
305 A prikere on a palfrey fro manere to manere,   *rider; manor, estate*
An heep of houndes at his ers as he a lord were;   *pack; behind him*
And but if his knave knele that shal his coppe brynge,   *servant; cup*
He loureth on hym and asketh hym who taughte hym curteisie?   *scowls at*
Litel hadde lordes to doon to yyve lond from hire heires
                        had no business alienating
310 To religious that han no routhe though it reyne on hir auters.

                        care; rain; altars
   'In many places ther thei persons ben, by hemself at ese,   *incumbents*
Of the povere have thei no pite—and that is hir pure charite,   *entire*
Ac thei leten hem as lordes, hir lond lith so brode.

                  consider themselves; extensive
   'Ac ther shal come a kyng and confesse yow religiouses,
                      hear the confessions of
315 And bete yow, as the Bible telleth, for brekynge of youre rule,
And amende monyals, monkes and chanons,   *nuns; (secular) canons*
And puten hem to hir penaunce—*Ad pristinum statum ire,*
                      return to their first state
And barons with erles beten hem, thorugh *Beatus vir*res techyng,
[Biyeten] that hir barnes claymen, and blame yow foule: *Take over; children*
Hii in curribus et hii in equis ipsi obligati sunt &c.

318 Blessed is the man (*opening of* Ps 1; *see vs.* 6).
319a Some [trust] in chariots, and some in horses . . . They are bound [and have
    fallen] &c (Ps 19: 8–9) (C).

297 on þis] R, C; in F.
    any] R (*cf.* C); þe F.
298 many] R, C; fele F.
299 no] F, C (*so* Sk); *om* R.
    chide] R, C; fyȝhte F; carpe
conj K-D *p.* 207 (C).
    fiȝte] R, C; chyȝde F.
302 lereth] loueþ *All* B-MSS; loweþ
    hym to *conj* K-D (C).
303 Romere] rennere F, ?A.
    bi str.] L&r, A; aboute W.
305 man. (1)] places C (C).

308 askeþ] lackeþ Hm (*so* K-D).
    tauȝte] lered *conj* K-D *p.* 187.
311 by h.] be þei purely *conj* K-D
p. 207.
312 pure] α, C (*so* K-D); *om* β.
    charite] W&r, C; charge F;
    chartre *conj* K-D.
313 h. lond l.] L&r, C (h.] ȝoure
    C); hire londes lyen wF.
317 hem] L&r; *om* W.
319 Biy.] Bynymen *conj* K-D *p.* 198;
    That W&r; & F (C).

320 'And thanne freres in hir fraytour shul fynden a keye   *refectory*
   Of Costantyns cofres, in which [the catel is]
   That Gregories godchildren [g]an yvele despende.   *wickedly spent* (*C*)
   'And thanne shal the Abbot of Abyngdoun and al his issue for evere
   Have a knok of a kyng, and incurable the wounde.   *blow from*
325 That this worth sooth, seke ye that ofte overse the Bible: *will be; look at*
   Quomodo cessavit exactor, quievit tributum? Contrivit Dominus
   baculum impiorum, et virgam dominancium cedencium plaga insanabili.
   'Ac er that kyng come Caym shal awake,
   Ac Dowel shal dyngen hym adoun and destruye his myghte.'   *strike; power*
   'Thanne is Dowel and Dobet,' quod I, '*dominus* and knyghthode?'
                                                              lord(ship), the nobility
   'I nel noght scorne,' quod Scripture; 'but if scryveynes lye,   *jeer; scribes*
330 Kynghod ne knyghthod, by noght I kan awayte,   *see, find out*
   Helpeth noght to heveneward oone heeris ende,   *a hair's end (=at all)*
   Ne richesse right noght, ne reautee of lordes.   *royalty, noble blood*
   'Poul preveth it impossible—riche men to have hevene.   (*see* I Tim 6: 9)
   Salamon seith also that silver is worst to lovye:
   Nichil iniquius quam amare pecuniam;
335 And Caton kenneth us to coveiten it naught but as nede techeth:
   Dilige denarium set parce dilige formam.
   And patriarkes and prophetes and poetes bothe
   Writen to wissen us to wilne no richesse,   *Wrote; counsel; desire*
   And preiseden poverte with pacience; the Apostles bereth witnesse
   That thei han eritage in hevene—and by trewe righte,   *i.e. the poor; inheritance*
340 Ther riche men no right may cleyme, but of ruthe and grace.'
                                                       Whereas; except by mercy
   '*Contra*,' quod I, 'by Crist! That kan I repreve,   *refute*
   And preven it by Peter and by Poul bothe:
   That is baptized beth saaf, be he riche or povere.'   *He who; saved*
   'That is *in extremis*,' quod Scripture, 'amonges Sarsens and Jewes—
                                                              pagans
345 They mowen be saved so, and [so] is oure bileve:
   That an uncristene in that caas may cristen an hethen,   *pagan; baptize*
   And for his lele bileve, whan he the lif tyneth,   *true; loses*
   Have the heritage of hevene as any man Cristene.
   'Ac Cristene men withoute moore maye noght come to hevene,

325a How is the oppressor come to nothing, the tribute hath ceased? The Lord
   hath broken the staff of the wicked, the rod of the rulers, [That struck the people
   in wrath] with an incurable wound . . . (*C*).
334a There is not a more wicked thing than to love money (Ecclus 10: 10).
335a Money esteem, but not for its own sake (Cato, *Distichs*, IV, 4).

321 the c. is] is þe c. *All* B-MSS (*C*).
322 gan] han *All* B-MSS; vngodly
   conj K-D p. 197 (*C*).
   -de] -ded *All* B-MSS.
327 Ac] LR; But WF.

345 so (2)] A (*so* K-D p. 89); þat *All*
   B-MSS.
346 an (1)] arn A; *so altered* C² (*so*
   K-D) (*C*).
348 any man] an heiȝ A (*so* K-D) (*C*).

350 For that Crist for Cristene men deide, and confermed the lawe   *because*
    That whoso wolde and wilneth with Crist to arise—
    Si cum Christo surrexistis &c—
    He sholde lovye and lene and the lawe fulfille.   *give*
    That is, love thi Lord God levest aboven alle,   *most dearly*
    And after, alle Cristene creatures in commune, ech man oother; *universally*
355 And thus bilongeth to lovye, that leveth to be saved.   *believes*
    And but we do thus in dede er the day of dome,   *unless; before*
    It shal bisitten us ful soure, the silver that we kepen,   *afflict; bitterly*
    And oure bakkes that mothe-eten be, and seen beggeris go naked,
                           cloaks; whilst (we)
    Or delit in wyn and wildefowel, and wite any in defaute. *know; need*
360 For every Cristene creature sholde be kynde til oother,
    And sithen hethen to helpe in hope of amendement.   *next; conversion*
    'God hoteth heighe and lowe that no man hurte oother,   *commands*
    And seith, "Slee noght that semblable is to ;nyn owene liknesse,
                           what resembles
    But if I sende thee som tokene," and seith "*Non mecaberis*—
365 Is slee noght but suffre, and al[so] for the beste,
    For *Michi vindictam et ego retribuam:*   *see VI 226a*
    "For I shal punysshe in purgatorie or in the put of helle *pit*
    Ech man for hise mysdedes, but mercy it lette." '   *prevent*

      ' This is a long lesson,' quod I, ' and litel am I the wiser!
370 Where Dowel is or Dobet derkliche ye shewen.   *obscurely*
    Manye tales ye tellen that Theologie lerneth,   *speeches; teaches*
    And that I man maad was, and my name yentred
    In the legende of lif longe er I were,   *Book of Life* (Rev 20: 12)
    Or ellis unwriten for som wikkednesse, as Holy Writ witnesseth:
                          not written down
    Nemo ascendit ad celum nisi qui de celo descendit.
375   'And I leve it wel, by Oure Lord, and on no lettrure bettre.
    For Salomon :he Sage that Sapience [made]   *wrote*

351a . . . if you be risen with Christ, [seek the things that are above . . .] (Col 3: 1).
355 The man that trusts to be saved has a duty to love.
364 Thou shalt not kill (Lk 18: 20) *is intended*, lit. Thou shalt not commit adultery (C).
374a [And] no man hath ascended into heaven, but he that descended from heaven (Jn 3: 13).
375 *Possibly* On Our Lord's own authority and not that of any better (written authority) *or else* There is no written text I believe more firmly.

355 to (2)] L&r; *om* W.
356 ar] L&r; at W.
365 also] al *All* B-MSS (al is F); so *conj* K-D *p.* 201 (C).
366 α; *om* β.
367 in (1)] α, A (*so* K-D); hem in β.

374 som] *om* Fg (*cf.* A) (*so* K-D).
375 And] R (?=α; For F), AC; *om* β.
   be] R (?=α; on F), AC (*so* K-D); quod I by WL&c (?=β).
376 made] AC (*so* K-D *p.* 81); tauȝte *All* B-MSS.

	God gaf hym grace of wit and alle goodes after	*the gift of mind, wisdom*
	To rule the reume and riche to make;	*make it rich*
	He demed wel and wisely, as Holy Writ telleth.	*judged*
380	Aristotle and he—who wissed men bettre?	*instructed*
	Maistres that of Goddes mercy techen men and prechen,	
	Of hir wordes thei wissen us for wisest as in hir tyme—	
	And al Holy Chirche holdeth hem bothe [in helle]!	*considers (C)*
	And if I sholde werche by hir werkes to wynne me hevene,	*according to*
385	That for hir werkes and wit now wonyeth in pyne—	*dwell; torment*
	Thanne wroughte I unwisly, whatsoevere ye preche!	
	'Ac of fele witty, in feith, litel ferly I have	*many; wonder*
	Though hir goost be ungracious God for to plese.	*spirit be unpleasing to*
	For many men on this moolde moore setten hir herte	*earth*
390	In good than in God—forthi hem grace failleth	*(material) goods*
	At hir mooste meschief, whan [men] shal lif lete,	*supreme need; abandon*
	As Salamon dide and swiche othere, that shewed grete wittes,	
	Ac hir werkes, as Holy Writ seith, was evere the contrarie.	
	Forthi wise witted men and wel ylettred clerkes	*educated*
395	As thei seyen hemself selde doon therafter:	*seldom practise*
	Super cathedram Moysi &c.	
	'Ac I wene it worth of manye as was in Noes tyme	*will become*
	Tho he shoop that ship of shides and of bordes:	*When; made; planks*
	Was nevere wrighte saved that wroghte theron, ne oother werkman ellis,	
		craftsman
	But briddes and beestes and the blissed Noe	
400	And his wif with hise sones and also hire wyves;	
	Of wrightes that it wroghte was noon of hem ysaved.	
	'God lene it fare noght so bi folk that the feith techeth	*grant*
	Of Holi Chirche, that herberwe is and Goddes hous to save	*shelter*
	And shilden us from shame therinne, as Noes ship dide beestes,	*shield*
405	And men that maden it amydde the flood adreynten.	*Whilst; drowned*
	The *culorum* of this clause curatours is to mene,	*conclusion; priests*
	That ben carpenters Holy Kirk to make for Cristes owene beestes:	
	Homines et iumenta salvabis, Domine, &c.	

382 *Either* Theologians inform us that (as far as) their words (went), A. & S. were the wisest &c *or* Theologians instruct us, drawing upon their words, as those of the wisest &c.

395a [The scribes and the Pharisees have sitten] on the chair of Moses (Mt 23:2).

407a Men and beasts thou wilt preserve, O Lord (Ps 35:7).

377 alle] R (? = α; of all F); a. hise
W&r (= β); and of C.
378 α, CA; *l. om* β.
þe] R; his F, A; alle C.
and] wel & hym F.
383 *b.* in h.] CA (*so* K-D *p.* 81); b.
ydampned *All* B-MSS (d. b. F).
389 men] β, C; man α.
herte] α, C (*so* K-D); *pl.* β.

391 men] þei *All* B-MSS (C).
393 was] L&r; were w.
395a -dram] RCr (*so* Vulg; *l. om* F);
-dra WL.
401 wriȝtes] LRFM, C; wightes w;
l. om g.

114

At domesday the deluvye worth of deth and fir at ones;   *deluge will occur*
Forthi I counseille yow clerkes, of Holy [Kirke] the wrightes,
410 Wercheth ye werkes as ye sen ywrite, lest ye worthe noght therinne!
    'On Good Friday, I fynde, a felon was ysaved   *read* (Lk 23: 39–43)
That hadde lyved al his lif with lesynges and with thefte;   *lies*
And for he beknew on the cros and to Crist shrof hym,
                     acknowledged; confessed
He was sonner ysaved than Seint Johan the Baptist   *sooner*
415 And or Adam or Ysaye or any of the prophetes,   *before; Isaiah*
That hadde yleyen with Lucifer many longe yeres.   *remained in hell*
A robbere was yraunsoned rather than thei alle   *ransomed; sooner*
Withouten penaunce of purgatorie to perpetuel blisse.
    ' Than Marie Maudeleyne wh[o myghte do] werse?   *Magdalen* (C)
420 Or who worse dide than David, that Uries deeth conspired?
                     Uriah's (2 Kg 11)
Or Poul the Apostle that no pite hadde
Cristene kynde to kille to dethe?   *people* (Ac 9)
And now ben thise as sovereyns with seintes in hevene—   *princes*
Tho that wroughte wikkedlokest in world tho thei were;   *most evilly; when*
425 And tho that wisely wordeden and writen manye bokes   *spoke; wrote*
Of wit and of wisedom, with dampned soules wonye.   *dwell*
    ' That Salomon seith I trowe be sooth and certein of us alle:
                     when applied to
Sunt iusti atque sapientes, et opera eorum in manu Dei sunt, &c.
Ther are witty and wel libbynge, ac hire werkes ben yhudde
                  wise; upright; hidden
In the hondes of almyghty God, and he woot the sothe—
430 Wher for love a man worth allowed there and hise lele werkes,
Or ellis for his yvel wille and envye of herte,   *malignity*
And be allowed as he lyved so, for by luthere men knoweth the goode.
                   judged; evil
    'And wherby wiste men which is whit, if alle thyng blak were,

427a There are just men and wise men, and their works are in the hand of God (Eccl 9: 1).
430 Whether in heaven a man will be assessed for his love and just actions ...

408–10 α (*cf.* C XI 251–2); *om* β.
408 delu.] R, C; flood F.
   deth] R, C; water F.
409 Kirke] *so* K-D; cherche RF.
   þe] *om* F.
410 werkes] *om* F.
   n. þer.] ydrenklid F.
412 with (2)] *om* HmF, A.
413 b. on] L&r, AC; beknede to WCr¹.
415 And] W&r, C; *om* F, A.
418 out*yn*] FG, AC (*so* K-D); outen any W&r (?=Bx).

419 who m. d.] AC (*so* K-D); what womman dide *All* B-MSS (C).
420 worse d.] R (?=α; *om* F); d. w. A; w. β.
   þan] W&r; þ. dyde F.
422 Cr.] AC (*so* K-D *p.* 151); Muche cr. β (*l. om* α) (C).
427a *Sunt*] αCr²³, C (*so* Vulg., *so* Sk.); *Siue* β (*sint* B).
430 for l.] L&r; fore WCr.
432 bi] LR; by þe W.
433 is] L&r (*l. om* F); were W.

And who were a good man but if ther were som sherewe?   *villain, evil-doer*
435 Forthi lyve we forth with lithere men—I leve fewe ben goode— *evil; believe*
For *"quant OPORTET vient en place il ny ad que PATI;"*
And he that may al amende, have mercy on us alle!
For sothest word that ever God seide was tho he seide *Nemo bonus.*
                                        No man is good (Lk 18: 19)
    '[And yet have I forgete ferther of fyve wittes techyng
440 That] Clergie of Cristes mouth comended was it [nevere];   *Learning*
For he seide to Seint Peter and to swiche as he lovede,
"Dum steteritis ante reges et presides &c.
Though ye come bifore kynges and clerkes of the lawe, *men learned in the law*
Beth noght abasshed, for I shal be in youre mouthes,
And yyve yow wit at wille [with] konnyng to conclude hem
                        intelligence; knowledge; confute
445 Alle that ayeins yow of Cristendom disputen."   *about*
    'David maketh mencion, he spak amonges kynges,
And myghte no kyng overcomen hym as by konnynge of speche.
                            through skill in
But wit ne wisedom wan nevere the maistrie   *victory, upper hand*
When man was at meschief withoute the moore grace.   *in peril*
450 'The doughtieste doctour and devinour of the Trinitee,   *theologian*
Was Austyn the olde, and heighest of the foure,   *(Who) was; greatest*
Seide thus in a sermon—I seigh it writen ones—   *discourse*
"Ecce ipsi idiote rapiunt celum ubi nos sapientes in inferno mergimur"—
And is to mene to Englissh men, moore ne lesse,
Arn none rather yravysshed fro the righte bileve   *orthodox faith*
455 Than are thise konnynge clerkes that konne manye bokes,   *clever; know*
Ne none sonner saved, ne sadder of bileve   *more constant in*
Than plowmen and pastours and povere commune laborers,   *herdsmen*
Souteres and shepherdes—swiche lewed juttes *unimportant, ignorant people*
Percen with a Paternoster the paleys of hevene   *penetrate*

436 For 'when *must* comes on the scene, there's nought but *to endure*' (*proverbial*).
441*a* When you shall stand before governors and kings [for my sake . . . be not
    thoughtful beforehand what you shall speak . . .] (Mk 13: 9, 11).
449 i.e. without grace rather than man's ability playing the greater role in saving
    him.
452*a* Lo, the unlearned themselves take heaven by force while we wise ones are
    drowned in hell (St Augustine, *Confessions*, Bk 8, ch. 8).

435 lither] L&*r*; oþere w.
439 A (*so* K-D); *om All* B-MSS (*C*).
440 þat c.] AC (*so* K-D); Cl. þo
    All B-MSS (þo *om* OC²).
    neuere] A (*so* K-D); euere C;
    litel WLR.
441*a Dum*] L&*r*, AC; *Cum* w.
444 *Line divided from* 445 *after*
    conclude *All* B-MSS (*C*).

at] LRF; *and* W&*r*.
with] and *All* B-MSS (*C*).
448 ne] L&*r*, C; and wF.
452*a ydiote*] FCr (*so* K-D); *ydioti*
    WLR.
453 englisshe] L&*r*; meene F; *om* W.
457 pouer] RL&*r*, C; oþere Wg.
458 suche] LRCr¹; *and* s. F&*r*; and
    oþere W.

460 And passen purgatorie penauncelees at hir hennes partyng

without punishment; death

Into the blisse of paradis for hir pure bileve,   *sheer faith*
That inparfitly here knewe and ek lyvede.   *?incompletely*
  'Ye, men knowe clerkes that han corsed the tyme   *learned men; cursed*
That evere thei kouthe or knewe moore than *Credo in Deum patrem*   *learnt*
465 And principally hir paternoster—many a persone hath wisshed.
  'I se ensamples myself and so may manye othere,
That servaunts that serven lordes selde fallen in arerage   *debt*
But tho that kepen the lordes catel—clerkes and reves.

(own) property; reeves

Right so lewed men and of litel knowyng,
470 Selden falle thei so foule and so fer in synne   *badly, grievously*
As clerkes of Holy Kirke that kepen Cristes tresor—   *guard, look after*
The which is mannes soule to save, as God seith in the Gospel:
"*Ite vos in vineam meam.*"'

Passus XI

Thanne Scripture scorned me and a skile tolde,   *derided; uttered a statement*
And lakked me in Latyn and light by me sette,   *disparaged*
And seide, '*Multi multa sciunt et seipsos nesciunt.*'
  Tho wepte I for wo and wrathe of hir speche   *resentment at*
5 And in a wynkynge w[o]rth til I [weex] aslepe.   *fell into a drowse; went to*

462 That possessed and existed in only an imperfect state of knowledge here on
    earth.
464 I believe in God the Father (Almighty) (*opening of* Apostles' Creed).
472*a* Go you [also] into my vineyard (Mt 20: 4).
3 Many know many things yet do not know themselves (pseudo-Bernard) (*C*).

461 blisse of] W&*r*; pleyn F; parfit b.
    of *sugg.* K-D *p.* 182.
464 þei] L&*r*; þe W.
    or k.] W&*r* (k. F; knowe Hm);
    on þe boke g (þe *om* Cot) (*C*).
469 men] laborers *conj* K-D *p.* 93 (*C*).
    kn.] β; kunnyng α.
471 kirke] LF; chirche WR.

Rubric *Passus vndecimus.*
2 se.] g, C (*so* K-D); she s. W&*r*.
5 warth] C (*so* K-D); wraþe W&*r*
    (*for* 5 *six spurious lines* F; *see* K-D
    pp. 222–3).
    t. I w.] *so* K-D; t. I was R
    (?=α); wee*x* I W&*r* (=β).

A merveillous metels mette me thanne,   *dream*
For I was ravysshed right there—for Fortune me fette
          carried off; fetched away
And into the lond of longynge and love she me broughte,
And in a mirour that highte Middelerthe she made me to biholde.
         '*the World*', *Middle Earth* (C)
10 Sithen she seide to me, 'Here myghtow se wondres,
And knowe that thow coveitest, and come therto, peraunter.'
         obtain it perchance
Thanne hadde Fortune folwynge hire two faire damyseles:
         young ladies (-in-waiting)
Concupiscencia Carnis men called the elder mayde,
         Lust of the Flesh (I Jn 2: 16)
And Coveitise of Eighes ycalled was that oother.
15 Pride of Parfit Lyvynge pursued hem bothe,
And bad me for my contenaunce acounten Clergie lighte.
         ?for the sake of my looks
Concupiscencia Carnis colled me aboute the nekke   *embraced*
And seide, 'Thow art yong and yeep and hast yeres ynowe *lusty; enough*
For to lyve longe and ladies to lovye;
20 And in this mirour thow might se myrthes ful manye   *delights*
That leden thee wole to likynge al thi lif tyme.'   *pleasure*
The secounde seide the same: 'I shal sewe thi wille;   *follow*
Til thow be a lord and have lond, leten thee I nelle   *abandon*
That I ne shal folwe thi felawship, if Fortune it like.'   *company*
25 'He shal fynde me his frend,' quod Fortune therafter;
'The freke that folwede my wille failled nevere blisse.'   *missed*
Thanne was ther oon that highte Elde, that hevy was of chere,
         Old Age; gloomy of face
'Man,' quod he, 'if I mete with thee, by Marie of hevene
Thow shalt fynde Fortune thee faille at thi mooste nede,   *greatest*
30 And *Concupiscencia Carnis* clene thee forsake.
Bittrely shaltow banne thanne, bothe dayes and nyghtes,   *curse*
Coveitise of Eighe, that evere thow hir knewe;
And Pride of Parfit Lyvynge to muche peril thee brynge.'
         (*You shall see*) *Pride, &c.*
'Ye? Recche thee nevere!' quod Rechelesnesse, stood forth in raggede
clothes,   *Recklessness, (who)*
35 'Folwe forth that Fortune wole—thow has wel fer til Elde. *a long way to go till*
A man may stoupe tyme ynogh whan he shal tyne the crowne.
         lose; i.e. his hair

16 *Apparently* bade me set small store by learning, lest I damage my looks by
excessive study.

6 m. me þ.] β (*cf.* C); me tydde to
dreme α.
7 For] α, C (*so* K-D); That β.
for f.] R (?=α), ?C; and βF.

8 & loue] R (?=α), C (*so* K-D *p.*
155); allone βF.
10 Si.] L&r *exc.* F; Sone W.
20 myrthes] L&r, C; myȝtes WHmCr¹.

‘ "*Homo proponit*," quod a poete, and Plato he highte,   *Man proposes*
"And *Deus disponit*," quod he, "lat God doon his wille."
                 God disposes (*proverbial, cf.* Prov 16: 9)
If Truthe wol witnesse it be wel do, Fortune to folwe,   *well done* (= *Do well*)
40 *Concupiscencia Carnis* ne Coveitise of Eighes
Ne shal noght greve thee graithly, ne bigile thee but thow wolt.’   *quickly*
    ‘Ye, farewel Phippe!’ quod Faunteltee, and forth gan me drawe,
                           Childishness
Til *Concupiscencia Carnis* acorded til alle my werkes.
    ‘Allas, eighe!’ quod Elde and Holynesse bothe,   *Oh!*
45 ‘That wit shal torne to wrecchednesse for wil to have his likyng!’
    Coveitise of Eighes conforted me anoon after
And folwed me fourty wynter and a fifte moore,   *fifth* (*winter*)
That of Dowel ne Dobet no deyntee me thoughte.   *I took no pleasure in*
I hadde no likyng, leve me, [o]f the leste of hem ought to knowe.
                      least (*C*)*; anything*
50 Coveitise of Eighes com ofter in mynde   *into* (*my*) *thoughts*
Than Dowel or Dobet among my dedes alle.
    Coveitise of Eighes conforted me ofte,
And seide, ‘Have no conscience how thow come to goode.
                 scruples; achieve wealth
Go confesse thee to som frere and shewe hym thi synnes.
55 For whiles Fortune is thi frend freres wol thee lovye,
And fe[stn]e thee in hir fraternitee and for thee biseke   *secure*
To hir Priour Provincial a pardon for to have,
And preien for thee pol by pol if thow be *pecuniosus*.’   *head* (*C*)*; rich, moneyed*
Pena pecuniaria non sufficit pro spiritualibus delictis.
By wissynge of this wenche I dide, hir wordes were so swete,
60 Til I foryat youthe and yarn into elde.   *lost; ran*
And thanne was Fortune my foo, for al hir faire biheste,   *promise*(*s*)
And poverte pursued me and putte me lowe.   *brought me down*
And tho fond I the frere afered and flittynge bothe   *changeable*
Ayeins oure firste forward, for I seide I nolde   *agreement*

42 Off with you, (Philip) Sparrow! (*contemptuous dismissal*).
58a [However], pecuniary penance does not suffice for spiritual faults [i.e. sins].
   A maxim of Canon Law; see the ref. in Pearsall, p. 210n.
63–4 ... and not to be relied upon when it came to fulfilling [*with pun on* ‘*arguing*
   against’] Our original agreement [i.e. that he would give me absolution for my
   sins].

41 graythly] α; gretly β (*C*).
   þe (2)] L&r; *om* W.
   but] LRF; b. if WM.
   wol r] L&r (knowe F); w. þi selue
   W (*C*).
43 til a.] R (?=α; with F), ?C; wiþ a.
   B; alle W&r (?=β).
46–9 *om* α.
49 of ... l.] if þe leste LMW (l.] list
   W); *cf.* K-D *pp.* 187, 193n (*C*).

56 festne] C (*so* K-D *p.* 90); fette R
   (?=α; sette F); fecche β.
   in] F, C (*so* K-D); to W&r.
58 -*osus*] -ous R (?=α; -ous holde F)
   B, *many* C-MSS.
58a *Pena*] α, C (*so* K-D); *Set p.* β.
59 dede] R (?=α), C (*so* K-D);
   wrou3te W&r (*incl.* F, *soph.*; *see*
   K-D *p.* 168n).
61 bi.] L&r, C; speche W.

65 Be buried at hire hous but at my parisshe chirche
    (For I herde ones how Conscience it tolde
    That there a man were cristned, by kynde he sholde be buryed).   *rights*
    And for I seide thus to freres, a fool thei me helden,   *considered*
    And loved me the lasse for my lele speche.   *honest*
70   Ac yet I cryde on my confessour that [so konnyng heeld hymself].
    'By my feith, frere!' quod I, 'ye faren lik thise woweris
                                            behave; wooers, suitors
    That wedde none widwes but for to welden hir goodes.   *control*
    Right so, by the roode, roughte ye nevere   *you would care*
    Where my body were buryed, by so ye hadde my silver!   *provided*
75 Ich have muche merveille of yow, and so hath many another,
                                            I greatly wonder at you
    Whi youre covent coveiteth to confesse and to burye
    Rather than to baptize barnes that ben catecumelynges.
                                            children; catechumens (C)
    Baptizynge and buryinge bothe beth ful nedefulle;
    Ac muche moore meritorie me thynketh it is to baptize;   *meritorious*
80 For a baptized man may, as maistres telleth,   *theologians*
    Thorugh contricion come to the heighe hevene—
    Sola contricio delet peccatum—
    Ac a barn withouten bapteme may noght so be saved—.   *baptism*
    Nisi quis renatus fuerit.
    Loke, ye lettred men, wheither I lye or do noght.'
84 And Lewte tho lo[ugh] on me, for I loured after.   *Equity; lowered*
85 'Wherfore lourestow?' quod Lewtee and loked on me harde.
    'If I dorste [amonges men,' quod I], 'this metels avowe!'
                                            dream; declare, make known
    'Yis, by Peter and by Poul!' quod he, ' and take hem bothe to witnesse:
                                            Yes indeed
    Non oderis fratres secrete in corde tuo set publice argue illos.'
    'They wole aleggen also,' quod I, 'and by the Gospel preven:
                                            adduce (texts); prove

81*a* Contrition alone (can) blot out sin (*theological maxim*).
82*a* Unless a man be born again [of water and the Holy Ghost . . .] (Jn 3: 5).
88 Thou shalt not hate thy brothers [secretly] in thy heart; but reprove him [*lit.* them] openly [lest thou incur sin through him] (Levit 19: 17; *cf.* Gal 2: 11, I Tim 5: 20).

67 That] At kirke *conj* K-D *p.* 199.
    After 67 *a spurious line Or* where he were parisshen riȝt þere he sholde be grauen *All* B-MSS (*see* K-D *p.* 193).
70 so . . . hyms.] *trsp.* K-D, *p.* 194; Conyngge hyghte hymselue F; h. hyms. (so) k. W&r.
80 as] LR; as þise w.
81 come] clene c. *conj* K-D, *p.* 198.

81*a* d. pecc.] YG&c (*so* Sk); &c WLMR.
82 a] L&r; *om* WCr.
84 þo] α (*cf.* C); *om* β. lowh] *after* C, *sugg.* K-D *p.* 90; loked W&r (-ed *om* C).
86 q. I] *om* G; *after* dorste W&r (C).
87 ȝis] w; *om* CB; ȝe L&r. take] LMRG; took W&r.

90 *Nolite iudicare quemquam.*'
   'And wherof serveth lawe,' quod Lewtee, 'if no lif undertoke it—   *rebuked*
Falsnesse ne faiterie? For somwhat the Apostle seide   *?for a (good) reason*
Non oderis fratrem.
And in the Sauter also seith David the prophete
95 *Existimasti inique quod ero tui similis &c.*   *See* X 283 *above, note.*
   It is *licitum* for lewed men to [l]egge the sothe   *lawful; affirm*
If hem liketh and lest—ech a lawe it graunteth;   *both Canon and Civil law*
Except persons and preestes and prelates of Holy Chirche:
   It falleth noght for that folk no tales to telle—   *befits; make public comments*
100 Though the tale were trewe—and it touched synne.   *if; concerned* (C)
   'Thyng that al the world woot, wherfore sholdestow spare   *refrain*
To reden it in retorik to arate dedly synne?   *teach in poetry; reprove*
Ac be neveremoore the firste the defaute to blame;
Though thow se yvel, seye it noght first—be sory it nere amended.
105 No thyng that is pryve, publice thow it nevere;   *private; make public*
Neither for love laude it noght, ne lakke it for envye: *praise; hatred*
Parum lauda; vitupera parcius.'

   'He seith sooth,' quod Scripture tho, and skipte an heigh and preched;
                                           rose up hurriedly
Ac the matere that she meved, if lewed men it knewe,   *put forward*
The lasse, as I leve, lovyen thei wolde   *less; believe; love*
110 The bileve o[f Oure] Lord that lettred men techeth.   *faith*
   This was hir teme and hir text—I took ful good hede: *theme; heed, note*
'*Multi* to a mangerie and to the mete were sompned;   *Many; feast; summoned*
And whan the peple was plener comen, the porter unpynned the yate
                                      fully; unlocked; gate
And plukked in *Pauci* pryveliche and leet the remenaunt go rome.'
                                    A few; wander off
                                    distress at
115   Al for tene of hir text trembled myn herte,
And in a weer gan I wexe, and with myself to dispute   *became perplexed*
Wheither I were chose or noght chose; on Holy Chirche I thoughte,
                                    chosen, elect

90 Judge not, [that you may not be judged] (Mt 7:1).
106*a* Praise little; blame less (attrib. to Seneca in Vincent of Beauvais, *Speculum Doctrinale*, 5.69).
112, 114 [For] many [are called, but] few [are chosen] (Mt 22:14).

96 legge] *conj* K-D, *p.* 184; segge   109 þey] F, C (*so* K-D *p.* 169); it þ.
  LRF; sigge W.   W&*r* (= Bx).
100 were] L&*r*; be W.   110 α, C (*so* K-D); *l.* om β.
  touched] L&*r* (t. to F); touche   The b.] R, C; But þei beleven F.
  WHm.   of o.] C (*so* K-D); on þe F;
102 To] W, C; And L&*r*.   þat R.
103 neu.] þou n. FHm (*so* K-D) (C).   men] m. hem F.
  þe (2)] L&*r*; *om* W.   117 chose] α, C; chosen β.
106 laude] LM; preise W; lakke R
  (?=α; *soph.* F); looue G (so K-D)
  (C).

That underfeng me atte font for oon of Goddes chosene.   *received (cf.* I 76)
For Crist cleped us alle, come if we wolde—   *called*
120 Sarsens and scismatikes, and so he dide the Jewes: *Pagans; schismatics*
    O vos omnes sicientes, venite &c;
And bad hem souke for synne sa[l]ve at his breste   *suck; a remedy (C)*
And drynke boote for bale, brouke it whoso myghte.   *cure; evil; enjoy*
    'Thanne may alle Cristene come,' quod I, 'and cleyme there entree
By the blood that he boughte us with and thorugh bapteme after: *redeemed*
    Qui crediderit et baptizatus fuerit &c.
125 For though a Cristen man coveited his Cristendom to reneye, *desired; abjure*
    Rightfully to reneye no reson it wolde.
    'For may no cherl chartre make, ne his c[h]atel selle   *villein; property*
Withouten leve of his lord—no lawe wol it graunte.   *leave; allow*
Ac he may renne in arerage and rome fro home,   *run into debt; wander*
130 And as a reneyed caytif recchelesly aboute.   *wretch forsworn*
Ac Reson shal rekene with hym and rebuken hym at the laste,
                                            make reckoning
And Conscience acounte with hym and casten hym in arerage,
                                          settle accounts
And putten hym after in prison in purgatorie to brenne,   *burn*
For his arerages rewarden hym there right to the day of dome,
                                   debts (i.e. sins, debita)
135 But if Contricion wol come and crye by his lyve   *life*
Mercy for hise mysdedes with mouthe or with herte.'
    'That is sooth,' seide Scripture; 'may no synne lette   *prevent*
Mercy al to amende, and mekenesse hir folwe;   *from amending all; if*
For thei beth, as oure bokes telleth, above Goddes werkes: *are*
    Misericordia eius super omnia opera eius.'
140   'Ye, baw for bokes!' quod oon was broken out of helle.
                                    bah!; one who was
'I Troianus, a trewe knyght, take witnesse at a pope   *Trajan; righteous, just*
How I was ded and dampned to dwellen in pyne   *torment*

120a All you that thirst, come to the waters (Is 55: 1).
124a He that believeth and is baptized shall be saved ... (Mk 16: 16).
125-6 For even if a Christian *wanted* to renounce his Christianity, Reason would
    not allow that he could legitimately do so.
139a His tender mercies are over all his works (Ps 144: 9).

118 fenge] OB (*cf.* I 76); fonge LR;
    fonged WCr.
121 salve] saue α, ?C; safly β (*C*).
127 chatel] C (*so* K-D *p.* 93); catel
    All B-, *many* C-MSS.
129 fro] αG, C (*so* K-D *p.* 162); so
    fro β.
130 a] β (*cf.* C); he α.
    reney.] β; renne(th) α.
    ab.] R&r; gon a. L; or romeþ a.
    F; rennen a. W.
131 Ac] LR, C; And W.

131b–2a] α, C (*so* Sk); *om* β.
133 in (1)] RY, C (*so* K-D); in a WL.
134 riȝte] R (?=α), C (*so* K-D *p.*
    168n); *om* βF.
136 or] L&r; and WHmF, ?C.
141 I] Cr, C (*so* K-D); Hiȝte W&r
    (That h. B); he was F (*C*).
    a (1)] Cr, C (*so* K-D); þe F;
    hadde ben a WLR.
    take] Cr¹, C (*so* K-D); toke
    Cr²³LR; took W.
142 I] Cr, C (*so* K-D); he W&r.

For an uncristene creature; clerkes wite the sothe—   *As; unchristened*
That al the clergie under Crist ne myghte me cracche fro helle   *snatch*
145 But oonliche love and leautee and my laweful domes.
                               justice; upright judgments
  'Gregorie wiste this wel, and wilned to my soule   *desired for*
Savacion for soothnesse that he seigh in my werkes.   *Salvation; truth; saw*
And after that he wepte and wilned me were graunted grace,   *according as*
Withouten any bede biddyng his boone was underfongen,   *praying*
150 And I saved, as ye may see, withouten syngynge of masses,
By love and by lernyng of my lyvynge in truthe,
Broughte me fro bitter peyne ther no biddyng myghte.
                        (Which) brought; praying
  'Lo! ye lordes, what leautee dide by an Emperour of Rome   *justice; for*
That was an uncristene creature, as clerkes fyndeth in bokes.
155 Nought thorugh preiere of a pope but for his pure truthe
                         simply for his upright life
Was that Sarsen saved, as Seint Gregorie bereth witnesse.   *pagan*
Wel oughte ye lordes that lawes kepe this lesson to have in mynde,
And on Troianus truthe to thenke, and do truthe to the peple.
                    administer (true) justice to
  'This matere is merk for many of yow—ac, men of Holy Chirche, *obscure*
160 The *Legend*[a] *Sanctorum* yow lereth more largere than I yow telle.
                            teaches; amply
Ac thus leel love and lyvyng in truthe   *faithful*
Pulte out of pyne a paynym of Rome.   *Took out by force; pagan*
Yblissed be truthe that so brak helle yates   *burst (open); hell's gates*
And saved the Sarsyn from Sathanas and his power,
165 Ther no clergie ne kouthe, ne konnyng of lawes!   *learning; knowledge*
Love and leautee is a leel science,   *trustworthy, true*
For that is the book blissed of blisse and of joye:
God wroughte it and wroot it with his owene fynger
And took it to Moises upon the mount, alle men to lere.   *gave; teach*
170   'Lawe withouten love,' quod Troianus, 'ley ther a bene—
                      bean (i.e. is worthless)
Or any science under sonne, the sevene arts and alle!

149 Without any (long process of) saying prayers, his request for favour was
accepted.
151–2 *Possibly* Through (his) love and through (his) learning of my just life,
(which latter it was that) brought . . .

148–9 *Divided before* Grace *All*   162 Pulte] Pytten F.
    B-MSS (*C*).   163 so b.] b. so F.
150 may] L&r, C; *om* w.   164 Sat . . . h.] sathenases F.
159–69 α (*cf.* C XII 93–7); *om* β.   167 *Om* F.
159 of ȝow ac] R; save F.   168 owne] F; on R.
160 *Legenda*] *so* K-D; legende RF.   169 vpon] on F.
    ȝow l.] lerneþ ȝ. F.   to] it to F.
161 Ac] & F.
    lyuyng] leel l. F.

—But thei ben lerned for Oure Lordes love, lost is al the tyme,
For no cause to cacche silver therby, ne to be called a maister,　　*procure*
But al for love of Oure Lord and the bet to love the peple.　　*better*
175 'For Seint Johan seide it, and sothe arn hise wordes:
Qui non diligit manet in morte.
Whoso loveth noght, leve me, he lyveth in deeth deyinge; *'is spiritually dead'*
And that alle manere men, enemyes and frendes,　　*(he says) that . . .*
Love hir eyther oother, and lene hem as hemselve.　*(Should) love; give (to)*
Whoso leneth noght, he loveth noght, Oure Lord woot the sothe
180 And comaundeth ech creature to conformen hym to lovye　　*be willing*
His neighebour as hymselve and hise enemyes after.
For hem that haten us is oure merite to lovye,　　　　*(it) is*
And sovereynly povere peple to plese—hir preieres maye us helpe. *above all*
For oure joy and oure [ju]ele, Jesu Crist of hevene,　*jewel, treasure*
185 In a povere mannes apparaille pursueth us evere,　　*guise, clothing*
And loketh on us in hir liknesse and that with lovely chere,　*expression*
To knowen us by oure kynde herte and castynge of oure eighen,
　　　　　　　　　　　　　　　　　　　'where we choose to look'
Wheither we love the lordes here bifore the Lord of blisse;
And exciteth us by the Evangelie that whan we maken festes,
　　　　　　　　　　　　　　　　　　　urges; Gospel; feasts
190 We sholde noght clepe oure kyn therto, ne none kynnes riche:
　　　　　　　　　　　　　　　　invite; no kind of rich men
Cum facitis convivia, nolite invitare amicos.
"Ac calleth the carefulle therto, the croked and the povere;
　　　　　　　　　　　　　　　　distressed; crippled
For youre frendes wol feden yow, and founde yow to quyte　*try to repay*
Youre festynge and youre faire yifte—ech frend quyteth so oother.
　　　　　　　　　　　　　　　　　　　repays thus
Ac for the povere I shal paie, and pure wel quyte hir travaille
　　　　　　　　　　　　　　　　　　　thoroughly; pains
195 That yyveth hem mete or moneie and loveth hem for my sake."

173 *i.e.* likewise if the motive is to obtain money or titles of respect.
175a He that loveth not abideth in death (I Jn 3: 14).
190a When thou makest a dinner [or a supper], call not thy friends [nor thy
brethren nor thy kinsmen nor thy neighbours who are rich] (Lk 14: 12; *see also*
vss 13–14).

179 Who] For ho a.
　　oure l.] R (?=a; *cf.* K-D *p.*
　168*n*); god βF.
180 And] L&r; he F; Crist W.
　　eche] L&r; ech a WHm.
181 His . . . hyms.] & his . . . hyms.
　　F; And souereynelyche pore
　　poeple L&r (þe p. p. WCr)
　　(?=Bx); *rec.* K-D, *p.* 188, *q.v.* (*C*).
　　hise] F; hir W&r.

183 And sov.] And *All* B-MSS; A.
　　nameliche C.
184 For] L&r; And w.
　　Iuel] *conj* K-D *p.* 184; euel R;
　　helthe FCr; heele W&r.
　　Ihes*u*] β; is i. α.
185 -eth] L&r; -ed wG.
195 and] L&r; or WF.

'Almighty God myghte ha[ve] maad riche alle men, if he wolde,
Ac for the beste ben som riche and some beggeres and povere.

(it is) for the b. that

For alle are we Cristes creatures, and of his cofres riche,   *from*
And bretheren as of oo blood, as wel beggeres as erles.   *one; earls*

200 For at Calvarie of Cristes blood Cristendom gan sprynge,

from; Christianity

And blody bretheren we bicome there, of o body ywonne, *delivered, redeemed*
As *quasi modo geniti* gentil men echone—   *noble*
No beggere ne boye amonges us but if it synne made.   *knave; caused*
Qui facit peccatum servus est peccati.
In the olde lawe, as the lettre telleth, "mennes sones" men called us,

205 Of Adames issue and Eve, ay til God-Man deide;   *God-(made)-man*
And after his resurexcion *Redemptor* was his name,   *Redeemer*
And we hise bretheren thorugh hym ybought, bothe riche and povere.

redeemed

Forthi love we as leve children shal, and ech man laughe of oother,

affectionate; rejoice at

And of that ech man may forbere, amende there it nedeth,

from, with; spare; make good

210 And every man helpe oother—for hennes shul we alle:

must we (go)—i.e. die

Alter alterius onera portate.
And be we noght unkynde of oure catel, ne of oure konnyng neither,

goods; knowledge

For woot no man how neigh it is to ben ynome fro bothe.   *taken (away)*
Forthi lakke no lif oother, though he moore Latyn knowe,

criticize no other person

Ne undernyme noght foule, for is noon withoute defaute.   *rebuke; bitterly*

215 For whatevere clerkes carpe of Cristendom or ellis,
Crist to a commune womman seide in commune at a feste

prostitute; openly (C)

201–2 And we became brethren-by-blood (*or* brethren *through* Christ's blood)
there, delivered from / redeemed by one body, 'As newborn babes' [I Pet 2: 2].
203a Whosoever committeth sin is the servant of sin (Jn 8: 34).
208 And so let us love each other as loving children do and each man take joy in
his fellows.
210a Bear ye one another's burdens; [and so you shall fulfil the law of Christ]
(Gal 6: 2).

196 α; *l. om* β.
   Almighty . . . r.] Al. g. hath m.
   r. R; God myghte ryche a maad
   all F (*C*).
197 Ac] R (?=α; But F) (*so* K-D);
   om β.
200 at] α, C (*so* K-D); on β (*om* Cot).
202 g.] C, *so* K-D; and g. *All* B-MSS.
203a pecc.] RFCr, C; *p. &c* WL.
204 *As two lines div. before* mennes

All B-MSS; *rec. as in* C *by* K-D *p.* 93.
   þe(2)] α, C (*so* K-D); holy β.
   -ed] L&r, C; -en W.
   vs] C (*so* K-D); vs echone *All*
   B-MSS (vs *om* CotF).
208 childern] α, C (*so* K-D);
   breþeren β.
   shal] L&r; *om* WCrF, ?C.
216 comm. (2)] come G (*so* K-D
   p. 148); conen Y.

That *Fides sua* sholde saven hire and salven hire of synnes.

Her faith (Lk 7: 50); *cure (C)*

'Thanne is bileve a lele help, above logyk or lawe.   *faith; trusty*

Of logyk ne of lawe in *Legenda Sanctorum*

220 Is litel alowaunce maad, but if bileve hem helpe;   *approval*

For it is overlonge er logyk any lesson assoille,   *explain*

And lawe is looth to lovye but if he lacche silver.   *(may) obtain s. (therby)*

Bothe logyk and lawe, that loveth noght to lye,   *(you) who l.*

I conseille alle Cristene, clyve noght theron to soore,   *stick; closely, tightly*

225 For some wordes I fynde writen, were of Feithes techyng,

That saved synful men, as Seint Johan bereth witnesse:

Eadem mensura qua mensi fueritis remecietur vobis.

Forthi lerne we the lawe of love as Oure Lord taŭghte;

And as Seint Gregorie seide, for mannes soule helthe,

Melius est scrutari scelera nostra quam naturas rerum.

230 'Why I meve this matere is moost for the povere;   *introduce; subject*

For in hir liknesse Oure Lord ofte hath ben yknowe.   *encountered*

Witnesse in the Pask wyke whan he yede to Emaus—

Easter week; went; Emmaus

Cleophas ne knew hym noght, that he Crist were,

For his povere apparaille and pilgrymes wedes,   *dress*

235 Til he blessede and brak the breed that thei eten.   *(Lk 24)*

So bi hise werkes thei wisten that he was Jesus,   *actions; knew*

Ac by clothyng thei knewe hym noght, ne by carpynge of tonge.

the way he spoke

And al was ensample, for sooth, to us synfulle here,   *an example*

That we sholde be lowe and loveliche of speche,   *humble; gracious*

240 And apparaille us noght over proudly—for pilgrymes are we alle.

And in the apparaille of a povere man and pilgrymes liknesse

Many tyme God hath ben met among nedy peple,

Ther nevere segge hym seigh in secte of the riche.

Whereas; man; class/clothes

'Seint Johan and othere seintes were seyen in poore clothyng,

i.e. the Baptist; seen

245 And as povere pilgrymes preyed mennes goodes.   *asked for alms*

Jesu Crist on a Jewes doghter lighte: gentil womman though she were,

descended, was born of

Was a pure povere maide and to a povere man ywedded.

(She) was a truly poor maid

'Martha on Marie Maudelayne an huge pleynt she made,   *great complaint*

226a With what [*in qua* Vulg] measure you mete, it shall be measured to you again
(Mt 7: 2).
229 It is better to examine our sins than the natures of things (*C*).

219 ne] L&*r*; or w.

225 were] LR; *þat* w. WG.

231 ofte] lome **C** (*so* K-D *p.* 53).

238 was] RFBM, **C** (*so* K-D); w. in
W&*r*.

for s.] R (?=a); *om* βF;

sothliche **C** (*so* K-D *p.* 157)

245 mennes] men R; men of here F.

248 she] L&*r*; *om* WCot (*so* K-D
p. 155).

And to Oure Saveour self seide thise wordes:
250 *Domine, non est tibi cure quod soror mea reliquit me solam ministrare?*
   And hastily God answerde, and eitheres wille ful [wel lo]wed,   *approved*
   Bothe Marthaes and Maries, as Mathew bereth witnesse;
   Ac poverte God putte bifore, and preised it the bettre:
   Maria optimam partem elegit, que non auferetur ab ea.
   'And alle the wise that evere were, by aught I kan aspye,
                                      as far as I can discover
255 Preisen poverte for best lif, if Pacience it folwe,   *accompany*
   And bothe bettre and blesseder by many fold than Richesse.   *time(s); Wealth*
   Although it be sour to suffre, ther cometh swete after;
   As on a walnote—withoute is a bitter barke,   *on the outside; husk, shell*
   And after that bitter bark, be the shelle aweye,   *removed*
260 Is a kernel of confort kynde to restore.   *strength; nourish, refresh*
   So is after poverte or penaunce paciently ytake,
   Maketh a man to have mynde in God and a gret wille
                             (Which) makes; thought(s) of
   To wepe and to wel bidde, wherof wexeth mercy,   *pray; grows; arises*
   Of which Crist is a kernell to conforte the soule.
265 And wel sikerer he slepeth, the segge that is povere,   *much more securely*
   And lasse he dredeth deeth and in derke to ben yrobbed   *(the) dark*
   Than he that is right riche—Reson bereth witnesse: *it stands to reason*
   Pauper ego ludo dum tu dives meditaris.
   'Although Salomon seide, as folk seeth in the Bible,
   Divicias nec paupertates &c,
270 Wiser than Salomon was bereth witnesse and taughte   *(One) wiser*
   That parfit poverte was no possession to have,
   And lif moost likynge to God, as Luc bereth witnesse:
                              (a way of) life; pleasing
   Si vis perfectus esse, vade et vende &c—

---

250 Lord, hast thou no care that my sister hath left me alone to serve? (Lk 10: 40).
253a Mary hath chosen the best part which shall not be taken away from her
   (Lk 10: 42).
260 *i.e.* a kernel with the power of building up one's natural strength.
267a Poor, I relax, while you, being wealthy, brood (Alexander of Ville-Dieu,
   Doctrinale, ed. D. Reichling (Berlin, 1893), *vs.* 1091).
269 Give me neither beggary [*mendicitatem* Vulg] nor riches (Prov 30: 8).
272 If thou wilt be perfect, go sell [what thou hast and give to the poor] (Mt 19:
   21).

251 ful . . . l.] riht wel alowede C: þere] L&r, C; þerafter w
   fulfylde F; folwed W&r (C).   (þ.] yet Cr).
253a que . . . ea] *om* R.   after] L&r, C; *om* w.
     auf. ab ea] YGF, C (*so* Sk); &c   261 is] *om* CB, C (*so* K-D *p.* 157).
   WL.   262 Mak.] α, C (*so* K-D); For it m.
255 -sen] L&r; -seden WM, ?C.   β.
   folwe] L&r; folwed W; wolde R;   265 segge] α, C (*so* Sk); man β.
   welde F (*cf.* 251 *above*).   272a &c] LR; *om* W.
257 Al] LMRF, C; For W.

127

And is to mene to men that on this moolde lyven,   *earth*

Whoso wole be pure parfit moot possession forsake,   *completely; must*

275 Or selle it, as seith the Book, and the silver dele   *give away*

To beggeris that goon and begge and bidden good for Goddes love. *ask alms*

For failed nevere man mete that myghtful God serveth,   *lacked*

As David seith in the Sauter; to swiche that ben in wille   (Ps 36: 25); *wish*

To serve God goodliche, ne greveth hym no penaunce— *privation, suffering*

Nichil inpossibile volenti—

280 Ne lakketh nevere liflode, lynnen ne wollen: *Nor does he lack necessaries*

Inquirentes autem Dominum non minuentur omni bono.

'If preestes weren wise, thei wolde no silver take

For masses ne for matyns, noght hir mete of usureres,

Ne neither kirtel ne cote, theigh thei for cold sholde deye,   *tunic*

And thei hir devoir dide, as David seith in the Sauter: *If; duty*

Iudica me, Deus, et discerne causam meam.

285 '*Spera in Deo* speketh of preestes that have no spendyng silver

'*Trust in God*' (Ps 36: 3)

That if thei travaille truweliche and truste in God almyghty, *labour honestly*

Hem sholde lakke no liflode, neyther lynnen ne wollen.

And the title that ye take ordres by telleth ye ben avaunced; sc. *of 'priest'*

Thanne nedeth yow noght to [nyme] silver for masses that ye syngen. *take*

290 For he that took yow youre title sholde take yow youre wages, *gave; give*

Or the bisshop that blessed yow, if that ye ben worthi.

'For made nevere kyng no knyght but he hadde catel to spende *wealth*

As bifel for a knyght, or foond hym for his strengthe.   *provided*

It is a careful knyght, and of a caytif kynges makyng,   *wretched*

295 That hath no lond ne lynage riche ne good loos of hise handes.

reputation (for valour)

The same I segge for sothe by alle swiche preestes   *about*

That han neither konnynge ne kyn, but a crowne one *learning; tonsure only*

And a title, a tale of noght, to his liflode at meschief.

mere name; time of trouble

279a Nothing is impossible to him who wills it (*cf.* Mt 17: 19).

280a [The rich have wanted, and have suffered hunger:] but they that seek the Lord shall not be deprived of any good (Ps 33: 11).

284 *Either* And they would be doing . . . *or, more likely*, If they were doing . . .

284a Judge me, O God, and distinguish my cause [from the nation that is not holy] (Ps 42: 1).

285 Trust in God [the Lord, *Domino* Vulg] (Ps 36: 3; *q.v.*).

288 And the title of priest / certificate of entitlement given when you are ordained proclaims that you have been set up in authority (*after* Sk).

298 And the mere empty name of 'Sir Priest' [*or*, guarantee of support (OED title *sb.* 8)] to earn a living with in time of distress.

281 wise] R (?=α; all wise men F)   289 nyme] C (*so* K-D *p.* 93); take *All*
(*so* K-D); parfite β.   B-MSS.

He hath moore bileve, as I leve, to lacche thorugh his croune
                                                expectation; obtain
300 Cure than for konnynge or "knowen for clene of berynge."
                                        (A) Benefice; good repute
I have wonder for why and wherfore the bisshop
Maketh swiche preestes, that lewed men bitrayen!
    'A chartre is chalangeable bifore a chief justice: *document; open to dispute*
If fals Latyn be in that lettre, the lawe it impugneth,   *calls in question*
305 Or peynted parentrelynarie, parcelles overskipped. *interlined; portions left out*
The gome that gloseth so chartres for a goky is holden.   *glosses; fool*
    'So is it a goky, by God! that in his gospel failleth   *makes mistakes*
Or in masse or in matyns maketh any defaute: *omission(s)*
Qui offendit in uno, in omnibus est reus.
And also in the Sauter seith David to overskipperis,
310 *Psallite Deo nostro, psallite; quoniam rex terrae Deus Israel, psallite sapienter.*
    'The bisshop shal be blamed bifore God, as I leve,
That crouneth swiche Goddes knyghtes that konneth noght *sapienter*
                                    tonsures, i.e. ordains; wisely
Synge, ne psalmes rede, ne seye a masse of the day.
Ac never neither is blamelees, the bisshop ne the chapeleyn;   *priest*
315 For hir either is endited, and that of "*Ignorancia*   *each of them; accused*
Non excusat episcopos nec ydiotes preestes."   *unlearned*
    'This lokynge on lewed preestes hath doon me lepe from poverte—
                                considering; made me digress
The which I preise, ther pacience is, moore parfit than richesse.'
                                    esteem; where; perfect

    Ac muche moore in metynge thus with me gan oon dispute—   *dream(s)*
320 And slepynge I seigh al this; and sithen cam Kynde
And nempned me by my name, and bad me nymen hede,   *called; take note*
And thorugh the wondres of this world wit for to take.
                                understanding; acquire
And on a mountaigne that Myddelerthe highte, as me tho thoughte,
I was fet forth by ensaumples to knowe,   *led, brought*

299–300 *Paraphrase*, He actually has more hope of getting a benefice through (the
    mere fact of) being ordained than through any (claim) to learning or reputation
    for piety (C).
303 The validity of a legal document can be questioned . . .
308a [And] whosoever [shall keep the whole law but] offend in one point, is
    become guilty of all (Js 2: 10).
310 Sing praises to our God, sing ye; . . . for [the] God [of Israel] is the king of all
    the earth: sing ye wisely (Ps 46: 7–8).
315–16 Ignorance [*sc.* of ordinands' deficiencies] does not excuse bishops (C).

300 of] L&r; *om* WCrBF (C).
305 parceles] L&r, C; or p. w.
314 Ac] LR, C; And W.
315 of] LR; is of Y; ys be F; is w.

323 þo] L&r; *om* wCotF.
324 ens.] forbisenes *conj* K-D *p.* 195
    (C).

325 Thorugh ech a creature, Kynde my creatour to lovye.
    I seigh the sonne and the see and the sond after,   *sand*
    And where that briddes and beestes by hir make thei yeden,   *mate(s); went*
    Wilde wormes in wodes, and wonderful foweles   *serpents*
    With fleckede fetheres and of fele colours.   *many*
330 Man and his make I myghte se bothe;
    Poverte and plentee, bothe pees and werre,   *war*
    Blisse and bale—bothe I seigh at ones,   *misery; at one time*
    And how men token Mede and Mercy refused.
    Reson I seigh soothly sewen alle beestes   *follow*
335 In etynge, in drynkynge and in engendrynge of kynde. *begetting offspring*
    And after cours of concepcion noon took kepe of oother *the process; notice*
    As whan thei hadde ryde in rotey tyme; anoonright therafter
                           copulated; rutting-time
    Males drowen hem to males amornynge by hemselve, *withdrew; in sadness* (C)
    And [femelles to femelles ferded and drowe]. *females; assembled together*
340 Ther ne was cow ne cowkynde that conceyved hadde   *cattle*
    That wolde belwe after bole, ne boor after sowe.   *bellow; boar*
    Bothe hors and houndes and alle othere beestes   *horses*
    Medled noght with hir makes that [mid] fole were. *Coupled; with foal, pregnant*
    Briddes I biheld that in buskes made nestes;   *bushes*
345 Hadde nevere wye wit to werche the leeste.   *a human being; build*
    I hadde wonder at whom and wher the pye   *from; magpie*
    Lerned to legge the stikkes in which she leyeth and bredeth. *lay; lays (eggs)*
    Ther nys wrighte, as I wene, sholde werche hir nest to paye;
                         craftsman; satisfactorily
    If any mason made a molde therto, muche wonder it were.
                  mould, pattern; ?comparable to
350   And yet me merveilled moore: many othere briddes *I marvelled further*
    Hidden and hileden hir egges ful derne   *covered; secretly*
    In mareys and moores for men sholde hem noght fynde,
                  marsh(es); moors; so that
    And hidden hir egges whan thei therfro wente,
    For fere of othere foweles and for wilde beestes.
355   And some troden hir makes and on trees bredden *copulated with; mated*

325 creature] so K-D *p.* 179; c. and W&r (and *om* F; *cf.* C).
327 m. þei] LR, ?C; makes WF.
330 se b.] R (=*a*; seyȝ y þere F), C (*so* K-D); boþe biholde *β*.
332 at] L&r, C; al at w.
337–9 *om* F.
337 r. þer] þei resten C (*so* K-D, *pp.* 90, 160, *trspd.*) (C).
338 am.] amornynges L; all mornynge Hm; amorwenynges WR&c (C).
339 femelles . . . d.] C (*see* K-D *p.* 164); in euenynges also þe

males *ben* fro femelles W&r *with varr.* (C).
341 belwe] bere C (*so* K-D).
    bole] F, C (*so* K-D *p.* 169); *pl.* W&r.
343 mid] wiþ W&r *exc* F (C).
346 *Divided from* 347 *as in* C (*so* K-D *p.* 93); *div. after* lerned *All* B-MSS.
348 neste] L&r, C; *pl.* WCr[1].
350 And] L&r (*om* F), C; Ac W.
    many] R (?=*a*), C; how m. W&r (=*β*); of m. FG.
355 hir m.] I toke kepe C (*so* K-D).

And broughten forth hir briddes so al above the grounde. *their young*
And some briddes at the bile thorugh brethyng conceyved, *bill; breathing*
And some caukede; I took kepe how pecokkes bredden.

trod; observed; peacocks

Muche merveilled me what maister thei hadde, *teacher*
360 And who taughte hem on trees to tymbre so heighe *build*
That neither burn ne beest may hir briddes rechen. *man; reach*
  And sithen I loked on the see and so forth on the sterres; *stars*
Manye selkouthes I seigh, ben noght to seye nouthe.

wonders (which); mention

I seigh floures in the fryth and hir faire colours, *wood*
365 And how among the grene gras growed so manye hewes,
And some soure and some swete—selkouth me thoughte. *wonderful*
Of hir kynde and hir colour to carpe it were to longe.
  Ac that moost meved me and my mood chaunged— *perturbed my heart*
That Reson rewarded and ruled alle beestes *watched over*
370 Save man and his make: many tyme and ofte
No Reson hem folwede, [neither riche ne povere].
And thanne I rebukede Reson, and right til hymselven I seyde,
 'I have wonder of thee, that witty art holden, *wise; considered*
Why thow ne sewest man and his make, that no mysfeet hem folwe.'

misdeed

375 And Reson arated me, and seide, 'Recche thee nevere

corrected; Trouble yourself

Why I suffre or noght suffre—thiself hast noght to doone.

'It's no concern of yours' (K-D)

Amende thow it if thow myght, for my tyme is to abide. *Improve (matters)*
Suffraunce is a soverayn vertue, and a swift vengeaunce.

Patience (cf. Lk 18: 1–8)

Who suffreth moore than God?' quod he; 'no gome, as I leeve.

puts up with; no one

380 He myghte amende in a minute while al that mysstandeth,

moment; is wrong, amiss

Ac he suffreth for som mannes goode, and so is oure bettre.

---

381 But he tolerates (evil) for the benefit of particular individuals, and (in doing so, shows himself) to be superior to our human notions.

---

356 so] *om* FHm, C (*so* K-D).
359 þei h.] L&r; hem made W.
362 on (1, 2)]g F, C (*so* K-D); vpon W.
370 and o.] me þouhte C (*so* K-D p. 91). ▬
371 *Divided from* 372 *after* reb. *All* B-MSS *exc* F (*soph.*) (*C*).
 noþer ... p.] C (*so* K-D); *om* Bx.

hem f.] W&r (=Bx); rewlyþ hem F; hem ruled C (*so* K-D p. 93).
373 of þee] o. þ. quod I *All* B-MSS; in my witt C (*C*).
377 it] *om* YG&c (*so* K-D p. 146).
379 -eth] L&r, C; -ede WYOC².
381 so] L&r; so it W.

The Vision of Piers Plowman

'Holy Writ,' quod that wye, 'wisseth men to suffre: *counsels*
Propter Deum subiecti estote omni creature.
Frenche men and fre men affaiteth thus hire children: *train*
Bele vertue est suffraunce; mal dire est petite vengeance.
Bien dire et bien suffrir fait lui suffrant a bien venir.
385 Forthi I rede,' quod Reson, 'thow rule thi tonge bettre, *advise; control*
And er thow lakke my lif, loke if thow be to preise.
For is no creature under Crist can formen hymselven,   *form, create*
And if a man myghte make hymself good,
Ech a lif wolde be laklees—leeve thow non other.   *without fault*
390 Ne thow shalt fynde but fewe fayne for to here   *willing*
Of here defautes foule bifore hem reherced. *vile faults; declared*
'The wise and the witty wroot thus in the Bible:
De re que te non molestat noli certare.
For be a man fair or foul, it falleth noght to lakke *is not right to disparage*
395 The shap ne the shaft that God shoop hymselve;   *form; figure*
For al that he wrought was wel ydo, as Holy Writ witnesseth:
Et vidit Deus cuncta que fecerat, et erant valde bona.
And bad every creature in his kynde encreesse, *species; increase*
Al to murthe with man that moste wo tholie *gratify; must endure (woe)*
In fondynge of the flessh and of the fend bothe. *temptation from*
400 For man was maad of swich a matere he may noght wel asterte
            quite escape
That som tyme hym bitit to folwen his kynde. *it befalls him; nature*
Caton acordeth therwith—*Nemo sine crimine vivit!*' *agrees*

    Tho caughte I colour anoon and comsed to ben ashamed,
            coloured, blushed

382*a* Be ye subject [therefore] to every [human] creature for God's sake (I Pet 2: 13).
384 Patience is a fair virtue, say-evil a poor vengeance:
    Say-well and suffer-well dispose a man to come through well.
393 Strive not in a matter which doth not concern thee (Ecclus 11: 9).
396*a* And God saw all the things that he had made, and they were very good (Gen 1: 31).
402 No man lives free of fault (*Distichs of Cato*, I, 5).

382-91 α (*cf.* C); *om* β.
382 wye] *so* K-D; weye RF.
   wiss.] R, *cf.* C; wyssheþ F.
384 *Beele*] F, C (*so* Sk); vele R.
   petite] C (*so* Sk); *pety* RF.
   soffrer] R; *suffre* F.
   soffrant] RF, *suffrable* C (*so* K-D).
385 quod] þe F.
   þou] F, C (*so* K-D); *om* R.
386 l. my l.] l. eny l. C (*so* Sk); my l. l. F.
   if þ.] þyn F; who C.
387 is] R, C; þere is F.

388 make ... g.] m. h. goed to þe poeple R; m. lakles hymselue F (*so* K-D) (C).
389 lif] man F; lede C.
390 for to] wolde F.
391 hem] here face·F.
392*a* noli] β; nolite R; non F.
396 wrou3t] α (*so* K-D); dide β.
397 And ... en.] And ... en. he bad sugg. K-D *p.* 194.
   eu.] β; to vch a R; ech F.
401 þat] α, C (*so* K-D); Th. ne β.

132

And awaked therwith. Wo was me thanne
405 That I in metels ne myghte moore have yknowen.   *dream*
And thanne seide I to myself, and [sherewe]de that tyme,   *spoke; cursed*
'Now I woot what Dowel is,' quod I, 'by deere God, as me thynketh!'
And as I caste up myne eighen, oon loked on me and asked
Of me, what thyng it were? 'Ywis, sire,' I seyde,
410 'To se muche and suffre moore, certes,' quod I, 'is Dowel.'
   'Haddestow suffred,' he seide, 'slepynge tho thow were,
                                        'waited patiently'; when
Thow sholdest have knowen that Clergie kan and conceyved moore thorugh
   Reson—   *what Cl. knows; grasped*
For Reson wolde have reherced thee right as Clergie seide.   *declared to*
Ac for thyn entremetynge here artow forsake: *interfering; abandoned*
Philosophus esses, si tacuisses.
415 'Adam, whiles he spak noght, hadde paradis at wille;
Ac whan he mamelede aboute mete and entremeted to knowe   *prated; food*
The wisedom and the wit of God, he was put fram blisse.   *expelled*
And right so ferde Reson bi thee—thow with thi rude speche   *dealt*
Lakkedest and losedest thyng that longed noght to doone.
                                        praised; was not fitting to
420 Tho hadde he no likyng for to lere the moore.   *wish; teach you*
   'Pryde now and presumpcion paraventure wol thee appele,
                                        perchance will accuse you
That Clergie thi compaignye ne kepeth noght to suwe.
                                        (Saying) that; cares; keep
For shal nevere chalangynge ne chidynge chaste a man so soone
                                        scolding; chasten
As shal shame, and shenden hym, and shape hym to amende.   *mortify; dispose*
425 For lat a dronken daffe in a dyk falle,   *fool; ditch*
Lat hym ligge, loke noght on hym til hym liste aryse.
                                        lie (there); feel like rising
For though Reson rebuked hym thanne, reccheth he nevere;   *cares*
Of Clergie ne of his counseil he counteth noght a risshe.
                                        values; rush (i.e. nothing)
[To blame] or for to bete hym thanne, it were but pure synne.
                                        beat; sheer malice

414*a* You would have been a philosopher if you had held your peace (*adap. fr.*
Boethius, *De Consolatione Philosophiae*, II, *prose* 7, 74–6).
419 Damned and praised what there was no call to.

406 sher.] chid*de* W&*r exc* F (*trsp.*)
   (*C*).
412 conc.] L&*r*, C; contreued WHm;
   kend Cr.
419 nou3t] L&*r*; þe no3t WF.
420 no] litel *conj* K-D *p*. 198.
422 þi] β (to thy Hm); in þi α.
   ne] L&*r*; *om* WHmF.
   to s.] β; efte to sitte α.

423 For] α, C; *om* β.
424 As] β; he R; þan F.
427a *As one line with* 429b β.
   recc. he n.] α (he] hym R), C (*so*
   Sk); *om* β.
428 α, *cf.* C (*so* Sk); *om* β.
429 To ... þanne] C, α (*so* Sk; To
   bl. *om* α; or *om* F, for *om* C).

430 Ac whan nede nymeth hym up, for doute leste he [ne] sterve,   *fear; die*
And shame shrapeth hise clothes and hise shynes wassheth,   *scrapes; shins*
Thanne woot the dronken daffe wherfore he is to blame.'
'Ye siggen sooth, by my soule,' quod I, 'Ich have yseyen it ofte.
    say truly; seen
Ther smyt no thyng so smerte, ne smelleth so foule   *strikes; sharply*
435 As shame, there he sheweth hym—for ech man shonyeth his felaweshipe.
    where; shuns; company
Why ye wisse me thus,' quod I, 'was for I rebuked Reson.' *lecture; because*
'Certes,' quod he, 'that is sooth,' and shoop hym for to walken.
    got ready, made as if to
And I aroos up right with that and [raughte] hym after, *moved, set off (C)*
And preyde hym [if his wille were, he wolde] telle me his name.

Passus XII

'I am Ymaginatif,' quod he, 'ydel was I nevere,   *idle, inactive*
Though I sitte by myself, in siknesse nor in helthe.
I have folwed thee, in feith, thise fyve and fourty wynter,
And manye tymes have meved thee to [m]yn[n]e on thyn ende, *reflect*
5 And how fele fernyeres are faren, and so fewe to come;
    many past years; (are) to come
And of thi wilde wantownesse [whan] thow yong were, *recklessness*
To amende it in thi myddel age, lest myght the faille *(the) power (to do so)*
In thyn olde elde, that yvele kan suffre *poorly; endure*
Poverte or penaunce, or preyeres bidde: *say*
Si non in prima vigilia nec in secunda &c.

9a If not in the first watch or the second . . . (*cf.* Lk 12: 38).

430 ne] *om All* B-MSS·(*C*).
432 daffe] wye *conj* K-D.
433 by m. s.] α (*after* q. I. F), C; *om* β.
434 foule] R (?=α), C (*so* K-D *p.* 168*n*); soure W&r (=β).
435 ech] Cr, C; no α; euery β.
shoneth] C; hym shonyeþ β (shendethe G); loueth α.
  h. felachipp] α; h. companye C; *om* β.
438 raughte] folwed *All* B-MSS (*C*).

439 if . . . wolde] C; of his curteisie to *All* B-MSS (of] for Hm) (*C*).

Rubric Passus xii ᵘˢ.
4 mynne] *conj* K-D *p.* 195; þynke *All* B-MSS.
6 whan] whiles *conj* K-D *p.* 195; þo *All* B-MSS.
7 faille] YR&r (f. after F) (*so* K-D); failled wL.
9 bidde] L&r; to b. WF.

10   'Amende thee while thow myght; thow hast ben warned ofte
    With poustees of pestilences, with poverte and with angres—
                                  violence; sorrows, afflictions
    And with thise bittre baleises God beteth his deere children: *rods*
    Quem diligo, castigo.
    And David in the Sauter seith, of swiche that loveth Jesus,
    " *Virga tua et baculus tuus, ipsa me consolata sunt:*
    Although thow strike me with thi staf, with stikke or with yerde,   *rod*
15 It is but murthe as for me to amende my soule."
    And thow medlest thee with makynges—and myghtest go seye thi Sauter,
                            dabble in verse-making
    And bidde for hem that yyveth thee breed; for ther are bokes ynowe
                                     pray; enough
    To telle men what Dowel is, Dobet and Dobest bothe,
    And prechours to preve what it is, of many a peire freres.'
                          prove; pair (of) friars (C)
20 I seigh wel he seide me sooth and, somwhat me to excuse,
    Seide, 'Caton conforted his sone that, clerk though he were,
    To solacen hym som tyme—a[lso] I do whan I make: *amuse; just as; versify*
    Interpone tuis interdum gaudia curis.
     'And of holy men I herde,' quod I, 'how thei outherwhile   *sometimes*
    Pleyden, the parfiter to ben, in [places manye].
25 Ac if ther were any wight that wolde me telle
    What were Dowel and Dobet and Dobest at the laste,
    Wolde I nevere do werk, but wende to holi chirche
    And there bidde my bedes but whan ich ete or slepe.' *say my prayers except*
    'Poul in his pistle,' quod he, 'preveth what is Dowel: *epistle*
    Fides, spes, caritas, et maior horum &c—
30 Feith, hope and charitee, and alle ben goode,
    And saven men sondry tymes, ac noon so soone as charite.
    For he dooth wel, withouten doute, that dooth as lewte techeth;
                            righteousness, faith
    That is, if thow be man maryed, thi make thow lovye,   *married; spouse*
    And lyve forth as lawe wole while ye lyven bothe.   *i.e. in chastity*
35 'Right so, if thow be religious, ren thow nevere ferther '*a monk or nun*'; *run*
    To Rome ne to Rochemador, but as thi rule techeth,
                         Roquemadour, in Guienne (C)

12*a* Such as I love I [rebuke and] chastise (Apoc 3: 19; *cf.* Prov 3: 12).
13*a* Thy rod and thy staff: they have comforted me (Ps 22: 4).
22*a* Give a place sometimes to pleasures amid your pressing cares (*Distichs of Cato*, III, 6).
29*a* . . . faith, hope, charity . . . [but] the greatest of these [is charity] (I Cor 13: 13).

17 yn.] L&*r* (*om* OC²); yknowe W.   23 I h.] I here R; h. y F.
19 preue] L&*r*; preuen W.   24 places m.] m. pl. β; m. a place α
21 his] L&*r*; me h. WHmCr¹.   (here prayeres after F).
22 also] so *conj* K-D *p.* 198; as
    W&*r*; and R.

And holde thee under obedience, that heigh wey is to hevene.
  'And if thow be maiden to marye, and mygth wel continue, *remain (a virgin)*
Seke thow nevere seint ferther for no soule helthe! *health of soul, sanctity*
40 For what made Lucifer to lese the heighe hevene, *lose*
Or Salomon his sapience, or Sampson his strengthe?
Job the Jew his joye deere he it aboughte; *dearly paid for it*
Aristotle and othere mo, Ypocras and Virgile, *Hippocrates*
Alisaundre that al wan, elengliche ended. *won, conquered; wretchedly*
45 Catel and kynde wit was combraunce to hem alle. *wealth; native intelligence; trouble*
  'Felice hir fairnesse fel hire al to sclaundre, *became a disgrace to her*
And Rosamounde right so reufulliche bisette *pitiably bestowed, used*
The beaute of hir body; in baddenesse she despended.
Of manye swiche I may rede—of men and of wommen—
50 That wise wordes wolde shewe and werche the contrarie: *do; opposite*
Sunt homines nequam bene de virtute loquentes.
  'And riche renkes right so gaderen and sparen, *men; gather; save*
And tho men that thei moost haten mynistren it at the laste; *spend, have the use of*
And for thei suffren and see so manye nedy folkes *allow (to exist)*
And love hem noght as Oure Lord bit, lesen hir soules: *commands; lose*
Date et dabitur vobis.
55 So catel and kynde wit acombreth ful manye; *hinder, cause trouble to*
Wo is hym that hem weldeth but he hem wel despende: *possesses; spends, uses*
Scient[es] et non facient[es] variis flagellis vapulab[un]t.
Sapience, seith the Bok, swelleth a mannes soule:
Sapiencia inflat &c.
And richesse right so, but if the roote be trewe. *its origin; honest*
  'Ac grace is a gras therfore, tho grevaunces to abate. *healing herb for them*
60 Ac grace ne groweth noght but amonges [gomes] lowe: *humble people*
Pacience and poverte the place is ther it groweth, *where*

50a They are evil men, who *speak* well of virtue (Godfrey of Winchester, epigram 169) (C).
54a Give; and it shall be given to you (Lk 6: 38).
56a Those who know [God's will] and do not act [according to it] shall be beaten with many whips (*cf.* Lk 12: 47).
57a Knowledge puffeth up; [but charity edifieth] (I Cor 8: 1).

40 For] W&r; And Y; Lo *conj* K-D p. 198.
42 dere he it] LR; d. it he OC²; ful deere W.
47 bysette] L&r (she b. F); to bileue w (*see* K-D p. 142).
48 badd. she] badd vse α.
55–7a α (55–6 C *also*); om β.
56 he; wel] F, C (*so* K-D); if he; wil R.
56a -tes (1, 2); -bunt] C (*so* Sk); -ti; -bit α.
59 fore] α, C; of β.
60 gomes l.] þe l. OC²; lowe W&r (C).
61 is] L&r (l. om F); hiȝte W.

And in lele lyvynge men and in lif holy.   *men of holy life*
And thorugh the gifte of the Holy Goost, as the Gospel telleth:
Spiritus ubi vult spirat.
    'Clergie and kynde wit cometh of sighte and techyng,   *from observation*
65 As the Book bereth witnesse to burnes that kan rede: *men*
Quod scimus loquimur, quod vidimus testamur.
Of *quod scimus* cometh clergie, a konnynge of hevene,
                                        From 'what we know'; from
And of *quod vidimus* cometh kynde wit, of sighte of diverse peple.
                                        From 'what we have seen'; from
Ac grace is a gifte of God, and of greet love spryngeth;
Knew nevere clerk how it cometh forth, ne kynde wit the weyes:
Nescit aliquis unde venit aut quo vadit &c.
70   'Ac yet is clergie to comende, and kynde wit bothe,   *to be commended; too*
And namely clergie for Cristes love, that of clergie is roote.
For Moyses witnesseth that God wroot for to wisse the peple
In the Olde Lawe, as the lettre telleth, that was the lawe of Jewes,
                                        writing, Scripture
That what wommman were in avoutrye taken, were she riche or poore,
                                        adultery
75 With stones men sholde hir strike, and stone hire to dethe.   (Lev 20: 10)
A wommman, as we fynden, was gilty of that dede;   *read*
Ac Crist of his curteisie thorugh clergie hir saved. *compassion, graciousness*
For thorugh caractes that Crist wroot, the Jewes knewe hemselve
                                        characters; recognized
Giltier as afore God and gretter in synne   (Jn 8: 3–9)
80 Than the womman that there was, and wenten awey for shame.
The clergie that there was conforted the womman.
Holy Kirke knoweth this—that Cristes writyng saved;
So clergie is confort to creatures that repenten,
And to mansede men meschief at hire ende.   *cursed (C); disaster*
85   'For Goddes body myghte noght ben of breed withouten clergie,
                                        i.e. in the Eucharist
The which body is bothe boote to the rightfulle,
                                        remedy; just, in a state of grace
And deeth and dampnacion to hem that deyeth yvele;

63*a* The Spirit breatheth where he will . . . (Jn 3: 8).
65*a* . . . we speak what we know and we testify what we have seen (Jn 3: 11).
69*a* But thou knowest [lit. he knows] not whence he [*sc.* the Spirit] cometh and
    whither he goeth (Jn 3: 8).
71 And particularly learning (acquired) for the love of Christ, who is the source of
    [all true] learning.

66 a] α (*so* K-D *p.* 146); and β.   78 For] L&r; And w.
74 were she] L&r (w.] wh. WF); *om*   caractes . . . wr.] cristes carectus α.
    Crg; wher *rec.* K-D *p.* 183.   81 The . . . was; þe] þus þoruh cl.
76 we f.] L&r (=β; I fynde W); *l. om*   þere; was þe F; *cf.* K-D *p.* 181.
    α.   82 saued] L&r; s. hire wM; hire s. F.

137

As Cristes caracte confortede and bothe coupable shewed
guilty, needing forgiveness
The womman that the Jewes broughte, that Jesus thoughte to save:
Nolite iudicare et non iudicabimini.
90 Right so Goddes body, bretheren, but it be worthili taken,
i.e. Holy Communion; unless
Dampneth us at the day of dome as dide the caractes the Jewes.
  'Forthi I counseille thee for Cristes sake, clergie that thow lovye,
For kynde wit is of his kyn and neighe cosynes bothe
To Oure Lord, leve me—forthi love hem, I rede.
95 For bothe ben as mirours to amenden oure defautes,
And lederes for lewed men and for lettred bothe.
  'Forthi lakke thow nevere logik, lawe ne hise custumes,   *criticize*
Ne countreplede clerkes—I counseille thee for evere!   *argue against*
For as a man may noght see that mysseth hise eighen,   *lacks*
100 Na moore kan no clerk but if he caughte it first thorugh bokes.
can (know); obtained
Although men made bokes, God was the maister,   *teacher*
And Seint Spirit the samplarie, and seide what men sholde write.
'copy' (exemplar), instructor
And right as sight serveth a man to se the heighe strete,
Right so lereth lettrure lewed men to reson.
literacy; (otherwise) uneducated
105 And as a blynd man in bataille bereth wepne to fighte,
And hath noon hap with his ax his enemy to hitte,   *luck*
Na moore kan a kynde witted man, but clerkes hym teche,   *unless*
Come, for al his kynde wit, to Cristendom and be saved—
Which is the cofre of Cristes tresor, and clerkes kepe the keyes,
110 To unloken it at hir likyng, and to the lewed peple   *unlock; ignorant*
Yyve mercy for hire mysdedes, if men it wole aske
Buxomliche and benigneliche, and bidden it of grace.
  '*Archa Dei* in the Olde Lawe, Levites it kepten;   *The Ark of God*
Hadde nevere lewed man leve to leggen hond on that cheste   *layman; lay*
115 But he were preest or preestes sone, patriark or prophete.
(But only a) priest

89a Judge not, that you may not be judged (Mt 7: 1).
107-8 No more can a man equipped only with the knowledge derived from common experience . . . Arrive at [the truths of] Christianity.
112 In a spirit of humble obedience and good will, and pray for it through the grace of God.

89 brouȝte] iugged *conj* K-D *p.* 198.
90 but] L&r; b. if WHmC².
91 dede þe carecte] α (*pl.* K-D *p.* 144); þe caractes dide β (þe *om* M).
99 eiȝen] β, C; siȝte α.
103 L&r, C; *l. om* w.
104 ler-] α, C (*so* K-D); led- β.

    'Saul, for he sacrificed, sorwe hym bitidde,   *because; befell* (I Sam 13: 12)
And his sones also for that synne mischeved,   *came to grief*
And manye mo other men that were no Levites,   (II Sam 6: 7)
That with *archa Dei* yeden, in reverence and in worship,   *went*
120 And leiden hond theron to liften it up—and loren hir lif after.
                            lost; accordingly, therupon
    'Forthi I conseille alle creatures no clergie to dispise,
Ne sette short by hir science, whatso thei don hemselve.   *set little store by*
Take we hir wordes at worth, for hire witnesses be trewe,
And medle we noght muche with hem to meven any wrathe,   *stir up*
125 Lest cheste cha[f]en us to choppe ech man other: *argument; rouse, heat*
    Nolite tangere christos meos &c.
    'For clergie is kepere under Crist of hevene;
[Com] ther nevere no knyght but clergie hym made.
Ac kynde wit cometh of alle kynnes sightes—   *natural understanding*
Of briddes and of beestes, [of blisse and of sorwe],
130 Of tastes of truthe and [oft] of deceites.   *From experiences; deceptions*
    '[Olde] lyveris toforn us useden to marke
                  Men of old; used to note, observe
The selkouthes that thei seighen, hir sones for tơ teche,   *strange sights*
And helden it an heigh science hir wittes to knowe. *(for) their minds to know*
Ac thorugh hir science soothly was nevere no soule ysaved,
135 Ne broght by hir bokes to blisse ne to joye;
For alle hir kynde knowyng com but of diverse sightes.
    'Patriarkes and prophetes repreveden hir science,   *condemned*
And seiden hir wordes ne hir wisdomes was but a folye;   *foolishness*
As to the clergie of Crist, counted it but a trufle: *Compared with; trifle*
    Sapiencia huius mundi stultitia est apud Deum.

125*a* Touch ye not my anointed (Ps 104: 15).
139–139*a* Considered it trivial when compared with Christian learning [= know-
    ledge of Christ and the Scriptures]: '[For] the wisdom of this world is foolishness
    with God' (I Cor 3: 19) (*C*).

116–25*a* α, *cf.* C XIV 61–69*a*; *om* β.
116 he s.] R, C; his myssacrifyse F.
119 ȝeden . . . worship] wentyn with
    worchepeful reuerencis F.
120 hond þ.] R, C; on h. F.
    to] & F.
121 to] R, C; ȝee F.
122 s. schort] R, C; settiþ lyght F.
123 we] R, C; *om* F.
    wyt.] F, C; *sg.* R.
124 med.] F, C; ne m. R.
    we] R, C; *om* F.
125 chaufe ous] C (*so* Sk); chasen vs
    R (? = α); be chased owt F.
    to . . . man] R, C (to] and C);
    þan ech man choppith F.
127 Com] Was *All* B-MSS (*C*).

129–30 *As one line from* Of . . . dec.,
    omitting of (2) . . . sorwe *All* B-MSS
    (*C*).
129 of (2) . . . s.] C (*C*).
130 oft of] of *All* B-MSS.
131 Olde l.] L. *All* B-MSS (*C*).
132 þe] L&*r*; For WHm; *om* Cr.
134 no] *om* gF, C (*so* K-D).
136 kn.] gF, C (*so* K-D); *pl.* W&*r*.
    cam] α, C (com B, *so* K-D);
    come W&*r* (= β; comethe G).
138 ne] L&*r*; and W.
    was] R (? = α; w. al F) Cr, C
    (*so* Sk); nas W&*r* (= β; were not
    G).
139 As] L&*r* (& as G), C; And W.

140   'For the heighe Holy Goost hevene shal tocleve,   *cleave asunder*
     And love shal lepe out after into this lowe erthe,
     And clennesse shal cacchen it and clerkes shullen it fynde: *purity (of life)*
     Pastores loquebantur ad invicem.
      'He speketh there of riche men right noght, ne of right witty,
                                            the (merely) clever
     Ne of lordes that were lewed men, but of the hyeste lettred oute:
                                        most learned men of all
145 *Ibant magi ab oriente.*
     (If any frere were founde there, I yyve thee fyve shillynges!)
     Ne in none beggers cote was that barn born,   *cottage; child*
     But in a burgeises place, of Bethlem the beste: *burgess's house*
     Set non erat ei locus in diversorio—et pauper non habet
       diversorium.
      'To pastours and to poetes appered the aungel,   *shepherds*
150 And bad hem go to Bethlem Goddes burthe to honoure,
     And songe a song of solas, *Gloria in excelsis Deo!*   *joyous hope, comfort*
     Riche men rutte tho and in hir reste were,   *were snoring (in sleep)*
     Tho it shon to shepherdes, a shewer of blisse.   *(i.e. the star); mirror, image*
     Clerkes knewen it wel and comen with hir presents,
155 And diden hir homage honurably to hym that was almyghty.
      'Why I have told thee al this—I took ful good hede
     How thow contrariedest clergie with crabbede wordes,
                               opposed learning; peevish
     How that lewed men lightloker than lettrede were saved,   *more easily*
     Than clerkes or kynde witted men, of Cristene peple.
                          naturally intelligent; from among
160 And thow seidest sooth of somme—ac se in what manere. *spoke truly about*
      'Tak two stronge men and in Themese cast hem,   *the Thames*
     And bothe naked as a nedle, hir noon sikerer than other;
                              neither of them safer
     That oon hath konnynge and kan swymmen and dyven,
                          One of them; knows how to
     That oother is lewed of that labour, lerned nevere swymme.   *ignorant*
165 Which trowestow of tho two in Themese is in moost drede— *do you think*
     He that nevere ne dyved ne noght kan of swymmyng,
     Or the swymmere that is saaf by so hymself like,   *safe if he please*
     Ther his felawe fleteth forth as the flood liketh, *Whereas; companion; floats*

142a . . . the shepherds said to one another . . . (Lk 2: 15).
145 . . . there came wise men from the east (Mt 2: 1).
148a But there was no room for them [*lit.* him] in the inn (Lk 2: 7); and a beggar
    does not use an inn!
151 Glory to God in the highest! (Lk 2: 14).

140–148a β, C; *om* α.   152–3 α, C (*so* Sk); *om* β.
141 lepe] L&*r*, C; lepen W.   155 her] L&*r*, C; *om* WCrF.
    þis] L&*r*, C; his OC²; þe W.   156 þe] R&*r*, C (*so* Sk); *om* wLMF.
147 begg.] L&*r*; burgeises W.   165 in th.] L&*r*, C; þat W.
    was] nas *sugg.* K-D *p.* 195.

And is in drede to drenche, that nevere dide swymme?'   *terror of drowning*
170 'That swymme kan noght,' I seide, 'it semeth to my wittes.'
                                      The one who can't swim
    'Right so,' quod the renk, 'reson it sheweth,   *man; it stands to reason*
That he that knoweth clergie kan sonner arise   *sooner*
Out of synne and be saaf, though he synne ofte,
If hym liketh and lest, than any lewed, leelly.   *desires; ignorant man; truly*
175 For if the clerk be konnynge, he knoweth what is synne,   *wise, instructed*
And how contricion withoute confession conforteth the soule,
As thow seest in the Sauter in salmes oon or tweyne,   *psalms; two*
How contricion is comended for it cacheth awey synne: *chases*
Beati quorum remisse sunt iniquitates et quorum tecta sunt peccata.
And this conforteth ech a clerk and kevereth hym fro wanhope,
                                   protects; despair
180 In which flood the fend fondeth a man hardest;   *tempts, puts to the test*
Ther the lewed lith stille and loketh after Lente,   *lies; waits for*
And hath no contricion er he come to shrifte—and thanne kan he litel telle,
                                      confession
But as his loresman lereth hym bileveth and troweth,
                             teacher instructs; thinks
And that is after person or parissh preest, and paraventure bothe unkonnynge
                         both of them perhaps unskilled
185 To lere lewed men, as Luc bereth witnesse:
Dum cecus ducit cecum &c.
    'Wo was hym marked that wade moot with the lewed!
                       allotted; must go with, follow
Wel may the barn blesse that hym to book sette, *the one who educated him*
That lyvynge after lettrure saved hym lif and soule. *an educated (way of) life*
Dominus pars hereditatis mee is a murye verset *heartening little text (C)*
190 That hath take fro Tybourne twenty stronge theves,
                       saved from hanging; confirmed
Ther lewed theves ben lolled up—loke how thei be saved!
                       Whereas; set swinging
    'The thef that hadde grace of God on Good Fryday as thow speke,
                       from; mentioned

178*a* Blessed are they whose iniquities are forgiven: and whose sins are covered (Ps 31: 1).
185*a* . . . if the blind lead the blind, both fall into the pit (Mt 15: 14; *cf.* Lk 6:39).
186 Misery was allotted to the man whose fate it is to be one of the ignorant.
189 The Lord is the portion of my inheritance . . . (Ps 15: 5).

170 β, C; *om* α.
178*a pecc.*] RF; *p. &c* Hm; *&c* WL.
179 keuereth] L&r (=β; couereþ W);
   kenneth α.
184 *divided from* 185 *before* vnk. *All*
   B-MSS; *re-div.* K-D (*cf.* C XIV
   124).

and] L&r (*om* F); þe whiche ben
   W.
   auenter b. Vnk.] R (?=α; a. þey
   be vnk. b. F), C; auenture vnk. WL.
187 þat] L&r, C; þat man þat W.
188 saued] L&r, C; saueþ WCr.
192 speke] L&r; spekest WHm.

Was for he yald hym creaunt to Crist on the cros, and knewliched hym gilty,
And grace asked of God, that to graunten is evere redy
195 To hem that buxomliche biddeth it, and ben in wille to amenden hem.
humbly pray for; desire
Ac though that theef hadde hevene, he hadde noon heigh blisse,
exalted (state of) glory
As Seint Johan and othere seintes that deserved hadde bettre.
Right as som man yeve me mete and sette me amydde the floor:
Just as if; were to give
I hadde mete moore than ynough, ac noght so muche worshipe
I would have; honour
200 As tho that seten at the syde table or with the sovereynes of the halle,
sat; lords, high ones
But sete as a beggere bordlees by myself on the grounde.
would sit; without a table
So it fareth by that felon that a Good Friday was saved: *with; on*
He sit neither with Seint Johan, Symond ne Jude,
Ne with maydenes ne with martires ne confessours ne wydewes,
205 But by hymself as a soleyn, and served on the erthe. *solitary; ground*
For he that is ones a thef is everemoore in daunger,
And as lawe liketh to lyve or to deye:
De peccato propiciato noli esse sine metu.
And for to serven a seint and swich a thef togideres—
It were neither reson ne right to rewarde both yliche. *equally, alike*
210 'And right as Troianus the trewe knyght tilde noght depe in helle
dwelt; (so) deep
That Oure Lord ne hadde hym lightly out, so leve I [by] the thef in hevene:
easily; concerning
For he is in the loweste of hevene, if oure bileve be trewe, sc. *part; faith*

193 *Either* That was because . . . (*anacoluthon*) *or* Was saved (*ellipsis*) because he
submitted in faith . . . and acknowledged his sin.
207a Be not without fear about sin forgiven (Ecclus 5: 5).

193 cre.] β; recre. R (?=α; *om* F) M.
on þe c. &] W&r (?=β; þe *om*
OC²); vpon a c. R (?=α); & F, C
(*so* K-D).
194 þat to gr.] W; and he L&r.
(line *om* α).
is . . . r.] L&r (?=β; it is r. W)
(C).
195 To hem] W; þam BoCot; That
L&r (?=Bx; *soph.* F) (C).
198 sette . . . fl.] L&r (amyddis his
hall F), C; am. þe fl. s. me W.

199 Ich] L&r, C; And W.
201 sete] *om* C (*so* K-D p. 152).
204 ne (2)] α, C; *om* β.
Conf. ne] with mylde C (*so* K-D
p. 93) (C).
205 þe] L&r, C; *om* w.
209 rew.] R (?=α), C (*so* K-D p. 168n);
r. hem βF.
210 tilde] L&r, C; dwelte w.
211 by þe þ.] *rec.* K-D; þe þ. be
WLMR&c (?=Bx; þeef *om* R).

And wel losely he lolleth there, by the lawe of Holy Chirche,
loosely, ?insecurely; rests, relaxes
Quia reddit unicuique iuxta opera sua.
   'Ac why that oon theef on the cros creaunt hym yald   *yielded*
215 Rather than that oother theef, though thow woldest appose,
question, inquire
Alle the clerkes under Crist ne kouthe the skile assoille: *reason; explain*
Quare placuit? Quia voluit.   *'Why? Because!'*
And so I seye by thee, that sekest after the whyes,   *'why's', reasons*
And aresonedest Reson, a rebukynge as it were,   *argued with; upbraiding*
And willest of briddes and of beestes and of hir bredyng knowe,
(manner of) breeding
220 Why some be alough and some aloft, thi likyng it were; *low down; high up*
And of the floures in the fryth and of hire faire hewes—
Wherof thei cacche hir colours so clere and so brighte, *From where; get*
And of the stones and of the sterres—thow studiest, as I leve,
How evere beest outher brid hath so breme wittes . . .   *powerful*
225   'Clergie ne Kynde Wit ne knew nevere the cause,
Ac Kynde knoweth the cause hymself and no creature ellis. *Nature (=God)*
He is the pies patron and putteth it in hir ere   *magpie's; ear*
That there the thorn is thikkest to buylden and brede.   *where; build*
And Kynde kenned the pecok to cauken in swich a kynde,
taught; couple; manner
230 And Kynde kenned Adam to knowe his pryve membres,
(the use of) his sexual organs
And taughte hym and Eve to helien hem with leves.   *cover themselves*
   'Lewed men many tymes maistres thei apposen,   *teachers; question*
Whi Adam ne hiled noght first his mouth that eet the appul,   *covered*
Rather than his likame alogh?—lewed asken thus clerkes.   *body below*
235 Kynde knoweth whi he dide so, ac no clerk ellis!
   'Ac of briddes and of beestes men by olde tyme
Ensamples token and termes, as telleth thise poetes,   *similitudes*
And that the faireste fowel foulest engendreth,   *breeds in the ugliest way*
And feblest fowel of flight is that fleeth or swymmeth. *weakest; in; flies*
240 And that is the pecok and the pehen—proude riche men thei bitokneth.
symbolize
For the pecok and men pursue hym may noght flee heighe: *if*

213a For thou wilt render [*lit.* he renders] to every man according to his works
    (Ps 61: 13).
216a Why did it seem good to him? Because he willed it (*cf.* Ps 134: 6, 113b: 3).

213 loselyche] L&*r* (lose-]lows- GC),
    C; loselly wCot.
213a Quia] LY&*c* (?=β); *Qui*
    WHmCr&*c*; And R (?=α; *soph.*
    F; *cf. Et* C).
214 Ac] R (?=α; But F), C; And β.
219–22 *so ordered* α (*so* K-D); 219
    and 220, 221 *and* 222 *trsp.* β.

228 Þat þ.] L&*r*; There W; That CB.
    to] þere to α.
230 And kende k.] α (*so* K-D); And
    k. β.
237 þis] LR; þe WF.
240 is] L&*r*, C; *om* w.
    þei] L&*r* (he F); *om* WHm.

For the trailynge of his tail overtaken is he soone.
And his flessh is foul flessh, and his feet bothe,
And unlovelich of ledene and looth for to here.   *cry; hateful*
245 'Right so the riche, if he his richesse kepe
And deleth it noght til his deeth day, the tail of alle is sorwe.
                                                      conclusion| ?tally (C)
Right as the pennes of the pecok peyneth hym in his flight, *feathers; hamper*
So is possession peyne of pens and of nobles   *burden, affliction; pence*
To alle hem that it holdeth til hir tail be plukked.
250 And though the riche repente thanne and birewe the tyme   *rue*
That evere he gadered so grete and gaf therof so litel,
Though he crye to Crist thanne with kene wil, I leve   *ardent desire*
His ledene be in Oure Lordes ere lik a pies chiteryng;
                                              cry will be; chattering
And whan his caroyne shal come in cave to be buryed.   *corpse; i.e. tomb*
255 I leve it flawme ful foule the fold al aboute,   *will smell; earth*
And alle the othere ther it lith envenymeth thorugh his attre.
                                           poisons; venom, infection
By the po feet is understande, as I have lerned in Avynet,
                                      peacock's; meant; Avianus (C)
Executours—false frendes that fulfille noght his wille
That was writen, and thei witnesse to werche right as it wolde.
                                              (even though); act
260 Thus the poete preveth that the pecok for his fetheres is reverenced;
Right so is the riche by reson of hise goodes.
  'The larke, that is a lasse fowel, is moore lovelich of ledene,
                                        smaller; pleasant; voice
And wel awey of wynge swifter than the pecok,
And of flessh by felefold fatter and swetter;   *many times; tastier*
265 To lowe libbynge men the larke is resembled.   *likened*
  ['Swiche tales he telleth, Aristotle the grete clerk];
Thus he likneth in his logik the leeste fowel oute.   *compares; smallest*
And wheither he be saaf or noght saaf, the sothe woot no clergie,
                                              saved; no learned men
Ne of Sortes ne of Salamon no scripture kan telle.
                                     Socrates; written authority
270 Ac God is so good, I hope that siththe he gaf hem wittes
To wissen us wyes therwith, that wisshen to be saved,   *guide; men*
(And the bettre for hir bokes to bidden we ben holden)

272 And we are bound to pray better, thanks to their books *or* And we are obliged
  to pray all the more [for them] because of [the value of] the books they wrote.

246 is] M; *om* W&r (C).   271 wyes] C (*so* K-D); wyȝen F;
247 as] LR; so as W.   wey*es* W&r (C).
260-1 W&r (*soph.* F); *rec.* K-D   wisshen] *so* K-D; w. vs Cr³;
  p. 183n.   wenen C; wissen vs W&r (C).
266 Swiche . . . cl.] A. þe g. cl. sw. t.
  he tell. *All* B-MSS; *re-arr.* K-D p. 194.

That God for his grace gyve hir soules reste—
For lettred men were lewed yet, ne were loore of hir bokes.'

would be; were it not for

275 'Alle thise clerkes,' quod I tho, 'that on Crist leven   *believe*
Seyen in hir sermons that neither Sarsens ne Jewes   *pagans*
Ne no creature of Cristes liknesse withouten Cristendom worth saved.'

human being; will be

' *Contra!* ' quod Ymaginatif thoo, and comsed for to loure, '*Not so!* '; *frown*
And seide, '*Salvabitur vix iustus in die iudicii;*
280 *Ergo—salvabitur!*' quod he, and seide no moore Latyn.
'Troianus was a trewe knyght and took nevere Cristendom,

just; received; baptism

And he is saaf, so seith the book, and his soule in hevene.   *saved*
Ac ther is fullynge of font and fullynge in blood shedyng,

baptism (of water, blood)

And thorugh fir is fullyng, and that is ferme bileve: *firm faith* (Mt 3: 11)
Advenit ignis divinus, non comburens set illuminans &c.
285 'Ac truthe that trespased nevere ne traversed ayeins his lawe,

righteousness

But lyveth as his lawe techeth and leveth ther be no bettre,

believes; i.e. religion

(And if ther were, he wolde amende) and in swich wille deieth—
Ne wolde nevere trewe God but trewe truthe were allowed.   *approved*
And wheither it worth or noght worth, the bileve is gret of truthe,
290 And an hope hangynge therinne to have a mede for his truthe;
For *Deus dicitur quasi dans vitam eternam suis, hoc est fidelibus.*
Et alibi, Si ambulavero in medio umbre mortis &c.

279–80 'The just man shall scarcely be saved' (I Pet 4: 18) on the day of judgment;
therefore—he *shall* be saved!
284*a* There came a divine fire, not burning but illuminating (*sc. at Pentecost*,
Acts 2: 3; *from Sarum Breviary*, Pentecost Antiphon (*Hort*)).
285 But a just man who never sinned or acted against his principles . . .
288 Righteous God would never / Would that righteous God should never permit
such genuine righteousness to go uncommended.
289–90 And whether it will (actually) turn out (so) or not, the faith (found) in a
just (pagan) is great (*or*, great trust can be put in truth) And (there is) a hope
depending on it (also) that he will have a reward for his righteousness.
291 For God is spoken of as giving eternal life to his own—that is to the faithful
(*cf.* Jn 17: 2); and elsewhere, For though I should walk in the midst of the shadow
of death [I will fear no evils] (Ps 22: 4) (*see* Addendum, p. 304).

275 on] L&r, C; in W.
283 Ac] R (=α; But F), C (*so* K-D);
For β.
288 trewe t.] R (=α; his wil F), C
(*so* K-D); truþe β.

289 worth (1)] L&r, C; be w. WHm
(C).
291 For] *Quia* g.
&c] R&r; *om* WLCr; *non timebo*
mala quoniam tu mecum es domine F.

The glose graunteth upon that vers a greet mede to truthe.   *gloss (C)*
And wit and wisdom,' quod that wye, 'was som tyme tresor
To kepe with a commune—no catel was holde bettre—
                                                rule; wealth, possession
295 And muche murthe and manhod'—and right with that he vanysshed.

Passus XIII

And I awaked therwith, witlees nerhande,   *almost out of my mind*
And as a freke that fey were, forth gan I walke   *man; doomed (to die)*
In manere of a mendynaunt many yer after,   *mendicant*
And of this metyng many tyme muche thought I hadde: *dream*
5 First how Fortune me failed at my mooste nede,   *greatest*
And how that Elde manaced me, myghte we evere mete;   *threatened*
And how that freres folwede folk that was riche,
And [peple] that was povere at litel pris thei sette,   *value*
And no corps in hir kirkyerd ne in hir kirk was buryed   *churchyard*
10 But quik he biquethe hem aught or sholde helpe quyte hir dettes;
                                                Unless (when) alive
And how this coveitise overcom clerkes and preestes;
And how that lewed men ben lad, but Oure Lord hem helpe,
Thorugh unkonnynge curatours to incurable peynes;   *ignorant parish priests*
And how that Ymaginatif in dremels me tolde   *dream*
15 Of Kynde and of his konnynge, and how curteis he is to bestes, *gracious*
And how lovynge he is to bestes on londe and on watre:
Leneth he no lif lasse ne moore;   *He gives no living creature*
The creatures that crepen of Kynde ben engendred;   *by; produced, created*
And sithen how Ymaginatif seide, ' *Vix iustus salvabitur*,'   *(see* XII 279 *above)*
20 And whan he hadde seid so, how sodeynliche he passed.

I lay down longe in this thoght, and at the laste I slepte;

292 *Either* The gloss upon that verse grants *or* The g. grants, on the strength of that v.
295 And (a source of) much happiness and human value.
10 Unless while still alive he bequeathes something to them or helps pay their debts,

Rubric Passus xiijus &c.
2 fey] BmBo, C (*so* K-D); faynt Cot;
  fere R (?=α; afeerd F); fre W&r
  (=β).
3 ȝere] RY, C (*so* K-D); a y. WLF.
8 peple] C (*so* K-D *p.* 93); folk W&r
  (poore f. F).

9 ne] L&r (*om* F); nor WCr.
10 hem] L&r, C; *om* WG.
  or ... qu.] LRY, C; to q. wiþ W.
14–20 β, *cf.* C; *om* α.
16 bestes] L&r; briddes W; eche lyf
  C (*so* K-D *p.* 152).
19 *iustus*] LY; *om* W.

And as Crist wolde ther com Conscience to conforte me that tyme,
And bad me come to his court—with Clergie sholde I dyne.　*manor-house*
And for Conscience of Clergie spak, I com wel the rather;
　　　　　　　　　　　　　　　　because; so much the sooner
25 And there I [merkede] a maister—what man he was I nyste—
　　　　　　　　　　　　　　　　observed; did not know
That lowe louted and loveliche to Scripture.　　*bowed; graciously*
　Conscience knew hym wel and welcomed hym faire;　*courteously*
Thei wesshen and wipeden and wenten to the dyner.　　*washed*
Ac Pacience in the paleis stood in pilgrymes clothes,　　*?courtyard*
30 And preyde mete *par charite* for a povere heremyte.　*for charity*
　Conscience called hym in, and curteisliche seide,
'Welcome, wye, go and wassh; thow shalt sitte soone.'
　This maister was maad sitte as for the mooste worthi,　*most honoured (guest)*
And thanne Clergie and Conscience and Pacience cam after.
35 Pacience and I were put to be mettes,　　　　*dinner-companions*
And seten bi oureselve at a side borde.　　　*sat; side-table*
　Conscience called after mete, and thanne cam Scripture
And served hem thus soone of sondry metes manye—
Of Austyn, of Ambrose, of alle the foure Evaungelistes:
Edentes et bibentes que apud eos sunt.
40　Ac this maister ne his man no maner flessh eten,
Ac thei eten mete of moore cost—mortrews and potages:　*stews; soups*
Of that men myswonne thei made hem wel at ese.　*wrongfully obtained*
Ac hir sauce was over sour and unsavourly grounde　*ill-tastingly*
In a morter, *Post mortem*, of many bitter peyne—　*after death*
45 But if thei synge for tho soules and wepe salte teris:
Vos qui peccata hominum comeditis, nisi pro eis lacrimas et
oraciones effuderitis, ea que in deliciis comeditis, in tormentis evometis.
　Conscience ful curteisly tho commaunded Scripture
Bifore Pacience breed to brynge and me that was his mette.　*companion*
He sette a sour loof toforn us and seide, '*Agite penitenciam*,'
　　　　　　　　　　　　　　　loaf; 'Do penance' (Mt 3: 2)
And siththe he drough us drynke: '*Dia perseverans*—

39a Eating and drinking such things as they have (Lk 10: 7).
45a You who feast upon men's sins—unless you pour out tears and prayers for
　them, you will vomit forth in torment what you eat with pleasure (*source*
　unknown).
49 Long-persevering (*cf.* Mt 10: 22) (*C*).

25 merkede] sei3 *All* B-MSS (*C*).　　　45a -fud-] GYOC²CCot, C (*so* K-D);
29 Ac] LRY; but GF; And W.　　　　　　-fund- W&r.
30 par] pur BF, C; for LR.　　　　　　47 mete] α (*cf.* C XV 55); macche WL;
35 mettes] α, C (*so* K-D); macches β.　　make GY.
36 a] L&r, C; þe w.　　　　　　　　　49 drough] L&r, C; brou3te w.
39 of a.] LR, C; and of w.　　　　　　　*Dia*] WLR, ?C; *diu* GO&c, some
40 ne] L&r; nor W; and Cr (*C*).　　　　C-MSS (*C*).
44 many] LR, C; m. a W.

50 As longe,' quod he, 'as lif and lycame may dure.'   *body; last, endure*
 'Here is propre service,' quod Pacience, 'ther fareth no prince bettre!'

excellent

 And he broughte us of *Beati quorum* of *Beatus vir*res makyng,
 And thanne he broughte us forth a mees of oother mete, of *Miserere mei, Deus*

dish; food

 Et quorum tecta sunt peccata
 In a dissh of derne shrifte, *Dixi et confitebor tibi.*   *secret confession*
55 'Bryng Pacience som pitaunce,' pryveliche quod Conscience;

portion; quietly

 And thanne hadde Pacience a pitaunce, *Pro hac orabit ad te*
 omnis sanctus in tempore oportuno.
 And Conscience conforted us, and carped us murye tales:

entertained; cheerful words

 Cor contritum et humiliatum, Deus, non despicies.
 Pacience was proude of that propre service,
 And made hym murthe with his mete; ac I mornede evere, *sulked constantly*
60· For this doctour on the heighe dees drank wyn so faste: *daïs; continuously*
 Ve vobis qui potentes estis ad bibendum vinum!
 He eet manye sondry metes, mortrews and puddynges,
 Wombe cloutes and wilde brawen and egges yfryed with grece.

Tripes; brawn; fat

 Thanne seide I to myself so Pacience it herde,
 'It is noght foure dayes that this freke, bifore the deen of Poules,

dean of St Paul's

65 Preched of penaunces that Paul the Apostle suffrede—
 In fame et frigore and flappes of scourges: *blows from*
 Ter cesus sum et a Iudeis quinquies quadragenas &c;
 Ac o word thei overhuppen at ech a tyme that thei preche *one; skip*
 That Poul in his Pistle to al the peple tolde—
 Periculum est in falsis fratribus!'

52 Blessed are they whose [iniquities are forgiven: and whose sins are covered] (Ps 31: 1); Blessed is the man [to whom the Lord hath not imputed sins] (Ps 31: 2).
53 Have mercy on me, O God (Ps 50: 1); *for 53a see 52 above.*
54 I said: I will confess [against myself my injustice to the Lord] (Ps 31: 5).
56 For this [*sc.* forgiveness] shall every one that is holy pray to thee in a seasonable time (Ps 31: 6).
57a A contrite and humbled heart, O God, thou wilt not despise (Ps 50: 19).
60a Woe to you that are mighty to drink wine (Is 5: 22).
66–66a, 69 In hunger and thirst . . .; Thrice was I beaten [with rods] . . . Of the Jews five times did I receive forty stripes [save one] . . .; [In] peril[s from] false brethren (II Cor 11: 27, 25, 24, 26).

50 he] aOC², C (*so* K-D); I W&r (*om* Cot).
 lif] R (=a; *om* F), C (*so* K-D); I lyue W&r.
52 *Trsp. with* 53 *All* B-MSS; *re-arr.* K-D *p.* 189.

53 vs] WLMR; *om rest.*
53a *div. fr.* 54 *after* dissh *All* B-MSS *exc.* F; *re-div.* K-D *p.* 189.

70   (Holi Writ bit men be war—I wol noght write it here   *bids*
    In Englissh, on aventure it sholde be reherced to ofte *lest perchance; spoken*
    And greve therwith that goode men ben—ac gramariens shul rede:
                                  those who are; scholars

Unusquisque a fratre se custodiat, quia, ut dicitur,
periculum est in falsis fratribus.

    Ac I wiste nevere freke that as a frere yede bifore men on Englissh *went*
    Taken it for his teme, and telle it withouten glosyng! *theme (in preaching)*
75 They prechen that penaunce is profitable to the soule,
    And what meschief and maleese Crist for man tholede). *pain; suffered*
      'Ac this Goddes gloton,' quod I, 'with hise grete chekes,
    Hath no pite on us povere; he parfourneth yvele. *acts badly*
    That he precheth, he preveth noght,' to Pacience I tolde, *lives out*
80 And wisshed witterly, with wille ful egre, *truly; fierce*
    That disshes and doublers bifore this doctour *platters*
    Were molten leed in his mawe, and Mahoun amyddes! *stomach; the Devil (C)*
    'I shal jangle to this jurdan with his juste wombe *jordan; bottle-belly*
    To telle me what penaunce is, of which he preched rather!' *earlier, before*
85   Pacience parceyved what I thoughte, and [preynte] on me to be stille,
                                    winked at
    And seide, 'Thow shalt see thus soone, whan he may na moore,
                              is capable of (eating)
    He shal have a penaunce in his paunche and puffe at ech a worde,
                            penance / pain; belch
    And thanne shullen his guttes gothele, and he shal galpen after; *rumble; yawn*
    For now he hath dronken so depe he wole devyne soone *expound*
90 And preven it by hir Pocalips and passion of Seint Avereys
                         Apocalypse; ?St Greed (C)
    That neither bacon ne braun ne blancmanger ne mortrews
                         brawn; chicken stew
    Is neither fissh ne flessh but fode for a penaunt.
    And thanne shal he testifie of a trinite, and take his felawe to witnesse
                         trinity, triad
    What he fond in a f[or]el after a freres lyvyng; *box concerning*

72–72a And thereby offend those (friars *sugg.* K–D) who *are* good men—but those
    who understand Latin shall read (it): 'Let every man guard himself from a
    brother [=friar], because, as they say, there is danger in false *brethren*.'
83 I shall argue with this chamber-pot, with his bottle-like belly (Sk).

72 þat, ben] L&r; *om* w; *see* K-D
    p. 147.
    rede] L&r; redde W.
79 he] and R (?=α; þus & F), ?C (C).
    to P.] compacience ?C (C).
80 witt.] L&r, C; ful w. w.
81 b. þ. doc.] R (?=α; on dees b.þ.d.
    F); b. þ. ilke d. β (*cf.* K-D *p.* 194).
84 To . . . me] And apose hym C (*so*
    K-D *p.* 93).

85 pr. on] *conj* K-D *p.* 195 *after* Sk
    ad loc; *cf.* 112 *below*); wynked on
    β; bad α (b. holde F).
    to] *om* RFCrCot.
91 he (2)] α, ?C; *om* β, *most* C-MSS.
92 ne] RY, C (*so* Sk); nor W; no L.
93 a] LRY, C; þe WF.
94 forel] C (*so* K-D); frayel W&r;
    sell F (C).

95 And but the first leef be lesyng, leve me nevere after!   *lies; believe*
And thanne is tyme to take and to appose this doctour
Of Dowel and Dobet and if Dobest be any penaunce.'
And I sat stille as Pacience seide, and thus soone this doctour,
As rody as a rose ruddede hise chekes,   *red; flushed*
100 Coughed and carped; and Conscience hym herde,   *spoke*
And tolde hym of a trinite, and toward us he loked.
'What is Dowel, sire doctour?' quod I; 'is Dobest any penaunce?'
'Dowel?' quod this doctour—and drank after—
'Do noon yvel to thyn evencristen—nought by thi power.'
105 'By this day, sire doctour,' quod I, 'thanne [in Dowel be ye noght]!
For ye han harmed us two in that ye eten the puddyng,
Mortrews and oother mete—and we no morsel hadde.
And if ye fare so in youre fermerye, ferly me thynketh   *infirmary*
But cheeste be ther charite sholde be, and yonge children dorste pleyne!
    strife; if
110 I wolde permute my penaunce with youre—for I am in point to dowel.'
    exchange; yours; ready
Thanne Conscience ful curteisly a contenaunce he made,   *gave a look*
And preynte upon Pacience to preie me to be stille,
And seide hymself, 'Sire doctour, and it be youre wille,
What is Dowel and Dobet? Ye dyvynours knoweth.'   *theologians, divines*
115 'Dowel?' quod this doctour; 'do as clerkes techeth;
And Dobet is he that techeth and travailleth to teche othere;
And Dobest doth hymself so as he seith and precheth:
Qui facit et docuerit magnus vocabitur in regno celorum.'
'Now thow, Clergie,' quod Conscience, 'carpe us what is Dowel.'   *say*
'I have sevene sones,' he seide, 'serven in a castel
120 Ther the lord of lif wonyeth, to leren hem what is Dowel.   *learn*
Til I se tho sevene and myself acorde
I am unhardy,' quod he, 'to any wight to preven it.   *lack the confidence*
For oon Piers the Plowman hath impugned us alle,
And set alle sciences at a sop save love one;   *morsel; only*
125 And no text ne taketh to mayntene his cause   *support his position*

117a [But] he that shall do and teach, he shall be called great in the kingdom of heaven (Mt 5: 19).

95 þe] L&r, C; he w.
leef] OC²Cot, C (*so* K-D *p.* 157);
lyue/lyne WLR.
97 best] L&r; wel W; bet C.
99 ruddud] Hm, C (*so* K-D); gan
rodye F; rubbede W&r.
102 dob.] α, C (*so* K-D); dowel L&r
(=β; it W).
103 dronk a.] R (=α; d. anon þerea.
F), C (d.] he d. C) (*so* K-D); took
þe cuppe and d. β.

104 Do] L&r, C; Is do WCr.
105 in . . . n.] *re-arr.* K-D *p.* 115; be
y. n. in d. W&r.
111 ful] α, C; *om* β.
he] LRFMHm, C; *om* W&r.
118 c. vs] Cot; ca*rpest* W&r; carpe
C (*so* K-D).
120 hem] YG; hym LRM; *om* W
(C).

But *Dilige Deum* and *Domine quis habitabit;*
And seith that Dowel and Dobet arn two infinites,
Whiche infinites with a feith fynden out Dobest,
Which shal save mannes soule—thus seith Piers the Plowman.'
130 'I kan noght heron,' quod Conscience, 'ac I knowe wel Piers.   *about this*
He wol noght ayein Holy Writ speken, I dar wel undertake.
Thanne passe we over til Piers come and preve this in dede.
                                                            demonstrate this in action
Pacience hath be in many place, and paraunter knoweth   *perhaps*
That no clerk ne kan, as Crist bereth witnesse:
Pacientes vincunt &c.'
135   'At youre preiere,' quod Pacience tho, 'so no man displese hym:
Disce,' quod he, '*doce; dilige inimicos.*
Disce, and Dowel; *doce,* and Dobet;
Dilige, and Dobest—[do] thus taughte me ones
A lemman that I lovede—Love was hir name.
140 "With wordes and with werkes," quod she, "and wil of thyn herte
Thow love leelly thi soule al thi lif tyme.
And so thow lere the to lovye, for the Lordes love of hevene,
Thyn enemy in alle wise eveneforth with thiselve.   *equally*
Cast coles on his heed of alle kynde speche;   (Prov 25: 22; Rom 12: 20)
145 Bothe with werkes and with wordes fonde his love to wynne,   *attempt*
And leye on him thus with love til he laughe on the;   *belabour*
And but he bowe for this betyng, blynd mote he worthe!" *submit; become*
    'Ac for to fare thus with thi frend—folie it were;   *behave, act*
For he that loveth thee leelly, litel of thyne coveiteth.
150 Kynde love coveiteth noght no catel but speche.
With half a laumpe lyne in Latyn, *Ex vi transicionis,*   *lamp*
I bere ther, in a bou[s]te, faste ybounde Dowel,   *box (for Host) (C)*
In a signe of the Saterday that sette first the kalender,
                                                    betokening; established
And al the wit of the Wodnesday of the nexte wike after; *?meaning; week*
155 The myddel of the moone is the myght of bothe.   *full; power*
And herwith am I welcome ther I have it with me.
    'Undo it—lat this doctour deme if Dowel be therinne;   *judge*

126 [Thou shalt] love [the Lord thy] God . . . (Mt 22: 37); Lord, who shall dwell
    [in thy tabernacle]? (Ps 14: 1) (C).
134a The patient overcome (*cf.* Mt 10: 22).
136 Learn, teach, love your enemies.
150 True affection desires nothing of yours but your conversation.
151 From the power of transitivity (C).

127 seiþ] demeþ *conj* K-D *p.* 200.
130 wel] *om* gM (*so* K-D *p.* 144).
133 kn.] L&r (he k. F); mouþed w.
135 At] LRF; Ac W.
138 do thus] þus W&r (*om* OC²) (C).
142 þe (2)] L&r; oure W.
145 werkes, wordes] *sg.* g (*cf.* C).

152 per . . . b.] *rec.* K-D *p.* 186.
    in] Cr; Inne W&r.
    a b.] *conj* K-D; aboute
    WCrLRFM; abounte HmY; abewte
    O&r (C).
155 is] L&r; as w.
    my3.] L&r; nyght WHmCB.

For, by hym that me made, myghte nevere poverte,
Misese ne mischief ne man with his tonge,   *Illness; pain, suffering*
160 Coold, ne care, ne compaignye of theves,
Ne neither hete, ne hayl, ne noon helle pouke,   *fiend of hell*
Ne neither fuyr, ne flood, ne feere of thyn enemy,   *fire; fear*
Tene thee any tyme, and thow take it with the:
Caritas nichil timet.
   'And ek, have God my soule! and thow wilt it crave,   *if; demand*
165 Ther nys neither emperour ne emperesse, erl ne baroun,
Pope ne patriark, that pure reson ne shal make thee
Maister of alle tho men thorugh myght of this redels—   *power; riddle*
Nought thorugh wicchecraft but thorugh wit; and thow wilt thiselve
Do kyng and quene and alle the comune after   *Make*
170 Yyve thee al that thei may yyve, as thee for best yemere,   *guardian (C)*
And as thow demest wil thei do alle hir dayes after: *judge, pronounce*
Pacientes vincunt.'
   'It is but a dido,' quod this doctour, 'a disours tale!

                           an old story; minstrel's
Al the wit of this world and wight mennes strengthe *wisdom; strong, energetic*
Kan noght [par]formen a pees bitwene the Pope and hise enemys,

                                 establish (C)
175 Ne bitwene two Cristene kynges kan no wight pees make
Profitable to either peple'—and putte the table fro hym,   *(he) pushed*
And took Clergie and Conscience to conseil, as it were,   *privately apart*
That Pacience tho most passe—'for pilgrymes konne wel lye.'

                    (Saying) that; should go away
   Ac Conscience carped loude and curteisliche seide,   *spoke up*
180 'Frendes, fareth wel,' and faire spak to Clergie,   *fare well; pleasantly*
'For I wol go with this gome, if God wol yeve me grace,
And be pilgrym with Pacience til I have preved moore.'   *experienced*
   'What!' quod Clergie to Conscience, 'are ye coveitous nouthe   *now*
After yeresyeves or yiftes, or yernen to rede redels?

                       presents; long; interpret
185 I shal brynge yow a Bible, a book of the olde lawe,
And lere yow, if yow like, the leeste point to knowe,   *teach; minutest*
That Pacience the pilgrym parfitly knew nevere.'   *thoroughly*
   'Nay, by Crist!' quod Conscience to Clergie, 'God thee foryelde.   *repay*

163*a* Fear is not in charity (1 Jn 4: 18) (*C*).
172 It's just the tale of Dido—an old romancer's yarn!

162 noither] L&r; *om* W.
164–171*a* α (*cf.* C); *om* β.
164 ek; it] e. so; love F.
165 erl] *so* K-D; neyþer E. F; erl
  kynge R.
166 *Div. from* 167 *after* make R.
  m. þee] the m. F; m. R.
167 Mayster] F; þe m. R.
169 *Line om* F.

170 þe for] þou f. F; for þe *conj* Sk
  (*C*).
171 *Line om* F.
171*a v.*] F; *v. &c* R.
174 per] C (*so* K-D *p.* 94); con *All*
  B-MSS.
  þe p.] L&r; *om* W.
178 þo] L&r; þow WCr¹M; *om* F.

For al that Pacience me profreth, proud am I litel;
190 Ac the wil of the wye and the wil of folk here   *will, attitude*
Hath meved my mood to moorne for my synnes.   *stirred my heart*
The goode wil of a wight was nevere bought to the fulle: *'is beyond price'*
For ther nys no tresour therto to a trewe wille.   *(compared) to*
   'Hadde noght Marie Maudeleyne moore for a box of salve   *ointment*
195 Than Zacheus for he seide, "*Dimidium bonorum meorum do pauperibus*,"
And the poore widewe for a peire of mytes   *couple of pennies*
Than alle tho that offrede into *gazophilacium?*'   *the treasury (Lk 21: 1–4)*
   Thus curteisliche Conscience congeyed first the frere,   *took leave of*
And sithen softeliche he seide in Clergies ere,
200 'Me were levere, by Oure Lord, and I lyve sholde,   *I'd prefer; if*
Have pacience parfitliche than half thi pak of bokes!'
   Clergie of Conscience no congie wolde take,   *farewell*
But seide ful sobreliche, 'Thow shalt se the tyme   *gravely*
Whan thow art wery forwalked, wilne me to counseille.'
                                    tired with walking (and) want
205 'That is sooth,' seide Conscience, 'so me God helpe!
If Pacience be oure partyng felawe and pryve with us bothe,
                                  partner, sharer; intimate
Ther nys wo in this world that we ne sholde amende,
And conformen kynges to pees, and alle kynnes londes—
                          dispose; every kind of nation
Sarsens and Surre, and so forth alle the Jewes—   *Moslems; ?pagans (C)*
210 Turne into the trewe feith and intil oon bileve.'   *convert; one religion*
   'That is sooth,' quod Clergie, 'I se what thow menest.
I shall dwelle as I do, my devoir to shewe,   *duty*
And confermen fauntekyns oother folk ylered
                            confirm children; or; instructed
Til Pacience have preved thee and parfit thee maked.'   *tried, tested*
215 Conscience tho with Pacience passed, pilgrymes as it were.
Thanne hadde Pacience, as pilgrymes han, in his poke vitailles: *bag; food*
Sobretee and symple speche and soothfast bileve,   *humble; genuine, real*
To conforte hym and Conscience if thei come in place
                            strengthen; should come
There unkyndenesse and coveitise is, hungry contrees bothe.

220   And as thei wente by the weye, of Dowel thei carped;   *talked*
Thei mette with a mynstral, as me tho thoughte.

195 The half of my goods I give to the poor (Lk 19: 8).

193 nys] WLR; is *rest.*
    þerto] L&*r*; forsoþe W.
194 marie] αG; *om* W&*r* (=β).
196 for] purely f. *conj* K-D *p.* 199.
204 for] L&*r*; of W.
    wilne] L&*r*; wille w.
205 seyde] LR; quod WF.

211 quod] seide *sugg.* K-D *p.* 195 (*cf.*
    205 *above*).
213 ooþer] *em.* K-D *p.* 194; and o.
    All B-MSS.
220 of] β, C; and of α.
    þei (2)] *om* α.

Pacience apposed hym first and preyde he sholde telle   *questioned*
To Conscience what craft he kouthe, and to what contree he wolde.
    trade; was going
  'I am a mynstral,' quod that man, 'my name is *Activa Vita.*   *Active Life*
225 Al ydel ich hatie, for of Actif is my name,   *idle people; hate; from A.*
A wafrer, wol ye wite, and serve manye lordes—   *wafer-seller*
And fewe robes I fonge or furrede gownes.   *obtain; furred*
Couthe I lye and do men laughe, thanne lacchen I sholde   *make; get*
Outher mantel or moneie amonges lordes mynstrals.   *Either*
230 Ac for I kan neither taboure ne trompe ne telle no gestes,   *stories*
Farten ne fithelen at festes, ne harpen,   *fiddle; play the harp*
Jape ne jogele ne gentilliche pipe,   *Jest; juggle; expertly*
Ne neither saille ne sautrie ne synge with the gyterne,
    dance; play psaltery, gittern
I have no goode giftes of thise grete lordes   *from*
235 For no breed that I brynge forth—save a benyson on the Sonday,
    except; blessing
Whan the preest preieth the peple hir Paternoster to bidde   *asks; pray, say*
For Piers the Plowman and that hym profit waiten—
    those (who); look to (his)
And that am I, Actif, that ydelnesse hatie;
For alle trewe travaillours and tiliers of the erthe,   *labourers; tillers*
240 Fro Mighelmesse to Mighelmesse I fynde hem with wafres.
    Michaelmas (29 Sept); provide
  'Beggeris and bidderis of my breed craven,   *desire*
Faitours and freres and folk with brode crounes.   *i.e. tonsured clerics*
I fynde payn for the Pope and provendre for his palfrey,   *bread; fodder*
And I hadde nevere of hym, have God my trouthe,
245 Neither provendre ne personage yet of the Popes yifte,
    prebend (pun); parsonage
Save a pardon with a peis of leed and two polles amyddes!
    Only; lump; heads (C)
Hadde ich a clerc that couthe write I wolde caste hym a bille   *draw up; note*
That he sente me under his seel a salve for the pestilence,
And that his blessynge and hise bulles bocches myghte destruye:
    plague-sores (C).
In nomine meo demonia eicient et super egros manus imponent et bene habebunt.
250 And thanne wolde I be prest to the peple, paast for to make,   *prompt; pastry*
And buxom and busy aboute breed and drynke   *willing*
For hym and for alle hise, founde I that his pardoun   *if I were to find*

245 Neither a clerical living nor a parsonage that lies in the Pope's gift.
249a In my name they shall cast out devils; . . . they shall lay their hands upon the
    sick; and they shall recover (Mk 16: 17, 18).

222 first] W&r; þoo OC²; *om* F, C   228 and] α, C (*so* K-D); to β.
    he] W&r, C; hym he LMR; hym.   229 lordes] LR, C; l. or W.
    F.   233 sautre] C (*so* K-D); saute WLR.
    tel(len)] FCr, C; hem t. W&r.   240 with] LR; w. my W.
225 ydel] L&r; ydelnesse WHmF.   245 the] L&r; *om* WG.

Mighte lechen a man—as I bileve it sholde.
For sith he hath the power that Peter hadde, he hath the pot with the salve:
Argentum et aurum non est michi: quod autem habeo,
tibi do: In nomine Domini surge et ambula.

255 'Ac if myght of myracle hym faille, it is for men ben noght worthi
To have the grace of God, and no gilt of the Pope.   *fault*
For may no blessynge doon us boote but if we wile amende,
Ne mannes masse make pees among Cristene peple,
Til pride be pureliche fordo, and that thorugh payn defaute.

                                                       destroyed; lack of bread
260 For er I have breed of mele, ofte moot I swete,   *from grain; sweat (in toil)*
And er the commune have corn ynough many a cold morwenyng;
So, er my wafres be ywroght, muche wo I tholye.   *made; hardship; endure*
'Al Londoun, I leve, liketh wel my wafres,
And louren whan thei lakken hem; it is noght longe ypassed   *scowl; lack*
265 There was a careful commune whan no cart com to towne
                                                      distressed population
With bake breed fro Stratford; tho gonnen beggeris wepe,
And werkmen were agast a lite—this wole be thought longe;
                                                    afraid; remembered
In the date of Oure Drighte, in a drye Aprill,   *year; Lord*
A thousand and thre hundred, twies thritty and ten,   *i.e.* 1370
270 My wafres there were gesene, whan Chichestre was maire.'
                                         scarce; mayor (of London) (C)
I took greet kepe, by Crist, and Conscience bothe,   *careful note*
Of Haukyn the Actif Man, and how he was yclothed.
He hadde a cote of Cristendom as Holy Kirke bileveth;
Ac it was moled in many places with manye sondry plottes—   *stained; patches*
275 Of pride here a plot, and there a plot of unbuxom speche,
                                                    disobedient, rebellious
Of scornyng and of scoffyng and of unskilful berynge;
                                                  unreasonable conduct
As in apparaill and in porte proud amonges the peple;   *demeanour, bearing*
Ootherwise than he hath with herte or sighte shewynge;
Hym wilnyng that alle men wende he were that he is noght,

254*a* [But Peter said]: 'Silver and gold I have none; but what I have, I give thee. In the name of the Lord [Jesus &c *Vulg*], arise and walk (Acts 3: 6).
278 Pretending to be, inwardly and outwardly, something that he isn't.

254 *Thus in* C; *so* K-D *p.* 94; *as two lines divided after* hadde W&r (*after* selfe Cr²³).
    hadde] hymself h. W&r (*trsp.* Cr²³).
    salue] s. sooþly as me þynkeþ W&r (so.] truly Cr²³).
256 þe (1)] β, C; no α.
    þe (2)] L&r; *om* W.
259 þat] L&r (?=β), C; alle R (?=α); *om* WCrMF.

266 bake] α (*so* Sk); *om* β; *see* K-D p. 147.
269 thretty] LR; twenty W&r.
271 grete] α (*so* K-D); good β.
278-9 K-D *div. after* Hym; *but cf.* C VI 32 (Me wilnynge).
278 he] L&r; he hym W.
279 wilnynge] R (?=α; wenynge F), ?C; willyng β.

280 Forwhy he bosteth and braggeth with manye bolde othes; *For which reason*
And inobedient to ben undernome of any lif lyvynge; *criticized by*
And so singuler by hymself as to sighte of the peple
Was noon swich as hymself, ne noon so pope holy;
Yhabited as an heremyte, an ordre by hymselve— *Dressed (C)*
285 Religion saunz rule and resonable obedience; *without*
Lakkynge lettrede men and lewed men bothe; *Reproaching, criticizing*
In likynge of lele lif and a liere in soule;
With inwit and with outwit ymagynen and studie
As best for his body be to have a bold name;
290 And entremetten hym over al ther he hath noght to doone;
  interfere; has no business
Wilnynge that men wende his wit were the beste, *Desiring that people think*
Or for his crafty konnynge or of clerkes the wisest,
Or strengest on stede, or styvest under girdel, *horse; most potent, virile*
And lovelokest to loken on and lelest of werkes, *handsomest; most trusty*
295 And noon so holy as he ne of lif clennere, *more chaste*
Or feirest of feitures, of forme and of shafte, *features; figure*
And most sotil of song other sleyest of hondes, *skilled in; most deft*
And large to lene lo[o]s therby to cacche; *praise; obtain*
And if he gyveth ought to povere gomes, [go] telle what he deleth;
  men; gives (as alms)
300 Povere of possession in purs and in cofre, *coffer, chest*
And as a lyoun on to loke and lordlich of speche; *lion; arrogant; haughty*
Boldest of beggeris, a bostere that noght hath,
In towne and in tavernes tales to telle
And segge thyng that he nevere seigh and for sothe sweren it,
  say; saw; truth
305 Of dedes that he nevere dide demen and bosten, *About; pronounce; boast*
And of werkes that he wel dide witnesse and siggen, *testify; declare*

284–5 . . . a religious order composed of only one member, Without any rule or
rationally ordained obedience to superiors.
287 [Giving the impression] of desiring to live honestly . . .
288–9 With his faculties of intelligence and sense given over to imagining and
brooding over What is best to do in order to acquire a reputation for physical
(?sexual) prowess.
298 Generous in giving, as a means of winning praise.

282 LRF, C; *run together with* 283
W&r.
  so] L&r (goo F); noon so WCr.
  as . . . p.] LRF, C (as to] in F);
  om W&r.
283 Was . . . hyms.] LRF, C; *om*
W&r.
  none (2)] L&r, C; *om* WCr.
  pope] RCrG, C (*so* Sk); pomp
WHmL.
285 and] L&r; or W.
289 bolde] α (*so* K-D *p.* 147); badde β.

291 -nyng] LR, C; -ynge WF.
292–8 α (*cf.* C VI 42–8); *lines om* β.
292 þe] he were þe F.
295 ne] ne non F.
296 forme . . . sh.] face ne of forme F.
298 loos] *sugg.* K-D; losse R (*l.* soph.
  F).
299 go telle] telle *All* B-MSS (*C*).
300 coffre] LR; c. boþe W&r.
301 on] β; *om* α.

'Lo! if ye leve me noght, or that I lye wenen,   *believe; suppose*
Asketh at hym or at hym, and he yow kan telle
What I suffrede and seigh and somtymes hadde,
310 And what I kouthe and knew, and what kyn I com of.'
Al he wolde that men wiste of werkes and of wordes
Which myghte plese the peple and preisen hymselve: *redound to his credit*
Si hominibus placerem, Christi servus non essem. Et alibi:
Nemo potest duobus dominis servire.
   'By Crist!' quod Conscience tho, 'thi beste cote, Haukyn,
Hath manye moles and spottes—it moste ben ywasshe!'   *stains*
315 'Ye, whoso toke hede,' quod Haukyn, 'bihynde and bifore,
                          observed; in front
What on bak and what on body half and by the two sides—   *front part*
Men sholde fynde manye frounces and manye foule plottes.'
                          creases; patches
   And he torned hym as tyd, and thanne took I hede;
                   quickly; looked closely
It was fouler bi fele fold than it first semed.   *many times*
320 It was bidropped with wrathe and wikkede wille,   *spattered; evil intent*
With envye and yvel speche entisynge to fighte,   *hostility; provoking*
Lying and lakkynge and leve tonge to chide;   *tongue willing to quarrel*
Al that he wiste wikked by any wight, tellen it,   *bad about*
And blame men bihynde hir bak and bidden hem meschaunce;
                   ask for bad luck for them
325 And that he wiste by Wille, [to Watte tellen it],
And that Watte wiste, Wille wiste it after,
And made of frendes foes thorugh a fals tonge:
'Or with myght of mouth or thorugh mannes strengthe
                 Either; slander; violence
Avenged me fele tymes, other frete myselve withinne   *gnawed, fretted*
330 As a shepsteres shere, ysherewed men and cursed hem.'   *tailor's scissors*
Cuius malediccione os plenum est et amaritudine; sub lingua
eius labor et dolor. Et alibi: Filii hominum dentes eorum
arma et sagitte et lingua eorum gladius acutus.

312*a* If I yet pleased men, I should not be the servant of Christ (Gal 1: 10); And in
    another place: No man can serve two masters (Mt 6: 24).
330 As with [*lit.* like] a tailor's scissors, and damned men and cursed them.
330*a* His mouth is full of cursing, and of bitterness, [and of deceit]: under his
    tongue are labour and sorrow (Ps 9B(10): 7). And in another place: The sons of
    men, whose teeth are weapons and arrows: and their tongue a sharp sword (Ps
    56: 5).

322 lak.] α (*so* K-D); laughynge β.
325 to . . . it] *so* K-D *p.* 94; to watekyn
    he tolde it C; tellen it watte WLR
    (w.] to w. R).
328 of] L&*r*; or G; or with W.
    mannes] L&*r*, C; mennes WHm.
329 *So div.* K-D *after* C; *div. from*

330 *after* selue *All* B-MSS.
    *A*uenged] R (?=α; but y avenge F),
    C; Auenge β.
330 men . . . hem] Hm; hem *om*
    W&*r*; m.] man W; men . . . h.] y
    grynte F; myn euencristene C
    (*so* K-D *p.* 90) (C).
330*a Et . . . ac.*] β, C (*Et al. om* C); *om* α.

'Ther is no lif that I lovye lastynge any while; *person; for any length of time*
For tales that I telle no man trusteth to me.
And whan I may noght have the maistrie, swich malencolie I take
             come out on top
That I cacche the crampe, the cardiacle som tyme, *heart-pains*
335 Or an ague in swich an angre, and som tyme a fevere *violent access*
That taketh me al a twelvemonthe, til that I despise *afflicts*
Lechecraft of Oure Lord and leve on a wicche, *Medicine (C); believe in*
And seye that no clerc ne kan—ne Crist, as I leve— *has knowledge*
To the Soutere of Southwerk, or of Shordych Dame Emme,
        (Compared) to; Cobbler (C)
340 And seye that [God ne] Goddes word gaf me nevere boote,
But thorugh a charme hadde I chaunce and my chief heele.'
        luck; health; recovery
I waitede wisloker, and thanne was it soilled *looked more carefully*
With likynge of lecherie as by lokynge of his eighe.
For ech a maide that he mette, he made hire a signe
345 Semynge to synneward, and somtyme he gan taste *suggesting s.; touch*
Aboute the mouth or bynethe bigynneth to grope,
Til eitheres wille wexeth kene, and to the werke yeden,
        desire; sharp; act; they went
As wel fastyng dayes as Fridaies and forboden nyghtes, *forbidden (C)*
And as lef in Lente as out of Lente, alle tymes yliche: *willingly; alike*
350 Swiche werkes with hem were nevere out of seson, *season*
Til thei myghte na moore—and thanne hadde murye tales, *sexy talk*
And how that lecchours lovye laughen and japen, *jest*
And of hir harlotrye and horedom in hir elde tellen. *old age*
Thanne Pacience parceyved, of pointes his cote *with specks*
355 Was colomy thorugh coveitise and unkynde desiryng. *grimy*
Moore to good than to God the gome his love caste, *possessions; directed*
And ymagynede how he it myghte have
With false mesures and met, and [mid] fals witnesse *measure; with*
Lened for love of the wed and looth to do truthe, *pledge*
360 And awaited thorugh w[itte]s wyes to bigile,

354–5 that his coat was grimy with specks (of sin) . . .
359–60 Lent (money simply out of) desire (to gain) the security (deposited by the
 borrower), and through no love of honest dealing (for its own sake), And sought
 with cunning ingenuity opportunities for cheating people.

331 I *louye*] L&r; me loueþ WCr.
333 swich] wFM, C; which R; with
 Lg.
334 þe (2)] L&r, C; and þe WBF.
340 God ne] no W&r; none of B;
 om HmF (C).
345 tyme] *om* F, C (*so* K-D).
348 wel] a, C (*so* K-D); w. in β.
 as] g, C (*so* K-D); and W&r.
 and] L&r (& other G), C; as W.
349 lef] a, C (*so* K-D); wel β.
351 had] L&r *exc* F, C; *om* w.
354 his] LR; of h. *rest* (h.]þis w).
355 Was] L&r; were M; That were W.
358 Wiþ] Thoruȝ *conj* K-D *p*. 200.
 mid] wiþ *All* B-MSS.
360 wittes] *so* K-D; whitus R; his
 wit F; which W&r (=β).
 wyes] *so* K-D; weyus R (?=α;
 fele wyȝes F); wey β.

And menged his marchaundise and made a good moustre:

mixed; adulterated; show

'The worst withinne was—a greet wit I let it!   *splendid device; thought*

And if my neghebore hadde an hyne, or any beest ellis,   *servant*

Moore profitable than myn, manye sleightes I made   *tricks*

365 How I myghte have it—al my wit I caste;   *exercised*

And but I it hadde by oother wey, at the laste I stale it,   *stole*

Or pryveliche his purs shook, unpikede hise lokes;   *picked; locks*

Or by nyghte or by daye, aboute was ich evere   *Either*

Thorough gile to gaderen the good that ich have.   *amass; wealth*

370 'If I yede to the plowgh, I pynched so narwe   *encroached*

That a foot lond or a forow fecchen I wolde   *foot of land; furrow*

Of my nexte neghebore, nymen of his erthe;   *From; take*

And if I rope, overreche, or yaf hem reed that ropen

reaped; gave advice to those

To seise to me with hir sikel that I ne sew nevere.   *appropriate; what; sowed*

375 'And whoso borwed of me aboughte the tyme   *had to pay for*

With presentes pryvely, or paide som certeyn—   *secretly; some definite sum*

So wolde he or noght wolde he, wynnen I wolde;   *make a profit*

And bothe to kith and to kyn unkynde of that ich hadde.

'And whoso cheped my chaffare, chiden I wolde

if anyone bought my wares

380 But he profrede to paie a peny or tweyne

Moore than it was worth, and yet wolde I swere   *further still*

That it coste me muche moore—swoor manye othes.

'In haly daies at holy chirche, whan ich herde masse   *holy days*

Hadde I nevere wille, woot God, witterly to biseche   *truly*

385 Mercy for my mysdedes, that I ne moorned moore   *lamented*

For losse of good, leve me, than for likames giltes;   *wealth; sins of my body*

As, if I hadde dedly synne doon, I dredde noght that so soore

As whan I lened and leved it lost or longe er it were paied.

So if I kidde any kyndenesse myn evencristen to helpe,   *showed*

390 Upon a cruwel coveitise my conscience gan hange.   *See (C)*

'And if I sente over see my servaunts to Brugges,   *Bruges (C)*

Or into Prucelond my prentis my profit to waiten,

Prussia; apprentice; see to

370–4 If I went ploughing, I encroached so closely that I would obtain for myself a
foot or a furrow's width of land (from my neighbour's adjacent strip) and take
from him his (very) earth; and if I was reaping, I would reach across (to my
neighbour's corn) or give instructions to the reapers to appropriate to me with
their sickles corn I had never sown.

363 an] α, C (*so* K-D); any β.
372b–373a β, C; *om* α.
373 rope] LCM, C; *repe* W&r.
375 whoso] what body *conj* K-D
    p. 195 (*but cf.* 196, 253).
377 walde he (1)] L&r; he w. W.
    he (2)] LM; *om* W.

383 In] L&r (& in F), C; On W.
386 for] R (?=α), C (*so* K-D p.
    168*n*); for my βF.
390 my cons.] α (*so* K-D); myn herte
    β (C).

To marchaunden with moneie and maken here eschaunges,   *do business; monetary exchanges*
Mighte nevere me conforte in the mene tyme   *meanwhile*
395 Neither masse ne matynes, ne none maner sightes;   *no kind of*
Ne nevere penaunce parfournede ne Paternoster seide   *(I) never performed*
That my mynde ne was moore on my good in a doute   *in (my) anxiety*
Than in the grace of God and hise grete helpes.'
Ubi thesaurus tuus, ibi et cor tuum.
   Yet that glotoun with grete othes his garnement hadde soiled
   Further; garment
400 And foule beflobered it, as with fals speche,   *foully muddied*
As, there no nede ne was, Goddes name an idel—   *in vain*
Swoor therby swithe ofte and al biswatte his cote;   *covered with sweat*
And moore mete eet and dronk than kynde myghte defie—   *nature; digest*
'And kaughte siknesse somtyme for my surfetes ofte;   *over-indulgence*
405 And thanne I dradde to deye in dedlich synne'—   *dreaded; mortal*
That into wanhope he w[orth] and wende nought to be saved,
   despair; fell; thought
The whiche is sleuthe, so slow that may no sleightes helpe it,
   sluggish; devices
Ne no mercy amenden the man that so deieth.   *i.e. in despair*
   Ac whiche ben the braunches that bryngen a man to sleuthe?
410 Is whan a man moorneth noght for hise mysdedes, ne maketh no sorwe,
   (It) is when
Ac penaunce that the preest enjoyneth parfourneth yvele,   *does badly*
Dooth non almesdede, dred hym of no synne,   *has no fear for his sin*
Lyveth ayein the bileve and no lawe holdeth.   *faith; keeps*
Ech day is halyday with hym or an heigh ferye,   *festival*
415 And if he aught wol here, it is an harlotes tonge.   *ribald jester's*
Whan men carpen of Crist, or of clennesse of soule,   *speak*
He wexeth wroth and wol noght here but wordes of murthe.   *angry*
Penaunce and povere men and the passion of seintes—
He hateth to here therof and alle that it telleth.

398*a* [For], where thy treasure is, there is thy heart also (Mt 6: 21).

393 mon.] my mon. F, C (*so* K-D).
  here] R (?=α; *om* F); her L; hire
  W.
394 tyme] L&*r*, C; while w.
399–408 α; *lines om* β.
399 þat gl.] þ. goome F.
  gar-] F; gra- R; *corr.* Sk.
400 as] al F.
401 As] & F.
  ne] *om* F.
  goddes . . . Id.] nempnede g.
  ydellyche F.
402 and . . . c.] abowte þe ale cuppe F.

404 for . . . surf.] *rec.* K-D; þoruh s.
  F; f. m. forfetes R.
406 worth] *so* Sk, *and see* K-D *p.* 185
  wrathe R; wente F.
  nauȝt] neuere F.
409 Ac] R (?=α), C; þe Hm; *om*
  W&*r*.
410 Is . . . m.] OC²B (a *om* B), C
  (*so* Sk); He þat w.
411 Ac] LY; And WR.
412 alm.] L&*r*, C; almesse W.
416 so.] L&*r*, C; *pl.* WCr.
418 and (1)] L&*r*, C; of WF.

420 Thise ben the braunches, beth war! that bryngen a man to wanhope.
    Ye lordes and ladies and legates of Holy Chirche
    That fedeth fooles sages, flatereris and lieris,   *maintain licensed jesters (C)*
    And han likynge to lithen hem [in hope] to do yow laughe— *listen to; make*
    Ve vobis qui ridetis &c—
    And yyveth hem mete and mede, and povere men refuse,   *food; rewards*
425 In youre deeth deyinge, I drede me soore
    Lest tho thre maner men to muche sorwe yow brynge: *kinds of*
    Consencientes et agentes pari pena punientur.
       Patriarkes and prophetes, prechours of Goddes wordes,
    Saven thorugh hir sermon mannes soule fro helle;   *speech, preaching*
    Right so flatereris and fooles arn the fendes disciples   *devil's*
430 To entice men thorugh hir tales to synne and harlotrie.   *obscenity*
    Ac clerkes, that knowen Holy Writ, sholde kenne lordes   *teach*
    What David seith of swiche men, as the Sauter telleth:
    Non habitabit in medio domus mee qui facit superbiam; qui loquitur iniqua ...
    Sholde noon harlot have audience in halle ne in chambre
    Ther wise men were—witnesseth Goddes wordes—   *take to witness*
435 Ne no mysproud man amonges lordes ben allowed.   *arrogant; approved*
    Clerkes and knyghtes welcometh kynges minstrales,
    And for love of hir lord litheth hem at festes;   *listen to*
    Muche moore, me thynketh, riche men sholde
    Have beggeres bifore hem, the whiche ben Goddes minstrales,
440 As he seith hymself—Seynt Johan bereth witnesse:
    Qui vos spernit me spernit.
    Forthi I rede yow riche, reveles whan ye maketh,   *give feasts*
    For to solace youre soules, swiche minstrales to have—
    The povere for a fool sage sittynge at th[i] table,   *in place of, as*
    And a lered man to lere thee what Oure Lord suffred   *teach*
445 For to save thi soule fram Sathan thyn enemy,
    And fithele thee, withoute flaterynge, of Good Friday the storye,
                                 play and sing for you

423a Woe to you that [now] laugh; [for you shall mourn and weep] (Lk 6: 25).
426a Those who consent [*sc.* to evil] and those who do [it] will be punished with
    the same penalty (*legal maxim* Sk; *exact source unknown*; see Alford, p. 395).
432a He that worketh pride shall not dwell in the midst of my house: he that
    speaketh unjust things [did not prosper before my eyes] (Ps 100: 7–8).
440a He that despiseth you despiseth me (Lk 10: 16; *cf.* Jn 5: 23).

423 in h.] C (*so* K-D *p.* 94); *om All*
    B-MSS.
      you] R (?=α) G, C (*so* K-D); yow
      to W&r.
425 me] R (?=α; *om* F), C (*so* K-D);
    me ful β.
427 pro.] C (*so* K-D); p. and *All*
    B-MSS (C).
428 sarm.] L&r; *pl.* w, ?C.
430 and] L&r, C; and to WGM.

432a qui] R (?=α; qui ... in. om F)
    Hm, C; & q. β.
433 ne] L&r, C; nor W.
436–53 α, C; *om* β.
437 here] F, C (*so* K-D); þe R.
441 riche] C (*so* Sk); r. at R; r. men
    at F.
443 thy] C (*so* K-D); þe F; þe heyʒ R.
446 storye] geste C (*so* K-D).

And a blynd man for a bourdeour, or a bedrede womman   *jester; bed-ridden*
To crie a largesse bifore Oure Lord, your good loos to shewe.
                                              bounty; fame; declare
     Thise thre maner minstrales maketh a man to laughe,
450 And in his deeth deyinge thei don hym gret confort
     That bi his lyve lithed hem and loved hem to here.   *while alive; listened to*
     Thise solaceth the soule til hymself be falle
     In a welhope, [for he wroghte so], amonges worthi seyntes,
                                              good hope; because
     There flatereres and fooles thorugh hir foule wordes
455 Leden tho that loved hem to Luciferis feste
     With *turpiloquio*, a lay of sorwe, and Luciferis fithele.
                                              foul speech (cf. Prol 39)

     Thus Haukyn the actif man hadde ysoiled his cote,
     Til Conscience acouped hym therof in a curteis manere,   *accused, found guilty*
     Why he ne hadde wasshen it or wiped it with a brusshe.   *(Asking) why*

Passus XIV

'I have but oon hool hater,' quod Haukyn, 'I am the lasse to blame
                                              untorn cloak
Though it be soiled and selde clene—I slepe therinne o nyghtes;   *at night*
And also I have an houswif, hewen and children—   *wife; servants*
Uxorem duxi, et ideo non possum venire—
That wollen bymolen it many tyme, maugree my chekes.
                                              stain; for all I can do

448 *Either* To ask for bounty for you before Our Lord (*sc.* at Judgment Day], to
   make manifest your good deserts *or* To ask for bounty / proclaim 'a bounty!' on
   Our Lord's (abiding) presence, to make known your good reputation.
3a I have married a wife; and therefore I cannot come (Lk 14: 20).

453 wel] R, ?C; wol good F, *some*
     C-MSS (*so* Sk).
        for . . . so] C (*so* Sk); *om* RF.
454 þere] a, C (*so* K-D); Ac WLY&c
     (? = β).
        -ereres] YG&c (*so* Sk); -eres
     WLR.

455 loued] a; louen β; liþed C (*so*
     K-D p. 90) (*C*).
456 lay] L&r, C; lady W.

Rubric Passus xiiijus &c.
1 hool] *om* LRF; *see* K-D p. 145.

5 It hath be laved in Lente and out of Lente bothe   *washed*
  With the sope of siknesse, that seketh wonder depe,   *soap; penetrates*
  And with the losse of catel, that looth me w[ere]   *so that; hateful*
  For to agulte God or any good man, by aught that I wiste; *offend against*
  And was shryven of the preest, that [for my synnes gaf me] *absolved by*
10 To penaunce, pacience, and povere men to fede,   *As a penance*
  Al for coveitise of my Cristendom in clennesse to kepen it.
                       Out of concern for
  And kouthe I nevere, by Crist! kepen it clene an houre,
  That I ne soiled it with sighte or som ydel speche,
  Or thorugh werk or thorugh word, or wille of myn herte,   *intention*
15 That I ne flobre it foule fro morwe til even.'   *sully; foully*
   'And I shal kenne thee,' quod Conscience, 'of Contricion to make
                       sc. *make something*
  That shal clawe thi cote of alle kynnes filthe—   *scrape (free) of*
  Cordis contricio &c;   *Contrition of heart (C)*
  Dowel shal wasshen it and wryngen it thorugh a wis confessour—
  Oris confessio &c;   *Confession of mouth*
  Dobet shal beten it and bouken it as bright as any scarlet,   *'buck'*
20 And engreynen it with good wille and Goddes grace to amende the,
                       dye fast
  And sithen sende thee to Satisfaccion for to sonnen it after: *dry in the sun*
  Satisfaccio.
   'And Dobest kepe[th] clene from unkynde werkes.
  Shal nevere my[te] bymolen it, ne mothe after biten it,   *defile, blemish*
  Ne fend ne fals man defoulen it in thi lyve.   *dirty, sully*
25 Shal noon heraud ne harpour have a fairer garnement   *herald; garment*
  Than Haukyn the Actif man, and thow do by my techyng,   *if*
  Ne no mynstrall be moore worth amonges povere and riche
  Than Haukyn wi[l] the wafrer, which is *Activa Vita.' Than will H. the waferer*
   'And I shal purveie thee paast,' quod Pacience, 'though no plough erye,
                      provide; dough; till
30 And flour to fede folk with as best be for the soule;
  Though nevere greyn growed, ne grape upon vyne,
  Alle that lyveth and loketh liflode wolde I fynde,   *sustenance; provide*
  And that ynogh—shal noon faille of thyng that hem nedeth.

7–8 . . . so that I would be unwilling Wittingly to offend God &c.
19 and steep in a solution of lye ('buck')—*sc.* to restore its original colour.

7 *Div. from* 8 *after* leese F, *after*
  agulte W&r; *re-div.* K-D *p.* 189,
  rec. p. 203 (*C*).
  that . . . w.] þ. looþ me was to
  leese F; looþ for W&r (l.] bothe
  YCB) (*C*).
9 for . . . me] g. m. f. my s. *All*
  B-MSS; *trsp.* K-D.
15 -bre] -bered FG.
21 sonne*n*] *a* (*so* K-D); sowen β.

21*a As one line with* 22 WLR (*om* F);
  re-div. K-D.
22 Dobest . . . w.] & D. & keep
  þe . . . werkis F; *om* W&r; *see*
  K-D *p.* 172 (*C*).
23 myte] myste L&r; cheeste w (*C*).
28 -kyn wil] *so* K-D; -kyn F; -kyns
  wif W&r.
  wh. is] *a* (*so* K-D *p.* 187); with his β.
32 Alle] L&r; To all W; For a. F.

We sholde noght be to bisy abouten oure liflode:
Ne soliciti sitis &c; Volucres celi Deus pascit &c; Pacientes vincunt &c.'

35 Thanne laughed Haukyn a litel, and lightly gan swerye,   *mildly*
'Whoso leveth yow, by Oure Lord, I leve noght he be blessed!'
'No?' quod Pacience paciently, and out of his poke hente   *bag; took*
Vitailles of grete vertues for alle manere beestes,
And seide, 'Lo! here liflode ynogh, if oure bileve be trewe.

40 For lent nevere was lif but liflode were shapen, *means of sustenance; created*
Wherof or wherfore or wherby to libbe.

'First the wilde worm under weet erthe,
Fissh to lyve in the flood, and in the fir the criket,
The corlew by kynde of the eyr, moost clennest flessh of briddes,

                                                          the natural vigour
45 And bestes by gras and by greyn and by grene rootes,
In menynge that alle men myghte the same   *As a sign*
Lyve thorugh leel bileve and love, as God witnesseth: *true faith*
*Quodcumque pecieritis a patre in nomine meo &c; Et alibi, Non
in solo pane vivit homo, set in omni verbo, quod procedit de ore Dei.'*
But I lokede what liflode it was that Pacience so preisede;
And thanne was it a pece of the Paternoster—*Fiat voluntas tua.*

                                                      piece; Thy will be done
50 'Have, Haukyn,' quod Pacience, 'and et this whan the hungreth,
Or whan thow clomsest for cold or clyngest for droughte;
                                        are benumbed; parch; drought
And shul nevere gyves thee greve ne gret lordes wrathe,   *fetters; afflict*
Prison ne peyne—for *pacientes vincunt.*
By so that thow be sobre of sighte and of tonge,   *Provided*
55 In [ond]lynge and in handlynge and in alle thi fyve wittes,

                                                    smelling; touching
Darstow nevere care for corn ne lynnen cloth ne wollen,
                                              You need; worry about
Ne for drynke, ne deeth drede, but deye as God liketh,
Or thorugh hunger or thorugh hete—at his wille be it.   *Either . . . or*
For if thow lyvest after his loore, the shorter lif the bettre:
Si quis amat Christum mundum non diligit istum.

34a ... Be not solicitous for your life, [what you shall eat], &c; [Behold] the birds
  of the air ... your heavenly Father feedeth them (Mt 6: 25, 26); The patient are
  victorious.
40 Life was never given [to any creature] without means of living also being pro-
  vided.
47a Whatsoever you shall ask the Father in my name, [that will I do] (Jn 14: 13);
  And in another place, Not in bread alone doth man live, but in every word that
  proceedeth from the mouth of God (Mt 4: 4).
59a If a man cares for Christ, he will not cleave to this world (source unknown).

34 K-D *rej. as spurious*, p. 193.   52 And] R (?=α; þere F), C; *om* β.
40 was] w. þere R, ?C.   55 ond-] C (*so* K-D p. 91); et- *All*
47 and . . . g.] as oure lord C.   B-MSS.
51 drouȝthe] α, C; drye β.   59 lyuest] L&r, C; lyue WCrG.

164

60   'For thorugh his breeth beestes woxen and abrood yeden: *came into being*
Dixit et facta sunt, &c.
Ergo thorugh his breeth mowen [bothe] men and beestes lyven,   *Therefore*
As Holy Writ witnesseth whan men seye hir graces: *grace (before meals)*
Aperis tu manum tuam, et imples omne animal benediccione.
  'It is founden that fourty wynter folk lyvede withouten tulying,
                          recorded; tilling
And out of the flynt sprong the flood that folk and beestes dronken;
                          (Num 20: 11)
65 And in Elyes tyme hevene was yclosed,   *Elias' time*
That no reyn ne roon—thus rede men in bokes,
                rained; (3 Kg 17: 1, Js 5: 17)
That manye wyntres men lyveden and no mete ne tulieden. *food; cultivated*
  'Sevene slepe, as seith the book, sevene hundred wynter,   *slept (C)*
And lyveden withouten liflode—and at the laste thei woken.
                    food; woke (alive)
70 And if men lyvede as mesure wolde, sholde nevere moore be defaute
                    moderation; lack
Amonges Cristene creatures, if Cristes wordes ben trewe.
Ac unkyndenesse *caristiam* maketh amonges Cristen peple,   *dearth*
And over-plentee maketh pryde amonges poore and riche;   *superfluity*
Ac mesure is so muche worth it may noght be to deere; *expensive, precious*
75 For the meschief and the meschaunce amonges men of Sodome
                disaster; misfortune
Weex thorugh plentee of payn and of pure sleuthe: *Arose from; bread*
Ociositas et habundancia panis peccatum turpissimum nutrivit.
For thei mesured noght hemself of that thei ete and dronke,
                Because; moderated
Diden dedly synne that the devel liked,   *(But) did . . .*
Vengeaunce fil upon hem for hir vile synnes;   *fell*
80 [So] thei sonken into helle, the citees echone.
  'Forthi mesure we us wel and make oure feith oure sheltrom; *defence (C)*
And thorugh feith cometh contricion, conscience woot wel,
Which dryveth awey dedly synne and dooth it to be venial.
And though a man myghte noght speke, contricion myghte hym save,
                lacked power of speech

60a [For] he spoke, and they were made (Ps 148: 5).
62a Thou openest thy hand: and fillest with blessing every living creature (Ps 144: 16).
76a Sloth and abundance of bread nourished the basest sin (*after* Peter Cantor, *ed.* Migne, *P.L.* 205, *col.* 331).

61 m. bothe] mowen *All* B-MSS;
   boþe *conj* K-D *p.* 182 (*C*).
74 Ac] LR; Therfore WCr.
   so] L&*r*; *om* W.
77 þat þ. e.] meete F; *cf.* K-D *p.* 173.
78 Diden] L&*r*; & d. swich F; Thei
   d. WCr.

79 Ven.] *so* K-D *p.* 188; *see l.* 80;
   So v. W&*r* (So] and B; & swich
   F).
80 So th.] þat þ. F; Thei W&*r*; *corr.*
   K-D.
81 oure (1)] we *conj* K-D *p.* 195.

85 And brynge his soule to blisse, by so that feith bere witnesse   *provided that*
That whiles he lyvede he bilevede in the loore of Holy Chirche.
Ergo contricion, feith and conscience is kyndeliche Dowel,
essentially make up
And surgiens for dedly synnes whan shrift of mouthe failleth.
oral confession
Ac shrift of mouth moore worthi is, if man be ynliche contrit,
inwardly contrite
90 For shrift of mouthe sleeth synne be it never so dedly—
destroys; mortal, grave
Per confessionem to a preest *peccata occiduntur*—
Ther contricion dooth but dryveth it doun into a venial synne,
only drives, reduces
As David seith in the Sauter, *et quorum tecta sunt peccata.*
Ac satisfaccion seketh out the roote, and bothe sleeth and voideth,
clears, removes
95 And as it nevere [n]adde ybe, to noghte bryngeth dedly synne,
That it nevere eft is sene ne soor, but semeth a wounde yheeled.'
visible; sore; healed/covered
'Where wonyeth Charite?' quod Haukyn. 'I wiste nevere in my lyve
Man that with hym spak, as wide as I have passed.'
'Ther parfit truthe and poore herte is, and pacience of tonge—
100 There is Charite the chief, chaumbrere for God hymselve.'   *chamberlain*
'Wheither paciente poverte,' quod Haukyn, 'be moore plesaunt to Oure
Drighte   *Our Lord*
Than richesse rightfulliche wonne and resonably despended?'   *honestly*
'Ye—*quis est ille*?' quod Pacience, 'quik—*laudabimus eum!*
Though men rede of richesse right to the worldes ende,
105 I wiste nevere renk that riche was, that whan he rekene sholde,
had to settle accounts
Whan he drogh to his deeth day, that he ne dredde hym soore,   *drew near*
And that at the rekenyng in arrerage fel, rather than out of dette.
into arrears
Ther the poore dar plede, and preve by pure reson
To have allowaunce of his lord; by the lawe he it cleymeth: *favour*
110 Joye, that nevere joye hadde, of rightful jugge he asketh,   *from a just judge*
And seith, "Lo! briddes and beestes, that no blisse ne knoweth,
And wilde wormes in wodes, thorugh wyntres thow hem grevest,   *you afflict*
And makest hem wel neigh meke and mylde for defaute,   *tame; lack*
And after thow sendest hem somer, that is hir sovereyn joye,
afterwards; supreme

91 Through sacramental confession sins are slain.
93 . . . and whose sins are covered (Ps 31: 1).
103 *Is* there such a man? [*Lit.* Yes—who is that man?] Quick, we'll praise *him*! (*C*).

85 by] LRFCr; for WM; *om r.*   95 nadde] *rec.* K-D *p.* 195; hadde
89 in-] RYOM (*so* Sk; *and see* K-D   *All* B-MSS.
  p. 145); y- WL.   98 Man] Wye *conj* K-D *p.* 195.

115 And blisse to alle that ben, bothe wilde and tame."

    'Thanne may beggeris, as beestes, after boote waiten,   *expect recompense*

    That al hir lif han lyved in langour and in defaute.   *pain; want*

    But God sente hem som tyme som manere joye   *Unless*

    Outher here or elliswhere, kynde wolde it nevere;

120 For to wrotherhele was he wroght that nevere was joye shapen!   *misfortune*

    'Aungeles that in helle now ben hadden joye som tyme,

    And Dives in deyntees lyvede and in *douce vie;*   *pleasure; delight, luxury*

    Right so reson sheweth that tho men that [riche were]

    And hir makes also lyvede hir lif in murthe.   *wives; pleasure*

125   'Ac God is of a wonder wille, by that kynde wit sheweth,

    To yyve many men his mercymonye er he it have deserved.   *reward*

    Right so fareth God by some riche: ruthe me it thynketh—

                  acts; in the case of; pity

    For thei han hir hire heer, and hevene, as it were,   *payment*

    And greet likynge to lyve withouten labour of bodye,

130 And whan he dyeth, ben disalowed, as David seith in the Sauter:

                  barred, not approved

    Dormierunt et nichil invenerunt; et alibi, Velud sompnum surgencium,

    Domine, in civitate tua, et ad nichilum rediges &c.

    Allas, that richesse shal reve and robbe mannes soule   *deprive*

    From the love of Oure Lord at his laste ende!

    'Hewen that han hir hire afore arn everemoore nedy;   *in advance; in need*

    And selden deyeth he out of dette that dyneth er he deserve it

135 And til he have doon his devoir and his dayes journee.   *duty; stint of work*

    For whan a werkman hath wroght, than may men se the sothe—

    What he were worthi for his werk, and what he hath deserved,

    And noght to fonge bifore, for drede of disalowyng.   *receive (pay); disfavour*

    'So I seye by yow riche—it semeth noght that ye shulle   *concerning*

140 Have hevene in youre here-beyng and hevene therafter,   *existence here*

119–20 ... it [perpetual suffering] would be a contradiction to their very nature; for he who was made never to experience joy was created for an evil destiny indeed!

125 But God's purpose is a strange one, to judge by the criteria of common sense ..

130a They have slept [their sleep]: and [all the men of riches] have found nothing [in their hands] (Ps 75: 6). And in another place, As the dream of them that awake, O Lord; so in thy city thou shalt bring [their image] to nothing (Ps 72: 20).

138 And [it is not proper for him] to receive his payment in advance, in case his work should be found unsatisfactory.

117 in (2)] *om* BG, C.

123 þo] L&r (no Y; þo þat Cot); þe w. that r. w.] þ. w. r. β; *om* R; shull redyly acounte F (*cf.* K-D *p.* 183n) (C).

125 a] L&r; *om* W.

126 men] L&r; man WCrGF. mercym.] L&r (m.ment F); mede W.

130a *et al.*] F, C (*so* K-D); And in anoþer stede also W&r (= Bx; A. a. in an. s. Hm). -num] W&r, C; -nium F (*so* K-D) (C).

140 beyng] LRMOCr²³C²; beryng YCr¹CB; dwellyng W (C).

Right as a servaunt taketh his salarie bifore, and siththe wolde clayme moore,
As he that noon hadde, and hath hire at the laste.   *wages; end (of the day)*
It may noght be, ye riche men, or Mathew on God lyeth:
De deliciis ad delicias difficile est transire!

  'Ac if ye riche have ruthe, and rewarde wel the poore,   *look after, care for*
145 And lyven as lawe techeth, doon leaute to hem alle,   *justice*
Crist of his curteisie shal conforte yow at the laste   *out of his mercy, grace*
And rewarden alle double richesse that rewful hertes habbeth.
                                    reward (with); pitiful
And as an hyne that hadde his hire er he bigonne,   *labourer; began*
And whan he hath doon his devoir wel, men dooth hym oother bountee—
                                    a further reward
150 Yyveth hym a cote above his covenaunt—right so Crist yyveth hevene
                                    agreed wages
Bothe to riche and to noght riche that rewfulliche libbeth;   *compassionately*
And alle that doon hir devoir wel han double hire for hir travaille—
                                    pay; effort
Here forgifnesse of hir synnes, and hevene blisse after.
  'Ac it is but selde yseien, as by holy seintes bokes,   *seldom seen*
155 That God rewarded double reste to any riche wye.
For muche murthe is amonges riche, as in mete and clothyng,   *pleasure*
And muche murthe in May is amonges wilde beestes,
And so forth while somer lasteth hir solace dureth.   *joy continues*
Ac beggeris aboute Midsomer bredlees thei soupe,   *sup*
160 And yet is wynter for hem worse, for weetshoed thei gange, *even; wet-shod; go*
Afurst soore and afyngred, and foule yrebuked   *Thirsty; hungry*
And arated of riche men, that ruthe is to here . . .   *scolded by*
Now, Lord, sende hem somer, and som maner joye,
Hevene after hir hennes goyng, that here han swich defaute!
165 For alle myghtestow have maad noon mener than oother,   *poorer*
And yliche witty and wise, if thee wel hadde liked.   *equally*
 'And have ruthe on thise riche men that rewarde noght thi prisoners;
                                      care for
Of the good that thow hem gyvest *ingrati* ben manye;
                          For; ungrateful (cf. Lk 5: 35)
Ac God, of thi goodnesse, gyve hem grace to amende.
170 For may no derthe be hem deere, droghte ne weet,   *injurious to them*
Ne neither hete ne hayll, have thei hir heele;   *health*
Of that thei wilne and wolde wanteth hem noght here.   *desire*
  'Ac poore peple, thi prisoners, Lord, in the put of meschief— *pit; distress*

143a *From* delights *to* delights is a difficult crossing (St Jerome, *Epistola ad Julianum, P.L.* 22, 965 (*cf.* Mt 19: 23).
161 Afflicted grievously by thirst and hunger, and ignominously abused.

141 as] L&r; so as W.   170 be] *om* OC²Cr²³.
159 soupe] L&r, C; slepe W.   weet] L&r; w. hem greue WCr.
160 gange] L&r, C; gone W; wandre F· 173 -oners l.] β; -ones lore R (?=α;
167 And] L&r; *om* F; But Lord W.   -oun lyȝn F).

Conforte tho creatures that muche care suffren
175 Thorough derthe, thorough droghte, alle hir dayes here,
Wo in wynter tymes for wantynge of clothes,
And in somer tyme selde soupen to the fulle;   *eat their fill*
Conforte thi carefulle, Crist, in thi riche—   *wretched; kingdom*
For how thow confortest alle creatures clerkes bereth witnesse:
Convertimini ad me et salvi eritis.
180 'Thus *in genere* of gentries Jesu Crist seide   *in the nature; nobility*
To robberis and to reveris, to riche and to poore,   *thieves*
To hores, to harlotes, to alle maner peple,
Thou taughtest hem in the Trinite to taken bapteme
                                             in (the name of) the Trinity
And be clene thorugh that cristnyng of alle kynnes synne,
185 And if us fille thorugh folie to falle in synne after,   *it befell us*
Confession and knowlichynge and cravynge thi mercy   *acknowledging (sin)*
Shulde amenden us as manye sithes as man wolde desire.   *times*
Ac if the pouke wolde plede herayein, and punysshe us in conscience,
                                     devil; against this; in our consc.
We sholde take the acquitaunce as quyk and to the queed shewen it—
                                                          evil one

Pateat &c: Per passionem Domini—
90 And putten of so the pouke, and preven us under borwe.   *repel; pledge*
Ac the parchemyn of this patente of poverte be moste,
                                        deed (of release); must be
And of pure pacience and parfit bileve.   *faith*
Of pompe and of pride the parchemyn decourreth,   *From; departs*
And principalliche of alle peple, but thei be poore of herte.
95 Ellis is al on ydel, al that evere we wr[ogh]ten—   *In vain; did*
Paternostres and penaunce and pilgrimage to Rome,

179a If you return ... you shall be saved (Is 45: 22).
189-90 We should take the document of acquittal immediately and produce it
before the devil (our accuser)—'Let it be manifest, &c [opening words of the
deed] through the passion of Our Lord (Jesus Christ)' ... and thereby repel the
fiend and prove ourselves to be secure under a pledge [sc. that of Christ's redemp-
tive death] (C).
193-4 The document (of release from sin through confession) in no way applies to
the proud, and utterly leaves out any but the humble.

176 w. tymes] β; wyntres tyme α.
178 ryche] L&r; richesse w (M).
182 α (so K-D); om β.
hores ... m.] harlotys & to
hoorys & to all oþer F.
184 be] L&r; to be WF.
186 and (2)] L&r; in W.
Conf., kn.] *trsp.* R (?=α; &
beknowleche it In conf. F).

188 Ac] LYM; And wRF.
pouke] α (*so* Sk): pope β (*cf.*
190, *and see* K-D *p.* 147).
189 We] F (*so* K-D *p.* 173); He
W&r (Ho R) (C).
194 alle] L&r; al þe WM; þe F.
195 we wr.] we writen L&r (we]þey F;
om W); we diden *conj* K-D *p.* 180 (C).
196 -age] L&r; -ages WCrG; -es F.

But oure spences and spendynge sprynge of a trewe welle;   *expenses*
Ellis is al oure labour lost—lo, how men writeth
In fenestres at the freres!—if fals be the foundement.   *windows; foundation*
200 Forthi Cristene sholde be in commune riche, noon coveitous for hymselve.
  'For sevene synnes ther ben, that assaillen us evere;
The fend folweth hem alle and fondeth hem to helpe,   *tries*
Ac with richesse tho ribaudes rathest men bigileth.
            evil ones; most quickly deceive men
For ther that richesse regneth, reverences folweth,
205 And that is plesaunt to pride, in poore and in riche.   *pleasing*
And the riche is reverenced by reson of his richesse
Ther the poore is put bihynde, and paraventure kan moore
            Where; though perhaps he knows
Of wit and of wisdom, that fer awey is bettre
Than richesse or reautee, and rather yherd in hevene. *royalty; sooner heeded*
210 For the riche hath muche to rekene, and right softe walketh; *very gingerly*
The heighe wey to heveneward ofte richesse letteth—   *obstructs*
Ita inpossibile diviti &c—
Ther the poore preesseth bifore, with a pak at his rugge—   *back*
Opera enim illorum sequuntur illos—
Batauntliche, as beggeris doon, and boldeliche he craveth
            With noisy eagerness; confidently
For his poverte and his pacience a perpetuel blisse:
Beati pauperes: quoniam ipsorum est regnum celorum.
215 'And pride in richesse regneth rather than in poverte: *holds sway sooner*
Or in the maister or in the man som mansion he haveth.   *dwelling-place*
Ac in poverte ther pacience is, Pride hath no myghte,.
Ne none of the sevene synnes sitten ne mowe ther longe,
Ne have power in poverte, if pacience it folwe.
220 For the poore is ay prest to plese the riche,   *always prompt*

197 Unless what we spend (on such) comes from an honest source [sincere repen-
tance].
211*a* Thus it is impossible for a rich man [to enter into the kingdom of heaven]
(cf. Mt 19: 23–4).
212*a* . . . for their works follow them (Rev 14: 13) (*C*).
214*a* Blessed are the poor [in spirit]; for theirs is the kingdom of heaven (Mt 5: 3;
but cf. Lk 6: 20, *which omits* 'in spirit') (*C*).

197 welle] L&*r*, ?C; wille WCrOC²C
(*C*).
203 þo r.] a, C (*so* K-D); þat
Ribaude L&*r* (=β; þ. r. he WCr¹).
204 reu.] R (?=a; r. it F), C (*so*
K-D); *sg.* β.
206 And] β, ?C; Ac R (?=a; But F).
210 riȝte s.] L&*r*, C; r. ofte him that
Cr; many tyme h. þ. W.
211 oft] L&*r* (but o. þe F); *om* WCr.
letteth] L&*r exc* F; hym l. WCr.

212 with] F, C (*so* K-D *pp.* 157, 169);
þe riche w. W&*r* (= Bx).
212*a* -*quu*-] C² (*so* Sk, K-D); -*qu*-
W&*r*.
215 And] β, ?C; Ac R (?=a; But F).
216 Or; or] a, C (*so* K-D); Arst; þan
β (þ.] or Cr).
219 it] L&*r* (*om* W; *l. om* Cr³), C;
hem F.

And buxom at his biddyng for his broke loves;

obedient; scraps ('broken loaves')

And buxomnesse and boost ben everemoore at werre, *arrogance; in conflict*
And either hateth oother in alle maner werkes.
If Wrathe wrastle with the poore he hath the worse ende,

gets the worse of it

225 For if thei bothe pleyne, the poore is but feble, *plead; weak*
And if he chide or chatre, hym cheveth the worse, *he succeeds*
For lowliche he loketh and lovelich is his speche
That mete or money of othere men moot asken.
'And if Glotonie greve poverte, he gadereth the lasse,

vex, trouble; collects

230 For his rentes wol naught reche no riche metes to bigge; *income; foods; buy*
And though his glotonye be to good ale, he goth to cold beddyng,

desire be for

And his heved unheled, unesiliche ywrye— *uncovered; uncomfortably twisted*
For whan he streyneth hym to strecche, the strawe is his shetes. *tries; sheets*
So for his Glotonie and his greete Sleuthe he hath a grevous penaunce,
235 That is welawo whan he waketh and wepeth for colde— *misery*
And som tyme for his synnes—so he is nevere mûrie *content*
Withoute mournynge amonge and meschief to bote.

an admixture of sadness; suffering

'And though Coveitise wolde cacche the poore, thei may noght come
togideres,
And by the nekke, namely, hir noon may hente oother.

especially; neither of them; grip

240 For men knowen wel that Coveitise is of a kene wille, *fierce*
And hath hondes and armes of a long lengthe,
And Poverte nys but a petit thyng, apereth noght to his navele—

little; that reaches; navel, middle

And lovely layk was it nevere bitwene the longe and the shorte.

good sport (i.e. wrestling)

And though Avarice wolde angre the poore, he hath but litel myghte,

afflict

245 For Poverte hath but pokes to putten in hise goodes, *bags; to put his goods in*

226 And if (Wrath) scolds or argues with (a poor man) he (Wrath) gets the worst
of it.

221 his b.] L&r, C; *pl.* W,
222 ben] *so* K-D *p.* 172; þey been F;
   ar*n* W&r, Cx (?=C).
225 For] L&r, C; And w.
227-237 α, C; *om* β.
228 mete] R, C; ony m. F.
230 wol] F, C; ne w. R.
231 gl. be to] glut be in F.
   to (2) ... b.] R, C; acold to
   bedde F.

232 vnh.] R, C; euele yhelyd & F.
234 his (1)] R, C; h. grete F.
235 wep.] R, C; w. sore F.
237 misch.] R; myche m. F.
238 þou3] α, C; if β.
   wolde] LRF (*cf.* C); *om* W&r.
240 a] L&r. C; *om* WCr.
241 a l.] L&r (a *om* R), C; an huge
   F; ful greet W.
243 And] A F, C.

Ther Avarice hath almaries and yren-bounden cofres.
> *cupboards; iron-bound chests*

And wheither be lighter to breke? Lasse boost it maketh—
> *which is easier; cause of boasting* (C)

A beggeris bagge than an yren-bounde cofre!

Lecherie loveth hym noght, for he yyveth but litel silver,

250 Ne dooth hym noght dyne delicatly ne drynke wyn ofte. *daintily, choicely*

A straw for the stuwes! It stoode noght, I trowe, *brothels*

Hadde thei noon [haunt] but of poore men—hir houses stoode untyled!
> *custom; untiled, roofless*

'And though Sleuthe suwe Poverte, and serve noght God to paie,
> *follow; satisfactorily*

Meschief is his maister, and maketh hym to thynke *Misfortune; teacher*

255 That God is his grettest help and no gome ellis, *nobody*

And he his servaunt, as he seith, and of his sute bothe. *retinue*

And wheither he be or be noght, he bereth the signe of poverte,

And in that secte Oure Saveour saved al mankynde. *garb, character* (C)

Forthi al poore that pacient is, may [asken and cleymen],

260 After hir endynge here, heveneriche blisse.

'Muche hardier may he asken, that here myghte have his wille *boldly*

In lond and in lordshipe and likynge of bodie, *bodily pleasure*

And for Goddes love leveth al and lyveth as a beggere. *abandons*

And as a mayde for mannes love hire moder forsaketh,
> *for love of a man; parts from*

265 Hir fader and alle hire frendes, and folweth hir make— *spouse*

Muche is that maide to love of [a man] that swich oon taketh,

Moore than a maiden is that is maried thorugh brocage,
> *by arrangement* (only)

As by assent of sondry parties and silver to boote,

Moore for coveitise of good than kynde love of bothe—

270 So it fareth by ech a persone that possession forsaketh *gives up property*

And put hym to be pacient, and poverte weddeth,

251–2 Fie upon the brothels! They could not continue to exist / would not have existed Had they [the prostitutes] been frequented only by the poor.

266–7 A girl greatly deserves love from a man who takes her on those terms [mutual affection]—More than does one whose marriage is arranged like a business transaction.

247 lasse] L&r, C; and l. WCr.
   it] L&r, C; he F; *om* WCr.
251–2 *om* a.
251 it] L&r; it ne B; þei W.
252 n. haunt] C (*so* K-D *p.* 182);
   none L; noght G; no þyng W&r.
259 al] L&r, C; euery W.
   asken . . . cl.] *trsp. All* B-MSS
   (*cf.* of pure right cl. C, *so* K-D).

266 Moche] L&r, C; M. moore WCr.
   þat (1)] a, C; suche a L&r (? = β;
   a G); *om* WCr.
   a man] C (*so* K-D); hym W&r;
   om Y.
267 More . . . is] LRMg; Thanne a m.
   is W.
269 good] catel C (C).
270 fareþ] preueþ *conj* K-D *pp.* 112,
   206 (C).

The which is sib to God hymself, and so neigh is poverte.'

'Have God my trouthe,' quod Haukyn, 'I here ye preise faste poverte.

constantly

What is poverte, Pacience,' quod he, 'proprely to mene?' *precisely, exactly*

275 '*Paupertas,*' quod Pacience, '*est odibile bonum—*
Remocio curarum, possessio sine calumpnia, donum Dei,
sanitatis mater, absque sollicitudine semita, sapiencie
temperatrix, negocium sine dampno, incerta fortuna,
absque sollicitudine felicitas.'

'I kan noght construe al this,' quod Haukyn, 'ye moste kenne me this on
Englissh.' *teach*

'In Englissh,' quod Pacience, 'it is wel hard, wel to expounen,

explàin, expound

Ac somdeel I shal seyen it, by so thow understonde.

provided you (try to) understand

Poverte is the firste point that Pride moost hateth; *quality, virtue (C)*

280 Thanne is it good by good skile—al that agasteth pride.

reason; scares, frightens off

Right as contricion is confortable thyng, conscience woot wel,

a comforting thing

And a sorwe of hymself, and a solace to the soule,

'*sorrowful in itself*'; *comfort*

So poverte propreliche penaunce [is to the body
And joye also to the soule], pure spiritual helthe,

285 And contricion confort, and *cura animarum:*

source of strength; guardian of souls

Ergo paupertas est odibile bonum.

'Selde sit poverte the sothe to declare, *sits the poor man* (sc. *on juries*)
Or as justice to jugge men enjoyned is no poore,
Ne to be mair above men, ne mynystre under kynges; *mayor*
Selde is any poore yput to punysshen any peple;
Remocio curarum.

290 *Ergo* poverte and poore men parfournen the comaundement— *carry out*
Nolite iudicare quemquam. '*Judge not*' (Mt 7: 1)

275 Poverty is a good—yet a hateful one:— the removal of anxieties; possession
without calumny; a gift of God; the mother of (good) health; a path free from
worry; mistress of wisdom; business without losses; amidst fortune's uncer-
tainty, happiness without worry (Vincent of Beauvais) (*C*).

272 and so . . . p.] R (? = α; & so neer
is þat persone F); and so to hise
seintes β.
273 I . . . ye] *rec.* K-D (ye] yow K-D);
y heere F; þat huyre R; ye β (*C*).
274 pac.] R (? = α; *om* F) (*so* K-D);
wiþ p. β; pacient ?C.

275a -*tatis*] L&c, C; -*tas* W.
283-4 is . . . the s.] and Ioye / Is to þe
b. W&r (*with varr.*) (*C*).
285 *trsp.* with 285a *All* B-MSS (*C*).
287 Or] L&r, C; For WCr¹M.
290a *quemq.*] Cot, C (*so* K-D); *q.q.*
þe þridde W&r.

'Selde is poore right riche but of rightful heritage:
Wynneth he noght with wightes false ne with unseled mesures,

weights; unsealed (C)

Ne borweth of hise neighebores but that he may wel paie:
Possessio sine calumpnia.

'The ferthe is a fortune that florissheth the soule *prospers*
295 With sobretee fram alle synne and also yit moore; *(away) from*
It afaiteth the flessh fram folies ful manye— *restrains*
A collateral confort, Cristes owene yifte: *accompanying*
Donum Dei.

'The fifte is moder of [myght and of mannes] hele, *strength*
A frend in alle fondynges, [of foule yveles leche],

temptations; healer, physician

300 And for the lewde evere yliche a lemman of alle clennesse:

foolish; constantly; chaste lover

Sanitatis mater.

'The sixte is a path of pees—ye, thorugh the paas of Aulton

pass; Alton (C)

Poverte myghte passe withouten peril of robbyng!
For ther that Poverte passeth pees folweth after,
And ever the lasse that he [led]eth, the [light]er he is of herte—
Cantabit paupertas coram latrone viator—
305 And an hardy man of herte among an heep of theves:
Forthi seith Seneca *Paupertas est absque sollicitudine semita.*

'The seventhe is welle of wisdom and fewe wordes sheweth,
For lordes alloweth hym litel or listneth to his reson.

approve; speech, arguments

He tempreth the tonge to trutheward, that no tresor coveiteth:
Sapiencie temperatrix.

310 'The eightethe is a lele labour and looth to take moore *honest*

291 A poor man seldom becomes rich except as the result of a lawful inheritance
(i.e. not through criminal means).
300 And a perpetual attraction to purity of life for all misguided men (*sc.* who
might turn to lechery if they were rich).
304a A traveller with an empty purse / Will sing when he shall meet a thief
(Juvenal, *Sat.* X, 22; *paup.*] *vacuus orig.*).
309 The man who does not long for riches tunes his tongue to tell the truth

291 pore riȝt] α, C (*so* K-D *p.* 155;
þe p. C); any p. W&r (=β; p.] p. man
Cr; poverte G).
298 *run together with* 299 *All* B-MSS;
rec. K-D *p.* 94.
myht . . . m.] C; *om All* B-MSS.
hele] α, ?C; helþe β, *many*
C-MSS.
299 of. . . . l.] C; *om All* B-MSS.
300 lewde] GOC²B (*so* K-D); lawde
YCR; lawe F; land wLM.
ylyche] F (=α; a l. R); a leche β.

300a -*tatis*] LR, C; -*tas* W.
304 ledeþ] C (lede K-D *pp.* 94, 182);
bereþ *All* B-MSS (l. *om* F).
lighter] *so* K-D *after* C; hard(i)er
W&r (C).
304a *trsp. with* 306 W&r; *in margin*
by 305 OC²; *corr.* K-D.
-*tor*] LRF; -*tore* W.
308 For] L&r, C; Therfore WCr.
309 He] L&r, C; For he WCr.
þat] α, C (*so* K-D); and β.

Than he may [sothly] deserve, in somer or in wynter,
And if he chaffareth, he chargeth no losse, mowe he charite wynne:

                                                   does business; accounts it

Negocium sine dampno.

    'The nynthe is swete to the soule, no sugre is swetter;
For pacience is payn for poverte hymselve,   *bread, food*
315 And sobretee swete drynke and good leche in siknesse.
Thus lered me a lered man for Oure Lordes love, Seint Austyn—
A blessed lif withouten bisynesse for body and for soule:
Absque sollicitudine felicitas.
Now God, that alle good gyveth, graunte his soule reste
That thus first wroot to wissen men what Poverte was to mene!'   *teach*
320 'Allas,' quod Haukyn the Actif Man tho, 'that after my cristendom

                                                   baptism

I ne hadde be deed and dolven for Dowelis sake!   *buried*
So hard it is,' quod Haukyn, 'to lyve and to do synne.   *miserable, cruel*
Synne seweth us evere,' quod he, and sory gan wexe,

                                     follows; wretched, sorrowful

And wepte water with hise eighen and weyled the tyme   *bewailed*
325 That evere he dide dede that deere God displesed—
Swouned and sobbed and siked ful ofte   *sighed*
That evere he hadde lond or lordshipe, lasse other moore,
Or maistrie over any man mo than of hymselve.   *power; more*
'I were noght worthi, woot God,' quod Haukyn, 'to werien any clothes,

                                                     wear

330 Ne neither sherte ne shoon, save for shame one   *shirt; shoes; modesty alone*
To covere my careyne,' quod he, and cride mercy faste,

                                      'corruptible body'; constantly

And wepte and wailede—and therwith I awakede.

328   .. over any man *other than*, *or*, more than (he had) over himself.

311 sothly] C (*so* K-D *p.* 94); wel
    All B-MSS.
313 is (2)] *om* g, *some* C-MSS.
316-17a *div. after* loue, bys. L&r
    exc MF; *after* heu., ladde WCr;
    after S.A. C (*so* K-D).
316 lered (2)] α, C; lettred β.

loue] L&r, C; l. of heuene
    WCrF.
317 bys.] L&r, C; b. ladde WCr(M).
    for (2)] *om* g.
319 þus] L&r, ?C; þis w.
325 e. he] L&r; he e. W.
327 or] L&r (*om* Cr); ouþer W.

Passus XV

Ac after my wakynge it was wonder longe
Er I koude kyndely knowe what was Dowel.
And so my wit weex and wanyed til I a fool weere;   *waxed; waned*
And some lakked my lif—allowed it fewe—   *blamed; approved*
5 And leten me for a lorel and looth to reverencen   *held; wastrel; unwilling*
Lordes or ladies or any lif ellis—   *person*
As persons in pelure with pendaunts of silver;   *fur; pendants*
To sergeaunts ne to swiche seide noght ones,   *serjeants-at-law*
'God loke yow, lordes!'—ne loutede faire,   *watch over; bowed graciously*
10 That folk helden me a fool; and in that folie I raved,
Til reson hadde ruthe on me and rokked me aslepe,
Til I seigh, as it sorcerie were, a sotil thyng withalle—
    magic; subtle, fine-drawn
Oon withouten tonge and teeth, tolde me whider I sholde   *(who) told*
And wherof I cam and of what kynde. I conjured hym at the laste,
15 If he were Cristes creature for Cristes love me to tellen.
    'I am Cristes creature,' quod he, 'and Cristene in many a place,
In Cristes court yknowe wel, and of his kyn a party.   *?partly (C)*
Is neither Peter the Porter, ne Poul with the fauchon,   *sword*
That wole defende me the dore, dynge I never so late.   *forbid; knock*
20 At mydnyght, at mydday, my vois is so yknowe   *familiar*
That ech a creature of his court welcometh me faire.'
    'What are ye called?' quod I, 'in that court among Cristes peple?'
    'The whiles I quykne the cors,' quod he, 'called am I *Anima*;
    give life to, animate; body
And whan I wilne and wolde, *Animus* ich hatte;   *am called*
25 And for that I kan and knowe, called am I *Mens*;
And whan I make mone to God, *Memoria* is my name;   *pray, recollect*
And whan I deme domes and do as truthe techeth,   *make (moral) judgments*
Thanne is *Racio* my righte name—"reson" on Englissh;
And whan I feele that folk telleth, my firste name is *Sensus*—   *perceive*
30 And that is wit and wisdom, the welle of alle craftes;
    source; skills, activities
And whan I chalange or chalange noght, chepe or refuse,
    claim; buy (=choose)

Rubric Passus xv ᴹˢ *&c: finit dowel &*
  incipit dobet.
5 leten] L&r; lete W.
8 ne] and a.
  seyde] L&r; s. I w(M).
15 for . . . l.] L&r; anoon WCr.

18 þe] R (?=a), C (so K-D p. 168n);
  his βF.
20 is so] RFY, C; so is WL.
  y-] LR, C; om W.
25 and] L&r, C; y F; om W.

176

Thanne am I Conscience ycalled, Goddes clerk and his notarie;   *scribe*
And whan I love leelly Oure Lord and alle othere,   *faithfully*
Thanne is "lele Love" my name, and in Latyn *Amor*;
35 And whan I flee fro the flessh and forsake the careyne,   *corpse*
Thanne am I spirit spechelees—and *Spiritus* thanne ich hatte.
Austyn and Ysodorus, either of hem bothe   *Isidore of Seville (C)*
Nempnede me thus to name—now thow myght chese   *named; choose*
How thow coveitest to calle me, now thow knowest alle my names.
Anima pro diversis accionibus diversa nomina sortitur: dum
vivificat corpus, anima est; dum vult, animus est; dum scit,
mens est; dum recolit, memoria est; dum iudicat, racio est;
dum sentit, sensus est; dum amat, Amor est; dum negat vel
consentit, consciencia est; dum spirat, spiritus est.'
40 'Ye ben as a bisshop,' quod I, al bourdynge that tyme,   *jesting*
'For bisshopes yblessed, thei bereth manye names—
Presul and *Pontifex* and *Metropolitanus*,   *Prelate; Pontiff; Metropolitan*
And othere names an heep, *Episcopus* and *Pastor*.'
    Bishop ('overseer'); Shepherd
'That is sooth,' seide he, 'now I se thi wille!   *purpose, intent*
45 Thow woldest knowe and konne the cause of alle hire names,
And of myne, if thow myghtest, me thynketh by thi speche!'
'Ye, sire,' I seide, 'by so no man were greved,   *provided; offended*
Alle the sciences under sonne and alle the sotile craftes
I wolde I knewe and kouthe kyndely in myn herte!'   *intimately*
50 'Thanne artow inparfit,' quod he, 'and oon of Prides knyghtes!
For swich a lust and likyng Lucifer fel from hevene:
Ponam pedem meum in aquilone et similis ero Altissimo.
'It were ayeins kynde,' quod he, 'and alle kynnes reson
That any creature sholde konne al, except Crist oone.   *alone*
Ayein swiche Salomon speketh, and despiseth hir wittes,   *pours scorn upon*
55 And seith, *Sicut qui mel comedit multum non est ei bonum,*
Sic qui scrutator est maiestatis opprimitur a gloria.
'To Englisshe men this is to mene, that mowen speke and here,

---

39a The Soul selects different names according to its different modes of operation.
As (the power which) gives life to the body, it is (called) 'soul'; as (that which)
wills, 'intention'; as (that which) knows, 'mind'; as (that which) reflects (on
things past, *or*, prays), 'memory'; as (that which) judges, 'reason'; (which)
perceives sensations, 'sense'; (which) loves, 'love'; (which) denies or consents,
'conscience'; (which) breathes (the breath of life), 'spirit' (Isidore of Seville,
Etymologies, XI, i, 13) (*P.L.* 82).
51a I shall place my foot in the north, and be like the most High (*cf.* Is 14: 13–14).
55–55a As it is not good for a man to eat much honey, so he that is a searcher of
majesty [*sc.* God's] shall be overwhelmed by [his] glory (Prov 25: 27).

36 spir.] L&r, ?C; a s. WF.   45 her] L&r, C; my WF.
    and] LRF, C; *om* W&r.   46 myne] L&r, C; me W.
38 now] L&r, C; and n. W.
39 now] L&r, C; *om* F; for n. W.
    alle] L&r, C; *om* WG.

The man that muche hony eteth his mawe it engleymeth,   *stomach; cloys*
And the moore that a man of good matere hereth,
But he do therafter it dooth hym doubie scathe.

                                        Unless; act accordingly; harm
60 "*Beatus est*," seith Seint Bernard, "*qui scripturas legit*
    Et verba vertit in opera fulliche to his power."
    Coveitise to konne and to knowe science
    Putte out of Paradis Adam and Eve:
    Sciencie appetitus hominem inmortalitatis gloriam spoliavit.
     'And right as hony is yvel to defie and engleymeth the mawe,   *hard; digest*
65 Right so that thorugh reson wolde the roote knowe
    Of God and of hise grete myghtes—hise graces it letteth.   *hinders, obstructs*
    For in the likynge lith a pride and licames coveitise
    Ayein Cristes counseil and alle clerkes techynge—
    That is *Non plus sapere quam oportet sapere.*
70   'Freres and fele othere maistres that to the lewed men prechen,
    Ye moeven materes unmesurable to tellen of the Trinite,

                                        adduce; unfathomable
    That oftetymes the lewed peple of hir bileve doute.   *doubt their faith*
    Bettre it were by many doctours to bileven swich techyng   *abandon*
    And tellen men of the ten comaundements, and touchen the sevene synnes,
                                        deal with
75 And of the braunches that burjoneth of hem and bryngen men to helle,   *shoot*
    And how that folk in folies mysspenden hir fyve wittes—   *misuse*
    As wel freres as oother folk, foliliche spenden   *(who) foolishly*
    In housynge, in haterynge, in to heigh clergie shewynge   *clothing; learning*
    Moore for pompe than for pure charite—the peple woot the sothe!
80 That I lye noght, loo!—for lordes ye plesen,   *flatter*
    And reverencen the riche the rather for hir silver:
    Confundantur omnes qui adorant sculptilia; Et alibi,
    Ut quid diligitis vanitatem, et queritis mendacium?
     'Gooth to the glose of the vers, ye grete clerkes;   *gloss on (C)*

60-1 Blessed is the man who reads the scriptures And turns (its) words into works
    as far as he is capable (St Bernard, *Tractatus de Ordine Vitae*, *P.L.* 184, 566).
63*a* The longing for knowledge deprived man of the glory of immortality (St
    Bernard, *Sermo* IV *in Ascensione Domini*, *P.L.* 183, 311).
67 For in the desire for knowledge [*with pun on* 'licking'?] lies a (form of pride)
    and fleshly greed . . .
69 . . . not to be more wise than it behoveth to be wise (Rom 12: 3).
81*a* Let them all be confounded that adore graven things (Ps 96: 7); And in another
    place, Why do you love vanity, and seek after lying? (Ps 4: 3).

62 sc.] L&*r*; *pl.* WF.   to bil.] (M) (*so* K-D); to leuen W;
63 *So* BxCx; *cf.* K-D *pp.* 113, 206.   *om r.*
63*a* -*am*] L&*r*; -*a* w.   swich] *om* a.
70 þe] LRY (*cf.* C); *om* WF.   78 into] a; and i. WL; and, to *om* G,
72 ofte] β (*l. om* a); lome *conj* K-D   C.
    p. 195.   82 þe (2)] L&*r*; þise WHm.
73 by] R (? a) (*so* K-D); to WF; *om r.*

If I lye on yow to my lewed wit, ledeth me to brennyng!   *burning*
For as it semeth ye forsaketh no mannes almesse—   *turn down; alms*
85 Of usurers, of hoores, of avarouse chapmen—   *greedy merchants*
And louten to thise lordes that mowen lene yow nobles   *bow; give*
Ayein youre rule and religion—I take record at Jesus,   *order; witness from*
That seide to hise disciples, "*Ne sitis acceptores personarum.*"
Of this matere I myghte make a long bible;   *book*
90 Ac of curatours of Cristen peple, as clerkes bereth witnesse,
    as regards priests
I shal tellen it for truthes sake—take hede whoso liketh!
  'As holynesse and honeste out of Holy Chirche spredeth
Thorugh lele libbynge men that Goddes lawe techen,   *upright*
Right so out of Holy Chirche alle yveles spredeth
95 There inparfit preesthode is, prechours and techeris.   *imperfect, faulty*
And se it by ensaumple in somer tyme on trowes: *trees*
Ther some bowes ben leved and some bereth none,   *leafy*
Ther is a meschief in the more of swiche manere bowes.   *disease; root*
Right so persons and preestes and prechours of Holi Chirche
100 Is the roote of the right feith to rule the peple;   *orthodox*
Ac ther the roote is roten, reson woot the sothe,
Shal nevere flour ne fruyt, ne fair leef be grene.   *f. or f. (grow)*
  'Forthi wolde ȝe lettrede leve the lecherie of clothyng,
And be kynde as bifel for clerkes and curteise of Cristes goodes,
    charitable with
105 Trewe of youre tonge and of youre tail bothe,   *sex(ual organs)*
And hatien to here harlotrie, and aught to underfonge   *receive at all*
Tithes of untrewe thyng ytilied or chaffared—
Lothe were lewed men but thei youre loore folwede
And amenden hem that thei mysdoon, moore for youre ensaumples
110 Than for to prechen and preven it noght—ypocrisie it semeth!
    practice; hypocrisy
For ypocrisie in Latyn is likned to a dongehill   *dung-hill*
That were bisnewed with snow, and snakes withinne,   *snowed over*

---

88 Do not be respecters of persons (*cf.* Js 2: 1, *also* Deut 1: 17) (C).
107 Tithe-offerings of produce obtained from dishonest farming or trade.
108–9 The uneducated would be reluctant to do anything other than follow your
    teaching And would amend their wicked ways . . .

88 *acc. pers.*] α, C; *p. a.* β.
92 spr.] spryngeth {M); *cf.* C.
94 spr.] L&r, C; spryngeþ W.
98 bowes] stokkes C; *cf.* K-D *p.* 157.
99 so] L&r; so bi W; so of Cr.
100 Is þe] R (?=α; þey sholde been F),
    C (*so* K-D); That aren β.
101 Ac] L&r (but GF), C; And
    WCrC² C.
102 fr.] f. wexe C; *cf.* K-D *p.* 90.

106 auȝt] R (?=α; looþ wrong F)
    (*so* K-D); noȝt β.
107 of vn-] L&r (=β); vn- *om* αG;
    but of WCr.
109 -den] L&r, ?C; -deden WHmBF.
    þei] R (=α; *so* K-D *p.* 168*n*; *cf.*
    C); *om* W&r.
111 For yp.] L&r; The which W.
    to a] to a lothliche C (*so* K-D
    p. 94).

Or to a wal that were whitlymed and were foul withinne.

washed with white lime (Mt 23: 27)

Right so manye preestes, prechours and prelates—

115 Ye [b]en enblaunched with *bele paroles* and with clothes, *whitened; fine words*
Ac youre werkes and wordes therunder aren ful w[o]lveliche. *wolf-like (C)*
Johannes Crisostomus of clerkes speketh and preestes:

Sicut de templo omne bonum progreditur, sic de templo omne
malum procedit. Si sacerdocium integrum fuerit, tota floret
ecclesia; si autem corruptum fuerit, omnium fides marcida est.
Si sacerdocium fuerit in peccatis, totus populus convertitur
ad peccandum. Sicut cum videris arborem pallidam et marcidam
intelligis quod vicium habet in radice, ita cum videris
populum indisciplinatum et irreligiosum, sine dubio
sacerdocium eius non est sanum.

'If lewed men wiste what this Latyn meneth,

120 And who was myn auctour, muche wonder me thinketh *authority*
But if many preest beere, for hir baselardes and hir broches, *swords*
A peire of bedes in hir hand and a book under hir arme.

set of rosary-beads; prayer-book

Sire Johan and Sire Geffrey hath a girdel of silver,
A baselard or a ballok-knyf with botons overgilte.

125 Ac a porthors that sholde be his plow, *Placebo* to sigge,

breviary; `psalms'; say

Hadde he nevere, [his] service to [h]ave,
[And save he have] silver therto, seith it with ydel wille.
'Allas, ye lewed men, muche lese ye on preestes!
Ac thing that wikkedly is wonne, and with false sleightes, *tricks*

130 Wolde nevere the wit of witty God but wikkede men it hadde—

115 You are made fair with fine words and with the finery you wear . . .
118 Just as all good comes out of the temple, so does all evil. If the priesthood has
integrity, the whole church flourishes; but if it is corrupt, the faith(ful) as a
whole wither up. If the priests live in sin, the whole people turns to sin. Just as,
when you see a tree pale and drooping, you know it has a diseased root, so when
you see a people undisciplined and irreligious, you can be sure their priests are
diseased (pseudo-Chrysostom, Homily 38 on St Matthew, (*P.L.* 56, 839).
120–1 . . . it (would) amaze me If many a priest did not carry instead of swords
and brooch-ornaments.
125–7 But a breviary that might be his working equipment, with which to say the
psalm 'I will please the Lord [in the land of the living (Ps 114: 9, Vespers,
Office of the Dead)]' He has never possessed, with which to provide his service,
And, except when assured of payment for doing so, says it unthinkingly / with a
bad grace (*C*).

115 ben] C; aren *All* B-MSS (*C*).
cl.] R (?=α; *soph.* F); cl. also
β; *bele* cl. C (*so* K-D *p.* 94).
116 wlueliche] R (?=α; foxly F)
(*corr.* K-D, *and cf.* C XVI 270b);
vnloueliche β.
121 pr.] αM (*so* K-D); *pl.* Cr; a pr. β.

123 a . . . of s.] of s. a g. *sugg.* K-D
p. 194 (*C*).
126–7 *As one line All* B-MSS: Hadde
he neuere seruice to saue siluer
þerto seiþ it with ydel wille (*with
varr.*; saue] haue R) (*C*).

The whiche arn preestes inparfite and prechours after silver,
Executours and sodenes, somonours and hir lemmannes.

sub-deans; mistresses

This that with gile was geten, ungraciousliche is spended.

got; evilly, scandalously

So harlotes and hores arn holpe with swiche goodes,

135 Ac Goddes folk for defaute therof forfaren and spillen.   *come to grief; die*
'Curatours of Holy Kirke, and clerkes that ben avarouse,   *avaricious*
Lightliche that thei leven, losels it habbeth,   *Easily; leave behind; wastrels*
Or deieth intestate, and thanne [entreth the bisshop]
And maketh murthe therwith, and hise meyne both,   *regales himself; retinue*

140 And seyen, "He was a nygard, that no good myghte aspare   *miser; spare*
To frend ne to fremmed—the fend have his soule!   *stranger*
For a wrecchede hous he held al his lif tyme,
And that he spared and bispered, spende we in murthe!"

hoarded; locked up; amusement

'By lered, by lewed, that looth is to spende—

145 Thus goon hire goodes, be the goost faren.   *when the spirit is gone*
Ac for goode men, God woot, greet doel men maken,   *sorrow*
And bymeneth goode meteyyveres, and in mynde haveth

lament; food providers

In preieres and in penaunces and in parfit charite.'
'What is charite?' quod I tho. 'A childissh thyng,' he seide—   *childlike*
'*Nisi efficiamini sicut parvuli, non intrabitis in regnum celorum*—

150 Withouten fauntelte or folie a fre liberal wille.'   *childishness; generous*
'Where sholde men fynde swich a frend with so fre an herte?
I have lyved in londe,' quod I, 'my name is Longe Wille—
And fond I nevere ful charite, bifore ne bihynde.   *total, perfect; 'anywhere'*
Men beth merciable to mendinaunts and to poore,   *compassionate*

155 And wollen lene ther thei leve lelly to ben paied.   *give; believe; honestly*
Ac charite that Poul preiseth best and moost plesaunt to Oure Saveour—

pleasing

As *Non inflatur, non est ambiciosa, non querit que sua sunt*—
I seigh nevere swich a man, so me God helpe,

149a Unless [you be converted and] become as little children, you shall not enter
into the kingdom of heaven (Mt 18: 3).
152 I have lived in this world, my name is Tall Will / 'Perseverance itself',
longanimitas.
157 ... is not puffed up, Is not ambitious, seeketh not her own (I Cor 13: 4–5).

133 þis] L&r; That WCr; Al F.
   sp.] L&r; desp. W.
135 Ac] R (=α; But F) (*so* K-D); And β.
136 and] α, C; as β.
138 e. þe b.] *trsp.* K-D; þe b. e. *All*
   B-MSS.
139 with] L&r; myd WCr.
   meyne] HmF; men W&r; *see*
   K-D p. 148.

142 he h.] L&r; h. he W.
143 spen(d)e] O&r; disp. W.
144 spen(d)e] L&r; desp. W.
152 I (2)] L&r; he WHmCr¹.
156 sau.] L&r (=β); God R (?=α;
   g. in heuene F)Cr²³; lord WCr¹.
157 sunt] L&r, C; s. &c W.

That he ne wolde aske after his, and outherwhile coveite   *sometimes*
160 Thyng that neded hym noght—and nyme it, if he myghte!   *he needed; take*
   'Clerkes kenne me that Crist is in alle places;   *teach*
Ac I seigh hym nevere soothly but as myself in a mirour:
Hic in enigmate, tunc facie ad faciem.
And so I trowe trewely, by that men telleth of charite,
It is noght chaumpions fight, ne chaffare, as I trowe.'
                       (a matter of) prize-fighting; trade
165   'Charite,' quod he, 'ne chaffareth noght, ne chalangeth, ne craveth;
As proud of a peny as of a pound of golde,
And is as glad of a gowne of a gray russet   *(a rough woollen material)*
As of a tunycle of Tarse or of trie scarlet.   *jacket; silk; choice*
He is glad with alle glade and good til alle wikkede,
170 And leneth and loveth alle that Oure Lord made.
Corseth he no creature, ne he kan bere no wrathe,   *curses; feel*
Ne no likynge hath to lye ne laughe men to scorne.
Al that men seyn, he leet it sooth, and in solace taketh,   *considers; content*
And alle manere meschiefs in myldenesse he suffreth.
175 Coveiteth he noon erthely good but heveneriche blisse.'
   'Hath he any rentes or richesse, or any riche frendes?'
   'Of rentes ne of richesse rekketh he nevere,   *cares*
For a frend that fyndeth hym, failed hym nevere at nede: *provides for*
Fiat voluntas tua fynt hym everemoore,   *'Thy will be done'* (Mt 6: 10)
180 And if he soupeth, eteth but a sop of *Spera in Deo.*
                  sups; 'Hope in God' (Ps 41: 6)
He kan portreye wel the Paternoster and peynte it with Aves,
              draw; i.e. say his rosary
And outherwhile he is woned to wenden on pilgrymages   *accustomed*
Ther poore men and prisons liggeth, hir pardon to have;
Though he bere hem no breed, he bereth hem swetter liflode,
185 Loveth hem as Oure Lord biddeth and loketh how thei fare.
   'And whan he is wery of that werk than wole he som tyme
Labouren in a lavendrye wel the lengthe of a mile,   *laundry*
And yerne into youthe, and yepeliche seche   *run; eagerly seek (out)*
Pride, with al the appurtenaunces, and pakken hem togideres,
190 And bouken hem at his brest and beten hem clene,   *cleanse with lye*
And leggen on longe with *Laboravi in gemitu meo,*   *lay on (i.e. labour at)*

162a [We see] here [*nunc* 'now' *Vulg*] [through a glass] in a dark manner; but then face to face (I Cor 13: 12).
165 Charity does not engage in trade, lay claims, make demands.
187 Work away for twenty minutes [the time taken to walk a mile] at the (inward) cleansing of his soul (*see* Sk *ad loc*).
191 'I have laboured in my groanings, [every night I will wash my bed: I will water my couch with my tears]' (Ps 6: 7).

160 n. hym] h. n. a, *some* C-MSS.
162 a] *om* a.
162a *Hic*] aM, C; *It(a)* G&r; *om* w.
177 ne] L&r, C; *nor* W.

187 a(1)] LR; þe C; *om* W&r.
188 seche] R (=a; þere seken F); scheþ C; speke β.

And with warm water at hise eighen wasshen hem after.
Thanne he syngeth whan he doth so, and som tyme seith wepynge,
Cor contritum et humiliatum, Deus, non despicies.'
195 'By Crist! I wolde that I knewe hym,' quod I, 'no creature levere!'
                                                                more dear
   'Withouten help of Piers Plowman,' quod he, 'his persone sestow nevere.'
                                                                will you see
     'Wheither clerkes knowen hym,' quod I, 'that kepen Holi Kirke?'
     'Clerkes have no knowyng,' quod he, 'but by werkes and by wordes.
   Ac Piers the Plowman parceyveth moore depper   *perceives; deeply*
200 What is the wille, and wherfore that many wight suffreth:
   Et vidit Deus cogitaciones eorum.
   For ther are ful proude herted men, pacient of tonge   *restrained in speech*
   And buxome as of berynge to burgeises and to lordes,   *deferential*
   And to poore peple han pepir in the nose,   *act superciliously*
   And as a lyoun he loketh ther men lakken hise werkes.   *where; criticize*
205 'For ther are beggeris and bidderis, bedemen as it were,   *beadsmen*
   Loken as lambren and semen lif-holy—   *(Who) look; lambs*
   Ac it is moore to have hir mete on swich an esy manere
   Than for penaunce and parfitnesse, the poverte that swiche taketh.   *assume*
   'Therfore by colour ne by clergie knowe shaltow hym nevere,
                                                       outward appearances
210 Neither thorugh wordes ne werkes, but thorugh wil oone,   *will alone*
   And that knoweth no clerk ne creature on erthe
   But Piers the Plowman—*Petrus, id est, Christus.*
   For he nys noght in lolleris ne in londleperis heremytes,   *vagabond hermits*
   Ne at ancres there a box hangeth—alle swiche thei faiten.   *on whom; cheat*
215 Fy on faitours and *in fautores suos!*   *on their patrons*
   For Charite is Goddes champion, and as a good child hende,   *well-behaved*
   And the murieste of mouth at mete where he sitteth.   *most cheerful; words*
   The love that lith in his herte maketh hym light of speche,
   And is compaignable and confortatif, as Crist bit hymselve: *sociable; bids*
   Nolite fieri sicut ypocrite tristes &c.
220 For I have seyen hym in silk and som tyme in russet,
   Bothe in grey, and in grys, and in gilt harneis—   *fur; gilded armour*
   And as gladliche he it gaf to gomes that it neded.   *equally gladly; men*
     'Edmond and Edward, either were kynges   *both*

194 . . . a contrite and humbled heart, O God, thou wilt not despise (Ps 50: 19).
200a And God saw their thoughts (*after* Lk 11: 17) (*C*).
212 Peter, that is, Christ; *cf.* and the rock [*petra*] was Christ (1 Cor 10: 4), *also*
   Thou art Peter, and upon this rock . . . (Mt 16: 18). See Huppé, *'Petrus'*.
219–219a And is good company and cheering (to be with), as Christ himself tells
   (us to be): '[And, when you fast], be not as the hypocrites, sad . . .' (Mt 6: 16).

193 þanne] α, ?C (*so* K-D); And þ. β.   209 hym] L&*r; om* WCr.
   seiþ] *om* C.   213 nys] loveþ F (*C*).
206 lyf] L&*r;* ful W.   223 eyther] L&*r,* C; boþe WHm.
207 on] α (*so* K-D); wiþ WCrLM; yn *r.*
   an] *om* gF.

And seintes yset—[s]til[le] charite hem folwede.   *considered; constantly*
225   'I have yseyen charite also syngen and reden,   (sc. *as a priest*)
Riden, and rennen in raggede wedes;
Ac biddynge as beggeris biheld I hym nevere.
Ac in riche robes rathest he walketh,   *soonest*
Ycalled and ycrymyled and his crowne yshave.
230 And in a freres frokke he was yfounden ones—   *once*
Ac it is fern ago, in Seint Fraunceis tyme;   *a long while*
In that secte siththe to selde hath he ben knowen.   *order; since then; seldom*
   'Riche men he recomendeth, and of hir robes taketh   *commends*
That withouten wiles ledeth hir lyves:
Beatus est dives qui, &c.
235   'In kynges court he cometh ofte, ther the counseil is trewe;   *honest*
Ac if coveitise be of the counseil he wol noght come therinne.
In court amonges japeris he cometh but selde,
For braulynge and bakbitynge and berynge of fals witnesse.
   'In the consistorie bifore the commissarie he cometh noght ful ofte,
     bishop's officer
240 For hir lawe dureth overlonge but if thei lacchen silver,   *lasts*
And matrimoyne for moneie maken and unmaken,   *marriage(s); (they) make*
And that conscience and Crist hath yknyt faste,   *that (which); bound firmly*
Thei undoon it un[digne]ly, tho doctours of lawe.   *unworthily*
   'Amonges erchebisshopes and other bisshopes and prelates of Holy Chirche,
245 For to wonye with hem his wone was som tyme,   *dwell; habit; once*
And Cristes patrimonye to the poore parcelmele dele.   *divide by portions*
Ac avarice hath the keyes now and kepeth for his kynnesmen
And for his seketoures and his servaunts, and som for hir children.

     executors
   'Ac I ne lakke no lif, but, Lord, amende us alle,   *disparage no person*
250 And gyve us grace, goode God, charite to folwe!
For whoso myghte meete with hym, swiche maneres hym eileth—

     afflict (ironic)

229 Wearing a cap, and with his head anointed, and with his hair tonsured.
234*a* Blessed is the rich man [that is found without blemish] (Ecclus 31: 8).
240 For their legal proceedings drag on interminably unless they receive bribes
   (to shorten them).

224 stille] *rec.* K-D *p.* 185 (*cf.* C
   XVI 346); tyl L&*r* (β); for wM;
   so α.
229 *After this a line* & clenlyche
   yclothed In cypres & In tartaryne
   g (*prob. spurious*).
232 knowe(n)] L&*r*; founde W, C
   (C).
237 lap.] þe commune *conj* K-D
   p. 94 *after* C (C).
243 -digne-] *conj* K-D *p.* 195;
   -worþi- *All* B-MSS.

244-8 α (*cf.* C XVI 363-6); *om* β.
244 *So printed* Sk; *as two lines
   divided after* bissh. (2) R.
   Amonges . . . o.b.] with B. &
   abbotys F.
246 patri.] parsy. F.
   dele] þey deltyn F.
247 Ac] R, C; But F.
   now] *om* F.
248 his (2)] *om* F.
   here] hise F.
251 with] L&*r*; myd W.

Neither he blameth ne banneth, bosteth ne preiseth,   *curses*
Lakketh, ne loseth, ne loketh up sterne,   *praises; sternly*
Craveth, ne coveiteth, ne crieth after moore:
In pace in idipsum dormiam &c.
255 The mooste liflode that he lyveth by is love in Goddes passion;
Neither he biddeth, ne beggeth, ne borweth to yelde;   *pay (back)*
Misdooth he no man, ne with his mouth greveth.   *Harms; offends*
    'Amonges Cristene men this myldenesse sholde laste,
In alle manere angres have this at herte—   *troubles; (they should) have*
260 That theigh thei suffrede al this, God suffrede for us moore
In ensample we sholde do so, and take no vengeaunce
Of oure foes that dooth us falsnesse—that is oure fadres wille.
For wel may every man wite, if God hadde wold hymselve,
Sholde nevere Judas ne Jew have Jesu doon on roode,   *crucified*
265 Ne han martired Peter ne Poul, ne in prison holden.
Ac he suffrede in ensample that we sholde suffren also,
And seide to swiche that suffre wolde that *Pacientes vincunt.*
    '*Verbi gratia,*' quod he—and verred ensamples manȳe.
     For example; instanced
    'In *Legenda Sanctorum,* the lif of holy seintes,
270 What penaunce and poverte and passion thei suffrede—   *pain*
In hunger, in hete, in alle manere angres.   *afflictions*
    'Antony and Egidie and othere holy fadres   *Egidius*
Woneden in wildernesse among wilde beestes;   *Dwelt*
Monkes and mendinaunts, men by hemselve
275 In spekes and in spelonkes, selde speken togideres.   *hollows; caves*
Ac neither Antony ne Egidie ne heremyte that tyme
Of leons ne of leopardes no liflode ne toke,   *From; sustenance*
But of foweles that fleeth—thus fyndeth men in bokes—   *fly; read*
Except that Egidie after an hynde cride,   *doe; called*
280 And thorugh the mylk of that mylde beest the man was sustened;
And day bi day hadde he hire noght his hunger for to slake,
But selden and sondry tymes, as seith the book and techeth.
Antony adayes aboute noon tyme   *daily; midday*
Hadde a brid that broughte hym breed that he by lyvede;   *bird*
285 And though the gome hadde a gest, God fond hem bothe.
     guest; provided for
    'Poul *primus heremita* hadde parroked hymselve,   *the first hermit; enclosed*

254*a* In peace in the selfsame I will sleep, [and I will rest] (Ps 4: 9).
255 His chief sustenance is love (nourished by) Christ's sufferings.

254*a* om *a.*
263 wel . . . man] e. man m. w. *a.*
268 verred] F (*so* K-D *p.* 172);
    verray W&r (*C*).
277 of] of þe *a.*

282 tymes] tyme *a.*
283 adayes] β (ech a daye Cr²³); on a
    day *a.*
285 fond] fedde *a.*
286 hym] β, C; in h. *a.*

That no man myghte hym se for mosse and for leves.
Foweles hym fedde fele wyntres with alle   *many; moreover*
Til he foundede freres of Austynes ordre.   *(Augustinian canons)*
290 Poul, after his prechyng, paniers he made,   *i.e. the Apostle; baskets*
And wan with hise hondes that his wombe neded.   *earned; what; stomach*
Peter fisshed for his foode, and his felawe Andrew: *companion*
Som thei solde and som thei soden, and so thei lyved bothe.   *cooked*
And also Marie Maudeleyne by mores lyvede and dewes,   *roots*
295 Ac moost thorugh devocion and mynde of God Almyghty.

        thinking, contemplating
I sholde noght thise seven daies siggen hem alle   *could not; in seven days*
That lyveden thus for Oure Lordes love many longe yeres.
'Ac ther ne was leoun ne leopard that on laundes wenten,   *glades*
Neither bere, ne boor, ne oother beest wilde
300 That ne fil to hir feet and fawned with the tailles;   *fell; tails*
And if thei kouthe han ycarped, by Crist, as I trowe,   *spoken*
Thei wolde have yfed that folk bifore wilde foweles.
For al the curteisie that beestes konne, thei kidde that folk ofte,

        are capable of; showed to
In likkyng and in lowynge, there thei on laundes yede.

        submitting (themselves); went
305 Ac God sente hem foode by foweles, and by no fierse beestes,
In menynge that meke thyng mylde thyng sholde fede.   *As a sign; creature*
As who seith religious rightfulle men sholde fynde,

        As if to say; upright; provide for
And lawefulle men to lif-holy men liflode brynge;

        men who keep (God's) law
And thanne wolde lordes and ladies be looth to agulte,   *commit sin*
310 And to taken of hir tenaunts more than trouthe wolde,   *their honest due*
Founde thei that freres wolde forsake hir almesses,

        If they were to find; give up
And bidden hem bere it there it was yborwed.
For we ben Goddes foles and abiden alwey,   *fools (C)*
Til briddes brynge us that we sholde [by lyve].   *live by*
315 For hadde ye potage and payn ynogh, and peny ale to drynke,

        stew; bread; cheap ale
And a mees thermyd of o maner kynde,   *dish; one*

289 ordere] o. or ellis frerys lyen B (C).
294 and] β, C; a. by α.
297 many . . . y.] β, C; amonges wilde bestes α.
303–4 α; om β.
303 curteisie . . . k.] kyȝndenesse þat þey cowde F.
    þat (2)] to F.

304 in low.] lovynge F.
    l. yede] londis wentyn F.
307 fynde] L&r (cf. C XVII 34a); fede WF.
    -ous] L&r; -ouses W.
308 br.] L&r; sholde b. WF.
312 was yb.] trsp. K-D p. 194.
313 foles] Cr²³; foweles W&r (C).
314 by l.] l. by All B-MSS.

Ye hadde right ynogh, ye religiouse—and so youre rule me tolde.
would have

Numquid, dicit Job, rugiet onager cum habuerit herbam?
Aut mugiet bos cum ante plenum presepe steterit? Brutorum
animalium natura te condempnat, quia cum eis pabulum commune
sufficiat; ex adipe prodiit iniquitas tua.

'If lewed men knewe this Latyn, thei wolde loke whom thei yeve,
take care whom they gave to
And avisen hem bifore a fyve dayes or sixe   *And take advice well in advance*
320 Er thei amortisede [moore] to monkes or chanons hir rentes.
conveyed; incomes from land
Allas! lordes and ladies, lewed counseil have ye   *ill-advised are you*
To yyve from youre heires that youre aiels you lefte,   *that which; forefathers*
And yyveth to bidde for yow to swiche that ben riche,   *pray*
And ben founded and feffed ek to bidde for othere!   *enfeoffed*
325 'Who parfourneth this prophecie, of the peple that now libbeth—
fulfils; among; live

Dispersit, dedit pauperibus?
If any peple parfourne that text, it are thise poore freres: *fulfil*
For that thei beggen aboute, in buyldynge thei spende,
And on hemself som, and swiche as ben hir laborers;
330 And of hem that habbeth thei taken, and yyveth hem that ne habbeth!
'Ac clerkes and knyghtes, and communers that ben riche,   *common people*
Fele of yow fareth as if I a forest hadde   *Many; behave*
That were ful of faire trees, and I fondede and caste   *tried; contrived*
How I myghte mo therinne amonges hem sette.   *more*
335 Right so ye riche—ye robeth that ben riche,   *clothe those who are*
And helpeth hem that helpeth yow, and yyveth ther no nede is;
As whoso filled a tonne ful of a fressh ryver,   *one who; tun; from*
And wente forth with that water to woke with Themese.   *moisten the Thames*
Right so ye riche, ye robeth and fedeth

317a Will the wild ass bray [says Job] when he hath grass? Or will the ox low when he standeth before a full manger? (Job 6: 5). The (very) nature of brute beasts is a condemnation of you, since with them common (?shared / ordinary) food suffices; your evil has originated from excess (*exact source unknown; see Sk ad hoc*).
320 Before alienating any more of their (income-yielding) properties in mortmain to (corporations of) monks and canons (regular).
323-4 And give (away your patrimony), in order that they should pray for you, to those who are wealthy AND, moreover, have been established and (already) endowed with lands for the purpose, precisely, of praying for others.
326 He hath distributed, he hath given to the poor (Ps 111: 9).

317a -quid] FCr²³ (*so* Vulg; *so* K-D);   323 ȝiu.] L&r; ȝ. it WCrFB.
-quam W&r, C.   328 sp.] R&r; sp. it WCrC; it sp.
    rugiet] a, C (*so* Vulg, K-D);   HmF.
    rugit β (*om* Y).   330 ne] L&r; nede BF; *om* w.
    hab. h.] aO, C (*so* Vulg); herb. h. β.   337 ful] a (*so* K-D *p.* 147); *om* β.
320 m. to] eny more for C; to *All*   fr.] ful R (?=a; *om* F).
B-MSS (sikirly vnto F) (*C*).
    rentes] L&r; *sg.* W.

340 Hem that han as ye han—hem ye make at ese.
    'Ac religiouse that riche ben sholde rather feeste beggeris   *entertain*
    Than burgeises that riche ben, as the book techeth:
    Quia sacrilegium est res pauperum non pauperibus dare.
    Item: peccatoribus dare est demonibus immolare.
    Item: monache, si indiges et accipis, pocius das quam accipis;
    Si autem non eges et accipis, rapis.
    Porro non indiget monachus, si habeat quod nature sufficit.
    'Forthi I counseille alle Cristene to conformen hem to charite—
    For charite withouten chalangynge unchargeth the soule,   *claiming; frees*
345 And many a prison fram purgatorie thorugh hise preieres he delivereth.
    Ac ther is a defaute in the folk that the feith kepeth,   sc. *the clergy*
    Wherfore folk is the febler, and noght ferm of bileve.   *firm in faith*
    As in lussheburwes is a luther alay, and yet loketh he lik a sterlyng: *bad*
    The merk of that monee is good, ac the metal is feble.   *imprint on*
350 And so it fareth by som folk now: thei han a fair speche,
    Crowne and Cristendom, the kynges mark of hevene,
    Ac the metal, that is mannes soule, with [many] synne is foule[d].   *debased*
    Bothe lettred and lewed beth alayed now with synne,
    That no lif loveth oother, ne Oure Lord, as it semeth.
355 For what thorugh werre and wikkede werkes and wederes unresonable,
    Wederwise shipmen and witty clerkes also   *Weather-wise, experienced*
    Have no bileve to the lifte, ne to the loore of philosophres.   *faith in; the sky*
    'Astronomiens alday in hir art faillen   *Astronomers*
    That whilom warned bifore what sholde falle after;
360 Shipmen and shepherdes, that with ship and sheep wenten,
    Wisten by the walkne what sholde bitide,   *sky; happen*
    Tilieris that tiled the erthe tolden hir maistres
    By the seed that thei sewe what thei selle myghte,
    And what to leve and to lyve by, the lond was so trewe;   *reliable*

342a For it is sacrilege not to give to the poor what is theirs (Peter Cantor, *ch.* 47, *quoting* St Jerome, Epist. 66, sect. 8). Also, to give to sinners is to sacrifice to devils (Peter Cantor, *ch.* 47, *after* Jer.). Also, monk, if you are in need and receive, you should still give rather than receive; but if you do not need and (yet) accept, you are stealing (Peter Cantor, *ch.* 48, *after* Jerome). (*P.L.* 205: *cols.* 147, 149, 152). Further, a monk is not in need if he has what suffices for nature (*cf.* I Tim 6: 8).
348 As Luxembourg coins [light coins of poor quality] are alloyed with base metal, and yet they look like (genuine) sterling (silver).
351 Tonsure and Christianity, the mark of the King of Heaven [*sc.* the sign of the cross made in baptism (Sk)].
364 And what to leave [? for seed-corn] *or* part with and what to keep for their own food, the earth yielded so reliably and consistently.

345 he d.] WHmLM (? = β; *soph.* Cr; he *om* r = g); is deliuered α (is) ben F).
352 with m.] w. *All* B-MSS; myd *conj* K-D *p.* 195 (C).
    fouled] foule alayed W&r (f.] ful OC²; so F) (C).
355 what] α, C; *om* β. unr.] vnseasonable Cr²³; unstable F (C).
363 selle] L&r, C; selde W.
364 to (2)] LMRF; what to W&r.

365 Now failleth the folk of the flood and of the lond bothe—
Shepherdes and shipmen, and so do thise tilieris:
Neither thei konneth ne knoweth oon cours bifore another.   *skill, procedure*
   'Astronomyens also aren at hir wittes ende:
Of that was calculed of the clem[a]t, the contrarie thei fynde.

                                     calculated concerning
370 Grammer, the ground of al, bigileth now children: *basis; perplexes*
For is noon of thise newe clerkes—whoso nymeth hede—   *takes notice*
That kan versifye faire ne formaliche enditen,
Ne naught oon among an hundred that an auctour kan construwe, *translate*
Ne rede a lettre in any langage but in Latyn or in Englissh.
375   'Go now to any degree, and but if gile be maister,
And flaterere his felawe [to fourmen under hym],   *teach*
Muche wonder me thynketh amonges us alle!
Doctours of decrees and of divinite maistres,   *Canon Law*
That sholde konne and knowe alle kynnes clergie,   *learning*
380 And answere to arguments and also to a *quodlibet*—

                    general intellectual problem (C)
I dar noght siggen it for shame—if swiche were apposed,   *questioned*
Thei sholde faillen of hir Philosophie, and in Phisik bothe.
   'Wherfore I am afered of folk of Holy Kirke,   *frightened by*
Lest thei overhuppen, as oothere doon, in Office and in Houres.

                              skip over parts
385 Ac if thei overhuppe—as I hope noght—oure bileve suffiseth;
As clerkes in Corpus Christi feeste syngen and reden   *feast of C. C.*
That *sola fides sufficit* to save with lewed peple—
And so may Sarsens be saved, scribes and Jewes.   *Moslems*
   'Allas thanne! but oure looresmen lyve as thei leren us,

                    but (that); teachers; should live
390 And for hir lyvynge that lewed men be the lother God agulten.
For Sarsens han somwhat semynge to oure bileve,   *resembling*
For thei love and bileve in o [Lede] almyghty,   *one (divine) person, lord*
And we, lered and lewed, [bileveth in oon God]—
Cristene and uncristene on oon [creatour] bileveth.

369 *clemat*, 'a region of the earth often considered with respect to its weather'
(*MED*) (*C*).
372 Who can write good verses or compose (letters/poetry) correctly.
387 That 'Faith alone suffices' to save uneducated people with (*Pange Lingua*,
st. 4) (*C*).
389–90 Alas, then, that our teachers should not live as they teach us to, And the
laity as a consequence of *their* (holy) lives be all the more reluctant to offend God.

369 þe clymat] C; clement α; þe
   element W&r (*pl.* g) (*C*).
372 L&r, C; *l. om* w.
373 Ne] L&r; Is OC²; *om* WCr.
376 to ... h.] to f. his speche & F;
   vnder h. to f. W&r (*C*).
385 Ac] LR; And W.

392 Lede] persone W&r; god Cr (*C*).
393 bileveth ... g.] in o*n* g. b. L&r
   (b.] almyȝty WCot); *trsp.* K-D *p.* 194.
394 α (*so* K-D); *om* β.
   cris.] & *so* cr. F.
   crea.] god α (*C*).
   bil.] ben leven F.

395 Ac oon Makometh, a man, in mysbileve   *into infidelity*
    Broughte Sarsens of Surree—and see in what manere.
     'This Makometh was a Cristene man, and for he moste noght ben a pope,
                                            because; might
    Into Surrie he soughte, and thorugh hise sotile wittes   *went*
    Daunted a dowve, and day and nyght hire fedde.   *Tamed; dove*
400 The corn that she croppede, he caste it in his ere;   *ate; put*
    And if he among the peple preched, or in places come,
    Thanne wolde the colvere come to the clerkes ere   *dove*
    Menynge as after mete—thus Makometh hire enchauntede,
                                        Seeking food; charmed
    And dide folk thanne falle on knees, for he swoor in his prechyng
405 That the colvere that com so com from God of hevene
    As messager to Makometh, men for to teche.
    And thus thorugh wiles of his wit and a whit dowve
    Makometh in mysbileve men and wommen broughte,
    That lered there and lewed yit leeven on hise lawes.   *still believe*
410   'And siththe Oure Saveour suffred the Sarsens so bigiled
                           allowed; (to be) thus deceived
    Thorugh a Cristene clerk acorsed in his soule—
    Ac for drede of the deeth I dar noght telle truthe,
    How Englisshe clerkes a colvere fede that Coveitise highte,
    And ben manered after Makometh, that no man useth trouthe,
415   'Ancres and heremytes, and monkes and freres
    Peeren to Apostles thorugh hire parfit lyvynge.   *Are as equals*
    Wolde nevere the feithful Fader that hise ministres sholde
    Of tirauntis that teneth trewe men taken any almesse,   *From; harm*
    But doon as Antony dide, Dominyk and Fraunceys,   *(should) do*
420 Beneit and Bernard [bo]the, whiche hem first taughte
    To lyve by litel and in lowe houses by lele mennes almesse.   *virtuous*
    Grace sholde growe and be grene thorugh hir goode lyvynge,
    And folkes sholden fynde, that ben in diverse siknesse,   *feel (v. MED s.v. 6c)*
    The bettre for hir biddynges in body and in soule.   *prayers*
425 Hir preieres and hir penaunces to pees sholde brynge
    Alle that ben at debaat, and bedemen were trewe: *strife; if*
    Petite et accipietis &c.

426*a* ... seek, and you shall find (Mt 7: 73).

395 *divided fr.* 396 *after* br. WCr (*cf.*
    408 *below*).
    Ac] LRB (But F); And W&*r*.
397 man] LRF (*cf.* C); *om* W&*r*.
399 Dau.] L&*r*; He d. WHmGF.
401–2 *om* α.
406 As] And α.
409 lered] L&*r* (l. men F); lewyd Hm;
    lyued þo WCrM.
    lew.] L&*r*; ler. Hm; lyu*e* WCrM.

412 Ac] LR (But F); *om* WCr; and *r*.
416 Peeren] β; Peres R; Been p. F.
    to] L&*r*; to þe WF.
420 and] or α.
    bothe] þe *All* B-MSS; *cf.* K-D
    p. 199 (C).
421 alm.] fyndynge α.
422 goode] lele α.
423 fynde] L&*r*; fare W(Hm).
425 br.] hem b. α.

"Salt saveth catel," siggen thise wyves;   *preserves; (here=) meat, fish*
Vos estis sal terre &c.
The hevedes of Holy Chirche—and thei holy were—   *heads; if*
Crist calleth hem salt for Cristene soules,
Et si sal evanuerit, in quo salietur?
430 Ac fressh flessh outher fissh, whan it salt failleth,   *lacks*
It is unsavory, for sothe, ysoden or ybake;   *ill-tasting; boiled*
So is mannes soule, soothly, that seeth no good ensample
Of hem of Holi Chirche that the heighe wey sholde teche
And be gide, and go bifore as a good banyer,   *guide; standard-bearer*
435 And hardie hem that bihynde ben, and yyve hem good evidence.
   embolden; example

  'Ellevene holy men al the world tornede   *converted*
Into lele bileve; the lightloker, me thynketh,   *more easily*
Sholde alle maner men, we han so manye maistres—
Preestes and prechours, and a pope above,
440 That Goddes salt sholde be, to save mannes soule.   *preserve/save*
  'Al was hethynesse som tyme Engelond and Walis,   *entirely pagan; Wales*
Til Gregory garte clerkes to go here and preche.   *made*
Austyn [cristnede the kyng at Caunterbury],
And thorugh miracles, as men mow rede, al that marche he tornede
   may; district, territory
445 To Crist and to Cristendom, and cros to honoure,
And follede folk faste, and the feith taughte   *baptized*
Moore thorugh miracles than thorugh muche prechyng,
As wel thorugh hise werkes as with hise holy wordes,
And [fourmed] what fullynge and feith was to mene.   *taught; baptism*
450   'Clooth that cometh fro the wevyng is noght comly to were   *weaving; fit*
Til it be fulled under foot or in fullyng stokkes,   *cleansing-frames*
Wasshen wel with water and with taseles cracched,   *teazles; carded*
Ytouked and yteynted and under taillours hande;   *tucked; stretched*
And so it fareth by a barn that born is of wombe: *child*
455 Til it be cristned in Cristes name and confermed of the bisshop,
It is hethene as to heveneward, and helplees to the soule.
   in respect of heaven, the soul

"Hethen" is to mene after heeth and untiled erthe—
   derives from; uncultivated
As in wilde wildernesse wexeth wilde beestes,   *spring up*

427a, 429a You are the salt of the earth. [But], if the salt lose its savour, wherewith
  shall it be salted? (Mt 5: 13).

427 catel] LR; þe c. WYF.
427a–90 *Lines om* F.
429a -tur] LR; -tur &c W.
430 Ac] LR; For WCr.
432 g. ens.] L&r; pl. W.
443 cristnede . . . C.] at C. cr. þe k. *All*
  B-MSS (þe k. cr. *sugg.* K-D p. 194).

449 And fo.] A. seide *All* B-MSS;
  Enformed *conj* K-D p. 195; *cf.* 376
  above).
454 And] L&r; Right W.
  of] L&r; of a wM.

Rude and unresonable, rennynge withouten keperes.　　*Untrained; keepers*
460　'Ye mynnen wel how Mathew seith, how a man made a feste:
　　He fedde hem with no venyson, ne fesaunts ybake,　　*pheasants*
　　But with foweles that fram hym nolde, but folwede his whistlyng:
　　Ecce altilia mea et omnia parata sunt—
　　And with calves flessh he fedde the folk that he lovede.
　　'The calf bitokneth clennesse in hem that kepeth lawes;
　　　　　　　　　　　　　　stands for purity (of life)
465　For as the cow thorugh kynde mylk the calf norisseth til an oxe,
　　　　　　　　　　　　　　feeds; until (it is) an oxe
　　So love and leaute lele men susteneth;
　　And maidenes and mylde men mercy desiren
　　Right as the cow-calf coveiteth swete melk—
　　So [muche] don rightfulle men mercy and truthe.
470　And by the hond-fedde foweles his folk understonde
　　That looth ben to lovye withouten lernynge of ensaumples.　　*unwilling*
　　Right as capons in a court cometh to mennes whistlynge—
　　　　　　　　　　　　　　chickens; court(yard)
　　In menynge after mete folweth men that whistlen—　　*Seeking food*
　　Right so rude men that litel reson konneth
475　Loven and bileven by lettred mennes doynges,　　*actions*
　　And by hire wordes and werkes wenen and trowen;
　　　　　　　　　　　　　　form opinions; hold beliefs
　　And as tho foweles to fynde foode after whistlynge,
　　So hope thei to have hevene thorugh hir [wiss]ynge.　　*instruction (C)*
　　And the man that made the feste the mageste bymeneth—　　*signifies*
480　That is God, of his grace gyveth alle men blisse.　　*(who) out of*
　　With wederes and with wondres he warneth us with a whistlere
　　　　　　　　　　　　　　tempests; portents
　　Where that his wil is, to worshipen us alle,　　*do honour to*
　　And feden us and festen us for everemoore at oones.
　　'Ac who beth that excuseth hem that arn persons and preestes
　　　　　　　　　　　　　　(Those) who
485　(That hevedes of Holy Chirche ben) that han hir wil here
　　Withouten travaille the tithe deel that trewe men biswynken—
　　　　　　　　　　　　　　the tenth part of the labour
　　Thei wol be wrooth for I write thus—ac to witnesse I take

462a Behold ... my [beeves and] fatlings [are killed] and all things are ready
　　(Mt 22: 4).
486 Without doing a tenth part [*with pun on* tithe(s)] of the hard labour that honest
　　men have to engage in.

459 keperes] R (?=α) (*so* K-D *p.*
　146); cropiers W&c; creperes L&c.
468 sw. m.] L&r; melk swete W.
469 muche d.] don *All* B-MSS (*C*).

470–83 R (?=α); lines om β.
478 wissynge] whistlynge R;
　techynge *conj* Sk (*C*).
484 aren] L&r; ben W.

Bothe Mathew and Mark and *Memento Domine David:*
Ecce audivimus e[a]m in Effrata &c.
What pope or prelate now parfourneth that Crist highte—   *carries out; bade*
Ite in universum mundum et predicate &c?
490   'Allas, that men so longe on Makometh sholde bileve!
So manye prelates to preche as the Pope maketh—   *(There are) so many*
Of Nazareth, of Nynyve, of Neptalym and Damaske.
That thei ne wente as Crist wisseth—sithen thei wilne a name—
                                                                                            (Alas) that; title
To be pastours and preche the passion of Jesus,
495 And as hymself seide, so to lyve and dye:
Bonus pastor animam suam ponit &c;
And seide it in salvacion of Sarsens and othere—
For Cristene and uncristene, Crist seide to prechours,
Ite vos in vineam meam &c.
   'And sith that thise Sarsens, scribes and Jewes
500 Han a lippe of oure bileve, the lightloker, me thynketh,   *portion; more easily*
Thei sholde turne, whoso travaile wolde to teche hem of the Trinite:
                                              be converted; if anyone would work
Querite et invenietis &c.
For alle paynymes preieth and parfitly bileveth   *(here=) Moslems*
In the [grete holy] God, and his grace asken,
And make hir mone to Makometh, hir message to shewe.   *pray*
505 Thus in a feith leveth that folk, and in a fals mene,
                                              one and the same f.; mediator
And that is routhe for rightful men that in the reawme wonyen,
                                                                          pity; just; dwell
And a peril to the Pope and prelates that he maketh,   *?dire disgrace*
That bere bisshopes names of Bethleem and Babiloigne.

488–8*a* Both Matthew [28: 19] and Mark [16: 15; *see* 489*a*] and 'O Lord, remember
   David'; 'Behold, we have heard of it [God's tabernacle] in Ephrata' (Ps 131: 6).
489*a* Go ye into the whole world and preach [the gospel to every creature] (Mk
   16: 15).
495*a* The good shepherd giveth his life [for his sheep] (Jn 10: 11).
498 Go you also into my vineyard (Mt 20: 4).
501*a* Seek, and you shall find (Mt 7: 7).
504 And pray to M., that he might make known their entreaty to God [*sc.* as
   mediator].

488*a* R (?=a); *om* β.
   eam] eum R; *corr.* Sk.
493 wilne] α (wilneþ C); wille β.
   a] LR; þe F, C; haue W&r.
495 so to] L&r (go to Cot); so C; to
   WGYF.
   dye] L&r, C; to d. W.
500 -loker] LRF; -lier W.
501 tr. w.] L&r; trauailled w(M).
502–8, 527–30 *copied after* 531–7 *All*

B-MSS (531–7 *om* α); *re-arr.* K-D
pp. 176–9 (C).
502 and ... b.] β, C (XVII 255); to
   on persone to [of F] helpe α.
503 In ... G.] In þe g. heye g. ?C;
   In þe holy gr. g. β; On [& on F] o
   god þei greden α (C).
   grace] α, C; g. þei β.
505 leueþ] OC²Hm; lyueth LRF, C
   (liue Cr); leue W&r.

'Whan the hye kyng of hevene sente his sone to erthe,
510 Many miracles he wroughte man for to turne,   *convert, cause to repent*
In ensaumple that men sholde se by sadde reson   *sober, serious argument*
Men myghte noght be saved but thorugh mercy and grace,
And thorugh penaunce, and passion, and parfit byleve;
And bicam man of a mayde, and *metropolitanus*,   *(=archbishop)*
515 And baptised and bishined with the blode of his herte   *?illuminated (C)*
Alle that wilned and wolde with inwit bileve it.   *'with mind and heart'*
Many a seynt siththen hath suffred to deye,
Al for to enforme the feith in fele contrees deyeden—   *teach; many*
In Inde, and in Alisaundre, in Ermonye and in Spayne,   *Armenia*
520 In doelful deth deyeden for hir feith sake.   *miserable, painful*
In savacion of the feith Seint Thomas was ymartired: *To preserve*
Amonges unkynde Cristene for Cristes love he deyede,
And for the right of al this reume and alle reumes Cristene.
    (cause of justice) in; kingdom
Holy Chirche is honoured heighliche thorugh his deying;
525 He is a forbisene to alle bisshopes and a bright myrour,
    example; image, pattern
And sovereynliche to swiche that of Surrye bereth the name,
    supremely; Syria, pagan lands
And naught to huppe aboute in Engelond to halwe mennes auteres,
    skip; sanctify; altars
And crepe in amonges curatours and confessen ageyn the lawe:
Nolite mittere falsem in messem alienam &c.
Many man for Cristes love was martired amonges Romaynes   *the Romans*
530 Er Cristendom were knowe ther or any cros honoured.
'It is ruthe to rede how rihtwise men lyvede—   *pitiful*

526–28a And supremely an example to bishops appointed to sees in Syria [*sc.* to go there and preach Christianity at the risk of their lives] And not to run all over England to consecrate altars And insinuate themselves (into the affairs of) parish-priests, and hear confessions unlicensed [by the ordinary]: 'Do not put your sickle to another man's corn' (*cf.* Deut 23: 25).

509–26 α, C; *lines om* β.
511 men] *om* F.
    by] C; þat by α (*C*).
513 beleve] F, C; byle R.
515 bisch.] *so* C-MSS XUI (?=C; busshopede C-MSS PT); ysygned F (*C*).
517 hath] haven F.
518 enf.] ferme F (*C*).
    deyeden] R, C; dyȝen F.
519 &c and (1, 2)] *om* F.
520 In] & in F.
521 þe f.] mannys saule C (*so* K-D).
522 Am.] R, C; And among F.
    loue] *om* F.
527 *Here* W&r *resume*.

And n. t.] α (*cf.* C); That β (*C*).
in] W&r (=β; *om* OC²), C; here in R (=α; *soph.* F).
mennes] β, C; *om* α, Hm.
528 in] α, C (*so* K-D); *om* β.
    and] WRF, C; *om* L&r.
529 am. rom.] R (?=α; in grete roome F), C (*so* K-D); in Romayne β.
530 Er] FR (=α), C (*so* K-D); Er any W&c (?=β).
    were] α, C (*so* K-D); was β.
531–67 *lines om* α; *after* 501a *and foll. by* 502–8, 527–30 β; *re-arr.* K-D; *see* (C) *on* 502–8.

How thei defouled hir flessh, forsoke hir owene wille,   *mortified*
Fer fro kyth and fro kyn yvele yclothed yeden,   *went about*
Baddely ybedded, no book but conscience,
535 Ne no richesse but the roode to rejoisse hem inne:
Absit nobis gloriari nisi in cruce Domini nostri &c.
     'And tho was plentee and pees amonges poore and riche;
And now is routhe to rede how the rede noble
Is reverenced er the roode, receyved for the worthier
Than Cristes cros that overcam deeth and dedly synne.
                              the cross of C., who . . .
540 And now is werre and wo, and whoso why asketh—
For coveitise after cros; the croune stant in golde.
Bothe riche and religious, that roode thei honoure
That in grotes is ygrave and in gold nobles.   *groats; engraved*
For coveitise of that cros [clerkes] of Holy Kirke
545 Shul torne as Templers dide—the tyme approcheth faste.   *be overturned*
     '[Mynne] ye noght, wise men, how tho men honoured   *Recall*
Moore tresor than trouthe? I dar noght telle the sothe;
Reson and rightful doom tho religious demede.   *judged*
Right so, ye clerkes, for youre coveitise, er [come aught] longe,
550 Shal thei demen *dos ecclesie*, and [depose youre pride]:
Deposuit potentes de sede &c.
     'If knyghthod and kynde wit, and the commune and conscience
Togideres love leelly, leveth it wel, ye bisshopes—
The lordshipe of londes [lese ye shul for evere],
And lyven as *Levitici*, as Oure Lord yow techeth: *the Levites*
Per primicias et decimas &c.
555   'Whan Costantyn of curteisie Holy Kirke dowed   *Constantine; endowed*
With londes and ledes, lordshipes and rentes,   *properties*
An aungel men herden an heigh at Rome crye,   *aloud*

535a But God forbid that I should glory, save in the cross of our Lord [J. C.]
     (Gal 6: 14).
541 Because of desire for the cross [imprinted on the noble]; the prize [they seek]
     is to be found in gold (C).
550–550a Shall they pass judgment on (those who hold) the temporal possessions
     of the Church . . . 'He hath put down the mighty from their seat' (Lk 1: 52).
554a By first-fruits and tithes (*cf.* Deut 12: 6).

538 rec.] L&r; and r. WCrB, ?C.   549 er c. au3t] C (*so* K-D *p.* 152); er
     þe (2)] L&r, C; *om* W.   W&r.
544 clerkes] C (*so* K-D *p.* 152; *cf.*   550 d. y. p.] d. 3ow for y. p. C (*so*
     549 *below*); men W&r.   K-D); y. p. depose W&r.
545 torne] ouert. B, C (*C*).   551 þe] W, C; *om r.*
546 Mynne] C (*so* K-D *p.* 152); Wite   & (3)] B, C (*so* K-D); by WCrM;
     W&r (*C*).   *om r.*
     wyse] L&r; ye w. wG.   553 of] L&r, C; of youre W.
548 þo] L&r, C; þe w.   lese . . . e.] C (*so* K-D); for e. s.
     dem.] W&r; damne*den* B, C (*so*   ye l. W&r (s.y.]y.s. g).
     K-D) (*C*).   554 3ow] L&r, C; *om* W.

"*Dos ecclesie* this day hath ydronke venym,   *poison*
And tho that han Petres power arn apoisoned alle!"
560 A medicyne moot therto that may amende prelates,   *is needed*
That sholden preie for the pees; possession hem letteth.   *hinders*
Taketh hire landes, ye lordes, and leteth hem lyve by dymes;   *tithes*
If possession be poison, and inparfite hem make,
Good were to deschargen hem for Holy Chirches sake,   *unburden*
565 And purgen hem of poison, er moore peril falle.
If preesthode were parfit, the peple sholde amende,
That contrarien Cristes lawe, and Cristendom dispise.
                          act against; (their) Christianity
   'Every bisshop that bereth cros, by that he is holden   *obliged*
Thorugh his province to passe, and to his peple to shewe hym,
570 Tellen hem and techen hem on the Trinite to bileve,
And feden hem with goostly foode, and nedy folk to fynden.
                              spiritual; provide for
Ac Ysaie of yow speketh and Osias bothe,   *Isaiah; Hosea*
That no man sholde be bisshop but if he hadde bothe
Bodily foode and goostly foode to gyve there it nedeth:
In domo mea non est panis neque vestimentum, et ideo nolite constituere me
   regem.
575 Osias seith for swiche that sike ben and feble,
Inferte omnes decimas in orreum meum, ut sit cibus in domo mea.
   'Ac we Cristene creatures, that on the cros bileven,
Arn ferme as in the feith—Goddes forbode ellis!—
                              God forbid that it be otherwise
And han clerkes to kepen us therinne, and hem that shul come after us.
580 And Jewes lyven in lele lawe—Oure Lord wroot it hymselve
In stoon, for it stedefast was, and stonde sholde evere—   *permanent*
Dilige Deum et proximum, is parfit Jewen lawe—   (*which*) *is; Jews', Jewish*
And took it Moyses to teche men, til Messie coome;
                              gave; the Messiah should come
And on that lawe thei leve, and leten it for the beste.   *believe; consider*

574a ... in my house there is no bread nor clothing: make me not ruler [of the
   people] (Is 3: 7).
576 Bring all the tithes into the storehouse that there may be meat in my house
   (Mal 3: 10).
582 Love God and your neighbour (*cf.* Mt 22: 37–40, Deut 6: 5, Lev 19: 18).

568 W&r (=β) *here have* 502–8 *and*
   RF (=α) *resume here.*
570 techen] shewen α.
571b–574a *in* α *only; om* β, *which*
   have 571a, 574b *as one line; see* Sk
   ad loc.
572 Ac] But F.
   of . . . sp.] as how þou spekist F.
574 foode (2)] *om* F.
   to] α (*so* K-D); and β.

575a sit] OC²Cr (*so* Sk); *om rest.*
576 decimas] L&r; *om* W.
578 ferme] for me R; formed F (*cf.*
   518 *above*).
579 vs (2)] WLMR; *om* r.
583 men] it hem α.
584 leue] R&r (bel. F), ?C (*so* K-D);
   lyue WL.
   and] α, C (*so* K-D); ȝit a. β.

585 And yit knewe thei Crist, that Cristendom taughte,
And for a parfit prophete that muche peple savede
Of selkouthe sores; thei seighen it ofte—   *strange*
Bothe of miracles and merveilles, and how he men festede,   *fed*
With two fisshes and fyve loves fyve thousand peple—   *loaves*
590 And by that mangerie thei myghte wel se that Messie he semede; *feeding*
And whan he lifte up Lazar, that leid was in grave,   *raised to life Lazarus*
And under stoon deed and stank, with stif vois hym callede,   *loud voice*
Lazare, veni foras,   *Lazarus, come forth* (Jn 11: 43)
Dide hym rise and rome right bifore the Jewes.   *(And) made; walk*
Ac thei seiden and sworen, with sorcerie he wroughte,
595 And studieden to struyen hym—and struyden hemselve,   *destroy(ed)*
And thorugh his pacience hir power to pure noght he broughte:
                                                  absolutely nothing
Pacientes vincunt.
    'Daniel of hire undoynge devyned and seide,   *prophesied*
Cum sanctus sanctorum veniat cessabit unxio vestra.
And yit wenen tho wrecches that he were *pseudo-propheta*   *a false prophet*
600 And that his loore be lesynges, and lakken it alle, *teaching; lies; disparage*
And hopen that he be to come that shal hem releve—   *redeem, rescue*
Moyses eft or Messie hir maistres devyneth.   *again; theologians foretell*
    'Ac pharisees and sarsens, scribes and Jewes
Arn folk of oon feith—the fader God thei honouren.
605 And sithen that the Sarsens and also the Jewes
Konne the firste clause of oure bileve, *Credo in Deum patrem*   *creed*
omnipotentem,
Prelates of Cristene provinces sholde preve, if thei myghte,   *endeavour*
Lere hem litlum and litlum *Et in Jesum Christum filium,*
                                              To teach them little by little
Til thei kouthe speke and spelle *Et in Spiritum sanctum,*   *make out*
610 And rendren it and recorden it with *remissionem peccatorum,*
Carnis resurreccionem et vitam eternam. Amen.'

598 When the Saint of Saints shall come, your anointing [*sc.* the special relation
    of the Jews with God] shall come to an end (*cf.* Dan 9: 24, 26).
606 I believe in God the Father Almighty (*first clause of the* Apostles' Creed).
608 And in Jesus Christ his (only) son. our Lord (*second clause of the* Apostles'
    Creed).
609 And (I believe) in the Holy Ghost (*seventh clause of the* Ap. Cr.).
610–10*a* And construe it and declare it, with 'the forgiveness of sins' (*tenth clause
    of* Ap. Cr.). The resurrection of the body and the life everlasting (*eleventh and
    twelfth clauses*).

586 And f.] α, C (*so* K-D); For β.   603 Iewes] WHm (*cf.* C); Grekis
590 þei] α (*so* K-D); men β.   L&r (C).
592 deed . . . stank] stanke and dede   608 Lere] LR, C; To l. WB.
    R; he stank ded F.   610 rendren] L, C (ren., rec. *trsp* C);
599 ȝet] L&r; *om* WCr.   reden W&r.

Passus XVI

'Now faire falle yow,' quod I tho, 'for youre faire shewyng!
For Haukyns love the Actif Man evere I shal yow lovye.
Ac yit am I in a weer what charite is to mene.'   *doubt, perplexity*
  'It is a ful trie tree,' quod he, 'trewely to telle.   *choice*
5 Mercy is the more therof; the myddul stok is ruthe;   *root; trunk*
  The leves ben lele wordes, the lawe of Holy Chirche;   *faithful*
  The blosmes beth buxom speche and benigne lokynge;   *kind*
  Pacience hatte the pure tree, and pore symple of herte,
  And so thorugh God and thorugh goode men groweth the fruyt Charite.'
10 'I wolde travaille,' quod I, 'this tree to se, twenty hundred myle, *travel*
  And to have my fulle of that fruyt forsake al other saulee.   *food*
  Lord!' quod I, 'if any wight wite whiderout it groweth?'
                                        from out of which place
  'It groweth in a gardyn,' quod he, 'that God made hymselve;
  Amyddes mannes body the more is of that stokke.
15 Herte highte the herber that it inne groweth,   *arbour, garden*
  And *Liberum Arbitrium* hath the lond to ferme,   *tend*
  Under Piers the Plowman to piken it and to weden it.'   *hoe; weed*

  'Piers the Plowman!' quod I tho, and al for pure joye
  That I herde nempne his name anoon I swowned after, *named, mentioned*
20 And lay longe in a lone dreem; and at the laste me thoughte *solitary (C)*
  That Piers the Plowman al the place me shewed,
  And bad me toten on the tree, on top and on roote.   *gaze*
  With thre piles was it underpight—I parceyved it soone. *props; supported*
  'Piers,' quod I, 'I preie thee—whi stonde thise piles here?'
25' 'For wyndes, wiltow wite,' quod he, 'to witen it fro fallyng— *keep*
  Cum ceciderit iustus non collidetur quia Dominus supponit manum suam—
  And in blowyng tyme abite the flowres, but if thise piles helpe. *(they) nip off*

8 The actual tree itself is called 'Patience and humble simplicity of heart' . . .
14 . . . is the root of that trunk (K-D's *punct.* (body;) *gives* the root is derived
  from that stock [*sc.* humanity]).
25*a* When the just man shall fall he shall not be bruised: for the Lord putteth his
  hand under him (Ps 36: 24).
26 . . . in the blossoming season *or* (*possibly*) in time of blustery weather.

Rubric Passus xvj ^{us} *&c & primus de*   16 to] L&r; þe W.
dobet.   17 Un.] And vn. α.
4 trewely] treuthe R; good t. F (*cf.*   to (2)] *om* gF.
  ruþe 5 *below*).   20 lone] *see* (*C*).
8 pore] LRF; pure W.   22 me] L&r; me to wYCB.
9 þoruʒ (2)] WLM; pure Hm; *om r.*   25 witen] kepen α.
11 to] R&r; for to WHmCr¹ LM.
  al o. s.] L&r; *pl.* WG.

The world is a wikked wynd to hem that willen truthe:
Coveitise comth of that wynd and crepeth among the leves
And forfreteth neigh the fruyt thorugh manye faire sightes.   *almost nips' off*
30 Thanne with the firste pil I palle hym doun—that is *Potencia Dei Patris.*
                                    strike; the power of God the Father
   'The flessh is a fel wynd, and in flouryng tyme,   *fierce; i.e. in youth*
   Thorugh likynge and lustes so loude he gynneth blowe   *sexual desire*
   That it norisseth nyce sightes and som tyme wordes,   *fosters; foolish*
   And wikkede werkes therof, wormes of synne,
35 And forbiteth the blosmes right to the bare leves.   *eats away*
   'Thanne sette I to the secounde pil, *Sapiencia Dei Patris*—
                          proceed; the wisdom of God the Father
   That is the passion and the power of oure prince Jesu.
   Thorugh preieres and thorugh penaunces and Goddes passion in mynde,
   I save it til I se it ripen and somdel yfruyted.   *somewhat in fruit*
40 'And thanne fondeth the fend my fruyt to destruye   *tries*
   With alle the wiles that he kan, and waggeth the roote,   *knows; shakes*
   And casteth up to the crop unkynde neighebores,   *throws; top*
   Bakbiteris brewecheste, brawleris and chideris,   *'Start-fight slanderers'*
   And leith a laddre therto—of lesynges are the ronges—   *rungs*
45 And feccheth awey my floures somtyme bifore bothe myne eighen.
   Ac *Liberum Arbitrium* letteth hym som tyme,   *hinders*
   That is lieutenaunt to loken it wel, bi leve of myselve: *guard*
   Videatis qui peccat in Spiritum Sanctum numquam remittetur
   &c; hoc est idem, qui peccat per liberum arbitrium non repugnat.
   'Ac whan the fend and the flessh forth with the world
   Manacen bihynde me, my fruyt for to fecche,   *threaten*
50 Thanne *Liberum Arbitrium* laccheth the thridde planke   *seizes*
   And palleth adoun the pouke pureliche thorugh grace   *devil; wholly*
   And help of the Holy Goost—and thus have I the maistrie.'   *victory*
   'Now faire falle yow, Piers!' quod I, 'so faire ye discryven   *describe*
   The power of thise postes and hire propre myghte.
55 Ac I have thoughtes a threve of thise thre piles—   *number (lit. bundle); about*
   In what wode thei woxen, and where that thei growed,
   For alle are thei aliche longe, noon lasse than oother,
                          of equal length; smaller
   And to my mynde, as me thynketh, on o more thei growed;   *one root*
   And of o greetnesse and grene of greyn thei semen.'   *size; colour*

47a You may see (by this that) 'He who sins against the Holy Ghost, it shall not
   be forgiven him' [Mt 12: 32]; which is the same (as saying), 'he who sins through
   his free will does not resist [sin, as he should]' (Sk *ad loc notes* Heb 12: 4).

27a *and* 28b *run together,* 27b *and*   45 byf-] RF, C; af-WL.
   28a *om* α.   48 whan] what α.
30 þat is] *om* G, C.   50 thridde] LRF (*cf.* C); firste W&r.
38 þoruȝ (2)] *om* g.   planke] α (*so* K-D *p.* 146); plante β.
43 brewe] R (?=α; & boosteris F)   51 pure] priue α.
   (*so* K-D); breke L&r (=β; b. þe w).   54 my.] L&r; *pl.* WHmF.

60 'That is sooth,' seide Piers, 'so it may bifalle.
 I shal telle thee as tid what this tree highte.   *at once; is called*
 The ground there it groweth, goodnesse it hatte;
 And I have told thee what highte the tree: the Trinite it meneth'—
                                                                    means, signifies
 And egreliche he loked on me, and therfore I spared   *sharply; refrained*
65 To asken hym any moore therof, and bad hym ful faire   *courteously*
 To di[ff]yne the fruyt that so faire hangeth.   *describe, explain (C)*
   'Heer now bynethe,' quod he tho, 'if I nede hadde,
 Matrimoyne I may nyme, a moiste fruyt withalle.   *take*
 Thanne Continence is neer the crop as kaylewey bastard.
                                                         top; a Cailloux pear (C)
70 Thanne bereth the crop kynde fruyt and clennest of alle—
 Maidenhode, aungeles peeris, and [ar]est wole be ripe,   *equals, peers; first*
 And swete withouten swellyng—sour worth it nevere.'   *becomes*
   I preide Piers to pulle adoun an appul, and he wolde,   *if*
 And suffre me to assaien what savour it hadde.   *allow; try*
75   And Piers caste to the crop, and thanne comsed it to crye;
                                                               ?reached; began
 And waggede widwehode, and it wepte after;   *(he) shook*
 And whan he meved matrimoyne, it made a foul noise,
 That I hadde ruthe whan Piers rogged, it gradde so rufulliche.
                                                         shook; cried; piteously
 For evere as thei dropped adoun the devel was redy,
80 And gadrede hem alle togideres, bothe grete and smale—
 Adam and Abraham and Ysaye the prophete,   *Isaiah*
 Sampson and Samuel, and Seint Johan the Baptist;
 Bar hem forth boldely—no body hym letted—   *He carried; hindered*
 And made of holy men his hoord *in Limbo Inferni*,   *the verge of Hell (C)*
85 There is derknesse and drede and the devel maister.
   And Piers, for pure tene, that a pil he laughte,   *anger; one; seized*
  'And hitte after hym, happe how it myghte,   *struck out*
 Filius by the Fader wille and frenesse of *Spiritus Sancti*,
 To go robbe that rageman and reve the fruyt fro hym.   *coward; take away*
90   And thanne spak *Spiritus Sanctus* in Gabrielis mouthe   *spoke*
 To a maide that highte Marie, a meke thyng withalle,
 That oon Jesus, a justices sone, moste jouke in hir chambre   *rest; i.e. womb*
 Til *plenitudo temporis* tyme comen were   *'the time of the fulness of time'*

70 Finally, the uppermost part bears a natural fruit, the finest / most pure of all.
88 The Son, by the will of the Father and grace [*lit.* generosity] of the Holy Spirit.

60 seide] LRF; quod W&r.
66 diffyne] discryue *All* B-MSS (C).
71 arest] erst *conj* K-D *p.* 195;
   ra*p*est W&r (C).
73 P.] L&r; P. þo W.
77 he] α (*cf.* C; *so* K-D *p.* 157); it β.
78 Þat I] LYR (I *om* R); And I W.
83 bol.] L&r, C; bodily WY.

86 þat] L&r (þo þ. F); of þ. WCr.
   la.] L&r (*and cf.* C); rauȝte W;
   caught Cr.
87 And] L&r, C; He w.
   happe] L&r, C; hitte WCr.
88 fader] faderes αCr, ?C.
93 tyme] α, C (*so* K-D); fully β.

That Piers fruyt floured and felle to be rype.   *should happen*
95 And thanne sholde Jesus juste therfore, bi juggement of armes,
                                           joust; (to settle) by trial-at-arms
    Wheither sholde fonge the fruyt—the fend or hymselve.   *Which; receive*
        The maide myldeliche tho the messager graunted,   *humbly; consented to*
    And seide hendeliche to hym, 'Lo me his handmaiden   *courteously*
    For to werchen his wille withouten any synne:
    Ecce ancilla Domini, fiat michi &c.'
100   And in the wombe of that wenche was he fourty woukes,   *girl; weeks*
    Til he weex a faunt thorugh hir flessh, and of fightyng kouthe,
                                               grew; child; learned
    To have yfoughte with the fend er ful tyme come.
    And Piers the Plowman parceyved plener tyme,   *the fullness of time*
    And lered hym lechecraft, his lif for to save,   *taught; medicine*
105 That though he were wounded with his enemy, to warisshen hymselve;   *cure*
    And dide hym assaie his surgenrie on hem that sike were,
                                           try; surgery, medical skill
    Til he was parfit praktisour, if any peril fille;   *practitioner; should befall*
    And soughte out the sike and synfulle bothe,
    And salvede sike and synfulle, bothe blynde and crokede,   *lame, maimed*
110 And commune wommen convertede [to goode]:
    Non est sanis opus medicus, set male habentibus.
        Bothe meseles and mute, and in the menyson blody—
    Ofte he heeled swiche, he ne held it for no maistrie,
                                           achievement, miraculous act
    Save tho he leched Lazar, that hadde yleye in grave
                                           Except when; cured Lazarus
    Quatriduanus quelt—quyk dide hym walke.
115 Ac a[r] he made the maistrie, *mestus cepit esse,*   *before; miracle*
    And wepte water with hise eighen—ther seighen it manye.   *saw*
    Some that the sighte seighen seiden that tyme
    That he was leche of lif, and lord of heigh hevene.
    Jewes jangled therayein that juggede lawes,   *objected violently to it*
120 And seide he wroghte thorugh wichecraft and with the develes myghte:
    Demonium habes &c.

99a Behold the handmaid of the Lord; be it done unto me [according to thy word]
   (Lk 1: 38).
110a They that are in health need not a physician, but they that are ill (Mt 9: 12).
111 Lepers and the dumb, and those suffering from a bloody flux.
114 Four days dead—made him walk alive (Jn 11: 39).
115 (Jesus) wept [*lit.* became sad] (*cf.* Mt 26: 37, Jn 11: 35).
120a He hath a devil [and is mad] (Jn 10: 20) (*C*).

110 to g.] and to g. turnede *All*   112 he (1)] L&r; *om* W.
   B-MSS (g. t.] crist t. hem F); and   115 ar] C (*see* K-D *p.* 90); as *All*
   clansed hem of synne C (*C*).   B-MSS.
110a *male h.*] F (?=α; *so* Vulg; *m h.*   119 þat] R (?=α; þo þ. F) (*so* K-D);
   &c R); *in* &c W&r (?=β; *in om*   and β.
   CrM; *infirmis* &c OC²) (*C*).   120a -*es*] L&r; -*et* W (*so* Vulg.).

'Thanne are ye cherles,' quod Jesus, 'and youre children bothe,
And Sathan youre Saveour—yowself now ye witnessen:
For I have saved yowself, and youre sones after,
Youre bodies. youre beestes, and blynde men holpen,   *helped*
125 And fed yow with fisshes and with fyve loves,   *loaves*
And lefte baskettes ful of broke mete—bere awey whoso wolde—'
     fragments of food
And mysseide the Jewes manliche, and manaced hem to bete,
     rebuked; boldly; threatened
And knokked on hem with a corde, and caste adoun hir stalles
     ... of those (who)
That in chirche chaffareden or chaungeden any moneie,   *traded*
130 And seide it in sighte of hem alle, so that alle herden,
' I shal overturne this temple and adoun throwe,
And in thre daies after edifie it newe,   *rebuild it*
And maken it as muche outher moore in alle manere poyntes *great; respects*
As evere it was, and as wid—wherfore I hote yow,   *wide; bid*
135 Of preieres and of parfitnesse this place that ye callen:
Domus mea domus oracionis vocabitur.'
Envye and yvel wil ar[ne] in the Jewes: *welled up (C)*
Thei casten and contreveden to kulle hym whan thei myghte;
     schemed; plotted
Eche day after oother hir tyme thei awaiteden,   *opportunity; watched for*
Til it bifel on a Friday, a litel bifore Pasqe.   *occurred; Passover*
140 The Thursday bifore, there he made his cene,   *held; supper (C)*
Sittynge at the soper he seide thise wordes:
'I am sold thorugh so[m] of yow—he shal the tyme rewe   *one (C); rue*
That evere he his Saveour solde for silver or ellis.'
Judas jangled therayein, ac Jesus hym tolde   *remonstrated, protested*
145 It was hymself soothly, and seide, '*Tu dicis*.' '*Thou hast said it*' (Mt 26: 25)
Thanne wente forth that wikked man and with the Jewes mette,
And tolde hem a tokne how to knowe with Jesus, *sign by which to recognize*
The which tokne to this day to muche is yused—
That is, kissynge and fair countenaunce and unkynde wille.   *looks*
150 And so was with Judas tho, that Jesus bitrayed: *then*
'*Ave, raby*,' quod that ribaud, and right to hym he yede,
     '*Hail, Rabbi*' (Mt 26: 49); *villain*

135a My house shall be called the house of prayer (Mt 21: 13).

121 Jesus] ihc R (=α [*cf.* C]; crist F)
(*so* Sk); ich WL (?=β).
122 ȝow] LRMY; ye W; youre *rest.*
123 self] selue α (*cf.* C) (*so* K-D); s.
seiþ crist β (self *om* HmB).
125 fisshes] L&r; two f. wM.
131 throwe] L&r; þr. it W; it þr. F.

136 ern] C, *so* K-D *p.* 186; aren R
(=α; *see* K-D *p.* 168n); was βF.
140 cene] α (*so* K-D); maundee β (*C*).
142 som] *so* K-D *p.* 144; summe α;
oon β (*C*).
147 how] *om* G; *cf.* K-D *p.* 148.
148 þe] α; And β.

And kiste hym, to be caught therby and kulled of the Jewes.
    Thanne Jesus to Judas and to the Jewes seide,
'Falsnesse I fynde in thi faire speche,
155 And gile in thi glad chere, and galle is in thi laughyng.   *cheerful expression*
Thow shalt be myrour to many, men to deceyve,
Ac the worse, and thi wikkednesse shal worthe upon thiselve: *redound upon*
Necesse est ut veniant scandala: ve homini illi, per quem
scandalum venit.
Though I bi treson be take, and [to] youre owene wille,   *treachery*
Suffreth myne apostles in pays, and in pees gange.'   *to go in peace* (C)
160   On a Thursday in thesternesse thus was he taken   *darkness*
Thorough Judas and Jewes—Jesus was his name
That on the Friday folwynge for mankyndes sake
Justed in Jerusalem, a joye to us alle.   *Jousted*
On cros upon Calvarie Crist took the bataille
165 Ayeins deeth and the devel, destruyed hir botheres myghtes—
      the power of both of them
Deide, and deeth fordide, and day of nyght made.   *destroyed*

    And I awaked therwith, and wiped myne eigñen,
And after Piers the Plowman pried and stared,   *peered*
Estward and westward I waited after faste,   *looked eagerly*
170 And yede forth as an ydiot, in contree to aspie   *seek, inquire*
After Piers the Plowman—many a place I soughte.
    And thanne mette I with a man, a myd-Lenten Sonday,
      fourth Sunday in Lent
As hoor as an hawethorn, and Abraham he highte.   *hoary, white(-haired)*
I frayned hym first fram whennes he come,   *inquired of*
175 And of whennes he were, and whider that he thoughte.   *intended (to go)*

    'I am Feith,' quod that freke, 'it falleth noght me to lye,   *man; befits*
And of Abrahames hous an heraud of armes.   *herald*
I seke after a segge that I seigh ones,   *man; once*
A ful bold bacheler—I knew hym by his blasen.' *young knight; blazon, arms*
180 'What berth that buyrn,' quod I tho, 'so blisse thee bitide?' *bears; warrior*
    'Thre leodes in oon lyth, noon lenger than oother,   *persons; body*
Of oon muchel and myght in mesure and in lengthe.   *size; power*
That oon dooth, alle dooth, and ech dooth bi his one. *That (which); self*
The firste hath myght and majestee, makere of alle thynges:

156 You shall be an example to many of (what it is to be) a deceiver of men.
157a For it must needs be that scandals come; but nevertheless woe to that man
  by whom the scandal cometh (Mt 18: 7).
159 Let my apostles alone, and let them go in peace (Sk).

152 of] β, C; þoruȝ α.
158 and to] C; and R; & þorgh F; at
  β; see K-D p. 94 (C).
159 pays] L&r, C; pees WCrGCF.
  pees] L&r (soph. F); pays WCr (C).

166 deth] L&r; deed W.
175 þouȝte] L&r; souȝte W (cf. 171).
176 n. me] R (=α; m.n. F), C; n. β.
178 I (1)] L&r; And W.

185 *Pater* is his propre name, a persone by hymselve.   *Father*
    The secounde of that sire is Sothfastnesse *Filius*,   *Truth the Son*
    Wardeyn of that wit hath, was evere withouten gynnyng.
                                 that (which); beginning
    The thridde highte the Holi Goost, a persone by hymselve,   *alone (distinct)*
    The light of al that lif hath a londe and a watre,   *on*
190 Confortour of creatures—of hym cometh alle blisse.   *Comforter*
    'So thre bilongeth for a lord that lordshipe cleymeth:
    Might, and a mene [his owene myghte to knowe],   *means; ?express (C)*
    Of hymself and of his servaunt, and what suffreth hem bothe.
    So God, that gynnyng hadde nevere, but tho hym good thoughte,
                               when it seemed good to him
195 Sente forth his sone as for servaunt that tyme,
    To ocupien hym here til issue were spronge—   *be active*
    That is, children of charite, and Holi Chirche the moder.
    Patriarkes and prophetes and apostles were the children,
    And Crist and Cristendom and alle Cristene Holy Chirche
200 In menynge that man moste on o God bileve,   *Signifying; one*
    And there hym likede and lovede, in thre [leodes] hym shewede.   *persons*
    And that it may be so and sooth [sheweth it manhode]:
    Wedlok and widwehode with virginite ynempned,
    In tokenynge of the Trinite was taken out of o man—   *Symbolizing*
205 Adam, oure alle fader; Eve was of hymselve,   *of us all; from*
    And the issue that thei hadde it was of hem bothe,
    And either is otheres joye in thre sondry persones,   *distinct*
    And in hevene and here oon singuler name.   *sole, single (C)*
    And thus is mankynde and manhede of matrimoyne ysprpnge,
210 And bitokneth the Trinite and trewe bileve.   *symbolizes; faith*
    'Might is in matrimoyne, that multiplieth the erthe,
    And bitokneth trewely, telle if I dorste,
    Hym that first formed al, the Fader of hevene.

191–3 Likewise, three things are proper for a lord who lays claim to dominion:
Power, and a means / intermediary to realise his power, Belonging to himself
and his servant, and (also) something which sustains / endures (the action)
of both (?) (C).

189 The . . . haþ] þat alle þe liȝt of þe
  lif α (of] & F).
192 a] LR, C; *om* W.
  his . . . k.] to k. h. o. m. W&r
  (o. *om* Cr, k. *om* R); to h. m. owiþ
  F; to se h. o. m. C; *trsp.* K-D (*see*
  pp. 113, 206) (C).
193 selue] α, C (*so* K-D); *om* β.
  suffreþ hem] FR (=α), C (*so*
  K-D *p.* 163); þei suffre β.
196 -pien] L&r, C; -pie w.
198 chil.] β, C; barnes α.
199 and alle] α, ?C; and β.

201 leodes] persones *All* B-MSS (C).
202 sh. it m.] m. it sh. W&r (*l. om*
  Cr²³OC²); *trsp.* K-D *p.* 194.
204 taken . . . m.] L&r (o *om* GMF;
  m.] mankynde F); out of m. t.
  WCr.
205 Adam; Eue] L&r; A. was; and
  E. WF.
209 þus] β (þis L); þat α.
211 Miȝte] L&r; Mighty WCr (C).
  in] α (*so* K-D *pp.* 145–6); *om* β
  (C).

The Sone, if I it dorste seye, resembleth wel the widewe:
Deus meus, Deus meus, ut quid dereliquisti me?
215 That is, creatour weex creature to knowe what was bothe.   *became*
As widewe withouten wedlok was nevere yit yseyghe,   *seen*
Na moore myghte God be man but if he moder hadde.
So widewe withouten wedlok may noght wel stande,
                   properly (be said to) exist
Ne matrimoyne withouten muliere is noght muche to preise: *offspring*
Maledictus homo qui non reliquit semen in Israel.
220 'Thus in thre persones is parfitliche pure manhede—
That is, man and his make and mulliere hir children,
                children born of woman(kind)
And is noght but gendre of a generacion, bifore Jesu Crist in hevene;
So is the fader forth with the Sone and Fre Wille of bothe—
Spiritus procedens a Patre et Filio &c—
Which is the Holy Goost of alle, and alle is but o God.   *one*
225 'Thus in a somer I hym seigh as I sat in my porche.   (Gen 18: 1 *ff*)
I roos up and reverenced hym, and right faire hym grette.   *greeted*
Thre men, to my sighte, I made wel at ese,   *entertained*
Wessh hir feet and wiped hem, and afterward thei eten   *Washed*
Calves flessh and cakebreed, and knewe what I thoughte.
230 Ful trewe toknes betwene us is, to telle whan me liketh.
              A most trusty covenant
 'First he fonded me, if I lovede bettre   *tested; (to see) if*
Hym or Ysaak myn heir, the which he highte me kulle.   *Isaac; bade*
He wiste my wille bi hym; he wol me it allowe;   (Gen 22)
I am ful siker in my soule therof, and my sone bothe.
235 'I circumcised my sone sithen for his sake—   *afterwards*
Myself and my meynee and alle that male weere   *household*
Bledden blood for that Lordes love, and hope to blisse the tyme. *bless*
Myn affiaunce and my feith is ferme in this bileve,   *trust; belief*
For hymself bihighte to me and to myn issue bothe   *promised*
240 Lond and lordshipe and lif withouten ende.

214*a* O God, my God . . .: why hast thou forsaken me? (Ps 21: 2, Mt 27: 46).
218–19*a i.e.* The idea of widowhood without marriage and that of marriage without
the female sex are both absurdities: 'Cursed is the man who has not left off-
spring in Israel' (*cf.* Gen 30: 23; found in *Pseudo-Matthaei Evangelium* (in
Evangelia Apocrypha, ed. Tischendorf, Leipzig 1876), beginning (Pearsall,
p. 303*n*)).
220 Thus human nature subsists in its totality in (at least) three persons.
222–3*a* And is nothing else than one species related through one common nature
. . . Such is the relationship accordingly between the three persons of the Trinity
—The Spirit proceeding from the Father and the Son (*C*).
233 He knew how I felt towards him [*sc.* how much I loved him]; he will hold it to
my credit [that I obeyed his command to sacrifice Isaac].

214 it] WLR; *om rest.*   222 a] WLR; *om rest* (*C*).
220 puir] α (þorgh3 F) (*so* K-D); *om* β.   231 I] I feiþ *conj* K-D *p.* 199 (*C*).
221 her] LRF (=? β, α), C; *om* W&r.   238 þis] his CB, C.

The Vision of Piers Plowman

To me and to myn issue moore yet he me grauntede—
Mercy for oure mysdedes as many tyme as we asken:
Quam olim Abrahe promisisti et semini eius.
  'And siththe he sente me, to seye I sholde do sacrifise,   *sent (word to)*
And doon hym worship with breed and with wyn bothe,
245 And called me the foot of his feith, his folk for to save.
                                                        i.e. support, founder
And defende hem fro the fend, folk that on me leveden.
  'Thus have I ben his heraud here and in helle,
And conforted many a careful that after his comynge waiten;   *look for*
And thus I seke hym,' he seide, 'for I herde seyn late   *talk lately*
250 Of a buyrn that baptised hym—Johan Baptist was his name—   *man*
That to patriarkes and to prophetes and to oother peple in derknesse
Seide, that he seigh here that sholde save us alle: *(the one) who was to*
Ecce Agnus Dei &c.'
  I hadde wonder of hise wordes, and of hise wide clothes;
For in his bosom he bar a thyng, and that he blissed evere.
                                                        bore something; blessed
255 And I loked in his lappe: a lazar lay therinne   *leper*
Amonges patriarkes and prophetes pleyinge togideres.
  'What awaitestow?' quod he, 'and what woldestow have?'
                                                        are you looking for
'I wolde wite,' quod I tho, 'what is in youre lappe.'
'Lo!' quod he—and leet me se. 'Lord, mercy!' I seide.
260 'This is a present of muche pris; what prynce shal it have?'   *value*
'It is a precious present,' quod he, 'ac the pouke it hath attached,
                                                        devil; claimed
And me therwith,' quod that wye, 'may no wed us quyte,   *pledge; release*
Ne no buyrn be oure borgh, ne brynge us fram his daunger;
                                                        surety; power
Out of the poukes pondfold no maynprise may us fecche   *pound; bail*
265 Til he come that I carpe of: Crist is his name   *speak*
That shal delivere us som day out of the develes power,
And bettre wed for us [wa]ge than we ben alle worthi—   *offer as security*
That is, lif for lif—or ligge thus evere   *(he must) lie*

242a As you [he *Vulg*] promised [*locutus* 'spoke' *Vulg*] to [our fathers;] to Abraham
  and to his seed [for ever] (Lk 1: 55, the Magnificat).
252a Behold the Lamb of God (Jn 1: 29).

241 me (2)] L&*r*, C; *om* W.
245 þe] WHmLR; *om rest.*
246 leueden] WLR; bil. B; beleveþ F
  (C).
248 -ten] L&*r*; -teden WY.
250 buyrn] α (*so* K-D); barn β.
252 vs] β, C; hem α.
254 For] β, C; And α.
  &] α, C; *om* β.

256 -inge] -ede R (? = α; -ende F),
  ?C (C).
262 with] RF&c, C; myde WL&c.
  wyȝe] FR (=α), C (*so* K-D);
  man β.
267 wagen] C; legge *All* B-MSS (*cf.*
  ligge 268 *and see* K-D p. 94).

206

Lollynge in my lappe, til swich a lord us fecche.'
270 'Allas!' I seide, 'that synne so longe shal lette   *obstruct*
    The myght of Goddes mercy, that myghte us alle amende!'
     I wepte for hise wordes. With that saugh I another
    Rapeliche renne forth the righte wey he wente.   *Quickly; very same*
     I affrayned hym first fram whennes he come,   *inquired of*
275 What he highte and whider he wolde—and wightly he tolde.   *with alacrity*

Passus XVII

    'I am *Spes*, a spie,' quod he, 'and spire after a knyght   *inquire*
    That took me a maundement upon the mount of Synay
                                gave; commandment
    To rule alle reames therewith—I bere the writ here.'   *realms*
     'Is it asseled?' I seide. 'May men see thi lettres?'
5   'Nay,' he seide, 'I seke hym that hath the seel to kepe—
    And that is cros and Cristendom, and Crist theron to honge.   *hang*
    And whan it is asseled so, I woot wel the sothe—
    That Luciferis lordshipe laste shal no lenger!'
     'Lat se thi lettres,' quod I, 'we myghte the lawe knowe.'
10 He plukkede forth a patente, a pece of an hard roche,   *rock*
    Whereon was writen two wordes on this wise yglosed: *glossed*

270-3 RF (= α) *have three spurious
    lines.*
273 he] we C (C).
275 What] α, C (*so* K-D); And w.
    W&r.

Rubric Passus xvii ᴴˢ *&c et iius de
Dobet.*
1 a . . . he] α, C (*so* K-D); q. h. a s.
    β.
3 þere] α, C; *om* β.
    writ] rolle F (C).
4 ass-] L&r, C; ens- WCrG.
    þi] WLRHm, *some* C-MSS; þe r,
    some C-MSS.

5 I] L&r, C; *om* W.
7 *As one line with* 8 α.
    ass-] L&r, C; ens- WCrG.
    I . . . s.] *om* α.
8 That . . . shipe] β, C; sathenas haþ
    lost his power F; sath. power R.
    After 8 *an extra l.* And þus my lettre
    meneþ men mowe knowe yt al FR
    (men . . . al *om* R).
9 þi l.] þat lettre α.
10 He pl.] α, C (He] A R; & he F);
    Thanne pl. he β.
11 was] LRF, C; were W&r.

Dilige Deum et proximum tuum—
This was the tixte trewely—I took ful good yeme.   *text; note*
The glose was gloriously writen with a gilt penne:
15 *In hiis duobus mandatis tota lex pendet et prophete.*
        'Is here alle thi lordes lawes?' quod I. 'Ye, leve me,' he seide.   *believe*
'And whoso wercheth after this writ, I wol undertaken,
Shal nevere devel hym dere, ne deeth in soule greve.   *harm; afflict*
For though I seye it myself, I have saved with this charme
20 Of men and of wommen many score thousand.'
        'He seith sooth,' seide this heraud, 'I have yfounde it ofte.
Lo! here in my lappe that leeved on that charme—   *(those) who*
Josue and Judith and Judas Macabeus,
Ye, and sixti thousand biside forth that ben noght seyen here!'   *seen*
25 'Youre wordes arn wonderfulle,' quod I tho. 'Which of yow is trewest,
And lelest to leve on for lif and for soule?   *most trustworthy*
Abraham seith that he seigh hoolly the Trinite,   *saw wholly*
Thre persones in parcelles departable fro oother,
And alle thre but o God—thus Abraham me taughte—   *one*
30 And hath saved that bileved so and sory for hir synnes,
                                        (those) who (were) sorry
He kan noght siggen the somme, and some arn in his lappe.
                                        say how many, the total
What neded it thanne a newe lawe to brynge,   *What need was there*
Sith the firste suffiseth to savacion and to blisse?
And now cometh *Spes* and speketh, that hath aspied the lawe,
                                        seen, examined
35 And telleth noght of the Trinite that took hym hise lettres—   *gave*
To bileeve and lovye in o Lord almyghty,   *believe in and love*
And siththe right as myself so lovye alle peple.
        'The gome that gooth with o staf—he semeth in gretter heele
                                        walks; better health
Than he that gooth with two staves, to sighte of us alle.
40 And right so, bi the roode, reson me sheweth
It is lighter to lewed men o lesson to knowe   *easier for; one; learn*
Than for to techen hem two, and to hard to lerne the leeste!   *while (it is) too*
It is ful hard for any man on Abraham bileve,

12, 15 Thou shalt love [the Lord thy] God ... and thy neighbour [as thyself];
    On these two commandments dependeth the whole law and the prophets
    (Mt 22: 37, 39, 40).
·28 Three separate persons distinguishable from each other.

15 *mand.*] *om* R.   24 Ye] *om a*, C.
    -*phete*] CrF, C (*so* Vulg); -*phetia*   26 on] L&r, C; *so* WHm.
    WLR.   32 neded] W&r (? = Bx), ?C; nedeth
16 Is] LRF, C; Ben W&r.   gF.
20 -sand] W, C; *pl. rest.*   bringe] a, C; bigynne β.
21 yfounde] W&r, C; founded YCB   34 hath] L&r, C; *om* WG.
    (*so* K-D *p.* 160).   38–48 β, *cf.* C; *om* α.
23 Ios.] Boþe I. F, C.   41 It] L&r, C; That it W.

And wel awey worse yit for to love a sherewe.   *much worse still*
45 It is lighter to leeve in thre lovely persones
    Than for to lovye and lene as wel lorels as lele.   *give (to); wastrels*
    Go thi gate, 'quod I to *Spes*; 'so me God helpe,   *way*
    Tho that lernen thi lawe wol litel while usen it!'   *practise*
    And as we wenten thus in the wey, wordynge togideres,   *talking*
50 Thanne seighe we a Samaritan sittynge on a mule,
    Ridynge ful rapely the righte wey we yeden,   *hastily; very same*
    Comynge from a contree that men called Jerico—   *district, place*
    To a justes in Jerusalem he [j]aced awey faste.   *joust; jogged (C)*
    Bothe the heraud and Hope and he mette atones   *arrived together*
55 Where a man was, wounded, and with theves taken.   *robbed by thieves*
    He myghte neither steppe ne stande, ne stere foot ne handes,   *stir*
    Ne helpe hymself soothly, for semyvif he semed,   *(barely) half-alive*
    And as naked as a nedle, and noon help abouten.
    Feith hadde first sighte of hym, ac he fleigh aside,   *hurried to one side*
60 And nolde noght neghen hym by nyne londes lengthe.   *approach*
    Hope cam hippynge after, that hadde so ybosted   *hopping*
    How he with Moyses maundement hadde many men yholpe;   *helped*
    Ac whan he hadde sighte of that segge, aside he gan hym drawe
    Dredfully, bi this day, as doke dooth fram the faucon!
                                   Fearfully; duck; falcon
65   Ac so soone so the Samaritan hadde sighte of this leode,   *as; man*
    He lighte adown of lyard and ladde hym in his handes,
                                   got down from his grey
    And to the wye he wente hise woundes to biholde,
    And parceyved by his pous he was in peril to dye,   *pulse*
    And but he hadde recoverer the rather, that rise sholde he nevere;
                                'immediate treatment'
70 And breide to hise boteles, and bothe he atamede.   *hastened; broached*
    With wyn and with oille hise woundes he wasshed,
    Enbawmed hym and bond his heed, and in his lappe hym leide,
                                Anointed; bound up
    And ladde hym so forth on lyard to *Lex Christi*, a graunge
                            the Law of Christ; farm-house
    Wel sixe mile or sevene biside the newe market;   *A good six m.*
75 Herberwed hym at an hostrie and to the hostiler called,
                                Lodged; inn; inn-keeper

60 And would not come any nearer him than the distance of the breadth of nine
    ridges in a ploughed field (*after* Sk).

49 þus] *om* CrF, C.   69 rather] L&r, C; rapelier W.
    wey] w. thus CrF, C.   70 a, *cf.* C (*so* Sk); *om* β.
53 jaced] C (*so* K-D); chac*ed All*   And] R, ?C; he F.
    B-MSS (*C*).   a-] R, C; hem F.
58 abowte*n*] FR, C; a. hym β (*C*).   72 lappe] bayard C; barm *conj* K-D
59 of] β (*cf.* C); on α, *some* C-MSS.   p. 195 (*C*).
66 handes] α, C; *sg.* β.   75 to] *om* α.

And [quod], 'Have, kepe this man, til I come fro the justes,   *look after*
And lo here silver,' he seide, 'for salve to hise woundes.'   *ointment for*
And he took hym two pens to liflode as it weere,

                         pence; in payment for his keep
And seide, 'What he [moore spendeth] I make thee good herafter,
80 For I may noght lette,' quod that leode—and lyard he bistrideth,
And raped hym to Jerusalemward the righte wey to ryde.

                         hastened; towards J.; direct
    Feith folwede after faste, and fondede to mete hym,   *tried*
And *Spes* spakliche hym spedde, spede if he myghte   *nimbly; succeed*
To overtaken hym and talke to hym er thei to towne coome.   *should come*
85   And whan I seigh this, I sojourned noght, but shoop me to renne,

                         delayed; set myself
And suwed that Samaritan that was so ful of pite,   *followed*
And graunted hym to ben his groom. 'Graunt mercy,' he seide,

                         offered; servant; Thank you
'Ac thi frend and thi felawe,' quod he, 'thow fyndest me at nede.'

                         companion
    And I thanked hym tho and siththe I hym tolde
90 How that Feith fleigh awey and *Spes* his felawe bothe
For sighte of the sorweful [segge] that robbed was with theves.
    'Have hem excused,' quod he, 'hir help may litel availle:
May no medicyne under molde the man to heele brynge—   *earth; health*
Neither Feith ne fyn Hope, so festred be hise woundes,   *festered*
95 Withouten the blood of a barn born of a mayde.   *child*
And be he bathed in that blood, baptised as it were,
And thanne plastred with penaunce and passion of that baby,

                         treated with a healing plaster
He sholde stonde and steppe—ac stalworthe worth he nevere *sturdy; will be*
Til he have eten al the barn and his blood ydronke.
100 For wente nevere wye in this world thorugh that wildernesse
That he ne was robbed or rifled, rood he there or yede,

                         plundered; rode; walked
Save Feith and [myselve and] *Spes* [his felawe],
And thiself now and swiche as suwen oure werkes.   *follow*
    'For Outlawe is in the wode and under bank lotieth,   *lurks*
105 And may ech man see and good mark take   *note*
Who is bihynde and who bifore and who ben on horse—

76 quod] seide *All* B-MSS; *cf.* K-D p. 194 (*C*).
79 m. sp.] sp. m. *All* B-MSS; *cf.* K-D p. 94.
82 -wede] W&r (*cf.* C); -weth LR.
83 spak] spark α.
87 groom] gome RFG (Bm).
89 I (2)] þus I F (*so* K-D p. 173) (*C*).
91 þe] L&r (*cf.* C); þat WCr²³. segge] *conj* K-D p. 195; man *All* B-MSS.
93 vnder] α, C (*so* K-D); on β (*C*).
96 be he] WLHm (?=β; *trsp. r.*); be α.
98–345 *defective* O.
102 myselve ... f.] his f. *Sp.* and mys. *All* B-MSS (my) y my G); *re-arr.* K-D p. 194 (*C*).
104 o. is] R (?=α; an o. is F); Outlawes β (an o. Cr²³) (*C*).
105 may] LRFCr; mowen W&r.

For he halt hym hardier on horse than he that is a foote.

                                         holds; (who is) on horse-back

For he seigh me that am Samaritan suwen Feith and his felawe

On my capul that highte *Caro*—of mankynde I took it—

                                           horse; Flesh; humanity

110 He was unhardy, that harlot, and hidde hym *in Inferno. fearful; rogue; Hell*

Ac er this day thre daies, I dar undertaken

That he worth fettred, that feloun, faste with cheynes,   *will be; chains*

And nevere eft greve gome that gooth this ilke gate:

                                      trouble (a) man; same way

O Mors ero mors tua &c.

   'And thanne shal Feith be forster here and in this fryth walke,

                                           forester; wood

115 And kennen out comune men that knowen noght the contree,

                                      guide (out of the wood)

Which is the wey I wente, and wher forth to Jerusalem;

                                   (Teaching them) which is . . .

And Hope the hostilers man shal be ther [an helyng the man lith],

                                          a-healing; lies

And alle that feble and feynte be, that Feith may noght teche,

Hope shal lede hem forth with love, as his lettre telleth,

120 And hostele hem and heele thorugh Holy Chirche bileve

                               lodge; H.C.'s faith, faith in H.C.

Til I have salve for alle sike—and thanne shal I returne,

And come ayein bi this contree and conforten alle sike

That craveth it or coveiteth it and crieth therafter.   *ask for; desire*

For the barn was born in Bethleem that with his blood shal save

125 Alle that lyven in Feith and folwen his felawes techynge.'

   'A, swete sire!' I seide tho, 'wher I shal bileve—   *am I to believe*

As Feith and his felawe enformed me bothe—   *instructed*

In thre persones departable that perpetuele were evere,

                              distinguishable; everlasting

And alle thre but o God? Thus Abraham me taughte;   *one*

130 And Hope afterward he bad me to lovye

O God with al my good, and alle gomes after,   *strength; men*

Lovye hem lik myselve—ac Oure Lord aboven alle.'

   'After Abraham,' quod he, 'that heraud of armes,

Sette faste thi feith and ferme bileve,

135 And as Hope highte thee, I hote that thow lovye   *bade; bid*

Thyn evenecristene everemoore eveneforth with thiselve.

                                     fellow-Christians; equally

111 But before three days from today [have passed]; (*cf.* Mt 27: 63).

113*a* O death, I will be thy death; [O hell, I will be thy bite] (Osee 13: 14).

107 a] LR; at C; *om* W; on *rest.*

110 vnh. þat] but an F; vn R.

113*a* α (*so* Sk); *om* β.

   &c] *morsus tuus* e(?)*r* F.

114–25 *om* α.

117 an . . . lith] þ. m. l. *anh.* W&*r*;

   trsp. K-D (*C*).

121 re-] L&*r*; *om* WHm.

123 or; and] L&*r*; *trsp.* W.

134 faste] L&*r*; fully WHm.

And if conscience carpe therayein, or kynde wit eyther,   *speak against it*
Or eretikes with arguments—thyn hond thow hem shewe: *heretics*
For God is after an hand—yheer now and knowe it.   *like; hear*
140 'The Fader was first as a fust with o fynger foldynge,   *fist; one; bent*
Til hym lovede and liste to unlosen his fynger   *unbend*
And profrede it forth as with a pawme to what place it sholde.
   (he) put; palm
The pawme is purely the hand, and profreth forth the fyngres,
   totally, integrally
To ministren and to make that myght of hand knoweth;
145 And bitokneth trewely, telle whoso liketh,   *stands for*
The Holy Goost of hevene—he is as the pawme.
The fyngres that fre ben to folde and to serve   *bend*
Bitoknen soothly the Sone, that sent was til erthe,   *to*
That touched and tastede at techynge of the pawme   *felt*
150 Seinte Marie, a mayde, and mankynde laughte: *assumed human nature*
Qui conceptus est de spiritu sancto &c.
 'The Fader is thanne as a fust with fynger to touche—
Quia "Omnia traham ad me ipsum &c"—
Al that the pawme parceyveth profitable to feele.
Thus are thei alle but oon, as it an hand weere,
And thre sondry sightes in oon shewynge.
155 The pawme for he put forth fyngres and the fust bothe,   *because; puts forth*
Right so, redily, reson it shewith,
How he that is Holy Goost Sire and Sone preveth.
   ?demonstrates, expresses
And as the hand halt harde and alle thyng faste   *holds; firmly*
Thorugh foure fyngres and a thombe forth with the pawme,
160 Right so the Fader and the Sone and Seint Spirit the thridde
Halt al the wide world withinne hem thre—
Bothe wolkne and the wynd, water and erthe,   *sky*
Hevene and helle and al that ther is inne.
Thus it is—nedeth no man to trowe noon oother—   *nothing else*
165 That thre thynges bilongeth in Oure Lord of hevene,
And aren serelepes by hemself, asondry were thei nevere,   *separately; apart*

144 To execute and perform that of which the hand's power has knowledge.
150a Who was conceived of the Holy Ghost (4th *art. of* Apostles' Creed).
151a For 'I will draw all things to myself' (Jn 12: 32).
154 And three distinct aspects in a single representation (*C*).

141 louede] β; lyþed F; leued R;
   lykede Hm, C (*so* K-D) (*C*).
142 profered] α, C (*so* K-D); profre
   β (put Cr).
143 purely] of F (*C*).
149 at] β, C; and α.
151 þanne] L&r (*om* F); pawme W.
155 he] L&r; it WF; þe paume R.
   put] α; putteþ β.

161 Halt] L&r; *om* W.
   Inne] *om* α.
   þre] LR; þ. holden W.
163 þ. is Inne] LRF; is þ. I. WHm;
   therin is *rest.*
164 is] *om* RFHmGCB.
   to] LRFC²Y; *om* W&r.
166 -lepes] LMR; -lopes W (*word
   misspelled most MSS*).

Namoore than may an hande meve withoute fyngres.   *move*
  'And as my fust is ful hand yfolden togideres,   *closed*
So is the Fader a ful God, formour and shappere—   *maker; creator*
Tu fabricator omnium &c—
170 And al the myght myd hym is in makynge of thynges.   *with*
  'The fyngres formen a ful hand to portreye or peynten;   *draw; paint*
Kervynge and compasynge is craft of the fyngres.   *Carving; designing*
Right so is the Sone the science of the Fader   *wisdom*
And ful God as is the Fader, no febler ne no bettre.
175   'The pawme is pureliche the hand, hath power by hymselve
    entirely; absolutely
Otherwise than the writhen fust, or werkmanshipe of fyngres;
    clenched; activity
For the pawme hath power to putte out the joyntes   *extend*
And to unfolde the fust, for hym it bilongeth,   *open; pertains to*
And receyve that the fyngres recheth and refuse bothe   *reach (to)*
180 Whan he feleth the fust and the fyngres wille.
  'So is the Holy Goost God, neither gretter ne lasse
Than is the Sire or the Sone, and in the same myghte,   *of the same power*
And alle are thei but o God, as is myn hand and my fyngres,   *one*
Unfolden or folden, my fust and my pawme—   *Open; shut*
185 Al is but an hand, howso I turne it.   *one; however*
  'Ac who is hurte in the hand, evene in the myddes,   *right; middle*
He may receyve right noght—reson it sheweth;   *take (in his hand)*
For the fyngres that folde sholde and the fust make,
For peyne of the pawme, power hem failleth   *pain; they lack power*
190 To clucche or to clawe, to clippe or to holde.   *seize; grasp*
  'Were the myddel of myn hand ymaymed or ypersshed,   *injured; pierced*
I sholde receyve right noght of that I reche myghte;
Ac though my thombe and my fyngres bothe were toshullen   *peeled*

169a Thou art Creator of all things . . . (*Jesu salvator saeculi*, st. 2) (*C*).

167 may an h.] α (*so* K-D); myn h.
  may β.
  fyngeres) LRFHm; my f. W&r.
168 (y)f-] L&r, C; yh- WHm.
172 and] or α.
  is] R (=α; þat is F) Cr; as β.
175 hath] L&r; and h. WC², *some*
  C-MSS; but he F.
177 þe p.] L&r, C; he WHm.
  þe] α, C (*so* K-D); alle þe β.
178 *run together with* 180 β.
  þe] α, C (*so* K-D); þe folden β
  (þe ful Cot; *om* Hm).
  for . . . b.] α (it] it to F), C (*so*
  Sk).
179 α, C (*so* Sk); *om* β.
  And (1, 2)] R, C; & to F.

180 Whan . . . fust] α (*cf.* C); *om* β.
  and] α; as GYCB; at W&r.
182 or] α, C (*so* K-D); and β.
  in] W&r (*om* Cr); of F, C.
183 are þ.] *trsp.* GF; thre Cr²³, C
  (*so* K-D *p.* 90).
185 *run together with* 186 WHmg.
  how . . . it] LRFCr(M), C; *om*
  W&r.
186 Ac . . . ha.] LRFCr(M), C; *om*
  W&r.
188–91 *om* F.
191 (y)persshed] LCr²³; ypersed R;
  yperissed W&r (*C*).
193 shullen] W&r; swolle
  RFHm(M)Cr²³; schiruerd C (*C*).

And the myddel of myn hand withoute male ese,   *pain*
195 In many kynnes maneres I myghte myself helpe   *ways*
    Bothe meve and amende, though alle my fyngres oke.   *repair; ached*
     'By this skile,' he seide, 'I se an evidence   *reasoning; indication*
    That whoso synneth in the Seint Spirit, assoilled worth he nevere,
                                      against; absolved

    Neither here ne elliswhere, as I herde telle—
    Qui peccat in Spiritum Sanctum &c—
200 For he priketh God as in the pawme, that *peccat in Spiritu*[m] *Sanctu*[m].
                                        as (it were)

    For God the Fader is as a fust; the Sone is as a fynger;
    The Holy Goost of hevene is as it were the pawme.
    So whoso synneth ayeyns the Seint Spirit, it semeth that he greveth *injures*
    God that he grypeth with, and wolde his grace quenche.
205 'For to a torche or a tapur the Trinite is likned—   *compared*
    As wex and a weke were twyned togideres,   *wick; twisted*
    And thanne a fir flawmynge forth out of bothe.   *flaming*
    And as wex and weke and warm fir togideres
    Fostren forth a flawmbe and a fair leye   *produce; flame*
210 [That serveth thise swynkeres to se by anightes],   *workmen; at night*
    So dooth the Sire and the Sone and also *Spiritus Sanctus*
    Fostren forth amonges folk love and bileve,   *Generate; faith*
    That alle kynne Cristene clenseth of synnes.
    And as thow seest som tyme sodeynliche a torche—
215 The blase therof yblowe out, yet brenneth the weke—   *flame; burns*
    Withouten leye or light, that [lowe] the macche brenneth;   *flame; wick*
    So is the Holy Goost God, and grace withoute mercy
    To alle unkynde creatures that coveite to destruye   *unnatural*
    Lele love or lif that Oure Lord shapte.   *created*
220 'And as glowynge gledes gladeth noght thise werkmen   *coals; cheer*
    That werchen and waken in wyntres nyghtes,   *work; watch/wake*
    As dooth a kex or a candle that caught hath fir and blaseth,   *hemlock-stem*
    Namoore dooth Sire ne Sone ne Seint Spirit togideres
    Graunte no grace ne forgifnesse of synnes
225 Til the Holy Goost gynne to glowe and to blase;   *blaze, burn (up)*

199a But he that shall sin [blaspheme *Vulg*] against the Holy Ghost [shall never
    have forgiveness . . .] (Mk 3 : 29).
204 . . . in the place where he grips (*see* C-Text).

197 he s.] α, C (*so* K-D); me þynkeþ   208 warme] α, C (*so* K-D *p.* 163);
    β.   hoot β.
199a -*um*, -*um*] CrC², C (*so* Sk); -*u*, -*o*   210 *From* C; *so* K-D *p.* 90; *om*
    W&r (*l. om* F) (C).   B-MSS (C).
    &c] *numquam &c* R (=α).   212 L&r, C; *l. om* WHm.
200 -*um*, -*um*] C (*so* Sk); -*u*, -*o All*   216 that lowe] þat *All* B-MSS (C).
    B-MSS (C).   217 þe] L&r, C; *om* W.
203 aʒeynes] α, C; in β (C).   220–46 *lines om* α.
205 For] α, C (*so* K-D); And β.   224 forg-] CrCG, C (*so* K-D); forʒ-
207 out of] of hem F, C.   W&r.

So that the Holy Goost gloweth but as a glede
Til that lele love ligge on hym and blowe.   *be (over)*
And thanne flawmeth he as fir on Fader and on *Filius*   *flames; Son*
And melteth hire myght into mercy—as men may se in wyntre   *power*
230 Ysekeles in evesynges thorugh hete of the sonne   *Icicles; eaves*
Melte in a mynut while to myst and to watre.   *minute's time*
  'So grace of the Holy Goost the greet myght of the Trinite
Melteth to mercy—to merciable and to noon othere.   *for (the) merciful*
And as wex withouten moore on a warm glede
235 Wol brennen and blasen, be thei togideres,
And solacen hem that mowe [noght] se, that sitten in derknesse, *comfort*
So wol the Fader foryyve folk of mylde hertes   *lowly, kind*
That rufully repenten and restitucion make,   *sorrowfully*
In as muche as thei mowen amenden and paien;   *make amends; pay*
240 And if it suffise noght for assetz, that in swich a wille deyeth,
                               adequate satisfaction
Mercy for his mekenesse wol maken good the remenaunt. *remainder due*
And as the weke and fir wol maken a warm flaumbe
For to murthen men with that in merke sitten,   *cheer; darkness*
So wole Crist of his curteisie, and men crye hym mercy,   *(out) of; if*
245 Bothe foryyve and foryete, and yit bidde for us   *further; pray*
To the Fader of hevene foryifnesse to have.
  'Ac hewe fir at a flynt foure hundred wynter—   *strike; from*
But thow have tache to take it with, tonder or broches,
Al thi labour is lost and al thi long travaille;   *effort*
250 For may no fir flaumbe make, faille it his kynde.
So is the Holy Goost God and grace withouten mercy
To alle unkynde creatures—Crist hymself witnesseth:
Amen dico vobis, nescio vos &c.
  'Be unkynde to thyn evenecristene, and al that thow kanst bidde—
Delen and do penaunce day and nyght evere,   *Give (alms)*
255 And purchace al the pardon of Pampilon and Rome,   *Pamplona*
And indulgences ynowe, and be *ingratus* to thi kynde, *unkind; fellow-men*
The Holy Goost hereth thee noght, ne helpe may thee by reson;

240–1 And if a penitent (who is truly sorry and tries) does not manage to make
    adequate (canonical) satisfaction, but dies wishing to do so, because of his
    humble intent, God's mercy will make good whatever remains to be paid.
248 Unless you have touchwood to light (from the spark), tinder or matches.
250 ... if the substance (needed for fire—*sc.* kindling) be lacking.
252a Amen, I say to you, I know you not (Mt 25: 12).

226 glede] L&r, C; glade W (C).
230 in] L&r, C; and WCr.
233 non] L&r, C; om WHm.
236 nat se] C (so K-D p. 152); se W&r.
242 warm] faire Y, C (C).
243 with] L&r, C; myd WCr[1].
    in] L&r, C; in þe WCr[23].
    merke] L&r, C; derke W.

248 tacche] a, C; towe β (C).
250 his] L&r, C; is WCBo.
256 ing.] β, C; ingrat a, some C-MSS
    (C).
    kynde] β, C; kynne aCr[3].

For unkyndenesse quencheth hym, that he kan noght shyne,
Ne brenne ne blase clere, for blowynge of unkyndenesse.   *bright*
260 Poul the Apostel preveth wheither I lye:
Si linguis hominum loquar &c.
    'Forthi beth war, ye wise men that with the world deleth,   *take care*
That riche ben and reson knoweth—ruleth wel youre soule;
Beth noght unkynde, I conseille yow, to youre evenecristene;
For manye of yow riche men, by my soule, men telleth,
265 Ye brenne, but ye blase noght, and that is a blynd bekene!—
                            lightless beacon (cf. Mt 5: 14-16)
Non omnis qui dicit Domine, Domine, intrabit &c.
    'Dives deyde dampned for his unkyndenesse   (Lk 16: 19-31)
Of his mete and his moneie to men that it nedede.   *With*
Ech a riche, I rede, reward at hym take,   *advise; heed from*
And gyveth youre good to that God that grace of ariseth.   *arises from*
270 For that ben unkynde to hise, hope I noon oother   *(those) who; expect*
But thei dwelle ther Dives is dayes withouten ende.
    'Thus is unkyndenesse the contrarie that quencheth, as it were,
The grace of the Holy Goost, Goddes owene kynde.   *nature*
For that kynde dooth, unkynde fordooth—as thise corsede theves,
275 Unkynde Cristene men, for coveitise and envye
Sleeth a man for hise moebles, with mouth or with handes.   *Kill; goods*
For that the Holy Goost hath to kepe, tho harlotes destruyeth—
                            preserve; villains
The which is lif and love, the leye of mannes body.   *flame*
For every manere good man may be likned to a torche,   *compared*
280 Or ellis to a tapur, to reverence the Trinite;   *taper*
And whoso morthereth a good man, me thynketh, by myn inwit,
                        murders; 'I truly believe'
He fordooth the levest light that Oure Lord lovyeth.   *puts out; dearest*
    'Ac yet in manye mo maneres men offenden the Holy Goost;
Ac this is the worste wise that any wight myghte   *way*
285 Synnen ayein the Seint Spirit—assenten to destruye   *by assenting to*
For coveitise of any kynnes thyng that Crist deere boughte.
                        that (which); redeemed

260a If I speak with the tongues of men, [and of angels, and have not charity]
    (I Cor 13: 1).
265a Not every one that saith (to me), Lord, Lord, shall enter [into the kingdom
    of heaven . . .] (Mt 7: 21).
274 For that which charitable people do / Nature (God) makes, uncharitable
    people / unnaturalness destroys.
276 . . . by slander or by actual physical violence.

265 &] *a*, C; *om* β (*C*).
267 a. his] LCM, ?C; and YR; ne F;
    and of his W&*r*.
270 þat] LRMCr¹; þei þ. W&*r*.
277 þo] L&*r*, C; þe WHmGC².
279 man] L&*r*, C; *om* W.

281 so] R&*r*, C (*so* K-D); þat CrM;
    om WL.
283 Ac] L&*r*; but C²F; for G; And
    WCrC, ?C.
    manye] *om* C (*so* K-D).

How myghte he aske mercy, or any mercy hym helpe,

That wikkedliche and wilfulliche wolde mercy aniente?   *destroy, annihilate*

  'Innocence is next God, and nyght and day it crieth   *nearest to*

290 "Vengeaunce! Vengeaunce! Foryyve be it nevere   *(cf. Gen 4: 10–11)*

That shente us and shedde oure blood—forshapte us, as it semed:

                                           unmade, uncreated (pret.)

Vindica sanguinem iustorum!"

Thus "Vengeaunce, vengeaunce!" verrey charite asketh;   *true; demands*

And sith Holy Chirche and charite chargeth this so soore,

                                 insists on; strongly

Leve I nevere that Oure Lord wol love that charite lakketh,   *(the man) who*

295 Ne have pite for any preiere [that he pleyneth ther].'   *in spite of; utters (C)*

  'I pose I hadde synned so, and sholde now deye,

                             put it that; were about to

And now am sory that I so the Seint Spirit agulte,   *offended*

Confesse me and crye his grace, God that al made,

And myldeliche his mercy aske—myghte I noght be saved?'   *humbly*

300 'Yis,' seide the Samaritan, 'so thow myghte repente   *thus, in such a way*

That rightwisnesse thorugh repentaunce to ruthe myghte turne.

                               justice; compassion

Ac it is but selden yseighe, ther soothnesse bereth witnesse,   *seen; truth*

Any creature be coupable afore a kynges justice,   *guilty*

Be raunsoned for his repentaunce ther alle reson hym dampneth.

                              redeemed; condemns

305 For ther that partie pursueth the peel is so huge

That the kyng may do no mercy til bothe men acorde   *reach agreement*

And eyther have equite, as holy writ telleth: *each; justice*

Numquam dimittitur peccatum &c.

Thus it fareth by swich folk that falsly al hire lyves

Yvele lyven and leten noght til lif hem forsake.   *desist; leave*

310 Drede of desperacion thanne dryveth awey grace,

That mercy in hir mynde may noght thanne falle;

Good hope, that helpe sholde, to wanhope torneth—   *'ill-hope', despair*

291*a* Revenge the blood of the just! (*cf.* Apoc 6: 10).

305 For where the (injured) party prosecutes, the accusation is so grave (Sk).

307*a* The sin is never forgiven [until what is stolen is restored] (St Augustine; *cf.* V 273*a*).

310 A panic fear, then, arising from pure despair *or* A terror amounting to despair (C).

287 LRFMCr, C; *l.* om W&r.

291 vs (1)] β, C; *om* α.
    seme*d*] α (-d]-þ F), C; were β.

295 that h. p. th.] þer þ. h. p. *All* B-MSS (C).

297 am] L&r, ?C; am I WHmM.
    I] W&r, C; *om* LR.

298 god] BxCx; crist *conj* K-D *p.* 206 (C).

300 so] α, C (*so* K-D); so wel β.

301 þoruჳ; myჳte] β, C; to; miჳtest α.

303 be] α, C (*so* K-D); þat is β.

305 *peel*] α, L (? = β), C; plee CrM; peple W&r.

308 lyues] lyue α.

310–11 α, C (*so* Sk); *ll.* om β.

310 þanne . . . a.] F (=α), C (*so* K-D); d. a. þanne R.

The Vision of Piers Plowman

Noght of the nounpower of God, that he ne is myghtful   *impotence*
To amende al that amys is, and his mercy gretter   *wrong*
315 Thanne alle our wikkede werkes, as Holy Writ telleth—
Misericordia eius super omnia opera eius—
Ac er his rightwisnesse to ruthe torne, som restitucion bihoveth: *is needed*
His sorwe is satisfaccion for [swich] that may noght paie.
'Thre thynges ther ben that doon a man by strengthe   *'force a man'*
For to fleen his owene hous, as Holy Writ sheweth.
320 That oon is a wikkede wif that wol noght be chastised:
Hir feere fleeth hire for feere of hir tonge.   *spouse; fear*
And if his hous be unhiled, and reyne on his bedde,   *unroofed; rain*
He seketh and seketh til he slepe drye.
And whan smoke and smolder smyt in his sighte,   *fumes; strike*
325 It dooth hym worse than his wif or wete to slepe.
For smoke and smolder smerteth hise eighen   *sting*
Til he be bler eighed or blynde and [the borre] in the throte, *hoarseness*
Cogheth and curseth that Crist gyve hym sorwe   *Coughs; (saying . . .)*
That sholde brynge in bettre wode, or blowe it til it brende! *should burn*
330 'Thise thre that I telle of thus ben to understonde: *be understood*
The wif is oure wikked flessh that wol noght be chastised,
For kynde clyveth on hym evere to contrarie the soule.   *nature; clings*
And though it falle, it fynt skiles, that "Frelete it made," *finds reasons*
And "That is lightly foryyven and foryeten bothe   *easily*
335 To man that mercy asketh and amende thenketh."
'The reyn that reyneth ther we reste sholde
Ben siknesses and sorwes that we suffren oughte,
As Poul the Apostle to the peple taughte:
Virtus in infirmitate perficitur.
And though that men make muche doel in hir angre,   *sorrow; pain*
340 And ben inpacient in hir penaunce, pure reson knoweth *tribulation*
That thei han cause to contrarie, by kynde of hir siknesse; *complain; virtue*

313 Not from God's lack of power, from his being unable . . .
315a His tender mercies are over all his works (Ps 144: 9).
317 (To God), the sorrow of a sinner who cannot do canonical penance (because he is dying) is satisfaction enough.
325 It makes sleep even harder for him than does his wife's nagging or the rain.
338a For power is made perfect in infirmity (II Cor 12: 9).

313 power] β, C; *per* α.
315a *eius*(1))] β, C (*so* Vulg); *domini* α.
317 β, *cf.* C; *l. om* α.
   suche] C (*so* K-D *p.* 152); hym W&r.
319 hous] L&r, C; *om* W.
321 hire] α, C (*so* K-D *p.* 155); fro h. β, *some* C-MSS.
324 sighte] ey3en F, C.
326 smerteth] α, C (*so* K-D *p.* 157); smyteþ in β (*in om* LGC).

327 þe borre] C, *sugg.* K-D *p.* 152; cow3he R (?=α; a bold c. F); hoors β (C).
328 hym] R&r, C (*so* K-D); hem wL.
330 þus b.] α, C; b. þ. β.
337 siken.] LR, C; *sg.* W&c.
   ou3te] α, C (*so* K-D *p.* 155); ofte β.
338a *-tur*] αCrBm, C; *-tur &c* W&r (*om* C).
341 cause] β, C; resoun α.

218

And lightliche Oure Lord at hir lyves ende   *easily*
Hath mercy on swiche men, that so yvele may suffre.
   'Ac the smoke and the smolder that smyt in oure eighen,   *strikes*
345 That is coveitise and unkyndenesse, that quencheth Goddes mercy.
For unkyndenesse is the contrarie of alle kynnes reson;
For ther nys sik ne sory, ne noon so muche wrecche   *miserable*
That he ne may lovye, and hym like, and lene of his herte   *if; give; from*
Good wille, good word—bothe wisshen and wilnen
350 Alle manere men mercy and foryifnesse,
And lovye hem lik hymself, and his lif amende.
   'I may no lenger lette!' quod he, and lyard he prikede,   *delay; spurred*
And wente awey as wynd—and therwith I awakede.

Passus XVIII

Wolleward and weetshoed wente I forth after   *Shirtless; shoeless*
As a recchelees renk that [reccheth of no wo],   *man; cares for; suffering*
And yede forth lik a lorel al my lif tyme,   *went; wastrel*
Til I weex wery of the world and wilned eft to slepe,   *desired; again*
5 And lened me to a Lenten—and longe tyme I slepte;   *idled till Lent*
Reste me there and rutte faste til *ramis palmarum*.
    Rested; snored; Palm Sunday
Of gerlis and of *Gloria, laus* gretly me dremed   *children; Glory, praise* (C)
And how *osanna* by organye olde folk songen,   *hosanna; to the organ*

343 ... that may suffer with such an ill grace *or* that may suffer evils in such a way.
1 With my skin towards the wool [*i.e.* with no shirt beneath my cloak] and with
   wet feet [with feet shod with wet *rather than* with wet shoes].
6 ... till Palm Sunday came (C).
7 C9th hymn by Theodulph of Orléans (*OBMLV* 81) (C).

344 *Here* MS O *resumes.*
345 þat] β (whiche C); þey F; *om* R.
349 goed] α, C; and g. β.
   bothe] L&r, C; and W.
   wilnen] α, C; willen β.

Rubric Passus xviii ᵘˢ &c et iiius de dobet.
2 reccheth ... wo] r. nat of sorwe C;
   of no wo r. L&r (r.] recched G;
   roughte WB); *trsp.* K-D *p.* 180.
6–8 *copied after* 9 *All* B-MSS; *re-ord.*
   K-D *p.* 176.

And of Cristes passion and penaunce, the peple that ofraughte.

suffering; reached to

10   Oon semblable to the Samaritan, and somdeel to Piers the Plowman,

resembling; somewhat

Barefoot on an asse bak bootles cam prikye,   *riding* (C)

Withouten spores other spere; spakliche he loked,   *spurs; lively*

As is the kynde of a knyght that cometh to be dubbed,   *nature, manner*

To geten hym gilte spores on galoches ycouped.   *slashed shoes* (C)

15   Thanne was Feith in a fenestre, and cryde '*A! Fili David!*'

window; Son of David (cf. Mt 21: 9)

As dooth an heraud of armes whan aventrous cometh to justes.

adventurous knights

Olde Jewes of Jerusalem for joye thei songen,   *sang*

Benedictus qui venit in nomine Domini.

Thanne I frayned at Feith what al that fare bymente,

asked; activity meant

And who sholde juste in Jerusalem. 'Jesus,' he seide,   *was to joust*

20   'And fecche that the fend claymeth—Piers fruyt the Plowman.'

the fruit of P.P.

'Is Piers in this place?' quod I, and he preynte on me.

winked, looked knowingly

'This Jesus of his gentries wol juste in Piers armes,   *in his nobility*

In his helm and in his haubergeon—*humana natura.*

coat of mail; human nature

That Crist be noght biknowe here for *consummatus Deus,*

25   In Piers paltok the Plowman this prikiere shal ryde;

P.P.'s jacket; horseman

For no dynt shal hym dere as *in deitate Patris.*'

'Who shal juste with Jesus?' quod I, 'Jewes or scrybes?'

'Nay,' quod Feith, 'but the fend and fals doom to deye.

Deeth seith he shal fordo and adoun brynge   *destroy*

30   Al that lyveth or loketh in londe or in watre.

Lif seith that he lieth, and leieth his lif to wedde   *lays; pledge*

That, for al that Deeth kan do, withinne thre daies to walke

And fecche fro the fend Piers fruyt the Plowman,

And legge it ther hym liketh, and Lucifer bynde,   *place*

17*a* Blessed is he that cometh in the name of the Lord (Mt 21: 9) (*C*).
24 . . . openly acknowledged as fully and truly God.
26 For no blow [that his human body receives in this combat] will injure him in the
    divine nature that he shares with his Father / God the Father (*not, as* S-P
    translate, 'in his divine nature as the Father', *p.* 154).
28 . . . and a false condemnation to death.

9 *copied after 5 All* B-MSS; *re-ord.*
    K-D.
14 on] F; or WHmLMR; and *r.,* C (*C*).
28 faith but þe . . . to deye] α (but]
    non b. F), C (*so* K-D); he þe foule
    . . . and deeþ β.

30 or (1)] L&*r,* C; and WRF.
    or (2)] L&*r,* C; and W.
31 lieþ] W&*r,* C; likthe LRF; liueth
    Cr²³ (*C*).
32 *So div. from* 33 C (*so* K-D
    p. 94); *div. after* daies *All* B-MSS.

35 And forbete and adoun brynge bale-deeth for evere: *baleful death (C)*
    O *Mors ero mors tua!'*
      Thanne cam *Pilatus* with muche peple, *sedens pro tribunali,*
    To se how doghtiliche Deeth sholde do, and deme hir botheres right. *of both*
    The Jewes and the justice ayeins Jesu thei weere,   *judge*
    And al the court on hym cryde '*Crucifige!*' sharpe.   *Crucify (him); loudly*
40 Tho putte hym forth a p[e]lour bifore Pilat and seide,   *Then; accuser (C)*
    'This Jesus of oure Jewes temple japed and despised,   *made fun of; scorned*
    To fordoon it on o day, and in thre dayes after   *destroy; in one*
    Edifie it eft newe—here he stant that seide it—   *Build; again*
    And yit maken it as muche in alle manere poyntes   *great; respects*
45 Bothe as long and as large a lofte and by grounde.'   *broad; on high*
      '*Crucifige!*' quod a cachepol, 'I warante hym a wicche!' *officer; declare*
      '*Tolle, tolle!*' quod another, and took of kene thornes,   *some sharp*
    And bigan of [gr]ene thorn a garland to make,
    And sette it sore on his heed and seide in envye,   *painfully; malice*
50 '*Ave, raby!*' quod that ribaud—and threw reedes at hym,
                              '*Hail, Rabbi*' (Mt 26: 49)
    Nailed hym with thre nailes naked on the roode,   *(They) nailed*
    And poison on a poole thei putte up to hise lippes,   *pole*
    And beden hym drynken his deeth-yvel—hise dayes were ydone— *bade; bane*
    And [seiden], 'If that thow sotil be, help now thiselve; *clever, cunning*
55 If thow be Crist and kynges sone, com down of the roode;   *from*
    Thanne shul we leve that lif thee loveth and wol noght lete thee deye!'
                                  believe
    '*Consummatum est,*' quod Crist, and comsede for to swoune,
                           '*It is finished*' (Jn 19: 30)
    Pitousliche and pale as a prison that deieth;   *Pitiable; prisoner*
    The lord of lif and of light tho leide hise eighen togideres.
60 The day for drede withdrough and derk bicam the sonne.
    The wal waggede and cleef, and al the world quaved. *shook; split; quaked*
    Dede men for that dene come out of depe graves,   *noise*
    And tolde why that tempeste so longe tyme durede.   *lasted*
      'For a bitter bataille,' the dede body seide;   *Because of*
65 'Lif and Deeth in this derknesse, hir oon fordooth hir oother.
                       Each is destroying the
    Shal no wight wite witterly who shal have the maistrie   *for certain*
    Er Sonday aboute sonne risyng'—and sank with that til erthe. *Before; to the*

35*a* O death, I will be thy death (Osee 13: 14).
46–7 Crucify him! Away with him! (Jn 19:15).
50 Hail, Rabbi (Mt 26: 49; *Judas' greeting to Jesus*).

40 pelour] C (*so* K-D); pilour *All*   48 grene] C (*so* K-D *p.* 152); kene
    B-MSS (C).   W&*r;* þat F.
41 Iewes] β, C; *om* α.   54 saiden] C (*so* K-D); *om All*
    iaped] L&*r,* C; haþ I. W; he I. F.   B-MSS (C).
42 on] W&*r,* ?C; in RFBGM.   59 The] β, C; Tyl þe F; Til R.
45 a] R (?=α), C; on FB; bi W&*r*   62 depe] β, C; here α.
    (=β).

Some seide that he was Goddes sone, that so faire deyde:
Vere filius Dei erat iste.
And some seide he was a wicche—'Good is that we assaye   *test, make sure*
70 Wher he be deed or noght deed, doun er he be taken.'   *Whether*
    Two theves also tholed deeth that tyme   *suffered*
Upon a croos bisides Crist—so was the comune lawe.
A cachepol cam forth and craked bothe hir legges,   *broke*
And hir armes after of either of tho theves.
75 Ac was no boy so boold Goddes body to touche;   *fellow*
For he was knyght and kynges sone, Kynde foryaf that throwe
                               As; granted; time
That noon harlot were so hardy to leyen hond upon hym.
                        scoundrel should be; bold
    Ac ther cam forth a knyght with a kene spere ygrounde,   *sharpened*
Highte Longeus, as the lettre telleth, and longe hadde lore his sight.   *lost*
80 Bifore Pilat and oother peple in the place he hoved.   *waited*
Maugree his manye teeth he was maad that tyme
To [justen with Jesus, this blynde Jew Longeus].
For alle thei were unhardy, that hoved on horse or stode,   *lacked courage*
To touchen hym or to tasten hym or taken hym doun of roode,   *handle; from*
85 But this blynde bacheler, that baar hym thorugh the herte.   *knight; thrust*
The blood sprong doun by the spere and unspered the knyghtes eighen.
                           unbarred, opened
    Thanne fil the knyght upon knees and cryde Jesu mercy: *fell*
'Ayein my wille it was, Lord, to wownde yow so soore!'
He sighed and seide, 'Soore it me athynketh!   *grieves*
90 For the dede that I have doon I do me in youre grace.   *put; mercy*
Have on me ruthe, rightful Jesu!'—and right with that he wepte.
    Thanne gan Feith felly the false Jewes despise—   *cruelly; scorn, upbraid*
Callede hem caytyves acorsed for evere: *wretches; cursed*
'For this foule vileynye vengeaunce to yow falle!   *low, base action*
95 To do the blynde bete hym ybounde, it was a boyes counseille.
                          make; knave's
Cursede caytyves! Knyghthood was it nevere   *A knightly action*

68a Indeed this was the Son of God (Mt 27: 54).
81 Despite his protests he was then forced . . . (S-P).

69 þat] β, C; *om* α.
73 A] β, C; Ac a α.
74 her] L&r, C; þe WCr.
75 boy] L&r, C; body WGCot.
76 þrowe] α (*so* K-D *p*. 161); tyme β, C (C).
82 *So* C (*so* K-D *p*. 94); To take the spere in his hond and Iusten wiþ Ihesus *All* B-MSS (C).
83 on horse] þer C.
   or] W&r, C; and g.
   st.] β, C; stede α.
84 hym (1)] β, C; *om* αCr.
   hym (3)] L&r, C; *om* w.
85 þat] α, C; þanne β (*om* WCrM).
86 vnsp.] β, C; opned α.
87 ihesu] R (=α; crist F), C (*so* K-D); hym β.
94 falle] WHmGC²; *bi*fall C; alle L&r.
96 -tyues] RFOBHmCr (?=Bx), C (*so* K-D); -tif WL&r.

To mysdo a deed body by daye or by nyghte.   *maltreat*
The gree yit hath he geten, for al his grete wounde.   *prize; i.e. Christ*
  'For youre champion chivaler, chief knyght of yow alle,
100 Yilt hym recreaunt rennyng, right at Jesus wille.   *Yields*
For be this derknesse ydo, Deeth worth yvenquisshed;   *at an end; defeated*
And ye, lurdaynes, han ylost—for Lif shal have the maistrye.   *villains*
And youre fraunchyse, that fre was, fallen is in thraldom,   *free condition; into*
And ye, cherles, and youre children, cheve shulle ye nevere,   *prosper*
105 Ne have lordshipe in londe, ne no lond tilye,   *ownership; cultivate*
But al barayne be and usurie usen,   *unproductive; practise*
Which is lif that Oure Lord in alle lawes acurseth.   *condemns*
Now youre goode dayes arn doon, as Daniel prophecied:
Whan Crist cam hir kyngdom the crowne sholde lese—   *lose*
Cum veniat sanctus sanctorum cessabit unxio vestra.'

110   What for feere of this ferly and of the false Jewes,   *wonder*
I drow me in that derknesse to *descendit ad inferna*,   *withdrew myself*
And there I saugh soothly, *secundum scripturas*,
Out of the west coste, a wenche, as me thoughte,   *region; woman*
Cam walkynge in the wey; to helleward she loked.   *toward hell*
115 Mercy highte that mayde, a meke thyng with alle,
A ful benigne burde, and buxom of speche.   *kindly lady; courteous*
  Hir suster, as it semed, cam softely walkynge   *quietly*
Evene out of the est, and westward she lokede—   *Directly; east*
A ful comely creature [and a clene], Truthe she highte;
120 For the vertue that hire folwede, afered was she nevere.   *Because of; power*
  Whan thise maydenes mette, Mercy and Truthe,
Either asked oother of this grete wonder—   *Each; about*
Of the dyn and of the derknesse, and how the day rowed,   *daylight dawned*
And which a light and a leme lay bifore helle.   *glow*
125 'Ich have ferly of this fare, in feith,' seide Truthe,   *wonder at; event*
'And am wendynge to wite what this wonder meneth.'
'Have no merveille,' quod Mercy, 'murthe it bitokneth.

    joy; signifies, portends

100 Admits that he has been defeated in the running (of the joust) (*C*).
109*a* 'When the Saint of Saints comes, your anoint[ed kingship] shall come to an
end (*cf.* Dan 9: 24) (*C*).
111 ... into the depths of hell [*lit.* he descended into Hell, *art.* 8 *of* Apostles'
Creed].
112 ... according to the Scriptures (*actually* Gospel of Nicodemus, *but cf.*
Ps 84: 11).

101 d. w. Ivenkesched] α, C (*so* K-D);
  his d. w. avenged β.
104 ʒe (2)] L&r; *om* W.
105 Ne] L&r, C; To WHm.
109 her] LY&r; of hir WHmCr¹M;
  þier G; þe R; to his F.
  lese] α (*so* K-D); cesse β (*om* L).
109*a* cessabit ... v.] β, C; *om* α.
117 softly] L&r, C; sooþly WYC²M;
  worthely Cr.
119 and a clene] C (*so* K-D *p.* 94);
  not in B-MSS (*C*).
121 Whan] β, C; And w. α.
124 which] β, C; swich α.

A maiden that highte Marie, and moder withouten felyng   *(sexual) contact*
Of any kynde creature, conceyved thorugh speche   *natural creature*
130 And grace of the Holy Goost; weex greet with childe;   *grew*
Withouten wem into this world she broghte hym;   *stain*
And that my tale be trewe, I take God to witnesse.
  'Sith this barn was ybore ben thritti wynter passed,
Which deide and deeth tholed this day aboute mydday—   *suffered*
135 And that is cause of this clips that closeth now the sonne,   *eclipse; encloses*
In menynge that man shal fro merknesse be drawe   *sign; darkness*
The while this light and this leme shal Lucifer ablende.   *glow; blind*
For patriarkes and prophetes han preched herof often—
That man shal man save thorugh a maydenes helpe,
140 And that was tynt thorugh tree, tree shal it wynne,   *that (which); lost*
And that Deeth down broughte, deeth shal releve.'   *raise up, restore*
  'That thow tellest,' quod Truthe, 'is but a tale of waltrot!   *absurdity*
For Adam and Eve and Abraham with othere
Patriarkes and prophetes that in peyne liggen,
145 Leve thow nevere that yon light hem alofte brynge,   *shall bring them above*
Ne have hem out of helle—hold thi tonge, Mercy!
It is but trufle that thow tellest—I, Truthe, woot the sothe.   *nonsense*
For that is ones in helle, out cometh it nevere;
Job the prophete patriark repreveth thi sawes: *disproves; words*
Quia in inferno nulla est redempcio.'
150   Thanne Mercy ful myldely mouthed thise wordes: *uttered*
'Thorugh experience,' quod he[o], 'I hope thei shul be saved.
For venym fordooth venym—and that I preve by reson.   *destroys*
For of alle venymes foulest is the scorpion;
May no medicyne [am]e[nd]e the place ther he styngeth,   *heal*
155 Til he be deed and do therto—the yvel he destruyeth,   *placed upon it*
The firste venymouste, thorugh vertu of hymselve.   *poison; power*
So shal this deeth fordo—I dar my lif legge—   *destroy; wager*
Al that deeth dide first thorugh the develes entisyng;   *tempting*
And right as thorugh [gilours] gile [bigiled was man],   *(a) deceiver's guile*
160 So shal grace that al bigan make a good ende

149a For in hell there is no salvation (*C*).
151 On the basis of practical experience I [found my] hope that . . .

129 kende] a, C; *kynnes* β.
138 often] L&r; ofte WHm.
141 doun] L&r, C; adown W.
147 but] a, C; but a β (a G).
   I] β, C; *om* a.
148 þat] L&r; he þ. WHmF.
   it] L&r, C; he wC²F.
151 heo] C (MSS PG&c) (*so* K-D);
   he aCr¹; she β
152 I p.] p. I WCot; p. Bo.
154 amende] C (*so* K-D *p.* 94); helpe
   All B-MSS..

156 vertue] a, C (*so* K-D); venym β.
157 fordo] β, C; do a.
158 dyd] L&r; fordide WHm.
159 thorugh . . . man] þoruȝ gile man
   was bigiled *All* B-MSS; þe gylour
   þorw gyle bygiled man formest
   C (*so* K-D *p.* 94) (*C*).
160 all b.] C²; b. al C;.he gan F;
   bigan W&r (*C*).
   ende] YGC², C (*so* K-D); sighte
   CBO; sleighte W&r (*C*).

[And bigile the gilour—and that is good] sleighte: *stratagem (C)*
Ars ut artem falleret.'

   'Now suffre we!' seide Truthe, 'I se, as me thynketh,   *let's be quiet*
Out of the nyppe of the north, noght ful fer hennes,   *cold region; from here*
Rightwisnesse come rennynge; reste we the while,   *Justice*

165 For he[o] woot moore than we—he[o] was er we bothe.'

   'That is sooth,' seide Mercy, 'and I se here by sowthe   *(the) south*
Where cometh Pees pleyinge, in pacience yclothed.
Love hath coveited hire longe—leve I noon oother   *desired*
But [Love] sente hire som lettre, what this light bymeneth   *means*

170 That overhoveth helle thus; she us shal telle.'   *hovers over*

   Whan Pees in pacience yclothed approched ner hem tweyne,
     near the two of them

Rightwisnesse hire reverenced for hir riche clothyng,   *saluted courteously*
And preide Pees to telle hire to what place she wolde   *wished to go*
And in hire gaye garnementes whom she grete thoughte?   *intended to greet*

175 'My wil is to wende,' quod she, 'and welcome hem alle
That many day myghte I noght se for merknesse of synne—
     because of the darkness

Adam and Eve and othere mo in helle,   ·   *more*
Moyses and many mo; Mercy shul [synge],
And I shal daunce therto—do thow so, suster!

180 For Jesus justede wel, joye bigynneth dawe: *Because; to dawn*
Ad vesperum demorabitur fletus, et ad matutinum leticia.

   'Love, that is my lemman, swiche lettres me sente   *beloved*
That Mercy, my suster, and I mankynde sholde save,
And that God hath forgyven and graunted me, Pees, and Mercy
     'freely assigned to'

To be mannes meynpernour for everemoore after.   *surety*

185 Lo, here the patente!' quod Pees, '*In pace in idipsum,*   *authority*
And that this dede shal dure, *dormiam et requiescam.'*
     document; be always valid

   'What, ravestow?' quod Rightwisnesse; 'or thow art right dronke!
     Are you mad? dead drunk

161a That God by stratagem should foil The shape-shifting Destroyer's guile
(Fortunatus' *Pange Lingua*, OBMLV 54, l. 8).

180a In the evening weeping shall have place: and in the morning gladness (Ps
29: 6).

185–6 See, here is the letter of authorization, and [a text from the Psalms signi-
fying] that this document shall have lasting validity: 'In peace in the selfsame I
will sleep, and I will rest' (Ps 4: 9).

161 *From* C (*so* K-D *p.* 90); *not in*
B-MSS (*C*).
165 heo (1, 2)] he W&*r*, C; she F;
corr. K-D.
167 com. p.] R (=*a*), C; p. c. *β*F.
169 loue] C (*so* K-D *p.* 94); he *All*
B-MSS.

172 for] L&*r*; by WHm; in C.
178 mercy] BxCx; merye *conj* K-D
p. 208 (*C*).
     synge] C (*so* K-D *p.* 92); haue
All B-MSS (*C*).
179 *β*, C; *line om a.*
182 my s.] *β*, C; *om a.*

Levestow that yond light unlouke myghte helle   *unlock*
And save mannes soule? Suster, wene it nevere!   *think, suppose*
190 At the bigynnyng God gaf the doom hymselve—   *gave; judgment*
    That Adam and Eve and alle that hem suwede   *followed, came after*
    Sholden deye downrighte, and dwelle in peyne after   *entirely, utterly*
    If that thei touchede a tree and of the fruyt eten.   *one; ate*
    Adam afterward, ayeins his defence,   *prohibition*
195 Freet of that fruyt, and forsook, as it were,   *Ate*
    The love of Oure Lord and his loore bothe   *teaching*
    And folwede that the fend taughte and his felawes wille   *i.e. Eve's*
    Ayeins reson—I, Rightwisnesse, recorde thus with Truthe   *declare*
    That hir peyne be perpetuel and no preiere hem helpe.
200 Forthi lat hem chewe as thei chosen, and chide we noght, sustres,   *quarrel*
    For it is botelees bale, the byte that thei eten.'   *incurable evil; mouthful*
    'And I shal preie,' quod Pees, 'hir peyne moot have ende,
    And wo into wele mowe wenden at the laste.   *happiness; turn*
    For hadde thei wist of no wo, wele hadde thei noght knowen;
205 For no wight woot what wele is, that nevere wo suffrede,
    Ne what is hoot hunger, that hadde nevere defaute.   *?hot/called; lack*
    If no nyght ne weere, no man, as I leve,
    Sholde wite witterly what day is to meene.   *properly; means*
    Sholde nevere right riche man that lyveth in reste and ese   *a very rich*
210 Wite what wo is, ne were the deeth of kynde.   *natural death, mortality*
    So God that bigan al of his goode wille
    Bicam man of a mayde mankynde to save,
    And suffrede to be sold, to se the sorwe of deying,
    The which unknytteth alle care, and comsynge is of reste.
                                     unknits; the commencement
215 For til *modicum* mete with us, I may it wel avowe,   *'a little'*
    Woot no wight, as I wene, what is ynogh to mene.
    'Forthi God, of his goodnesse, the firste gome Adam,   *man*
    Sette hym in solace and in sovereyn murthe;   *content; supreme joy*
    And siththe he suffred hym synne, sorwe to feele—   *allowed (to)*
220 To wite what wele was, kyndeliche to knowe it.   *directly; i.e. suffering*
    And after, God auntrede hymself and took Adames kynde   *ventured; nature*
    To wite what he hath suffred in thre sondry places,

215–16 For till we experience 'too little', we none of us can know the meaning of
    'enough'.

189 it] β, C; þow it α.
190 At . . . god] L&r exc F, C
    (bi.]b. of þe world C); For god þe
    bigynnere W.
192 peyne] RF&c, ?C; pyne WL&c
    (cf. 199 below).
193 of] F (?=α), C; om βR (C).
198 β, C; line om α.
    I] L (?=β), ?C (C-MS I) (so
    K-D); And W&r, most C-MSS (C).

202 preie] α, C; preue β (C).
208 wite] L&r, C; neuere w. WHm.
213 to (2)] β, C; and α.
216 is yn.] L&r (=β; y. i. WHm),
    C; is nouȝte R; it is F.
218 murþe] β, C; ioye α.
220 was] β, C; is α.
    to] L&r, C; and W.

Bothe in hevene and in erthe—and now til helle he thenketh,   *to; i.e. to go*
To wite what alle wo is, that woot of alle joye.
225 'So it shal fare by this folk: hir folie and hir synne
Shal lere hem what langour is, and lisse withouten ende.   *teach; pain; joy*
Woot no wight what werre is ther that pees regneth,   *war*
Ne what is witterly wele til "weylawey" hym teche.'   *misery ('alas!')*

Thanne was ther a wight with two brode eighen;   *wide*
230 Book highte that beaupeere, a bold man of speche.   *i.e. 'Bible'; elder*
'By Goddes body!' quod this Book, 'I wol bere witnesse
That tho this barn was ybore, ther blased a sterre   *when; star*
That alle the wise of this world in o wit acordeden—   *one judgment agreed*
That swich a barn was ybore in Bethleem the citee
235 That mannes soule sholde save and synne destroye.
'And alle the elements,' quod the Book, 'herof beren witnesse.
That he was God that al wroghte the wolkne first shewed: *heaven(s)*
Tho that weren in hevene token *stella comata*   *a comet*
And tendeden hire as a torche to reverencen his burthe;   *kindled*
240 The light folwede the Lord into the lowe erthe.
The water witnesseth that he was God, for he wente on it;
Peter the Apostel parceyved his gate,   *going*
And as he wente on the water wel hym knew, and seide,   *recognized*
"*Iube me venire ad te super aquas.*"
245 And lo! how the sonne gan louke hire light in hirselve   *lock up*
Whan she seigh hym suffre, that sonne and see made.   *sea*
The erthe for hevynesse that he wolde suffre   *grief*
Quaked as quyk thyng and al biquasshed the roche.   *a live; shattered*
'Lo! helle myghte nat holde, but opnede tho God tholede,
   when; suffered
250 And leet out Symondes sones to seen hym hange on roode.   *Simeon's (C)*
And now shal Lucifer leve it, though hym looth thynke.
   believe; seem hateful
For *Gigas* the geaunt with a gyn engyned
To breke and to bete adoun that ben ayeins Jesus.   *(those) who*
And I, Book, wole be brent, but Jesus rise to lyve   *burnt; unless*
255 In alle myghtes of man, and his moder gladie,   *powers; cheer*

244 [Lord, if it be thou], bid me come to thee upon the waters (Mt 14: 28).
252 For Gigas the giant has contrived with an engine (of war) . . . (C).

224 þat . . . of] L&r (of] what G),
   C; and what is WHm.
233 wise of] β (w.] w. men Cr), C;
   men in α.
   -deden] LROHm, C; -den W&r.
238 -mata] L&r, C; -meta WHmCr²³G
   (C).
239 hir] L&r; it W, C.
241 -eth] R&r, C; -ed wLM; *om* C.

246 see] β, C; mone α.
250 sones] L&r (*om* Y), C; *sg.*
   WHmB.
251 leue] W&r, C; leese F; *om* R.
252 β, C; *line om* α.
   engyned] L&r; haþ e. W.
253 β, C; *om* α (C).
255 of] of a α.

And conforte al his kyn and out of care brynge,		
And al the Jewene joye unjoynen and unlouken;	*Jews'; dissolve*	
And but thei reverencen his roode and his resurexion,		
And bileve on a newe lawe, be lost, lif and soule!'	*(they shall) be*	
260 'Suffre we!' seide Truthe, 'I here and see bothe	*Let us be quiet*	
A spirit speketh to helle and biddeth unspere the yates:	*bids unbar; gates*	
"*Attolite portas.*"		
A vois loude in that light to Lucifer crieth,		
"Prynces of this place, unpynneth and unlouketh!	*undo; unlock*	
For here cometh with crowne that kyng is of glorie." '	*(he) who*	
265 Thanne sikede Sathan, and seide to helle,	*sighed*	
'Swich a light, ayeins oure leve, Lazar it fette;	*leave/belief; fetched*	
Care and combraunce is comen to us alle!	*confusion*	
If this kyng come in, mankynde wole he fecche,		
And lede it ther Lazar is, and lightliche me bynde.	*easily*	
270 Patriarkes and prophetes han parled herof longe—	*spoken*	
That swich a lord and a light shal lede hem alle hennes.'	*from here*	
'Listneth!' quod Lucifer, 'for I this lord knowe;		
Bothe this lord and this light, is longe ago I knew hym.		
May no deeth this lord dere, ne no develes queyntise,	*harm; cunning*	
275 And where he wole, is his wey—ac ware hym of the perils!	*let him beware*	
If he reve me of my right, he robbeth me by maistrie;	*deprive; sheer force*	
For by right and by reson the renkes that ben here	*people*	
Body and soule beth myne, bothe goode and ille.		
For hymself seide, that sire is of hevene,	*lord*	
280 That if Adam ete the appul, alle sholde deye,		
And dwelle [in deol] with us develes—this thretynge he made.	*pain; threat*	
And [sithen] he that Soothnesse is seide thise wordes,	*since*	
And I sithen iseised sevene [thousand] wynter,		
I leeve that lawe nyl noght lete hym the leeste.'		

261a Lift up your gates, [O ye princes] ... (Ps 23: 9).
283–4 And (since) I was then put in possession [*sc.* of these souls] ... I am convinced that [his own] decree will not permit him [to overcome us by sheer strength].

258 reu.] L&r, C; reuersen WCr¹.
261 A] α, C (*so* K-D); How a β.
261a portas] α, ?C (*so* K-D); p. &c β.
262 crieþ] W&r (-þ]-d GOC); sayd Cr²³, C.
265 helle] α, C (*so* K-D); hem alle β.
266 it] L&r (is B), C; out WCr.
267 comb-] L&r, C; encomb- WB.
269 it] β, C; hem α.
    lazar is] α, C (*so* K-D); hym likeþ β.
271 a (2)] L&r, C; *om* WHmC².
    schal] αC, C; sholde β.
274 þis lorde] α, C (*so* K-D); hym β.

276 reue] L&r, C; reueþ WYC²; reuees C.
    of] αCr, C; *om* β.
    he robbeþ] β, C; & robbe α.
279 *Line om* g.
280 þat] α (*cf.* C); *om* β.
281 in deol] *not in* B-MSS; *cf.* C (C).
282 sithen] *conj* K-D *p.* 199; *om All* B-MSS (C).
283 I] R; *om* W&r (C).
    i-] I RWHmLM; y was F; is YGOC²; he CrCB (C).
    thousand] C (*so* K-D *p.* 90); hundred *All* B-MSS.

285   'That is sooth,' seide Satan, 'but I me soore drede;

For thow gete hem with gile, and his gardyn breke,   *got; broke (into)*

And in semblaunce of a serpent sete on the appultre,   *sat*

And eggedest hem to ete, Eve by hirselve,   *urged*

And toldest hire a tale—of treson were the wordes;   *treachery, deceit*

290 And so thou haddest hem out and hider at the laste.

It is noght graithly geten, ther gile is the roote!'   *duly obtained*

    'For God wol noght be bigiled,' quod Gobelyn, 'ne byjaped.   *fooled*

We have no trewe title to hem, for thorugh treson were thei dampned.'

       valid claim

    'Certes, I drede me,' quod the Devel, 'lest Truthe wol hem fecche.

295 Thise thritty wynter, as I wene, he wente aboute and prechèd.

I have assailled hym with synne, and som tyme I asked   *once*

Wheither he were God or Goddes sone—he gaf me short answere;

And thus hath he trolled forth thise two and thritty wynter.   *wandered*

And whan I seigh it was so, slepynge I wente   *in (her) sleep*

300 To warne Pilates wif what done man was Jesus;   *'make of' (Sk; q.v.)*

For Jewes hateden hym and han doon hym to dethe.

I wolde have lengthed his lif—for I leved, if he deide,   *prolonged*

That his soule wolde suffre no synne in his sighte;

For the body, while it on bones yede, aboute was evere   *walked alive*

305 To save men from synne if hemself wolde.   *(they) themselves*

And now I se wher a soule cometh [silynge hiderward]   *gliding*

With glorie and with gret light—God it is, I woot wel!

I rede we fle,' quod he, 'faste alle hennes—

For us were bettre noght be than biden his sighte.   *await, endure*

310 For thi lesynges, Lucifer, lost is al oure praye.   *lies; prey*

First thorugh the we fellen fro hevene so heighe;

For we leved thi lesynges, we lopen out alle with thee;   *believed; fled*

And now for thi laste lesynge, ylorn we have Adam,   *lost*

And al oure lordshipe, I leve, a londe and a watre: *on*

Nunc princeps huius mundi eicietur foras.'

314*a* Now shall the prince of this world be cast out (Jn 12: 31).

287 on] L&*r*; vpon WCr.

290 so] β, C; al so α.

294 wol] BxCx; do *conj* K-D *p.* 206 (C).

295 he . . . ab.] α, C (he] and C) (*so* K-D); haþ he gon β.

296 tyme] β, C; *om* α.

    I] C; y- W&*r*; y have hym F; *om* CrGC²B.

297 gaf] LR, C; yaf WF.

298 haþ he] β, C; he h. αCr.

299 slep.] L&*r*; lep. WHmCr².

302 I (1)] β, C; And I α.

    leued] β, C; leue α.

303 suff.] β; nauȝt s. α.

306 syl. h.] C (*so* K-D *p.* 94); h. seillynge *All* B-MSS (*C*).

308 we] L&*r*, C; þat we WB.

312 *run together with* 313 β.

    þi] L&*r*, C; on þi WCr.

    we (2) . . . þe] α (w. þe *om* F) (*so* Sk); *om* β.

313 And . . . les.] α, C (thi l.] a later C) (*so* Sk); *om* β.

The Vision of Piers Plowman

315 Eft the light bad unlouke, and Lucifer answerde,   *Again; unlock*
 '*Quis est iste?*
What lord artow?' quod Lucifer. The light soone seide,   *are you*
 '*Rex glorie*,
The lord of myght and of mayn and alle manere vertues— *strength; powers*
Dominus virtutum.
320 Dukes of this dymme place, anoon undo thise yates,   *at once; gates*
That Crist may come in, the Kynges sone of Hevene!'
   And with that breeth helle brak, with Belialles barres—   *burst open*
For any wye or warde, wide open the yates.
   Patriarkes and prophetes, *populus in tenebris*,
325 Songen Seint Johanes song, '*Ecce Agnus Dei!*'
                Behold the Lamb of God (Jn 1: 36)
Lucifer loke ne myghte, so light hym ablente.   *blinded*
   And tho that Oure Lord lovede, into his light he laughte,
                those; caught up
And seide to Sathan, 'Lo! here my soule to amendes   *in satisfaction*
For alle synfulle soules, to save tho that ben worthi.
330 Myne thei ben and of me—I may the bet hem cleyme. *better, more validly*
Although reson recorde, and right of myselve,
         declare; my own (principle of) justice
That if thei ete the appul, alle sholde deye,
I bihighte hem noght here helle for evere.   *promised*
For the dede that thei dide, thi deceite it made;   *caused it*
335 With gile thow hem gete, ageyn alle reson.   *got; against*
For in my paleis, Paradis, in persone of an addre,   *form; serpent*
Falsliche thow fettest there thyng that I lovede.   *brought away from*
   'Thus ylik a lusard with a lady visage,   *serpent; woman's face*
Thefliche thow me robbedest; the Olde Lawe graunteth *Like a thief*
340 That gilours be bigiled—and that is good reson:
Dentem pro dente et oculum pro oculo.

316, 317a, 319 Who is this [King of Glory]? The Lord of hosts, he is the King of
Glory (Ps 23: 10) (*C*).
324 The people [that walked] in darkness [have seen a great light] (Is 9: 2, *qu.*
Mt 4:16).
325 Behold the Lamb of God (Jn 1: 36).
340a Eye for eye, tooth for tooth (Ex 21: 24, *trsp.*).

316–18 *as two lines divided after iste* α.
316–17a *as two lines div. after iste*
  β; *rec. & trsp.* K-D *p.* 183n; *cf.* C (*C*).
  Quis . . . glor.] What l. a. q. Luc.
  Quis est iste Rex gl. þe l. s. seide
  W&r *exc* F.
318 *as one line with* 319 WL; *re-div.*
  K-D.
    þe] α, C (*so* K-D); And β.
    mayne] L&r, C; man WR; mani
    BmBo.

319 *om* YF; *as one line with* 320 R.
320 Dukes] β, C; *sg.* α (þow d. F).
322 brak] β, C; braste α.
323 opene] L&r (=β), C; opned α
  WHm, *some* C-MSS.
331 Al] L&r, C; And WHm.
332 þei] L&r, C; he WHm.
337 þere] L&r, C; *om* WYO.
339 þe] L&r; and þe W.

Ergo soule shal soule quyte and synne to synne wende,   *Therefore; pay for* (C)

And al that man hath mysdo, I, man, wole amende it.   *done wrong*

Membre for membre [was amendes by the Olde Lawe],   *satisfaction*

And lif for lif also—and by that lawe I clayme

345 Adam and al his issue at my wille herafter.

And that deeth in hem fordide, my deeth shal releve,   *destroyed; restore*

And bothe quyke and quyte that queynt was thorugh synne;

And that grace gile destruye, good feith it asketh.   *should destroy; requires*

So leve it noght, Lucifer, ayein the lawe I fecche hem,   *believe; against*

350 But by right and by reson raunsone here my liges: *ransom; subjects*

Non veni solvere legem set adimplere.

    'Thow fettest myne in my place ayeins alle reson—

Falsliche and felonliche; good feith me it taughte,   *felonously*

To recovere hem thorugh raunsoun, and by no reson ellis,   *no other method*

So that with gile thow gete, thorugh grace it is ywonne.   *that* (*which*)

355 Thow, Lucifer, in liknesse of a luther addere   *treacherous, evil*

Getest bi gile tho that God lovede;   *Got; those*

And I, in liknesse of a leode, that Lord am of hevene,   *human being*

Graciousliche thi gile have quyt—go gile ayein gile!   *let guile go against g.*

And as Adam and alle thorugh a tree deyden,   *one*

360 Adam and alle thorugh a tree shal turne to lyve;

And gile is bigiled, and in his gile fallen:

Et cecidit in foveam quam fecit.

Now bigynneth thi gile ageyn thee to turne

And my grace to growe ay gretter and widder.   *ever; wider*

The bitternesse that thow hast browe, now brouke it thiselve;   *brewed; enjoy* ('*brook*')

365 That art doctour of deeth, drynk that thow madest!   (*You*) *who*

    'For I that am lord of lif, love is my drynke,

And for that drynke today, I deide upon erthe.   *because of/for the sake of*

I faught so, me thursteth yet, for mannes soule sake;   *fought; I thirst*

May no drynke me moiste, ne my thurst slake,

---

347 And both give life to and make satisfaction for that which was quenched through sin [*sc.* eternal life for man and its loss through the fall].

350*a* I am not come to destroy the law but to fulfil (Mt 5: 17).

361*a* ... he is fallen into the hole he made (Ps 7: 16).

---

342 am. it] α (it wel am. F), C; am. β.

343 was ... L.] by þe o. l. w. am. *All* B-MSS (by] in Cr); *trsp.* K-D p. 194.

344 cl.] α (*so* K-D); cl. it β.

347 quykke] L&r, C; quykne w; quyt F.

348 -struye] W&r (=β); -stroyeth α Cr; -stroyed CB.

349 it] L (?=β) α, C; I W&r; thow M. noȝt] β, C; neuere α.

350 by (2)] W&r (*cf.* C); *om* αg (*exc.* C).

354 with] α, ?C; þoruȝ β, *some* C-MSS.

is] β, C; was α.

360 turne] α, C (*so* K-D); t. ayein β.

363 wid.] β, C; grettere α.

364 L&r, C; *l. om* W.

now] α, C (*so* K-D); *om* β.

370 Til the vendage falle in the vale of Josaphat,   *vintage take place*
That I drynke right ripe must, *resureccio mortuorum.*
And thanne shal I come as a kyng, crouned, with aungeles,
And have out of helle alle mennes soules.
   'Fendes and fendekynes bifore me shul stande   *'fiendlings', minor devils*
375 And be at my biddyng wheresoevere [be] me liketh.
Ac to be merciable to man thanne, my kynde it asketh,   *merciful; nature*
For we beth bretheren of blood, but noght in baptisme alle.
                              by blood. baptism
Ac alle that beth myne hole bretheren, in blood and in baptisme,   *entire*
Shul noght be dampned to the deeth that is withouten ende:
Tibi soli peccavi &c.
380   'It is noght used on erthe to hangen a feloun   *customary*
Ofter than ones, though he were a tretour.   *once; traitor*
And if the kyng of that kyngdom come in that tyme   *came*
There the feloun thole sholde deeth oother juwise,   *suffer; judgment*
Lawe wolde he yeve hym lif, and he loked on hym.   *should grant; if*
385 And I that am kyng of kynges shal come swich a tyme
There doom to the deeth dampneth alle wikked;   *(final) judgment*
And if lawe wole I loke on hem, it lith in my grace   *lies*
Wheither thei deye or deye noght for that thei diden ille.
Be it any thyng abought, the boldnesse of hir synnes,   *redeemed*
390 I may do mercy thorugh rightwisnesse, and alle my wordes trewe.
And though Holy Writ wole that I be wroke of hem that diden ille—
                              avenged upon
Nullum malum impunitum &c—
Thei shul be clensed clerliche and [clene] wàsshen of hir synnes   *clearly*
In my prisone Purgatorie, til *parce* it hote.
And my mercy shal be shewed to manye of my bretheren;

371 When I shall drink new wine [from grapes] thoroughly ripened—the resurrection of the dead (*C*).
375 . . . wherever it pleases me that they should be.
377 For men and I are brothers through the human nature we share, but not all are my brothers through baptism.
379*a* To thee only have I sinned . . . (Ps 50: 6).
383 'Where the criminal is due to suffer death or a sentence of death' (*C*).
389–90 Should there be any circumstance to mitigate the gravity of their sins, I have the power to show mercy as part of justice, and (still preserve) the truth of all I have said.
391*a* No evil shall go unpunished [and no good unrewarded] (*cf.* IV 143).
393 . . . till (a command to) spare (them) bid it be otherwise (*C*).

374 fendek.] L&*r*, C; fyndek. WC.
375 evere be] euere *All* B-MSS; best conj K-D *p.* 196 (*C*).
376 Ac] α, C (*so* K-D); And β.
    to be] β, C; not so F; *om* R.
    þanne β, C; *om* αY.
    it] L&*r* (?=β); *om* WO, C; þanne it R (?=α; may not F).

380 on] R (?=α), C; in βF.
383 other] CrM, C (*so* K-D); or o. W&*r*.
    Iu-] wC² (G), C; els CrM; *om r*.
384 and] α, C; if β.
390 may] L (?=β) α, C; *om* W&*r*.
392 clene] *not in* B-MSS (*C*).

395　For blood may suffre blood bothe hungry and acale,
　　　Ac blood may noght se blood blede, but hym rewe.'
　　　Audivi archana verba que non licet homini loqui.
　　　'Ac my rightwisnesse and right shal rulen al helle,　　　*'strict justice'*
　　　And mercy al mankynde bifore me in hevene.　　　　　sc. *shall rule (C)*
　　　For I were an unkynde kyng but I my kyn helpe—　　　*unless*
400　And nameliche at swich a nede ther nedes help bihoveth:
　　　Non intres in iudicium cum servo tuo.
　　　　'Thus by lawe,' quod Oure Lord, 'lede I wole fro hennes
　　　Tho [leodes] that I lov[e] and leved in my comynge.　*people; believed*
　　　And for thi lesynge, Lucifer, that thow leighe til Eve,　*lie; told to*
　　　Thow shalt abyen it bittre!'—and bond hym with cheynes.　*pay dearly for*
405　　Astroth and al the route hidden hem in hernes;　　*crew; corners*
　　　They dorste noght loke on Oure Lord, the [lothli]este of hem alle,
　　　　　　　　　　　　　　　　　　　　　　　　　　most fearsome
　　　But leten hym lede forth what hym liked and lete what hym liste.
　　　　　　　　　　　　　　　　　　　　　　　　　leave; wished

　　　Manye hundred of aungeles harpeden and songen,
　　　'*Culpat caro, purgat caro, regnat Deus Dei caro.*'

410　　　Thanne pipede Pees of poesie a note:
　　　'*Clarior est solito post maxima nebula phebus;*
　　　Post inimicicias clarior est et amor.
　　　' After sharpest shoures,' quod Pees, ' moost shene is the sonne;
　　　Is no weder warmer than after watry cloudes;
　　　Ne no love levere, ne lever frendes　　　　　*more precious; dearer*
　　　Than after werre and wo, whan love and pees ben maistres.
415　Was nevere werre in this world, ne wikkednesse so kene,　　*fierce*
　　　That Love, and hym liste, to laughynge ne broughte,
　　　And Pees, thorugh pacience, alle perils stoppede.'

395-6a For one may put up with one's kinsmen going both hungry and cold,
　　But not with seeing one's kin bleed, without feeling pity. I heard secret words
　　which it is not granted to man to utter (II Cor 12: 4) (C).
400-400a And especially in dire straits, when there is a great need for help: '. . .
　　enter not into judgment with thy servant' (Ps 142: 2).
409 Flesh sins, flesh frees from sin, / As God now reigns, God flesh within (*Aeterne
　　rex altissime*, st. 4, Matins Ascension Hymn, Roman Breviary).
410a After much cloud the sun we brighter see / Love brighter, also, after enmity
　　(Alanus de Insulis, *Liber Parabolorum*, P.L. 210, 581-2) (C).

396 se] β, C; se his α.
399 kyn] α, C; kynde β.
402 ledis] ?C (*so* K-D *p.* 94); *om All*
　　B-, *most* C-MSS (C).
　　I louye] C (*so* K-D); I louede α;
　　me louede β (C).
403 til] WL&c, C; to RF&c.
406 lothlieste] boldeste *All* B-MSS;
　　leste Cx (C).

407 what (1, 2)] LR; whom W;
　　which C.
410a clarior . . . am.] R&r (=αg), C
　　(*so* Sk); *om* Cr; &(c) WHmLM.
411 -est] α, C; -e β.
413 R *defective as far as* XX 26.
416 þat] FCBMCr¹, C (*so* K-D);
　　That ne W&r.
417 -ed] L&r, C; -eþ WF(M).

'Trewes!' quod Truthe; 'thow tellest us sooth, by Jesus!   *Truce!*
Clippe we in covenaunt, and ech of us kisse oother.'
                             Let us embrace; concord
420   'And lete no peple,' quod Pees, 'parceyve that we chidde;
                                  notice; quarrelled
For inpossible is no thyng to Hym that is almyghty.'
    'Thow seist sooth,' seide Rightwisnesse, and reverentliche hire kiste,
Pees, and Pees h[i]re, *per secula seculorum*.   *for ever and ever*
Misericordia et Veritas obviaverunt sibi; Iusticia et Pax osculate sunt.
    Truthe trumpede tho and song *Te Deum laudamus;*
                             'We praise you, God' (C)
425 And thanne lutede Love in a loud note,   *(sang to the) lute*
'Ecce quam bonum et quam iocundum &c.'
Til the day dawed thise damyseles carolden,   *dawned; danced* (C)
That men rongen to the resurexion—and right with that I wakede,
And called Kytte my wif and Calote my doghter:
430 'Ariseth and reverenceth Goddes resurexion,   *do honour to*
And crepeth to the cros on knees, and kisseth it for a juwel!   *creep*
For Goddes blissede body it bar for oure boote,   *bore; salvation*
And it afereth the fend—for swich is the myghte,   *frightens; power*
May no grisly goost glide there it shadweth!'   *where its shadow falls*

423a Mercy and truth have met each other: justice and peace have kissed (Ps 84: 11).
424 We praise you God (*the* Te Deum *hymn*).
426 Behold how good and how pleasant it is [for brethren to dwell together in unity] (Ps 132: 1).
428 Until the bells of Easter Morning were rung . . .

419 cusse] L&r, C; clippe W.
420 lete] L&r, C; leteþ W.
422 seyde] LM, C: quod W&r.
423 hire] *so* K-D *after* C (heore C-MS P&c); here W&r; there G.
425 loue] L&r, C; *soph.* F; *om* WHm.
427 carolden] F (?=α), C (*so* K-D *pp.* 155, 165); dauncede W&r (=β), *some* C-MSS (C).

430 Ariseth] L&r, C; And bad hem rise W.
    reu.] L&r; goo r. F, C; reuerence WCrGC.
431 -peth] L&r; -pe WCrG, C.
    -seth] L&r; -se WCrGF, C.
434 shadweth] L&r, C; walkeþ W.

Passus XIX

Thus I awaked and wroot what I hadde ydremed,
And dighte me derely, and dide me to chirche,   *dressed tidily; went*
To here holly the masse and to be housled after.
In myddes of the masse, tho men yede to offryng,   *when; went*
5 I fel eftsoones aslepe—and sodeynly me mette   *again; I dreamed*
That Piers the Plowman was peynted al blody,   *painted*
And com in with a cros bifore the comune peple,
And right lik in alle lymes to Oure Lord Jesu.   *limbs, features*
   And thanne called I Conscience to kenne me the sothe: *teach*
10 'Is this Jesus the justere,' quod I, 'that Jewes dide to dethe? *jouster*
Or it is Piers the Plowman! Who peynted hym so rede?'
   Quod Conscience, and kneled tho, ' Thise arn Piers armes—
Hise colours and his cote armure; ac he that cometh so blody *coat-of-arms*
Is Crist with his cros, conquerour of Cristene.'   *Christians' conqueror*
15 'Why calle ye hym Crist?' quod I, 'sithen Jewes called hym Jesus?
Patriarkes and prophetes prophecied bifore
That alle kynne creatures sholden knelen and bowen
Anoon as men nempned the name of God Jesu.   *At once; uttered*
Ergo is no name to the name of Jesus,   *Therefore; (compared) to*
20 Ne noon so nedeful to nempne by nyghte ne by daye.   *necessary*
For alle derke develes arn adrad to heren it,   *terrified*
And synfulle aren solaced and saved by that name;
And ye callen hym Crist; for what cause, telleth me?
Is Crist moore of myght and moore worthi name   *of greater power*
25 Than Jesu or Jesus, that al oure joye com of?'
   'Thow knowest wel,' quod Conscience, 'and thow konne reson,   *if*
That knyght, kyng, conquerour may be o persone.   *one single*
To be called a knyght is fair, for men shul knele to hym;
To be called a kyng is fairer, for he may knyghtes make;
30 Ac to be conquerour called, that cometh of special grace,
And of hardynesse of herte and of hendenesse—   *courage; courtesy*
To make lordes of laddes, of lond that he wynneth, *commoners; with land*
And fre men foule thralles, that folwen noght hise lawes. *vile slaves*

---

3 To be present throughout Mass and receive Holy Communion at the end of it
(*C*).

*Rubric Passus xixus; explicit dobet et
   incipit dobest.*
8 lymes] L&*r*, C; þynges W.
  -su] L&*r exc* F, C; -sus WCr.
12 P.] W&*r*; cristis F, C (*C*).

15 ȝe] L&*r*, C; *om* W.
  q. I] *om* C; *cf.* K-D *p.* 152.
  called] **g** (*exc* C²) Hm, C (*so*
  K-D); calle WC² &*r*; named F.
24 wor.] worthiere F, ?C.

'The Jewes, that were gentil men, Jesu thei despised—
35 Bothe his loore and his lawe; now are thei lowe cherles.　　*base serfs*
As wide as the world is, wonyeth ther noon　　*dwells*
But under tribut and taillage as tikes and cherles;　　*taxation; villeins*
And tho that bicome Cristene bi counseil of the Baptiste
Aren frankeleyns, free men thorugh fullynge that thei toke

　　　　　　　　　　　　　　　　　franklins; baptism
40 And gentil men with Jesu—for Jesus was yfulled　　*baptized*
And upon Calvarie on cros ycrouned kyng of Jewes.
　'It bicometh to a kyng to kepe and to defende,　　*befits; protect*
And conqueror of his conquest hise lawes and his large.
And so dide Jesus the Jewes—he justified and taughte hem
45 The lawe of lif that laste shal evere,　　*'eternal life'*
And fended from foule yveles, feveres and fluxes,　　*defended*
And from fendes that in hem was, and false bileve.
Tho was he Jesus of Jewes called, gentile prophete.　　*Then; by; noble*
And kyng of hir kyngdom, and croune bar of thornes.　　*bore*
50 　'And tho conquered he on cros as conquerour noble;
Mighte no deeth hym fordo, ne adoun brynge,　　*destroy; defeat*
That he n'aroos and regnede and ravysshed helle.　　*But that he; plundered*
And tho was he conquerour called of quyke and of dede,
For he yaf Adam and Eve and othere mo blisse　　*gave*
55 That longe hadde yleyen bifore as Luciferis cherles.　　*lain (in hell); serfs*
And took [Lucifer the lothly], that lord was of helle,　　*terrible, fearsome*
And bond [hym] as [he is bounde], with bondes of yrene.　　*bound; chains*
Who was hardiere than he? His herte blood he shadde　　*bolder; shed*
To maken alle folk free that folwen his lawe.
60 And sith he yeveth largely al his lele liges　　*gives to; loyal subjects*
Places in Paradis at hir partynge hennes,
He may wel be called conquerour—and that is 'Crist' to mene.

　　　　　　　　　　　　　　　　　what 'Christ' means (C)
　'Ac the cause that he cometh thus with cros of his passion
Is to wissen us therwith, that whan we ben tempted,　　*instruct*

43 And (it befits) a conqueror to maintain and guard his laws and his munificence
by virtue of his act of conquest.

34 -su] -sus WHmC².
36 wonyeth . . . n.] L&r (n.]
n. therInne MCr), C; n. of hem
þer w. W.
38 bap.] L (?=Bx), C; baptisme
W&r (om Hm) (C).
39 free] W&r; & f. FO, C.
40 -sus] L&r, C; -su WHmC²F.
43 his (1)] F (?=α), C (so K-D); om
W&r (?=β).
46 fended] L&r, C; def. WCr.
47 was] L (?=β) F (?=α), C (so
K-D); were W&r (so Sk).

56–9 F (=α), C; om W&r (=β)
(so K-D p. 165n) (C).
56 And . . . lo.] C (so K-D); A.
þanne t. he lotthly l. F.
57 hym . . . bounde] C (so K-D); his
as his bondeman F.
58 he (1)] C (so K-D); he þat F.
59 lawe] C (so K-D); pl. F.
60 ʒeveþ] F (?=α), C; yaf W&r
(=β); cf. K-D p. 118 (C).
64 we] YFBoCot, C (so K-D); þat
we W&r.

65 Therwith to fighte and fenden us fro fallynge into synne,   *defend ourselves*
   And se bi his sorwe that whoso loveth joye,
   To penaunce and to poverte he moste puten hymselven,
   And muche wo in this world wilnen and suffren.   *desire, will*
   'Ac to carpe moore of Crist, and how he com to that name,   *speak*
70 Faithly for to speke, his firste name was Jesus.   *Truly*
   Tho he was born in Bethleem, as the Book telleth,   *When*
   And cam to take mankynde, kynges and aungeles   *human nature*
   Reverenced hym right faire with richesses of erthe.
   Aungeles out of hevene come knelynge and songe,
   Gloria in excelsis Deo &c.
75 'Kynges come after, knelede and offrede sense,   *incense*
   Mirre and muche gold withouten mercy askynge   *myrrh; thanks, reward* (C)
   Or any kynnes catel, but knoweliched[en] hym sovereyn
   Both of sond, sonne and see, and sithenes thei wente   *sand; afterwards*
   Into hir kyngene kith by counseil of aungeles.   *their respective kingdoms*
80 And there was that word fulfilled the which thow of speke—   *spoke of*
   Omnia celestia, terrestria, flectantur in hoc nomine Iesu.
   'For alle the aungeles of hevene at his burthe knelede,
   And al the wit of the world was in tho thre kynges.   *wisdom; those*
   Reson and Rightwisnesse and Ruthe thei offrede,
   Wherfore and why wise men that tyme   *For which reason*
85 Maistres and lettred men, *Magi* hem callede.
   'That o kyng cam with Reson, covered under sense.   *hidden (in the form of)*
   The seconde kyng siththe soothliche offrede
   Rightwisnesse under reed gold, Resones felawe.   *companion*
   Gold is likned to Leautee that laste shal evere,   *fidelity, justice*
90 And Reson to riche[ls]—to right and to truthe.   *incense* (C)
   'The thridde kyng tho kam, and knelede to Jesu,
   And presented hym with Pitee, apperynge by mirre;   *under the appearance of*
   For mirre is mercy to mene, and mylde speche of tonge.
   Ertheliche honeste thynges was offred thus at ones   *Objects of earthly value*

74*a* Glory to God in the highest (Lk 2: 14).
80*a* That in the name of Jesus every [knee] should bow, of those that are in heaven,
   on earth, [and under the earth] (Phil 2: 10).

65 fend.] L&r, C; defend. WHmFCot.
   into] L&r, C; to W.
68 wylnen] F (?=a), C; willen L&r
   (=β; to w. W).
73 ryght] F (?=a), C (*so* K-D); *om* β.
75 Kynges] L&r, C; K. þat W.
   sense] Cot (?*by corr.*) (*so* K-D
   p. 160); *om* W&r (=β); *cf.* F
   below (C).
76 Mirre] W&r, C; Ensens & m. F.
   mercy] W&r, C; mercede Cot
   (*by corr.*); mede CrM (*by corr.* M)
   (C).

77 -lechid] F (?=a) G, C (*so* K-D);
   -liche MCr¹; -lichynge W&r (C).
78 sonde] L&r (soule B), C; lond
   WHmCr¹ (=w).
90 And . . . rich.] And . . . riche golde
   L&r (l. *om* W), C; For it shal turne
   tresoun F (*so* K-D p. 161) (C).
91 & kn.] F (?=a), C; knelynge β
   (C).
94 Erthely] F (?=a), C (*so* K-D
   p. K-D p. 165n); Thre yliche β.
   was] LF, C (*so* K-D; *cf.* 47);
   were W&r (*so* Sk).

95 Thorugh thre kynne kynges knelynge to Jesu.   *kings of three races* (Sk)
   'Ac for alle thise preciouse presents Oure Lord Prynce Jesus
   Was neither kyng ne conquerour til he [comsede] wexe   *began to grow*
   In the manere of a man, and that by muchel sleighte—   *great skill*
   As it bicometh a conquerour to konne manye sleightes,   *know*
100 And manye wiles and wit, that wole ben a ledere;   *stratagems*
   And so dide Jesu in hise dayes, whoso hadde tyme to telle it.
   'Som tyme he suffrede, and som tyme he hidde hym,
   And som tyme he faught faste, and fleigh outherwhile,   *readily; fled*
   And som tyme he gaf good and grauntede heele bothe,   *money; health*
105 Lif and lyme—as hym liste he wroghte.   *he pleased; did*
   As kynde is of a conquerour, so comsede Jesu   *is the nature of*
   Til he hadde alle hem that he for bledde.   *bled for*
   'In his juventee this Jesus at Jewene feeste   *youth; 'a Jewish feast'*
   Water into wyn turnede, as Holy Writ telleth,   (Jn 2: 1–11)
110 And there bigan God of his grace to do wel.
   For wyn is likned to lawe and lifholynesse;   *holiness of life*
   And lawe lakkede tho, for men lovede noght hir enemys;   *was defective then*
   And Crist counseileth thus—and comaundeth bothe—   *as well*
   Bothe to lered and to lewede, to lovyen oure enemys.
115 So at that feeste first, as I bifore tolde,
   Bigan God of his grace and goodnesse to dowel;
   And tho was he cleped and called noght oonly Crist but Jesu—
   A fauntekyn ful of wit, *filius Marie.*   *child; son of Mary*
   For bifore his moder Marie made he that wonder,   *performed; miracle*
120 That she first and formest sholde ferme bileve   *foremost; firmly*
   That he thorugh Grace was gete, and of no gome ellis.   *conceived; person*
   He wroghte that by no wit but thorugh word one,   *cunning device; only*
   After the kynde that he cam of; there comsede he Dowel.
   'And whan he was woxen moore, in his moder absence,   *grown; mother's*
125 He made lame to lepe and yaf light to blynde,   *run; sight*
   And fedde with two fisshes and with fyve loves   *loaves*
   Sore afyngred folk, mo than fyve thousand.   *Very hungry*
   Thus he confortede carefulle and caughte a gretter name,   *the distressed; got*
   The which was Dobet, where that he wente.

100 And as (it befits) him who wishes to be a leader to know . . .
121 That he had been conceived by the (power of God's) Holy Spirit (*Grace*) and
   not by any human agency.
123 In accord with the nature of God his Father [who *created* by his word].

96 prynce] L&r, C; kyng W.
97 com.] C (*so* K-D *p. 91; cf.* 106);
   gan to *All* B-MSS.
101 h. t. to] durste C (*so* K-D *p.* 94).
111 lif] W, C; l. of L&r (*C*).
114 Bothe] L&r (*l. om* C²), ?C; *om*
   WHmF, *some* C-MSS.
115 at þat] WHm, C; atte L&r.

117 þo] L&r, C; þanne WHm.
   cl. &] L&r, C; *om* W.
   only] CrF(M), C (*so* K-D
   p. 157); holy W&r.
118 -ekyn] F (?=α), C (*so* K-D
   p. 165); fyn β (*C*).
120 s. ferme] C, ?α (s. f. þe F); f. s. β.
124 was w.] L&r, C; wo. w. WHm.

238

130 For deve thorugh hise doynges and dombe speke and herde,   *the deaf; actions*
    And alle he heeled and halp that hym of grace askede.   *helped; for mercy*
    And tho was he called in contre of the comune peple,   *by*
    For the dedes that he dide, *Fili David, Ihesus.   Son of David (cf.* Jn 12: 13)
    For David was doghtiest of dedes in his tyme,   *Because; bravest*
135 The burdes tho songe, *Saul interfecit mille et David decem milia.   damsels*
    Forthi the contree ther Jesu cam called hym *fili David,   Therefore*
    And nempned hym of Nazareth—and no man so worthi
    To be kaiser or kyng of the kyngdom of Juda,   *emperor*
    Ne over Jewes justice, as Jesus was, hem thoughte. *judge; it seemed to them*
140   'Wherof hadde Cayphas envye, and othere of the Jewes,
    And for to doon hym to dethe day and nyght thei casten;   *schemed*
    And killeden hym on cros wise at Calvarie on Friday,   *by crucifixion*
    And sithen buriede his body, and beden that men sholde   *ordered*
    Kepen it fro nyghtcomeris with knyghtes yarmed,
145 For no frend sholde it fecche; for prophetes hem tolde   *So that*
    That that blissede body of burieles sholde risen,   *from its tomb*
    And goon into Galilee and gladen hise Apostles   *cheer*
    And his moder Marie—thus men bifore demede.

                                   believed (MED *s.v.* 11, b–c)
    'The knyghtes that kepten it biknewe hemselven   *guarded; admitted*
150 That aungeles and archaungeles er the day sprynge   *dawned*
    Come knelynge to that corps and songen   *dead body*
    Christus resurgens—and it aroos after,   ' *Christ rising* ' (Rom 6: 9)
    Verray man bifore hem alle, and forth with hem he yede.   *True; went*
    'The Jewes preide hem of pees, and [preide] the knyghtes
155 Telle the comune that ther cam a compaignie of hise Apostles   *people*
    And biwicched hem as thei woke, and awey stolen it.

135 Saul slew his thousands, and David his ten thousands (I Sam 18: 17).
144 Guard it with armed men against any who might come by night.
154 The Jews begged them to say nothing about it, and beseeched the knights . . .
156 And cast a spell on them as they were keeping watch . . .

130 &(1)] F (?=a), C (*so* K-D
    pp. 158, 165); to here and β.
    & h.] F (?=a), C; he made β
    (*om* B).
140 Whereof . . . e.] perfore h. kay.
    F (?=a), C (p.] Herof C); Wh.
    Cay. h. β.
    of pe] konynge F (?*soph.*); *om* C.
142 &] F (?=a) B, C; *om* W&r
    (?=β).
145 freend s. it] F (?=a), C (*so* K-D);
    frendes s. hym β.
146 sh. r.] L&r, C; r. sh. WHm.
148 dem.] deuyned C (*so* K-D *p.* 90)
    (C).

149 bekn.] F (?=a), C (*so* K-D); b.
    it β.
150 pat] F (?=a), C; pe β.
151-2 *So divided* F (?=a)Cot, C (*so*
    K-D); *as one line* β (C).
152 res.] r. a mortuis FCot (m.]
    m.&c Cot); rex res. ?C (*res.* X).
    and . . . a.] C, ?a (and hit) &
    anoon he F) (*so* K-D); *om* β.
153 man] L&r, C; men W.
    he y.] y. C; wente F.
154 of] F (?=a), C; be W; *om rest.*
    and p. pe] C (*so* K-D *pp.* 95,
    152); bisouʒte pe β; al po propre F.

'Ac Marie Maudeleyne mette hym by the weye
Goynge toward Galilee in godhede and manhede,
And lyves and lokynge—and she aloud cride   *alive; looking (about)*
160 In ech a compaignie ther she cam, "*Christus resurgens!*"
Thus cam it out that Crist overcoom, recoverede and lyvede:
Sic oportet Christum pati et intrare &c.
For that wommen witeth may noght wel be counseille! *know; remain secret*
  'Peter parceyved al this and pursued after,
Bothe James and Johan, Jesu for to seke,
165 Thaddee and ten mo, with Thomas of Inde.   *Thaddeus; India (C)*
And as alle thise wise wyes weren togideres   *men*
In an hous al bishet and hir dore ybarred,   *locked up*
Crist cam in—and al closed bothe dore and yates—   *gates*
To Peter and to hise Apostles, and seide, "*Pax vobis;*" *Peace unto you*
170 And took Thomas by the hand and taughte hym to grope, *touch*
And feele with hise fyngres his flesshliche herte.
  'Thomas touched it, and with his tonge seide,
"*Dominus meus et Deus meus.*
Thow art my lord, I bileve, God Lord Jesu!
175 Thow deidest and deeth tholedest and deme shalt us alle, *suffered; judge*
And now art lyvynge and lokynge, and laste shalt evere!"
  'Crist carpede thanne, and curteisliche seide,   *spoke*
"Thomas, for thow trowest this and treweliche bilevest it, *because; think*
Blessed mote thow be, and be shalt for evere.
180 And blessed mote thei be, in body and in soule,
That nevere shul se me in sighte as thow seest nowthe, *at this time*
And lelliche bileve al this—I love hem and blesse hem: *faithfully*
Beati qui non viderunt et crediderunt."
  'And whan this dede was doon, Dobest he [thou]ghte,
And yaf Piers power, and pardon he grauntede:
185 To alle maner men, mercy and foryifnesse;
[To] hym, myghte men to assoille of alle manere synnes,

16!*a* Ought not Christ to have suffered these things and so to enter into his glory?
(Lk 24: 26).
173 My Lord and my God (Jn 20: 28).
182*a* Blessed are they that have not seen and have believed (Jn 20: 29).

161*a*-2 β, C; *om* F.
162 þat] LCrG, C (*so* K-D); þat þat
  W&r (*so* Sk).
169 his] L&r, C; þise WHm; þe B.
173 *Dom. m. & d.*] F (?=a) CrCot,
  C (*so* Vulg; *so* K-D); *Deus m. et*
  dom. W&r (?=β).
    meus (2)] β, C; *m. & doun he fel*
  to grownde F.
174 god] L&r, C; my g. W; my lord
  B.

180 be] F (?=a) GC², C (*so* K-D
  p. 158); alle be W&r (?=β).
181 seest] O, C (*so* K-D); hast Cr¹;
  doost W&r (?=Bx).
182*a* & cr.] F (?=a), C (*so* K-D); &
  cr. &c rest. (*so* Sk); &c WCrLM.
183 thouhte] C (*so* K-D p. 152);
  tauᵹte β; took sone F.
186 To hym] Hym BxCx (C).
  synnes] L&r, C; *sg.* WHm.

Passus XIX

In covenaunt that thei come and kneweliche to paye
To Piers pardon the Plowman—*Redde quod debes.*
  'Thus hath Piers power, be his pardon paied,
190 To bynde and unbynde bothe here and ellis,
And assoille men of alle synnes save of dette one.
  'Anoon after an heigh up into hevene
He wente, and wonyeth there, and wol come at the laste,   *dwells*
And rewarde hym right wel that *reddit quod debet—* *'makes satisfaction'*
195 Paieth parfitly, as pure truthe wolde.   *complete integrity*
And what persone paieth it nought, punysshen he thenketh,
And demen hem at domesday, bothe quyke and dede— *judge; living*
The goode to the Godhede and to greet joye,
And wikkede to wonye in wo withouteñ ende.'

200   Thus Conscience of Crist and of the cros carpede,   *spoke*
And counseiled me to knele therto; and thanne cam, me thoughte,
Oon *Spiritus Paraclitus* to Piers and to hise felawes.
In liknesse of a lightnynge he lighte on hem alle   *alighted*
And made hem konne and knowe alle kynne langages. *kinds of languages*
205 I wondred what that was, and waggede Conscience,   *nudged*
And was afered of the light, for in fires liknesse
Spiritus Paraclitus overspradde hem alle.   *covered*
  Quod Conscience, and knelede, 'This is Cristes messager,
And cometh fro the grete God—Grace is his name.
210 Knele now,' quod Conscience, 'and if thow kanst synge,
Welcome hym and worshipe hym with *Veni Creator Spiritus!*'
  Thanne song I that song, and so dide manye hundred,
And cride with Conscience, 'Help us, God of grace!'
  And thanne bigan Grace to go with Piers Plowman,
215 And counseillede hym and Conscience the comune to sompne: *summon*
'For I wole dele today and dyvyde grace   *share; apportion*
To alle kynne creatures that kan hise fyve wittes— *have use of their*
Tresour to lyve by to hir lyves ende,

187–8 On condition that they should come and acknowledge satisfactorily [i.e.
    meet the terms of] Piers the Plowman's pardon—'Pay what thou owest' (Mt
    18: 28).
191 *i.e.* the binding obligation to make satisfaction—*not* the sin of debt.
202 The Comforter, the Holy Ghost (Jn 14: 26, *A.V.*).
211 Come Holy Ghost, Creator come (Pentecost Vespers Hymn, C9th *Anon*).

187 -che] L&r; -ched WHm, ?C.
189 be] L&r, C; by WC²BoCot; for F.
190 elles] L (?=β) F (?=α), C; e.
    where W&r.
204–7 **om** F.
206 lyk-] L&r, C; light W.
209 god] F (?=α), C (*so* K-D *p.* 165);
    g. and β.
211 *V.C.Sp.*] *om* F.

212–13 **om** F.
212 and] L&r, C; *om* W.
213 god] crist *conj* K-D *p.* 118 (*C*).
216 dyuyde] L&r, C; ȝyue diuine
    WHm.
217 kan] LF (?=β / α), C; han
    W&r.
    hise] F (?=α), C (*so* K-D); hir β.

241

And wepne to fighte with that wole nevere faille.
220 For Antecrist and hise al the world shul greve,　　　　*Anti-Christ* (C)
　　And acombre thee, Conscience, but if Crist thee helpe.　　*overwhelm*
　　'And false prophetes fele, flatereris and gloseris,　　*many; deceivers*
　　Shullen come and be curatours over kynges and erles.　　*spiritual rulers*
　　And thanne shal Pride be Pope and prynce of Holy Chirche,
225 Coveitise and Unkyndenesse Cardinals hym to lede.　　*guide*
　　Forthi,' quod Grace, 'er I go, I wol gyve yow tresor,
　　And wepne to fighte with whan Antecrist yow assailleth.'
　　And gaf ech man a grace to gye with hymselven,　　*guide, direct*
　　That Ydelnesse encombre hym noght, ne Envye ne Pride:
　　Divisiones graciarum sunt.
230 　Some [wyes] he yaf wit, with wordes to shewe—　　*men; declare*
　　Wit to wynne hir liflode with, as the world asketh,　　*earn their living*
　　As prechours and preestes, and prentices of lawe—　　*students*
　　They lelly to lyve by labour of tonge,　　*honestly*
　　And by wit to wissen othere as grace hem wolde teche.　　*instruct others*
235 　And some he kennede craft and konnynge of sighte,
　　With sellynge and [by] buggynge hir bilyve to wynne.　　*buying; living*
　　And some he lered to laboure on lond and on watre,　　*taught*
　　And lyve by that labour—a lele lif and a trewe.　　*honest*
　　And some he taughte to tilie, to dyche and to thecche,　　*plough; thatch*
240 To wynne with hir liflode bi loore of his techynge.
　　And some to devyne and divide, [diverse] noumbres to kenne;　*make out*
　　And some to compace craftili, and colours to make;　　*design skilfully*
　　And some to se and to seye what sholde bifalle,
　　Bothe of wele and of wo, telle it [wel] er it felle—　　*before it occurred*
245 As astronomyens thorugh astronomye, and philosofres wise.
　　And some to ryde and to recovere that unrightfully was wonne:
　　　　　　　　　　　　　　　　　　　　　　that (which)
　　He wissed hem wynne it ayein thorugh wightnesse of handes,　*back; strength*

229*a* [Now], there are diversities of graces, [but the same Spirit] (1 Cor 12: 4).

219 *as one line with* 227, 219b–227a *om* g.
224 & þan s. P.] F (?=*a*), C; And P. s. *β*.
　and] F (?=*a*) Cr²³, C; *om β*.
228 gye] LM, F (?=*a*) w (gide WCr), C; go g.
229 ne(1)] F (?=*a*), C; *om β*.
229*a* sunt] F (?=*a*) Cr, C; *s. &c β*.
230 wyes] *conj* K-D *p.* 118; men ?C; *om All* B-MSS (C).
232 of] *β*, C; of þe F (?=*a*) G.
236 by] *not in* B/C-MSS (C).
237 *run together with* 238 *β*.
　on (1) . . . w.] F (?=*a*), C (*so* K-D); *om β*.

238 & . . . lab.] F (?=*a*), C (*so* K-D); *om β*.
239 dyche] coke *rec.* K-D *pp.* 174–5 (C).
241 div. n.] noumbres W&r (membres CB), C; figures *conj* K-D *pp.* 118, 207 (C).
　kenne] *β*, C; knowe F.
244 t. it w . . . f.] t. it er it f. *All* B-MSS (t.] to t. F); and be ywaer bifore C (*so* K-D *p.* 95) (C).
246 vnriȝt-] L&r (vn- *om* Hm), C; wrong- W.
247 wynne] L&r (*l. om* F), C; to w. WOB.

    Spiritus Iusticie spareth noght to spille hem that ben gilty,   *put to death*
305 And for to correcte the kyng if he falle in [any kynnes] gilt.

                                        kind of crime, fault
    For counteth he no kynges wrathe whan he in court sitteth *takes account of*
    To demen as a domesman—adrad was he nevere   *judge (v & n)*
    Neither of duc ne of deeth, that he ne dide the lawe; *duke ('powerful noble')*
    For present or for preiere or any prynces lettres,
310 He dide equyte to alle eveneforth his power.   *according to*
    Thise foure sedes Piers sew, and siththe he dide hem harewe
    With Olde Lawe and Newe Lawe, that love myghte wexe   *grow up*
    Among thise foure vertues, and vices destruye.
    'For comunliche in contrees cammokes and wedes   *rest-harrows*
315 Foulen the fruyt in the feld ther thei growen togideres;   *Choke; where*
    And so doon vices vertues—[f]orthi,' quod Piers,   *therefore*
    'Hareweth alle that konneth kynde wit by conseil of thise doctours,
    And tilieth after hir techynge the cardynale vertues.'   *according to*
    'Ayeins thi greynes,' quod Grace, 'bigynneth for to ripe,

                             Before; seeds; ripen
320 Ordeigne thee an hous, Piers, to herberwe inne thi cornes.' *Prepare; store*
    'By God! Grace,' quod Piers, 'ye moten gyve tymber,   *must*
    And ordeigne that hous er ye hennes wende.'
    And Grace gaf hym the cros, with the croune of thornes,
    That Crist upon Calvarie for mankynde on pyned;   *suffered on*
325 And of his baptisme and blood that he bledde on roode
    He made a manere morter, and mercy it highte.   *a kind of mortar*
    And therwith Grace bigan to make a good foundement,   *foundation*
    And watlede it and walled it with hise peynes and his passion, *wattled*
    And of al Holy Writ he made a roof after,
330 And called that hous Unite—Holy Chirche on Englissh.   *Unity*
    And whan this dede was doon, Grace devysede   *designed*
    A cart highte Cristendom, to carie home Piers sheves, *(=Baptism); sheaves*
    And gaf hym caples to his carte, Contricion and Confession;   *horses*
    And made Preesthod hayward, the while hymself wente   *overseer (C)*

309 In spite of bribes, entreaties, or royal interventions.

304, 305 *As three lines divided after*
   spille, corr. BxCx; *cf.* K-D *pp.* 119,
   95 (*C*).
305 the . . . g.] The k. if he f. in g. or
   in trespas β; þey men falle ageyn
   þe k. F; The k. and the k. f. in eny
   thynge gulty Cx (*C*).
308 þe] LF (?=α/β), C; *om* W&r.
310 po.] knowyng C (*so* K-D *p.* 92).
313 þese] F (?=α), C; þe L&r; þo
   WHm.
316 *So divided from* 317 C (*so* K-D
   p. 95); *div. after* wor. β, *after* ver.
   F (?=α).

   v. forthy] C (*so* K-D); v. worþi β;
   w. fayre ver. F.
318 after] to *conj* K-D *p.* 118 (*C*).
320 Ord.] β, C; Peers ord. F.
   P.] WHmCr³, C; quod P.
   LMCr¹²; *om* gF.
323 croune] garland *conj* K-D *p.*118 (*C*).
328 L&r, *with varr.* (=β; h. peynes
   sg. W), C; & he peyntyde þe wallis
   wiþ þe woundis of h. pass. F.
332 hoem P.] C (*so* K-D *pp.* 163,
   165); hoom F (?=α); P. β (*C*).
333 hym] β, C; peers F.
   c. and c.] *om* F.

335 As wide as the world is, with Piers to tilie truthe
And the lo[nd] of bileve, the lawe of Holy Chirche.

   Now is Piers to the plow. Pride it aspide
And gadered hym a greet oost: greven he thynketh   *intends to harass*
Conscience and alle Cristene and Cardinale Vertues—
340 Blowe hem doun and breke hem and bite atwo the mores;   *in two; roots*
And sente forth Surquidous, his sergeaunt of armes,   *Presumption*
And his spye Spille-Love, oon Spek-yvel-bihynde.
   Thise two coome to Conscience and to Cristen peple,
And tolde hem tidynges—that tyne thei sholde   *were going to lose*
345 The sedes that [Sire] Piers sew, the Cardynale Vertues:
'And Piers bern worth ybroke, and thei that ben in Unitee   *barn; will be*
Shulle come out, and Conscience; and youre [caples two],
Confession and Contricion, and youre carte the Bileeve   *Creed*
Shal be coloured so queyntely and covered under oure sophistrie,
   ingeniously
350 That Conscience shal noght knowe by Contricion
Ne by Confession who is Cristene or hethene;
Ne no manere marchaunt that with moneye deleth
Wheither he wynne with right, with wrong or with usure.'   *gain; usury*
   With swiche colours and queyntise cometh Pride y-armed,
   banners/deceptions
355 With the lord that lyveth after the lust of his body—   *pleasure*
'To wasten on welfare and on wikked kepynge   *luxury; living*
Al the world in a while thorugh oure wit!' quod Pryde.
   Quod Conscience to alle Cristene tho, 'My counseil is to wende
Hastiliche into Unitee and holde we us there,
360 And praye we that a pees weere in Piers berne the Plowman.   *P. the P.'s barn*
For witterly, I woot wel, we beth noght of strengthe   *assuredly*
To goon agayn Pride, but Grace weere with us.'
   And thanne kam Kynde Wit Conscience to teche,
And cryde, and comaundede alle Cristene peple

336 F (? =a), C (*so* K-D *p.* 165); *om* β.
   londe] C; loore F.
   the] C; & þe F.
337 pr.] C (*so* K-D *p.* 91); and p. *All*
   B-MSS.
   ost] F (? =a), C (*so* K-D); o. to
   LMCr?g (? =β; o. for to W).
339 *Line om* g.
   Con. and . . . cr.] β, C; & C. &
   cristendom F.
341 Surquidous] β (? =Bx);
   surquidoures F, C (*C*).
   his s.] β; *pl.* C; were sergawntys F
   (*C*).
344 *So div. from* 345 C (*so* K-D
   p. 95); *div. after* sedes *All* B-MSS.

345 sire] C (*so* K-D *p.* 95); *om All*
   B-MSS.
   sewe] C (*so* K-D); plouhman
   seew all F (? =a); þere hadde
   ysowen β (*C*).
346 bern] β, C; doore F.
347 c. two] two c. BxCx; *trsp.* K-D
   p. 118.
349 owre] L&r, C; your CotCr¹; *om*
   WF.
356 on (2)] L&r, ?C; in W, *many*
   C-MSS; *om* GC²F.
   w. kep.] L&r, C; w. lyuyng W;
   w.nesse he meyntiþ F.
362 *Here* O *resumes.*

365 For to delven and dyche depe aboute Unitee   *dig and make a ditch*
    That Holy Chirche stode in [holynesse], as it a pyl weere.   *might stand; fort*
      Conscience comaundede tho alle Cristene to delve,
    And make a muche moot that myghte ben a strengthe
                            great moat; fortification
    To helpe Holy Chirche and hem that it kepeth.
370   Thanne alle kynne Cristene—save comune wommen—   *except prostitutes*
    Repenteden and refusede synne, [right] save thei one,   *only excepting them*
    And [a sisour and a somonour] that were forsworen ofte;   *juror; perjured*
    Witynge and wilfully with the false [thei] helden,   *deliberately*
    And for silver were forswore—soothly thei wiste it!
375   Ther nas no Cristene creature that kynde wit hadde—
    Save sherewes one swiche as I spak of—   *evil-doers only*
    That he ne halp a quantite holynesse to wexe: *helped; measure; grow*
    Some by bedes biddynge and some by pilgrymage   *saying prayers*
    And other pryve penaunce, and somme thorugh penyes delynge.
                            private; almsgiving
380   And thanne wellede water for wikkede werkes,
    Egreliche ernynge out of mennes eighen.   *Bitterly running*
    Clennesse of the comune and clerkes clene lyvynge
    Made Unitee Holy Chirche in holynesse stonde.
    'I care noght,' quod Conscience, 'though Pride come nouthe;   *now*
385 The lord of lust shal be letted al this Lente, I hope.   *prevented*
    Cometh,' quod Conscience, 'ye Cristene, and dyneth,   *dine*
    That han laboured lelly al this Lenten tyme.
    Here is breed yblessed, and Goddes body therunder.
    Grace, thorugh Goddes word, gaf Piers power,
390 Myght to maken it, and men to ete it after
    In helpe of hir heele ones in a monthe,   *(spiritual) health*
    Or as ofte as thei hadde nede, tho that hadde ypaied
    To Piers pardon the Plowman, *redde quod debes.*'   *pay your debt*
      'How?' quod al the comune. 'Thow conseillest us to yelde   *give up*

388 Here are consecrated Hosts and Christ's body beneath (their appearance of bread).
393 ' Pay what thou owest ' (Mt 18: 28).

365 and] Y&r, ?C; a WGLM.
  di*chen*] OCHmBFCr, ?C; dych
  W&r.
366 in h.] C (*so* K-D *p.* 152); in
  vnitee W&r; strong F (*C*).
371 right] *not in* B/C-MSS (*C*).
372 *From* C (*so* K-D *pp.* 95, 193*n*);
  a spurious line And false men
  flatereris vsurers and þeues *All*
  B-MSS, *foll. by a spurious half-line*
  Lyeris and questemongeres *and*
  then 372b *as above.*
373 þei] C; *om* B-MSS; *cf. above.*

376 *om* C-MSS.
378 by (1, 2)] Cr, C; þoruʒ W&r (*C*).
  -age] L&r; -ages W, C.
379 other] L&r, C; oþere WO.
  pen.] L&r, C; *pl.* W; paines CrM.
380 wel.] W&r, C; walmed F.
382 of þe] L&r, C; out of WHm.
383 st.] YF, C (*so* K-D); to st. W&r,
  some C-MSS.
389 gaue] L&r, C; yaf WC²B.
390 Mighte] C, C (*so* K-D); And m.
  CrF; Myʒtes L&r; And myʒtes
  WHm.

395 Al that we owen any wight er we go to housel?' *Holy Communion*
 'That is my conseil,' quod Conscience, 'and Cardinale Vertues;
 (that of the) C.V.

That ech man foryyve oother, and that wole the Paternoster—
Et dimitte nobis debita nostra &c—
And so to ben assoilled, and siththen ben houseled.'
 absolved; take communion

 'Ye? Baw!' quod a brewere, 'I wol noght be ruled,
400 By Jesu! for al youre janglynge, with *Spiritus Iusticie*, *arguing*
Ne after Conscience, by Crist! while I kan selle *know how to*
Bothe dregges and draf, and drawe at oon hole *ale-leavings*
Thikke ale and thynne ale; that is my kynde, *nature, way*
And noght hakke after holynesse—hold thi tonge, Conscience! *grub about for*
405 Of *Spiritus Iusticie* thow spekest muche on ydel.' *to no purpose*
 'Caytif!' quod Conscience, 'cursede wrecche!
Unblessed artow, brewere, but if thee God helpe.
But thow lyve by loore of *Spiritus Iusticie*, *Unless; teaching*
The chief seed that Piers sew, ysaved worstow nevere. *will you be*
410 But Conscience be the comune fode, and Cardinale Vertues,
Leve it wel, thei ben lost, bothe lif and soule.'
 'Thanne is many [leode] lost!' quod a lewed vicory. *man; ignorant vicar*
'I am a curatour of Holy Kirke, and cam nevere in my tyme
Man to me that me kouthe telle of Cardinale Vertues,
415 Or that acountede Conscience at a cokkes fethere! *valued*
I knew nevere Cardynal that he ne cam fro the Pope; *who did not*
And we clerkes, whan thei come, for hir comunes paieth, *clergy; food*
For hir pelure and hir palfreyes mete and pilours that hem folweth.
 feed; robbers
The comune *clamat cotidie*, ech a man til oother, *'cries out daily'*
420 "The contree is the corseder that cardinals come inne, *worse off*
And ther thei ligge and lenge moost lecherie there regneth!" *dwell; remain*
 'Forthi,' quod this vicory, 'by verray God! I wolde
That no cardynal coome among the comune peple, *came*

397a And forgive us our trespasses . . .
402 Both the sediment and the liquid covering it at the bottom of the cask (after the ale has been drawn off).

397 That] Or F (? = a), *some* C-MSS
 (*so* K-D *p.* 155) (*C*).
402 at] O, C (*so* K-D); it at LY&c
 (? = β); it out at W; out an F (*C*).
403 þat] F (? = a) (*so* K-D *p.* 165); for
 þ. β; and þ. C (*C*).
407 þe g] β, C; *trsp.* F, *some* C-MSS.
410 be the] be þyn F; be C², ?C; þe
 W&r (*C*).
 fode] F (? = a) C², ?C; fede W&r
 (seed OG), *some* C-MSS; *cf.* K-D
 p. 208 (*C*).

411 þei ben] þou art F (*so* K-D
 p. 165); we be C (*C*).
412 many] L, C; m. a W&r.
 leode] man BxCx; lif *conj* K-D
 p. 118 (*C*).
415 fe*d*re] F (? = a), ?C (*so* K-D
 p. 156); f. or an hennes β, *some*
 C-MSS (*incl.* X).
420 þat] þere F, *some* C-MSS.

But in hir holynesse helden hem stille   *remained quiet/always*
425 At Avynoun among Jewes—*Cum sancto sanctus eris &c*—   *Avignon (C)*
    Or in Rome, as hir rule wole, the relikes to kepe;
    And thow Conscience in kynges court, and sholdest nevere come thennes;
    And Grace, that thow gredest so of, gyour of alle clerkes;   *go on about; guide*
    And Piers with his newe plough and ek with his olde
430 Emperour of al the world—that alle men were Cristene.
    'Inparfit is that Pope, that al peple sholde helpe,   *Faulty*
    And s[ou]deth hem that sleeth swiche as he sholde save.   *pays*
    A[c] wel worthe Piers the Plowman, that pursueth God in doynge,
                                      well be it (for)
    Qui pluit super iustos et iniustos at ones,
435 And sent the sonne to save a cursed mannes tilthe   *sends; bad; fields; crops*
    As brighte as to the beste man or to the beste womman.
    Right so Piers the Plowman peyneth hym to tilye   *takes pains; plough*
    As wel for a wastour and wenches of the stewes   *prostitutes*
    As for hymself and hise servaunts, save he is first yserved.
440 [So blessed be Piers Plowman, that peyneth hym to tilye],
    And travailleth and tilieth for a tretour also soore   *criminal; as hard*
    As for a trewe tidy man, alle tymes ylike.   *honest upright*
    And worshiped be He that wroghte al, bothe good and wikke,
    And suffreth that synfulle be til som tyme that thei repente.
445 And God [the Pope amende], that pileth Holy Kirke,   *robs*
    And cleymeth bifore the kyng to be kepere over Cristene,   *guardian*
    And counteth noght though Cristene ben killed and robbed,   *cares*
    And fynt folk to fighte and Cristen blood to spille   *provides, maintains*
    Ayein the Olde Lawe and Newe Lawe, as Luc bereth witnesse:
    Non occides: mihi vindictam &c.
450 It semeth, bi so hymself hadde his wille,   *provided that*
    That he ne reccheth right noght of al the remenaunt.
    'And Crist of his curteisie the cardinals save,

425 With the holy, thou wilt be holy (Ps 17: 26).
430 . . . and that all men were (true, not just nominal) Christians [*sc.* as they would
    be if Piers *were* Emperor].
434 Who . . . raineth upon the just and the unjust (Mt 5: 45).
449a Thou shalt not kill (Ex 20: 13; *qu.* Lk 18:20); Revenge is mine (Deut 32: 35;
    qu. Heb 10: 30).

425 jewis] F (?=α), C (*so* K-D); þe
    I. β.
428 gred.] L&r, C; graddest W.
429 P.] P. plowman F (*C*).
    ek w. h.] þe F; and also his C.
431 peple] LB, ?C; þe p. F&r; þe
    world WCr.
432 soudeth hem] C (*so* K-D *p.* 90);
    sendeth hem L&r (h.] swiche W).
    s. as] L&r, C; hem þat W.
433 Ac] C, ?α (But F) (*so* K-D);
    And β.

438–9 *Lines om* F.
440 *From* C (*so* K-D *p.* 90; *cf.* 437
    above); *not in* B-MSS.
444 til . . . r.] L&r, C; *erasure* W.
445 the p. a.] a. þe p. BxCx (*C*).
449 beriþ w.] F (?=α), C (*so* K-D);
    þerof witnesseþ β.
449a &c] β; & ego retribuam F, *some*
    C-MSS.
451 ne] L&r; *om* WHm, ?C; (*cf.*
    K-D *p.* 152).

And torne hir wit to wisdom and to welthe of soule! *minds/cunning*
For the comune,' quod this curatour, 'counten ful litel
455 The counseil of Conscience or Cardinale Vertues
But if thei sowne, as by sighte, somwhat to wynnyng.
Of gile ne of gabbyng gyve thei nevere tale, *lying; take no account*
For *Spiritus Prudencie* among the peple is gyle,
And alle tho faire vertues, as vices thei semeth.
460 Ech man subtileth a sleighte synne to hide, *devises a stratagem*
And coloureth it for a konnynge and a clene lyvynge.'
          disguises it as; wise act
Thanne lough ther a lord, and 'By this light!' seide, *laughed*
I holde it right and reson of my reve to take *sensible; from*
Al that myn auditour or ellis my styward *accountant; steward*
465 Counseilleth me bi hir acounte and my clerkes writynge.
          Advise me (to); records
With *Spiritus Intellectus* thei toke the reves rolles,
        the sp. of Understanding
And with *Spiritus Fortitudinis* fecche it—wole [he, nel he].' *i.e. by force*
And thanne cam ther a kyng and by his croune seide,
'I am kyng with croune the comune to rule,
470 And Holy Kirke and clergie fro cursed men to defende. *evil*
And if me lakketh to lyve by, the lawe wole I take it
Ther I may hastilokest it have—for I am heed of lawe: *most promptly*
For ye ben but membres and I above alle.
And sith I am youre aller heed, I am youre aller heele, *of you all; protection*
475 And Holy Chirches chief help and chieftayn of the comune.
And what I take of yow two, I take it at the techynge
Of *Spiritus Iusticie*—for I jugge yow alle.
So I may boldely be housled, for I borwe nevere,
Ne crave of my comune but as my kynde asketh.'
480 'In condicion,' quod Conscience, 'that thow [the comune] defende,
And rule thi reaume in reson, right wol and truthe

456 Unless they (C. & the C.V.) visibly result in some sort of financial gain (*cf.* Chaucer's *Gen. Prol.* 275).
461 And passes off sharp practice as prudence and honest dealing.
468 *by*, with reference to (Sk) *or, more likely, an oath.*
478-9 So I may confidently (go forward and) receive Holy Communion, for I *never* borrow Or make demands from my subjects except as my position as king requires.

456 þei] hit C (*so* K-D).
 sowne] F (?=a), C (*so* K-D);
 sowe L (?=β); seiȝe W *& most.*
460 to] F (?=a), C (*so* K-D); for to β.
466 tooken] F (?=a), C (*so* K-D *p.* 172); seke β.
467 wollche nullehe] C (*so* K-D);
 wole Y; whole Cr; I w. L&r (I w. after W); to presoun F.

470 de-] L&r, C; *om* WHm.
471 I] þat I C², C.
473 For] L&r; And W, ?C.
480 þe comune] ?C (*so* K-D *p.* 90);
 konne *All* B-MSS (k. hem F).
481 right] W&r, C; as r. Cr; in r. FHm.
 wyll &] Cr (*so* K-D *p.* 160); wel and in W&r (w. *om* FHm), C (C).

That thow [have thyn askyng], as the lawe asketh: *request; requires*
Omnia sunt tua ad defendendum set non ad deprehendendum.'
   The viker hadde fer hoom, and faire took his leeve—   *far (to go)*
485 And I awakned therwith, and wroot as me mette.   *as I (had) dreamed*

Passus XX

Thanne as I wente by the way, whan I was thus awaked,
Hevy chered I yede, and elenge in herte;   *Sad-faced; desolate*
For I ne wiste wher to ete ne at what place,
And it neghed neigh the noon, and with Nede I mette,
5 That afrounted me foule and faitour me called.   *accosted; rudely; knave*
  'Coudestow noght excuse thee, as dide the kyng and othere—
That thow toke to thy bilyve, to clothes and to sustenaunce,
                                                        (Saying that) what
Was by techynge and by tellynge of *Spiritus Temperancie*,
And that thow nome na moore than nede thee taughte,   *took*
10 And nede ne hath no lawe, ne nevere shal falle in dette
For thre thynges he taketh his lif for to save?—
That is, mete whan men hym werneth, and he no moneye weldeth,
                                                        refuse; possesses
Ne wight noon wol ben his borugh, ne wed hath noon to legge;
And he ca[cch]e in that caas and come therto by sleighte,   *take (something)*

482a What's yours is yours to keep (in trust) / Not seize according to your lust
(?*legal maxim; cf.* 482b *above*).
13 And nobody will stand surety for him, and he has nothing to pledge (against
a loan).
14 If in those circumstances he obtains anything by underhand means ...

482 *So* C, F (h. thyn a.] þ. lykyng h.
F. l. a.] C; *pl.* F); Take þow mayst
in reson as þi lawe askeþ β (C).
482a *sunt tua*] F (?=α), C; *t. s.* β.

Rubric Passus xx ᵘˢ *de visione &*
primus de Dobest.
3 For] F (?=α), C; *om* β.
6 Coudestow] L (?=β), C; & seyd c.
F; Kan*stow* W&r.

8 Was] C (*so* K-D) ?α (& þat was F);
As LMCr, *some* C-MSS; And
W&r, *some* C-MSS.
9 þat] F (?=α), C; *om* β.
10 And] β, C; For F.
11 he] þat he F, *some* C-MSS.
14 cacche] C (*so* K-D); caste F;
cauȝte W&r (C).

15 He synneth noght, soothliche, that so wynneth his foode.   *obtains*
    And though he come so to a clooth, and kan no bettre chevyssaunce,
                                           bargain (i.e. can't pay)
    Nede anoon righte nymeth hym under maynprise.
    And if hym list for to lape, the lawe of kynde wolde   *if he wish; drink*
    That he dronke at ech dych, er he [deide for thurst].
20 So Nede, at gret nede, may nymen as for his owene,   *take*
    Withouten conseil of Conscience or Cardynale Vertues—
    So that he sewe and save *Spiritus Temperancie.*   *Provided; follow; keep*
       'For is no vertue bi fer to *Spiritus Temperancie*—   *far; (compared) to*
    Neither *Spiritus Iusticie* ne *Spiritus Fortitudinis.*
25 For *Spiritus Fortitudinis* forfeteth ful ofte: *fails, goes wrong*
    He shal do moore than mesure many tyme and ofte,   *'act immoderately'*
    And bete men over bittre, and som body to litel,   *too severely*
    And greve men gretter than good feith it wolde.
       'And *Spiritus Iusticie* shal juggen, wole he, nel he,   *tends to judge*
30 After the kynges counseil and the comune like.   *According as*
    And *Spiritus Prudencie* in many a point shal faille
    Of that he weneth wolde falle if his wit ne weere.
    Wenynge is no wysdom, ne wys ymaginacion: *Supposition, opinion*
    Homo proponit et Deus disponit—
    [God] governeth alle goode vertues;
35 And Nede is next hym, for anoon he meketh   *makes (men) humble*
    And as lowe as a lomb, for lakkyng that hym nedeth;
    For nede maketh nede fele nedes lowe-herted.   *necessarily humble*
    Philosophres forsoke welthe for thei wolde be nedy,
    And woneden wel elengely and wolde noght be riche.   *very wretchedly*
40   'And God al his grete joye goostliche he lefte,   *great spiritual joy*
    And cam and took mankynde and bicam nedy.   *human nature*
    So he was nedy, as seith the Book, in manye sondry places,
    That he seide in his sorwe on the selve roode,   *the cross itself*
    "Bothe fox and fowel may fle to hole and crepe,

17 (The fact of) his need immediately 'stands bail for him'.
32 Concerning that which he thinks would happen if his wisdom did not exist (*C*).
33a Man proposes, God disposes (*provbl.*).
42 needy in many ... *or* as says the book in many ∴..

19 dei(*d*)e f. þ.] C; f. þ. d. *All* B-MSS;
   see K-D *p.* 95.
24 Neither] L&*r*, C; Ne W.
27 **Here R resumes.**
   s. body] R (=α; *pl.* F), C (*so*
   K-D); some of hem β.
33a–35 *as two lines div. after* alle α,
   C; *after* vertues β; *rec.* K-D *p.* 95.
34 God] C (*so* K-D); and *All* B-MSS
   (*etc* a. BmBo).
35 And] R (?=α; *om* F) CrG, C;
   Ac W&*r* (?=β).

36 þat] α, C (*so* K-D); of þat β,
   some C-MSS.
37 α (n.f.] fele for F; h.] of herte F),
   C (*so* K-D); *om* β.
38 Fil.] α, C (*so* K-D); Wise men β.
   welth] αC²G, C; wele W&*r*
   (?=β).
39 wel e.] α (wol e. F), C (*so* K-D);
   in wildernesse β.
42 So . . . n.] α (he w. so n. F), C
   (*so* K-D); So n. he w. β.

45 And the fissh hath fyn to flete with to reste,   *fin; swim*
   Ther nede hath ynome me, that I moot nede abide *Whereas; seized; endure*
   And suffre sorwes ful soure, that shal to joye torne."
   Forthi be noght abasshed to bide and to be nedy,
   Sith he that wroghte al the world was wilfulliche nedy,   *voluntarily*
50 Ne nevere noon so nedy ne poverer deide.'   *poorer*

      Whan Nede hadde undernome me thus, anoon I fil aslepe, *reproached*
   And mette ful merveillously that in mannes forme
   Antecrist cam thanne, and al the crop of truthe   *upper growth*
   Torned it [tid] up-so-doun, and overtilte the roote,   *quickly; upturned*
55 And made fals sprynge and sprede and spede mennes nedes.   *prosper*
   In ech a contree ther he cam he kutte awey truthe,   *region*
   And gerte gile growe there as he a god weere.   *made*
      Freres folwede that fend, for he gaf hem copes,
   And religiouse reverenced hym and rongen hir belles,
60 And al the covent cam to welcome that tyraunt,
   And alle hise as wel as hym—save oonly fooles;
   Whiche fooles were wel gladdere to deye
   Than to lyve lenger sith Leute was so rebuked,   *Fidelity*
   And a fals fend Antecrist over alle folk regnede.   *reigned*
65 And that were mylde men and holye, that no meschief dradden,
                                                       suffering; feared
   Defyed alle falsnesse and folk that it usede;   *practised*
   And what kyng that hem conforted, knowynge h[ir] gile,   *supported*
   They cursed, and hir conseil—were it clerk or lewed.
      Antecrist hadde thus soone hundredes at his baner,
70 And Pride bar it bare boldely aboute,   *bore; displayed*
   With a lord that lyveth after likyng of body,
   That cam ayein Conscience, that kepere was and gyour   *leader*
   Over kynde Cristene and Cardynale Vertues.   *true*
      'I conseille,' quod Conscience tho, 'cometh with me, ye fooles,
75 Into Unite Holy Chirche, and holde we us there.
   And crye we to Kynde that he come and defende us
   Fooles fro thise fendes lymes, for Piers love the Plowman.
   And crye we on al the comune that thei come to Unitee,
   And there abide and bikere ayeins Beliales children.'   *fight*

45 to (2)] β, C; or to α.
48 bide] wLMC², C; bidde R&r
   (?=αg), *many* C-MSS; bowe F (C).
51 had] L&r, C; haþ W.
54 hit tyd] C (*so* K-D *p.* 95); it
   W&r; *om* FCrGC.
55 made] α (*so* Sk); *om* β.
60 cam] αC (*so* K-D); forþ c. β.
62 *So divided from* 63 C (*so* K-D
   p. 95); *after* lyue *All* B-MSS (*cf.*
   C-MS T).
   gl.] α, C (*so* K-D); leuere β.

63 leute] RFBHmCr¹, C (*so* Sk);
   Le(n)ten W&r.
64 a] L&r, C; as a W.
65 And] L&r, C; Saue W.
   were] β, C; we α.
67 here] C (*so* K-D); hem W&r;
   hym F.
   gyle] α, C (*so* K-D); any while β.
70 bare] F (?=a) (*so* K-D *p.* 159);
   om W&r, C (C).
78 on] α, C (*so* K-D); to β.

253

80 Kynde Conscience tho herde, and cam out of the planetes,
  And sente forth his forreyours—feveres and fluxes, *foragers, harbingers*
  Coughes and cardiacles, crampes and toothaches, *heart-attacks*
  Rewmes and radegundes and roynouse scalles,
  Biles and bocches and brennynge agues,
85 Frenesies and foule yveles—forageres of Kynde *vile diseases*
  Hadde ypriked and prayed polles of peple; *preyed on; heads*
  Largeliche a legion lees hir lif soone. *Fully; lost*
   There was 'Harrow!' and 'Help! Here cometh Kynde, *Alas!*
  With Deeth that is dredful, to undo us alle!'
90 The lord that lyved after lust tho aloud cryde
  After Confort, a knyght, to come and bere his baner.
  'Alarme! Alarme!' quod that lord, 'ech lif kepe his owene!'
               To arms; everybody
   Thanne mette thise men, er mynstrals myghte pipe,
  And er heraudes of armes hadden discryved lordes, *named*
95 Elde the hoore; he was in the vauntwarde, *grey-haired; vanguard*
  And bar the baner bifore Deeth—bi right he it cleymede. *claimed*
   Kynde cam after hym, with many kene soores, *sharp*
  As pokkes and pestilences—and muche peple shente; *plague-sores*
  So Kynde thorugh corrupcions kilde ful manye. *diseases; killed*
100 Deeth cam dryvynge after and al to duste passhed *dashed*
  Kynges and knyghtes, kaysers and popes. *emperors*
  Lered ne lewed, he lefte no man stonde
  That he hitte evene, that evere stired after.
  Manye a lovely lady and [hir] lemmans knyghtes *lover-knights*
105 Swowned and swelted for sorwe of Dethes dyntes. *died; blows*
   Conscience of his curteisie to Kynde he bisoughte
  To cesse and suffre, and see wher thei wolde *desist; whether*
  Leve Pride pryvely and be parfite Cristene.
  And Kynde cessede tho, to se the peple amende.
110 Fortune gan flatere thanne tho fewe that were alyve, *those*
  And bihighte hem long lif—and lecherie he sente *promised*
  Amonges alle manere men, wedded and unwedded,

83-4 Colds and running sores and unwholesome scabs, Boils and swellings and burning agues.
102-3 No man whatever whom he struck with a direct blow was left standing or ever stirred again.

83 sc.] L&r; scabbes W, C (C).
87 Lar.] α, C (*so* K-D); That l. β.
 lese] L (?=β), C; lose R (?=α);
 loste WF; loren Y.
 hir] þe C.
91 Con.] β, C; *om* α.
93 þanne] α, C (*so* K-D); And þ. β.
95 ho.] β, C; horel α.
 he] L&r (*l. om* g), C; þat W.
97 hym] α, C; *om* β; *cf.* K-D *p.* 161.

102 ne] L&r, C; and WCr[12].
 left] α, C; leet β.
104 and . . . k.] C, ?α (h.l.] l. R;
 and . . . k.] for h. levis sake F)
 (*so* K-D *p.* 152); and l. of k. β.
105 de*thes*] L&r, C; hi*se* W.
106 to] þo C.
109 þo] W&r, C; sone F (*so* K-D
 pp. 172, 161).

And gaderede a greet hoost al agayn Conscience.
This Lecherie leide on with laughynge chiere   *pressed on; expression*
115 And with pryvee speche and peyntede wordes,
And armede hym in ydelnesse and in heigh berynge.   *lofty demeanour*
He bar a bowe in his hand and manye brode arewes,   *broad-tipped arrows*
Weren fethered with fair biheste and many a fals truthe.   *promise; troth*
With untidy tales he tened ful ofte   *indecent; hurt*
120 Conscience and his compaignye, of Holy Kirke the techeris.

Thanne cam Coveitise and caste how he myghte   *schemed*
Overcome Conscience and Cardinale Vertues,
And armed hym in avarice and hungriliche lyvede.   *'in miserly fashion'*
His wepne was al wiles, to wynnen and to hiden;
125 With glosynges and with gabbynges he giled the peple.   *deceptions; lies*
Symonye hym s[ue]de to assaille Conscience,   *followed*
And preched to the peple, and prelates thei hem maden
To holden with Antecrist, hir temporaltees to save;   *temporalities*
And cam to the kynges counseille as a kene baroun,   *bold*
130 And kneled to Conscience in Court afore hem alle,
And garte Good Feith flee and Fals to abide,
And boldeliche bar adoun with many a bright noble   *brought down*
Muche of the wit and wisdom of Westmynstre Halle.
He jogged til a justice and justed in his eere,   *rode up to; jousted*
135 And overtilte al his truthe with 'Tak this up amendement.'   *overturned*
And to the Arches in haste he yede anoon after,
And tornede Cyvyle into Symonye, and siththe he took the Official:
   gave to, bribed
For a menever mantel he made lele matrymoyne   *fur; true wedlock*
Departen er deeth cam, and a devors shapte.   *Dissolve; made*
140 'Allas!' quod Conscience, and cryde tho, 'wolde Crist of his grace
That Coveitise were Cristene, that is so kene to fighte,   *bold in fighting*
And boold and bidynge the while his bagge lasteth!'   *steadfast; money-bag*
And thanne lough Lyf, and leet daggen hise clothes,   *be 'dagged' (C)*

135 'Take this (bribe) to amend your judgment [in my favour]'.
137 (He) made civil law subservient to simoniacal purposes, and then gave (some bribe) to the court-official (*after* Sk).
143 And then (the Pride of) Life laughed, and had his clothes curiously cut (C).

114 w.] α, C (*so* K-D); w. a β.
   lau.] L&r, C; langlynge WHm.
117 br.] WHmF, C; blody L&r (C).
119 w.] α (& w. F), C (*so* K-D); W. hise β.
120 kerke] αCr (*so* K-D); chirche β, Cx.
126 s*eude*] R (=α), C (*so* K-D *p.* 198); sente β (soughte Hm) F (C).
127 preched . . . pe.] presed on þe pope C (*so* K-D *p.* 92 (C).
   hem] *om* MCr, C.

130 kn. to] knokked C (*so* K-D *p.* 92) (C).
132 br.] β, C; rede α.
134 til] L&r, C; to WHmCr³.
135 vp] on Cr³, C.
138 men. m.] α, C (*so* K-D); M. of Men. β.
139 a] α, C; *om* β.
141 to f.] α, C (*so* K-D); a fightere β.
142 þe] α, C; *om* β.

	And armed hym in haste in harlotes wordes,	*lascivious speech*
145	And heeld Holynesse a jape and Hendenesse a wastour,	*joke; Courtesy*
	And leet Leautee a cherl and Lyere a fre man;	*considered; noble*
	Conscience and counseil, he counted it folye.	
	Thus relyede Lif for a litel fortune,	*rallied; (good) fortune*
	And priked forth with Pride—preiseth he no vertue,	*esteems*
150	Ne careth noght how Kynde slow, and shal come at the laste	*slew*
	And kille alle erthely creature save Conscience oone.	*alone*
	Lyf lepte aside and laughte hym a lemman.	*took; mistress*
	'Heele and I,' quod he, 'and heighnesse of herte	*Health; presumption*
	Shal do thee noght drede neither deeth ne elde,	*make; old age*
155	And to foryyte sorwe and yyve noght of synne.'	*forget; care nothing for*
	This likede Lif and his lemman Fortune,	
	And geten in hir glorie a gadelyng at the laste,	*(they) begot; base fellow*
	Oon that muche wo wroughte, Sleuthe was his name.	
	Sleuthe wax wonder yerne and soone was of age,	*grew; quickly*
160	And wedded oon Wanhope, a wenche of the stuwes.	*Despair; brothels*
	Hir sire was a sysour that nevere swoor truthe—	*juror*
	Oon Tomme Two-tonge, atteynt at ech a queste.	*found false; inquest*
	This Sleuthe was war of werre, and a slynge made,	*wary, cautious (in)*
	And threw drede of dispair a dozeyne myle aboute.	*despairing fear*
165	For care Conscience tho cryde upon Elde,	*anxiety, trouble*
	And bad hym fonde to fighte and afere Wanhope.	*try; frighten (off)*
	And Elde hente good hope, and hastiliche he shifte hym,	
		seized; moved himself
	And wayved awey Wanhope and with Lif he fighteth.	*drove*
	And Lif fleigh for feere to Phisik after helpe,	
170	And bisoughte hym of socour, and of his salve hadde,	*help; remedy*
	And gaf hym gold good woon that gladede his herte—	*a-plenty*
	And thei gyven hym ageyn a glazene howve.	*in return; glass hood (C)*
	Lyf leeved that lechecraft lette sholde Elde,	*believed; stop*
	And dryven awey deeth with dyas and drogges.	*remedies; drugs*
175	And Elde auntred hym on Lyf—and at the laste he hitte	*set off against*
	A phisicien with a furred hood, that he fel in a palsie,	
	And there dyed that doctour er thre dayes after.	
	'Now I se,' seide Lif, 'that surgerie ne phisik	

172 . . . an imaginary protection (Sk), a nostrum, a placebo.

144 in h. in] L&r, C; an h. wiþ W.
147 and] L&r, C; a. his W.
 it] R&r (it a LMHm; it but F),
 C (*so* K-D); at a flye W.
149 -ked] L&r; -keþ W, C.
151 -ture] LY (? = β) R (? = a), C
 (*so* K-D); -tures W&r (*so* Sk).
152 l. as.] β, C; seiþ *occide* a.
155 sorwe] deþ MCr; зowthe C; *cf.*
 K-D *p.* 209.
158 wo] β, C; *om* a.

162 a] L&r (*om* F), ?C; en- W, *some*
 C-MSS, *incl.* X.
163 was] W&r (=Bx), C; wex g (*so*
 K-D *p.* 95).
 war] sley C (*so* K-D).
167 shifte] shrof C (C).
170 ha.] L&r, C; he h., WF.
171 And] L&r, C; He W.
174 dry.] β, ?C; to d. a, *some* C-MSS.
 dyas] β, C; dayes a.

May noght a myte availle to medle ayein Elde.'   *engage against*
180 And in hope of his heele good herte he hente   *took*
And rood so to Revel, a riche place and a murye—
The compaignye of confort men cleped it som tyme—
And Elde anoon after hym, and over myn heed yede,
And made me balled bifore and bare on the croune: *bald in front*
185 So harde he yede over myn heed it wol be sene evere.   *visible*
　'Sire yvele ytaught Elde!' quod I, 'unhende go with the!
                                            ill-bred; discourtesy
Sith whanne was the wey over menne heddes?   *men's*
Haddestow be hende,' quod I, 'thow woldest have asked leeve!'   *leave*
　'Ye—leve, lurdeyn?' quod he, and leyde on me with age,
                                            sluggard; struck at
190 And hitte me under the ere—unnethe may Ich here.   *scarcely*
He|buffetted me aboute the mouth and bette out my|wangteeth,   *beat; molars*
And gyved me in goutes—I may noght goon at large.   *shackled; freely*
And of the wo that I was inne my wif hadde ruthe,   *plight; sorrow*
And wisshed wel witterly that I were in hevene.   *most assuredly*
195 For the lyme that she loved me fore, and leef was to feele—
                                            member; loved to feel
On nyghtes, namely, whan we naked weere—   *particularly*
I ne myghte in no manere maken it at hir wille,
So Elde and he[o] hadden it forbeten.   *she; enfeebled*
　And as I seet in this sorwe, I saugh how Kynde passede,   *sat*
200 And deeth drogh neigh me—for drede gan I quake,   *drew*
And cryde to Kynde, 'Out of care me brynge!   *affliction*
Lo! how Elde the hoore hath me biseye: *visited*
Awreke me if youre wille be, for I wolde ben hennes!'   *Avenge*
　'If thow wolt be wroken, wend into Unitee,   *avenged*
205 And hold thee there evere, til I sende for thee;
And loke thow konne som craft er thow come thennes.'   *see; learn*
　'Counseille me, Kynde,' quod I, 'what craft be best to lerne?'
　'Lerne to love,' quod Kynde, 'and leef alle othere.'   *leave all else*
　'How shal I come to catel so, to clothe me and to feede?'
210　'And thow love lelly, lakke shal thee nevere   *If; faithfully*
Weede ne worldly mete, while thi lif lasteth.'   *Clothing; food*

189 'Oh, yes—permission, rascal?' [or, *perhaps*, 'dear rascal'].

179 medle] L&r, C; mede W.
181 so to] L&r, C; forþ to a W.
183 anoon] *om* C.
　hym] α, C (*so* K-D); me β.
187 men] L; menne C; mennes W&r.
190 may] L&r, C; myʒte W.
191 me] L&r, C; me so W.
　and ... my] L&r (o. m.] me on
　þe g), C; þat out my W.
　wange t.] α, C (*so* K-D); t. β
　(t. he bette W).

194 wel] α (often F), C; ful β.
198 heo] C (MSS MF); hee C-MS X,
　α (þe gowte & she F) (*so* K-D); she
　sooþly β.
202 me] β, C; my lif α.
207 be] R (=α; *soph.* F), C; is β.
208 leue] αCr¹, C (*so* K-D); leef of β
　(l.] loue Y).
210 la.] α, C (*so* K-D); quod he l. β.
211 Wede; mete] α, C (*so* K-D);
　trsp. β.

And there by conseil of Kynde I comsed to rome
Thorugh Contricion and Confession til I cam to Unitee.
And there was Conscience conestable Cristene to save,   *constable*
215 And bisegede soo[r]ly with sevene grete geaunts   *grievously (C)*
That with Antecrist helden harde ayein Conscience.
   Sleuthe with his slynge an hard saut he made.
Proude preestes coome with hym—passynge an hundred
In paltokes and pyked shoes and pisseris longe knyves
220 Coomen ayein Conscience—with Coveitise thei helden.
   'By the Marie!' quod a mansed preest, was of the march of Irlonde,
                                  ?defrocked; province
'I counte na moore Conscience, by so I cacche silver,   *esteem; provided*
Than I do to drynke a draughte of good ale!'
And so seiden sixty of the same contree,
225 And shotten ayein with shot, many a sheef of othes,   *oaths*
And brode hoked arwes—Goddes herte and hise nayles—
And hadden almoòst Unitee and holynesse adown.
   Conscience cryede, 'Help, Clergie, or ellis I falle
Thorugh inparfite preestes and prelates of Holy Chirche!'
230 Freres herden hym crye, and comen hym to helpe—
Ac for thei kouthe noght wel hir craft, Conscience forsook hem.
   Nede neghede tho neer, and Conscience he tolde
That thei come for coveitise to have cure of soules.   *i.e. church livings*
'And for thei are povere, paraventure, for patrymoyne hem failleth,
235 Thei wol flatere, to fare wel, folk that ben riche.   *prosper*
And sithen thei chosen chele and cheitiftee, poverte—   *cold; destitution*
Lat hem chewe as thei chose, and charge hem with no cure!
                                    burden; cure of souls
For lomere he lyeth, that liflode moot begge,   *oftener; a living*
Than he that laboureth for liflode and leneth it beggeres.   *gives to*
240 And sithen freres forsoke the felicite of erthe,   *renounced*

219 [Dressed up like blades] in jackets and peaked shoes, and wearing long
    tapering daggers (*see* Sk).
234 . . . because they lack endowments (to provide a steady income).
237 Let them lie on their beds as they've made them, and don't burden them with
    the responsibilities of a parish.

212 þere; I] I; *om* C.
214 was C.] β, C; was R; he was mad
   a F.
215 soorly] sooþly BxCx; sikerly *conj*
   K-D *p.* 117 (*C*).
217 saut] LRFHmC², C; assaut
   W&r.
218 p. an h.] a, C; mo þan a
   þousand β.
221 þe (1)] R (=a), C (*so* K-D); *om*
   βF.
     yrl.] L&r, C; walys W.

225 wiþ] hym w. YOCB, C (*C*).
227 -nesse] churche C (*C*).
228 ellis] *om* C.
233 for] β, C; for no a.
234 hem f.] L&r, C; þei faille WHm.
235 to] L&r, C; and WHm.
   folke] L&r, C; wiþ f. W; of f. F.
236 ch. p.] WLR, ? C (*C*).
238-9 β, C; *ll. om* a.
240 And] β, C; For a.
   þe] β, C; *om* a.

Lat hem be as beggeris, or lyve by aungeles foode!'
 Conscience of this counseil tho comsede for to laughe,   *at; advice*
And curteisliche conforted hem and called in alle freres,   *cheered*
And seide, 'Sires, soothly welcome be ye alle
245 To Unitee and Holy Chirche—ac o thyng I yow preye: *one; beg*
Holdeth yow in unitee, and haveth noon envye
To lered ne to lewed, but lyveth after youre reule.
And I wol be youre borugh, ye shal have breed and clothes *will guarantee*
And othere necessaries ynowe—yow shal no thyng lakke,   *enough*
250 With that ye leve logik and lerneth for to lovye.   *Provided that*
For love lafte thei lordshipe, bothe lond and scole—   *abandoned*
Frere Fraunceys and Domynyk—for love to be holye.
 'And if ye coveite cure, Kynde wol yow telle   *wish to be parish priests*
That in mesure God made alle manere thynges,   *proportion*
255 And sette it at a certein and at a siker nombre,   *definite; fixed*
And nempnede hem names newe, and noumbrede the sterres:
Qui numerat multitudinem stellarum et omnibus eis &c.
 'Kynges and knyghtes, that kepen and defenden,   *protect*
Han officers under hem, and ech of hem a certein. *definite (number of men)*
And if thei wage men to werre, thei write hem in noumbre;
260 Wol no tresorere taken hem wages, travaille thei never so soore,
[But thei ben nempned in the noumbre of hem that ben ywaged].
Alle othere in bataille ben yholde brybours—   *thought (to be mere) robbers*
Pylours and pykeharneys, in ech a parisshe ycursed.
 'Monkes and moniales and alle men of religion—   *nuns*
265 Hir ordre and hir reule wole to han a certein noumbre;   *requires (them)*
Of lewed and of lered the lawe wole and asketh
A certein for a certein—save oonliche of freres!   *except only from*

256a [Praise ye the Lord . . .] who telleth the number of the stars: and calleth them
  all by their names (Ps 146: 4).
259 And if they undertake to pay the wages of soldiers, they keep a written record
  of their (exact) number.
261 Unless they are included by name in the payroll of enlisted men.
263 Pillagers (of the fallen) and plunderers of (dead men's) armour.
267 A fixed number to each particular category.

242 þo] β, C; *om* α.
249 yow] W&r (ye CrO), C; þow R;
 for ȝee F.
  lakke] α, C (*so* K-D *p.* 162);
 faiſle β.
253 telle] α, C (*so* K-D); teche β.
255 it] L&r, C; hem WCrF.
  at (2)] L&r, C; in FG; *om* WCr.
256 hem] α, C (*so* K-D); *om* β.
  n. and] β; and n. α; and C (C).
256a et . . . &c] WL; et o. e. nomina
 &c YB (n.] n. vocat Cot); *om* R
 (?=α), C.

260 *here in* L&r, C; *after* 263 *in*
 WHmB.
  Wol] W&r, C; Ellys w. F; Or
 they w. CrM; And þerfore w. B.
  no tr.] LRF, C; no man tresore W.
 take h. w.] α (h.] hym R), C
 (*so* K-D); hem paie β (wages
 h. p. C²).
261 *From* C (*so* K-D); *om* W&r; but
 he kunne rekene ariȝt her names in
 his rollis C² (C).
263 par.] α, C (*so* K-D); place β.

Forthi,' quod Conscience, 'by Crist! kynde wit me telleth   *plain reason*
It is wikked to wage yow—ye wexen out of noumbre!
                                  are grown to excessive numbers
270 Hevene hath evene noumbre, and helle is withoute noumbre;
Forthi I wolde witterly that ye were in the registre   *list*
And youre noumbre under notarie sygne, and neither mo ne lasse!'
                                   officially recorded
    Envye herde this and heet freres go to scole   *ordered; university*
And lerne logyk and lawe—and ek contemplacion—
275 And preche men of Plato, and preve it by Seneca   *from*
That alle thynges under hevene oughte to ben in comune.
                                 (owned) in common
    He lyeth, as I leve, that to the lewed so precheth;
For God made to men a lawe and Moyses it taughte—   *t. it to Moses*
Non concupisces rem proximi tui.
280 And yvele is this yholde in parisshes of Engelonde;   *badly; observed*
For persons and parissh preestes, that sholde the peple shryve,
Ben curatours called to knowe and to hele.
Alle that ben hir parisshens penaunces enjoigne,   *bid (to do)*
And ben ashamed in hir shrift; ac shame maketh hem wende
285 And fleen to the freres—as fals folk to Westmynstre,   *dishonest*
That borweth, and bereth it thider, and thanne biddeth frendes
                                 sc. to bribe jurors
Yerne of foryifnesse or lenger yeres leve.
Ac while he is in Westmynstre he wol be bifore   *forward (to spend)*
And maken hym murie with oother menne goodes.   *entertain himself; men's*
290 And so it fareth with muche folk that to freres shryveth;
As sisours and executours—thei shul yyve the freres

270 *i.e.* the number of the blessed is fixed (predetermined), that of the damned is indeterminate (*C*).
272 And the number (allowed) you noted in a formal document, and your (actual) numbers in agreement with it.
279 Thou shalt not covet thy neighbour's goods [*domum* house *Vulg*] (Ex 20: 17).
284 And (their parishioners) should experience in confession the sense of shame (which is part of true penance), but their (fear of) shame causes them to go (away) . . .
287 Eagerly for a remission (of the debt), or for a longer period of grace (in which to repay it) (*see* Sk).

269 out of] β, C; of on R; ouer ony F.
272 -rie] LRFGHm, C; -ries W&r.
273 go] R&r, C (*so* K-D); to go WLC.
277 He] α, C (*so* K-D); And yet he β.
283 pen.] α, C; *sg.* β.
    en.] R (=α), C; to en. βF.
284 been] F (=α; beth R), C (*so* K-D); shulden b. L&r (=β; sh. W).

287 leue] R (=α; bleue þere F) L (?=β), C; loone W&r (of l. B) (*C*).
289 -ken] β, C; -keþ α.
    me*n*] R (?=α), C; mennes βF (*cf.* 187).
290 to] αCr, C (*so* K-D); to þe β.
291 schul] α, C (*so* K-D); wol β.

A parcel to preye for hem, and [purchace] hem mur[th]e   *portion; obtain*
With the remenaunt that othere [renkes] biswonke,   *men; toiled for*
And suffre the dede in dette to the day of doome.
295   Envye herfore hatede Conscience,   *for this reason*
And freres to philosophie he fond hem to scole,
The while Coveitise and Unkyndenesse Conscience assaillede.
In Unitee Holy Chirche Conscience held hym,
And made Pees porter to pynne the yates   *fasten; gates*
300 Of alle taletelleris and titeleris in ydel.   *To; tatlers*
Ypocrisie and h[ii] an hard saut thei made.   *they; assault*
Ypocrisie at the yate harde gan fighte,
And woundede wel wikkedly many a wise techere
That with Conscience acordede and Cardynale Vertues.
305   Conscience called a leche, that coude wel shryve,   *doctor*
To go salve tho that sike were and thorugh synne ywounded.
Shrift shoop sharp salve, and made men do penaunce   *prepared*
For hire mysdedes that thei wroght hadde,
And that Piers [pardon] were ypayed, *redde quod debes.*   *pay what you owe*
310   Some liked noght this leche, and lettres thei sente,
If any surgien were in the sege that softer koude plastre.   *more gently*
Sire Leef-to-lyve-in-lecherie lay there and gronede;   *Love-to-live-in-l.*
For fastynge of a Fryday he ferde as he wolde deye: *acted*
'Ther is a surgien in this sege that softe kan handle,
315 And moore of phisik bi fer, and fairer he plastreth—   *(knows) far more*
Oon Frere Flaterere, is phisicien and surgien.'
   Quod Contricion to Conscience, 'Do hym come to Unitee;
For here is many a man hurt thorugh Ypocrisye.'
   'We han no nede,' quod Conscience, 'I woot no bettre leche
320 Than person or parissh preest, penitauncer or bisshop—   *confessor*
Save Piers the Plowman, that hath power over alle,
And indulgence may do, but if dette lette it.

294 And leave the dead man (still) in debt till doomsday (Sk; *q.v.*).
296 And made provision for friars to study philosophy at universities (C).
300 Against [*Of* 'to', *v.* OED *s.v.* XVI, 58] all gossip-mongers and idle chatterers.
322 . . . unless the sinner's unfulfilled penitential obligation prevent it.

292 pur.] make BxCx (C).
   hem] R (?=α; *om* F), C;
   hemself β.
   murthe] murye *All* B-MSS (C).
293 rem.] C; residue and þe r. W&r
   (=Bx; and þe r.] of þe good F)
   (C).
   renkes] men BxCx (C).
296 hem] L&r, C; þanne W.
301 hiij] *em.* K-D; he W&r; *l. om* F;
   þey C.
   saut] LR, C; assaut W.
   made] ȝeuen C (*so* K-D *p.* 91) (C).

302 L&r, C; *l. om* W.
306 To go] W; To FC²CB, C; Go
   L&r.
   were] α, C; ben β (C).
309 par.] C (*so* K-D *p.* 95); þe
   ploughman B; þe C; *om* W&r.
311 in the s.] αCr, C (*so* Sk); þe
   segge W&r (*om* B; s. *corr. to* sege
   L).
312 leef] β; lif αHmCr, Cx (C).
314 þis] þe C.
321 alle] αG, C (*so* K-D); hem a. β.

I may wel suffre,' seide Conscience, 'syn ye desiren,   *permit; since*
That Frere Flaterere be fet and phisike yow sike.'   *fetched; treat*
325 The frere herof herde and hiede faste   *hurried*
To a lord for a lettre, leve to have to curen   *heal/act as a parish-priest*
As a curatour he were, and cam with his lettre
Boldely to the bisshop, and his brief hadde,   *authority obtained*
In contrees ther he coome, confessions to here—   *districts; should come*
330 And cam there Conscience was, and knokked at the yate.
    Pees unpynned it, was porter of Unitee,   *unlocked; (who) was*
And in haste askede what his wille were.
    'In faith,' quod this frere, 'for profit and for helthe *benefit (with pun)*
Carpe I wolde with Contricion, and therfore cam I hider.' *Speak*
335   'He is sik,' seide Pees, 'and so are manye othere;
Ypocrisie hath hurt hem—ful hard is if thei kevere.'   *recover*
    'I am a surgien,' seide the frere, 'and salves can make.
Conscience knoweth me wel and what I kan do bothe.'
    'I praye thee,' quod Pees tho, 'er thow passe ferther,
340 What hattestow? I praye thee, hele noght thi name.' *are you called? conceal*
    'Certes,' seide his felawe, 'Sire *Penetrans-domos*.' *Surely; companion*
    'Ye? Go thi gate!' quod Pees, 'by God, for al thi phisik, *way*
But thow konne any craft, thow comest nought herinne! *some skill*
I knew swich oon ones, noght eighte wynter passed,   *once; ago*
345 Coom in thus ycoped at a court there I dwelde,   *manor-house; was staying*
And was my lordes leche—and my ladies bothe.   *physician (pun on lover)*
And at the laste this lymytour, tho my lord was oute, *licensed mendicant*
He salvede so oure wommen til some were with childe.' *salved/greeted*
    Hende-Speche heet Pees tho, 'Opene the yates. *Good Manners; bade*
350 Lat in the frere and his felawe, and make hem fair cheere. *welcome*
He may se and here here, so may bifalle,   *hear here; happen*
That Lif thorugh his loore shal leve coveitise,   *teaching; abandon*
And be adrad of deeth and withdrawe hym fram pryde,
And acorde with Conscience and kisse hir either oother.'
        each of them; the other
355   Thus thorugh Hende-Speche entred the frere,
And cam in to Conscience and curteisly hym grette. *greeted*
    'Thow art welcome,' quod Conscience, 'kanstow heele sike?
Here is Contricion,' quod Conscience, 'my cosyn, ywounded.
Conforte hym,' quod Conscience, 'and take kepe to hise soores. *inspect*
360 The plastres of the person and poudres ben to soore, *dressings; harsh*

323 (However), I suppose that since you wish it, I can allow . . .
341 Sir Piercer-of-Homes' (*alluding to* 2 Tim 3: 6, *and with possible sexual pun*).

327 le.] α, C (*so* K-D); *pl.* β.
329 coome] Wα, C; c. in L&r
  (?=β).
337 fr.] α, C (*so* K-D); segge β.
343 any] α (more F), C (*so* K-D);
  som*me* L&r (=β; som oo*þer* W).
344 passed] L&r, C; hennes WG.

349 þo] α, C; *om* W&r (=β; to
  YCrO).
351 her so] α, C (*so* K-D); so it β.
356–*end defective* Bm.
  in] *om* Cr, C.
357 syke] α, C (*so* K-D); þe s. β.
360 ben] R (=α), C; biten βF.

And lat hem ligge overlonge and looth is to chaunge hem; *(he) lets; remain*
Fro Lenten to Lenten he lat his plastres bite.'
'That is overlonge!' quod this lymytour, 'I leve—I shal amende it'—
And gooth, gropeth Contricion, and gaf hym a plastre *handles*
365 Of 'A pryvee paiement, and I shal praye for yow, *secret*
And for al [hem] that ye ben holden to, al my lif tyme, *bound*
And make yow [and] my Lady in masse and in matyns
As freres of oure fraternytee for a litel silver.'
Thus he gooth and gadereth, and gloseth there he shryveth—
'plays down (sin)'
370 Til Contricion hadde clene foryeten to crye and to wepe,
And wake for hise wikked werkes as he was wont to doone. *watch (in prayer)*
For confort of his confessour contricion he lafte, *sorrow for sins; left*
That is the soverayneste salve for alle[s]kynnes synnes. *all kinds of (C)*
Sleuth seigh that, and so dide Pryde,
375 And comen with a kene wille Conscience to assaille. *came; fierce intent*
Conscience cryed eft [Clergie come] helpe hym,
And [bad] Contricion [come] to kepe the yate.
'He lith adreynt,' seide Pees, 'and so do manye othere; *drowned (in torpor)*
The frere with his phisyk this folk hath enchaunted, *bewitched*
380 And plastred hem so esily [that hii] drede no synne!'
'By Crist!' quod Conscience tho, 'I wole bicome a pilgrym,
And walken as wide as the world lasteth, *extends*
To seken Piers the Plowman, that Pryde myghte destruye,
And that freres hadde a fyndyng, that for nede flateren
385 And countrepledeth me, Conscience. Now Kynde me avenge, *oppose*
And sende me hap and heele, til I have Piers the Plowman!' *luck; health*
And siththe he gradde after Grace, til I gan awake. *cried aloud*

384 (And who might bring about) that friars should have some proper endowment,
instead of being led to resort to flattery through their need for money.

361 And] R (=α), C (*so* K-D); He
βF.
364 goth] R (=α), ?C (*so* K-D *pp.*
156, 168*n*); g. and βF, *some* C-MSS.
366 And . . . h.] And for al BxCx
(And *om* WHmLMR; al] hem Cx)
(C).
367 and my] my BxCx (C).
368 fre.] LR, C; *sg.* WHmO.
371 to d.] bifore C.
373 -ayneste] -eyne C (*so* K-D *p.* 91).
skynnes] kynne W&r (= Bx;
kinnes CrG) Cx (C).
376 Cl. come] C; and bad Cl. *All*
B-MSS (C).
hym] W&r, C; *om* g.

377 bad . . . come] C (*so* K-D *p.* 92);
also Con. for *All* B-MSS.
kepe] helpe k. C.
378 adr.] Cot, C; and dremeþ W&r
(C).
379 haþ] β, C; h. so α.
380 And . . . hii] And p. h. so e. þei
All B-MSS; And doth men drynke
dwale that men C (C).
382 wal.] wenden C (*so* K-D).
la.] W&r; askeþ F; regneth Cx
(renneþ *sugg.* K-D *p.* 91).
383 my.] α (he m. F), C (*so* K-D);
may β.
*Colophon Explicit hic dialogus petri
plowman.*

Commentary

On division of material in the Commentary,
see INTRODUCTION, *section VIII*

A TEXTUAL AND LEXICAL

TITLE There is no authoritative title for any version of the poem; Langl. nowhere names the work, and the various titles for the whole or parts may be scribal in origin. The long title in Sk *The Vision of William concerning Piers the Plowman, together with Vita de Dowel, Dobet, et Dobest, secundum Wit et Resoun* is unambiguous and informative, but does not adequately indicate the continuing importance of Piers throughout the poem. K-D modify Sk slightly. I follow Crowley, the poem's first publisher, in calling it *The Vision of Piers Plowman*; Skeat's fears about the ambiguity of this form have no real basis today.

PROLOGUE

Rubric The rubric *prologus* is generally absent from MSS of all three versions; I follow Skeat in printing from the A-MS R, Bodleian MS Rawlinson Poetry 137.

2 *shep* A (Ka; *var. she*(*e*)*p*(*e*)), C (*var. shepherde*, so SkC) may support H's rare *schep* 'shepherd' as orig. B. *habite* (3) then = '(general) appearance' rather than 'clothing' (unless we read 3a in apposition with 2b and see hermit's/shepherd's garments as identical—against which cf. Bn *ad loc*). However H may here show contamination from an A exemplar (cf. *a schroude*, also *trowe* 34) and the harder sense may support the originality of *sheep* perh. as a bold revision of A (? later reversed in C).

10 *sweyued* L&c 'flowed' is perh. a scribal var. of *sw(e)yed* (= *swiȝede* A) 'sounded' induced by *sweuene* (11); *murye* goes somewhat better with sound than movement. However Langland (?revising) cd. have intended to suggest 'flowing along from the waking to the dream world', which an echo of *sweyued* in *sweuene* would re-inforce. (Bn, foll. Sk's small edition, glosses *sweyued* without authority as 'sounded', thus confusing two separate words carefully distinguished in earlier Sk.)

13 I assume omission of *Ac* in Bx (cf. L&r) and mistaken correction with *And* in WCMH.

34 Wr's em. from A seems inevitable. An allit. pattern *aaaxy* is possible (K-D p. 138) but comparison with A suggests Bx substitution of easier, more explicit *synnelees. trowe* H (= A) cd. be due to contamination from an A exemplar (G's is perh. coincidental).

50–2 are not in AC; they were either om. at C revision or are spurious (cf. the allit.), an archetypal expansion of 49.

Commentary

63 H's *mete* (= A; cf. C², C-MS I) again looks like contamination from an A exemplar. Such instances from H are not generally noticed hereafter.

82 ?Bx (β) scans *aaaxy*, but AC's agreement (and cf. α) points to *poraille* as scribal.

83 F's var. *vikerys* makes explicit the distn. betw. the incumbent and his unbeneficed substitute/assistant (see Bn p. 91).

108–9 *MED* s.v. 2b glosses *impugnen* 'find fault with', quoting these ll. The C var. *repugnen* (*OED* 2 'resist, object to &c') suggests a meaning 'dispute the authority of' for **B** (*MED* 2a), ?whence K-D place in parenthesis and treat the sent. as anacoluthon. This is unnecessary, and the C var. may be interpreted as making explicit a sense rendered hard by the distance betw. *of the c.* and the vb. *imp.* and the prob. rareness of the constr. Transl. (a) seems preferable as Langl. is more concerned with the electoral college's power to create St P.'s successor (a power held to have been orig. invested in St P. by Christ; cf. the var. *þat] þe*, which implies understanding the l. thus) than with its capacity to invest the pope with Petrine authority generally, as K-D's punct. requires; cf. *eleccion* 110, even more emphatic in C. *OED* s.v. 4 quotes 108 meaning 'assume or take for granted'; Bn's 'took (on themselves)' (*OED* s.v. 2) does not fit with *in hem*, which points to the cardinals' (sin of) presumption that they really do possess the power in question.

117 Bx's defective alliteration directs reconstruction after C; but I take C's *hire* as revision.

122 *lede] man* is the poss. **B** orig., if F's *lyf* is taken as having come in from 120.

143 I conj. an orig. *can* subst. by more familiar *gan* in all B-MSS; I do not find *gan* easier than *comsed* (conj. K-D p. 195), but it is easier than *can* in sense *gan*, a chiefly N/N Midl. usage, *MED* s.v.; cf. A-MS V at IX 109, where *conne] gonne r.* is not a stave word.

148 Emendation of Bx is directed by the ease of the error and the superior sense of C; the number describes the whole gathering, not just a portion of it.

152 K-D needlessly read *dedes*; but there is no tautology, since *drede* 'danger, source of fear' is well-instanced by *MED* 5a from Chaucer, who actually combines both words as in Langl.: 'I sey nat thow shalt be so coward, that thow doute ther wher as is no drede' (*CT Mel* B 2517).

159 *Seide* perh. absolute 'spoke' (*OED* s.v. 3 (e)); if not, *quod he* 160 is pleonastic but need not be scribal (though C *om*, lightening the l., perh. as rev. of a difficult use of *seyen*). *selue* β perh. reflects the conjecturally omitted stave word *salue*.

201 *reik* Bn after A. G. Mitchell (*MÆ* 8 (1939) p. 118) and C. T. Onions (*MLR* 3 (1908), 170–1) from C-MS Bodl. 814 (*reed* most C-MSS).

206 I supply the needed stave word by conj. *to] so* substn. through unconscious infl. of the expected word. F's *slen] doon* (adop. K-D) I see as attempt to improve allit. (line not in C).

PASSUS I

4 The def. art. seems preferable on grounds of sense; presumably the Bx scribe missed the ref. back to *tour* Prol 14.

12 The W and L varr. respectively perh. indicate split variation from orig. *vpon*, which I read.

41 The complex variation in this line easily explains corruption of an ostensibly easy word. Here as frequently G appears to have been corr. from either a B-MS superior to Bx or from an A or C MS regarded as containing superior B-readings.

44 The puzzling variation here cd. be explained by correction of α from C or revision of Bx by C so as to coincide with α's presum. unoriginal reading.

112 I include this line from A following K-D as it seems necessary to the sense. I conj. loss of orig. final *one* (which gives the best sense) through unconscious infl. of the common collocation *loken on*. K-D more drastically conj. *liʒt* for Ka *siʒt* as the AB orig.

118 C's reading at this point is closer to F's *lord hymselue made*] *lyed . . . m.* (βR), and may indicate contamination of F from C.

154 Something of a crux. K-D wd. take Cr (= C) as a correction from a superior B-MS; Bx *fille* can be seen as resulting from misreading *yeten* 'begotten' (= become incarnate) as p.p. *y-eten* (with loss of *y-* in W). Alternatively, Cr may here incorporate a C reading, C having been revised to tone down the bold and slightly grotesque metaphor. Retaining *fille* avoids anticipating the sense of 155 (which *is* explicitly an incarnational statement) and enriches the image of love as a plant drawing sustenance from the earth.

160 *inmiddes* (cf. C IX 122) I read as a rare prepositional use of the adverb (see MED *s.v.* 2), easily supplanted. Scan as T-type (see Appendix).

PASSUS II
28 I see Bx substn. of the commoner form of the pronoun; AC point to *heo* as the second stave.

47 Perhaps Bx substn. through stylistic objection to repeating *alle* 45.

84 Bx's line cd. allit. vocalically on *and* with C a revision to improve the metre but on balance it might seem better to emend with K-D and see *wraþe* as unconscious scribal substitution.

91 K-D's rec. *wenes* 'hopes' wd. account for *wenyngis* F, *wedynges* R (possibly split variants of ?α *wendynges*) as well as H's *wendys*. β's agreement with C establishes Bx, which may be orig.; see XV 103).

143 Bx's b-half-line is so feeble it suggests a damaged exemplar; K-D's restoration has the support of only one A-MS (most have a metrically defective line) but seems justified.

166 G's reading *feytliche* cd. be seen as corruptly reflecting a difficult orig. B *feyntly* ('deceptively', = ?A); it cd. also be a spelling variant of *feetly* 'neatly', itself closely related to *fetisly* (a revision?).

180 *lede* seems unconscious scribal substn., perh. induced by *leden* 182.

PASSUS III
10 A two-stave line; C's allit. on *m* cd. support F's *mente* as the α and perh. orig. reading, co-incidentally subst. in R by *broʒte*, to agree with β; but more probably F is intelligent correction and C a revision.

46 K-D, reading A's *baude*, see scribal censorship; but this cd. be authorial, the revision being a suggestive euphemism.

62 C's reading, here adopted after K-D, is greatly superior in precision, and cd. easily have been corrupted to the presumed Bx reading.

69 Bx looks like the substn. of a more general for a particular term, perh. to avoid repetition (*writen* 70).

75 I read this as an (awkward) two-stave line; cf. K-D, who emend.

210 Bx *to* could have come in from 211, where it appears three times.

255 K-D read *lowe lewed folk*, seeing split variation. I take *lowe* as a corruption of *lewed* and conj. an orig. archaic *ledes* replaced by *folk/men*.

296 Bx cd. theoretically be two-stave; but the rarity of the stave-word preserved in C suggests *pauiloun* as orig. B, archetypally replaced by the nearest gloss.

298 It is hard to see why orig. *ledeþ* should have been found lexically or contextually difficult, as might an orig. *lordeþ* (which cd. have suffered substitution to avoid repetition). But this is not instanced before the C16th in transitive form (cf. X 86 for intrans.).

303 No emendation is needed, since *come into* gives a 'liaisonal' key-stave (see Appendix).

319 I emend from C, keeping the Bx word-order and seeing *wole* as perh. unconscious substn.

322 Bx is perh. explained as unconscious visual error; it does not make sense as it stands.

346 I conj. *tidy* (a favourite word of Langl.) in *OED* sense 3a 'good, useful'. K-D's conj. *trewe* seems to bear an uncharacteristic sense here, and it is hard to see why it was subst. by Bx *good*.

351 F's *tale* could be correction or improvement, but it gives acceptable sense.

PASSUS IV

12 A two-stave line with extra (non-structural) stave-letter in the b-half.

21 K-D p. 107 prefer the difficult A *wytful*] *witty-wordes*; but A could have been revised precisely because it *was* difficult. K-D recognize that Bx lies behind C's *auyseth-þe-byfore*, which is possibly a further attempt at explicitness.

36 F's *leete* is of doubtful authority, but it is unusual enough to have been the original replaced archetypally by unmetrical *wol*; this is not the case with C's *hem likeþ*, which K-D (p. 181) here read. I scan the line as two-stave on *þ*.

38 I omit as plainly scribal the line following in all B-MSS; K-D elaborately reconstruct.

91 could have alliterated irregularly in AB and been finally regularized in C, which K-D (p. 205n) regard as preserving the AB orig.

145 My conjectured verbal form *Englyssed* is more likely to have generated the B-variants than the AC reading, which K-D see as orig. B, and which seems unlikely to have been corrupted. Restoration in C of an A reading may be coincidental or indicate Langland's practice of referring back to the first version of his poem.

158 K-D's conj. seems necessary if confusion with Wisdom's crooked companion Witty (27 above) is to be avoided.

PASSUS V

9 is metrically imperfect in AxBx (and perh. AB), revised in C, after which K-D emend (orig. AB *mette me* could easily have suffered substitution in both earlier archetypes through eyeskip from *seigh* 10).

23 F's reading may be no more than an independent improvement, but is prob. closer to the orig. than the manifestly corrupt Bx half-line (no **AC** evidence).

44 I have not regularized the spelling of *leuen*, which may be an attempt to play on the senses 'live' / 'believe' (*leue* appears in A-MSS WE (altered to *lyue* W, see Ka p. 274)).

47 *stewid* could be (1) the rare verb meaning 'restrain, check' [*OED* stew 1] or (2) a spelling variant of *stowed* 'placed, established (in order)'. The likelihood of a pun on sty*ward* points to (1) (cf. the sp. of A-MS R (Ka) and C-MS G (SkC)).

70 I take *hated* not as scribal substn. for **A**'s unusual expression 'to have envy of (= hate)' as do K-D but as a revision (confirmed by **C**) to avoid confusion of Pride's sin with that of Envy proper.

76 I see **A**'s difficult *co(u)pe* as having been revised to the less easily corrupted Latin formula from the general confession in the Introit of the Mass. There is no need to see this as scribal (*so* K-D p. 107).

93 K-D print hereafter two lines from **A** (V 74–5) *And blamide hym behynde his bak to brynge hym in fame | To apeire hym be my power I pursuide wel ofte* which they believe lost from the **B** orig. by homoteleuton (*ofte*). But they could have been omitted by Langl. as not adding much to the sense. **C** VI 69a may be an echo of **A**, an echo of the lines supposed lost from **B** or a re-writing of **B** V 88a, 91b.

110 *al the web*: 'the whole piece of cloth (from which the coat was cut)' (Sk).

111 ?Bx here looks typical scribal substitution of an easier reading.

124 *þe beste* (K-D *goode* after Ka) is also found in four A-MSS, which may suggest that this was the reading of Langl.'s own A-MS used for revising, and so tacitly accepted by him.

127 K-D p. 102 argue that *megre* is scribal because Envy has been described as swollen; but E's lean physique is not incompatible with his becoming swollen through emotional turmoil (*bolneth* 118 does not imply *fatness*).

149–50 The corresponding **C** lines (VII 126) have the same division.

165 K-D's highly meaningful conjectural reading restores the metre, damaged in Bx by what could have been a gloss as much as an unconscious substitution.

171 The line is also defective metrically in Cx (identical), unless we find a 'liaisonal' stave between *breed_and*; see Appendix.

174 K-D's second stave, supplied from **C** VI 158, which gives a smoother line, could be revision.

183 Here a two-stave line (?revised in **C**); original **B** could have been *wey] cause*.

194 The line is unsatisfactory in both sense and metre as it stands; possibly the original third stave in **B** was *leue þou*, the reading of A-MS W, with Bx loss of *leue* through attraction to preceding *lepe* and of *þou* to foll. *þe*.

208 K-D correct the imperfect first stave from A-MS U, which has the hard reading *prochid* 'approached, brought together', thus seeing *p* as the line-stave in both **B** and **A**. But the revised C-line alliterates unmistakably on *b*, perhaps confirming LRF's *bat*. Possibly **B** had its first stave on *b*, its second and third on *p*, an imperfection calling forth the revision in **C**. At any rate, the attestation of the verb *brochen* in **BC** argues against emending on the strength of one A-MS (possibly an attempt to correct the metre). Given such confusion, it seems best to leave **W** as it stands.

209 *pyned*, attested in A- and B-MSS, enables a witty pun (the cloth is being 'racked'); the majority variant *pynned* could be scribal smoothing, its acceptance in **C** indicating the triumph of prose clarity over poetic daring.

214 Perhaps Bx points to an original *whan so I*.

253 My conjecture, prompted by K-D's *for pure nede* (p. 196) yields a sense 'have no choice but to borrow'.

259–60 I follow K-D (pp. 188–9) in re-arranging these lines (unmetrical in Bx) to scan *aaaxy*; They divide however after *Rep.*, omitting *on þis grounde* as scribal.

266 My reconstruction perhaps accounts better for the *h*-variants than K-D's; a possible *so God fro pyne my soule hele/saue* I see as less likely to have suffered censorship than the strong oath suggested here.

268 Extra line: printed after Sk by Bn, who nonetheless queries it; I reject as spurious with K-D.

275 K-D needlessly emend *noȝt ... sooþ* to *þat I liȝe* (after **C**); with stave on *-s* the line scans normatively, or as two-stave on *l*.

277 K-D reject as spurious on insufficient grounds. The metre is correct and the line *not* a mere translation of the Latin.

282 Emendation of *goddes* to *his* provides correct alliteration (on vowels) while making the line a closer translation of 281*b* (cf. F's attempt to improve the b-half-line by adding a stave on *m*). *goddes* could be Bx scribal explicitness induced visually by *god* 284 (in the vicinity of *mercy*). K-D omit the line as spurious.

284 I conjecture the less usual form *inniddes*, lost from Bx by omission of the alliterating portion; K-D following **C** read *amyd*.

304 The omitted words look like a scribal attempt to fill out a short line, *quod he* (no doubt supplied by the WF scribes) having been probably omitted in Bx.

308 *sowestre* 'sempstress' (well-attested for **A**, less well for **C**) could be the **B** original.

310 Against AC *knaues* Bx *prentice(s)* seems scribal substitution of a term both neutral and explicit.

328 The missing line is here reconstructed from A V 176a, C VI 385b (see K-D p. 79). I presume for the second half-line in **B** the revised form found in **C**, which gives fuller sense than the vapid one in **A**. Possibly for *oon* **B** read *ooþer* (= 'one or the other'), providing a word-play on *oþes* in the a-half, but the better C-MSS read *oon*.

330 R (?representing *a*) seems to preserve (in agreement with **C**) the **B** original in a slightly corrupt form (*þe = þei, by- om*).

338 The linking of *bargayne* with *beverage* (see also the latter in *MED* s.v. (b)) suggests for the former its normal sense or even a special sense 'undertaking' (= 'bet') rather than 'contention, wrangling' (*MED s.v.* 5). *MED* cites the passage under both words but fails to note the contradictory glosses.

345 *waxed* must mean 'polished' rather than 'stopped up' here to enable the pun on *horn* (hunters' horns were polished to improve their tone; see *OED wax* v.² 1, quots.).

363 *warp* seems the harder reading, but the C evidence is difficult to construe as revision back to A. *warpe* in A-MS W (see Ka) shows an A-scribe anticipating the Bx tradition in supplying an extra stave-word through failure to scan *was* as the second stave-word. Hm's *spak* could be a happy correction; but arguably the scribal line is better poetry.

364 This corrupt line is tentatively reconstructed: C's a-half-line suggests that *wit* as well as *wif* appeared in the original B a-half, giving it one stave more than A (the evidence is the reading of LRF&c). I assume loss of *wit* in WCr¹ through the proximity of *edwyte* (Hm's *wytte* coincidentally supplanting a group original *wif*; see K-D *ad loc*) while in the LRF traditions it was *wif* that was lost. Factors facilitating the losses could have been the seemingly overloaded quality of the a-half-line and scribal judgment that either *wif* or *wit* but not both was needed as subject for *edwyte*. (For the b-half-line I do not find sufficient AC evidence to justify emending Bx, as do K-D). I believe the reconstructed a-half to contain the full sense of B, but the exact wording remains uncertain.

370 Unlike K-D I take *and halidome* on the strength of LRF&c and see C's *almyhty* as a revision of it and W's reading as simple omission.

377 Like K-D I find *dyned* unsatisfactory, but take it as Bx visual error for the bold *dyued*, with loss of *in* from *into* following misreading of the verb. F's *wente*, a verb of motion, is consonant with my conjecture, as also with K-D's *hyed* (taken from the next line, see K-D p. 182), which is however less likely to have given rise to *dyned* than is *dyued*.

378 The emended line scans on vowel-staves. The presence of C's *bifore noen* in the first half-line may point to the original B word-order, with Bx inversion of adverbial phrase and verb.

394 will scan as a double clustered line of Type IIb (*aaabb*) with a 'liaisonal' stave *d* in *quod̯ h*é (see Appendix). K-D's reading gives the sense 'I am terribly afraid lest I should meet my death today' (*sc.* because of his state of despairing sinfulness). The Bx reading makes Sloth's words an expression of further *wanhope* rather than of terror of judgement. In the *a* half-line I presume loss of *quod he* in β through the influence of *deye-day* attraction.

400 My conjectured third stave emphasizes the affirmation of Sloth that he failed not only in *satisfaction* but also in *contrition*: even though he had confessed orally, his shrift would be invalid.

406 The B-variants could be both scribal improvements of an original *fettred in*.

420 *oon* W&c is perhaps an auditory error (?from orig. *construen*), *wel* a visual error for *mel*.

441 I conj. *be* in sense 'through' (*MED be* 7), substituted archetypally by *for* through alliterative influence of *foule* and retained in C (cf. K-D's conj. *by cause of my*] *f. m.f.s.*).

456 Adoption of the well-attested (and easily corrupted) A form improves alliteration and stress.

466 The line scans *xaax* in all three archetypes or, with only one stress in the a-half, as two-stave (R's corruption appears an attempt to correct). Singlular *þee* goes better with the verbs in 465, 467 than *ʒow*.

468 The proper name seems to provide a better grammatical fit with the first person verb, and *me] þis* in ?A, C (also HmF) perhaps lends support.

469 The textual evidence favours *knowe*, but if *owe* (A-MS N, *β*; so K-D) means not 'possess' but 'owe' (cf. L's gloss *debeo*) it will seem the stronger reading.

487 The intrusive *and* Bx destroys the sense: 'God became "like" us through the Incarnation'.

488 I see W's agreement with C (?induced by *secte* 490 below) as coincidental and C probably a revision of B, here authentically preserved in Bx.

492 *liʒt* W&c, Cx seems a visual error induced from 493; *siʒt* is both harder and improves the alliteration, but could possibly be a Bx attempt to supply a stave on *s* after corruption of a possible original *som* to *a* in the b-half. For coincidental agreement of C and W cf. 488.

512 On the evidence of the A-MSS' *seke] go to* (see Ka *ad loc*) and C's *go to* I conjecture a B-original *go seke] go wiþ hem* and loss of the b-half-line attested in AC through insertion of *wiþ hem*.

603 *unrosted*: i.e. uncooked, in their natural state.

PASSUS VI

11 *sandel* 'fine silk' (Bn); 'a kind of costly fabric, app. of linen or cotton' (*MED*).

26 Bx is not patently scribal here, but the AC agreement (note however revision of C here) may indicate orig. **B** *laboure* (vb), 'improved' by the Bx scribe because it appears merely to repeat *swynke* 25.

28 K-D here read A for the b-half-line (scribally emphatic); but the latter's sense is wider than A's, which refers only to those whose ravages harm agricultural workmen, whereas Bx includes clergy and commons generally, who look to the knightly class for protection against disorder. I therefore see Bx as revision and original.

33–4 The evidence of C-MS M points to A's *conseyuede* as original **B**, a reading corrupted (mechanically or deliberately) to the easier *comsed* in four A-MSS, the other C-MSS and all surviving B-MSS (thus presum. the Bx reading). If the meaning is 'grasped' (Ka p. 446, ref. to *OED s.v.* vb. 9) then Bx *quod he* 34 should be kept; if it is 'uttered' (*MED* 8c), which I prefer, we may omit *q.h.*

37, 38, 41 The variation between singular and plural pronouns in P.'s address to the Knight may indicate an incomplete attempt at regularization to the pl. in the B-archetype, or else the variation may be non-significant and F's regularization to the sg. purely scribal.

114 *hired* Bn reads as in 312, 'paid' (*MED s.v.* (c)), *thereafter* 'accordingly'. I read *hired* in *MED* sense (a) and the adv. as temporal: those who help to sow the crop will help to harvest it (and so, also, enjoy it; cf. 119); they will surely be *paid* before then.

123 K-D emend the metrically imperfect b-half-line from C's *how þei myghte noʒt werche*. It would be easier to see *mone* as unconscious scribal substn. for *pleynt* (cf. *And pleynide hem to peris wiþ suche pitous wordis* A

VII 115). C would then be a revision to make the line alliterate perfectly on *m* and to give it more substance as well.

137 Transposition of the b-half easily transforms a 'prose line' (K-D p. 88) to a (two-stave) verse line. K-D reject for A's *þei shuln ete as good as I, so me god helpe*.

138 I propose *garisoun* as an unusual word easily liable to substitution by the unmetrical near-synonym *amendement*. Its sense is appropriate to deliverance from both sickness and imprisonment (see 136) and its form hints at possible suggestion by the original A half-line *gare hem to arise* (A VII 132).

150 K-D (p. 173) see F's unique reading as original (derived from a superior lost B-MS); but unconscious archetypal substitution of the commoner *make* for *put*, though conjectural, is easier than presuming that Bx varied from a reading not especially difficult in itself.

192 K-D, p. 210, suspect a line missing hereafter from AC evidence: *And lame menis lymes wern liþid þat tyme* (A VII 180), *And lame men he lechede with longes of bestes* (C VIII 189).

197 This line appears twice in C, (1) at VIII 197: *Tho was peers proude and potte hem alle a werke*, the a-half indicating Bx's order as present in the C-reviser's B-MS, (2) at VIII 203 *And p.w.p. þerof and potte h.a. to swynke*, directly before the line corresponding to A VII 185, B VI 198, and confirming the order found in A's a-half-line. I follow K-D in printing the form as in A and C (2). Agreement of A VII 185/C VIII 204 may indicate scribal activity in B VI 198, but the appearance for forms (1), (2) of A VII 184, B VI 197 may be a piece of evidence that in revising Langl. had before him a MS of A.

215 The very rare *abaue* must have generated the Bx *abate*, anticipated in A-MS L.

223b appears to conflate A VII 209–10 and is reflected in C VIII 233. For discussion see Russell, 'Aspects', p. 42, K-D pp. 89, 108.

249 *men w.*, echoing *wight w.* 247, may be unorig. K-D p. 85 read A's *it als*.

273 R's puzzling *morareres* may be a desperate attempt to patch up α *mor : : : eres* (= *more lieres*). That C alliterates on *l* confirms A as = B, as K-D argue.

279 Bx *Til*] AC *Er* seems an unconscious scribal substitution of a more familiar expression.

282 K-D, p. 205n, reject the metrically defective AxBx readings as scribal and find the original of both in C. This seems likely, as *hauer cake* would have seemed a more natural and so easier expression than the metrical but uncolloquial *cake of otes*.

298 *peysen* 'pacify' (*OED s.v.* pease) seems the easier reading, but could be original (K-D p. 88).

323 The omission of *yer* from several AB-MSS may be orig., as more appropriate to the tone of the prophecy. But its insertion in C and the fact that it is to be understood anyway may warrant printing it.

PASSUS VII

19 The textually secure AB reading *þe pope* looks intrinsically suspicious because the Pardon is explicitly Truth's, and even if the Pope is to be seen as Truth's agent, he can hardly send the Archangel Michael as Truth does in the letter which presumably accompanies the pardon itself. C's revision to

no treuthe may point to an original A reading with stave on *p: pardon nolde he*]
þe p. n. hem, the ambiguity of which led to scribal substitution of *pope*,
which was then retained in **B**. At any rate, the sceptical attitude to papal
pardons voiced at 173ff calls in question whether Langl. could ever have
written *pope* at 19b.

39 K-D p. 188 find the b-half-line corrupt (both A and C alliterate on *l*)
and conj. *leue þow noon ooþer* (dislocated from 45b). A reading with *l*-stave
that could have generated Bx is *þat for lucre pleteden*. The word *lucre* is
unrecorded before Chaucer and Gower *c.* 1386–90 (*MED*) but Langl. could
have known it from the Vulg. (Tit 1: 11, I Pet 5: 2) and its novelty would make
it all the more prone to substitution, with subsequent smoothing to prose order.

45b *leue þow* could be a corruption of *preve ʒe* 'you (will) find by ex-
perience [that this is so]'. K-D p. 188 emend to *pleden at þe barre* (presum. on
the basis of C IX 44b); but a judge or juror would not *plead* (*iustice* =
'counsel' is dubiously attested, MED *s.v.* 6(c), and C anyway refers to bar-
risters).

49 K-D's restoration from the A text (p. 88) is supported by C's *And for
þe loue of oure lord lawe for hem declareth*, which omits to mention *lerning*.
But C could be a simplification back towards A of an unwieldy B original,
with *ylerned haþ] h.yl.*

51 *in] and* or *he, and om* would give better readings than Bx; but I cannot
agree with K-D that A here = **B**, since no reason for the substitution appears.

59b K-D's reconstruction both derives from A's *wyten* 'know' (A VIII 61)
and explains Bx *blame* (a misunderstanding of the conjectured *wyteþ* fol-
lowed by padding and an 'explanatory' line occasioned by the misconstruc-
tion (I reject with K-D as spurious). In the reconstructed text *witeth* can still
mean 'blame'.

69 I reconstruct from the form of WLR and the order of Y&c (? = **g**) to
achieve a more likely rhythm, after K-D (*it ʒyue*).

81a Here as often in *PP* the exact form of the Biblical quotation in **B** is
obscured by the variety of MS corruption. F's version (as generally) has the
advantage of coming closest to Vulg. (cf. 138a).

95 F could agree with A against Bx, C because of correction from a
B-MS superior to C's, contamination from A, or independent coinciding
variation.

121 K-D conj. *werche] slepe* on grounds of superior sense (p. 193),
detecting 'corruption by rhyming inducement of preceding *slepen*.' But there
is no preceding *slepen*.

138a F correctly quotes Vulgate *E. derisorem & exibit cum eo iurgium
cessabitque cause & contumelie*. But Bx's agreement with A suggests that F's
correct form is scribal.

155 Apparently a revised line with two staves on *d*; cf. K-D.

166 This type of small change provides strong presumptive evidence of
Langland's propensity for revision even in the case of seemingly indifferent
particulars; cf. also 193.

171 An acceptable two-stave line as it stands (so **ABC**). The easy correc-
tion *triennals boþe* gets no support from the archetypes.

174–5 K-D punctuate as a question; I follow SkBn in reading as a state-
ment with inversion.

PASSUS VIII

Title After *Visione* R has *Petri Plowman. Incipit Dowel, Dobet & Dobest.*
L's marginal note *Ps viijus de visione, & hic explicit, & incipit inquisicio prima de dowel* points to scribal understanding of a major division in the poem at this point; but it is impossible to be sure how much of the titles and colophons is to be regarded as original. Certainly the connective *Thus* at the beginning of Passus VIII argues against making too sharp a break.

18 The Bx line is not suspect in itself but becomes so in the light of F, A and C. It seems an unquestionable instance of F's preserving the correct reading of B against the rest (including R), through contamination from A or C or, less probably, through correction from a MS superior to Bx at some points (perhaps one itself corrected at these points; see on MS F K-D pp. 165–72). The Bx error could have arisen through censorship of the oath and subsequent transposition of the third stave-word to first position. The presence of the new asseveration word in first position in the re-written C line here supports acceptance of F as original B and not—as it otherwise might seem— a mere borrowed A or C reading.

23 K-D, p. 109, emend the whole b-half on dubious grounds, replacing Bx by A. But arguably the greater explicitness of Bx is more in keeping with the syllogistic flavour of the speech than the anacoluthon of A. The presence of *certes* in C (X 25b) perhaps suggests approval by the revising poet (and so possible originality, though the exact form of B is undeterminable).

34 is awkward to translate, since the last phrase seems to refer back to *is*, though a more appropriate sense would be 'and so he cannot help doing [i.e. moving, to carry out his steering]'—*so* referring back to *meve* 33.

35 *rau3te* looks like the preterite of *rechen*, but the sequence of verbs (*arise*, and *wolde* in the apodosis 36) would seem to require a present (a verb *raught* is recorded from the late C16th, modelled after the preterite form).

43, 45 In these F, A agreements it is possible that the F-scribe or a predecessor compared an A-text with his B-exemplar; cf. 18 above and 81, 102, 103 and (*C*) below.

50 The omitted line could be a borrowing from A by F with characteristic sophistication, or a correction from a superior B-MS. The sense does not strictly require it; but this fact may also account for its unconscious omission in Bx. The original form of the line can only be conjectured. *fowle* seems a scribal intensifier and *þere* an addition typical of F. K-D print A.

62 The Bx b-half looks suspicious in the light of F, which is close to AC. C could represent a reversion to A, with all this might imply for the evidential value of AC agreements against a supposedly erroneous Bx. F's variant may be 'creative correction' on the basis of an A- or C-MS; but its tone goes better with the delicate irony of 58–9 than the heavy obviousness of the Bx reading.

70 The absence of C-evidence makes determination of originality difficult here. A's rare *dri3t* could easily have suffered substitution in Bx by the easier *wi3t*, with subsequent insertion of a new stave-word replacing *doute* and so ruining the metre. F's line is a clever attempt to correct Bx and does not look original.

81 F's line, corresponding to A IX 71, could be borrowed from an A-MS.

K-D's view that it was present in **B** has no C-evidence to support it (cf. K-D p. 171, C X 79).

87 K-D, p. 109, object to the 'inferior doctrine' of Bx and reject for **A**'s *Whiles he haþ ouȝt of his owene he helpiþ þere nede is* (*And helpeth alle men of þat he may spare* C X 84). But **C** is not a reversion to **A** and need not point to corruption in Bx (K-D do not explain why such corruption should have arisen). I read Bx therefore as revision of **A**, itself revised in **C**.

93 Perhaps Langl. originally wrote *sufferte* (imperative), as several A-MSS read (cf. 93).

96 A crosier, not a cross, seems clearly intended as the bishop's symbol of authority.

100 The line just scans as it stands; possibly **B** read *ordeyned hem amonges*.

101–10 show much disordering with omissions in RF: 104 om RF (= α), 100–1 om F, 101b–7a om R. F's divergences from R probably represent attempts to correct errors coming from α.

102 C X 101 is slight evidence that the F, A line after 102 was in **B**. But it could have been borrowed by F from **A**: it is lacking in A-MSS VA, and if Langl. revised from an A-MS lacking the line, he could have omitted it in **B**. Indeed, he could have done so deliberately, since it adds little to the sense of 102. The C 'evidence' could be due to revision at C X 100.

106b in F could show contamination from **A**. That 107b repeats the sense of the original **A** IX 98 would account for the latter's revision in **B** to a form not tautologous but recapitulatory.

107 Bx, C agreement might support a view of F as a borrowing from **A** to correct a metrically defective line in the immediate B-exemplar. My tentative reconstruction rests on the possibility that loss of original *rede* was induced by homoarchy from *reme* and *thre* caught up from the next line (C's revised line scans as two-stave, on vowels, the b-half incorporating Bx).

112b It is hard to see how **B**, if F preserves it, could have been corrupted to Bx, in which case Bx is original here and F's reading almost certainly derived from **A**, with characteristic alteration of *erþe* to the more poetic *molde*. The implications of this striking instance of A-contamination in F for F's supposed textual value are not considered by K-D, who here accept Bx.

114 F, C agreement could be fortuitous or reflect contamination from a C-MS rather than preserving by correction the true **B** reading. Bx scans adequately as two-stave and agrees with Ax, but the strong likelihood of *noot*] *woot* corruption lends support to A-MS V as representing the AB originals corrupted in AxBx respectively.

127 C's *teche* appears harder than the A/B variants with *hym* and so more probably original, Bx having supplied the pronoun in prose position, perhaps through auditory error. However, *hym* could have been lost mechanically from the A-MSS which lack it. Perhaps we should place the semi-colon after *wite* instead of *teche* and read 128 without *And* as does F.

PASSUS IX

15 K-D propose *boldeþ* for unmetrical Bx *ruleþ* on the basis of a line not found in the Ax tradition but preserved in A-MS J: *Dobest is in hire bowre & boldyth þat leuedy* (after **A** X 13; see Ka p. 49). This is slender evidence, but in the absence of better conjecture could be accepted, *ruleþ* then appearing as Bx 'improvement' on a (not entirely appropriate) use of *boldeþ*. Other possiblities for the third stave are *buldeþ* 'edifies' (*MED s.v.* 4a) or *biddeþ* 'directs' (*MED s.v.* 4b), here used absolutely. Both seem appropriate to a bishop and the latter could have been easily supplanted by a more familiar near-synonym. It also provides a characteristic wordplay with *bit*; accordingly I adopt it. *Dobest*] *he*, also possible, would allow *ruleþ* to be kept. (The line is lacking in Ax, C, and A-MS J, which here follows with another line (see Ka p. 49), may not be original at this point).

23 Conflicting evidence from AC makes it hard to determine **B** here. If F's agreement with A is due to contamination, Bx's *to* may be seen as corruption of **B** *for to* (so C) or as an imperfect original later corrected by C (without *for* Bx scans *aaxy* on *f*/*þ*; cf. K-D).

26–7 K-D read A's *beestes*] *þynges* Bx, C and *þe first of alle þynges* A] *of . . . maked* Bx, *of . . . forth groweth* C (p. 110). But Bx is not metrically defective (*of al* is a 'liaisonal' stave) and is doctrinally superior to A, and hence a probable revision. God's creative power need not be limited to animals, and to call him creator of all *again* is not merely to repeat but to emphasize a point in danger of being lost in A (which is itself near-heretical in calling God 'first of all *things*'). F, though sharing the word *þing* with A is actually much closer in meaning to Bx. In the light of C, a possible **B** original easily corrupted to the F, Bx forms is *of al þat on erþe groweþ*. In Bx *euere* could be caught up from *neuere* 28. The line scans better without it.

31 Bx *shafte* is the harder reading in itself, but CrC both agree more closely with Ax and correspond better to *of membres and of face* C which stresses man's physical resemblance to God (seen in post-incarnational terms) as against his inner, spiritual likeness (*shafte* = nature, creation). In favour of *shafte* is its appearance at XIII 296, *q.v.*

32 *spak* is easier than *warp* and so possibly scribal here (though Bx still scans either as two-stave on *w* or normatively on *f*/*þ*). But cf. V 86, 363 (C) above for discussion of *spak*/*warp*.

32–3 K-D p. 171 restore from F, A the supposedly lost line in A's form *And al at his wil was wrouȝt wiþ a speche* (A X 34). But F's line could come by contamination from A. Lines 33–45 reveal extensive revision and expansion, and 33 can be seen as the beginning of this rather than as scribal smoothing after omission of a line. Nonetheless, I conjecture on F, A evidence *Ac he*] *And* as giving superior sense and repair the metre by reading *likkest* as unconscious substitution for *moost lik* or as an attempt to avoid repeating 31.

38 I conjecture *no* omitted through visual attraction to *no . . . p.* 39 and reconstruct on different lines from K-D (*q.v.* p. 188) but with the same aim, to recover a text in which only one of the three 'elements necessary for writing' is absent. I opt for *penne* as corresponding more closely to God's *miȝt* than *parchemyn*, as in K-D's reconstruction, p. 188, *q.v.*

41 K-D reconstruct (p. 189) to retain *by hym* and omit *as . . . telleþ*. I follow them in reading the Latin from F against the plainly erroneous Bx. The evidence for corruption is the faulty metre.

67–8 K-D, p. 174, undertake major reconstruction on A/C evidence. But Bx reads as characteristically Langlandian with its play on *fynden* 'read', 'provide' and *fauten*/-*eth*. They argue plausibly that *fauntes* was omitted from first-stave position in 67 (probably through attraction to fau*ten*) but equally this could be due to its inclusion under the phrase *faderlese children* in 68 (**C**, which lacks that phrase, can be read as a reversion to **A**).

77 I conjecture for the metre *preve*, a verb slightly unusual but of highly apt meaning. K-D's *purchace* is possible but seems mechanically and semantically less likely; vocalic scansion is possible.

87 could be an awkward two-stave line; but the prose order of Bx directs transposition for the sake of the metre. K-D read *ne wol*] *nel* with HmBR, but the stave-letter seems to be *k*.

88 K-D, p. 199, conj. *So*] *As, shul*] *that* on grounds of defective metre. But scanned vocalically the line reads scarcely more awkwardly than theirs and stresses two key-words *oure, us*.

91 I accept with modification K-D's conj. and see loss of first stave through ju-*gged*/*Judas* attraction.

96 K-D (pp. 147–8) read after RF and state (wrongly) on p. 184 that both RF and WL&c fail to scan normatively. But WL scan so on *f/v*, or as two-stave on *d*, making their emendation to a repetitive and overloaded line otiose.

98a *verbo* αL, though incorrect, could be original here.

108 An example of scribal disarrangement of an entire line towards prose order (see K-D p. 194).

111 *clerkes* fits well in a list of what are surely honorific ranks of society.

121 K-D, p. 89, read *cursed*] *yuel* after **A** (cf. **C** X 213), but wrongly scan Bx as *axay*, whereas it will scan vocalically. *yuel* could indeed have been caught up from 123 below, but the evidence of revision in the order of the first two words should give us pause in emending. Note that F's *Are con.*] *Con. b.* Bx, *Ben c.* **A** again suggests contamination from an A-MS. The A line after 121, which K-D see as omitted from Bx through preoccupation with the following rubric, re-appears in **C** with revised b-half. But A X 142–8 have been omitted in the process of revision to **B**, and the line in question, immediately preceding, forms syntactically a part of this, so that its restoration in **C** could be through reversion to the A-text.

122a The Latin line occurs in the WL form in various A/C MSS; it is hard to discern the original between the correct and incorrect forms.

124 The B- and some A-MSS attest *Seem* meaning Seth son of Adam (Gen 5: 3–8) but confused with Sem son of Noah (Gen 5: 31). Some A-MSS correct to Seth (so **C**) but Bx *Se(e)m* may be original.

163 K-D's conj. (p. 205) requires a sense not recorded before the C16th but one more appropriate than 'submissive' (rec. C14th). The word's rarity would account for the substitution.

166 The sense in Bx is acceptable, but the order probably scribal on A/C evidence.

179 I scan as a two-stave line, revised in **C** because perhaps ambiguous ('secular' vs. 'regular').

188 **B** is uncertain, though the A/C *l*-phrases, with legal sense, support rejection of Bx as scribal explicitness prompted by failure to grasp sense. Langl.'s point seems to be that as well as freedom from canonical sin a couple must have the right spiritual attitude (mutual love) and be married without impediment if intercourse is to be pleasing to God. A X 206–8 is plainer.

PASSUS X

19 K-D p. 110 see A's *construe*] *contr*. rightly as the harder reading. But Bx may represent an original revision (cf. C) precisely to avoid the ambiguity (*construe* also = 'interpret').

21 The plural seems certain from AC and *Thei* 22. I retain the sg. *kan* as probably original (so C).

50 M's *glee* looks like a felicitous independent correction; *game* would account for Bx *murþe*.

57 K-D, p. 102, read *g. in* 'bite persistently in' arguing that *g. wiþ* is nonsensical (pp. 102–3); Stanley (pp. 445–6) gives reasons for accepting Sk's interpretation 'defame [God] with their words', drawing attention to X 66 below. If A originally meant what K-D claim, BC may indicate an unwillingness on Langl.'s part to press it.

60 A's sense ' take him in ' is repeated in C's *haue hym yn*, but Bx may be a B revision, *nym* bearing the rarer sense ' betake oneself, go ' (*OED s.v.* 2). The cruelty is thus emphasized still further. But as Langl. probably had in mind Is 58: 7 (*q.v.*), the source of 84*a* below also, AC may be right.

61 *hunsen*, the presumed unusual B form of *honiss[h]en*, easily explains corruption to *hunten*, less easily to *hoen/heon*, itself probably the archetypal reading (and, possibly, an original B revision), of which w, the group ancestor of WHmCr, is a deliberate correction fortuitously formed like an easy corruption of *hunsen*.

69 *opere kynnes* could be a revision, though a weak one, of A *kete* 'keen, acute' here (Sk p. 238) and C a later attempt to give it a more exact meaning.

73 The natural sense of the idiom (see *MED s.v.* 2a) would give 'because of pure ill-will *towards* the clergy'; but the friars themselves are clerks, so another possibility is 'out of sheer clerkly [i.e. intellectual] malice [*sc.* against the unlearned, the "simple faithful"]'.

78–9 Omission from β through censorship is an interesting possibility. In 78b F's agreement with C could be by contamination or coincidence: R is bold enough to have invited revision; it does not look scribal. In 79 C's *oure* would seem preferable if the original point was that children (like the 'good men' in C) became victims of God's wrath in the plague because of the sins of their parents. But it could be a revision, the original meaning 'so great was God's wrath that he destroyed the children for their sins [however slight these were, a sign that his anger against *us* is great indeed]'. The rare verb *forgrynt* (presum. = 'grinds to nothing') is not recorded in *OED* or *MED*. Conceivably R is original in omitting *noght*, if we read *deyneth* as short for *dedeyneth* 'disdains' (cf. C-MSS SK at XI 61).

86 *ledes* C is harder than *londes* Bx, but the reading of B, unless a purely coincidental variation towards the set phrase (see *MED lede* n. (2), 2(a)), may point to the original, from which the *ledes* component was lost by visual error in Bx and the *londes* component deliberately in the revision to C.

90 My conjecture supplies a two-stave line, but is directed by the revised C-line *Yf þow haue lytel, leue sone, loke by þy lyue* (C XI 74).

108 *wye* A (varied to *man* in many A-MSS) provides the key to the missing stave-word (on *w*) and so prompts the emendation K-D offer (pp. 89, 205, also Ka p. 156); for *biwile* cf. *SGGK* 2425.

110 *deeþ*, possibly a revision, could be a marginal or supralinear gloss misread as a correction.

129 *β*'s grammar is smoother, but *α*, A suggest the awkwardness was original: Study is finishing one thought and moving abruptly to another.

131 The tricks are those of the hunted fox, who doubles back to throw off his pursuers (cf. *SGGK* 1708, vb.). I conjecture for the metre *ablende* (found in XVIII 137), giving a more satisfactory stress-pattern than K-D's *for to* (p. 196), on *þ/f*.

139 F and C² (here visibly corrected) could show contamination from A at this point; but they agree with W&r, C in reading *loke* 138 (*mele* A), *loute* 144 (*knele* A), so correction from a superior B-MS here seems intrinsically more likely.

171 Possibly B read *bibles*, mistakenly glossed *bokes* at an early archetypal stage and then further corrupted in Bx (>W&r).

173 Transposition to *opere l. m.* would restore the metre, but the AC evidence points to deeper corruption, perhaps induced by *alle* 174.

186 Absence of the line from C could indicate its corruption and authorize restoration of the A line (so K-D). I see C as further revision and explain Bx's form by conjecturing loss of *that . . . ther* (found in A as the second stave-phrase) through eyeskip to the line-end, which contained the unusual *leþi* (posited as a genuine revision of A's less exact *lewed*). My reconstruction retains A's sense and accounts for Bx's form.

190 AC alliterate on *d* and *here doctour is dere loue* C XII 136b points to a word like *scole* A, *kynne* Bx being a scribal substitution of a commoner expression. I conjecture *kennyng* (*MED s.v.* sense *b*) 'training, discipline' (cf. sense *a* in 194 below) as supplying the needed meaning and readily accounting for Bx's corruption.

197 K-D needlessly reject *bidde for* as scribal substitution of an easier reading for A's *blissen*. But the play on the senses of *biddeth/bidde for* seems characteristically Langlandian revision.

209 A includes astronomy (= astrology) under sorcery, an apter reading than Bx's, which is a slip or officious 'correction'; the metre is improved if only unvoiced *þ* is stave.

210 W's plural is more logical but probably scribal; Langl. probably regarded all three as one 'science' characterized by proneness to sinister uses.

211 K-D see Bx 211 as run together with 212 and reconstruct from 211b on the basis of A XI 160–1: *. . . of Albertes makynge, | Nigromancie and perimancie þe pouke to raise.* Confusion will have come into Bx from miscopying *makynge* for *wittes* in 211, followed by re-writing of 212b (with tell-tale imperfect metre). On the other hand, Langl. may have chosen to excise his criticism of Albertus Magnus (which had no foundation in fact) and also to delete the reference to black magic as imprudent. The new 212 is now two-stave. A further piece of evidence that the censorship may be scribal rather than authorial is that 212b anticipates 215b. On balance, the argument for reconstruction seems to me indecisive here.

224 K-D prefer A's illogical *heuene*; but *worlde* looks unmistakably like a revision.

240 The suspect Bx metre leads K-D to conjecture, in the absence of any

AC evidence, and while discussing other possibilities, p. 201, an omitted stave *and his make* after *man*. But the line is contrasting human and non-human, not male, female and non-human. Following their search for 'the least violent' emendation, I conjecture *animales*, a rare word at this time, but therefore all the more liable to substitution (see *OED*'s example from Trevisa's *Barth. c.* 1398: '*Animall*, a beest'). *boþe* could be Bx substitution for *als* induced by loss of the latter through assimilation to *animal*es and eyeskip to *boþe* 239, bo*kes* 241 in end-position. But it can be defended stylistically as different in meaning from 239.

244 I conjecture a needed stave and see β (? = Bx) as perhaps deriving from a marginal gloss (of pre-Bx origin?) mistaken for a correction.

246 *lewed* reads badly, since the sense is surely that *all* need faith to be saved. The group reading *men* may reflect a Bx *ledes* corrupted in the other MSS (perhaps by inducement from the implied contrast with *clerkes* 245).

247 Sk (IV, i. p. 247) translates *dispute* as 'dispute against', a sense attested though less common than 'expound, maintain, defend (by reasoning)' (see *MED s.v.*). It requires a subtle intellect to argue for rather than against faith.

249 I conjecture a word needed for metre and sense: the second of the three states or ways is being described in order (256 shows the parallelism); cf. *sithen* 361.

270 will scan vocalically (if awkwardly) on *If, a-, a-*.

272 I see Bx as unconscious substitution destroying a needed stave-word. K-D's conj. *wis*] *lered* is more drastic.

289–300 correspond to A XI 204–10 and form a major piece of evidence for the existence of α, the exclusive common ancestor of RF. They are omitted from β, the exclusive common ancestor of W&r, but their appearance in C V 147–55 points to their existence in **B**, since C reproduces (153–5) the lines in praise of monasteries and universities which appear in RF but not in A. K-D pp. 63–9 discuss the relation between RF and W&r and conclude against the earlier view of some scholars (p. 64n) that one or other family represents an earlier or later stage of *PP* in the process of revision from A to **B** or from **B** to C. Instead 'the distinctiveness of W[&r] and RF with respect to content is a matter of loss rather than insertion of lines and passages'.

295 I accept K-D's dismissal of the following α line as spurious (p. 193). Though metrically correct, it expands *strueþ* (the last word in the corresponding A line) so as to destroy the metre in 295 preceding (> *axaa*). The line-division as in A is confirmed by C. The unusual *roileþ* (see *OED s.v.* and Sk's note, IV, i, 94) is presumably the original of *rolleth*, which means much the same. C's *roteth*, replacing a word liable to corruption, seems influenced by the meaning of *strueþ* following. In theory, both the line's omission from C and its addition to A could be due to revision, but its over-emphasis renders it suspect. Such spurious lines are much commoner in F than in α.

299 K-D's conj. presupposes corruption in Bx, Cx; but to deny the existence of *chide* in the C original where revision has occurred we must posit a substitution for *carpe* (or *querele*, say) by *chide* at the Cx stage (coinciding with the Bx error), possibly even contamination from a corrupt B-MS. Alternatively, Langl. could have tolerated an imperfect line on occasion (thus 298 preceding is imperfect unless we scan on *k* or awkwardly on vowels; cf. also below).

301 could scan vocalically, or *clerk* could be a Bx substitution for *scolere* (cf. *Wars of Alexander* 641, *Purity* 1554).

302 K-D p. 179 rightly suspect the pointless repetition of Bx *loueþ* and reconstruct after C's a-half-line. In support of *lereþ* is C's b-half-line *and lykyng to lerne* (V 156) which adduces the notion of 'learning' as a cause of not 'fighting'.

305 K-D p. 93 see Bx's first *manere* as substitution of an easier expression. But possibly Langland did not solve the metrical problem till C: Bx's *aabb* scansion is paralleled in A's XI 213 *fro toune to toune.* C introduces a distinction without a difference, for the metre.

319 I suggest as the needed verb *biyeten* 'acquire possession of' (*MED s.v.* 1(a)), easily lost by visual inducement from *beten* 318a preceding.

321 I here propose the prose order as original, since it restores the metre.

322 K-D's conj. is brilliant but more radical than the visual error, with subsequent corruption of the verb, that I posit; *Greǵories* is possible.

342 K-D reject *by . . . b.* for A's *pistil þat peter is nempnid.* The Latin supporting A XI 234 is not from St Peter's epistles but from Mk 16: 16. Langl. may have realized his error and decided to refer generally to the Apostles' teaching on baptism (I Pet 3: 21, Eph 5: 26–7 &c).

346 A's is much the harder reading here; but C² could be contaminated from an A-MS.

348 Again, A is harder; but Langl. could have thought its sense too strong theologically and have toned it down; cf. his attitude to the Good Thief's rank in heaven.

364 Various MSS correct (to *necabis* &c), but the mistake seems likely to be authorial, as A reads *mecaberis* (see the Vulgate Luke).

365 Prompted by K-D's conj. I suggest that *also* lost its stave sound through unconscious influence from the common phrase *al for the b.*

419 Bx's metre is just acceptable; but CA agreement points to anti-feminism in Bx.

422 *Muche* looks scribal: the point is *that* the (future) Apostle Paul killed Christians, not how many he killed. The tight brevity of the line may have invited expansion.

423 Bx's two-stave pattern looks original in the light of A XI 291 (two-stave, and cf. *þise* in 292); C, retaining *þese*, adds a stave to normalize. K-D's *swiche*, p. 195, is not necessary.

439–40 Bx is certainly corrupt here. On the evidence of C XII 275–6 *And fonde y neuere in faith for to telle treuthe* / *That* . . . I follow K-D in restoring from A, though there is no evidence to show whether B was closer to A or to C.

444–5 look corrupt and more than one reconstruction is possible in the light of C. In the uncertainty, I conjecture *with*] *and* for the needed stave and re-divide for the style.

455 K-D p. 86 read A's *kete* for *konnynge*; but revision is likely (a) because *kete* was obscure and (b) to obtain a play on the senses 'know-ledgeable', 'clever' through closeness to *konne.*

464 There is no real tautology if we read the two verbs as meaning respectively 'learnt' and 'knew', and so no need to emend. The clerks look back to the time when they knew no more than the *lewed*.

469 An easier emendation than K-D's is *ledes*; but the line will scan as two-stave.

41 Most C-MSS confirm β, but α is much harder and easily corrupted. W's *þiselue* appears in many C-MSS (C XI 309) but the line in its W form is suspiciously overweighted.

49 I modify K-D's reconstruction (p. 187), seeing *if* as corruption of *of* through misinterpreting the grammar of original *leste*, but retaining *ouȝt*.

60 K-D (p. 111) conj. *foryede*, not finding the required sense of *foryat* supported by the exx. in *MED*; but see *s.v.* vb. 4(c).

86 The position of Bx *quod I* looks suspicious as it gives an a-half-line with a seven-syllable dip before the first stave. I suggest either that it is unoriginal or that it belongs after the second stave (on *m*).

87a Langl.'s plural *fratres* enables a glancing blow at the friars; 90*a* gets the quot. right.

103 I read the first stave on *neuére*, with wrenched stress. FHm look like scribal attempts to supply a voiced fricative, as in some C-MSS likewise.

106 G's *looue* may be the hardest reading and most Langlandian in its chime with *loue* and *laude* suggested by the following Lat. *lauda*.

121 RF's arrestingly concrete *saue* is an ambiguous form of *salue* (cf. XX 370), corrupted to *safly* in the larger group, to the abstract *sauere* in some C-MSS (so K-D); cf. also 217.

141–2 Cr, C avoid the abrupt shift to direct speech in 143a of Bx. Cr was corrected from either a B-MS better (at this point) than Bx or from a C-MS (in which case Bx, however awkward, could be original).

148–9 K-D's elaborate reconstruction here is unnecessary; simple re-division will suffice.

181–3 I follow K-D in reading from F here for its manifestly superior sense but reject their reconstruction (p. 188). F's singular is more natural after *ech* 180 and scansion on the very appropriately stressed *His, hym, hise / enemyes* renders their conj. *euenecristene*] *neyȝhebore* otiose.

196 K-D reconstruct *Alle myȝte god haue maad riche men if he wolde*. I reason to original α by identifying loss of *myȝte* in R and *Almiȝty* in F (split variation). In favour of retaining *Almiȝty* is its appropriateness to the sense: God *could* have done this, being all-powerful.

216–17 The majority *commune* 216 furnishes a characteristic *adnominatio* (cf. *sauen/saluen*) with slightly stretched meaning 'publicly', 'openly' (so *MED s.v.* 11 (e)). This would make G (cf. Y) an inaccurate expansion from the exemplar, not correction from a superior MS. *saluen* was no doubt suggested by 'Fides tua te *salvam* fecit' (Lk 7: 50).

251 I reconstruct from C, seeing F's *fulfylde* as sophisticated and R as having varied with W&r through visual error (attraction of *ful* to *wed*, easily visible in the text on either side of the brackets) with loss of *wel* being accomplished through attraction of preceding *wille* and the whole corruption perhaps activated by the over-weighted quality of the half-line.

281 ? α *wise* gives correct metre but less good sense than β, which seems echoed in C XIII 100. Possibly *siluer* is Bx substitution for *paiement* or *pitaunce*; to avoid conjecture I follow K-D.

299–302 K-D p. 114 elaborately reconstruct, rejecting 301–2 as spurious. 302 scans as two-stave, though possibly *mansed pr.* was the second stave (cf. *luther lyvynge* C XIII 116). In 301 the emphatic explicitness *could* be authorial. 298–9 K-D rej. as 'untranslatable as they stand'. I have translated them and find them easier to translate than their emended lines (*q.v.*). (K-D's discussion here, though ingenious, illustrates the danger of assuming that Langl. always wrote at the top of his bent). For an echo of the phrasing of 301 (perhaps supporting its authenticity) cf. C XIII 186a.

324 K-D's brilliant conj. is supported by the **AB** variants to VIII 29 and a supralinear gloss would explain the substitution. But the line will scan vocalically as two-stave (cf. 302).

337–9 K-D p. 90 see *riȝt þer* 337 as visual error for *reste þei* C. But the situation may be more complex. C XIII 146 *As when þei hadde roteyed; anon they resten after* is itself two-stave and may represent Cx corruption of orig. *anonriȝt] anon*, itself retained from **B**. The idea of resting could then be a C revision designed to tighten up the line, *ruteyed* having given the whole sense of B *ryde . . . tyme*. For 338–9 K-D offer a bold and brilliant conjecture that **BC** *mornyng* adj. (so Hm) was misunderstood in both Bx and Cx stages as a noun, generating in Bx a line suspicious because of defective metre and sense. I see the B-variants as more easily generated if **B** read *a-mornyng* (= *on* + gerund). In the apparent absence of any worthwhile B-evidence, 339 is impossible to reconstruct, so I follow K-D in reading C XIII 148.

343 K-D p. 173 adopt F's *saue man oone* (cf. C XIII 153a *Saue man and his make*). I suspect possible contamination from C or else independent substitution to emend the exemplar's defective metre. While we cannot rule out a two-stave line in Bx with play on two senses of *wiþ*, it seems likelier that *mid* was replaced by its commoner synonym through presence of the latter in 343a.

352–3 K-D transpose, and emend *And* to *manye*. But 353 could scan vocalically *aaabb/xy* or, more likely, *aaax*, with *þei* Bx for *hy* **B**.

370 Reconstruction from C is unsatisfactory in the absence of **B** evidence, but Bx must be corrupt.

372 *quod I* is intrusive and looks scribal; C revises this two-stave line (cf. 355 above).

376 K-D rej. *it*; but Reson seems to be saying, '*You* put things right *if* you can (but you can't)!'

388 I see R's *to &c* as padding of a short line, F's *lakles* as caught up from 389. C's revised line has different sense and metre.

406ff K-D reject 406–7, 409 and read after C. But C's extensive revision in XIII 217–21 need not indicate Bx corruption, only a desire to strengthen lines thought weak in sense and to replace the proclaimed certainty of **B** with an attitude of greater tentativeness. *sherewede* (cf. XIII 330) I conjecture as a possible stronger term liable to substitution by a milder one.

430 I conj. omission of a small needed stave-word, easily lost in this construction (see *doute* n. in *MED*) in preference to K-D's *nede] doute* (p. 198).

435 On the strength of C I discriminate α as Bx, shortened in β.

438–9 are thoroughly revised in C, which K-D read in place of Bx (p. 93). I cannot see why C's equivalent to 438b *and reuerensed hym fayre*, with its implied verb of 'asking' generating the indirect question of 439, should have been corrupted to a verb of motion (*folwed*). I see the latter as replacing an original verb of motion with appropriate sense and stave-letter (though rare it is recorded in *OED, reach v.* 15). (An awkward vocalic scansion is also possible). I accept with K-D that 439 is a prose line and reconstruct from C's *And yf his wille were, a wolde his name telle*. This is unsatisfactory, but the shape of the C line makes a closer approximation to the likely **B** original hard to arrive at.

PASSUS XII

60 I conjecture *gomes* as the needed stave-word lost through scribal absorption in the idea of humility. Another possibility is *goode lowe*, since 61–2 make plain that it is not merely the poor but the virtuous poor, the poor in spirit, patient poor or humble that Langl. has in mind.

127 On the basis of C²'s *kynge*] *kn.* K-D conj. a third stave *kyng ne* (easily lost through homoearchy; see also *ky-* in 128). Also possible is *no kyn kn.*, but on the basis of *comeþ* 128 I conj. a first stave *Com*, lost through unconscious influence of the easier expression.

129–30 I reconstruct to preserve Bx as far as possible, conjecturing a needed stave in the dental of *oft* of 130 (easily lost through homoeoarchy *oft* > < *of d* . . .). K-D p. 199 reject *and . . . dec.* as scribal expansion; but C XIV 80b points to an antithesis-pattern in the B-original which K-D's reading destroys. Langl. seems to conceive *kynde wit* as learning from error also.

131 K-D p. 115 needlessly reconstruct as *Dyuyneris toforn us viseden and markeden.* The staves they fail to find in Bx are on *us, use-* and *Olde* may be conjectured as supplying the appropriate word for defining the *lyueris*— the men of pagan antiquity 'repreved' by the Christian Fathers (137). K-D's two verbs say virtually the same (see *OED visen v.*) and *Dyuyneris* in any case is forced: it is not augury but observation, developing into empirical science, that Langl. has in mind.

162 K-D p. 179 conj. *sadder*] *sik.* in view of *heuegore* C. But *sik.* 'in a safer position' is hardly worse sense than *sadder, heuegore*, although all three may be thought rather weak.

163 scans as either two-stave on *k* or normatively on vowels. K-D's adoption of F's *can*] *haþ* Bx, C (from a grossly sophisticated F line) gives a strange and unidiomatic phrase.

194–5 W looks like an intelligent scribal attempt to correct the metre and grammar of Bx. I retain W's stave word and read the rest from L in the absence of sufficient evidence to reconstruct the original. The revised C XIV 134 may point to *gracious* as the lost stave word. K-D's conj. *graiþ is hem euere* (p. 202) is very plausible. Lack of α here is a great handicap.

204 The line will scan on *ne*; C could be revision to bring the stresses onto words of higher semantic rank.

211 The C-text is itself uncertain (*of þe þeef/þat thef*) but supports K-D's powerful reconstruction, which convincingly accounts for the B-text variants.

246 The pun on *tail* links the rich with the peacocks encumbered by their long tails (cf. 249). K-D p. 202 unaccountably reject this for a pun on *taille* ('account', 'reversion') to which they emend after LR (p. 201), reading accordingly *is al of*] *of alle is*. The sense runs, 'the end of the rich / the account they must make to God at their judgement is an entirely miserable one.'

271 The sense of Bx '[intellect to those] who teach us to be saved, means to instruct us therewith' is possible, but C's *wenen* 'hope, think to' suggests that *wissen* (2) is a corruption of *wisshen*, with *weyes* a corruption of an original perhaps spelt *w[e]yʒes*.

289 K-D p. 209 ingeniously reconstruct BxCx *And wh. it w. of truþe or n.*, *þe worþ of bileue is gret*, finding the former's sense 'obscure' and interpreting the latter 'And the intrinsic value of faith is great, whether it actually comes to be faith in the true religion or not.' But the archetypes' syntax is no more awkward than K-D's, and the meaning given is straightforward and clear (see Skeat's and the footnote translation). It is impossible to believe that a medieval Christian could have easily maintained the view K-D attribute to Imaginatif, since faith was seen as a divine gift and so must be, if only implicitly, faith in the true religion.

PASSUS XIII

16 A two-stave line on *l* Bx; possibly the original alliterated on vowels, with archetypal corruption of *animales* 'living creatures' to *bestes*, caught up from 15 (cf. C's *vch a lyf*).

25 My conjecture is a relatively unusual word more likely to have been substituted by *seiʒ* than K-D's proposed *mette* (after C XV 31, which I take as a revision).

40 K-D pp. 179–80 ingeniously reconstruct *of þise men . . . eet*] *ne his man . . . eten*, which leaves unexplained the pl. *þei, hir* (42, 43), which they nonetheless print while denying the existence of the Doctor's 'man'! Langl.'s contrast is between 'merely nourishing meat' (*flessh*) and 'tasty, elaborately cooked dishes' (*mortrews* &c).

49 I retain *Dia* as a possible original pun on the sense 'potion' (cf. XX 174).

79 According to K-D the minority but original C reading is harder and gives better sense than the majority B/C reading (α is seen as partly preserving B but corrupting *compacience* with β). But the Bx ?Cx agreement on *to P.* is striking, and paradoxically *comp.* may be brilliant scribal improvement, α's apparent agreement with part of the minority C-reading (*and*] *he*) being explainable as a group misreading of the syntax of 78–9. The line is a serious crux.

94 *frayel* Bx seems a misreading induced by the food references (such baskets held figs &c). *leef* 95 implies that the *forel* (box) contained a *book* with an account of friars' eating-habits favourable to the gluttonous Doctor.

120 Adopting *hem* with K-D makes Cl.'s seven sons the learners—they are teaching themselves—not the teachers of Life (the majority agree with W's *sense*). The speech is somewhat dark.

138 I conjecture loss of a third stave *do* through attraction to preceding *Do*.

152 K-D's brilliant emendation adequately accounts for the puzzling variants and provides a suitably potent meaning at the heart of this riddle:

the sacramental body of Christ as the supreme symbol of *kynde loue* and essential Dowel.

170 Elliptical, if we read R as meaning 'inasmuch as they recognize you as the best governor.'

194–5 Perhaps to be divided after *box*, with *salue* as stave in the next line.

283 *pope holy:* 'pretending to great holiness ... sanctimonious, hypocritical' (*OED*).

284 *yhabited* (*In h.* OC²&c) should mean 'dressed'; in its echo of Prol 3 it links Haukyn with Will. A possible punning sense 'with the habits of' (implying his sense of superiority; cf. *singuler* 282) is unrecorded (but why should *cote* suggest hermit's dress?).

299 will scan awkwardly on vowels, but the equivalent C line (VI 47) scans on stopped *g*. I conjecture this stave letter for B, *go* having been lost through attraction to *gomes*.

330 Bx could well be a visual or auditory error for the reading preserved in C (so K-D).

340 I conjecture Bx omission of *God* through attraction to *Goddes* and subsequent corruption of *ne* to *no* on the basis of C VI 84 *For god ne goddes word ne grace helpe me neuere.*

390 The metrically superior α line does not give a sense much different to β's, though it is harder to translate. H's point is that after acts of kindness he was troubled by *negative* scruples: would he stand to lose by his generosity? These scruples serve to vitiate the original act and turn it into a further occasion of sin.

427 I agree with K-D (p. 91) that Bx looks scribal here, but not because it is more explicit than C; it actually gives a different meaning. Langl. does not mean the patriarchs and prophets of the OT but modern bishops and priests, their successors in the office of proclaiming God's word: the phrase is in apposition to *prechours.*

455 K-D p. 90 read *liþed* after C, seeing *loued* as induced from 451 above; the converse is also possible, as *liþed* also appears in that line.

PASSUS XIV

7–9 In the absence of firm evidence I leave 7 and 9 as two-stave lines and in 7 adopt F's reading as the basis for a syntactically meaningful re-division.

22 I follow K-D in rejecting as spurious the line after 22 in F: *& þey þou slyde or stumble sore soone vp þou ryȝse;* but the parallelism of the three D's seems to require a line here, and F's 22 looks like an original line omitted from Bx through distraction by the rubric (so K-D)—as evidenced by the running together of 21*a* with the first word of 22.

23 K-D conjecture *myx*; I suggest an original *myȝt* 'mite' misread *myst* in Bx; cf. Chaucer, *WBProl* 360, where mites and moths are associated as threats to fabrics.

34 scans correctly and does not break the sense; it *could* be scribal expansion of the Latin.

48–9 K-D plausibly reconstruct after C XV 248–51; but Bx makes sense and is metrically tolerable: the third stave of 48 is on *-lode* (*aaabb*); 49 has only two staves in the line because of the Latin.

61 Like K-D I adopt *boþe* from C as the needed stave-word, but see its loss as due to attraction of *mowen* to *men* rather than of *breeþ* to *beestes* (which would make *mowen* scribal).

77 scans very awkwardly on *f/v*; possibly **B** read *hii*] *þei*(1) and scanned vocalically; K-D rec.

123 I diagnose simple transposition to prose order- (here *β* = Bx) as having corrupted the metre.

130a K-D emend to the correct form, but the incorrect BxCx form may be an original error induced by the presence of *som(p)num* 'sleep' in the earlier, uncompleted quotation (*q.v.*).

140 K-D p. 186 conj. *herberwyng* 'lodging' as hard enough to generate the variants; but *herebeyng* is even harder, perhaps even a coinage of Langland's; it occurs at C XVI 9.

189 Sk takes *He* Bx as referring to Christ (?at the Last Judgment); but the context indicates that Langl. is thinking of the sinner's continuing remorse *post confessionem* and envisages divine forgiveness as a document empowering the penitent to require his malign accuser to cease his suit against him.

195 I explain *wryten* as a visual error perhaps suggested by the contextual references to documents &c; K-D's conj. *diden* leaves the form of Bx unexplained.

197 The C-MSS also divide over *welle*, a reading which is visually specific not doctrinally exact.

247–8 Langland's point—that the poor have less to worry about than the rich because they possess less—requires *boost* to mean 'cause or occasion for boasting' not 'noise'. A robber finds it a greater challenge to steal from the rich, and so is likely to leave the poor alone.

259 scans vocalically as reconstructed; I diagnose transposition in Bx to stress the stronger idea, and see C (which K-D adopt) as revision, with new stave-sound, of a line seen as corrupt.

269–70 are both two-stave, with a long dip in 270 (the latter could also have the anomalous pattern *abba* or have read *fors. p.*). I see *catel* as C revision (the b-half in C is also revised).

273 I reconstruct on the assumption of split variation in *a* and *β* from the reading of Bx.

283–5 The corruption in these lines is hard to identify in the absence of C evidence. K-D discuss fully on p. 203 and conjecturally read *... is to þe body | And Ioye to pacient pouere.* My reconstruction pretends to no greater certainty, though I find it likelier that the stave of 284 was *s* and that the reference to the body in 283b might authorize conjecturing *soule* in 284a. I follow K-D's arguments in transposing 285 and 285a.

300 The required meaning of *lewde* seems forced in context; the variants may indicate damage in the archetype concealing original *leode*.

304 Bx could scan vocalically; but K-D p. 182 give good reasons for suspecting the line and for reconstructing after C.

PASSUS XV

16–17 K-D pp. 209–10 emend *cristene* to *of cr.* and trsp. 16 *and ... pl.*, 17 *and ... p.* But if *a party* 17 can mean 'partly' (Sk) BxCx should stand. The sense is that all souls were created by Christ (= God), some are Christians, all are 'known' in heaven (because Christ died for all), and some will enter there (the just).

84 A two-stave line with awkward caesura before (or after) *ye*. K-D conj. *me þynkeþ] it s*.

109 R's syntax, though awkward, gives better flow than W&r's (which is possible with a comma after *hem*). Possibly split variation to α and β conceals orig. *hem þei þat*.

115 Possibly B read *ben] aren* and *bele* (2) is C-revision, but cf. Kane and Donaldson.

123 Possibly a by-pronunciation of *girdel* with /dʒ/ existed; stave on *s* seems forced.

126-7 For another attempt to recover the original, see K-D pp. 189, 204. I offer my less drastic version as capable of accounting for the form of Bx, with corruption of *haue* to *saue* in β, omission of the whole phrase *And . . . have* through unconscious assimilation to *haue* 126 having resulted in misunderstanding of the syntax and subsequent mislineation. K-D use the OC² variant *for spendyng at ale] seiþ . . . wille*, which looks scribal to me.

213 F's reading is here typical 'improvement', though K-D base their conj. *lyueþ* upon it. Their objection to 'unalliterating *is*' (p. 185) is answered by finding the stave on *n* (*nys* WR supported by *ne is* LM).

232 W's *founde*, coincidentally agreeing with C's revision, may have come in from 230b.

234 The anomalous metre (*aabb*), not in itself a sure sign of unoriginality, prompts K-D to conj. *wel hir] hir*, which seems weak. Possbily *ledeþ* is a corruption of *wole leden* (*wole* lost through attraction to *wiles*) or, more radically, *weldeþ*, which is hard enough to have suffered substitution by the common collocation *lede . . . lyf*.

237 K-D's plausible conj. makes *court* the manor-court; but *laperis* is more easily seen as a visual error or visually motivated substitute for *carperis* (unrecorded before C15th).

267-8 I reject K-D's redivision after *wolde* (p. 188) and accept F's *verred*, seeing it as preserving α where R varies with β. But *q. he* is not scribal smoothing (K-D p. 193*n*): it serves to indicate that Anima has finished, for the examples are *verred* by him, not by God, the subject of *seide*, whose words (reported or direct) end with *vincunt*. 268 is another two-stave line.

289 I find the third stave on the medial *f* between *of*, *Au-*. K-D read after B, which recalls C XVII 15b *yf frere austynes be trewe* ('? if what the Austin friars claim is true'). If C XVII 15a corresponds to B XV 288a, we could surmise archetypal loss of the second *frere* through haplography and explain B's phrase as a scribal attempt to correct the metre, perhaps under influence from C.

295 scans normatively with caesura after *mynde* or else as two-stave, rendering K-D's conj. *meditacion] dev*. ('private devotional exercise') needless.

313 is two-stave; K-D p. 201 conj. *by] be(n)*, *behestes] foweles* (<pre-Bx *bestes*). Cr²³'s correction shows how Bx *foweles* could have been induced by proximity of *briddes* 314 (and infl. of Mt 6: 26). Langland's notion is of total dependence on God's bounty ('folly' in worldly terms).

314 I correct damage to metre caused by variation to prose order; cf. 284.

320 On C evidence I find Bx loss of *moore* 'further', induced by *mort-* or mon*kes*. K-D's conj. (p. 115) *monyales*] *ch.* is unnecessary.

352 I propose the needed third stave-word on the evidence of C's *of many of þese techeris* XVII 78. The Bx b-half is suspiciously long even in the absence of *many*, and OC²'s variant *ful*] *foule* might point to an original *fulled*, the *ful-* component corrupted to *foule* for emphasis in Bx with *alayed* then caught up from 353 through attraction to following copy (the second *alayed* is removed in C).

355 K-D adopt Cr²³'s commonplace substitution for an original meaning 'disordered (like men's actions)'.

369 I see *clement* RF not as 'nonsense' (K-D) but as an easy corruption of Bx *clemet* (= *climat*) through unconscious association with *element*, the actual further corruption recorded in β. Unemended, the β line reads as two-stave.

376 Transposition (to prose order here) corrects the metre. K-D rec. 376–7 after C.

388 K-D p. 194 read *Grekes*] *Iewes* on the strength of 603 (*q.v.*), where the majority have *Gr.* against *Iewes* WHm. But it seems incredible that Langl. should class the (Christian) Orthodox with two groups (Jews, Moslems) united by monotheism, not faith in Christ. *Pace MED, Grekes* at 603 more probably means 'pagans' as opposed to Moslems and Jews (cf. *gentel sarresines* C XVII 132: ?'pagans'; see variants).

392 K-D p. 198 conj. *lord*] *p.*; but *lede* (*MED* 1(c)) was both used of God in alliterative poetry (*Patience* 281) and has the necessary ambiguity (sense 1(a) 'person') to have generated Bx's *persone*; cf. XVI 181.

394 will scan vocalically, but the proposed reading gives better sense and metre, and *oon g. b.* could be visually induced from the Bx form of 393b (*q.v.*).

417 K-D p. 196 needlessly read *þise*] *h.*, observing that the third stave cannot be found otherwise. It is on *þat.*

420 I agree with K-D (p. 199: *Boþe B. and B.*] *B.a.B.*) that *boþe* was omitted through failure to grasp its sense 'likewise', but prefer it as the third stave-word (whether preceded or followed by the caesura), since Bx *þe* is easily accounted for through attraction of *bo-* to earlier *Be- / Be-*.

469 K-D p. 198 conj. *menen r. m. after*] *don r. m.* My conj. links the line more closely with the simile in 468: just men *need* mercy and truth to grow to spiritual maturity as much as the calf needs milk to grow into an oxe.

470 K-D needlessly emend *his* to *is*; but the verb is imperative in mood not indicative and *his* refers to God.

478 Developing Sk's sugg. (p. 415) I conj. a reading easily corrupted through homoteleuton.

479 Since *bym.* is transitive, its subject must be *man*; R's *by þe man* I diagnose as a visual error induced by eyeskip to *bymen-* at the line-end.

499 K-D p. 194 seriously conj. *Grekes* (= 'the Eastern Church')] *Iewes*, as if Langl. could have believed the Orthodox were ignorant of the doctrine of the Trinity (cf. 388, 603).

502–8 etc On the grounds of inconsequence in the argument and on the showing of C, K-D diagnose 'early corruption by dislocation in the archetypal text of **B** XV 50*1*–66 and emend by reconstruction as the criterion of sense and the suggestion of revised C direct' (pp. 178–9). Their supporting arguments are powerful but hard to summarize. Lacking an alternative explanation, I gratefully accept their brilliant solution. The resulting text is superior as argument to Bx, which is surely corrupt; but it is not clear that C, which links 529 and 568 as does Bx, points to the reconstruction as giving original **B**. While accepting K-D's principle that 'correction by the criterion of sense is an editorial imperative' here (p. 178) I remain less certain than they that a passage which received 'perfunctory revision' in C could not also have originally contained 'incoherent or otherwise feeble argument' (p. 178).

503 In the light of C, I accept β as archetypal, but emend its awkward word-order to accord with C's, and see *heye* as a revision.

505 The OC² form (supported by Hm following erasure; see K-D) is probably archetypal, allowing both meanings ('believe', 'live in') which are separated out by the two other variants.

511 If α here preserved **B** (?revised in C) the meaning would be 'so that men should see that salvation could not be achieved through (the power of even) steadfast reasoning (alone) ... but only through mercy, &c.' If α is scribal, as seems likelier, C gives the sense 'so ... see through a serious argument [*sc*. Christ's life and death] that ... etc'. In theory, C can bear the α meaning, but Langl.'s point seems to be that Christ's miracles confirmed the authority of his teaching, which was that salvation *per se* and evangelization *per consequens* require suffering (implying that if today's apostles were to suffer they might also work miracles—such as converting the Moslems).

515 The probable Cx form was as in R, with the form of C-MSS PT being a prosaic easier reading partially induced by *busshopes* at 277 below. The sense 'illuminated [*sc*. with knowledge of God]' *could* allude to Confirmation (the coming of the Holy Spirit to enlighten as well as strengthen) but this would be theologically confusing, since Christ did not send the Paraclete till after his resurrection, and Langl. would be making the doubtfully orthodox claim that he both redeemed ('baptized') *and* enlightened ('confirmed', 'illuminated') through the act of the Passion itself. F's variant tantalizingly suggests an (unrecorded) form *bisigned* 'marked with a sign', which goes well with 'blood of his heart' (alluding to the Paschal Lamb, opening of Longeus' eyes, etc). *bishined* continues suspect because of its form (the preterite of this strong verb is *bishon*).

518 Various C-MSS agree with F (?pointing to contamination); but Langl. must surely mean to refer to missionaries, not established churchmen.

527 *That* β represents smoothing after omission of 509–26. The elliptical αC reading requires us to understand some action of which Abp. Thomas was an exemplar—presumably risking his life 'in salvation of men's souls.'

545 Since *turn* (*OED* v. 10) bore the necessary sense 'turn upside down' (= 'be upended, put down') B may be a scribal correction coinciding with revised C.

546 Possibly B scanned on *w*, with substitution of *men* (2) for *wyes* in Bx; but C-MS G also has *Wyte*] *M*., a reading even more easily induced by the existence of *wise* in **B**.

548 On B's agreement with C, see 545 above; this more emphatic reading looks like scribal coincidence with revised C (C XVII 215 also revises *demen* 550 to *dampne*, thus pointing to earlier revision of 548).

Commentary

566 As a consequence of the K-D re-arrangement adopted, *peple* here must now mean 'the Christian people', who 'despise' (i.e. fail to live by) their own Christian principles, whereas in Bx it seems to mean the Moslems, who despise *Christianity* (because they see Christians failing to live by the standards they proclaim), and *contrarien* must mean 'oppose' in Bx, not 'offend against'. The awkward fact that C XVII 251ff apparently agrees with Bx will tell against the case for re-arrangement, unless we argue that the C-reviser here perforce followed his corrupt B-MS in the absence of his original.

603 The MSS point to Bx here reading *Grekes* (meaning Gentiles, not the Orthodox) rather than *Iewes*. But C XVII 315b *boþe sarrasyns and Iewes*, though a revised line, may suggest that B originally read *Iewes*, which fits better with the preceding line and with 605, which refer only to monotheists. WHm must be taken as felicitously varying towards the presumed original (Cr's *Grekes* counts against *Iewes* as a w-group reading).

PASSUS XVI

20 The original reading of *lone | loue* cannot be settled on palaeographical or, indeed, semantic grounds. 'Love-dream' consorts well with 'pure joy' (18) while 'lone dream' highlights the solitary, interior and mystical quality of the inner vision.

33 K-D pp. 113, 206 conj. *anoþer*] *som* BxCx to amend the metre; but *som* is scarcely 'easier' than *ano.* as they aver, and Langl. may be counting *-seþ* as the first (*s*) stave.

66 K-D p. 195 conj. *dyuyse* as the first *f/v* stave word; but *diffyne* 'describe in detail' (*MED* 1 (b)) is as apt, harder and perhaps more prone to visual mistaking (*-yne*>*yue*, *-ff-* >long *ss*).

71 Adopting K-D's conj., I propose a shape of the word more likely to have generated *raþest*.

108–10 K-D rec. pp. 183, 194. I also suspect the lines, but see no way of telling whether the C line on which their rec. hinges (XVIII 143) preserves B or is revised. I take 110 as a two-stave line padded by the Bx scribe to make more explicit, with destruction of metre.

110a I read α as original, and see OC² as a substitution for a less usual expression.

136 K-D's excellent conj. is strongly supported by the C-variants; *arn* α would account for R.

140 *maundee* 'act of washing the disciples' feet (= commandment to love)' is scarcely less hard than *cene*, but could be the β-scribe's substitution for a word known to mean *soper* (141).

142 Vowel scansion as in β is possible, but it is less likely that α substituted for Bx *oon* than that B had archaic *som*, thoughtlessly corrupted in α, more thoughtfully modernized in β.

157 is revised in C XVIII 176 as *Wo to tho þat thy wiles vysen to the worldes ende*, which conceals any presumed original different from Bx but nonetheless serves K-D in reconstructing. Taking *worse* as 'losing part, disadvantage' (*OED s.v.* B (4)) would mean that not only must Judas suffer damnation, his action will also fail in its intent (since Christ's death is the means of man's salvation). But putting a comma after *worse*, as in the text, makes Jesus warn Judas that, though he may achieve a bad eminence as mirror for evildoers, *he* will be the worse for it—by being damned as the price of infamy.

158 K-D conj. *iewene w.*] *o. w.* after *wille iewes* C; but Bx is satisfactory, C looks revised and the proposed phrase, though certainly harder, seems forced and unidiomatic here.

159 The two 'peace' words, as Sk notes, are identical except for spelling; presumably differences in pronunciation (with half-rhyme effect) would differentiate sense in context.

161 K-D p. 185 conj. *ynome*] *his name* on the strength of F's *þan taken*. But this looks like either repetition induced visually by 160 (end) or characteristic sophistication of an exemplar reading perhaps *ys nome* (misread as *ynome*). *his name* is scarcely more 'pointless' (as K-D aver) than the repetition which they posit as original. Langl. is *naming* his hero, whom he goes on in 164 to call by his *title* 'Christ'.

192 The corresponding C line (XVIII 203) shares Bx's corrupt order; but since the immediately preceding line has been revised, it seems scarcely credible that Langl. missed the error. Prose-order corruption presumably occurred again at the Cx stage.

193 perhaps translates '[to make known his own power]—That of himself, and that of his agent, and what they are both capable of experiencing / suffering'. No impersonal use of *suffre* is recorded and *hem boþe* may be no more than a version of *þei boþe*. β corrects.

198–201 Wr puts a comma after *chirche* 199, Sk, K-D a stop, which renders unintelligible already difficult lines. C XVIII 211 which, though identical in form with B XVI 210 (*q.v.*) actually corresponds to XVI 200 shows that the three nouns of 199 should be taken as imparting to *In menynge þat* 200 the sense '(Which are to be understood as) signifying that.' In Sk, K-D these nouns share with *Patr.* etc 198 the complement *children*. This makes some sort of theological sense: Christ and his religion *are* the offspring of God, Holy Church *is* his daughter (cf. II 29–30). But if HC is also 'mother' of the 'children of charity' (197) the theological notion operative in Langl.'s mind must be that of Christ as the Church's bridegroom, not (*qua* divine) her father. (The latter meaning would require *Of*]*And* in 199, for which there is no evidence.) Bx here may be an original passage which Langl., even if he found it unsatisfactory, was unable finally to put right. The point being made seems a rather strained quasi-allegorical parallel between two arbitrary triads which does not bear close inspection (the OT figures are 'children' of the *Christian* Church only by retrospective adoption).

201 I conj. the needed stave-word on the strength of 181 (cf. also XV 392 (*C*)). K-D's conj. *and he*] *and* leaves a line with poor vocalic alliteration and improved grammar (though still poor style). Possibly Langl. found it sufficient to let *louede* (without pronoun subject) be 'carried' by the force of the strong impersonal idiom *hym likede*.

211 More probably *in* was lost from Bx by β rather than intruded by α through mistaking adjectival *miȝté* for the noun. *Might*, the procreative power of the human couple, is cautiously compared to God's *creative* power (cf. 192).

221 See Sk's lengthy discussion *ad loc* of the variants produced by the strange expression.

222 is difficult to translate exactly (line om C). I take *bifore . . . hev.* as an asseveration, since the context excludes Langl.'s meaning that 'human nature remained merely human *prior* to the Incarnation' (when it became joined to God's in Christ's person). Presumably he is stressing identity of substance ('gendre', 'generacion') in the divine Persons while trying to find in the relationship some sort of metaphysical (not temporal) priority. The analogy is perforce inadequate because the relation of human child to parents is contingent while that of Holy Ghost to Father and Son is, in Christian teaching, necessary. But Langl. has ended by thinking of human nature in metaphysical rather than empirical terms.

231 I find the third stave in the *f* of *if I* (cf. *afyngred, afurst* etc).

246 MS W reads *leueden*; K-D's reading *leneden* is harder and goes well with the metaphorical *foot* 245.

256 R, agreeing with C-MS T, may preserve a common B/C original corrupted to *-ende* and thence to *-inge* (variously in the MSS).

273 K-D read C's *we* for *he*; but as Sk notes *ad loc* the reference could be to Abraham (and C a revision to avoid ambiguity).

PASSUS XVII

3 K-D p. 182 conj. *riȝt h.*] *here* to give a third *r*-stave (cf. C XIX 3b). Levelling of /wr/ to /r/ is C15th, but perhaps Langl. pronounced disyllabically (*we - rit*) when metre required.

46 *lene* could have originally read *leue*, giving a better parallel with 36.

53 Sk could be right that *jaced* is a C revision to improve the alliteration; the word did not cause the C-scribes difficulty, which seems odd.

58 *hym* β seems an auditory error, also found in some C-MSS, for an original *abouten* (C-MS X).

72 Orig. *barm* could have been supplanted by *lappe* through inducement from *ladde* 73; *or* scan on vowels and *l* to obtain a T-type line with unusual blank second stave *or* on *b* and *l* to obtain a Type IIb line with blank third stave.

76 scans as two-stave in Bx, but *quod*] *s.* makes it easier to stress *haue.*

89 scans either vocalically or on *þ* with intervocalic *þ* in *siþþe I.* as the third stave.

93 K-D pp. 111–12 conj. *mone*] *molde* BxCx. But the idea is that no mere herbal (earthly) remedy can cure sinful man, only a heavenly one.

102 Also possible would be *fyn* Sp.] Sp. (cf. 94), but K-D's re-arr. gives an *s*-stave supported by the re-written C, which also has *mys.* in the a-half-line.

104 I see R as confirmed by the sg. verb 107, FCr²³ as scribal explicitness (destroying the personification) and W&r as due to misreading of the number of *lotieþ.*

115 K-D p. 183 read *outcomen*] *out c.*, a harder variant (Cr²³); but Langl.'s point may be the special value of *faith* as a guide to salvation for the ordinary unlearned layman.

117 K-D may be right to omit *-s man*, which could have come in from the b-half-line.

141 On the strength of XVI 201 I accept an (?idiolectal) impersonal use of *loue*, seeing R as probably a misreading of an original identical with β, and F's nonsense variant as perhaps an attempt at the same correction achieved in Hm (?from **C**, which revised to the more normal usage). It is very hard to see *louede* arising from original *likede*.

143 Unlike K-D, p. 158, I see **C**'s *the pethe of* as revision of *purely*, which occurs a second time in 175 (confirmed by **C** XIX 140).

154 K-D trsp. *in oon s.*] *s. in oon*. I read *shéwýnge* not as a pres. participle but as a noun, '[mental] representation, image' and suspect possible loss of a final word *one* 'only, solely', perhaps through attraction to preceding *oon* or through incomprehension after misreading of *sh.* as participial.

191 The context requires 'pierced'; an ambiguous Bx form like L's accounts for both R and W.

193 Agreement of some α and β MSS here is caused by variation to a lexically easier word.

199a–200 If Bx *-u, -o* were original the phrase would be untranslatable. The correct **C** forms indicate Langl.'s awareness that Lat. *in* here means 'against'; indeed he uses English *in* with that sense (*MED* 9(a)) in 198 (and cf. 203 in β).

203 The unoriginal β variant could be due to attraction from 198a influenced by preceding *synn-* and attraction of *ayeyns* to foll. *seint* (a coincidence with **C** is less likely).

210 Support for K-D's view that this line was in **B** is the lack of revision (except in small details) in **C** XIX 166–228, which correspond closely to **B** XVII 203–65. 220 also reads more naturally if 210 is included, but the evidence is not conclusive.

216 I conj. as a third stave-word *lowe* (adv.) lost by attraction to an original *lowe* n.] *leye* in the preceding half-line or to *yb*lowe 215a; the word-play is Langlandian. K-D read *liþ fir in the macche* after **C**, which is more drastic.

226 K-D's conj. p. 207 *gl. unglade*] *gl.* requires the unlikely convergent variation of all B-MSS, W alone retaining a trace of the presumed original. But W's variant looks like a simple mechanical error. More credibly, **B** read *grace þe*] *þe*, Bx's version being retained (?deliberately) in **C** or lost in Cx through identical causes—eyeskip to *grace* 224. As it stands the line is a rare two-stave type with five-syllable anacrusis, no dip after the a-stave, and caesura between *Go.* and *glow.* (cf. *Beowulf* 1407).

242 Y is presumably an error coinciding with **C**'s revision. **C**'s *warm f.*] *fir* may be due to dissatisfaction with a second stave (*wol*) followed apparently by the caesura before completion of the sense-unit, a type very rare in Langl.

248 *tow* β looks an attempt to improve by avoiding a word synonymous with *tonder*. Perhaps *tache* means 'kindling' generically, with the other two words specifying further.

256 The English form of the word is not recorded except here, which makes α harder; but β is confirmed by the better C-MSS, and accords with Langl.'s style.

265 is followed in **C** by a line *Minne ʒe nat riche men to which a myschaunce* (going on *That* dives . . .) which K-D print as originally in **B** and om in Bx. But at the **C** line following (*Of . . . nedede* **C** XIX 231) major revision becomes evident (**C** XIX 166–228 had had only a dozen trivial changes; see above 210(**C**)) and this may have begun right after 265a, perhaps to make mention of Dives less abrupt. There seems no reason why the line should have been lost.

287 A striking case where Cr seems to have been corrected from a good B-MS, since it agrees with LM (= β), RF (= α) and C and not with w its group ancestor and g.

295 Scansion of *pléynéþ* in Bx position can be avoided by conjecturing attraction of originally final *þer* (= at the Last Judgment) to preceding preiere.

298 K-D's conj. corrects the metre but their explanation (*god*> <*made* attraction) is too weak to explain the substitution. More likely would be the Bx scribe's objection to Christ as creator combined with awareness that the 'Samaritan' *is* Christ. This seems a classic instance of a Bx corruption retained in C (though it could have recurred in Cx). More drastic solutions are scansion on vowels or reading *created*] *made*, with substitution in both archetypes here accounted for by the novelty of the verb (first found in Chaucer).

327 α and β, scanning *aaaxy* (on *b*) both look like attempted glosses of the unusual *borre* (preserved in C), one by a verb (converted to a noun in F's sophistication), the other by an adjective. But either could be original and C revised.

PASSUS XVIII

14 *and* C could be revision, with which *r*. coincide, while WL, R point to the harder αβ (= Bx) reading preserved correctly (or by correction) in F. Obtaining the spurs, not the shoes, was part of the knighting ceremony.

31 LRF's *likthe* 'is willing, satisfied [to accept the challenge of Death's threat]' is possibly a harder original that could have generated *lieþ* wg; but C supports *lieþ*.

40 Bx *pilour* could be original and revised in C, but looks like unconscious visual error or substitution of a vaguely abusive for a precise legal term.

49–50 K-D punctuate *enuye*; (reading *seide* as 'spoke'); I take *quod* 50 as pleonastic.

53 K-D p. 91 read *to lette and*] *yuel*, and *lengþe*] *were y*. after C. This, the harder reading, could have suffered Bx substitution through misreading of *poison*, which must be ironic in C; but C could be revision due to changed understanding of the function of the vinegar (Mk 15: 36, Jn 19: 29).

54 *seiden* seems syntactically necessary. A two-stave line scanning on vowels (*If, help*).

76 The improbability of scribal substitution of *throwe* for Bx *tyme* points to coincidental convergence of β with C (C being revised or substituted in Cx by the same error).

82 Unmetrical Bx is plainly corrupt, whether or not through objection to Longinus as a Jew (and so 'enemy of God, villain'), as K-D suggest (he was honoured as a Christian saint, feast day Mar 15). *Javelot* is rare enough to have been substituted by *spere*, but is unrecorded before 1440.

94 *alle* L&r looks like an intensifier of scribal origin; the immediate curse of Faith is on the Jews present at the scene and their offspring.

119 C supplies the needed stave-word. K-D p. 91 also see Bx *ful* (*om* C) as scribal.

149 K-D p. 90 read C's *parfit* for *prophete*, diagnosing a misread contraction. But Bx could be original, illustrating in one man both categories named at 144, and C revision.

159–61 The text seems to require reconstruction here on account of the grossly defective metre of 159 and the unsatisfactory sense of 160 (which could, however, be a compressed, inexplicit original later expanded and made explicit in C). K-D p. 90 diagnose omission of 161 by eyeskip (*good* 160, 161) and in 159 prosification through imperfect recollection; they reconstruct after C. I see 159 as revised in C and suspect loss of the needed stave-word *gilours* through homoarchy, with transposition to prose order in 159b. In 160 *ende* YGC² may be due to independent perception of the poor sense of the group-ancestor **g**. C² gives in *al* a good reading which could be a happy guess or even a contamination from C.

178 K-D argue the corruption of original *merye* in the first archetypal phase, whence its presence in C, while original *synge* was smoothed to *haue* in the second archetypal phase but retained in C. This gives good sense, but *mercy* BxCx is nonetheless acceptable.

193 I interpret F as here preserving α (varied in R to coincide with β). This gives vocalic scansion with stresses on the important small words *of* and *a* 'one particular'.

198 is uncertain through absence of α evidence. L may be seen as preserving β, the rest (**w**, **g**, M) having erred through the influence of the stock phrase and misconstruction of the grammar (as happened also in most C-MSS). L is here strikingly faithful to its exemplar, which could have been β itself.

202 β is attractive, but a positive, certain tone seems less appropriate to Peace than one of humble hope.

238 scans as two-stave on *t*, the first stave coming from medial *t* in liaised *þat_weren*.

253 After this K-D read after C XX 265 *And to haue out of helle alle þat hym likeþ*, which they suppose lost from B. But this could be a C-revision; B XVIII 255 is omitted from C.

281 On the strength of the revised C XX 306 *Sholde deye with doel and here dwelle euere*, I conj. the missing stave *in deol*, lost through attraction to *dwelle . . . deueles*. K-D p. 197 conj. *driȝten*] *he*.

282 will scan as two-stave in Bx but the evidence of C XX 309 *And sethe he is a lele lord* . . . supports K-D's plausible conj. of omission caused through repetition of *siþen* in 283.

283 K-D follow F (cf. the passive construction in C). The MS variation points to a syntactically difficult Bx reading, partly preserved in R and F respectively, R converging with WL in capitalizing the past part. marker *i-* (taken as the pronoun). I interpret *isesed* as the α (and prob. Bx) reading, with either transposition of α *was* to position after *i* (*y*, pronoun) in F and its total omission in R, or else independent correction by F (which seems likelier).

294 alliterates imperfectly on *ddt*, unless we conj. *driȝt(en)* corrupted to *truþe* in Bx and either not noticed in revision to C or else re-corrupted in Cx. K-D's conj. is unattractive because the meaning 'have them fetched' is incompatible with Christ's active, personal role in the deliverance.

306 The harder C reading looks like the B original, corrupted in Bx to a more familiar word and unconsciously transposed.

315–18 Divergent corruptions appear in α and β, caused by difficulty over the lineation. K-D convincingly make the Latin phrases independent metrical units (cf. 261*a*), thus giving normative alliteration to 317, which now resembles the corresponding C XX 363, also scanning on *l*.

351 scans as two-stave on vowels; K-D p. 195 conj. *maugree*] *ayeins*.

375 could scan as two-stave on *m*, but a more natural scansion is on *b* (as in C, which revises the b-half). I diagnose loss of *be* through assimilation to preceding *be*, *bi*-.

379 is an awkward two-stave line (less awkward if *þat is* is seen as Bx scribal explicitness). K-D see *is* as more explicit than *dureþ*, which they conj.; but the reverse is true.

392 I presume easy loss of the adj./adv. through assimilation to preceding *clen*-, *cler*-. K-D p. 198 more radically conj. *keuered*] *wasshen* to provide the third stave.

394 K-D read *halue* before *breþeren* after C, which I take as revised. C certainly makes explicit the (implied) distinction between pagans/pre-Christians and Christians.

402 The presumed **B** reading could have been corrupted by unconscious analogy (a) of tense (*loue* > *leuede*), in Bx stage; (b) of person (*I* > *me*), at sub-archetypal stage, in β only. If *ledis* (C-MS T) is scribal correction and not original, the line scans as two-stave, with the disyllabic Southern form of *louye* as in C-MS X.

406 Since vocalic scansion seems improbable here, a third stave-word on *l* is needed. A possible word is *lordlieste*, the first element dropping out in the first archetypal phase through attraction to preceding *lord* and *lieste* remaining as *leste* in C and undergoing substitution by *boldeste* in Bx. But I prefer *lothlieste* (cf. C XXI 56), the appropriate meaning of which ('fearsome', *MED s.v.* 1(a)) was somehow missed, or which was unconsciously supplanted by a quasi-synonym induced by *dorste*. K-D p. 94 read *leeste* after C; but this seems too feeble (and illogical) to be original (whether **B** or C) and could be the error noted above, which went unnoticed in revision, or a Cx corruption induced by *luste* in the next line. The context implies the notion of diabolical *power* rendered impotent by Christ.

427 C-evidence indicates the likely process of substituting a synonym for a word with unsuitable secular overtones (see *MED s.v.*). F here could well represent α.

PASSUS XIX

12 F here may be a correction to improve the metre, a contaminated reading from a C-MS, or the α reading (preserving Bx). But its sense renders *ac* 13 meaningless (*ac* is also attested by the better C-MSS). Alternatively, *Piers* could be a β substitution to improve the grammatical logic. If *Piers* is original, it must mean specifically 'Jesus' human nature [as opposed to his triumphant divinity: Christ = conqueror].'

38 L preserves by pure descent from β the obviously correct reading corrupted in **wg**, M and F (coincidentally?) through apparent reluctance to see those baptized by John as properly Christians (**wg**M give bad grammar and nonsense, F improves the grammar, but not the sense, through omitting *þe*). Langl. presumably means that those baptized by John were Christians inasmuch as Christ himself received baptism from John and also insofar as John 'counselled' them to follow Jesus.

Textual and Lexical

56–9 F here represents α, and in the absence of R I correct from C according to F's known tendency to sophisticate its exemplar's readings.

60 K-D re-arr. the BxCx line but normative metre can be found if *-ly* is taken as the second *l*-stave. Alternatively, the line is two-stave (on *l* or on vowels). β *yaf* is matched by several C-MSS.

75 Some reference to incense seems imperative. K-D p. 160 convincingly explain the loss of the word from Cxβ (not Bx) and take F as α, Cot as later correction. FCot could both be scribal improvements, but this seems unlikely (if F's lineation represents Bx, the omission in both β and Cx is more readily accounted for, and the presumption that C was unrevised in XXI and XXII strengthened). Another α MS could be determinative for **B** and C.

76 K-D argue well (p. 160) for Cot's *mercede* as the original that generated *mede* and *mercy* (though the former appears CrM correction of the β-type exemplar). Cot's convincing correction in 75 would seem to lend weight to the view that a superior **B** tradition is here being used; but in itself *mercede* is not harder than BxCx *mercy* in sense 'thanks', to which CotCrM could be dissatisfied scribal responses.

77 The reading adopted is found in C-MSS ITM, and such a form in Bx could have been misread as the present part. with *-ande* ending (transcribed as *-ynge* in β). F here prob. = α.

90 The problem of 90a, noted by Sk, is resolved by K-D through adopting F (as preserving a superior **B** tradition to that of BxCx). I see F as enterprising re-writing of an α line with the same corruption as βC. I conj. the rare word *richels* (more commonly spelled *rekels*), the form of which invited substitution by *riche*, with *golde* then obtruded as an 'appropriate' noun. The syntax of the restored line parallels (in reverse order) 89a, while the preserved 90b repeats (with variation) the referents of 89a and 90a respectively.

91 I see β as visually corrupted from 95b below; cf. 77 (*C*) above.

101 will scan on vowels, but if the original stave was *d*, a conjectured *dwelte*] *h. t. to* could have been substituted by the combined influence of *tyme, hidde* 102 and *telle it* 101b. There is no evidence that *durste* C was not revision, or even (since its sense is poor) Cx 'correction' of a defective half-line.

111 W's agreement with C is happy coincidence. The majority (= Bx) reading could be original.

118 F here could = α rather than showing C-contamination. β could reflect an original *fauntekyn ful of fyn wit*, later revised in C (since *k/f* confusion seems odd).

148 K-D explain Bx as visual error for **B** (= 'prophesied'); but *deme* (*MED s.v.* 11, b-c) affords an apt sense 'believe, expect' and C could be revision, not preserved **B**.

151–2 The CotF agreement in the form of the Latin may point to Bx (preserved in F from α, not necessarily from another B-source, in Cot by correction possibly from a lost α MS) and revised in C with a third *r*-stave (though C is uncertain). On the cause of loss of 152b in β, see K-D p. 165.

186 Notwithstanding the complexity of the variants (see K-D *ad loc*), WL agreement with Cx points to Bx, which I correct by diagnosing loss of *To* in 186 through assimilation to initial *To* in 185 above. The sense is that Christ gives has pardon to all men universally, but the power to absolve—the

Commentary

agency of the pardon—he gives to the Apostle Peter (see 189 below). K-D's elaborate construction allows the same sense but is neither justified nor necessary.

213 K-D's conj. posits that Langl. overlooked the line in revising or that the Bx corruption recurred in Cx, which also reads *god*. Conceivably *aabb* was acceptable to Langland.

230 K-D convincingly find substitution of *men* for *wyes* at Cx stage. C-MS T reads like Bx.

236 Following K-D's conj. *By*] *Wiþ*, I find Bx loss of the stave-word needed through easy assimilation to following *bu-* (orig. *by-*?), *bi-*, either unrestored in C or lost again in Cx.

239 K-D's restored verb (= 'make hay cocks') makes sense of the complex B/C variants, but is not quite demonstrative. The text remains in doubt here.

241 K-D's conj. leaves BxCx agreement unexplained while creating a difficulty of meaning which they acknowledge. I posit loss of the third stave-word through double homoarchy; it could have been restored (marginally) in Langland's scribal revising-copy and again omitted in Cx. C-MS T's omission of *to kenne* enables a two-stave line, but the phrase seems to have been in Cx.

244 Vocalic scansion is awkward and seems excluded by C's clear *w*-alliteration. C revises 245b to give a new meaning. I find loss of the needed stave-word (with sense 'accurately, correctly' or 'long') through attraction to *wele, felle*.

252 K-D here read C's *Ne no boost ne debat be among hem alle*, which I take as possible revision. On the strength of C's b-half-line I conj. *be*] *were*, and see Bx 'improvement' of the tense as destroying the metre.

254-5 K-D pp. 193, 95 see 254 (a two-stave line not in C) as one of the spurious lines and reconstruct 255 after C. The thought in 254 does not strike me as scribal. In 255 I find the sense *craftes* rather than *grace* appropriate and so exclude the simpler reconstruction *of my gifte c*. Inattention to copy would explain the *craftes/grace* error.

279 F's *frut* may be a sophistication of *αBx seed*, but lacking R I read with *β*.

297 The point is that the man of fortitude 'goes to law' only by enduring mishaps and injustices; *β pleiþ* destroys the metaphor.

303 scans as two-stave. *þoruȝ* is needed if the text is to make sense: *for* meaning 'on the part of' would be very strained here.

304-5 In reconstructing 305 I see Cx's b-half as careless copying of the presumed original, with scribal dittography after mislineation had destroyed the metrical form. I see Bx's 305b as scribal making explicit of the presumed original—i.e. by attempting to indicate *what* kind of fault might render a king subject to justice.

318 I scan the line as *aaaxy* with second stave on *after*. K-D's conj. (*OED s.v.* prep. 20) is more than possible if the presumed form were *til* (before mute *h*), which could easily have been assimilated to preceding *til*-with subsequent smoothing.

323 K-D's conj. is supported by the ease with which preceding *cros* could have suggested the familiar *croune* (cf. XVIII 48). But *gr-/cr-* alliteration remains possible.

332 Either F shows contamination from **C** or this is a case of split variation in αβ.

341 β reads better than F, C, but the improvement could be scribal. C, which is hard, may be revision, and so F could show C-contamination rather than standing for α.

345 β may be explained as misreading of *sere* as *pere* and replacement of the simple preterite *sew* with subsequent displacement of the adverb.

350–1 K-D p. 119 reconstruct as one line, omitting *by . . . Conf.*, which they ingeniously explain as an early intruded gloss. But there is nothing wrong with either the metre or the sense of the BxCx reading. 351 scans as two-stave. Langl. is describing the corruption ('colouring') not only of the Church's *creed* (the cart) but also of its *sacrament* of penance (the *caples*), so crucial to its ethical integrity (see esp. 252–3). K-D's analysis presupposes non-revision of **B** here, it does not prove it.

366 Bx gives poor sense here. The image is plainly one of a fortified tower standing in a moat (367–9, and cf. 383 below).

371 I conj. a stave-word lost through alliterative attraction of *synne* to *saue*. K-D's conj. (p. 118) *forsoke] refusede* is unacceptable, since it makes a mere anacrusis of the key word *Rep.* in a way uncharacteristic of Langland.

378 Cr could here be contaminated from **C**; but one or other *by* is needed for the metre, and both may be original.

397 F could here show contamination from a C-MS like MFSG. If it here = α, it could be original. *Or* is the harder reading if the sense is 'Beforehand', but the usage is dubious.

402 If O is right here, it is probably by happy coincidence.

403 Its intrinsic quality and the nature of the other variants point to F (= α) as original. Cx *and* seems no revision but a scribal intrusion; so does β *for*, perhaps an attempt to supply an *f*-stave (whereas Langl. apparently alliterated voiced and unvoiced labial and dental fricatives indifferently; see K-D pp. 132–3).

410 I see F as preserving part of α (= Bx) and sophisticating to the possessive the definite article supported by β and several C-MSS. Possibly C²'s *be* (?obtained by correction or mere misreading of *pe* and also supported in the C-tradition) is the original, corrupted in β and some C-MSS through visual confusion of the noun *fode* with the verb *fede*.

411 F's reading has been determined by preceding *pyn* 410. C's *we*, possibly revision, points to a plural rather than a singular verb.

412 K-D's conj. enables a pun, but *leode* is preferable because of the ease of its assimilation to following *lewed* and substitution by the commoner synonym under influence from *many*.

429 scans as two-stave on vowels. I see F as scribally corrected to scan normatively.

443 scans either as two-stave on *b* or was corrupted in both archetypes to the commoner order, the original having read *wikke and good*.

445 scans as two-stave on *p* in emended form, though vowel scansion on *ám- hóly* is possible. I see unconscious variation to prose order in both archetypes.

481–2 In 481 the difficulty of the grammar disappears if we see Cr as preserving the original in 481b except for an intrusive *as* induced through wrongly taking *Take þow mayst* 482 rather than *right wol* as the main verb. In 482 I see F as preserving α but characteristically sophisticating *askyng* to scan on *l*. The α word-order I see as either original and varied to prose order in Cx, or, more probably, revised in C. The offered reading involves no major reconstruction and accounts for αC, while β's reading appears smoothing after the corruption of the presumed original form to Bx *r. w. and in* 481b.

PASSUS XX

14 C's reading fits the tense-sequence of the main verb; the Bx preterite subjunctive is probably due to anticipatory misreading of *come* (pres. indic.) as pret. subj.

32 The sense is perhaps that the very wisdom which enables men to anticipate eventualities may lead them to misjudge what is actually going to happen.

48 *bide* seems harder in context and supported by 46. The theme here seems to be endurance rather than mendicancy.

70 The ease with which *bare* in the α exemplar could have been misconstrued as dittographic error supports the case for F's correctness here.

83 W coincides here with Cx substitution of the more familiar word or else revised C coincides with W's scribal variant.

104 The *hire* in F's sophisticated variant may reflect its original presence in α.

117 *blody* (apparently = Bx) seems wrong when compared with C. Perhaps its inaptness struck the WHmF scribes independently.

126 F's agreement with β no doubt has the same cause as β's error—misreading of Bx *seude* (so R, = α) as *sende* and alteration of this to the dominant form *sente*.

127 could be revised in C or censored in Bx (so K-D); yet there is no censorship of the even stronger attack on the pope at XIX 445.

130 Sk's 'submitted (hypocritically)' for *kneled* fits well, and motivation for supposed Bx 'improvement' (so K-D) is obscure.

167 *shifte* could easily be Bx corruption of *shrivede* (= *shrof* C); but it makes sense, and C could be revised.

215 The presumed original *soorly* could easily have suffered from visual error since the usual form of the adverb was *soore*.

219 K-D's conj. (p. 184) *purses and*] *and pisseris* is based on GC²'s *and gypsers*. But this pair of MSS could have coincidentally substituted for an exemplar form misread as *and purses*. K-D's dismissal (p. 117n) of Skeat's explanation of the Bx phrase as a cant term for soldiers or armed retainers is nugatory. The word could hardly have entered and persisted through the B/C traditions if unintelligible to the scribes who copied it, and *ballok knyf* XV 124 lends support to Sk's explanation. The text of III Kg 14: 10, 16: 11 is for, not against Sk: the turning to cant use of a Biblical expression would be both characteristic of a clerkly poet and brilliantly apt in this precise context, the attack on a perverted clergy.

225 Agreement of YOCB (? = g) with C may be coincidental, and C a revision for clarity.

227 If *churche* is due to the Cx scribe it is an attempt to improve the sense, for *holynesse* in XIX 366 is a *moat* and so cannot be 'brought down'. Such a scribal change would be remarkable; a revision would be less so, improving sense while spoiling the style.

236 K-D p. 117 plausibly explain *cheitiftee poverte* as containing a gloss (*pov.*); but it could have been a gloss within the line, not a scribal one. Most B-MSS omit *-tee*; the B group are corrupt and F is sophisticated.

256 *newe* was certainly in Bx and could have been revised out by C or omitted in Cx. But C translates the Latin, which omits it, more closely.

261 The sense is incomplete without this line, which seems to have been omitted in Bx. C²'s line, with a small change in the b-half, would fit in well, but its discrepancy from C suggests it is just a scribal effort which comes reasonably near the mark.

287 *leue / lene* LR could be a visual error for *lone* (the more explicit reading). But if L = β and R = α, Bx is established, and agreement with C establishes **B**.

292–3 are reconstructed by K-D p. 119 as one line, 292b reading *and pleye wiþ þe remenaunt* after F's b-half *with the remnaunt make mery ʒe*. I see the latter and F's 293a *Of þe residue of the good* as either sophistication or contamination from a C-MS, and worthless in establishing the text. In 292 I conj. a needed stave-word which could have been substituted in BxCx by part of the common collocation *maken merye* (induced from 289a above) after misreading of þ in *murþe* as *y* (the simplest of visual errors). Directed by C, I see *þe residue and* Bx 293 as possibly scribal expansion and conj. *renkes* as the likely stave-word in 293b, which scans as two-stave.

301 *ʒeuen* C could be a revision; otherwise, the Bx reading (also in C-MS T) was an easy substitution.

306 The original could have read *To, Go* or *To go*. C supports *To*, but following *go* could have been lost in Cx through attraction of *To* to *þo*.

308 is two-stave in BxCx. K-D's conj. p. 119 *fetes*] *dedes* is attractive. Also possible are *wrong*] *mys-* (with *wrong* lost through assimilation to *wroʒt* and smoothing towards the common expression) and *hi*] *þei* (still two-stave, but with better stress-pattern).

312 β seems correct here on criteria of sense; the error in αCx seems induced by *lyue*.

360–1 αC give better metre. *biten* has come in from 362 by eyeskip, F here coinciding with β as in 361, where the understood but omitted pronoun invites insertion (so C-MS T).

366 I find split variation in the archetypes from their respective originals, Bx losing *hem*, Cx losing *al*.

367 K-D p. 160 solve this crux by adopting F's *of ʒow memory* (emending *m.* to *memoria*) as the original (?by correction). This is easier than the archetypes, but suspect for that reason (their view that *my lady* arose as misreading of contracted *memoria* is quite unconvincing). S-P's rendering 'the friars [will] pray for you with the same zeal that they pray to Our Lady' is excellent, but depends on reading *Of*]*As* in 368 after C-MSS XU, which may be scribally smoothed here (cf. *All þe*] *As* F). The solution here adopted depends on remembering Flatterer's way with women (346 above). He is offering membership of the fraternity to both master and mistress. I presume *and* lost through assimilation to preceding *And*. C could be unrevised here, or the loss repeated in Cx.

373 Presumption of an omitted *s* (lost in BxCx through distraction from the two -*ynnes* endings) obviates the need for drastic emendation such as that of K-D (p. 119).

376–7 I read with **C**, finding Bx anticipation of *bad* 377. But revision cannot be ruled out, and Bx 367 could be two-stave.

378 K-D p. 175 detect split variation in the B/C archetypes from their respective originals and read *adreynt and dremeþ*. But if Cot's reading is by correction from a superior **B** source and not the reading of its group ancestor, then while it points to **B** as reading *adreynt* (so *confirming* Cx) it necessitates *rejection* of Bx. Diagnosing a two-stave line, I accept CotC as harder than Bx, though contamination of Cot from **C** cannot be ruled out and **C** may be revised.

380 K-D reconstruct 380a after **C**, seeing Bx as a substituted easier reading. This is not necessary, as simple Bx *þei] hii* would account for the lost stave (the line scans vocalically, with *hem* as first stave). **C** looks like a vivid revision, presenting in the image a dramatic reversal of Christ's drink of love (the Friar-doctor being an agent of death).

ADDENDUM

XII 291 Bx *vitam eternam* should perhaps be emended to *eternam vitam* (so K-D, without comment) and the line translated 'God is called *Deus* because his name spells salvation to his people—i.e. "*dans eternam vitam suis*" gives "*devs*"'. E. Faral, *Les Arts Poétiques du XIIe et du XIIIe Siècle* (Paris, 1924), p. 65, notes a gloss in a MS of Evrard the German's *Laborintus* offering this etymological *interpretatio* of the word *Deus*, and Langl. could have known it. (I am grateful to Professor Burrow for this note.)

II 33 has in Bx the un-Langlandian scansion *aabb*. Possibly *in the heighe hevene* is a variation towards a common collocation from an original *on lofte in hevene*.

B LITERARY AND HISTORICAL

PROLOGUE

1–22 The opening lines echo several earlier alliterative poems (for details see Bn *ad loc*), esp. *Wynnere and Wastoure* (cf. 22).

3 On false hermits, see Jusserand, *Wayfaring Life*, 140–3.

5 Malvern Hills, the setting of the vision, but not (as Sk notes) of the visionary events themselves, was prob. Langl.'s early home; see Kane, *Evidence*, pp. 38–41.

6 On Fairy Land as a source of marvellous dreams, cf. *Sir Orfeo*, ed. Bliss, ll. 133ff.

11 Medieval dream vision poems, deriving from the C13th *Roman de la Rose*, generally have the dreamer in bed; Langl. follows *Wynnere* and *The Parlement of the Thre Ages* in setting his visions mainly outdoors and motivating them by the dreamer's fatigue after wandering (Passus XIX, set in church, is exceptional).

17ff On Langl.'s picture of society generally see the many refs. under *PP* in Mann, *Estates Satire*, also Jusserand, *Life*.

38–9 Bn notes the allusion to Eph. 5: 3–5. Langl.'s hostility to false minstrels echoes the *Wynnere*-poet (cf. esp. *WW* 24–8).

44 *Roberdesmen* was a contemporary name for thieves of no fixed abode; cf. Robert the Robber, V 461ff.

46 *palmeres* = more specifically pilgrims to the Holy Land, who returned with palm branches. On pilgrims, see Jusserand, *Life*, III, ch. III, pp. 338–403.

47 The shrine of St James at Compostella, N. Spain; the relics of apostles and martyrs in Rome.

54 The shrine of Our Lady at Walsingham, in Norfolk, the most famous English shrine after that of Thomas Becket at Canterbury.

58 The Dominicans, Franciscans, Carmelites and Augustinians; cf. VIII 9 and esp. XIII 62–83 for the collocation of greed, gluttony and insincere preaching. See Jusserand, *Life*, 279–309.

68ff The pardoner was empowered by the Pope to supply an indulgence remitting part of the temporal punishment imposed for sin in return for some payment towards the general work of the Church. He required the local bishops' licence to preach etc in their dioceses. Langl. attacks the prevalent corruption of the practice, which came to be popularly seen as a means of buying absolution without contrition or sacramental penance. On pardoners, see Juss., *Life*, III, ii, pp. 309–37.

75 *rageman*: a long parchment document with a ragged edge; see Bn *ad loc*.

80 Sk (small edition) translates 'against the b.', Bn 'with the b.'s permission' (with evidence that pardoners cd. obtain the seal without the bp.'s knowledge), S-P 'for the b.'s benefit' (sense of *by* unsupported by *MED* however). My tr. (cf. *MED bi* 8b (a)) allows the bp. responsibility for granting the pard. the seal but *not* any authority to preach in his diocese (a duty of the parish priest; pardoners were laymen or in minor orders); but Bn's tr. is equally consonant with 78–9 and overcomes Sk's objections to the (natural) sense of *bi* here.

87 Specifically the 'curial' bishops, who received their office as a reward for serving the king (see Bn); but all absentee bishops may be the target here.

96 The steward was the lord's chief official on the manor, and could deputize for him in the manor courts; see Bennett, *Manor*, pp. 157–61.

99 *Consistorie*: (a) the Bp.'s court, for cases involving ecclesiastics (b) the Pope's solemn council of cardinals (c) here (fig. and iron.) Christ's court on Judgment Day (cf. Mt 25: 41).

100–6 The divine ratification of Peter's authority is described in XIX 183–90, the giving of the Cardinal Virtues (Prudence, Temperance, Fortitude and Justice) in XIX 274–309.

107–11 perh. allude to the rebel group of French cardinals who in Sept. 1378 elected an antipope (Clement VII, a Frenchman), thus causing the Great Schism (see Bennett, 'Date', p. 56).

114 *Kynde Wit* refers to natural and practical reason as opposed to speculative intellect. It is here shown as responsible for the proper ordering of society (see Quirk, *art.*).

122, 126 On *leaute* interpreted as justice in society, see P. M. Kean, *arts.* (1964, 1969).

132–8 These anonymous Leonine verses, which appear in an early C14th sermon MS (see Bn), sum up concisely Langl.'s view of proper social order. *Pietas* could mean 'mercy' (= ME *pite*), but a wider contrast seems intended between law viewed as a purely human institution subject to the will and caprice of earthly rulers and Law as a reflex of divine justice. The good Christian ruler will indeed show mercy but he must also be constantly aware of the need to rule *religiously*—with an abiding sense of what is owed to God by his earthly deputy. Mercy is not being represented as an arbitrary *deflection* of (strict) justice, rather justice is to be seen as 'law administered with Christian goodness'. The play on 'measure' and 'reap' is lost in translation. *Ius* here = 'the law', 'legal justice' rather than justice absolutely. Of the Biblical texts alluded to, Mat. 7: 1–2 is esp. important.

139–42 The words of the goliard or vagabond clerk echo and complement those of the lunatic earlier, and perh. reflect the author's shrewd practical sense (see Wright's *Pol. P.* i. 278 for an earlier form, and Bn).

145 The ignorant common people's utterance of this dangerous absolutist maxim from Roman Law suggests their helplessness and contrasts with the educated goliard's attitude.

146ff Langl. here re-tells a traditional fable, also used topically by Bp. Brinton in a sermon of 18 May 1376 (ed. Devlin). Langl.'s sceptical and ironic treatment is original; the topical application should not be overdone (see Intro. p. xxv): Langl.'s tale has general validity.

196 Richard II was a boy of ten when he was crowned king in July 1377.

225 The song may allude to the 'wise woman' Dame Emme of Shoreditch referred to in XIII 339. Bn thinks the Emma in question may be Canute's queen (see his note).

PASSUS I

3 The traditional image of the Church as a beautiful woman may also owe something to the literary personification of a simple or complex idea as an authoritative female instructor, from Philosophy in Boethius' *Consolation* to Raison in the *Roman de la Rose* and De Guilleville's *Pèlerinage de la vie Humaine*, a work known to Langland (see Bn for details).

12 The reference to God as Truth is deeply Biblical; see esp. Ps 30: 6, Jn 14: 6; in this application it means both 'the real object of knowledge' and 'the object and source of faith and trust, fidelity.'

20 *three thynges*: HC bases her doctrine on the fundamental postulate that God created man as a physical creature with legitimate needs to be properly satisfied according to a natural law. The example of Lot's daughters (incest) graphically illustrates the disobedience to God that comes through actively or passively ignoring the law of nature.

35 *Mesure*: to live according to nature and reason is to live moderately, and so avoid the ills that come from all excesses. The Deadly Sins later to be described may be seen as aberrations, whether through excess or defect, from a central norm of moderate sufficiency. As the cardinal virtue of Temperance, the idea of *mesure* derives from Plato, but the common medieval notion of virtue or goodness as a mean derives from Aristotle (*Nic. Eth.* II. 6–9).

66–70 The figures of Cain the first murderer and Judas the supreme traitor sum up the nature of diabolic activity as Langl. sees it—to obstruct God's love and pervert God's truth. Bn notes the scriptural source in Jn 8: 44. The elder-tree 68 was popularly thought to be the tree on which Judas hanged himself.

85 HC now enunciates the nature of Truth as the supreme value: it is to *live* in and by faith in God and 'fidelity' towards one's fellow man. That 'knowing Truth' is not to be equated with merely intellectual understanding is boldly illustrated by the example of the fallen angels. This notion that Truth (== God himself) can only be 'known' by being 'lived', with its implied warning of the danger of mere knowledge, is the central doctrine which the poem develops through the figure of Piers Plowman.

124–5 On the traditional belief in devils and spirits infesting earth (prob. deriving from Eph 6: 12) and afflicting mankind, see Lewis, *Image*, pp. 135–6.

142–5 As Bn well puts it, 'Truth and love have . . . become identical.' It is by loving God that we are to obtain a direct 'natural' knowledge of him; this leads inevitably to an exposition of the doctrine, of which HC is the appropriate custodian, that man only knows God because God has revealed himself to man, first in the Law and Prophets of the OT (*Moyses* 151), finally through his Son (167). On God's love for man as the 'motive' of the Incarnation, see Jn 3: 16.

148ff On the rich imagery of this passage, see P. M. Kean, 'Incarnation'. The remedy for the bite of the diabolical serpent is seen as having to be made from the powdered skin of a serpent (tyriacon = *triacle*). Following traditional exegesis of Num 21: 8–9, Langl. sees the Incarnation as God's way of becoming the serpent, which (through his sacrificial death and sacramental life in the eucharist of the Church) provides the healing remedy for man's wounded nature. For valuable commentary on this passage see also Bn (many refs.).

185–7a HC underlines the lesson that true religious 'works' are not a matter of empty observances or even passive and selfish 'holiness' but of active, urgent *concern* for the welfare of individuals in need. Her attack focuses with especial sharpness on the sin of avarice, which is antithetical to the nature of a God whose supreme generosity is revealed in the Incarnation, and she singles out as the most hateful form of avarice that of churchmen, who have a particular vocation to charity over and above the general obligation binding on all Christians. This shows unambiguously that HC, the ideal or spiritual or divine aspect of the Church is not to be casually identified with the formal institutional structure and its official functionaries.

PASSUS II

5–7 Bn identifies Will's *left* as the *north* (the 'devil's quarter', cf. I 118*a*) because he is facing *east*. But the left side traditionally bore the association 'bad, inferior', regardless of 'direction' (see *OED s.v.* and cf. *luft* at IV 62, also V 578).

8–19 alludes to the Whore of Babylon (Apoc 17: 4–5) and probably also Alice Perrers, Edward III's extravagant mistress (cf. 10). Her marriage to William of Windsor, the king's deputy in Ireland, in 1376, is perhaps alluded to in 18 (see Bn).

14 Reading this as *specifying* the sapphires of 13 accords better with the grammar, but Bn's 'pearls' for *Orientals* may find confirmation in *margaritas* in Apoc 17: 4. Langl. here refers to the healing properties attributed to some jewels in medieval lapidaries (see Evans and Serjeantson).

16 The redness of gold was traditional (cf. *Sir Orfeo* 150) but its factual basis, as Bn notes, was the addition of copper as an alloy (cf. pure Anglo-Saxon gold, which was yellow).

20 *mayde* 'virgin' looks sarcastic in the light of Conscience's accusation at III 121–33. On Mede generally, see A. G. Mitchell, and on her literary antecedents, Yunck.

23 Since 1309 the popes had resided at Avignon, which became the court of final appeal for all ecclesiastical cases and, as the church's administrative, so also a major financial centre.

25–6 The Fals who is a liar and the father of Meed is the same as Wrong (I 63–4). The Fals who is proposing to marry Meed may be regarded as Wrong's representative(s), son(s) (see 41), 'incarnation(s)' almost, anticipating Antichrist in XX 53.

30 HC is God's daughter, as Meed is the devil's (cf. Jn 8: 44). See also XVI 197.

33 Bn renders *leef* 'portion' (*MED* n. (1), 2d). In context 'beloved' (ib. n. 2) is more natural.

39 Ps 14 promises salvation to the man who speaks and lives truth and 'hath not put out his money to usury, nor taken bribes (*munera* "Meed") against the innocent'. The context of the Biblical quotations Langl. uses is always relevant to his pattern of thought. On their importance see Alford, 'Role'.

56 repeats Prol 18, reminding that lovers of Meed are found in all sections of society.

59–60 specify officials especially prone to taking 'bribes against the innocent': *sisour*, member of the sworn assize or inquest, the precursor of the modern jury; *somonour*, the official who summoned defendants for trial in the church courts, which dealt with a variety of offences against morality and such matters as wills, etc; *sherreve*, the chief administrative officer of the crown in each shire; *bedel*, a minor manorial official with duties roughly those of the village policeman (summoning tenants to court, collecting fines, etc; see Bennett, *Life*, p. 181); *baillif*: chief representative of the lord on a manor (ib. pp. 163-6). *brocours*: either retail-traders or agents in business transactions between two parties.

61 *Forgoers*: purveyors concerned with 'pre-empting for the king' and 'impressing labour and materials for [his] building operations' (Bn); *Arches*: the provincial court of the Archbp. of Canterbury sat at St Mary Arches in Bow Street.

63 *Symonie*, as Bn notes, seems conceived as a Canon Lawyer linked with his counterpart, Cyvylle.

69 *chartre*: a 'deed of conveyance of landed property' (*OED s.v.* 2(b)), the lands being (loosely) equated with five of the Seven Deadly Sins in 80–89 (the metaphor changing at 93). Bn documents the origins of the literary figure.

74a The standard opening of a charter. This and passages like XI 303-5 attest Langl.'s knowledge of legal forms and procedures (cf. Kirk, art.).

87 Usury as 'lending at exorbitant interest' was forbidden to Christians, and 'distress-loans' to people at need, commonly at 43% interest, were officially made by Jews only; loans (*mutua*) with 'compensation' for loss arising (*interesse*) were permissible for Christians (see Gilchrist, pp. 64-5, 68).

96 Only one solid meal was allowed on fast-days and full time was reckoned as noon (the usual time for the main meal was evening; see Bennett, *Life*, p. 236).

100–1 The end-rhyme, unique in the poem, may be accidental.

105 Alluding to the custom of annual tenure, Langl. sees a *life* of sin as one which must terminate with the sinner yielding up his soul in payment for his sins, with perhaps the suggestion that a life passes as quickly as a year (cf. *Dr Faustus*, 1. 1144).

109 Bn notes that friars were not usually pardoners; but this one could have been, and the word *doctrine* strongly implies an order or profession— i.e. the Paulines.

111 The reeve, an official with a wide range of duties in the manorial economy, was elected by the peasants from their own number (see Bennett, *Life*, pp. 166–78).

113 These words (?spoken by Wrong) parody the normal dating formula ('... of Our Lord'; cf. XIII 268) and point to Wrong's affinity / identity (see (*C*) on 25-6) with Satan.

115 Theology, as Bn notes, takes over HC's role; he personifies her doctrine systematized and applied to society. His claim at 119 should perhaps be understood 'Meed is ideally, *ought* to be, the offspring of Amends (= satisfaction for sin, which God will reward in heaven)'. In reality, as Meed's words and actions show, payment and reward are unjust. The context of the Luke quotation is Christ's statement of the right of apostolic preachers to get food and shelter in return for their work. That it is at Theology's behest that Meed goes to London—where she nearly succeeds in becoming accepted by the king—may seem a tart comment on the probability of ideal justice being realized in the world.

144 *floryn*: gold coin worth six shillings introduced by Edward III in 1344 (illustration in Poole, *Medieval England*, pl. 34).

163 If Langl. is here punning on *foles* then the worldly wise who follow Wrong are 'fools in the eyes of God', whereas the *fooles* of XX 61–2 (a passage recapitulating Passus II) are, though 'foolish in the eyes of the world, wise in God's eyes', and do *not* follow Antichrist (= Wrong).

171 *provisours*: clergy appointed directly to benefices by the Pope. The Statute of Provisors (1351) only slightly reduced petitions for benefices from English clerics to the papal court—petitions accompanied by payments (see McKisack, pp. 280–3).

173–4 These officers of the bishop were, like the manorial officials of 59–60, prone to corruption (accepting bribes or inflicting blackmail), and would count as simoniacs (so Bn) because they were churchmen abusing their office. *official*: the bishop's representative in the consistory court.

176 These matters, which came within the jurisdiction of the church courts, were the special concern of the Archdeacon. He could be bribed to overlook adultery and to effect divorce under the guise of canonical annulment. *derne usurie* may here be the practice of *occulta* as opposed to *manifesta usura*, i.e. not publicly licensed lending, but lending (at exorbitant rates) under the pretence of a trading transaction—e.g. the purchase of wheat from a vendor (actually, debtor) who was paid in excess of the real value, the excess constituting a secret loan on which interest became due (see Gilchrist, refs. under usury, esp. p. 108).

180 *commissarie*: legate of the bishop exercising jurisdiction in far-flung parts of the diocese.

181 They will provision themselves at the expense of fornicators, by fining them (Sk).

189 *Soothnesse*, truth, *veritas*, may signify especially the perspicaciousness of integrity.

206 Bn questions *doom*, as no judgment has been passed; but the tone of 193–8 makes plain that the king sees the wrongdoers' condemnation as assured once they come to trial.

211 This is the first of the attacks on friars which run through *PP*. For balanced comment on their condition at this time, see McKisack pp. 309–10, etc.

217 seems echoed by Chaucer in *CYT* (*CT*, G 658).

229 Bn interestingly notes that this was the exact length of Edward III's French campaign of 1359–60, 'a period when rumour was rampant' (and spread by minstrals and messengers).

PASSUS III

22 Cf. the golden cup of the Whore of Babylon (Apoc 17: 4).

24 *moton*: a gold coin worth about five shillings, bearing the impression of a lamb.

31 Judicious bribery will help procure employment for them in the church courts.

36ff The abuse of confession by a friar is recapitulated in XX 364ff. The essence of the abuse on the penitent's part is formally confessing without contrition (*shamelees*).

45 *noble*: a gold coin worth 6s 8d (Poole, pl. 34*e*).

58 The seven capital sins (deadly = mortal, 'destroying sanctifying grace in the soul'). *lecherie's* brief treatment in V 71–4 may be due to Langl.'s already having personified the sin here in Mede. Her special fondness for it underlines her affinity with the Whore of Babylon, with her cup of fornication (Apoc 17: 4).

63 i.e. enrolled as a member of his order by letters of fraternity 'entitling the [benefactor] to special privileges and benefits' (*MED fraternite* 1(c)). In XX 367, which recapitulates this scene, Friar Flatterer makes the same promise.

66 *pride* is the other deadly sin only briefly treated in V 62–70, again perhaps because partly anticipated in the person of Meed.

76–86 Bn suspects this passage as 'not clearly related to its context.' Abrupt it is, but it describes the presence at Meed's trial of those who had followed her to London (II 56; III 80 echoes II 187). Meed had bribed the men of law and clergy (III 20, 29); now she bribes the civic authority.

76 The municipal government of which the mayor was head had the special duty 'to check dishonest dealing' (see Poole, pp. 251–5 and fig. 56; pl. 24 depicts the civic mace and the punishment of dishonest traders).

83 *regratrie* here includes not simply *selling* retail but (the illegal practice of) *buying* in price rings from the producers so as to depress the price they obtained and make large profits at the expense of the poor.

93 Solomon was regarded as the author of the *sapience* (= wisdom) *bokes Proverbs*, *Ecclesiastes* and *Wisdom*; Langl. here loosely attributes to him an utterance of Job (the greatest 'wisdom-writer', see *Jerusalem Bible* pp. 723–5). See also Prov 15: 27, which is very close (. . . *Qui autem odit munera vivet*) and cf. 336 (*C*) below).

100 *yeresyeve*: a toll or payment ('or rather a . . . bribe . . . to connive at extortion', Sk) taken by a royal officer (sheriff, judge etc) upon entering office and renewed annually (on New Year's day). Cf. VIII 53 (metaphorical) and XIII 184.

127 The reigning king when these lines first appeared in the A-text was Edward III, and even in B it is he and not the young Richard who must be in mind, though the latter was crowned in July 1377. His *fader* is therefore Edward II, murdered in 1327. Edward, however, was not destroyed through avarice, and the lines are ironically more applicable to *Richard's* father, Edward the Black Prince, d. 1376, 'whose troubles arose from the failure of Don Pedro [the Cruel of Castile] to supply him with the money he had promised' (Sk)—i.e. for restoring him to his throne (see McKisack, p. 144).

128 Benedict XI was said to have died by poison (1306), but the allusion is to the Donation of Constantine, 'poison' to the Church (Sk; see XV 558–9 (*C*)).

138 *grote*: 'great' silver coin (worth fourpence) introduced in 1351 (Poole, p. 293, pl. 35*a*).

146–8 The king's personal seal accompanied a letter granting abbey or cathedral chapters permission to proceed to an election or a bishop leave to appoint to a benefice. As Bn notes, it could be circumvented by a provisor (see (*C*) on II 171) who had secured a prior claim through a papal bull (obtained by payment, hence by simony). Sk quotes aptly from Wyclif *ad loc.*

158 *lovedaies* were set apart for the amicable settlement of differences in the manor court. Bribes often played a part in this. Cf. also V 421.

160–2 On corruption in the law at this period, see McKisack, pp. 205–7.

165 *coupleth* suggests 'married, united' not just 'linked'; cf. I 195–7.

176 Sk notes Meed's respectful *ye* used to the King and the familiar (disrespectful) *thow* 178 used to Conscience, who replies in kind at 347.

190–208 allude to Edward III's Normandy campaign and identify Conscience with the King's policy of abandoning his claim to France in return for Aquitaine and a money-payment of three million crowns (Treaty of Brétigny, 8 May 1360). She argues (207–8) that the King should have maintained his claim, because of the great wealth to be got from France. 191–4 refer to the severe hailstorm and cold of 'Black Monday' (April 14 1360), which contributed to Edward's decision to make peace. 196 alludes to English plunder of copper utensils on the way back to Calais (Bn). *marchal*: commanding officer of the king's army.

211 *aliens:* either mercenaries or foreign messengers or traders (Bn).

230–1 Conscience's denial and distinction recall scholastic procedure (cf. also VIII 20).

234ff From the psalm quoted by HC at II 39 Consc. develops his doctrine of integrity to refute Meed's specious argument that all forms of *mede* are simple rewards for service. 241*a* is the vs. of Ps 14 alluded to by HC in II 37.

243–5 probably allude to Lk 6: 35: the unjust seek immoderate gain, the just receive (from God) reward beyond what is strictly due (Bn).

258 Consc. does not recognize legitimate profit (*lucrum*) in trade, which was allowed by the theologians; but he may imply it under *permutacion* (see *commutatio*, *ST* II, 2, 77: 4).

259ff The scriptural moral of the 1st Book of Kings (= I Sam), ch. 15, is that Saul was punished for disobeying God through listening to the voice of the people (15: 24), who kept the cattle, etc for sacrifice. Consc. interprets Saul's sin as avarice, thereby perhaps implying that Edward III might have incurred divine wrath if he had refused peace and persisted in his claim to the 'richeste reaume' (208).

263 *dede*: the attacks upon the Israelites in the wilderness (Ex 17: 8, 16).

276–7 refer to the destruction of Saul and his sons after defeat by the Philistines (I Kg 31: 2, 4).

280 *culorum*: the *ende* (281b) of the phrase *in saecula saeculorum* 'for ever and ever' with which many prayers *ended*. It is unclear what implication exactly Consc. finds in the *cas* and therefore what he might fear.

285–9 After killing Agag, Samuel anointed David (I Kg 16: 13), who was to succeed Saul as king. The prophecy is general and millennial; no direct contemporary application appears.

297ff are not in A (which ends at 300). Sk associated the lines with the jubilee of 1377, Edward III's fiftieth year as king. Bn instead links the prophecy of just times to come with Is 2: 2–5 (cf. 308*a*, 324*a*). It is a vision of an ideal state of affairs, possibly in the 'last days' before the Second Coming of Christ. In X 314ff the reign of general justice foretold is to be preceded by the coming of *Caym* (326), perhaps the Antichrist who actually appears in XX 53. By contrast, the portents of 325–9 seem benign, and the prevailing optimistic tone recalls that of the Chancellor's speech at the opening of Parliament in Jan 1377, when Prince Richard entered as president, and the atmosphere at his coronation (see McKisack, pp. 395–6, 399).

320 The Court of *King's* Bench was the chief criminal court, originally presided over by the sovereign. The Court of *Common* Pleas was the high court for civil actions.

325–30 Riddling prophecies were common at the time (e.g. those of 'John of Bridlington' in Wright, *Pol. P.* vol. 1; cf. also VI 322–30, XIII 151–6). The passage is discussed by Sk and Bn, who notes (after Bradley) that a sheaf contained 24 arrows (= here 12, and cf. *six* suns) and that sun, moon and arrows occur in Hab 3: 11. If we develop Bradley's hint (with Bn's gloss) we may see the ship as symbolizing the church (*navis*, whence 'nave'), seen perhaps in the form of Christ's cross (the mast). The number twelve may suggest the Apostles come to judge the tribes of Israel (Mt 19: 28). The six suns remain a vague dire portent. The *myddel of a moone* may be the Paschal full moon (as at XIII 155) 'with the events of the crucifixion' (Sk). The under-lying sense may be that when Christians are prepared to love one another and lay down their lives for their friends (Christ's discourse at the Last Supper, (Jn 15: 12–13) *Ante diem festum Paschae*, Jn 13: 1), that is, live out the Christian faith, the Jews will be converted and the pagans (?Moslems) at that sight ('Christians living virtuously in peace and charity', Bn) will believe in Christ (sing *Gloria*, Lk 2: 14). The signs at 326 seem to suggest that this will occur only at the end of the world, i.e. that ideal justice will not be established in our time (cf. also Bloomfield, *Apoc.* pp. 211–12). *Makometh*: Bn aptly notes his association later with the *coveitise* of clerks (XV 395, 413–14).

336 Meed's quotation, which comes from a mere eight verses after that of Consc., shows that she knows how to employ Scripture for her own purposes. It is not, *pace* Bn, inaccuracy she is guilty of in attributing *Proverbs* to Solomon (see Prov. 1: 1, and 1: 2 calls the work *sapientiam*) but dishonesty: she quotes only partially, in order to justify *giving* gifts (unobjectionable in itself; cf. 346) not *receiving* them (*sc.* as bribes). Consc. seems to attack only *hem that* taketh *mede* (*accipientium ... munera*; cf. the just of Ps 14: 5, *Qui ... munera ... non accipit*).

PASSUS IV

5 Conscience, the soul in its capacity to say 'no' or 'yes' to a course of action (XV 31–2, 39*a*) must get from Reason, the power to make (moral) judgments (XV 28, 39*a*), 'the knowledge on which to act' (Bn, who gets them the wrong way round, however).

17 If *Caton* here = the (supposed) author of the *Distichs of Cato* (?C4th), then he must stand for 'practical common-sense morality, day-to-day prudence' (see X 191–9) not 'elementary learning' (Bn).

27 These are 'merely worldly knowledge and intelligence', associated with Meed (34) and Wrong (63ff).

29 The Exchequer Court dealt with 'cases arising from the audit of the revenue'; Chancery, the Lord Chancellor's court, was coming to be a court of equity dealing especially with grievances arising from the other courts (McKisack, p. 199).

36*a* Psalm 13 as a whole describes the ways of evil-doers who have no fear of God.

41 Conscience, who *knew* ('recognized') this pair at 32 does not *know* ('acknowledge') them here (Bn notes the allusion to Mt 7: 23, where *vos* . . . *qui operamini iniquitatem* echoes *omnes qui operantur iniquitatem* in Ps 13: 4).

45 *sone* is retained from **A**, written when the Black Prince was alive. It is the *importance* of Reason's place that matters in the allegory: it is a 'central' one.

47 *parlement* is not clearly distinguishable from the great council of lords temporal and spiritual meeting as a court to hear complaints and petitions from private individuals (cf. Prol 144; see McKisack, pp. 193–4).

48 The diabolical figure Wrong (see (*C*) on II 25–6, 113) is here personified as a king's purveyor, forcibly requisitioning and engaging in rape and violence. His acts are echoed by (as they are echoes of) those of the first robber Lucifer (described in XVIII 286–91, 335–40).

55 *maynteneth* implies that he arms as well as aiding and abetting his retainers.

56 *Forestalling*: buying up goods before they came to market (perhaps with the aid of threats) so as to re-sell them at a profit.

58 The tally-stick, marked with notches indicating the amount due, was split in such a way that buyer and seller each retained one half as a record of the transaction. Peace complains that the debt was never honoured.

75 In the game of handy-dandy one player shakes an object between his hands and then shuts his fists, the other having to guess which hand it is in. Wrong will pay Wisdom 'with closed hands' (i.e. secretly), as he may go on to bribe the judges.

82 The attempt to *overcome* the King is recapitulated at XX 122 by the attempt of Coveitise to *overcome* Conscience (noted by Bn).

116 Pernelle, enjoined by Reason at V 26–7, appears ready at V 62ff to do just this. But Reason's conditions are ideal ones, and only if they are realized will he have 'ruth' on Wrong; and since he will never do that, the implication is that the conditions will remain unfulfilled.

117 The *act* of spoiling (meaning the *agents*, the parents) will be chastised: *they* ought to be beaten for *not* beating their offspring.

121–2 St Benedict was the founder of monasticism, St Bernard of Clairvaux founder of the Cistercian order, St Francis founder of the Friars Minor. St Francis did not prescribe an enclosed life for his followers; Bn seems right that Langl. means roughly 'all orders should observe their rule', but his view that *prechours* 122 = the Dominicans (Order of Preachers) is too specific: as at V 42, all preaching clergy (including parish priests) are meant.

124–5 Elliptical: instead of keeping expensive mounts, hawks etc, in the manner of secular lords, bishops should help to house and feed the poor as is their duty.

126–7 St James should be 'visited' not through (repeated) pilgrimages to his shrine (at Compostela in Galicia, in N.W. Spain) but through the works of charity specified in his own definition of 'Religion clean and undefiled . . . to *visit* the fatherless and widows etc' (Js 1: 27, noted by Bn). 127 seems to acknowledge a single pilgrimage at the end of one's life or a perpetual (spiritual) pilgrimage (Bn).

128–33 refer to clerics taking money to the officials of the papal court in consideration of benefices etc. The curia was at Avignon (II 23) but the phrase was a set one. The excepting of provisors at 133 sorts oddly with lines like II 171; but if Bn is right that no satire is meant here then the word covers those who 'go to receive benefices or offices already given' (with no implication of simony). *Dovere*: pilgrims could here be examined to ascertain whether they were carrying gold or silver abroad.

143–4 The Latin phrases come from Innocent III's definition of the just judge who leaves no evil man unpunished and no good one unrewarded (*De Contemptu Mundi* iii 15). This (divine) standard of justice is that invoked by Consc. in distinguishing two 'meeds' (III 232–45): if I were king, says R. (if Reason ruled), this standard would prevail and have the results described in 147–8. The response to *this clause* of clergy and lawyers in 149–53 contrasts with that of the people and the *grete* ('the lords judging', Bn) at 157–9.

168 The sheriff's clerk was open to being bribed to refrain from serving writs (Bn).

172 Reason's actions accord with his nature as later defined at XV 27–8.

175 Property reverted to the Crown if there were no heirs. The king implies that lawyers dishonestly produce bogus heirs so that he is defrauded of reversions.

177–end The passus ends with Meed apparently defeated; but the King's commitment to Reason and Consc. indicates how things ought to be rather than how they are or will be. Conscience's recognition of realities at 182–4 is elaborated in Passus V, where the quest of the *commune* (= the folk of the field of Prol 17ff) for Truth will not prove easy (159): in V 556 they offer Piers *huyre* 'payment, meed' to show them the way to Truth.

PASSUS V

8 Bn sees *bedes* 'prayers' (cf. 401) as 'rosary-beads'. But Will says the Creed, the muttered clauses presumably acting like the *sweying* of water in Prol 10 to 'bring him asleep'.

11 Reason (?an archbishop) preaches a sermon to the whole realm urging general repentance. The action of this passus, beginning with the sermon, is analyzed by Burrow, ' Action ' (see p. xliii, n. 16).

13 The 'Black Death' (bubonic, the more lethal pulmonary or pneumonic, and septicaemic plague) reached England in 1348, with further outbreaks in 1361–2, 1375–6 (see McKisack, pp. 331–3 and Ziegler, esp. pp. 27–9). Langl. agrees with Brinton, Bromyard and other contemporary writers in seeing the plague and other disasters as divine punishment for sin.

14 alludes to a memorable tempest on St Maur's day, Jan 15 1362 (a Saturday) which occurred during the second plague and lasted five days. It is seen as an act of God putting down the pride of men and serving as a threat of the Last Judgment and warning to repent.

28–9 Beating his wife may save her from exposure to jeers or being ducked in the pond.

31 The mark was not a coin but a money of account, worth 160p, = (Bn) a skilled workman's wage for a fortnight. On *grote* see III 138 (*C*).

39a The quotation continues 'but he that loveth him correcteth him betimes' (cf. 38).

45–7 The threat of royal intervention in lax monasteries anticipates the famous prophecy at X 314–25 (in C part of Reason's sermon here) which made Crowley in the C16th see Langl. as a precursor of the Reformation. Langl. advocates not suppression but right observance.

49 alluding to possible popular treason is omitted in C, written after the Peasants' Revolt.

50 Bn's 'deal gently with' for *have pite on* is unjustified in the light of XIX 431, 445, *q.v.*

55 is from the Parable of the Virgins but Langl. may have thought of the (more appropriate) Mt 7: 23 *Quia nunquam novi vos*, said to those *qui opera-mini iniquitatem* (cf. (*C*) on IV 41).

57–8 Bn's 'the Holy Spirit' for St Truth is over-specific. *Qui &c* is formulaic and need not have Truth as antecedent. Reason is the living voice of HC, who at I 12–14 describes Truth as (God) the Father.

61 *Wille*: 'a momentarily personified abstraction of the human will' (Bn), but since the poet-dreamer is called Longe Wille at XV 152 perhaps the repentance (and so the sins) are meant as his own and he stands as a representative of sinful humanity (cf. 184–5 below).

62–461 The tradition of the Deadly Sins is traced by Bloomfield, *Sins*. Contemporary parallels appear in confessional treatises on sins and their remedies (e.g. Chaucer's *ParsT* 385–958) and sermons (e.g. no. 9 in W. O. Ross, *Middle English Sermons*, EETS 209 (1940), which relates the sins to the seven petitions of the Our Father, as in the York Paternoster Play).

65–6 The hair-shirt worn as a lining (Bn) will tame (the desires of) her flesh, which is (as) fierce (as a hawk or other wild creature; cf. VI 31).

71–4 The B.V.M. is invoked as patron of chastity (cf. *SGGK* 1769) and intermediary between God and the sinner (see 635 below). Bn notes Saturday fasting as a special devotion to her.

76 *mea culpa*: from the *Confiteor*, the prayer of penitence at the opening of Mass.

122 *diapenidion*: sugar twisted into a thread, used to relieve phlegm in the throat.

147–8 Bn finds a play on the senses 'church properties and dues', 'endowments'. Less specifically, the first *spiritualte* means 'church dues', the second 'spirituality' (ironic): pre-occupation with the money they can get from the laity distracts both friars and parish priests from their true spiritual concerns.

158–9 Dame Pernele's situation would be considered in the chapter-court before being brought before one of the church courts.

164–6 Bn reads as authorial, but it is better as tart comment from the speaker's experience of such ladies. Gregory IX (Pope 1227–41) strictly forbade the practice of abbesses' hearing their nuns' confessions. Wrath denies that they could keep them secret.

167–79 With the favourable view of monks here cf. X 303ff.

184–5 St Peter warns against the devil as a roaring lion, an apt image of wrath. The *me* and *my* need not be scribal slips (Bn) but are bold re-inforcements of the idea that the dreamer is representative man, prone to all the sins.

199 The metaphor is that of learning to read from a book (*leef* = folium).

201 Weyhill, near Andover, Hants, had a large autumn fair, as did Winchester.

205 *Donet*: the Latin grammar of Donatus (C4th). Having learned to 'read' in the book of fraud (199–200) he advances to the subtler lessons in deception.

206 He racked or stretched the cloth in a frame, lengthening but also weakening it.

211–14 Loosely spun yarn is easier to rack. Her further deception is to use a pound weight of 1¼ lbs (paying the spinners for only one pound's worth of wool). Coveitise's own auncer 'weighed truth' but the device was banned generally because it was thought open to fraudulent use and only the balance (= scales) was permitted. Cf. also Deut 25: 14–15.

216–21 Thin ale sold at 1d a gallon, thick (the best) at 4d. By bringing it in by cupfuls from her chamber Rose could mix both secretly and sell the mixture at the higher price (the customers having already *sampled* the best ale; see also Stanley, pp. 439–40).

227 Bromholm Priory near Walsingham (see (*C*) on Prol 54) had a relic of the true cross, to which Coveitise will pray for release from his *dette* (of sin).

235 Presumably he knows *no* French (Bn), 'Norfolk' standing for a region so remote from the capital that knowledge of French was not to be expected there. This and the above reference may imply that he is a Norfolk man.

236–48 On usury see II 87, 176 (*C*). Lending at interest was highly developed in Lombardy because its economic prosperity made surplus cash available (see Gilchrist, p. 93). In C IV 194 Langl. specifies the Lombards of Lucca as living 'by lone as Iewes' (*ib.* p. 301). Either usury or coin-clipping is protested against as a horrible crime in a petition of the Commons of 1376 (*Rotuli Parliamentorum* II 332). 240 describes Cov. as lending for love of money itself (the cross on the coins, see Poole, pls. 32, 34) and not for charity (the cross of Christ; cf. amplification of the image in XV 536–43). Cov.'s aim is for the borrower to lose his pledged security by failure to pay on the day assigned. 243–4: he lent *goods* and bought them back at less than true value to conceal the interest charged (Bn); cf. *derne usurie* II 76 (*C*). 246 *lese*: i.e. in interest.

247–8 *Lumbardes l.*: 'bills of exchange used by Lombard bankers . . . in forwarding money to the papal camera' (Bn). An early form of international credit transfer. Cov. presumably doctored the bills and paid in less at Rome than he got in England, keeping the difference for himself.

249 *mayntenaunce*: either Cov. bought the protection of lords or lent to them to enable them to maintain their position.

251–2 The knight might have to forfeit clothes laid in pledge or sell back those bought by feigned sale (Bn; see 243–4 above).

275 The *Glossa Ordinaria* (quoted SkBn) interprets these vss. of the 4th penitential psalm as meaning that God will not compromise his truth by letting sin pass unpunished, and demands satisfaction from the sinner in the form of mercy shown to others.

305–6 These spices could be chewed, possibly, without breaking the fasting rule. Trevisa (*cit. MED s.v.*) says fennel comforts the stomach and abates nausea (*wlatenesse*).

312–13 The women are prostitutes (Cock's Lane was a haunt of theirs). *Pridie* 'on the day before', a phrase from the consecration prayer, was the

317

point in the mass at which a priest who had forgotten the bread and wine had to recommence (Bn); hence the name may mean 'incompetent priest'.

320–36 Hikke and Clement, the parties to the barter (the 'new fair'), ask the chapmen to assess the value of cloak and hood. Helped by an umpire, Robin, they make the exchange, Clement paying the agreed difference in value with a drink (?all round). Whoever has second thoughts is to pay a fine of a gallon of ale.

342 Like *evensong* 339 this expression points up Glutton's failure in his religious duty (cf. the gluttonous Doctor of Divinity at XIII 103, also 395 below).

370 These are the 'great oaths' that accompanied Gloton at 307; cf. *PardT C* 629–60).

372 On the usual medieval meals, see Bennett, *Life*, pp. 234–7.

391 'Bless me father, for I have sinned': the words with which the penitent began his confession.

396 This, the earliest vernacular reference, presupposes the existence of ballads about Robin Hood (see H. C. Sargent & G. L. Kittredge, *English and Scottish Popular Ballads* (1932), 254–5). The Earl of Chester (1172–1232) was another popular hero.

406 These are two of the seven corporal works of mercy; see Mt 25: 36.

415 i.e. not once a year, which he was obliged to do.

419 Both psalms describe the kind of conduct required for salvation.

422 Gratian's Decretals and the commentaries on them made up the Canon Law (Bn).

433 The hawk's lure was usually 'a bundle of leather and feathers resembling a bird' (*MED* s.v.). Sometimes it had a piece of meat attached, and Sloth may mean by *ligge &c* 'unless there is something in it for me.'

443 *Vigilate* alludes to either Mk 13: 33–7 (Sk) or Mt 26: 41 (Bn).

451 Sloth vows devotion on Sunday, as Lechery had for Saturday (73), Glutton for Friday (383).

453–5 *matyns*: at dawn, followed by mass. He will not drink between midday and evensong at 3 p.m.

460 A famous cross formerly stood on Rood Eye (Cross Island) in the Dee at Chester.

461 Sloth's resolution, which echoes and accepts Reason's injunction at 57, closes the confessions of the Sins and states the major theme of the rest of V—'pilgrimage' as conversion of the inward man, change of heart.

462–77 A transition from confession to absolution. Robert is not 'an eighth sin' or 'a generic name for a slothful waster' (Bn). Rather, he sums up all the sinners as those who owe *debita* to God: all have stolen like Lucifer (477) and must beg mercy from the crucified saviour. The wording of 473 echoes 61, linking Robert with Wille, the human will of which all the sins are expressions. In a sense Robert 'is' Wille, humanity in debt to God and totally dependent on divine mercy.

466 *Dismas*: the penitent thief's name, found in the Gospel of Nicodemus.

468 Having *no* means of satisfaction, he depends on God's mercy, like the creditors in Lk 7: 42 (Bn).

475 The penitential staff points to the idea of pilgrimage as satisfaction for sin (510).

478ff Bn notes liturgical echoes, 'in particular the services of Holy Week.'

487a Genesis describes the creation of the first man, John the 'new creation' of man through a life of charity (cf. HC at I 85–91, 148ff). *Pace* Bn, the reference *is* to the Christian (in John's epistle) and not to Christ himself.

488 *oure sute* perhaps plays on the senses 'in our cause, action-at-law' (Bn), 'in pursuit of us'. Both chivalric and legal meanings are apposite to Christ's encounter with Lucifer in XVIII 249ff, esp. 349–350a, 368, 401.

488–501a is recapitulated and amplified in XVIII 36–63, 324–6 and XIX 157–60.

489 Christ's death occurred at 3 p.m. according to the Synoptic Gospels, and the phrase for this, *nona hora* 'ninth hour' later took on the meaning *noon* 'midday'.

490 The thought is that the divine nature did not suffer crucifixion; cf. XVIII 26.

491a St Paul's quotation from Ps 67: 19 alludes to the belief that Christ descended into the underworld (and released the souls of the just from Limbo).

492 The image may be that of the sun, the eye of heaven, becoming temporarily blind.

493–4 The time of the midday meal, 'when most light is', becomes that at which the patriarchs, in the 'darkness' of hell, receive the saving effects of Christ's sacrificial blood, freshly shed.

494a This quotation from the lesson of the Monday in the fourth week of Advent is here linked with the narrative of the Harrowing of Hell deriving from the Gospel of Nicodemus. It is repeated in the account of that event in XVIII 324.

498 i.e. Mary Magdalen, 'out of whom he had cast seven devils' (Mk 16: 9).

499a Langl.'s point is that the resurrected Christ, by *first* appearing to the Mary who was the type of sinners, and not to the (Blessed) Mary, the type of holiness, provided special comfort for sinners.

501 is the first use of the metaphor of chivalric deeds for the Incarnation and its climax the Crucifixion and Resurrection; cf. XVIII 22–6.

504 Christ is man's *brother* through the human nature he had (cf. XI 199–203, XVIII 377). *fader* seems unsuited to God the Son; but if *with* in 487, 488 above is taken literally (cf. also the hard Latin at XVIII 26) it seems that Christ *qua* divine is being thought of as consubstantial with his Father and so (somewhat confusingly) identical in person with him (it is good poetry but bad theology).

507 Ps 70, esp. 1, 5, 14, is a hymn of hope in God. Bn suggests a source for the horn image in the Easter *Exultet*, but the phrase *horn of salvation* is more likely the source. It occurs in Ps 17: 3 (the *next* vs. of which appears in the mass after the priest's communion) just after the words *sperabo in eum*, and this explains the image.

514 *beestes* was perhaps suggested by *iumenta* 509a above. They are like lost sheep (cf. Mt 9: 36, Ps 77: 52–3).

515–31 This pilgrim is a type figure (cf. Chaucer's Knight) who has been to nearly all the shrines and brought back stamped pewter ampullae from Canterbury (Jusserand, *Life*, p. 338); souvenirs of the relics at St Catherine's convent in Sinai; shells commemorating a miracle of St James (see Anderson, pl. 60); patterns of cross and (St Peter's) keys from the Holy Land and Rome respectively; a copy of the cloth image of Christ's face supposedly taken by Veronica when she wiped it on the way to Calvary (also kept at Rome); see Anderson, pl. 39, for the scene. 527 *Babyloyne*: near Cairo, where 'a faire churche of oure lady' (Mandeville) commemorated the Flight into Egypt. 528 *Armonye*: Mt Ararat, where Noah's ark had rested and supposedly did still; *Alisaundre*: where St Catherine was martyred.

542 *fourty wynter*: probably 'many a long year' (Bn); at VI 83 Piers is 'old and hoor'.

552 alludes to the parable of the vineyard (Mt 20: 8).

558 Pilgrims' offerings had made the shrine a veritable treasure-house (despoiled at the Reformation).

563–5 allude to Christ's summary of the Old Law (Mt 22: 37–39 run together with 7: 12).

567ff 'Honour thy father and thy mother', the fourth commandment (Ex 20: 12); 570, the second; 573–4, the ninth and tenth; 577, the seventh and fifth (the sins they forbid, theft and murder, are to be passed on the left: cf. (*C*) on II 5–8); 579, the third; 580–4, the eighth, alluding to the perils of bribery leading to perjury (Bn).

585–608 Observing the commandments of the Old Law prepares the soul for Christianity; as Bn notes, God's mercy is shown to those who do so (Ex 20: 6). On the background and sources of the castle image (possibly derived from Robert Grosseteste's *Chasteau d'Amour*) see Bn 589 alludes to the opening of the Athanasian Creed: faith (in Christ and his Church) is necessary for salvation. 601–4 Repentance or Conversion (*Amende-yow*) procures the grace through which alone heaven can be opened. 606–8 alludes to Col 3: 14, Mt 18: 3; 606 echoes I 163–4 and refers to the indwelling of God's spirit in the Christian. With 607 cf. XV 149. In the context the image of a chain seems to suggest (loving) servitude rather than a chain of office.

609–17 stress the new peril of *spiritual* pride (as opposed to worldly pride, the Pride of Life) that may threaten a Christian who 'does well', and the continuing need for total dependence on God's grace. 615: time spent in purgatory making reparation for sin.

618–24 The seven virtues which are remedies (in order) against Gluttony (and Sloth), Pride, Envy, Lechery, Wrath, Avarice.

632 The wafer-seller anticipates Haukyn in XIII 226; they were of ill-repute (Bn).

635 Mercy, a moat in the allegory of 586, is now seen as an intermediary, the B.V.M.

639–41 Linking pardoner with prostitute (?his concubine, *suster*) underlines the low view Langland had of the former's profession (cf. also XIX 370).

PASSUS VI

7 *scleyre*: the veil covering head and chin worn by ladies of rank (Poole, pl. 108).

10–12 The embroidery done by English ladies was thought the best in Europe; see Boase in Poole pp. 508–9 and pl. 107a (early C14th).

16 alludes to Mt 25: 63, 'Naked, and you covered me' (one of the corporal works of mercy).

21 On conceptions of the knight in contemporary literature, see Mann, *Estates* pp. 106-15.

30 Beasts of the warren like foxes and hares could be hunted only by manorial lords, but the peasants could hunt deer ('beasts of the forest') over 'warren-land' (Bennett, *Life*, p. 94).

38 As Bn notes, a knight could *tene* his tenants (observe the wordplay) by tallage (arbitrary rates of rent), heriot (a customary claim on the best chattel of a dead tenant) and amerciaments (discretionary fines).

48 *charnel*: vault under the church for bones brought to light when a graveyard was dug over for new burials.

57 It appears from 59-61 that Piers' pilgrim garb is no special dress but his ordinary working clothes. His pilgrimage is to be not a journey but a way of life.

62 *busshel*: the amount of seed required to sow a half-acre.

63-4 imply a literal pilgrimage for a literal pardon; but 102-4 make clear that P. understands by 'pilgrimage' a life of labour performed in charity, so this may be figurative.

75-7 The text is closely echoed by Apoc 3: 5. Langl. seems certain about the fate of such characters, whose 'sin's not accidental, but a trade' (*Measure for Measure* III i 147); cf. V 639-41 (*C*) above. The exact sense of 77 may be 'they have not yet felt God's wrath; may they repent (before they do).'

85-6 As Bn notes, men usually made their will before a pilgrimage. Here the action is equally apt if what is envisaged is preparation for death.

87-90 P. bequeathes his soul to God who made it, alluding perhaps to the last petition of the Paternoster and the Creed article on Christ as judge of living and dead. The *rental* was a register of rent due from tenant to landlord: the record P. believes in is the Creed, with its final clauses promising forgiveness, resurrection and eternal life.

91-5 P. paid his parish-priest tithe from his corn and from any profit arising from the trades described in 547-8 (*catel*). As Truth's servant, he paid promptly (93 echoes V 551) and so trusts in Truth's repayment. He hopes to be remembered in the *Memento* prayer for the faithful departed in the Canon of the Mass.

99 alludes to Deut 24: 12-13 (Bn); cf. V 423-6.

100 *residue*: the third of the legacy remaining after the widow had received one third and divided the other among the children. P. swears by the famous wooden Rood of Christ crowned on the cross in the Cathedral at Lucca.

103 This second allegorical pilgrim's staff (cf. V 475) concretely symbolizes Piers' spiritual intention: to *labour* for his fellow-Christians. The plough-pusher is a stick with pointed or forked end (see fol. 6 in Hassal, *Book* (Ka p. 447)).

113 *oversen*: Piers' role is that of overseer, 'reeve' (Bn), 'head-harvestman' (Sk).

117 *pure tene* recurs at VII 115, XVI 86, both referring to P. This is the righteous anger, called *ira per zelum* by Gregory (*Moralia*, ch. 45, in *P.L.* 75, 726), which was found in Christ (*ST* II, 2, 158: 2; III, 15: 9). Cf. also Theology at II 115.

122 *aliri*: *MED* suggests they are pretending to be paralysed, but Bn's view that they tie 'the calf against the back of the thigh, so that it appears to be cut off' seems supported by 124.

133–8 mirrors social conditions after the Black Death had caused a scarcity of labour leading to huge rises in workmen's wages and inducing some not to work at all (see Ziegler ch. 15, McKisack pp. 331–42).

148 Robert is probably a 'wandering hermit' (Bn) as in Prol 3; cf. 187 below.

154 Bretons seem to have had a reputation for boastfulness (cf. allit. *Morte Arthure* 1348).

155 *forpynede*: 'tortured, tormented', but if elliptical for 'tormented in hell' (cf. Chaucer's *GP* 205) it can be rendered 'damned'.

164 Courtesy is seen as a characteristic of knighthood (cf. 33, Chaucer *GP* 70–1, 99).

182 Such bread was used to feed horses (193); cf. 283, 303 below.

212–17 Hunger urges feeding the (able-bodied but idle) beggars with food so unattractive they will become convinced it is better to work.

221–1a Paul sees concern for one's neighbour as commanded by Christ (hence the probable Bx reading; see variants). But the AC reading makes such concern part of natural law. In 207 P. sees all men as his brothers because Christ *died* for all, here (it is implied) because God *created* all. Christ's epitome of the commandments (Mt 22: 37–40) is the 'eternal law' in which 'natural law is contained' (*ST* I, 2, 71: 6).

226 urges charity without regard to desert and probably echoes Lk 6: 30.

229–30 shows P. uncertain whether to provide able-bodied beggars with just the mere necessities (Bn). Hunger's firm rejoinder on the divine command to work reassures him.

232 Genesis is the 'giant' book of the Bible (the longest after Psalms) and describes the 'engendering' or creation of mankind (Bn).

238 According to early tradition, the 'four living creatures' of Ezech 1: 10, Apoc 4: 7 were interpreted as symbolizing the Evangelists: Matthew a man, Mark a lion, Luke an ox, John an eagle (cf. also XIX 264–8 and see Mâle, *Image*, pp. 35–7). The ref. itself is to Lk, but (as Bn notes) the word *piger* occurs in the corresponding account in Mt 25: 26 as well as in the Prov quotation, and this may have confused Langl.'s recollection of the source.

248–9 The natural interpretation is to see 'teaching' and 'tilling' as forms of the active life, 'travailling in prayers' as the contemplative (cf. VII 118–30). Bn questions this, but there are no grounds for reading further meanings into the text at this stage. For discussions, see Donaldson, *C-text*, pp. 156–61, Hussey, 'Lives', Dunning, 'Structure'.

250–2a Hunger misinterprets the Psalm, which says that the man who fears the Lord shall eat, &c—i.e. that *righteousness* will be blessed with prosperity, not that *labour* is blessed.

257ff Bn sees as addressed to P.'s 'servants', but *myself bothe* 255 shows this is not so.

269–70 Phisik's expensive clothes are either payment in kind or evidence of the large fees he charges. Hunger's attribution of most illness to excess (= gluttony) helps to equate *hele* with the opposite virtue to gluttony, temperance.

288 The *droghte* is that of March (cf. Chaucer *GP* 2), the time for manuring the fields (Bn).

289 *Lammesse* (Loaf-mass) *tyme* = harvest: on Aug 1 a loaf of new wheat was offered at mass.

299 *neghed neer* is here probably litotes for 'came' unless, as Bn notes, this is a reference to the release by merchants of wheat hoarded from the previous year.

301 recalls V 303 and perhaps hints recognition of excess as inevitable after a long period of restricted supply.

307 The landless labourers are crofters or town-workmen (Bn); with the phrase cf. XV 534.

311 For similar examples of pretentious 'restaurant French' cf. the Wakefield *Prima Pastorum*, 238–43.

314a The *Disticha Catonis* are maxims in four books dating from the C4th. They formed a part of the grammar school course and were studied after Donatus (see V 205).

317–19 *lawes*: the Statute of Labourers (1351), designed 'to ensure a supply of cheap labour by pegging wages [which increased by over 90% between 1340 and 1360] at pre-plague rates' (McKisack, p. 335), was much resented. Enforcement was at first successful, though 319 implies that Hunger was the only effective answer to peasant discontent.

320–end The prophecy is serious, as Bn contends, but not offered as genuine prediction of disaster in five years' time. The passages Bn adduces to show Langland's belief in astronomy show only that contemporary astronomy is unreliable (XV 356–9, cf. X 207–9) though it was once a true, God-given art (XIX 243–5). Saturn 325 is the malign planet linked with natural disasters like flood and drought. Bn ventures interpretations of 326–7 which do not really fit the enigmatic and arbitrary details: 'eclipse' seems too quotidian for the [m]one (or *sonne*) *amys*, and a possible alchemical sense of *multiplie* very hard to apply to a *mayde* of unknown identity. The obscure details may be intended merely to suggest mysterious future happenings which will discipline mankind: *chaste* 322 is the operative word which makes the prophecy consonant with Reason's earlier interpretation of calamities that have already taken place (V 13–20). 328 says that in the future God's instrument of chastisement will not be, as it was then, *deeth*, but *derthe* (the two are associated in Apoc 6: 8). The prophecy of famine can be read as a warning against the sin currently in question, avarice (and perhaps also sloth) just as the plague was interpreted at V 13–15 as a punishment specifically for pride (cf. also the warning to wasters at 130–5 above). The passage is thus prophecy more in a Biblical sense—warning and reminder of God's presence—than in the popular sense of 'prediction'.

PASSUS VII

3 *a pena et a culpa*: 'from punishment and from guilt'. In strict theory, guilt was forgiven in sacramental confession and only the canonical temporal punishment (e.g. fasting) could be remitted through a pardon or indulgence, and such punishment, if incomplete, might have to be completed in purgatory. But in practice it was widely believed that a papal pardon obtained, say, through making a pilgrimage, absolved the sinner from both punishment and guilt. It was therefore especially prudent to go on pilgrimage towards the end of one's life. Truth's 'pardon' seems to be granted not for a specific act but for a life lived in truth and love.

18–22 Bn finds here 'the view that trade was dangerous for the soul'; but III 257–8 show that Langl. did not hold this view but condemns the merchants specifically for impiety and false swearing (20–2), which he no doubt thought endemic to their trade. In 19 we should read ironically (in the light of 173ff), 'only an ideal pope would not, the actual pope (probably) would.'

24ff The letter may imply that trade, overtly disapproved of, is covertly allowed in special cases (so Bn). Or Truth may mean that merchants, to make satisfaction for *dishonest* trading, should use (legitimately-earned) profits for charitable ends. Cf. Lk 16, esp. 9. On these charitable works see Willard, 'Origin', Thomson, 'Piety' and Rosenthal, *Gift-Giving*.

42–3a urges another class of men who have misused their skill to use the same skill now to make amends (compare 50 with 34): lawyers should give their services free to the helpless (?widows, orphans) and be paid by the crown (?or perhaps by God). Aquinas (*ST* II, 2, 71 : 2) sees this as an act of mercy. The source of 43 remains unknown.

44–59a is a digression on law and lawyers; the narrative resumes at 60, after which begins a digression on false beggars 71–97.

44 *Johan* is less effective in context if it means 'common fellow' than if it is a female name.

52 Classing *wit* 'knowledge', 'intelligence' as an elemental gift of God Langl. can argue that it belongs to men in common and cannot be bought or sold (cf. XIII 150).

67 Such beggars are guilty of *false* suggestion (a legal notion); cf. 65.

73–3a refers to the *historiae* which make up the *Historia Scholastica* of Peter Comestor (d. 1179), a re-telling of sacred history (ed. *P.L.* 148, 1049–7722, and see Daly). The quotation is adapted from the *Historia Tobie*.

75a is actually from Jerome's Commentary on Eccl 11 : 6 (*P.L.* 23, 1103); see Bn *ad loc*.

78 *reste*: i.e. in heaven; by charitable acts he shortens his time in purgatory.

81 *usure* (cf. III 240) has a favourable sense (like *mede* at III 244–5). A man's generosity to beggars is an investing of the wealth (God has) given him. God will take the interest but restore it to him in heaven (Bn aptly quotes Prov 19 : 17).

84a is from Jerome's Epistle 125 (*P.L.* 23, 1085). Logically this is the *Book* of 83, but in fact the latter looks forward to the (strictly) biblical *Book* of 86.

85–6 The *solas* comes from the accounts of God's direct provision for his saints (see XV 269ff). Ps 36 is one of total trust in God; it prohibits or condemns begging only by implication: 'the Lord . . . will not forsake his saints' (vs. 28); cf. XI 277.

98–104 The operative idea is not the suffering of the physically handicapped but the patience and humility with which they bear it; this is what wins God's favour.

110–14 The lines from the Athanasian Creed echo Mt 25 : 46, which

concludes a passage (vss. 31ff) on the Last Judgment specifying forms of
'doing well', specifically the corporal works of mercy. Truth's words ratify
HC's teaching at I 128–33, but the priest fails to recognize this divine promise
of salvation/threat of damnation as a pardon.

115 Interpretations of the tearing of the pardon are surveyed by Frank,
Scheme pp. 28–9. Frank, 'Pardon Scene', convincingly interprets the tearing
as a symbolic act of rejecting (inefficacious) paper pardons; cf. Rosemary
Woolf, 'Tearing', and Schroeder, *art.*

116–17 Ps 22 is one of faith in God's support and *mercy* (= ultimate
forgiveness, 'pardon').

120 *plough*: 'striving', 'concern' recalls the image of penance as the
pilgrim's staff at V 475. But P. is not going to depend on God's provision
necessarily in the sense of *abandoning* 'tellynge' for 'travaillynge in preieres',
active for contemplative life (VI 248–9); *cessen* 118 taken with *so harde*
means 'desist (for a time)' rather than 'renounce (permanently)'. P.'s later
function is spiritual, but the hyperbolic language of 120–30 need not mean he
is choosing to be a hermit, only that he is giving priority to prayer over work.
Bn sees P. as taking prayer and penance as the *bona [opera]* of the pardon
(though prayer was normally contrasted with works, and what the latter are
is suggested by 110–14 (*C*)). We may see P. as resolving to replace agricultural
work as his main activity with prayer and penance.

123 *othere manye* = 'many other (holy men)'; the relevance to this of
Ps 33: 20, which SkBn quote, is not clear.

136 The priest taxes P. not with atheism but folly, i.e. presumptuousness in
being so confident, though a mere ploughman, about the meaning of scripture,
like a skilled exegete (*divinour*).

137 *Lewed* has ironic bite, since P. understands the pardon's spiritual
meaning better than the *lered* priest who can construe its Latin (106). P.'s
knowledge of the Latin Bible presumably has a symbolic not a realistic
significance.

140–1 For naturalistic waking of the dreamer by noise *within* the dream
cf. Chaucer's *Parlement of Foules* 693–5. *south:* 'so it is almost noon' (Bn).

144–201 are both 'epilogue' (Bn) and prologue / passage of transition
to the poem's second main section. Its two themes are the validity of dreams
(149–67) and the validity of pardons (174–95) and it concludes by suggesting
that dreams can be true and by declaring that the only true pardon is Truth's.

146 *pencif in herte* suggests a love-melancholy, which turns to *pure joye*
the next time the Dreamer meets Piers (XVI 18–20).

148 The *propre wordes* are *Dixit insipiens* 136.

152 Langl. again sets one authority (a weightier one) against another, as
at 72–4 ('Gregory' against 'Caton'). The latter regularly stands in *PP* for
mundane prudence as opposed to (sometimes imprudent) Christian charity
and faith.

154 explicitly makes the dream Nabuchodonosor's (Dan 2: 36ff), but it is
his ?son Baltasar (Belshazzar) who 'lees his lordshipe' (Dan 5: 30).

162–4 As Sk notes, this is not what the Bible says of Jacob's reaction. But
Langl. may be reading into Gen 37: 11 ('but his father considered the thing
[= the dream] with himself') the implication that Jacob believed it might
come true.

Commentary

171 Such masses were said for the repose of a person's soul for a period of two / three years after his death. The bishops' letters license the preaching of indulgences (Bn).

174–9 Bn sees as 'orthodox enough', but they seem not without irony. Firstly Langl. affirms the Pope's power to grant salvation to men *without* penance on their part, and supports this with an appeal to Christ's words entrusting the 'power of the keys' to St Peter. But his protestation of belief 177 seems ironic since he *secondly* affirms that pardon causes souls to be saved (only when linked) *with* penance and prayer (180–1 reads like ironic understatement). His true aim then would seem to be to *deny* the view of the papal plenitude of power first affirmed; if that makes Langl. 'unorthodox', such he is.

192–3 The provincial was head of all the houses of a religious order in a particular area or province, who could admit a lay person to all the privileges of the order in his province (see also (*C*) on III 63).

194 Dowel here seems to personify the *bona*, the good deeds of the man facing judgment; but at 200 it is more suggestive of Christ the king speaking for the just (Mt 25: 31ff, *q.v.*). A third sense, 'a way of life in which to do good deeds' is introduced in the opening of Passus VIII.

PASSUS VIII

1–5 That VIII is a new prologue to the poem's second major part is confirmed by the echoes in 2, 1 of Prol 1, 2 (season, clothing). The Dreamer wanders not to 'hear wonders' but to 'seek Dowel'. *russet*, worn by shepherds (Sk) = the *shroudes* of Prol 2.

9 The Franciscan Order produced such leading masters of divinity as Scotus and Ockham.

20–26 *as a clerc*: Will answers in scholastic style with a (foreshortened) syllogistic argument: a two-part major premiss, an assertoric proposition (from scripture, = statement of fact) and an apodictic proposition (*whoso . . . yvele*, necessarily true); an apodictic minor premiss (*Dowel . . . togideres*); a conclusion. The latter is only partly true: indeed Dowel cannot always be with the friars, but *if* 'Dowel' is incompatible with sinning, and *if* even the just sins, Dowel cannot be 'at home' with any man—i.e. is no man (cf. 5).

21 *Sepcies*: cf. also Eccl 7: 21, 8: 12. 24 recalls Boethius, *De Cons. Phil.* IV, pr. ii: 'But for to mowen don yvel and felonye ne mai nat ben referrid to good' (*Boece*, ib. 247–9).

29 *forbisne*: Sk traces to Augustine's Sermo 75, ch. 3 (*P.L.* 5, 475), but Langl. develops his image independently and he may be original here.

30ff A *distinctio*: he accepts the truth of Will's major premiss but distinguishes the just man's sins as venial not mortal and so not contrary to Dowel. Though orthodox, he does not give due weight to the need to avoid venial sin, the links between venial and mortal, and the danger (in fighting *wanhope*, an aspect of *accidia*) of falling into spiritual complacency (cf. *sleuthe* 52). Langl. finds laxity characteristic in friars.

54–5 The notion of free-will in animals may come from Gandulph of Bologna (C12th); see my 'Philosophy' pp. 145–9. He is close to *De Cons. Phil.* IV pr. ii; cf. also XII 161ff (*C*).

58 Will cannot grasp the argument or feel it on the pulses. It is less that the friar's reasoning is hard (it is not) than that it fails to answer Will's need; cf. 111 below.

71 *muche*: cf. Longe *Wille* XV 152. To see an aspect of oneself personified as a double appears common in dream experience (see Freud, *Interpretation*, pp. 505–6).

75 *Thought*: the mind as knowing power rather than 'memory' (Spearing, *Dream-Poetry*, p. 148; cf. *id.* pp. 85, 223, which take Chaucer's 'Thought' in *HF* II 523, translating *mente* 'mental power, mind' in *Inf.* 7–9, as 'memory'; see C XVI 185, 'Philosophy' p. 151 and n. 99).

76 *seven yeer*: probably an indefinite period of time, as at IV 86, V 204.

79–108 Dowel is the virtuous secular life; Dobet the life of the devout clergy; Dobest that of the conscientious episcopacy. For discussion, see Kean, 'Justice', pp. 79–84.

91 *religion*: perhaps covers priesthood generally (*OED s.v.* 1b) though the passage is cited by *OED* under 1(a) 'religious order'. *rendred, &c*, in A, cannot allude to Wycliffe; it means 'read aloud and expounded'.

94–5 misreads *suffertis* as imperative and misses Paul's irony (cf. also I Cor 4: 10).

115–24 concisely dramatize the experience of a period of 'thought' terminating in 'knowledge' or 'understanding' (*OED wit* 11).

PASSUS IX

2 *Kynde*: Nature's creator, *natura naturans*, not created Nature, *natura naturata*.

3–4 The traditional fourth element was fire, and if Sk is right, Langl. means by 'air' Latin *aether* 'the upper air', which he took as fiery (?because fire rises upward). Goodridge's suggestion that this may be the 'breath of life' (*spiraculum*) of Gen 2: 7 is unlikely, since Langl. calls this *spirit* at XV 36, 39a.

6–7 The allegory of God as lover of the human soul was traditional; see the famous version in *Ancrene Wisse* in Bennett-Smithers pp. 239–40, their note p. 413 and Gaffney, *art.* The figure is developed as a chivalric one in XVIII 10ff.

10–16 *Anima* seems envisaged as a (royal) ward entrusted to the care of a great lord.

17–22 *Constable*: 'governor or warden of a royal castle' (*MED s.v.* 3(b)). Like Sk I tr. *Inwit* 18 as 'Conscience' (*MED* 4) though at 53 'Mind' or 'the collection of inner faculties' (*MED* 1a, 3a); see also Quirk, 'Use'. Since the word's neutral sense could expose it to a bad use, as in XIII 288 (= *MED* 3a, in opposition to *outwit*), that sense is ruled out here, where Inwit is *wis* and his sons not just the senses, the *(out)wits*, but the right uses (of sight, speech, hearing, touch and motion). The parallel in *The Ayenbite of Inwit* (1340) is incorrectly described by Sk. There Inwit is the house guarded by *wyl of skele* 'rational will' (? = free will, conscience); see the edn. by R. Morris (*EETS* 23 (1866) p. 263). See further Harwood and Smith, 'Inwit'.

35 The point here is not that *Faciamus* is a plural verb (Sk) but that it means 'Let us *make*' (implying for Langl. an action) in contrast with *Dixit* 32a, the (merely) verbal command that created the beasts. So the question of the Persons of the Trinity is not the issue. Goodridge, following Sk's misleading note, makes no sense of the passage and gives a note which makes no sense in itself. What the action (*myght* 37 expressing itself in *werkmanshipe* 45) was appears from the verbs *Formavit, inspiravit, aedificavit* in Gen 2: 7, 22. In 43 *with* thus = 'along with, in addition to' *not* 'by means of', and the purpose of the 'writing' analogy is that in addition to the 'slime of the earth' (= *parchemyn*) and his knowledge (*wit*) God 'needed' the active exertion of his power in 'forming, breathing, building', as it were instrumentally (= *penne*).

53 If *Inwit* here means 'man's rational (judging) power' rather than 'conscience' in the narrower sense it is easier to see how it can be both abused by gluttons and lacked by idiots, children and women without protectors. Yet 59, which suggests 'conscience', is hard to reconcile with the allegory of 10–24, where Inwit's role was to *save* 'protect' (23) Anima, not lead (58), a function earlier given to Dobest (16). See further my art. on 'Anima' and 'Inwit'.

64a Sk notes occurred in graces before and after meals. But Langl. already seems to be using drunkenness as a general symbol of *synful lif* (63), the opposite of charity.

65–6 *fordo; shoop*: the drunkard who destroys his reason, in virtue of which man is God's 'likeness', uncreates the creator's work. The juxtaposition of ideas of destroying, creating and redeeming anticipates the fervent lines against murder (XVII 274–82) as does the notion of the Creator/Redeemer forsaking (withdrawing his grace from) his rebellious creature.

73–4 The four doctors of the Western Church, Ambrose, Augustine, Jerome and Gregory. *Luc:* as Goodridge notes, Acts 6: 1 speaks of widows, but an apter scripture would be Js 1: 27, which links widows and fatherless, echoing Deut 16: 11–14 etc.

90–2 Wit condemns bishops who patronize bawdy minstrels but will not feed ragged beggars. Their failure is a Judas-like betrayal of Christ (Judas was, in fact, the apostles' purse-keeper (Jn 13: 29), which sharpens the point of the comparison).

95–8a After a long discourse on man's origin, rational nature and duty to his kind, Wit gives his first definition of Dowel, Dobet and Dobest. Like his third and fourth (200–3, 204–7) it specifies inward dispositions: Dowel = fear of God / keeping the Law; Dobet = fear of God from love of God / loving friend and enemy / suffering (? = patience); Dobest = (?) contemplative withdrawal / active works of charity / humility bringing power over evil. At 108 comes a definition of Dowel only, as faithful marriage, an outward, objective state, though one reflecting an inner disposition (cf. VIII 81–4). This objective definition introduces the second theme of IX, the right and wrong sexual relations between men and women, the sustainers of the social fabric.

114, 117 *thus* seems to imply Langl. sees the existing marriage arrangements as divinely instituted. As customary and proper, he sees them as right and good in contrast to the irregularities and disorders to be described.

118 *witnesse* means not 'present at' (whence Sk finds a ref. to the Marriage at Cana, Jn 2: 2) but 'bearing testimony to'—i.e. the paradisal quality of marriage, the allusion being to Gen 2: 18–25; cf. the very similar thought in *Purity* 697–704.

121 Wr (p. 533) refers to an unspecified legend that 'Cain was born during

Literary and Historical

the period of penitence and fasting to which our first parents were condemned for their breach of obedience'. I have not traced the legend.

123 alludes to the destruction of Cain's progeny in the Flood. The verbs are preterite in that case; but if Langl. is speaking metaphorically of *sherewes* as Cain's kin (a common expression) they could be present.

124–6 Some early Latin Christian writers, e.g. Augustine in *De Civitate Dei* 15: 23 (Corpus Christianorum Series Latina 48, pp. 490ff), interpreted 'the sons of God' and 'the daughters of men' in Gen 6: 2, 4 as respectively Seth's offspring and Cain's. This tradition appears in Comestor's *Historia* (Gen ch. 31) from which, as Sk notes, Langl. probably got the idea of God's prohibition to Seth. Cf. Wilson, *Gawain-Poet*, pp. 88–92.

149 Langl. may specify the elder as the tree on which Judas was believed to have hanged himself. He associates Judas and Cain at I 66–8, *q.v.* They are also linked intriguingly in the Towneley play *Suspensio Iude*, where Judas calls himself a 'Cursyd Clott of Camys kyn' (ed. Pollard and England, *EETS* 71 (1897), l. 17). The fruit-tree imagery anticipates that of the Tree of Charity in XVI.

154–5 Wit argues that to marry for the wrong reasons is to act 'against God's will' by re-enacting the sin of the Sethites (*thei* 154), who 'imped their apples' on the Cainite 'elders'. The analogy lends force to the word *unkyndely* 157 and the pun in 160, which highlights the perversion of values involved in confusing virtue with wealth.

161 The idea here of Christ as fount of nobility anticipates the picture of him as conqueror, ennobler of his followers in XIX 32ff. Cf. Chaucer in *WBT* (D 1117–18).

167 Wit's comment on the effect of the Black Death upon marriages may be compared with Reason's on the upbringing of children (V 35–6).

169 seems to imply, unless *no* is rhetorical exaggeration, that fewer children were born. Marriages and births rose after the Black Death in 1348, the 'pestilence' presumably alluded to, but by the time of the B-text the previous trend of decline had returned (Postan, ch. 3 'Population', p. 43).

170–2 allude to the custom at Dunmow in Essex of awarding a flitch of bacon to a couple married for a year who could swear they had never quarrelled.

179 *seculer* Sk wrongly takes to cover the secular clergy. *OED s.v.* 2 gives ample contemporary support for the meaning 'lay' (as opposed to clerical) and there is no support in Langl. for the uncanonical view that priests might marry.

181 *lymeyerd*: a twig smeared with thick glue to trap birds. There may be a pun on *yerde OED* 11, meaning 'penis' (cf. the witty play on *wepene* and *wreke* in 182–3).

183a The second line is found in a couplet from John of Bridlington (quoted by Sk), but the source is probably older.

186 *untyme* may refer to fasting-times or, more generally, to any period when either partner might not be in a state of grace. 187–8 specify the conditions for virtuous intercourse: chastity, charity and canonical wedlock.

192 The words of St Paul which Langl. quotes give a somewhat negative reason for marrying, which does not seem to accord with 117–18; but he may also have been remembering Gen 2: 18, *Non est bonum esse hominem solum ... &c.*

200–end On these definitions, see the analysis at 95–8 (*C*) above.

329

PASSUS X

12 The Earthly Paradise was believed to be full of precious stones which 'grew'; see Gen 2: 12 for the basis of the idea and cf. *Pearl* 73ff.

18 *card*: comb out impurities in wool and straighten the fibres for spinning with a metal instrument with the hooks of teasels attached to it. Intellectual ability will not succeed unless ' dressed ' with ambitious greed.

30–50 An attack on the decline of minstrelsy (on which see Poole, pp. 605–10, Strutt, *Sports*, pp. 152–66). Lords and even high clergy patronize bawdry rather than religious poetry.

66 This is graphically illustrated by the gluttonous Doctor at XIII 100ff.

68a True charity (*eam* [the ark] is glossed *caritatem* in C) is found amongst the humble and simple country people. Ephrata is Bethlehem in the famous messianic prophecy of Micah 5: 2, and as the place of Christ's birth in a stable, an apt symbol of humility. Goodridge's interpretation, 'We *hear* God spoken of among the wealthy (at Ephrata) but we only find him among the poor, in country places' has no basis in the text.

71 Friars who raised such *questions* 'problems' in the early C14th are the Franciscan Peter Aureole and the Dominican Durandus of St Pourçain (see Leff, pp. 272–9).

73 The Cross just north of the east end of St Paul's was used for open-air preaching.

75–84a reflect the social upheaval caused by the Plague. Study links the clerics' intellectual pride with ordinary worldly pride (cf. Reason at V 13–20). Her twin themes are laymen's theological pride (fostered by friars' preaching and influence) and the decay of the social fabric.

79 *girles*: the outbreak of 1361–2 was 'known as the *mortalité des enfants*' (McKisack, p. 331). Children suffer for their parents' *giltes*; cf. IX 143–4, and see Ex 20: 5).

95 A celebrated specimen of a friar of this type occurs in Chaucer's *SumT*.

96–102 A vivid glimpse of domestic life in the manor house (on which see Colvin, in Poole, pp. 41–50). Langl. attacks eating in private less as an undesirable social innovation than as a practice destructive of charity (see 99).

117 Study's striking reference to Ymaginatif, who only appears at XI 408, shows Langl. carefully planning his poem and using each of Will's interlocutors for a definite purpose in the task of bringing him to know Dowel. Ymag. does not explain why men suffer death but he does defend *clergye* (divine learning which teaches about God), attacked by the lay *maistres* 115 and by Will XI 367–73 when he rebukes Reason.

118 The Romans passage exhorts 'to be wise unto sobriety'. Sk's quotation from Aug.'s *De Baptismo contra Donatistas* attacking the 'human temptation' to wish 'to know a thing as it is in itself (*aliquid sapere quam res se habet*)' is strikingly like a critique of the *kynde knowyng* Will insists on in VIII 58 and 111. On the latter phrase see the art. by Davlin.

129–30 Study's stress not just on the absolute supremacy of God's will but on the need to accept it in faith may reflect Bradwardine's stand earlier in the century against Ockham's followers (see Leff, pp. 286–99). Her attack on the quest for distinctions between Dowel and Dobet implies that those who really do well do not need to ask and that the way to do well is 'love' (189–90, 205–6 below).

148–9 Because Will's request for *kynde knowyng* is now made in *mekenesse* 'humility' Study undertakes to guide him. He has too precipitately sought *wit*, which is inseparably 'wedded' to, can only be reached by, *study*. After a course of study, he will be able to confront *clergye* 'learning', 'wedded' to God's written word (*scripture*).

152 The basic university arts course consisted of the *trivium* (grammar, rhetoric, logic: mastery of language and reasoning) and the *quadrivium* (arithmetic, geometry, astronomy, music: substantial sciences). Scripture formed part of the advanced course for a theology degree. The seven arts are, as it were, her younger sisters.

156 Will's improved disposition is shown in his valuing wisdom more than gold (Prov 8: 10).

159–69 recalls P.'s directions to the pilgrims. *left half* 164: cf. V 578.

174 *musons*: the time and rhythm of *mensurable* music (as opposed to *immensurable*, e.g. plainchant), denoted by various signs. See the long note in Sk.

175 Plato did write poems, but Langl. means 'writer', as of Aristotle at XII 260.

186 Study's disquiet about Theology (the academic subject, not quite identical with the authoritative figure of II 115, the approved teaching tradition of the Church) may reflect contemporary unease caused by the speculations of advanced thinkers like Holcot, Buckingham and Adam of Woodham (see Leff, pp. 291–3).

208 Geomancy is 'divination by means of earth, dots and figures written in the ground, etc' (*MED*). See Chaucer *KtT* (A 2045) and Robinson's note.

211–12 *fibicches: MED's* sugg. '? some kind of alchemical manipulations or tricks' (foll. Quirk's deriv. from *Pebichios*, an early alchemist) is supported by 212. cf. Chaucer's *CYT*.

217 *kyndely* belongs metrically in the a-half (= 'kindly') but also looks across to the b-half to form the phrase *kyndely to knowe*.

230–57 Clergie's def. of Dowel (*It* 230) is 'to believe in God'; of Dobet, 'to live out one's belief (by acts of charity)'; of Dobest, 'to rebuke sinners' (implying the right to do so, i.e. the previous two, and perhaps holy orders).

238a is from the Athanasian Creed, clause 15, said at Prime on Sundays.

241 refers to the fifteen books of Augustine's *De Trinitate* (completed 417 A.D.). Bk. IV ch. 15 sect. 20 attacks the pride of intellectuals who mock 'the mass of Christians who live by faith alone.' Clergy wishes to establish that it is necessary for all to believe in the doctrine of the Trinity but not for any to understand it (for none can).

259–327 Clergie now launches into a long digressive diatribe against unworthy religious.

264 *bosard*: 'an inferior kind of hawk, useless for falconry' (*OED*). Langland's image compares the ignorant priest to a bird lacking the falcon's keen sight and training.

265 *person* (Lat *persona*): 'a holder of a parochial benefice in full possession of its rights and dues, a rector' (*OED s.v.* parson), here distinguished from vicars, acting in place of the rector, and curates, temporary paid assistants to the rector or vicar (see McKisack, pp. 302–3).

278–80 Ophni and Phinees, sons of Heli the priest, stole the sacrificial meats for themselves, arousing God's anger. When Israel was fighting the Philistines, they brought the ark of the covenant into the battle. They were killed and the ark taken. When Heli heard the news he fell backwards and broke his neck. Clergie's point is that unless priests desist from rapacity, the mere fact of their being priests will not save them from God's wrath in the end.

284 Sk may be right that these 'homespun scholars' are laymen who can read, since this meaning fits well with the sense of 286–8.

290–1 St Gregory the Great (pope 590–604), one of the Four Doctors (IX 73), author of the influential work of allegorical exegesis, the *Moralia in Job*. The exact source of this passage is untraced, but Sk notes a text in Gratian from a Pope Eugenius, 'As a fish without water loses life, so does a monk without a monastery' and it appears in the *Legenda Aurea* ch. 21 sect. iv, which Langl. uses at XV 269ff. (cf. Chaucer *GP* A 179–81).

297–8 Orsten, 'Vision', quotes from Bishop Brinton 'si sit vita angelica in terra, aut est in studio, vel in clanstro'.

301–3 Clergie contrasts unfavourably the lax monasteries with the rigorous universities. cf. the genial view of monks in V 169–79; on monasteries at the time, McKisack pp. 305–9.

310–13 The rector, individual or corporation (e.g. a monastery) owned the greater (predial or agrarian) tithe. Cl. speaks of (absentee) monastic rectors who do not repair their churches (310) and of incumbents (possibly canons regular rather than monks) who simply exploit their property like lay lords.

314–27 This famous 'prophecy' of the Reformation is really an apocalyptic threat that the pride and negligence of religious will be chastised by king and nobles, who will resume the lands given to the orders in former times.

319a alludes to the fall of the rich monks who now ride about in state (305–6).

320–2 Clergie's point is that if friars have a share in church (esp. monastic) wealth they will have no need to beg, with the evils that brings (cf. XX 384). The passage looks forward to XV 549–67. On the allusion to the Donation of Constantine (the endowing of the Roman Church with property) see note on that passage. 'Gregory's god-children' are esp. monks, since he was a monk before (reluctantly) becoming pope.

323 Abingdon Abbey, now in Oxfordshire, was one of the oldest and richest in England.

325–7 Isaiah foretells the fall of the King of Babylon through pride. Clergie associates the monks with him as receivers of large revenues from their many lands (*exactor*, *tributum*). Cain (? = Antichrist) suggests upheaval before the new age.

328 Will's naïve question, provoked by Clergie's (apparent but not real) equation of the future reforming king with Dowel, occasions the return to the theme laid aside by Cl. at 258 and a transition to Will's argument with Scripture.

341–3 could allude to I Pet 3: 21, Gal 3: 27–9; A, misattributing to Pet., quotes Mk 16: 16.

344 *in extremis*: at the point of death, a pagan, Moslem or Jew desiring baptism may have no Christian at hand to administer it. The disputation has continued in scholastic style: Scr. has not refuted Will's scriptural proof-text but distinguished the narrower sense in which it can be absolutely true (i.e. when baptism can be all that is both necessary and sufficient for salvation). What Christians need is *to lovye* (355).

364 *Non mecaberis*: 'thou shalt not commit adultery', confused with 'thou shalt not kill' (*Non occides*) perhaps through unconscious confusion with *necare* 'kill' (see Sk).

371–4 Scr. has only said that charity, shown in good deeds, is necessary for salvation. Will is oppressed by the fact that theologians have found in the Scriptures the dread doctrine of predestination; so he goes on to attack learning as useless and dangerous.

383 Aristotle would be in hell as a pagan, Solomon for his idolatry in his later years (3 Kg 11: 1–11). Dunning, 'Salvation', p. 52, shows that medieval theologians had developed a doctrine of baptism by the Holy Ghost (direct infusion of grace into a man of perfect good will), *Baptismus flaminis* ('thorugh fir is fullyng' XII 284).

403 The image of the Church as the ark of salvation breasting the waves of the world and time goes back to I Pet 3: 20, which compares Noah's family, 'the eight souls . . . saved by water' to Christians saved by baptism. The laity might be saved (through the clergy's preaching) while the clergy are damned (through not living up to their own preaching).

408 The fiery flood of the last days (I Pet 3: 10) foreshadowed by Noah's flood.

414 alludes to Christ's promise in Lk 23: 43. In *The Gospel of Nicodemus* the patriarchs to their surprise meet the thief in paradise; see the ME translation, ed. Hulme, 1573ff.

419 She was seen as the type of sinners since the 'seven devils' cast out of her (Mk 16: 9) came to be interpreted symbolically as the Seven Deadly Sins.

438 The statement is less dispiriting in context, where it compares men to God, of whom alone it can be properly said that he is 'good'.

452a The original translates (Keble): 'The unlearned (*indocti*) start up and *take heaven by force* [alluding to tradl. interpretation of Mt 11: 12], and we with our learning and without heart (*sine corde*), lo, where we wallow in flesh and blood' (*P.L.* 32, 757). If Langl. was not using some other Augustinian source, then he has omitted *sine corde* (which had left learning *per se* blameless) and replaced 'flesh and blood' with 'hell'. He thus attacks learning as dangerous in itself. Possibly the distortion was meant to be recognized by some readers, who would appreciate Will's extremism.

PASSUS XI

3 The opening of the pseudo-Bernardine *Cogitationes Piissimae de cognitione humanae conditionis* (*P.L.* 184, 485).

7 Fortune is described in Chaucer's *Boece* Bk II, pr. 1 as 'thilke merveylous monstre . . . sche useth ful flaterynge famylarite with hem that sche enforceth to bygyle, so longe, til that sche confounde with unsuffrable sorwe hem that sche hath left in despeer unpurveied' (ed. Robinson, p. 329).

9 *Middelerthe*: the earth thought of as placed between heaven and hell (a *mountaigne* at 323, here almost = the field of folk). *merv. met.* 6 recalls *merv. swevene* Prol 11, *wondres* 10 recalls Prol 4. The world's pleasures are gathered into a panoramic spectacle before him, as in a magic mirror (cf. *MerT*, E 1582ff). Js 1: 23–4 links failure to know oneself (see 3 above) and the image of a mirror in describing mere hearers not doers of the word, who are like men who look in a mirror and then forget what they look like (their true features, nature). Will becomes such a man, hearing the word but not doing. The idea of a mirror of nature was perhaps sugg. by the title of Vincent of Beauvais' encyclopaedia, the *Speculum Naturale*.

13–15 Jn describes these three as 'all that is in the world' (cf. Study, X 161–4). King Life is the main character in the mid-C14th morality *The Pride of Life* (ed. Davis). Life reappears in XX, which recapitulates this sequence (Elde at 95, Fortune at 110).

27 Elde appears in *The Parlement of the Thre Ages* (ed. Offord) of *c.* 1370, which Langl. could have known. His speech 265–94 is close to this one and in 290 he warns Youth and Middle Eld, 'Makes ʒoure mirrours bi me'.

34, 42 *Rechelesnesse*: an attitude of total abandonment to what may come, not bad in itself if attuned to Truth (39, alluding perh. to Mt 6: 25–34); but *Faunteltee* is childish irresponsibility, into which such an attitude can degenerate; see Donaldson, *C-Text*, pp. 171ff.

47 implies Will was young before his 'wit' began to 'torne' and wasted forty years following his youth (this goes well with *elde* 60 and makes him about 65). Sk takes 45 as his total age, partly from XII 3 (not quite parallel), which makes poorer sense in itself (Will becoming guilty of these sins even as a child) and goes less well with 60, which does not mention a further 20 or so years spent with Fortune.

58 *pol*: each friar individually will pray for him; cf. VII 192–3, III 63.

76–7 Both were more profitable and there was always hope of gifts from the dead man's relatives or a legacy. *catecumelynges*: properly young people receiving instruction (either converts or) in preparation for confirmation; baptizands were mostly infants.

87 Lewte's Peter text may be I Pet 1: 22, on sincere brotherly love, with its implied corollary, sincere rebuke (the wording is close).

100 *synne*: i.e. sins told to them in the secrecy of the confessional.

101–6 Lewte, 'Fairness, Justice' licenses Will to satirise notorious abuses but not to expose individuals' faults. Since Scripture confirms him, this may express the poet's own view of the legitimate scope of satiric and polemical poetry.

120–2 The image is of Christ offering his blood as a healing potion for sinners to drink (cf. XVIII 364–73).

127–36 boldly compares the Christian who lapses to the villein who quits his manor. He has no right to do so, and will have to pay for it in the end, just as the lapsed Christian will have to face his creator's judgment. On villeins, see McKisack pp. 326–8.

140 The quiet harmonious dialogue of Will and Scr. is broken by a contemptuous cry against the *bokes* 139 of which Scr. is custodian. Not all of Trajan's speech, which runs to 318, is strictly apt to the Roman Emperor, but he is a figure from heaven with supernatural authority and knowledge. *oon* 319, perh. recalling *oon* 140, may confirm the limits of the speech.

Emperor A.D. 98–117, he was famed for his justice and integrity. The story of his release from hell through the prayers and tears of Pope Gregory goes back to early lives of the latter. The point of the story is that just pagans, dead or living, have hope of being saved through God's special mercy; cf. the Middle English alliterative poem *St Erkenwald*.

160 The *Legenda Aurea* of Jacobus a Voragine (1230–98), Archbishop of Genoa, tells the story in the life of St Gregory (46: 10).

163 Here God's power breaking through hell's gates (cf. XVIII 322–3) is hard to distinguish from the man's *truthe*, which enabled *him* to 'break out of hell' (140 above).

166ff do not contradict Scripture's *bokes*: she taught Will the same lesson (X 344). Trajan's argument that learning without love is valueless does not *condemn* learning *per se*, and is close to Aug. (X 452 (*C*) above). Gradually the teaching on love intensifies.

185 alludes to Mt 25: 35ff. Christ is served in 'one of these my least brethren' (25: 40). This is developed at 198–203 below, with which cf. VI 207–9. Trajan recalls Piers' teaching and looks forward to Christ's own words at XVIII 376–9.

202 *quasi modo geniti* opens the Introit for the Mass of the Sunday within the Octave of Easter. The Lesson of the day contains the passage from I Jn 5: 6 on the water and blood from Christ's side (symbolizing baptism and eucharist) and may have suggested 200.

203 *synne* makes the sinner a slave, and it is not the slave but the son who will inherit eternal life; see Jn 8: 34–6 (noted Sk).

204 The phrase 'sons of men' (*filii hominum*) is confined to the OT (Sk).

229a I have not traced the quotation in Gregory, but Robertson and Huppé (*PP and Scriptural Tradition*, Princeton 1951) remark the following, which is close: 'Melius est enim scire infirmitatem nostram, quam naturas rerum. Laudabilior enim est animus cui nota est infirmitas sua, quam qui ea non respecta, siderum viam *scrutatur*, et terrarum fundamenta, et coelorum fastigia ...' (attrib. to Aug. by Peter Lombard, *Collectanea*, in *P.L.* 191, 1601). The lines, for which Lomb. gives no source in Aug., are the source of a passage in ch. V of the pseudo-Bernardine treatise quoted in XI 3 (*q.v.*).

240 *pilgrymes*: wanderers, *peregrini*, until we find our true home, heaven (cf. Heb 13: 14).

248 Langl. confuses Mary Magdalen with Mary of Bethany because Jn 11: 2 calls her 'she that anointed the Lord with ointment' (cf. Lk 7: 38) and the latter was commonly identified with Mary of Magdala.

253 *poverte* has the extended sense 'poverty of spirit, humility' (cf. 239 above) which is aptly used of one 'who, sitting at the Lord's feet, heard his word.' Exegetes often took Martha as representing the active, Mary the contemplative form of life.

255 introduces the theme of Patient Poverty, to be developed in XIII.

284a Sk finds 'unconnected with the subject'. But Ps 42 is the entrance psalm at Mass and vs. 1 ends 'ab homine iniquo et doloso erue me.' Such men the celebrant should avoid, not take gifts from, and they are mentioned again in the *Lavabo* psalm of the Offertory as 'impiis ... In quorum manibus iniquitates sunt: dextera eorum repleta est *muneribus*' (Ps 25: 10). Now since this same psalm begins also with the words *Iudica me*, it is easy to see how Langl. (or possibly the Bx scribe) completed it wrongly from Ps 42.

285 Ps 36 speaks of God protecting the just in need, not specifically priests.

290 *he*: 'the pope' (Sk); but it is probably parallel with *bisshop* (*Or* 291 = *vel*, not *aut*) since he and not the pope would presumably have ordained him (see 301 below).

310 Those who skip portions of the Mass or Offices do not 'sing wisely'.

312 strikingly fuses the image of knighting (292–5) with that of ordination, though (cf. Sk) *MED* sense 3(a) for *knyght* 'servant' is possible here.

316 *ydiotes* is here adjectival and takes a plural like a French adjective.

357–8 Aristotle's *Historia Animalium* VI, ii, does not seem the source of the passage (see Peck's translation in the Loeb edn. p. 231). Perhaps Langl. had in mind the billing of pigeons, which Aristotle notes as preliminary to copulation (VI, ii, end, p. 233). Trevisa's translation of Bartholomaeus Anglicus (ed. M. C. Seymour *et al.*) tells how 'the pohenne . . . hidiþ hire eiren [eggs] fro þe male, for he brekeþ hem and he may hem fynde, as Aristotil seiþ' (Bk 19, ch. 107); see also Sk's addition 'to occupy him the more in his lecherie' (from Batman uppon Bartholomè, 12, 31). Aristotle merely calls the peacock 'jealous and conceited' (*Hist. An.* 488b 23).

368–74 For discussion, see my art. 'Philosophy', p. 148.

375–6 On God's 'glorious, and secret, and hidden' works see Ecclus 11: 4.

386 cf. Ecclus 11: 7.

410 This new definition of Dowel takes up elements of Wit's at IX 95–8*a* (*C*) etc. Will has not yet learnt patience, but he has learnt to appreciate its value.

PASSUS XII

1 *Ymag.*: the word's form suggests equivalence to *vertu imaginatif* in *MED* sense 1(c): 'the ability to form images of things not experienced, e.g. of past or future events' (see refs.). For thorough discussion of earlier interpretations, see Harwood, 'Imag.'. Imag. is not a name Anima applies to himself in XV (though 'Thought' is); perhaps Langl. saw it as intermediary between the bodily senses and the rational soul, providing images from which the intellect draws ideas by abstraction. Harwood sees Ymag. as personifying 'the mind's power for making similitudes' (p. 249).

9a refers in context to Christ's Second Coming, the time of which is unknown. Ymag. equates the three watches of the night with the Three Ages of Man: 'if death does not come at the first or second, it will come at the third: be prepared', an interpretation found in the *Glossa Ordinaria* (*P.L.* 114, 298), noted by Robertson and Huppé, p. 149.

12a comes from the Lord's words to the Laodiceans, who were 'neither cold nor hot'. The warning to come suddenly at 3: 20 links the quoted phrase with that from Lk. Will is to grasp that public and private afflictions are God's signs to sinners to repent in time.

13a Ymag. interprets the shepherd's 'rod and staff' (for guiding the sheep) as instruments for beating: 'God's corrections turn to consolations' (Sk).

19 Friars often went about in pairs, e.g. those at VIII 8.

29–31 Ymag. defines Dowel as *faith* (following *lewte*, keeping God's law), Dobet as *hope*, Dobest as *charity*. His expansion of Dowel develops into a defence of learning (*clergie*).

36 For illustrations of Our Lady's shrine at Roquemadour, see Jusserand, *Life*, pp. 338, 365.

40–1 The answer to the question may be 'self-esteem' (?which makes girls wish to marry).

43–4 Aristotle was said by Eumelus to have killed himself by drinking hemlock ('The Myth of Aristotle's Suicide', ch. xiv in Chroust). Hippocrates in *The Seven Sages* (ed. K. Brunner, *EETS* 191 (1932), 1040ff) dies of dysentery sent as a divine punishment for murder. Virgil was said to have died in a sudden tempest, also to have had himself cut to pieces as part of a magical attempt at self-rejuvenation, which failed (Comparetti, p. 367). Alexander in common medieval tradition was poisoned. These four represent respectively Philosophy, Medicine, Literature and Earthly Empire.

46 *Felice the Fair*: heroine of the popular romance *Guy of Warwick*. She tells Guy 'Yuel were min fairhed sett on þe, / & y swiche a grome toke' (Auch. MS, ed. Zupitza, p. 24). She contemplates suicide when Guy leaves her on pilgrimage (p. 408) and dies of grief soon after his death. Fair Rosamond, Walter Lord Clifford's daughter, Henry II's mistress, allegedly poisoned by Queen Eleanor (1177), was buried at Godstow nunnery.

50a The Latin continues *Non hos sed verbum pectore fige tuo*, 'Fix not the men in your heart, only their words' (Wright, *Poets*, vol. 2, p. 130, *cit*. Alford, 'Quotations').

54a The context makes clear that 'unto whomsoever much is given [*sc*. the rich and the wise, cf. 6: 38], of him much shall be required' (Lk 12: 48); see 57–8.

60 The image of grace as a herb growing from humility (Patient Poverty) anticipates that of the Tree of Charity at XVI 5–9, and looks back to I 152.

63–9a refer closely to Jn 3: 8–16. The *greet love* 68 is God's for the world (Jn 3: 16).

75 Stoning is specified in Deut 22: 23–4 as the punishment for an espoused girl who is willingly unchaste.

77 *clergie*: Sk refers us to St Augustine (Homily 33 on St John, vii, 6, Library of Fathers, Oxford 1848, p. 477) which states that Christ 'is the Lawgiver ... What else doth he signify ... when with his finger he writeth on the ground? For with the finger of God was the law written ...' Line 73 strongly suggests that Langl. had this in mind. The interpretation of the *caractes* as announcing the Pharisees' sins comes from Jerome (*Dial. adv. Pelag., P.L.* 23, 553).

84 *mansede* may here imply 'excommunicated'. Such a man receiving Holy Communion (see 90–1 below) 'eateth and drinketh judgment to himself' (I Cor 11: 29).

89a perh. suggested by the meaning of Jn 8: 1–11 and the wording of I Cor 11: 31, *q.v.*

90 The pl. *bretheren*, out of place here, may be unconsciously retained from I Cor 11: 2, 33.

95 The comparison of *clergie* and *kynde wit* to mirrors was perhaps suggested by Js 1 : 23–4 (see also XI 9): both sense-perception and learning can be means to self-knowledge.

105–6 as Sk notes may allude to the action of the blind king John of Bohemia, killed at the Battle of Crécy, Aug 26 1346 (see Froissart, tr. Lord Berners, ch. 130).

113 *Levites*: see Num 1: 50–1, 3: 31; II Kg 15: 24.

125 Ps 104: 15, referring to the Israelites, is applied by Ymag. to priesthood (anointing forms part of ordination).

136, 139a This sort of *kynde knowyng* does not avail for salvation because it concerns only the empirically knowable (= the natural world). *Sapiencia* (here = *science* 137), the wisdom of those who know only the natural world, is counted as true *folye* because it gives no knowledge of God. Paul advises the Corinthians to become fools (i.e. humble) that they may be wise in the eyes of God (vs. 18).

146–7a Ymag. means that the statement 'there was no room in the inn' implies that Joseph and Mary were seeking a room at an inn and therefore cannot have been beggars. He wishes to deny the claim that mendicancy can be traced back to Christ himself.

149 The associating of *poetes* with *pastours* may be due to recollection that David, the Bible's 'poet' par excellence, was a shepherd (I Kg 16: 11) or to knowledge of Virgil's Eclogues, esp. the Fourth, with its 'prophecy' of a Saviour, often taken in the Middle Ages in a Christian sense.

157 *contrariedest*: i.e. at X 439–72a.

161ff Sk sees as imitated from Boethius (*Boece* IV pr. 2, 103); but the comparison is not close. Langl. speaks not of a natural power (use of feet) but acquired skill (*clergie*).

177–8a Ymag. alludes to vs. 5: confessing sin to God with contrition brings forgiveness.

189 Ps 15 begins aptly 'Preserve me, O Lord . . .' and ability to read this enabled a man to claim benefit of clergy and so escape hanging for certain offences on a first conviction (the 'neck-verse', as it came to be called, was more usually Ps 50: 1).

190 A permanent gallows stood at Tyburn, the chief place of execution.

192 Ymag. refers us back to Will's argument at X 411–18.

193 The variant *recreaunt* (MSS RM) makes the metaphor unequivocally chivalric but loses the pun on 'believing': the thief's 'defeat', through his faith, turns to 'victory'.

207a Ecclus goes on to warn against presuming on God's mercy.

216a The phrases, for which Sk finds parallels in Peter Comestor, etc., may echo the emphasis in contemporary theology on God's absolute power (on which see Leff, pp. 288ff). The passage from *Hist. Schol.* ch. 24 speaks of the futility of seeking the cause of the divine will, since it is itself the highest of all causes.

243 Peacocks were still eaten at this time, but their popularity was waning.

257 *Avynet*, as Wr notes, means generically a collection of fables. Avienus was a C4th writer of Latin fables. Wr quotes the morality of Fable 39 in Robert's *Fables Inédits* (on the peacock who lost his voice) which constrasts the fate of the earthly rich, who will be poor in heaven, with that of those who live poor but just on earth, who will enjoy riches in heaven. The detail of the peacock's feet is untraced.

262–7 Aristotle in his *Historia Animalium* IX. 25 (ed. D'Arcy Thompson, Oxford 1910) notes that the lark is edible, but does not make the moral comparison he is credited with. *logik* 267 seems chosen for the metre and perhaps because of his fame as a dialectician.

270–80 Ymag.'s stress is on *salvabitur* rather than *vix*, implying that *if* Aristotle, Socrates etc. are found just at judgment day their salvation is assured.

283–4a On the three kinds of baptism see Dunning, 'Salvation', cit. at X 383. Baptism of blood is that of the martyr.

292 As Sk notes, the *Glossa Ordinaria* glosses the words *mecum es* 'you are with me' (which complete Ps 22: 4) as follows, '*i.e. in corde per fidem*'. This suggests the view that pagans of just life possess an *implied* faith in Christianity, *sc.* they would (have) believe(d), if they knew about it, and this faith ('baptism by fire') may justify them in the sight of God; see also p. 304.

PASSUS XIII

1–20 summarizes XI and XII from the inner dream to the end of Vision 3. Will's *wo and wrathe* XI 4 have become *fey witlesnesse*, a long-lasting mental anguish overshadowed by forebodings of death and damnation. His distress makes him sleep and Conscience, absent since Vision 1, comes to comfort him.

24 Will's eagerness for *clergie* is the fruit of Ymaginatif's instruction. But after meeting the Doctor he has his earlier misgivings shockingly confirmed and withdraws from learning into the company of a spiritual virtue, Patience, to seek the *kynde knowyng* of Dowel he has sought in vain elsewhere.

39a Christ's instruction to his disciples is dramatically realized: the just man's food is to be 'every word that proceedeth from the mouth of God' (Mt 4: 4), i.e. the Scripture and the Fathers (noted Owen, p. 103; cf. XIV 47a).

45–5a warns (supported by an unidentified authority) that friars who profit from dishonestly-won wealth will themselves be punished after death unless they do penance and say mass for the souls of their dead benefactors. The notion of 'eating sins' (as Sk notes from Warton) may come from Huon de Méri's *Tournoiment de l'Antichrist* (see Owen, pp. 104–7).

60a The preceding vs (Is 5: 21) accounts for the one quoted: 'Woe to you that are wise in your own eyes, and prudent in your own conceits' (appropriate for the Doctor).

82 *Mahoun*: a corruption of Mahomet, popularly believed (though not by Langl.) to be worshipped by the Moslems as a god; here = 'the Devil himself'.

83 *jurdan*: a possible allusion to the Dominican friar William Jordan (see Marcett) does not seem in tune with Langland's methods and views as a satirist (see XI 101–6).

90 *Pocalips*: the parodistic *Apocalypse of Golias* attributed to Walter Map, which has a description of greedy abbots (ed. Wright, *Mapes*, 11 341–80). *Averys*: either a corruption of Aurea or Avoya (Sk) or an imaginary 'saint' with a name suited to the Doctor, whose own 'passion' (cf. penaunce 87) can be imagined as over-eating.

94–5 *leef* suggests the *forel* contained a book defending the friars' way of life.

108–9 Will's point seems to be that if the friar leaves the sick in his infirmary to eat 'penitents' food' while he eats *mortrews &c* there will be violent protests. It is not clear who exactly *yonge children* refers to.

115–17a After defining Dowel at 104 as 'Do no evil' (an improvement on the friar at VIII 45) he equates it implicitly with obedience to the clergy; Dobet with the clergy *qua* teachers; and Dobest with doing as one preaches, a confused mixture.

119–29 This *ad hoc.* allegory makes the seven arts Clergie's sons (cf. X 152, though the *castel* image recalls rather IX 1–24). The comment on Piers (who did not attack learning *per se*) presupposes knowledge of the latter ulterior to that supplied in the text (e.g. recognition of an implicit symbolic value in the Plowman). Ps 14 is a psalm about 'Dowel', negatively and positively expressed (vss 3, 5). On *infinites* 'limitless, boundless things' see the art. by Middleton.

134 A proverbial phrase *vincit qui patitur* 'he conquers who suffers' is recorded (Sk). Connecting patience with Dowel suggests the infl. of Romans 2: 7, 10, where *boni operis* recalls the *bona egerunt* of the Pardon.

136–8 Patience does not 'set science at a sop': learning and teaching are steps to Dobest.

150–71 See Sk and the important arts. by Kaske (revd. vsn. in Blanch) and Schweitzer, Smith, 'Riddle' and Goodridge 'Appendix C'. The grammatical 'power of transitivity' is that 'by which a verb "rules" its direct object in the accusative case' (Kaske, p. 236). This may be a pun on *transitus* 'passage' in Ex 12: 11 (Schweitzer, p. 315) involving an allusion to the Pasch (which celebrated the Hebrews' deliverance from Egypt) and hence to Christ's passion, death and resurrection. *laumpe lyne* plays on grammatical and liturgical significances, alluding to the phrase from Priscian's grammar *Tene hanc lampadem* 'illustrating grammatical "rulership" by the verb *ex v. t.*' (Kaske, pp. 240–1) and *half* the priest's words to the baptizand in the rite of solemn baptism during the Easter vigil 'Accipe lampadem ardentem et irreprehensibilem: custodi baptismum tuum: serva mandata . . .' (*Sarum Manual*, qu. Schweitzer), the candle symbolizing good works (cf. Mt 5: 15–16). On *bouste* see Text. Comm., Kaske p. 250. Schweitzer explains 153 as referring to the sacramental *sign* of confirmation, administered on Holy Saturday, the vigil of Easter, from the date of which the dates of the Church's moveable feasts were reckoned. 154 refers to the significance or meaning of the mass of the Wednesday of Easter Week, i.e. the fulfilment of Christ's promises in the Second Coming and Judgment (Schw.). In 155 the full or Paschal moon (= Easter) stands for the power of baptism and confirmation, both sacraments deriving their efficacy from Christ's redemptive sacrifice (Schw. p. 326; cf. Kaske, p. 245).

163a The other relevant text is I Cor 13: 4–7, esp. *Charitas patiens est*, which illuminates the link between Patience and (his own def. of Dobest) *Dilige* 'Love' (138).

167 *redels*: 'The general solution' (as Sk notes) is 'Charity, exercised with Patience.'

172 *dido*: the well-known story of Dido, Queen of Carthage (Sk).

174–6 probably allude to the Great Schism of 1378 and the continuing war between France and England. France supported the Avignonese contender to the Papacy, Clement VII, and England the Roman Urban VI, so the two issues were closely entangled (McKisack, pp. 145–7).

178 On this trait of pilgrims cf. Prol 46–9.

193 echoes I 85–93: truth and a well-disposed human will are closely connected.

194 See Lk 37: 50: the woman (often identified with the Magdalen) has Many sins . . . forgiven her because she hath loved much.' The implication is that those who give 'all their living' (Lk 21: 4) for love of God will be saved.

209 Either both expressions = Moslems or one (cf. Saracen *OED* 2) means 'pagans'.

224 On Haukyn see the important art. by Maguire, which makes him an inferior form of *Activa Vita*, 'Practical Life' (p. 198), 'based on, and judged by, purely temporal conceptions of goodness' (in Blanch, pp. 195, 200).

224–6 *mynstral, wafrer* are linked in *PardT* (C 479) and a pun is likely here since the words were near-synonyms (cf. *wafferariis & menestrallis* in Webb, *Roll*, and see *MED minstral* 2 'servant, functionary'). H. is a real *waferere* but (perhaps to his credit) no minstrel (cf. Prol 33–9).

246 The lead seal (*bulla*) of the papal pardon was stamped with the heads of SS Peter and Paul.

249 *bocches*: boils or tumours in groin, armpit etc, commonest symptom of plague.

254 H. visualizes the apostolic healing power as a pot of curative ointment.

259 recalls XII 11, VI 328–30.

266 The bakers of Stratford-atte-Bowe supplied bread for the people of London.

270 John de Chichester was mayor of London during the great dearth of 1370.

273 alludes to the white robe of baptism (*cristendom*) worn by the infant or neophyte.

274 recalls the 'spotted garment which is carnal' of Jude 23 (Frank).

312 H.'s gospel, unlike Paul's, is *secundum hominem* 'according to men, worldly' (Gal 1: 11); he serves worldly interest (mammon): cf. also 397–8*a* below.

337–41 H. has sought charms from these (unknown, but no doubt famous) characters instead of God's help. Failure to pray is a cause of physical as much as symptom of spiritual sickness.

348 *forboden nyghtes*: fast-days and vigils ('Holi tyme and solenne dayes', *Speculum Christiani*, ed. G. Holmstedt (EETS 182 (1933) p. 228), but may include periods of pregnancy, menstruation etc (*ib.*).

391–2 Bruges was a great market-town and centre of the Flemish cloth-trade; Prussia 'the chief distributor of English cloth in Poland and west Russia' (McKisack, p. 359).

398*a* The contrast of spiritual and worldly values in the Sermon on the Mount is relevant to understanding H. (see Alford, 'Coat').

409 *braunches*: sin is seen as a tree with branches and twigs (*Ayenbite*, p. 17, *ParsT*, I 388).

422 *fooles sages*: wise fools licensed to make sharp satirical comments.

431–5 Ps 100 mentions walking 'in the unspotted way' and excluding the proud and perverse from one's *house*.

436 *kynges minstrales*: a privileged class: 'The permanent salary of the royal minstrels of Edward III was 7½d a day' (Strutt, *Sports*, p. 164).

PASSUS XIV

1–15 As Sk well puts it: 'H.'s one garment symbolizes the carnal nature of man, which requires shrift in the same way that a garment needs to be washed'; see Alford, 'Coat'.

16–21a The sacrament of Penance has three parts: contrition of heart; oral confession to a priest; satisfaction through prayers and good works; see Chaucer's *ParsT*.

43–4 The cricket here is probably the salamander (see *MED s.v.*). Langl.'s view of the curlew may be influenced by associating it with the quails of Ex 16: 13. Gower (*C.A.* VI 943) says the same of the plover.

62 Ps 144: 15–16 was a commonly used grace at meals.

68–9 The Seven Sleepers of Ephesus (*Legenda Aurea*, ch. 100) were Christians who were said to have slept in a cave from the Decian persecution to the time of Theodosius (448 A.D.), nearly 200 years, when they miraculously woke, in proof of God's power over life and death.

75 See as well as Gen 18, 19, Ezek 16: 49, Comestor's source. Gluttony and lechery were commonly linked: see I 27–37, and cf. *ParsT*, I, 839.

81 *sheltrom*: the shield-wall defence formation. The imagery recalls Eph 6: 11–17.

84 A man unable to make oral confession (e.g. because sick or wounded) may be saved from damnation if he is truly contrite.

103 Patience quotes Ecclus 31: 5, '*Quis est hic? et laudabimus eum . . .*'

103ff For a solemn contrast between the condition of rich and poor cf. Js 5: 1–11.

122 *Dives*: the 'rich man' (*dives*) of Lk 16: 19; cf. XVII 266.

130 Ps 72 actually deals not with the dangers of riches but the prosperity of sinners.

143 *Mathew*: the allusion is to Mt 19: 23–6 (cf. 211a below).

179a Is 45 describes God as creating both peace and evil (*malum*, implying in context affliction), but it also includes a solemn promise of justice and salvation (23).

189–92 P. describes the power of Christ's passion (sacramentally applied to the sinner in confession) in terms of the sovereign's words in a letter patent; but to be written at all, such words need a 'parchment', man's own humility (191, 194); cf. XVII 4ff, also *Ancrene Wisse* (in Bennett-Smithers p. 239/ 470, 471).

200 This is a doctrine not of communism but of charity, concern for others restraining the quest for personal wealth (see the attack on communism in XX 273–8a).

208–9 *fer . . . bettre; rather yherd*: P. here distinguishes the 'gift of nature' *wit* from the 'gift of fortune' *richesse* (cf. *ParsT* 452–3) in sharp contrast to Ymag., who linked them as *combraunces* (XII 45).

212a, 214 *Opera* shows that P. sees heaven as a reward not for earthly poverty *per se* but for patient bearing of poverty, though he quotes the first beatitude in a form closer to Lk than Mt. See also *Patience* 34–45, 528–31, which links patience and poverty, and 275 (*C*) below.

217ff P. describes poverty as a general remedy against the deadly sins (envy is left out). As *humylitee, or mekenesse* (*ParsT*, I, 475) it is the *specific* against pride, the 'root' of all seven; but P. strongly stresses the objective advantages (as he sees them) of material poverty as against riches.

254–5 contrast with Haukyn's admission at XIII 331–41 above; cf. *WBT*, D 1201–2.

258 *secte*: a relevant meaning here is 'livery': because Christ was one of the poor, the latter belong objectively and irrespective of their virtues to the section of society he belonged to (see esp. Js 2: 1–6 and cf. Lk 7: 25).

261–72 perhaps allude to St Francis, the 'rich young man' who *did* marry Poverty (see 271). Sk notes the reference to Mt 19: 21, Eph 5: 31.

275 The definition of poverty comes from the *Gnomae* of Secundus, quoted in Vincent of Beauvais' *Speculum Historiale*, bk. X, ch. 71 (Chaucer paraphrases in *WBT*, D 1195–1200). *donum Dei* is not in Vincent but from the opening of Augustine's *De Patientia* (see Schmidt, 'Two Notes').

279 *point*: cf. *Patience* 1, 531.

292 As Sk notes, liquid measures used by brewers and taverners had to be sealed with the Alderman's seal to attest their true capacity.

300a Poverty is the 'mother of (good) health' because it protects from excess, for Langl. evidently a chief cause of illnesses; cf. VI 269–70 (*C*).

301 The Alton road or 'pass', on the Surrey–Hampshire border (then forest), was a haunt of outlaws who lay in wait for the merchant-trains travelling to Winchester.

304a–6 Seneca praises poverty in his Epistles 2 and 8, the latter being close to the phrase from Vincent (see Sk). Chaucer quotes the Juvenal at *WBT*, D 1193–4.

312a He does business without worrying about 'loss' or risking damnation (i.e. since profit is not his aim, he does not risk his soul to gain the world).

316–19 *Austyn … mene*: for an explanation of this passage see my 'Two Notes'.

324 The phrase recalls V 361, linking Haukyn with Will (see V 462–77 (*C*)).

332 Haukyn's loud weeping wakes Will as had the quarrelling at VII 140. On the links between Haukyn and the *Visio* see Maguire, *art*.

PASSUS XV

3, 10 *fool*: cf. XX 61–4. Will's seeming a fool before the world shows how he has changed.

18 *Peter*: traditionally though of as gate-keeper of heaven (cf. Mt 16: 19); *fauchon*: a symbol of his martyrdom (by beheading) and perh. alludes to the 'sword of the spirit' (Eph 6: 17).

23–39 For an analysis of Anima's names see my 'Philosophy', 151–2.

37 On the mention of Augustine here, see my 'Philosophy', 142–3. On Isidore (*c*. 560–636), Bishop of Seville and author of the encyclopaedic *Etymologies*, see Leff, pp. 51–2.

49 In spite of his language and Anima's sharp rejoinder, Will is clearly much better able now to learn, after his sojourn with Patience.

Commentary

51a Isaiah's address to the King of Babylon was traditionally applied to Satan (Lucifer, Is 14: 12; cf. also Lk 10: 18).

60 St Bernard may be taken as representing faith, humility and love, not reason and intellect, as the *kynde* way to know God; see Leff, pp. 134–5. Anima in 64–9 repeats his teaching, which stems from Augustine and Paul. *licames coveitise* 67 is the 'wisdom of the flesh' (*sapientia carnis*) which 'is an enemy to God' (Rom 8: 7).

70 On these *freres* see X 71 (*C*).

82 *glose*: the *Glossa Ordinaria* gives Cassiodorus' gloss on Ps 4: 3, which identifies idols with lies and false earthly goods that cannot fulfil what they promise (*P.L.* 113, 849). His *Expos. in XX Primos Psalmos* quotes without attribution the passage from Augustine given by Sk, which contrasts *truth* (which makes blessed) with vanity and falsehood (= love of worldly goods) (*P.L.* 114, 759).

83 *brennyng* need not imply that heretics were burnt in England before the statute of 1401 (Sk). The phrase may be rhetorical, perhaps reflecting knowledge of the practice in France.

88 Sk notes that the words of Jesus Langl. has in mind may be in Lk 14: 12.

111–14 perhaps alludes to a known Latin similitude; the imagery recalls Mt 23: 27, Acts 23: 3.

116–17 *wolveliche*: cf. Mt 7: 15, and the immediately following image of the evil tree in vss 16–20; this, not Is 24: 2, is pseudo-Chrysostom's source (though see Sk on 129).

124 'A fashionable ornamental dagger or a knife with a knobbed (= testicle-shaped) haft, covered with gilt-studs.'

149 *childissh*: cf. 216 below and Piers' words at V 607–8.

152 gives us his stature, his persevering character and perhaps his name (cryptogrammatically).

155 *paied*: i.e. rewarded by God. Their charity has an element of prudent self-interest.

168 *Tarse*: 'a rich and costly stuff of Oriental origin' (*OED*), from Tharsia (?Turkestan).

179–80 have a nexus of associations with texts on spiritual feeding (Jn 4: 34, Mt 4: 4, Ps 41: 4), and cf. XIV 49.

188–9 perhaps refer to doing penance specifically for the extravagant sins of youth.

200a Langl. heightens the effect by replacing the *he / Jesus* of Lk 11: 17, Mt 9: 4 by *God* and naming *Christ* only at 212.

223 Edmund the martyr, King of the East Angles (d. 869); Edward the Confessor (d. 1066).

227–9 Charity is nowadays more likely to be found in a rich abbot or bishop than a friar.

231 *fern ago*: St Francis had died a century and a half before in 1226. On his order's development see Keen, *Europe*, pp. 156–61.

234 comes from the praise of the just rich man quoted XIV 102, drawn on at XIV 144–53.

242 *yknyt*: see Mt 19: 6, evaded by divorces obtained under guise of annulment.

254a The apparent antecedent in Vulg is 'the light of [God's] countenance', but in this context *Goddes passion* is the source of the peace of Charity.

266 perhaps alludes to Lk 24: 26; cf. also Mt 26: 54, referring to Is 53.

269–97 The main source is *Legenda Aurea* chs. 21, 128, 18, 56. *Antony* (d. 356): an early desert father and reputed founder of monachism. *Egidius (Giles)*: lived as hermit and monk in Provence, d. 700. 285 According to the life of Paul, Antony was his guest when a raven brought bread. 286 *primus heremita*, the opening description of Paul (d. 342) in *L.A.* ch. 18. 289 Anima repeats the Austin Friars' claim to have been founded by Paul the Hermit. 290 Paul the Apostle's trade was tent-making (Ac 18: 3); like Chaucer in *Pard Prol*, C 445, Langl. may be confusing him with the Hermit, who did make baskets (Jerome, *P.L.* 23, 28), but there was confusion about Paul's trade. 294 Mary Magdalen, according to legend, came to Marseilles and after converting the pagans lived 30 years in solitude on angels' music; (*dewes*: cf. Rawlinson lyric *Maiden in the mor lay* in Sisam).

317a The comment is close to one Sk quotes from St Bruno's *Expos. in Job* 6: 5.

325 *prophecie*: 'utterance made by the prophet-king David'.

348 The importation of these coins, forged abroad, was forbidden as treason by Edward III.

369 *clemat* here *MED* glosses 'one of the regions [of the earth] dominated by certain zodiacal signs', 1 (b); sense (c) 'often considered with respect to its weather' seems apt in context, where weather-forecasting is being discussed.

372 cf. the complaint against bad poets in *Wynnere* 20–30, seen as a sign of social decay.

374 He means that *few* know French; cf. Trevisa's comment in 1387, in Sisam, p. 149.

380 *quodlibet*: 'any question in philosophy or theology proposed as an exercise in argument or disputation' (*OED*). The discussion was presided over by a *maistre*.

387 The phrase from the *Pange, lingua* sung at Lauds on Corpus Christi is especially apt since the hymn is by the greatest *of divinite maistres*, Thomas Aquinas. Anima's point is that the priest's defective performance of the liturgy will not harm the lay-people as long as they have true faith.

396–409 As Wr notes, Hildebert's life of Mohammed makes him ambitious *pontificari* 'to become patriarch' (= Langl.'s *ben a pope* 397). 399 *dowve*: so in Vincent of Beauvais' *Speculum Historiale*, bk. 23, ch. 40. *com from God* 405 alludes to the descent of the Holy Spirit as a dove at Christ's baptism (Mt 3: 16).

423–6 Anima brings together healing and reconciliation as fruits of devout prayer, echoing Haukyn at XIII 255–9 and the Doctor at XIII 172.

436 As Sk notes, Matthias, elected to replace Judas (Ac 1: 25–6), in fact made them twelve.

442–3 Augustine was sent by Gregory the Great to preach to the heathen English in 597 and in the same year converted Ethelbert, king of Kent.

444 *rede*: in Bede's *Ecclesiastical History of the English Nation*, I, 26 and 31.

464 The calf as Sk notes is regarded as clean in Lev 11: 3, Deut 14: 4.

488a As Sk suggests, the meaning is that the possibility of finding 'charity' (*eam*: see (*C*) on X 68*a*) in heathen lands (= receptivity to the Gospel) is a motive for missionary effort.

491 Clerics were sometimes appointed by the Pope to (non-existent) titular sees *in partibus infidelium* (such as the places named), territory held by the Moslems. They rarely if ever actually visited these places.

507 *peril*: because such 'bishops' do not fulfil Christ's commands (quoted above) to preach.

528*a* is adapted from Deut 23: 25 in the light of Mt 9: 37–8 to become a means of criticizing the 'bishops' who interfere with the rights and duties of parish clergy.

541 They seek a 'corruptible' crown (I Cor 9: 25) not a 'crown of justice' (II Tim 4: 8). The obverse of the noble and groat showed a crowned king's head (Poole, pls. 34, 35).

545–8 The Order of Knights Templars was suppressed by Clement V in 1312 under pressure from the French king, who wanted their vast wealth in France (see Keen, pp. 217–18). *dar* 547 may allude to the French charges against them 'of cloaking under oaths of secrecy a system of organized vice and communal sacrilege' (Keen, p. 217). *religious* 548: the Templars united 'monastic austerity with the martial spirit of chivalry' (Keen, p. 122).

558 The grammar is confusing since the subject of *hath ydronke* should be *ecclesia* not *Dos*. Anima means that through receiving worldly wealth and power the Church, which had flourished spiritually in apostolic poverty, suffered corruption from the head downwards. The Donation was an C8th forgery purporting to be a letter from the Emperor Constantine to Pope Silvester I in 315 granting him lands and privileges (see Southern pp. 91–3 and Smalley, *Friars*, pp. 154–7, on contemporary citations of the Donation).

561 Anima objects that worldly pre-occupations prevent the clergy from prayer and charity.

572 Isaiah refers to a secular ruler; Osee is confused with Malachias perhaps because the prophecies are similar, Os 5:1 threatening priests in terms close to Mal 2 and 3.

599 *wrecches*: Anima is pitying rather than attacking the Jews: he urges their conversion and that of the *Sarsens* 'Moslems' because, if the missionaries of old converted the *heathen* English, it should be all the easier to convert people who are already monotheists.

PASSUS XVI

4 *tree*: for a penetrating and suggestive discussion see Aers, pp. 79–109, who also surveys and criticizes earlier work.

15 *Herte*: cf. HC at I 142ff (and cf. 6 above), also Piers at V 606–7.

16 *Lib. Arb.*: 'Free Judgment'; see my 'Philosophy', esp. 134–43, and '"Free Wit"'.

19 *swowned* suggests (like *ravysshed* XI 7) 'a spiritual vision or imaginatif' (*The Chastising of God's Children*, ed. J. Bazire and E. Colledge, Oxford 1957, pp. 169–70) like the *gostly drem* in *Pearl* 790 (see E. Wilson, art.).

25*a* *collidetur*: the 'bruising' notion perhaps sugg. the imagery of 79–82.

27–52 There is symmetry in the opposition of each enemy of Charity to a person of the Trinity: the created world and the world's Creator; the flesh and God-made-flesh; the evil spirit and the Holy Spirit.

35 If *blosmes* and *leves* here are closely related to 6–7 the sense is that fleshly lust destroys kindness in the soul, leaving (perhaps only nominal) adherence to the Church's teaching (not necessarily 'the bare text of God's scriptures', Salter, *PP*, p. 75; see also Aers, pp. 91–2).

36 The Latin phrase occurs in the heading of Augustine's *De Trinitate* VI, i, which discusses I Cor 1: 24. cf. also the Macro morality *Wisdom* (ed. M. Eccles, EETS 262(1969), 5–16).

53 Will's grateful blessing on Piers (cf. also 1) contrasts with his dissatisfied rejoinders to earlier instructors.

61–3 That the tree 'means' the Trinity and grows in goodness is not incompatible with Anima's description of it as 'Patience' growing in man's heart: Piers' account is of charity's source and origin (in the divine nature), Anima's of its manifestation (in man).

68–72 descr. the three possible human states in rising order of excellence: marriage, widowhood (see 76 and cf. I Cor 7: 8–9), virginity. On the 'grades of chastity' see Bloomfield's article. *bastard* 69 perhaps = grafted, cultivated, not growing naturally (*MED s.v.* 2(c)). *swellyng* 72: i.e. with desire or pregnancy; *peeris* seems a pun.

81–2 These names stand for all the just from Adam to Christ's precursor, the Baptist.

84 The Limbo of the Fathers was believed to be continuous with Hell (*ST* 3: 52, *Suppl.* 69: 4, 5; and see (*C*) on 254 below).

88 The syntax leaves it doubtful whether *Filius* is in apposition to *pil* or *Piers*.

92 *jouke* 'roost': a bold metaphor from the action of hawks, rich in suggestion.

93 *plenitudo temporis* is quoted from Gal 4: 4–5, *q.v.*

95 *juste* takes up *justice(s)* 92: the metaphor is from the outset legal as well as chivalric.

103–5 The notion of Jesus under a tutor may have been suggested by Gal 4: 1–5; cf. Lk 1: 80.

112, 115 *maistrie* alludes to Christ's description of his act as 'for the glory of God' (Jn 11: 4, 40).

120a occurs before Lazarus' raising, and is provoked by Christ's claim to power over death.

149 *kissynge*: the common salutation among friends in England at this time.

170. Will becomes more of a fool (*ydiot MED* (b)) in the world's eyes as he *sees* more.

172 *myd-Lenten Sonday*: 'Laetare Sunday', after the opening of the Introit of the Mass of the day, *Laetare, Jerusalem* 'Rejoice, J.' (cf. 163 above). The subject of the Epistle (Gal 4: 22–32) is Abraham and his two sons, which St Paul interprets allegorically.

181 The blazon recalls the wording of 57: the Trinitarian theme of the inner vision has spread into the containing outer dream.

208 *oon singuler name*: i.e. humanity (on earth), divinity (in heaven). As Sk notes, the analogy occurs in *De Trin.* XII, v, 5, but Augustine rejects it as a misleading opinion.

211 Faith goes on to extend the analogy so that each of the Persons of the

Trinity corresponds to a grade of human nature as seen on the tree in the inner dream.

223 *Fre Wille*: Langl. adapts from Augustine the analogy between the Holy Ghost and the human will, the faculty that loves (*De Trin.* X, xii, 19 and XV, xxi, 41); cf. *frenesse* 88. This explains also why Piers links the Third Person with *Liberum Arbitrum* 50–2.

244 As Sk notes, Langl. confuses Abraham's sacrifice (Gen 15: 9) with Melchisedech's (Gen 14:18), referred to in the Canon of the Mass in the prayer *Supra quae*.

245 *feith*: Abraham is the OT personification of faith and as the recipient of God's promise of salvation an apt *heraud*, as is John the Baptist, whose own 'heralding' of Christ fulfilled God's promise to Abraham (cf. Rom 4, esp. 11, 16–20, and Mt 3: 9–11).

254 *bosom*: a vividly concrete metaphorical *shewyng* of Limbo, drawing on Lk 16:22. Aquinas (*ST Suppl.* 69, 4) specifies Limbo (= 'Abraham's bosom') as the place of rest of the just before Christ's advent, free from the pains of punishment but deprived of the beatific vision of God, and so 'Hell', not *per se* but *per accidens*.

270–1 Will's words recall Haukyn's at XIV 322–8. Now he weeps 'religious tears' (see on this Vernet, pp. 120–5).

PASSUS XVII

1 On *Spes* 'Hope' and *spire*, a probable pun on Fr *espier* 'spy' / *espeir* 'hope' see St-Jacques, ' "Spes" '.

5 *seel*: the ratification of God's promise that will come with Christ's saving death.

10 Letters patent were sealed with the Great Seal; cf. XIV 191. *hard roche*: the stone tables of the Law (Ex 31: 18).

11–15 The *text* runs together Deut 6: 5 and Lev 19: 18 (Vulg has *amicum* 'friend', trans. 'neighbour' in A.V. to accord with Lk 10: 27, which allows for *sherewe* 44 below). The *gloss* is 'splendid' as Christ's own authoritative interpretation of the law.

19, 22 *charme*: contrast Haukyn's irreligious resort to magic at XIII 341.

41, 45 Goodridge (Intro. p. 42) finds Will unable to reconcile the doctrine that faith justifies with the command to do good works and practise charity. But Will's problem is simply finding *lighter* 'easier' Faith's message than the 'Law' of *Spes*.

50ff The Samaritan parable in Lk 10: 30–36 answers the lawyer's question 'Who is my neighbour?' after Christ has answered his question 'What must I do to possess eternal life?' The meaning is 'Show Charity, Dobest', the superlative act of the Samaritan (= Christ) corresponding to the positive and comparative degrees of doing well embodied in Faith and *Spes*. Most of the elements of Langl.'s version not found in the Gospel go back to patristic exegesis via the medieval homilists and especially the liturgy of the 13th Sunday after the Octave of Pentecost and the interpretations of liturgical commentators; see the illuminating art. by St-Jacques, 'Liturgical Associations'. The uniquely Langlandian 'chivalric' view of the Samaritan-Christ may derive from the Gospel account of Christ's entry into Jerusalem riding an ass and the imagery of the Easter sequence *Victimae Paschali*, esp. the lines

Mors et vita duello | conflixere mirando 'There together Death and Life |
Met in strange and wondrous strife' (cf. 113*a* below).

57 *semyvif*: a brilliant coinage (for the metre) which translates Vulg
semivivo (Lk 10: 30).

73 *Lex Christi*: see Gal 6: 2, which makes 'bearing one another's burdens'
(= charity) the fulfilment of Christ's law; cf. XI 210*a*. It is under this law
(= Christian life in the Church, cf. 120 below) that sick humanity will
recover.

96 *bathed*: the main Scriptural sources are I Jn 1: 7, I Pet 1: 2, Apoc 7: 14.

109 *Caro*: a traditional interpretation going back to Bede and familiar
through liturgical commentaries; see St-Jacques, *art. cit.*

113*a* occurs in an antiphon at Lauds on Holy Saturday.

140–204 The extended analogy may be original, but the source of the
basic fist-image is presumably the line (which the C-text here quotes) *mundum
pugillo continens* 'holding the world in his fist' applied to the Creator, *supernus
artifex*, in the Anon. C6th hymn 'Quem terra, pontus, aethera' used at
matins in the Office of the BVM (no. 59 in Raby, *OBMLV*).

151*a* was spoken by Jesus himself, but cf. the Father's voice at Jn 12: 28.

169*a* comes from a Compline hymn for the Sunday after Easter (*Hereford
Breviary*, ed. Frere and Brown, I, 342).

204 *quenche* effects a transition from the 'hand' to the 'torch' image; cf.
I Thess 5: 19.

205ff The development of the image may be original. *torche*: a twist of
hemp soaked in wax; *tapur*: a wax candle.

252*a* The bridegroom's words come from a parable especially apt in
context, since it is *oil* (= *kyndenesse*, charity) that the foolish virgins lack to
fill their lamps.

256 *ingratus* perhaps comes from Paul's description in II Tim 3: 2ff of the
ingrati who *resistunt veritati* 'resist the truth' (vs. 8); cf. 265*a* below, which
comes from a passage warning against the same 'false prophets' whom Paul
is attacking.

259 *blowynge* takes up the earlier metaphor of the three winds (XVI
25ff). The wind of *unkyndenesse* 'uncharitableness' which blows out God's
flame of love is the absolute negation of *Goddes owene kynde* (273: 'God is
love', I Jn 4: 8). Langl. sees charity as like gratitude: due to others in return
for God's showing mercy towards us.

274 Lack of charity is shown supremely in murder of a man's body or
reputation, an undoing of God's creation (a human being, virtue) which
stands at the opposite pole to God's own incarnation and sacrificial death
(see 291, 286), the acts of charity which establish the new creation.

310ff describes the dilemma of the man whose life of (freely committed) sins
leaves him at the end despairing of God's mercy and so failing to show in his
last moments the contrition needed to turn God's (wrathful) justice into mercy.

318 *Thre thynges*: a proverb in Pope Innocent III's *De Contemptu Mundi*,
I, 18 which draws on Proverbs 19: 13, 27: 15 (comparing wife and leaky roof),
10: 26 (smoke) (Sk).

330–end The Samaritan distinguishes the three conditions in which men
succumb to sin—through the weakness of their bodily nature, through being
weakened by outward afflictions, and through deliberate evil in the will. The

skilful use of *kynde* in 332, 341 shows how sins arising from the first two sources may find forgiveness while those due to *unkyndenesse*, being the 'contrarie' of 'reson', extinguish the fire of God's grace, just as wet wood, though kindled, cannot foster the flame and goes out.

4 Will's weariness of the world and desire to sleep signalize spiritual advance: he has left *bely-joy* (VII 119) for *mynde of God Almyghty* (XV 295) like the *Goddes foles* of XV 269ff. In this vision, the content of the canonical and apocryphal gospels is mediated through phrases and images drawn from the liturgy of Lent and Eastertide.

6–8 On *Dominica in ramis palmarum* clergy and people processed round the church carrying blessed palm-branches and on re-entering sang the hymn, clergy and adults chanting the verses (*Hosanna* occurs in vs. 1) and children (choir and others) the response *Gloria, laus*.

10 Christ entering Jerusalem (Mt 21: 1–9, Palm Sunday Gospel) is the embodiment of Charity figured in the Samaritan of his own parable and the poet's fictional creation.

11 Christ rides 'without boots' but not 'without a remedy for man's sin'; without spurs to 'prick' his mount, he is yet the knight par excellence seeking the supreme battle against Death (personified 37; on *Mors et vita duello* see XVII 50 (*C*) above).

17a *Benedictus &c*, which ends the *Sanctus* in every mass, also ends the second Palm Sunday antiphon *Pueri Hebraeorum*.

22 *armes*: perhaps heraldic sense, with a pun; but Christ is not wearing the *blasen* Faith described at XVI 181: rather, like such knights as Lancelot, he disguises his divinity in the form of the humble ploughman, *habitu inventus ut homo*, 'in habit found as a man' (Phil 2: 7).

36 *sedens &c*: 'sitting in the place of judgment' (Mt 27:19), one of a cluster of Latin phrases from the Holy Week Gospels which keep the intense emotional experience of the liturgy firmly in the consciousness of the poet's audience.

46 *wicche*: one of many details from the *Gospel of Nicodemus* (ME vsn, ed. Hulme, 215–16).

79 *Longeus*: so named in *Gosp. Nic.* 625 after Jn 19: 34 (*lancea* 'spear', Gk *longché*). He was revered as a Christian martyr; see Peebles, *Longinus*, V. A. Kolve, *The Play Called Corpus Christi* (Calif., 1966), 218–21.

81 *manye teeth*: a variant on *chekes* (cf. VI 40) perhaps alluding to the tearing out of his teeth and tongue for refusing to worship idols (*Legenda Aurea*, ch. 47).

100 *recreaunt*: etymologically 'unfaithful, giving up one's faith', here punning paradoxically on the fact that Longeus' *faith* in Christ saved him (*Leg. Aur.*, and cf. XII 193).

109a The exact source is untraced. Faith's point is that since the Jews have rejected Jesus as the Messiah, God will reject them as his chosen people, withdrawing his protection to let them lose their independence and become subject to hatred and persecution. On the condition of Jews in the Middle Ages, see Southern, p. 17, Cohn, pp. 76–81.

111 *derknesse*: see Mt 27: 45. Sk finds a possible allusion to the service of

Tenebrae, said in the darkened church on the Wednesday, Thursday and Friday of Holy Week.

113ff The motif of the Four Daughters of God derives from Ps 84: 11 (quoted at the climax of the passus, 423*a* below). The 'directions' may owe something to Is 43: 6; a precise symbolic meaning for them is unlikely. Their debates, as Sk notes, are adapted from Robert Grosseteste's *Chateau d'Amour*; cf. also *Ludus Coventriae*, ed. K. S. Block, EETS 120 (1922), 99–103, and *The Castle of Perseverance*, ed. M. Eccles, EETS 262 (1969), pp. 95–111 and bibl. note p. 200, also Owst, *Literature and Pulpit* (1966) pp. 90–2.

122 *wonder*: the Harrowing of Hell is dramatized in miracle plays (York 37, Towneley 25, Chester 17). The main sources are *Gosp. Nic.* 1160–1548, *Leg. Aur.* ch. 54.

140 alludes to Fortunatus' hymn *Pange, lingua*, 1.6 (Raby, no. 54) sung during the Adoration of the Cross at Mass on Good Friday. In medieval legend the wood of the cross was said to be that of a tree grown from seeds of the tree of knowledge in Gen 2: 17.

142 *waltrot* may be Langland's reversal of *troteuale*, found in Robert Mannyng of Brunne's *Handlyng Synne*, ed. F. J. Furnivall, EETS 119, 123 (1901–3), ll. 9244 etc; see Sk. Both words are of doubtful origin but seem to mean ' an idle tale '; cf. *trufle* 147, ? a pun.

149*a* continues 'miserere mei Deus et salva me' (Office of the Dead, Nocturn 3, resp. 7, from *SB*, II, 278).

153–6 See Bartholomaeus Anglicus, *De Prop. Rer.* (ed. Seymour), pp. 1249–50.

161 The 'strategem' is God's assuming human form, as Lucifer did a serpent's (287), with the important difference that the Incarnation, though a mystery, is reality, not deception: *grace* is God's *sleighte*, not *gile*; see 355–7.

165 It is apparent how God's justice is prior to his mercy, but not how it is prior to his truth, unless perhaps the latter is equated with his self-revelation to man.

180*a* In vs 4 the psalmist praises God for saving his 'soul from hell', the immediate cause of his rejoicing.

185 Love's *patente* is the New Covenant sealed in Christ's blood, which fulfils (not replaces) that of *Spes* (XVII 10). It brings mankind rest and peace because Love is the 'plant of peace' (I 152); cf. XV 254*a* (*C*). The verse is the opening antiphon of Holy Saturday, Matins.

213 alludes to the doctrine of Christ's *kenosis* 'self-emptying' in Phil 2: 6–11.

220 The familiar phrase brings home that the price of knowledge like this is suffering: to 'know' like man, God must become man, so to know God man must become like God.

229 *two brode eighen*: symbolizing the literal and spiritual sense of Scripture (Kaske, ' "Book" ', p. 127) or else perhaps the Old and New Testaments.

236 *elements*: the theme of the witnessing elements goes back to Gregory's commentary on Mt 2:1–2 (Kaske, *id.* p. 119).

250 In *Gosp. Nic.* Caryn and Lentin, sons of the Simeon of Lk 2: 25 who uttered the *Nunc dimittis*, are raised from the dead at Christ's resurrection and tell the story of the Harrowing in written form.

252ff *Gigas* 'giant' = Christ, whose breaking down of the gates of hell (recalling Samson's carrying off the gates of Gaza, Jg 16: 3), is about to be witnessed. Sk's note is supported by iconographic evidence (see Anderson, *Imagery*, fig. 11); but Kaske ('*Gigas*') finds a reference to Ps 18: 6, uniformly interpreted as referring to Christ, who is a giant because of his indomitability and more-than-human nature.

254–9 On these lines see Donaldson's convincing arguments in 'Grammar'.

261 Ps 23 was sung at Matins on Holy Saturday. The phrase is used in *Gosp. Nic.* and *Leg. Aur.*; on its use in semi-dramatic church ceremonies see K. Young, *The Drama of the Medieval Church* (Oxford, 1933), ch. V, index.

281 *thretynge*: Gen 2:17, 3:19 specifies death, not damnation; cf. 333 below.

283 *sevene*: perhaps chosen for the metre; the commoner figure was four or five.

299–300 follows the legend developed from Mt 27: 19 that the Devil in a dream urged Pilate's wife to save Jesus in order to stop him dying to redeem mankind; see no. 30 in *York Plays*, ed. L. Toulmin Smith (Oxford, 1885), 11 158–76, Kolve, *Play*, pp. 228–30.

338 *lusard* here = serpent (cf. *addre* 336, 355), though the standard medieval representation was of a standing lizard-like creature with a woman's face.

341 Christ gives his soul in payment for Adam, but answers Lucifer's original *gile* by giving him tit for tat: hell cannot *hold* his soul. *synne to synne wende* seems to mean that only the unjust will henceforth go to hell, the abode of sin.

361a comes from a psalm in praise of the justice of God's judgments.

370–1 *Josaphat* 'Jehovah has judged' (Joel 3: 2, 12) was traditionally understood as the place assigned for the Last Judgment. The vintage metaphor comes from vs. 13, but Langland, drawing on other harvest and vintage images from the Gospels (e.g. Mt 13:39) has transformed Joel's grapes of wrath into grapes of righteousness: God will save as well as judge.

379a As Goodridge well remarks, 'since sin is only an offence against himself . . . [Christ] may forgive it if he chooses'. Ps 50 asks for and expresses hope in God's mercy.

380–4 alludes to the custom at law of pardoning a criminal who had somehow managed to survive hanging. Sk notes Edward III's pardon of one Walter Wynkeburn, hanged at Leicester in 1363, as the actual incident alluded to. The point of the illustration is that the King of Kings can hardly be *less* just than a human king: man has already suffered *juwise* once (death) and there is no call for a second 'hanging' (damnation): a spell in prison (Purgatory) will suffice to satisfy justice.

393 *til parce it hote*: see the helpful article on this phrase by J. Alford.

396a The poet implicitly identifies himself with St Paul through the verb *Audivi*, referring here to the privileged Apostle's experience of mystical 'visiones et revelationes Domini' (II Cor 12: 1) when he was 'ravished' or 'caught up' (*raptus*, vss 2, 4) into heaven. This is Langl.'s boldest claim for the value and validity of his own 'visions and revelations'.

398 does not necessarily imply that all men *will* be saved (any more than 373, which refers to judgment rather than election); but Christ retains the right, as judge and king, to show mercy to all men, thus giving them a chance to gain heaven.

400a The whole of Ps 142, with its cry for deliverance from hell, is relevant here.

405 *Astroth*: Ishtar, the Babylonian Venus (Jer 7: 18); in medieval usage, a devil.

410a The quotation from Alanus may have been connected in Langland's mind with Tob 3: 22, a passage of special relevance in this context (noted Sk).

424 The *Te Deum*, the great hymn of praise formerly attributed to St Ambrose, would not have been sung at the Offices during the penitential season of Lent. Its triumphant appearance here signalizes the end of Lent and the dawning of Easter, the greatest feast of the Christian Church.

429 For discussion of these names and their possible pejorative associations see Mustanoja, 72–4, Alford, 'Coat', p. 136.

431–end alludes to the penitential practice of creeping on one's knees to venerate the cross (also part of the Liturgy of Good Friday). Will's cry to perform this act on Easter morning expresses his profound grasp of the continuing cost of Christ's victory over death—participation by his followers in the suffering that made that victory possible; cf. XIX 63–8. The ringing last line affirms the popular belief that the shadow of a cross would ward off evil spirits.

PASSUS XIX

3 *housled*: all were required to receive Communion yearly, preferably at Easter. Will's intention implies that he has confessed and is in a state of grace.

4 *offryng*: i.e. at the Offertory, when the people brought their offerings to the priest.

7 *with a cros*: cf. V 12. This time it is not Reason preaching God's wrath and the need for repentance but Conscience who, in the light of Christ's passion, speaks of God's love and mercy and the reward awaiting those who do repent.

17 *knelen*: see Phil 2: 10, quoted at 80a below.

23–5 cf. Aquinas: 'in this name *Christ* are understood both the divinity which anoints and the humanity which is anointed' (*ST* 3: 16, 5)—i.e. Christ = 'God-made-man'.

37 *taillage*: on the civil disabilities of the Jews see Cohn, pp. 79–80, Gilchrist, p. 111.

39 *frankeleyn*: 'a landowner and member of the gentry ranking immediately below the nobility; a freeman, a gentleman' (*MED, s.v.*); cf. *generosus*, Intro. p. xiv.

44 *justified* perhaps means 'brought them the means of justification', the *lawe of lif*.

62 Langl. need not have thought *Christ* meant *conquerour* (Sk): he merely associated the ideas of 'the Anointed One' with the (anointed) king and emperor, moving on to the notion of 'conqueror' as the superlative degree of ' knight ' (see 27–30 above).

75 *Leg. Aur.* calls the Magi kings, naming them Caspar, Balthasar and Melchior (ch. 14).

86 *covered under*: the *Leg. Aur.* proposes gold = royalty / love, incense =

divinity / prayer, myrrh = humanity / mortification of the flesh. Langl.'s symbolic meanings are his own but the virtues fit a king-conqueror. The 'contradiction' Sk finds is removed by reading *richels* 90 (see textual commentary).

103–4 *faught; gaf* are metaphors, to keep the 'conqueror'-analogy: the allusion is presumably to Christ's arguing, driving out the sellers from the Temple, turning water to wine (cf. 108).

111–12 Consc. interprets this miracle (water = law, wine = love, the new law; cf. Jn 13: 34) as signifying the extension of love to all men, including enemies.

116–200 Consc. makes Dowel Christ's act of *power* (changing water to wine 116), Dobet his acts of *compassion* (healing etc 128), Dobest his acts of *pardon* to all mankind to come (through giving Peter his own power 183).

165 An early tradition made Thomas the apostle of India; see *Leg. Aur.* ch. 5 on his life.

184 *Piers* here seems startlingly identified with the Apostle Peter, at 188 with the Plowman, though at 11 he was Christ. This can only mean that those who imitate Christ become one with him as he is with the Father; cf. the teaching in Jn 14, esp. 20–3.

189–91 refer to Mt 16: 19, so *and ellis* means 'in heaven [as well as earth]' rather than 'in the future [as well as here and now]'. This statement of St Peter's unique authority is not in itself an affirmation of the medieval doctrine of the Pope's 'plenitude of power' in things earthly and heavenly, though it is the ultimate source of that doctrine.

209 The Holy Ghost is the grace-bringer in line 3 of *Veni, creator* (Raby, no. 88).

214 Sk is quite mistaken to say that Piers here 'is still Christ', since Christ has ascended, the scene appears to be Pentecost and Piers can only be St Peter.

220 The idea of an Antichrist goes back to 1 Jn 2: 18, 22 etc; on medieval developments see Cohn, pp. 33–6.

248 *Folvyles lawes* may be a pungently ironic allusion to the violent practices of the notorious Folville family, a criminal gang active in Leicestershire in the early years of Edward III (see McKisack, p. 204). Knights are to *recover* stolen goods from men like the Folvilles by the same methods the criminals use—'main force'.

260–3 recapitulate Passus VI–VII: the ploughing *now* has an allegorical (spiritual) sense because Piers is now head of a community directed to a spiritual end, without specific concern for the material basis of life: he is to *tilie truthe*.

264 The image of oxen, as Sk notes, is especially apt since the ox was the traditional 'symbol' of the Evangelist Luke; see VI 238 (*C*).

274–5a seem to imply that the Bible is to be used to interpret itself: and this is precisely what the Fathers did in their commentaries on it.

276 The Cardinal Virtues are the basic, 'natural' (as opposed to the infused, supernatural) virtues, on which the others depend (*cardo* 'hinge'). The Christian view of them was influenced by Is 11: 2–3, the list of the gifts of the spirit, prophetically applied to Christ. Of these, Aquinas regarded counsel, fortitude and piety as 'corresponding' to the cardinal virtues prudence, fortitude and justice. *Prudence*: 'foresight, sagacity' (fr. *providentia*); *Temperance*: not plain 'moderation' but restraint of the passions, as necessary foundation of asceticism; *Fortitude*: the virtue that resists pain and fear; *Justice*: rectitude of judgment, a virtue close to *truth*, and so to God (cf. 300–1); Consc. describes it as the *chief seed* 409.

311–13 Harrowing breaks the earth and covers the seeds against birds: the natural virtues need the help of revealed truth (the Bible interpreted by the Fathers) to foster *the plante of pees, moost precious of vertues*, which alone is powerful enough to destroy the choking weeds of vice. Langl. here, by way of expansive recapitulation, develops into full allegory the tightly compressed metaphor of I 152.

330 *Unite* is English, but Langl. aims to arouse attention to the doctrine of the Church as Christ's body (his vital source here is Eph 4: 1ff). The word had a poignant significance in 1378, the year in which Christendom was rent by the Great Schism.

335 As Sk well notes, *Piers* now signifies '[Christ's] faithful pastors and teachers', whom the Holy Spirit will accompany everywhere they preach and who will meet opposition from 'Antichrist', from the period of the Neronian persecutions to the present day and till the end of time.

337–end recapitulate in reverse the actions of the Second and (to some extent) the First Vision (esp. Passus V–VI, III–IV). The Deadly Sins return in force to assail Piers' barn and eventually (in XX) they prevail.

348 links the corruption of the sacrament of confession (by friars, it will be made clear) with the growth of false belief, moral evil (vice) leading to intellectual evil (heresy).

360 *pees*: cf. Paul's wish in Eph 4: 3 for '*unity* of the Spirit in the bond of *peace*'.

366 The castle of the church, the whole Christian community, is now under siege from a diabolical army, just as in IX 1–24 the individual soul had been under attack from 'the Prince of this World'.

370–4 recapitulate moments in Visions 1 and 2, esp. II 59, V 641. As the action draws near the present, the world depicted increasingly recalls the field of folk; 380–3 echoes the repentance of the folk of the field in V.

394–5 allude to Christ's words in Mt 5: 23–4; cf. also I Cor 11: 8.

399–404 recall the deceptions practised by Coveitise's wife in V 215ff.

425–6 The vicar's attack is upon the venal cardinals who associate with Jewish money-lenders and merchants instead of looking after the churches in Rome from which they took their formal titles, churches possessing important relics. Avignon, the residence of the papacy until 1377, was the centre of papal taxation and litigation. The papacy raised loans from bankers, who may have included Jews (see refs. under Avignon in Gilchrist); in addition, Jewish merchants were major suppliers to the papal court and a Jew transported to Avignon in June 1379 the cardinals who supported the antipope Clement (Bennett, 'Date', p. 63).

431–51 This contrast between Piers, the ideal of what a pope should be, and the graceless reality, may contain allusions (432, 435–8) to both the Great Schism of 1378 and the wars which broke out between Urban VI and the antipope Clement VII in April 1379 (see Bennett, 'Date', p. 60). The vicar's expression '*the* Pope' ironically leaves open who is the 'true' pope, but

England in fact supported the Roman Pope Urban against Clement, who had French support and who returned to Avignon in September 1378.

466 On the 'spirit of understanding' (ironic here) see 276 (*C*). The attitudes of the lord and king here are perversions of the knight's in VI 55 and the king's in IV 194–5.

PASSUS XX

10–11 In the maxim *Necessitas non habet legem* 'nede hath no lawe' it is dire need or extremity that is meant: the man who uses force or theft to preserve his life does not incur *dette* (sin).

18 *the lawe of kynde* here means less *lex naturalis* 'natural law', the principles of (moral) conduct forming part of man's nature as created by God, than 'the instinct of self-preservation' (also ordained by God and prior to and, in some circumstances, superior to any other man-made *lex*).

23 cf. XIX 276 (*C*); Nede sees Temperance as intrinsically incapable of perversion (one cannot, by definition, be *too* temperate).

35 Need's nearness to God derives from its capacity to induce humility; cf. also 40.

43 These words were not spoken at the Crucifixion (see Mt 8: 20), but that may be fittingly seen as Christ's moment of *moost nede*; cf. also Psalms 39: 18, 40: 2, 68: 30.

53 Antichrist corresponds to Mede in Vision I, his victory answering her defeat; but if Mede was worldly and carnal, he is diabolic. The allegory develops Mt 13: 24–30, 39.

76 *crye ... Kynde*: cf. IX 24. The situation is desperate because the devil has human allies; in Passus IX Anima was entrusted to Inwit's protection until called by Kynde (at death). Conscience's only weapon against human pride is an appeal to the inescapable realities of old age, disease and death (the *deeth of kynde*, cf. XVIII 210).

109–10 *to se* is not ironical (Sk) since it means not 'at seeing' but '(in order) to see' (cf. 106–8). 110 nonetheless refers to the confidence, expressed is dissipation, of the survivors of the plague. The assault of the Deadly Sins which now opens recapitulates and reverses the confessions of the latter in V, as 126–39 does the defeat of Mede in Passus IV.

143 *daggen*: cutting the edges of garments into elaborate patterns in the fashionable style was attacked by moralists as both vain and wasteful.

167 *Elde* Sk oddly remarks 'had fòrmerly fought under Death's banner on the side of the Vices'; but he had been in Kynde's army *against* the Pride of Life (95ff).

172 The proverbial glass helmet, like the physicians' nostrums, provides no real protection.

183 *myn heed* dramatically brings Will back into the action. Old age is inevitable and universal. Will stands clearly as a representative of common humanity.

203 *ben hennes*: Will has learnt by *kynde knowyng* 'the knowledge derived from experience' to desire what the ascetics of XIX 249 knew from the outset —detachment from the transience of worldly things.

207 Will's blunt question about the 'best' gets an equally direct and authoritative answer from Kynde (= Truth = God), but it is only now, after a whole life, that he has learnt the meaning of this *craft*.

250 Conscience attacks the friars for turning from their founders' intentions towards the study of a subject which has had the effect of weakening both faith and social order (cf. XV 70–2 and 276 below). 'Logic' probably means 'philosophy'.

270 alludes to the notion that there is a fixed number of the blessed (cf. Apoc 7: 4), with a probable pun on *Hevene / evene*, while in hell there is *nullus ordo* 'no order' (Job 10: 22). Consc. argues that since friars are mendicants they have no natural limit on their numbers in the form of the number of religious houses available.

275 Neither philosopher taught pure communism, though Plato (*Republic* III 416e) required the guardians of his ideal state to possess no more property than was strictly necessary, and Seneca (*Epistles* IX 3) stated that avarice destroyed the golden age (when ownership was in common). The peasant leader John Ball taught the doctrine of primeval common possession (Berners' Froissart, vol. 2, ch. 381) and was not unsympathetic to the mendicants (McKisack, p. 421); but Owst found no such doctrine in the extant sermons of friars (*Pulpit*, p. 288).

296 On some of these friar-philosophers see Leff, pp. 279–94.

311 *in the sege*: 'present at the siege' (i.e. somewhere outside the barn). Sire Leef is *within* Unitee; Friar Flatterer enters from outside.

323 Conscience's tolerance, already shown at 242, is a form of *hendenesse* (145; cf. 349); though he was not deceived by Mede, he succumbs to a hypocritical friar. This is perhaps Langl.'s strongest statement of the danger represented by the friars' fluent address. For a general discussion of Conscience in *PP* and esp. in XX, see Jenkins, 'Conscience'.

355 succinctly makes clear that the friars win men's confidence through their persuasive talk. *Hende-Speche* is both the politeness of Christians generally and, from the other standpoint, the 'glib and oily art' of the mendicants themselves.

365–8 recapitulate the words of the flattering friar to Mede at III 35–50.

381 Conscience should not be taken over-literally as intending to 'leave' the (corrupted) Church. That would be entirely against his nature as the true conscientious Christian, attuned to the good though not infallible. His resolution resembles that of Piers to set out as a pilgrim at VI 58. His last cry is an expression of total dependence on God the Trinity (*Kynde*, 'the Creator' [Father], *Piers*, 'God Incarnate' [the Son], Grace [the Holy Spirit], the final and sole supports of the individual conscience and the Christian community alike.

ADDENDUM to XVIII 109*a*: source identified as pseudo-Augustine, *Contra Judaeos* (*P.L.* 42: 1124), used in lesson for 4th Sunday in Advent (Derek Pearsall, *PP: An Edition of the C-text* (1978), p. 324).

Appendix

LANGLAND'S ALLITERATIVE VERSE

This Appendix, which supersedes that in the first and second printings of this book, is intended only as a concise guide to the scansion of the poem. A full account is given in my study *The Clerkly Maker: Langland's Poetic Art* (1987). For discussion of the metrical question from a textual standpoint, see Kane and Donaldson (pp. 131–40).

Langland's alliterative line consists of between two and five stressed syllables (*lifts*) separated by one or more unstressed syllables (*dips*). A dip may often precede the first lift, and may sometimes be omitted between lifts, usually at the caesura:

Sŏmmĕ *p*úttĕn hĕm tŏ thĕ *p*lóugh,//*p*léidĕn fūl sélde   (Prol 20).

Lifts that carry alliteration are *full staves* (*p*útten, *p*lóugh, *p*léiden). Lifts without alliteration are *blank staves* (sélde). A *mute stave* is a syllable within a dip that carries alliteration but no stress, its purpose being to satisfy half the metrical requirement (alliteration) while the other half (stress) is satisfied by the lift that follows, which is accordingly a blank stave:

And *w*ónnen that thise *w*ástours *w*ith glótonye d estrúyeth   (Prol 22).

Here the mute stave *with* is shown without a stress mark. Mute staves are found especially in the position after the half-line break. The very rare *liaisonal stave* arises when the consonant of a preceding word is treated as if it belonged with the vowel of a following word, thereby generating a required full stave:

Fírst he fónded me, *if* Í lovede béttre   (XVI 231).

Except for a few lines with prose quotations in them and some where the text remains doubtful, Langland's lines conform to *ten regular metrical patterns*, to each of which I give a descriptive name. These fall into *three* clear classes or *types*:

Type I (Standard)

a *Normative*

I *sh*óop me into *sh*róudes as I a *sh*éep wére   (Prol 2) *aa/ax*

b *Enriched*

In a *s*ómer *s*éson, whan *s*ófte was the *s*ónne   (Prol 1) *aa/aa*

c *Extended*

With *d*épe *d*íches and *d*érke and *d*rédfulle of síghte   (Prol 16) *aaa/ax*

359

d *Enriched extended*

And *l*éne thee *l*éde thi *l*ónd so *l*éaute thee *l*óvye   (Prol 126) *aaa/aa*

e *Blank extended*

A *d*éep *d*ále bynéthe, a *d*óngeon therínne   (Prol 15) *aax/ax*

Type II (Clustered)

a *Single clustered*

And *b*ére hire *b*rás at thi *b*ák to Cáleis to sélle   (III 196) *aaa/xx*

b *Double clustered*

And *s*ómme *s*érven as *s*érvaunts *l*órdes and *l*ádies   (Prol 95) *aaa/bb*

Type III (Reduced)

a *Minimal*

The *n*ótaries and yé *n*óyen the péple   (II 127) *ax/ax*

b *Enriched reduced*

How thow *l*érnest the péple, the *l*éred and the *l*éwed   (IV 12) *ax/aa*

c *Crossed*

And who so *l*éveth noght this be *s*óoth, *l*óke in the *S*áuter glose   (V 275) *ab/ab*

In addition, a very rare type of line, apparently unique to Langland, may be described as *transitional* between Type I with 'muted' post-caesural stave (e.g. Prol 22 above) and Type IIb, which has a second stave-letter in the *b* half-line (e.g. Prol 95 above):

Ne nevere *w*éné to *w*ýnne *w*ith cráft that I *k*nówe   (V 469) *aa(a)bb*

The presence of the muted stave-word *with* establishes that V 469 is not of the *aabb* variety, found in other writers but not used by Langland. The existence of this 'T-type' line in the *Piers Plowman* text in MS Bodley 851 (ed. Rigg-Brewer) at III 158, VII 38, 245 etc (lines not found in the A, B and C texts) is evidence that this version of the poem, known as the 'Z' text, is authentic (see Additional Note to Introduction, p. xliii).

There is occasionally some doubt as to which precise type a particular line belongs to, and Langland sometimes wrenches stress as well as muting staves. The most difficult examples are discussed in the Textual and Lexical Notes; for fuller discussion see ch. 2 of *The Clerkly Maker*.

Index of Proper Names

Supplementary Bibliography

A large number of studies of *Piers Plowman* have appeared since the first printing of this edition and the publication of A. J. Colaianne's Annotated Bibliography in the same year. Only a selection of the most important of these is given here, the titles being arranged under subject headings for convenience.

EDITIONS

Derek Pearsall: *Piers Plowman by William Langland: An Edition of the C-text* (York Medieval Texts, 2nd series, 1978); reviewed by A. V. C. Schmidt in *N&Q* 225 (1980), 102–10.

A. G. Rigg and Charlotte Brewer, eds.: *Piers Plowman: the Z Version* (Toronto, Pontifical Institute of Mediaeval Studies, 1983).

BACKGROUND AND LITERARY RELATIONS

David Aers: *Chaucer, Langland and the Creative Imagination* (1980); reviewed by A. V. C. Schmidt in *EC* 32 (1983), 238–46.

Janet Coleman: *Piers Plowman and the Moderni* (Rome, 1981).

Peter Dronke: 'Arbor Caritatis', in P. L. Heyworth (ed.), *Medieval Studies for J. A. W. Bennett* (Oxford, 1981), 207–53.

Pamela Gradon: 'Langland and the Ideology of Dissent', *Proceedings of the British Academy* 66 (1982 for 1980).

Anne Middleton: 'The Audience and Public of *Piers Plowman*', in D. Lawton (ed.), *Middle English Alliterative Poetry and Its Literary Background* (Cambridge, Brewer, 1982), 101–23.

GENERAL CRITICAL AND INTERPRETATIVE STUDIES

Anna P. Baldwin: *The Theme of Government in Piers Plowman* (Cambridge, Brewer, 1981).

T. P. Dunning: *Piers Plowman: An Interpretation of the A Text*, 2nd edn. rev. and ed. by T. P. Dolan (Oxford, 1980).

Margaret E. Goldsmith: *The Figure of Piers Plowman* (Cambridge, Brewer, 1981).

Priscilla Martin: *Piers Plowman: The Field and the Tower* (1979).

Myra Stokes: *Justice and Mercy in Piers Plowman: A Reading of the B Text Visio* (London, 1984).

R. Adams: 'The Nature of Need in *Piers Plowman* XX', *Traditio* 34 (1978), 273–301.

J. A. W. Bennett: 'The Passion in *Piers Plowman*', ch. IV of his *Poetry of the Passion* (Oxford, 1982), 85–112.

J. Burrow: 'Langland *Nel Mezzo del Cammin*', in Heyworth (ed.), *Medieval Studies* . . ., 21–41.

P. Gradon: '*Trajanus Redivivus*: Another Look at Trajan in *Piers Plowman*', in D. Gray and E. G. Stanley (eds.), *Middle English Studies Presented to Norman Davis* (Oxford, 1983), 93–114.

A. J. Minnis: 'Langland's Ymaginatif and late-medieval theories of imagination', *Comparative Criticism: A Year Book*, 3 (Cambridge, 1981), 71–103.

G. H. Russell: 'The Poet as Reviser: the Metamorphosis of the Confession of the Seven Deadly Sins in *Piers Plowman*', in *Acts of Interpretation: Essays . . . in Honour of E. Talbot Donaldson*, ed. M. J. Carruthers and E. D. Kirk (Norman, Oklahoma, 1982), 53–65.

A. V. C. Schmidt: 'Langland and the Mystical Tradition', in M. Glasscoe (ed.), *The Medieval Mystical Tradition in England* (Exeter, 1980), 17–38.
'The Treatment of the Crucifixion in *Piers Plowman* and in Rolle's *Meditations on the Passion*', *Analecta Cartusiana* 35 (1983), 174–96.
'The Inner Dreams in *Piers Plowman*', *Medium Ævum* LV (1986), 24–40.

J. Simpson, 'From Reason to Affective Knowledge: Modes of Thought and Poetic Form in *PP*', *Medium Ævum* LV (1986), 1–23.

STYLE AND METRE
G. Kane: 'Music "Neither Unpleasant nor Monotonous"', in Heyworth (ed.), *Medieval Studies* . . ., 43–63.

A. V. C. Schmidt: 'Langland's Structural Imagery', *EC* 30 (1980), 311–25.
'*Lele Wordes* and *Bele Paroles*: Some Aspects of Langland's Word-Play', *RES* 34 (1983), 137–50.
The Clerkly Maker: Langland's Poetic Art (Cambridge: D. S. Brewer, 1987).

J. Simpson: 'The Transformation of Meaning: A Figure of Thought in *Piers Plowman*', *RES* 37 (1986), 161–83.

Glossary

(Compiled with the assistance of Judith V. Schmidt)

The aim of this glossary is to list *each separate sense* of those words which are likely to cause difficulty, with at the minimum a reference to its first appearance. It is meant to be used in conjunction with the marginal glosses and footnote translations.

The following abbreviations are used:
a. adjective, *av.* adverb, *c.* conjunction, *comp.* comparative, *i.* intransitive, *imper.* imperative, *n.* noun, *p.* participle, *pl.* plural, *p.p.* past participle, *p.t.* past tense, *prep.* preposition, *pres.* present, *prn.* pronoun, *refl.* reflexive, *sg.* singular, *subj.* subjunctive *t.* transitive, *v.* verb.

a, one, single XVI 86; on XVI 172
abave, confound VI 215
abide, stay VIII 65; endure XX 46
abidynge, long-suffering XIX 296
abien pay for III 251; **abye** IX 89
abiggen, pay II 128
abite, nip off XVI 27.
ablende (*v*), blind X 131; **ablyndeth,** blinds X 262
abosted, boastingly defied VI 154
aboughte, IX 143, *p.t. of* **abi(gg)en; abought** (*p.p.*), XVIII 389
ac, (*c*) but Prol. 5 et passim.
acale, chilled XVIII 395
accidie, attack of sloth V 360
acombre, oppress II 51; *p.p.* overcome I 32
acorden, agree V 329
acorse, condemn Prol. 99; **acurseth,** XVIII 107
acounte, settle IV 11; *p.t.* valued XIX 415
acountes, reckoning VI 89
acouped, accused XIII 458
acquitaunce, document of acquittal XIV 189
aday, at morn VI 308; **adayes,** daily XV 283
addre, serpent XVIII 336
adreynten (*v.i.*), drowned X 405; **adreynt** (*p.p.*), XX 378
af(f)aite(n), subdue, discipline V 66, VI 31
afereth, frightens XVIII 433
affiaunce (*n*), trust XVI 238
aforthe, afford VI 198
afrounted, accosted XX 5
after, according to XII 188; like XI 261
afurst, a-thirst X 59
afyngred, very hungry VI 267
agasteth, frightens XIV 280; **agast** (*p.p.*), XIX 301

agein, in return for X 199
agrounde, on the earth I 90
agulte, offend/sin against XIV 8; *p.t.* XVII 297
aiels, forefathers XV 322
a·thes (*n*), harrows XIX 275
alarme, to arms! XX 92
alay (*n*), alloy XV 348; *v.p.p.* XV 353
alday, continually XV 358
aleggen, adduce (texts) XI 89
aliry, across VI 122
alkenamye, alchemy X 212
aller, of all XIX 474
alleskynnes, of all kinds (of) XX 373
al(l)owaunce, approval, favour XI 220
allowed (*p.p.*), assessed X 430
almaries, cupboards XIV 246
alough, low down XII 220
also, as III 331; **als,** likewise III 72
amaistrye, dominate II 148
amende, improve V 265
amendement, conversion X 361
amendes, compensation V 325
amercy (*v*), fine VI 39
amonge (*av*), mixed in XIV 237
amornynge, a-mourning, in sadness XI 338
amortisede, conveyed in mortmain XV 320
ampulles, phials V 520
ancres, anchorites Prol. 28
and, if IV 88 et passim; whilst X 405
angres, afflictions XII 11; *v.* V 116
aniente, annihilate XVII 288
anoonright, immediately XI 337
apaied, pleased, satisfied VI 195; **apayed** VI 108
apeire (*v*), harm, damage V 46, 564
apendeth, pertains I 100
apereth, reaches XIV 242
apertly, plainly, manifestly I 100

apeward, ape-keeper V 631
appele, accuse XI 421
appose, (put) question(s) to III 5; *p.t.* disputed with VII 139
ar, before XVI 115 (=**ere**)
arate, reprove, correct XI 102
arerage, debt, arrears X 467
arere, backwards V 348
aresonedest, argued with XII 218
arest (*av*), first XVI 71
armes, (coat of) arms, form V 501
arn, are XVII 31
arne (*p.t. of* **ernen**), welled up, ran XVI 136
arraye, prepare IV 16
artow (=**art thow**), art thou V 256
arwes, arrows III 326
askes (*n*), ashes III 98
asketh, requires Prol 19
aspie, seek XVI 170
assay, trial X 253; **assayen,** try III 5
asseled, sealed XVII 4
assetz, adequate satisfaction XVII 240
assoilen, absolve Prol. 70; solve, explain III 237
asterte, escape XI 400
astronomiens, astronomers XV 358
at, from III 25, XI 346
atamede, broached XVII 70
atones, at the same time XVII 54
athynketh, grieves XVIII 89
attachen, arrest II 200; *p.t.* claimed XVI 261
atteynt (*p.p.*), found false, attainted XX 162
attre, venom XII 256
auditour, accountant XIX 464
aught, something V 433
auncer, steelyard V 214
auntrede, ventured XVIII 221; set off XX 175
auter, altar V 108
avaunced, promoted, advanced I 191
aventrous, adventurous (*sc.* knights) XVIII 16
aventure, an, in case, lest perchance III 66
avoutrye, adultery XII 74
avowe, declare III 257; **avowes** (*n*), vows V 398
awayte, see, observe X 330
awreke, avenge VI 173; **awroke** (*p.p.*), VI 201
axe, ask IV 103
ayeins (*prep.*), against III 92; towards IV 44; in return for V 431; *av.c.* before XIX 319

baberlipped, thick-lipped V 188
bablede, mumbled V 8
bacheler, young knight XVI 179
baches, valleys V 514
baddely, badly XV 534
baddenesse, wickedness XII 48

bagge, money-bag XX 142
baillies, bailiffs II 2
bakbite, slander II 81
bakkes, cloaks X 358
baksteres, bakers Prol 219
bale, evil IV 89; misery XI 332; **bale-deeth,** baleful death XVIII 35
baleised, beaten with a **baleys** (*q.v.*) V 173
baleys, rod, birch X 178; **baleises** XII 12
balkes, ridges (on ploughed land) VI 107
balled, bald XX 184
ballok-knyf, knife with knobbed haft XV 124
banne, curse I 62; denounce X 7
banyer, standard-bearer XV 434
bar, bore II 3 (*p.t.* of **beren**)
barayne, unproductive XVIII 106
bare, openly displayed XX 70
bark, husk XI 258
barn, child II 3 et passim
baselard, dagger III 305; sword XV 121
batauntliche (*av*), with noisy eagerness XIV 213
batred, slapped III 199
baude, bawd III 129
baw, bah! XI 140
bayard, bay horse IV 53
beaupeere, elder XVIII 230
bedbourde, intercourse IX 187
bede (*v*), pray, intercede VIII 104
bede (*n*), prayer XI 149
bedelles, beadles, tipstaffs, II 60, III 2
beden, bade III 27 (*p.t.* of **beden** and **bidden**)
bedeman, beadsman, one who prays III 41
bedes, prayers V 9
bedreden, bed-ridden VII 100
beem, beam, plank X 262
beere, bore V 138 (*p.t. pl.* of **beren**)
beflobered (*v.p.t.*), muddied XIII 400
beighes, necklaces Prol. 161
bekene (*n*), beacon XVII 265
beknew, acknowledged X 413
belsires, ancestor's IX 143
belwe (*v*), bellow XI 341
ben, are VI 130
benes, beans VI 182
benigneliche, with good will XII 112
benyson, blessing XIII 235
beren, bear Prol. 161; **bere** (*p.t.*), III 196; **berth** XVI 180
bernes, barns VI 183
beryng, manner X 254
bete, beat V 33; **bette** (*p.t.*), X 178
bete, relieve VI 237 (*see* **boote**)
beth, are III 27 (= **ben**); be X 443, XIII 420
bette, beat X 178 (*p.t.* of **beten**)
bible, book XV 89
bicche, bitch V 347
bicome, went V 642
bidde, pray V 227; **-ynge,** prayer(s), III 219
bidderes, beggars Prol. 41

368

biddeth, directs IX 15
bidraveled, beslavered V 191
bidropped, spattered XIII 320
bienfait, good turn V 430; *pl.* good deeds
V 612
biennals, biennial masses VII 171
bigge (*a*), strong VI 213
bigge (*v*), buy XIV 230; *see* **buggen**
biggyng, trading V 128
bigile, deceive X 120; perplex XV 370
bigirdles, purses VIII 88
bigruccheth, complains VI 67
biheste, promise III 127
bihighte, promised III 29; *see next entry*
bihote (*v*), promise VI 231
bihynde, behind, overdue V 427
bikenne, commit, commend II 56
bikere, fight XX 79
biknowe, acknowledge V 196
bile, bill XI 357
biles (*n*), boils XX 84
bil(e)eve, creed V 7, XIX 348
bileve(n) (*v*), give up VI 179
bilieth, tell lies against X 22; *p.t.* II 22
bille, petition IV 47
bilongeth, is due IX 78
bilove, make beloved VI 229
bilowen, told lies about II 22
bilye, tell lies against V 408
biquasshed (*v.t.* or *i.*), shattered XVIII
248
birewe, regret XII 250
bisette, bestow V 260; *p.t.* XII 47
biseye, visited XX 202 (*p.p.* of **bisen**)
bisherewed, cursed IV 168
bishetten, shut (something) up II 214; *p.p.*
XIX 167
bishined, ? illuminated XV 515 (*see note*)
bisitte(n), oppress II 141; afflict X 357
bislabered, soiled V 386
bismere, calumny V 88; *pl.* XIX 296
bisnewed, snowed over XV 112
bispered, locked up XV 143
biswatte (*p.t.*), covered with sweat XIII
402
biswynke, labour for; **biswonke** (*p.t.*), XX
293; **biswynken,** work at XV 486
bit, commands IX 15 (= **biddeth**)
bit, begs VII 66 (= **biddeth**)
bitelbrowed, with beetling brows V 188
bitit, it befalls XI 401; **bitidde** (*p.t.*), XII
116
bitter (*n*), bitterness V 118
bittre (*av*), grievously X 278
bityme, early V 638
biwicched, cast a spell on XIX 156
biwiled, deceived X 109
biyete (*n*), offspring II 41
biyeten, take over X 319
biyonde, abroad IV 128
blame (*v*), slander V 129
blancmanger, chicken stew XIII 91
blasen, coat-of-arms XVI 179

blenche, turn aside V 580
blente, blinded V 495 (*p.t.* of **blenden**)
blered, dimmed, bleared Prol. 74
blisse (*v*), bless XVI 237
blisse (*n*), happiness, joy VIII 65
blisful, blessed II 3
blody, consanguineous VI 207
bloo, pale III 98
blosmede, blossomed V 139
blowyng tyme, blossoming time XVI 26
blustreden, wandered aimlessly V 514
bocches, plague-sores XIII 249
bocher, butcher V 323; *pl.* Prol. 219
body half, front part XIII 316
boldede, emboldened III 199
boldnesse, strength, force V 612
boldely, confidently XIX 478
bole, bull XI 341
bolk, belch V 391
bolle, bowl V 107
bolneth, swells V 118
bonched, struck Prol. 74
bondeman, labourer, serf V 191
boon, bone VII 92
boone, request XI 149
boost, arrogance XIV 222
boot (*v*), bit (*p.t.* of **biten**) V 83
boot (*n*), boat VIII 30
boote, remedy IV 89 *et passim*
bootned, healed VI 191
borde, table VI 265
bordlees, without a table XII 201
borgh, surety IV 89; **borwe** XIV 190
borre, hoarseness XVII 327
borwe, stand bail for IV 109; borrow I 77
bosard, oaf X 264
botelees, irremediable XVIII 201
bother, of them both II 67; **botheres** XVI
165
botons, studs XV 124
botrased, buttressed V 589
boughte, redeemed II 3 (*p.t.* of **biggen**)
bouken, cleanse with lye, buck XV 190
bour, private room III 14
bourdeour, jester XIII 447
bourdynge, jesting XV 40
bouste, box, pyx XIII 152
bowe (*v*), sink VIII 48; submit XIII 147
bowes, boughs V 575
boweth (*v. imper. pl.*), proceed, turn V
566
boy, rogue, knave Prol. 80
brak, broke I 113 (*p.t.* of **breken**)
brast, burst VI 178 (*p.t.* of **bresten**)
brawen, brawn XIII 62
brech, breeches V 174
bred corn, seed-corn VI 62
bredful, brimful Prol. 41
breide, hastened XVII 70
breken, break VI 30; **breketh** X 84
breme, powerful XII 229
bren (*n*), bran VI 182
bren (*v*), burn III 267 (*imper.* of **brennen**)

brent, burnished   V 267
brevet, letter of indulgence   Prol.74
brew, brewed   V 215 (*p.t.* of **browen**)
brewecheste (*a*), trouble-brewing   XVI 43
briddes, young (birds)   XI 356
brocage, arrangement   XIV 267
broche (*v*),sew   V 208
broches (*n*), matches XVII 248
brocours, brokers   II 60; *sg.* go-between III 46; agent   V 129
brode (*av*), extensively   X 313
broke, torn   V 107 (*p. p.* of **breken**)
broke (*n*), brook   VI 135
brol, brat   III 205
brotel, fragile   VIII 43
brouke, partake of   XI 122; enjoy   XVIII 364
browe, (*p. p.*), brewed   XVIII 364
brugge, (draw-)bridge   V 592
brunneste, darkest   VI 306
brybours, robbers   XX 262
bugge, buy   Prol. 168 (= **biggen**); **-ere,** purchaser   X 304; **-ynge,** buying   XIX 236
bukkes, male deer, bucks   VI 30
bulles, mandates   III 148
bummed, tasted   V 219
burde, lady   III 14
burdoun, staff   V 517
burel, coarse, half-educated   X 284
burgages, tenements   III 86
burgeises, burgesses   Prol.217
burgh, town   II 98
burieles, tomb   XIX 146
burjoneth (*v*), shoot   XV 75
burnes, men   III 267; **buyrn** XVI 180
busked, went, betook themselves   III 14
buskes (*n*), bushes   XI 344
but (if), unless   Prol.66, I 181
but (*av*), only   V 74
buxom, obedient, willing   I 110
buxomnesse, obedience   I 113
by, concerning   V 178; in accordance with Prol.80; with   I 28
byjaped, fooled   XVIII 292
bymeneth, signifies   Prol. 209
bymolen, (*v*), stain   XIV 4
bynam, took away from   VI 241; **bynomen,** (*p. p.*),   III 31
by wille, wilfully   IV 70

cabane, shelter   III 191
caccheth, take   II 36; obtain   XIII 298
cachepol, officer   XVIII 46
cairen, wander   Prol. 29; proceed   IV 24
cammokes, rest-harrows   XIX 314
can, proceeded to (= **gan**)   Prol. 143
canonistres, canon-lawyers   VII 150
canoun, Canon Law   V 422
caples, horses   II 162; **capul** (*sg.*)   XVII 109
caractes, letters, characters   XII 78
carded, combed   X 18

cardiacle, heart-attack   XIII 334
care, trouble, distress   IX 153
cared, wanted, were concerned   II 162
carefulle, full of anxiety   I 203; *av.*   V 76
carolden, danced   XVIII 426
caroyne, carcass, corpse   Prol. 189
carped, told   II 192; **carpen,** cry out   X 51
carpynge, talking   Prol. 204; speech   XI 237
cast, (*n*), purpose   III 19
casten, (*v*), arranged (*p. t.* of **casten**); make   VI 16; contrived   XV 333
catecumelynges, catechumens   XI 77 (*see note*)
catel, wealth   Prol. 205; food   XV 427
caukede, trod, mated with   XI 358
caytif, wretch   V 196; *a.* wretched   XI 294
cene, supper   XVI 140
certein (*a*), definite   XX 258
certes, assuredly   II 152
cesseth, cease!   IV 1
chafen (*v*), heat   XII 125
chaffare (*n*), trade   Prol. 31; goods   V 243
chalangeable, open to dispute   XI 303
chalangen, claim   Prol. 93; charged   V 172
chalangynge, accusing   V 87; criticising XI 423; claiming   XV 344
chambre, private room   III 10
chanons, canons   X 316
chapeleyns, priests   VI 12
chapitle, chapter (-court)   III 320
chapman, merchant   Prol. 64
chargeth, (*v*), accounts   XIV 312; insists on   XVII 293; burden   XX 237
charnel, charnel-house   VI 48
chaste (*v*), discipline, chastise   VI 51
chastilet, small castle   II 85
chaumbrere, chamberlain   XIV 100
Chauncelrie, Chancery   Prol.93
che(e)ste, angry quarrelling   II 85, et passim
cheitiftee, destitution   XX 236
Cheker, the Exchequer   Prol. 94
chekes, cheeks   VI 40
chele, cold   I 22
Chepe, Cheapside   V 315
chepe (*v*), buy   XV 31; **-pyng,** market   IV 56
chere, face, look   IV 165
chered, looking, of appearance   XIX 265
cherissynge, spoiling   IV 117
cherl, villein, serf   XI 127
chervelles, chervil   VI 294
chese (*v*), choose   XV 38
chesibles, chasubles   VI 12
chetes, escheats, reversions   IV 175
cheveden, succeeded   Prol.31 (*p.t.* of **cheven**)
chevysaunces, loans at interest   V 245; bargain   XX 16
chewen, eat up, consume   I 193
cheyne, chain   V 607
chibolles, spring-onions   VI 294

chiden, complain I 193; quarrel III 178; **chidde** (*p.t.*), XVIII 420
chidynge, scolding V 87
chief, foremost Prol.64
chiknes, chickens IV 38
childissh, childlike XV 149
chirie-tyme, cherry-time, summer V 159
chiteryng, chattering XII 253
chivaler, knight XVIII 99
choppes, blows IX 169
chymenee, fireplace X 100
chyveled, trembled V 190
clausemele, clause by clause V 420
claweth, grasp X 281; scrape XIV 17; seize XVII 190
cleef (*v.i.*), split XVIII 61 (*p.t.* of **cleven**)
clemat, weather-region XV 369
clene, pure V 511
cler, bright V 585
clergie, learning, the learned III 165
clergially, learnedly Prol. 124
clermatyn, a fine white bread VI 304
cleymeth (*v*), claim I 93; *p.t.* XX 96
cliket, latch-key V 604
clippe, grasp XVII 190; embrace XVIII 419
clipse, eclipse XVIII 135
clokke, limp III 34
clomsest, are benumbed XIV 51
closeth, encloses XVIII 135
clouted, patched VI 59; **cloutes,** rags II 221
clyngest, are parched XIV 51
clyve, adhere XI 224
coffes, mittens VI 60
cofres, treasure-chests XI 198
cokeney, egg VI 285
cokeres, leggings VI 60
coket, a fine white bread VI 304
cokewold, cuckold IV 164
collateral (*a*), accompanying XIV 297
colled, embraced XI 17
colomy, grimy (with soot) XIII 355
coloppes, bacon and eggs VI 285
coloureth, disguises XIX 461
colvere, dove XV 402
combraunce, trouble XI 45
comeres, callers II 231
comly, fit XV 450
commissarie, bishop's officer XV 239
commune, common people Prol.115; **communers** XV 331
communes, food Prol. 117
commune womman, prostitute V 641
compaignable, companionable XV 219
compased, established X 180
compasynge, designing XVII 172
comsed, began III 104; **comseth,** arises I 139
comsynge, beginning XVIII 214
comune, in, in public XI 216
conceyve, take in, grasp VIII 58
conclude, confute X 444

conestable, constable XX 214
conformen, dispose XIII 208
confort (*n*), benefit IV 151
confortatif (*a*), agreeable XV 219
conforted, entertained XIII 57; supported XX 67
congeien, dismiss III 174; **congeye,** IV 4
congie (*n*), farewell XIII 202
conjured, required on oath XV 14
conseyved, uttered VI 33
contenaunce, appearance Prol. 24; looks V 181
contrarieth, acts contrary to V 54
contrees, districts XX 329
contreve, devise, invent Prol. 118
conynges, rabbits Prol. 189
coped, clothed, robed II 231
coppes, cups III 22
corlew, curlew XIV 44
correctours, (those) who correct X 281
corrupcions, diseases XX 99
cors, (living) body I 139, XV 23
corsaint, saint's shrine V 532
corseder, the worse off XIX 420
corseth (*v*), curses VI 316
costes, regions II 86, VIII 12
cote, coat V 109; **c. armure,** coat-of-arms XIX 13
cotes, cottages VIII 16
counseil, secret, confidence V 166
countee, county II 86
counteth, cares III 142
countreplede, argue against XII 98; oppose XX 385
coupable, guilty XII 88
coupe, sin, guilt V 298, 474
coupes, bowls III 22
courbed (*v*), bent I 79
cours, impulse III 56; skill XV 367
court, manor-house V 585, XX 345
courtepy, short coat V 79; *pl.* VI 188
coveited, desired XI 125
coveitise, greed II 86; anxious concern XIV 11
covenaunt, condition V 333; agreement XIV 150
covent, convent V 153
covere (*v*), roof III 60
cowkynde, cattle XI 340
crabbede (*a*), ill-tempered X 106
cracched, carded XV 452 (*see note*)
cracchen, scratch Prol. 154; snatch XI 144
craft, power I 139; skill II 4
crafty (*men*), crafts-, tradesmen III 225
craked (*v*), broke XVIII 73
craven (*v*), ask, require III 222; *p.t.* VI 92
creaunt (*a*), believing XII 193
Cristendom, Christian faith, baptism V 588
croce, crosier VIII 96
croft, small field V 572
crokke, pot XIX 282

371

crop, upper growth, top XVI 42, XX 53

cropen (*v*), crept (*p.t.* of **crepen**) Prol. 186; **crope,** III 191

crouch, cross-ornament V 522

crowne, air XI 36; tonsure XI 297

crownynge, the tonsure Prol. 88

cruddes, curds VI 282

cuppemele, by cupfuls V 221

curatours, parish-priests I 195; spiritual rulers XIX 223

cure, benefice XI 300

curen (*v*), act as parish priest XX 326

curious, artfully cut XIX 289

cursed, condemned, excommunicated III 142; wicked XIX 435

curteisie, generosity I 20; graciousness XII 77

daffe, fool I 140, XI 425

daggen (*v*), tailor curiously XX 143

dampne, damn V 470; condemn XVII 304

damyseles, attendant ladies X 12

daunten, subdue III 288; make much of X 37

dawe (*v*), dawn XVIII 427

debate (*n*), quarrel, strife V 97, XV 426

decourreth, departs XIV 193

dedes, bonds V 241

dedeynous, arrogant VIII 84

dedly, mortal I 144, IX 207

deef, deaf X 132

deele, give, distribute I 199

deere, dearly VI 291

deeth, plague X 81

deeth-yvel, bane XVIII 53

defaute, deficiency II 140; lack VI 206

defence, prohibition XVIII 194

defendeth, forbids III 64

defie, digest Prol.230; *i.* V 383

defouled, mortified XV 532

delicatly, luxuriously V 375

deluvye, deluge X 408

delven, dig VI 141; **delveres,** Prol. 224

demen, judge Prol. 96; claim III 188; believed XIX 148

dene, din XVIII 62

departable, distinguishable XVII 128

departed, divided VII 157

depper (*av*), more deeply X 184, XV 199

deprave, revile, abuse III 179, V143

dere (*v*), harm VII 34; *n* XIV 170

derely, tidily, properly XIX 2

dereworthy, precious I 87

derk, dark Prol.16; **derkliche,** obscurely X 370

derne (*a*), secret II 176; *av.* XI 351; intimate IX 189

deschargen, unburden XV 564

despended, spent V 263

despiseth, pours scorn on XV 54

deve, deaf XIX 130

devinour, expositor VII 136, X 450

devoir, duty XI 284, XIII 212

devoutrye, adultery II 176

devyne, interpret Prol. 210; ponder X 184; *p.t.* foretold V 597

devyse, indicate V 547; consider XIX 280; *p.t.* designed XIX 331

deyned, deigned VI 308

deyntee, pleasure XI 48

deys, dais, upper table VII 17, X 56

diapenidion, cough-medicine V 122 (*see note*)

dide, made I 99 et passim; betook XIX 2

dido, an old tale XIII 172

dighte, prepare VI 291; *p.t.* dressed XIX 2

digneliche, honourably VII 172

disalowed, disapproved XIV 130

disalowyng, disfavour, disapproval XIV 138

discryve, describe V 78; *p.t.* named XX 94

disours, minstrel's XIII 172

divined, expounded VII 153; **divinour,** VII 136

do (it), appeal to I 86, III 188

doel, lament V 380; pain VI 120

doelful, painful XV 520

doke, duck V 74, XVII 64

doles, alms III 71

dolven, buried VI 180 (*p.p.* of **delven**)

done, what, what make of XVIII 300

Donet, grammar V 205 (*see note*)

donge, dung III 310

doom, judgment II 206

doon, do Prol. 224; make V 94; put IX 11; (*causative*) have (something) done III 60-2

dorste, dared Prol. 178

doted, foolish, silly I 140

doughtier, braver V 101

doute, fear Prol. 152, XI 430

downrighte, utterly XVIII 192

dowve, dove XV 399

doynges, actions XIX 130

dradden, feared (*p.t. pl.* of **dreden**) XX 65

draf, hog's-wash X 11; ale-leavings XIX 402

drat, fears IX 93 (= **dredeth**)

drawe forth, advanced X 37

dred, fear, treat with respect I 34

dredful, terrible XX 89

dredfully, fearfully XVII 64

dremels, dream XIII 14

drenche, drown VIII 51

drevelen, slobber X 41

dright, man VIII 70; Lord XIII 268

drogges, drugs XX 174

droghte, dry weather VI 288

dronkelewe, drunken VIII 84

drough, betook V 205; drew V 350

372

drow, withdrew XVIII 111 (*p.t.* of
  drowen)
drury, love-gift I 87
drye (*n*), dryness XIV 51
drynkes, potions VI 274
dryvele, slobber X 11; prate X 56
duc, duke, magnate XIX 308
dureth, lasts VI 56; remain valid XVIII
  186
dyas, remedies XX 174
dyche (*v*), make a ditch XIX 365
dykeres, ditch-diggers Prol. 224
dym, dark III 193; weak-sighted X 181
dymes, tithes XV 562
dyngen, beat, strike III 312, X 327, XV
  19; thresh VI 141
dynt, blow XVIII 26
dysshere, dish-seller V 316
dyvyde, apportion XIX 216

echone, each one I 17
edifie, build XVI 132
edwyted, reproached V 364
eft, again III 348; next time IV 107
eftsoone(s), again V 474
egre, fierce XIII 80
egreliche, sharply XVI 64; bitterly XIX
  381
eighe!, (*excl.*) oh! XI 44
ek, also II 93, 237; XIII 164
elde, old age V 190, XII 8, XX 154
elenge, wretched Prol. 194, X 96, XX 2
elengeliche, wretchedly XI 44, XX 37
eller(e), elder-tree I 68, IX 149
ellis, at other times Prol. 91; otherwise
  VIII 114, XIV 195
enbawmed, anointed XVII 72
enblaunched, whitened XV 115
enchauntede, charmed XV 403; XX 379
encreesse, increase XI 397
endited, accused, indited XI 315; (*pres.*)
  compose poetry or letters XV 372
enformeth, teaches III 241, XV 518; XVII
  127
engendreth, breeds XII 238; *p.p.* XIII 18
engendrour, procreator, beginner VI 232
engendrynge, begetting XI 335
engleymeth, cloys XV 57
Englyssed, translated into English IV 145
engreyned, fast-dyed II 15, XIV 20
enjoyned, joined II 66, IX 4; enjoin
  (upon) XIII 411, XX 283
ensamples, examples IV 136; parables
  VII 128
entente, aim, intention VIII 129
entisynge, provoking XIII 320; tempting
  XVIII 158
entremetten, interfere XIII 290; *p.t.* XI
  416
entremetynge, interfering XI 414
envenymes (*n*), poisons II 14
envenymeth (*v*), poisons XII 256
envye, enmity, hostility V 610

equité, justice XVII 307
er, before Prol. 155 et passim
erchebisshopes, archbishops XV 244;
  -dekenes, archdeacons II 174
erd, land, habitation VI 200
erende, message III 41
eretikes, heretics XVII 138
erie (*v*), plough VI 4; **erye,** XIV 29
eritage, inheritance X 339
ernynge, running XIX 381
ers, buttocks V 173; rear X 306
erst, first V 461
ertheliche, earthly, material XIX 94
eschaunges, monetary exchanges V 245
eschuwe, avoid VI 53
ese, comfort I 19, X 297
esily, at ease, comfortably II 38
ete, eat V 119; **eten** (*p.t.*), V 603
Evangelie, Gospel XI 189
evencristen, fellow-Christian II 95
evene, right, exactly XVII 186
eveneforthe, equally XIII 143; according
  to XIX 310
evesynges, eaves XVII 230
evidence, example XV 435; indication
  XVII 197
ewages, sea-coloured sapphires II 14
exciteth, urges XI 189
expounen, expound XIV 277
eyleth, afflicts, troubles VI 128
eyr, air Prol. 128

faderlese, fatherless IX 68
faille, lack IX 81; *p.t.* missed XI 26
faire (*av*), properly I 4; courteously I 58
Fairye, land of enchantment Prol. 6
faiteden, practised deceit Prol. 42 (*p.t.* of
  faiten)
faiterie, deceit XI 92; **faityng,** X 38
faithly, truly XIX 70
faitours, deceivers, knaves II 183
falle (in), come upon IV 156
falleth, pertains I 166
falshede, dishonesty, deceit Prol. 71
famed, slandered III 186 (= **defamed**)
fange, take V 558
fantasies, extravagant amusements Prol.
  36
fare (*n*), activity XVIII 18
faren, proceeded V 5 (*p.p.* of **faren**)
faren, behave XI 71
fareth, it happens VIII 38, XII 202
faste (*av*), firmly III 140; constantly XIV
  273
fauchon, sword XV 18
faucons, falcons VI 31; *sg.* XVII 64
faunt, child XVI 101; *pl.* VI 283
fauntekyns, little children XIII 213; *sg.*
  XIX 118
faunteltee, childishness XI 42, XV 150
fauten, lack IX 67
Favel, Flattery, Deceit II 6

373

fayn, pleased, content II 158; desirous II 78; *av.* gladly VIII 128

feble, weak V 175; w. with sickness V 406

feele, perceive XV 29; feel XIX 171

feere, spouse XVII 321; *pl.* companions II 6

feet, action, deeds I 186

feffement, deed of endowment II 73

feffeth, endows II 79

feires, chances of selling IV 56

feith, honesty III 157; feithful, honest VI 251

feitures, features XIII 296

fel (*n*), skin I 15

fel (*a*), fierce XVI 31; felle V 168

felawe, companion VII 12

felaweshipe, company I 114, III 119

fele, many III 342, IX 73

feledest, felt V 490

felefold, many times V 490

felly, fiercely XVIII 92

felonliche, felonously XVIII 352

femelles, females XI 339

fend, fiend, devil I 40

fendekynes, fiendlings, minor devils XVIII 374

fenden, defend XIX 65; *p.t.* XIX 46

fenestre, window XVIII 15; *pl.* XIV 199

fer, far VIII 80

ferded, assembled XI 339

ferden, fared IX 144; *sg.* dealt XI 418

fere (*n*), companion IV 27 (= feere)

fere (*v*), frighten VII 34

ferly, wonder, marvel Prol. 6, X 387, XIII 108, XVIII 110

ferme, to, to tend XVI 16

fermed, strengthened X 74

fermerye, infirmary XIII 108

fernyere (*av*), formerly V 434; *n.* past years XII 5

ferthe, fourth VII 72

ferye, festival XIII 414

fesaunts, pheasants XV 461

fest, fastened II 124 (*p.p.* of festen, fasten)

festen (*v.t.*), feed XV 483, 341; *p.t.* XV 588

festes, feasts, dinner-parties X 94; festynge XI 193

festne (*v*), secure XI 56

festred, festered XVII 94

festu, mote X 275

fet, fetched XI 324 (*p.p.* of fetten)

fetisli(che), gracefully, elegantly II 11

fette, fetched II 65 (*p.t.* of fetten)

fey, doomed to die XIII 2

feynen, pretend to be X 38

feyntise, faintness V 5

fibicches, tricks X 211

fikel, treacherous, deceiving II 25

fil, fell XIV 79 (*p.t.* of fallen)

fir, fire III 98

firses, (pieces of) furze V 345

fithele, fiddle IX 103; *v.* XIII 231

fithelere, fiddler X 94

flappes, blows, strokes XIII 66

flapten, threshed VI 184

flatte, dashed V 444

flawme (*v*), smell XII 255

flawmynge, flaming XVII 207

fleigh, flew, rushed XVII 59 (*p.t.* of fleen)

flete, swim XX 45; fleteth, floats XII 168

flex, flax VI 13

flicche, side of bacon, flitch IX 171

flittynge, changeable XI 63

flobre, sully XIV 15

florissheth (*v.t.*), prospers XIV 294

flowen, flew II 234 (*p.t. pl.* of fleen)

flux, discharge V 177

fobberes, tricksters II 183

fold, times XI 256

fole, foal XI 343; *pl.,* II 163

foliliche, foolishly XV 77

follede, baptized XV 446 (*p.t.* of fullen)

folwen, pursue, follow I 40

folwere, follower V 542

fond, provided for XV 285 (*p.t.* of fynden)

fond (*v*), try, test VI 219

fondlynges, bastards IX 194

fondynge, temptation XI 399

fonge, receive XIV 138, XVI 96

fo(o)ld, earth VII 53, XII 255

fool sage, wise fool XIII 443; *pl.* XIII 422

foon, foes V 95

for, to prevent I 24; in spite of V 382

forbar, spared III 274 (*p.t.* of forbere)

forbere, spare XI 209

forbete, beat down XVIII 35; *p.p.* enfeebled XX 198

forbisne, parable VIII 29; example XV 525

forbiteth, eats away XVI 35

forbode, that forbid (*lit.* forbidden) III 152

forbrenne, burn up III 98

forceres, boxes X 211

fordide, destroyed XVI 166 (*p.t.* of fordoon)

fordo(on), destroy V 20; *p.p.* XIII 259

foresleves, fore-part of sleeves V 80

foreward, agreement IV 14

forfaren, come to grief XV 135

forfeteth, fails XX 25

forfreteth, nips off XVI 29

forglutten, greedily consume X 83

forgoeres, purveyors II 61

forgrynt, destroys (= forgrindeth) X 79

formaliche, according to rule XV 372

formest, first of all X 215; foremost XIX 120

formour, creator IX 27

forpynede, wretched, damned VI 155

forreyours, harbingers XX 81

forsake, abandon V 425, XIV 264; turn down XV 84

forshapte, unmade, uncreated XVII 291

forsleuthed, spoilt through neglect V 439

forstalleth, buys up in advance IV 56

374

forster, forester XVII 114
forsworen, perjured XIX 372
forth (n), way, course forward III 157
forth (av), on X 435; also, further XIII
  209
forthi, therefore Prol. 111
forthynketh, it me, I regret IX 130
forto, till V 567
forwalked, tired with walking XIII 204
forwandred, worn out with wandering
  Prol. 7
forwanye, weaken V 35
forwhy, for which reason XIII 280
forwit, foresight V 164
foryaf, granted XVIII 76
foryat, forgot XI 60
foryelde, reward VI 276; repay XIII 188
foryete, forgotten I 398; foryyte XX 155
foryifnesse, remission XX 287
fostren, produce XVII 209
foughten, fought Prol. 42
foule (av), foully III 186; badly X 470;
  viciously XI 214; rudely XX 5
founde, try XI 192 (= fonde)
founde, thought up X 71 (p.p. of fynden)
foundement, foundation XIV 199, XIX
  327
fourmen, teach XV 376
fraternitee, religious brotherhood XI 56
frayned, asked I 58, V 525, VIII 3
fraytour, refectory X 320
fre(e), noble II 77; generous, X 74;
  freeborn XIX 33
freet, ate XVIII 195 (p.t. of freten)
freke, man IV 13, X 247, XI 26, XIII 2,
  XVI 176
frele, weak III 122; changeable VIII 43
freletee, frailty III 55, XVII 333
fremmed, stranger XV 141
frendes, relatives IX 115
frendloker, in a friendlier manner X 225
frenesse, generosity, grace XVI 88
frenetike, crazed X 6
freres, friars Prol. 58
frete, eat II 96; p.p. XIII 329
fretted, adorned II 11
frith, wood XVII 114, XII 221
fro, from III 110, VI 88, VIII 97
frokke, gown V 80
frounces, creases XIII 317
frythed, hedged V 581
ful (av), very Prol. 20, VI 44, XI 20
fullynge, baptism XII 283
fullyng stokkes, cleansing-frames XV 451
furlang, ten-acre field V 418
furwes, furrows VI 104
fust, fist V 84, XVII 140, 151
fuyr, fire XIII 162
fyle, concubine V 158
fyn, fin XX 45
fyn (a), subtle X 247; good XVII 94
fynde, find (in books) IX 68; read X 298
fynden, provide IX 68, XV 571

fyndyng, provision, endowment XX 384
fynt, finds IV 131; provides VII 129 (=
  fyndeth)

gabbe, lie III 180; gabbynge XIX 457
gadelynges, rascally fellows IV 51; sg.
  XX 157
gaf, gave XIV 9 (p.t. of gyve)
gailers, gaolers III 138
galoches, shoes XVIII 14
galpen, yawn XIII 88
game(n), play Prol. 153, V 407; delight,
  entertainment IX 102
gan, did I 173(as auxiliary forming simple
  past tense)
gange, go II 168, XIV 160, XVI 159
garisoun, cure VI 138
garnement, garment XIII 399
garte, made I 122, V 61, VI 301, XV 442
gat, begot I 33 (p.t. of geten)
gate, way I 205, III 156
gateward, gate-keeper, porter V 595
gaynesse, extravagance X 83
geaunt, giant VI 232
gedelyng, scoundrel IX 104
gendre, species XVI 222
generacion, (act of) generation XVI 222
gentile, noble, good I 185
gentilliche, courteously III 13; elegantly
  XIII 232
gentries, nobility XIV 180, XVIII 22
Geomesie, geomancy X 208
gerles, children I 33, X 79, X 177, XVIII 7
gerner, granary VII 130
gerte, made XX 57 (= garte)
gerthes, girths IV 21
gesene, scarce XIII 270
gest, guest XV 285
gestes, stories, narrative(s) X 23, XIII 230
geten, begot XX 157 (p.t. of geten); p.p.
  IX 193
Gile, guile, deceit II 145; Gyle, II 188
gileth, cheats VII 68
gilour, deceiver II 121
gilt, guilt, sin IV 101; giltlees Prol. 34
girdeth (imper. pl.), strike II 202
girte, vomited V 373
glade (v), cheer VI 119; gladie XVIII 255
glazene (a), of glass XX 172; v. glaze III
  61
gleede, glowing coal II 12, V 284; pl. XVII
  220
glee, singing Prol. 34
gleman, minstrel IX 102, X 156, V 347
glorie, presumption X 115, XX 157
glose (n), gloss, commentary V 275
glosed, expounded Prol. 60; glossed X
  172
glosynges, deceptions XX 125
glubberes (n. as a.), gulpers IX 61
gnawen, revile X 57
go me to, let one go to X 192
goky, fool XI 306

375

goliardeis, buffoon Prol. 139
gomes, men II 74; sg. V 368
gommes, (kinds of) gum II 227
good(e), wealth, goods III 169, V 296
goode, to, to good conduct III 223, V 634
goodliche, generously I 182; well XI 279
gorge, throat X 57
goost, spirit I 36, IX 46, X 388
goostliche, spiritual(ly) XX 40
gossib, friend V 303
gothelen (v), rumble V 341, XIII 88
grace, favour III 108; mercy IV 141;
  success V 96; luck V 150
gracious, pleasing VI 227
gradde, cried aloud XX 387 (p.t. of
  greden)
graffen (v), graft V 136
graithe, direct I 205
graithly, quickly XI 41; duly XVIII 291
gramariens, scholars XIII 72
gras, herb XII 59
graunge, farm-house XVII 73
grave, stamped IV 130; v. engrave III 49
gravynge, engraving III 64
grece, fat XIII 62
greden, cry out II 74; call for III 71
gree, prize XVIII 98
greete, weep V 380
greetnesse, size XVI 59
grene, unmatured VI 281
greten, greet V 336
greven, injure Prol. 153; offend Prol.
  203; take offence Prol. 139; feel
  aggrieved VI 315
greyn, grain VI 119; seeds XIX 276
greyne, colour XVI 59
griped, clutched III 182
groom, servant XVII 87
grope, feel, handle XIII 346, IX 170
grotes, groats III 138, XV 543
growed, grew XVI 56
grucche, complain Prol. 153, VI 216
grym, terrible V 354. -ly, fiercely X 259
grys, pork Prol. 227; pigs VI 281
grys, fur of grey squirrel XV 221
gyde, guide VI 1
gyed, guided II 188
gyn, device XVIII 252
gynful, treacherous X 208
gynnyng, beginning II 30, IX 28
gyour, guide XIX 428
gyterne, gittern XIII 233
gyved, fettered XX 192; gyves (n), XIV
  52

habbeth, have IV 147, XV 137
haddestow, had you XI 411, XX 188
hailse, greet V 100; p.t. did obeisance to
  VII 161
hakeneyman, horse-hirer V 311
hakke, grub about XIX 404
half, hand, side II 5, III 181
haliday, holy day V 579

halidome, the holy relics V 370
halie (v), draw VIII 97
halp, helped XIX 131 (p.t. of helpen)
hals, neck Prol. 170, VI 61
halsede, adjured I 73
halt, holds XVII 107 (= holdeth)
halwe, sanctify XV 527
handwhile, short time XIX 274
handy dandy, by secret bribery IV 75 (see
  note)
hanged on, taken III 181
hanselle, gift, treat V 319
hap, luck XII 106; pl. V 96
happe, happen III 286, VI 46, XVI 87
happily, perhaps V 615
hardie (v), embolden XV 435
hardier, more boldly XIV 261; hardiliche,
  boldly VI 29; hardy, bold IV 60
harewen (v), harrow XIX 270
harlottes, ribald fellows IV 118, VI 52;
  villains XVII 276
harlotrie, obscene talk, story IV 115, V
  407
harmede, did harm, injury III 141
harmes, trouble, injury IV 31
harneis, armour XV 221
harrow!, alas! XX 88
hastilokest, most promptly XIX 472
hastow, have you (= hast thow) III 106
hater, cloak XIV 1; haterynge, clothing
  XV 78
hatie(n), hate VI 50, X 95
hatte, is called V 573
haubergeon, mail-coat XVIII 23
haunten, indulge in Prol. 77, III 53
havylons, tricks X 131
hawes, hawthorn berries X 10
hayward, overseer XIX 334
hede, heed VI 15, XI 111, XV 91
heed, head I 164; pl. heddes XX 187
he(e)le, recovery XIII 341; health XIV
  171, XVII 38; protection XIX 474
heeled, healed VI 192
heep, crowd Prol. 53; number V 328
heeris, hair's X 331
heet, ordered XX 273 (p.t. of hoten)
heighe (a), great, ultimate V 274
heighe (av), loudly IV 162; aloud II 74;
  properly, duly V 579
heighnesse, exaltedness XX 153
heigh prime, the end of prime VI 112 (see
  note)
helden, thought Prol. 180 (p.t. of holden)
hele (n), crust VII 195
hel(i)en, cover XII 231; conceal V 166,
  XX 340
hem, them Prol. 45; themselves Prol. 20
hemselven, themselves III 216
hende, courteous V 257; av. –liche
  graciously III 29; hendenesse, courtesy
  XIX 31

376

hennes (*av*), (from) hence III 109; **–goyng**, departure hence (= death) XIV 164
hente, seized V 5 (*p.t.* of **henten**)
heo, she II 28, III 29
heragein, against this IX 145, XIV 188
herber, arbour XVI 15
herberwe (*n*), shelter X 403; *v.* store, XIX 320; *p.p.* lodged XVII 75
here, hear Prol. 4
here-beyng, existence here XIV 140
hernes, corners, nooks II 234
heron, on this X 281
hestes, commandments II 83; *sg.* command III 113
hethynesse, (a) pagan country XV 441
heved, head XIV 232
heveneriche, the kingdom of heaven Prol. 27, XIV 260
hevy, gloomy XI 27, XX 2
hevynesse, grief XVIII 247
hewe, workman V 552; *pl.* **hewen**, IV 55
hewe (*v*), strike XVII 247
heyre, hair-shirt V 65
hiede, hurried XX 325; **hyed**, V 378
highte, commanded Prol. 102 (*p.t.* of **hoten**)
hii, they Prol. 66, XX 301
hiled, covered V 590; **hileden**, XI 351
hippynge, hopping XVII 61
hir(e), their Prol. 28 et passim; of them XI 315; **her**, I 10
hire (*prn*), her II 1; *refl.* herself V 62
hire (*n*), reward, payment III 72
hitte, threw down V 322
hoked, crooked Prol. 53
hokes, hooks V 594
holde, hold on to V 45; observe VII 20
holden (*p.p.*), practised V 223; considered III 212; obliged V 274
hole, entire XVIII 378; **holly**, wholly III 113
holpen, helped (*p.t.* of **helpen**) VI 116; *p.p.* VII 70
holwe, hollow(ly) V 187
homliche, at home X 95
honeste, honourable XIX 94
hool, untorn XIV 1
hoolly, entirely XVII 27
hoor, white-haired, hoary VI 83, XVI 173; **hore**, VII 98
hoper, seed-basket VI 61
hoppe, dance III 200
hors, horses XI 343
hostiler, inn-keeper XVII 75; ostler V 332
hostrie, hostelry, inn XVII 75
hote, command II 200
hoten, called II 21 (*p.p.* of **hote**, **hatte**)
houped, shouted VI 172
houres, the 'Hours' of the breviary I 183
housbondrie, thrift I 57
housel, Holy Communion XIX 395
housled, be, receive Communion XIX 3

housynge, house-building XV 78
hoved, waited about Prol. 211, XVIII 80
howve, coif III 295; *pl.* Prol. 211; hood XX 172
hucche, clothes-trunk IV 116
hukkerye, retail trade V 223
hulles, hills IX 139
hungrily, hungrily V 187; in miserly fashion XX 123
hunsen, abuse X 61
huyre (*n*), pay V 556
hyed, hurried V 375; **hyedest** III 194
hyere, higher II 28
hyne, servant Prol. 39; thing of low worth IV 118

i–, *past participle marker*
ido, done V 545
idolve, dug V 545
idyked, ditched V 545
if, in case V 241
ik, I V 224
ilke, same I 83
impe, graft IX 149; *n.pl.* grafts V 136
impugnen, find fault with Prol. 109
infinites, infinite things XIII 127
ingong, entrance V 629
inmiddes, in the midst of V 284
inobedient, resistant XIII 281
inparfit, imperfect, faulty XV 50
inparfitly, imperfectly, incompletely X 462
intil, into XIII 210
Inwit, conscience, moral sense IX 18; intelligence, understanding IX 67
irens, irons, fetters VIII 103
iseised, put in possession of XVIII 283

jaced, jogged XVII 53
jangle, argue Prol. 130; quarrel II 95, VIII 121; utter IV 155
jang(e)leres, idle chatterers Prol. 35, X 31
jangling, protestation IV 180; crying out IX 82
jape (*v*), jest, mock II 95; *n.* XX 145; japed, deceived I 67
japeres, jesters, buffoons Prol. 35
jogged, rode up XX 134
jouke, rest XVI 92
journee, day's stint XIV 135
joutes, stews V 156
juele, jewel XI 184
jugged, concluded I 185; interpreted VII 162
jurdan, chamber-pot XIII 83
juste, bottle-shaped XIII 83
juste (*v*), joust XVI 95, XVIII 19
juttes, nobodies X 458
juventee, youth XIX 108
juwise, judgment, sentence XVIII 383

kaiser, emperor XIX 138; **kaysers** IX 111

377

kan, know, have acquaintance with, know how to (passim)
kaughte, snatched Prol. 107
kaurymaury, coarse garment V 78
kaylewey bastard, Cailloux pear XVI 69
kemben, comb X 18
kene, sharp IX 182; bold XX 129
kenne, teach I 81; guide, direct XVII 115
kennyng, instruction X 194
kepe, care III 280; protect VI 27; govern VIII 101; notice XI 336
kepe (*n*), notice, heed XI 336; XIII 271
kepere, guardian XII 126; XIX 446
kepynge, living, behaviour XIX 356
kerneled, crenellated V 588
kerse, cress X 17
kerve (*v*), cut VI 104
kerveres, carvers X 180; **kervynge** XVII 172
kevereth, protects XII 179; recover XX 336
kex, dried hemlock-stem XVII 222
kidde, showed V 434 (*p.t.* of **kithen**)
kirk, church III 60, V 1, VI 91; **kirkyerd,** churchyard XIII 9; **kirkeward,** towards church V 298
kirtel, under-jacket V 79, XI 283
kith, kindred XIII 378; country XIX 79
kitten (*v*), cut (*p.t. pl.* of **kutten**) VI 188
knappes, buttons VI 270
knave, servant IV 17; fellow Prol. 44
knele, kneel X 307; **knelynge** Prol. 73
knewliched, acknowledged XII 193; **knoweliched** V 474; **knowlichynge** XIV 186
knowes, knees V 353
knytten, fasten Prol. 169
konne, learn XV 45; know XV 53; know how to VI 68
konnynge (*a*), clever, learned III 34; *n.* knowledge XI 165; wise act XIX 461
kouthe, knew Prol. 182; knew how to V 24
kultour, coulter III 308
kuttepurs, cutpurse V 630
kyen, cows, kine VI 140
kynde (*n*), kind Prol. 186; nature V 588; stock IX 126; people X 422; natural strength XI 260
kynde (*a*), natural I 138; right, own VIII 72
kyndely, kyndeliche, properly, in the right way I 81; naturally V 538; essentially XIV 87
kyngene, of kings XIX 79
kyngryche, kingdom Prol. 125
kynnes, of kind XIV 184 et passim
kynrede, kindred IX 174

lacche, capture II 204; catch V 349; obtain VI 228; seize XVI 50
lachesse, negligence, sloth VIII 37

ladde, led Prol. 112; carried V 247 (*p.t.* of **leden**); **lad,** (*p.p.*) led, guarded IX 16
laddes, ordinary people XIX 32
lafte (*v.i.*), remained III 197; *v.t.*, left XX 251
laike (*v*), play Prol. 172
lakke (*v*), criticise, disparage II 48; blame VI 225
lakkes (*n*), defects X 260
laklees, faultless XI 389
lambren, lambs XV 206
lang, long II 182
langour, pain XIV 117, XVIII 226
lape, lap up V 357; drink XX 18
lappe, portion II 35
large (*a*), wide, full X 164; liberal XIII 298; *n.* bounty XIX 43
largely, generously XIX 60; fully XX 87
largenesse, generosity V 623
largere (*av*), more amply XI 160
largesse, bounty XIII 448
lasse (*a*), lesser II 46; smaller XII 262; *av.* less X 263
lat, leads IX 58 (= **ledeth**)
lat (*imper.*), let V 337; **late** (*subj.*), let Prol. 155
latter, later I 199
laude (*v*), praise XI 106
laughte, seized Prol. 150 (*p.t.* of **lacchen**); took III 25; assumed XVII 150
laumpe, lamp XIII 151
launde, clearing, plain VIII 66; X 163
laved, washed XIV 5
lavendrye, laundry XV 187
layes, songs, lays VIII 67
layk (*n*), contest, sport XIV 243
lazar, leper XVI 255
leautee, justice Prol. 122; loyalty II 21; right III 294; equity XI 84
leche, physician I 204, II 224
lechen (*v*), cure XIII 253; XVI 113
lechecraft, medicine VI 254, XVI 104
lede, person XV 392; *pl.* servants X 86
lede (*v*), draw II 182; lead, rule IV 148; manage X 20
ledene (*n*), voice, cry XII 244, 253, 262
ledere, leader I 161; guide XII 96
leed, lead V 591, XIII 82, 246
leef, leaf III 341, XV 102; part VII 176
leef (*a*), pleasing IX 58; fond XX 195; *av.* dearly III 18; *n.* beloved II 33
leel, faithful XI 161; **leelly** (*av*), I 78
le(e)re, face I 3
lees, lost (*p.t.* of **lesen**) VII 159
leet, caused (*p.t.* of **leten**) XX 143
leet, considered XX 146
leeve, dear IV 39
legende, book X 373
legge (*v*), lay V 240; wager II 34; affirm XI 96; **l. on,** lay on XV 191
legistres, legal experts VII 14
leide, pressed XX 114
leith, lays V 349

378

leighe, said falsely to XVIII 403
lele, honest X 430 (*pl.* of leel)
lelly, faithfully VII 124
leme, gleam, light XVIII 124
lemman, lover V 411; XIV 300
lene, give, grant Prol. 126, I 181; lend V 240
lenede, leaned Prol. 9; idled XVIII 5
lenge (*v*), remain I 209, XIX 421; *p.t.* dwelt VIII 7
lenger, longer III 340
lengthed, lengthened XVIII 302
lent (*v*), grants IX 106, X 62 (= lendeth)
Lenten, season of Lent Prol. 91, XIII 349, XVIII 5
leode, man I 141; persons XVI 181
lepe, run V 569; digress XI 317
lere, learn I 146; teach III 69
lered, educated, learned IV 12, X 232
lerned, learnt V 199; taught V 295
lese, lose II 35, III 159
lese, glean VI 66
lesynge, loss V 111
lesynge, lie IV 19; *pl.* II 125
let, considers X 187 (= leteth)
leten, consider XV 576; *p.t.* IV 160; give up V 458; leave IV 191
leten, caused II 159
lethi, empty, vain X 186
lette, impede, prevent III 32; *p.t.* III 198; letted, XIX 385; delay IX 131
lettere, hinderer I 69
lettre, written assurance X 91; *pl.* letters of warrant IV 132
lettred, educated I 136, VII 132
lettrure, learning Prol. 110; scripture X 27; literacy, education XII 104; text X 375
lettyng, delay VI 7, X 219
leve (*n*), permission Prol. 85, III 15
leve (*a*), dear V 556
leve (*v*), believe I 38; leveden (*p.t. pl.*), I 118
leve (*v*), leave I 103; abandon VII 150
leved, leafy XV 97
level, (use of the) level X 181
leven, live V 44 (= lyven)
levere (*a*), dearer V 38; preferable X 11
levere (*av*), more dearly I 143, XV 195
leves, leaf's III 340
levest (*av*), most dearly V 563, X 353
leveste (*a*), dearest I 151
levynge, leavings V 357
lewed, uneducated, ignorant Prol. 72; useless, worthless I 189
lewednesse, ignorance III 32
Lewte, Equity XI 84
leyd, laid (in pledge) III 202; leyen, lain III 38
leye (*v*), strike, lay on XIII 146
leye (*n*), flame XVII 209
leyes, fallow lands VII 5
libbe (*v*), live III 227

lich, like IX 63
liche, body X 2
liere, liar I 38; lyeres, IX 119
lif, living creature III 294
liflode, living Prol. 30; livelihood I 37; source of sustenance V 87; means of life V 458
lifte, sky XV 357
lige, liege, bound IV 184
liggen, reside Prol. 91; liggeth, lies III 176; liggynge, lying II 52
light, lightly, at low value IV 161
lighte, descended XI 246; alighted XIX 203
lighter, easier XIV 248, XVII 41
lightliche, easily Prol. 150
lightloker, more nimbly V 569
likame, body Prol. 30, I 37
likerous, luxurious Prol. 30; dainty VI 266; lascivious X 163
liketh, pleases I 43, II 232
likne, compare (disparagingly) X 42, 274
likynge (*n*), pleasure XI 21; *a.* pleasing XI 272
lippe, portion V 246, XV 500
liser, selvage, edge of cloth V 206
lisse, delight IX 29; joy XVIII 226
list, it pleases Prol. 172, III 158, XX 18
liste, strip of cloth V 517
lith, lies (= lyeth), I 126
lithen, listen to XIII 423
lither, evil X 166; *pl.* X 435
litlum and litlum, by little and little XV 608
lixt, liest V 161
lobies, lubbers, ungainly fellows Prol. 55
loke, behold I 112; protect I 209; govern VII 166; watch over XV 9
lokynge, considering XI 317
lolled, hung V 189, XII 191; lolleth, rests XII 213; lollynge, lying XVI 269
lomb, lamb V 553, VIII 86
lomere, more often XX 238
lond, land (passim); londleperis, vagabond XV 213
lone, solitary XVI 20
longe, tall Prol. 55, XIV 243
longen, belong II 46
loof, loaf XIII 48
loore, teaching V 38, IX 71
lo(o)resman, teacher XII 183; *pl.* IX 88, XV 389
loos, reputation XI 295, XIII 448; praise XIII 298
looth, reluctant, unwilling III 161, XI 222, XV 471; hateful IX 58
lopen, leapt I 117; ran Prol. 223; lope, if he ran (*pt. subj.* of lepen)
lordlich, haughty XIII 301
lordshipe, domain II 46, III 20; *pl.* properties XV 556
lorel, wastrel VII 137, XV 5, XVIII 3; *pl.* XVII 46

379

loren, lost XII 120; lore XVIII 79 (*p.p.* of **lesen**)
losedest, praised XI 419
losels, wretches, wastrels Prol. 77, VI 122
losely, loosely XII 213
losengeries, deceitfulness VI 143; flattery X 49
loseth (*v*), praises XV 253
lotebies, concubines III 151
lotheth, is hateful Prol. 155
lother, the more unwilling XV 390
lothliche, loathsome I 117
lothlieste, most fearsome XVIII 406
lotieth, lurks XVIII 104
lough, laughed XIX 462, XX 143
loure, scowl, frown V 131, XII 278; *p.t.* II 224; **lourynge,** V 82, 337
lous, louse V 194
loutede, bowed III 36, 116, X 142
lovedaies, days of settlement out of court III 158, V 421, X 20, 304
lovelich, amiable, pleasing V 553, VIII 86; *av.* XIII 26
lovelokest, handsomest I 112, XIII 294
loves, loaves VI 283
lowe, humble V 553; gentle V 591; *av.* XII 265; **lowenesse,** III 291
lowen, lied V 94
luft, worthless wretch IV 62
lurdaynes, villains XVIII 102; *sg.* sluggard XX 189
lusard, serpent XVIII 338
lussheburwes, light coins XV 348 (*see note*)
lust, pleasure XIX 355
lutede, sang to the lute XVIII 425
luther, bad, vicious V 117, X 432, XV 348
lyard, grey horse XVII 66
lybbynge, living Prol. 223, VII 60, XII 265
lyme, limb V 98; *pl.* features XIX 8
lymeyerd, lime-rod, snare IX 181
lymitours, licensed mendicants V 137, XX 347
lynage, descendents IX 48; ancestry XI 295
lynde, lime-tree I 156, VIII 66
lyne, measuring-line X 181
lyth, limb (= body) XVI 181
lythe(n), listen to VIII 67, XIII 423
lyveris, people living XII 131
lyves (*av*), alive XIX 159

macche, wick XVII 216
maceres, mace-bearers III 76
magesté, majesty IX 52, XV 479, XVI 184
maires, mayors III 76; XIII 270, XIV 288
maistrie, advantage, upper hand V 102; miracle XVI 115; *pl.* acts of power IV 26; arts XIX 257
make (*n*), spouse III 119; mate XI 327
make (*v*), compose poetry XII 22; **makynges,** verse-making XII 16

maleese, pain XIII 76; **male ese,** XVII 194
males (*n*), bags V 230
mamelen, go on (about) V 21; *p.t.* XI 416
manacen, threaten XVI 49; *p.t.* VI 170
manere, kind of XIX 326
manere (*n*), estate, manor X 305; **manoirs** V 242; **manoir,** manor-house V 586
manered, disposed, mannered XV 414
manged, eaten VI 258
mangerie, feast XI 112; feeding XV 590
manhod, humanity, human nature XII 295
mankynde, human nature XVII 150, XIX 72
manlich, charitable V 256; **manliche** (*av*), generously X 89; forthrightly X 282, XVI 127
mansed, wicked II 40; vicious, ? excommunicated X 276, XX 221
mansion, dwelling-place XIV 216
march(e), province XV 444, XX 221
marchal, marshalling officer III 201
marchaunden, do business XIII 393; **marchaundise,** goods, wealth V 285; **marchaunts,** merchants VII 18
mareys, marsh(es) XI 352
marke, observe XII 131
marked, allotted XII 186
massepens, mass-pence III 224
maugree (*n*), disfavour VI 240; ill-luck IX 155; *av.* in spite of V 40
maundement, commandment XVII 2
mawe, stomach V 123, VI 174
mayn, strength XVIII 319
mayné, household, retainers V 97
maynpernour, surety IV 112
maynprise (*n*), bail IV 88; *v.* II 197
mayntene, support, maintain III 185
maze, dismay Prol. 192; vain wanderings I 6
me, one, people X 192; **men,** XI 13, 204
mede, reward, hire, payment II 20 et passim; **medeth** (*v*), reward III 216
medled, mixed, had intercourse with XI 343; **medlest,** concern XII 16
me(e)ne (*n*), intermediary I 160, IX 34, XV 505
me(e)ne (*a*), lesser I 108; humble X 64
mees, mice Prol. 147
mees, (dish of) food XIII 53, XV 316
meete (*v*), measure Prol. 215
megre, thin V 127
meke, humble I 173; **meke** (*v*) humble V 69
mele, meal, ground grain XIII 260
melk, milk V 439
melleth, speaks III 105
mene (*v*), mean III 97; refer to V 276
mened, complained III 170, VI 2
menever, furred XX 138
menged, adulterated XIII 361
mengen, commemorate VI 95

380

menske (v), honour III 184
menynge, in, (as if) seeking XV 473
menyson, flux XVI 111
mercer, silk-dealer V 251
merciable, merciful V 504, XVII 233.
merciede, thanked III 20
mercy, thank you I 43, X 145
mercyment, fine I 162
mercymonye, reward XIV 126
meritorie, meritorious XI 79
merk(e) (a), dark I 1; obscure XI 159;
merknesse, darkness XVIII 136
merk, imprint XV 349
merkede, observed XIII 25
meschief, ill-luck III 177; danger X 449;
disease XV 98
mesel(e)s, lepers III 133, VII 101
mesondieux, hospitals VII 26
mestier, occupation VII 7
mesurable, moderate III 256; fitting VI
198
mesure, moderation I 35; measure I 177
mesurelees, immoderate III 246
met (n), measure XIII 358
mete (n), food I 24
mete (v), measure, mete out I 177
metelees, without food VII 142
metels, dream VII 143
meten (v), dream Prol. 11; metyng,
dream XIII 4
meteyyveres, food-providers XV 147
mettes, dinner-companions XIII 35
meve, move VIII 33; urge VIII 121; stir
up XII 124; mevestow, do you arouse
X 261
meynee, troop I 108, III 24, X 93;
household XVI 236
mildely, humbly III 20
mirre, myrrh XIX 92
misese, illness XIII 159; myseisé, sick VII
26
mitigacion, compassion V 470
mnam, pound VI 241
mo, more Prol. 147, IV 10
modiliche, angrily IV 173
mody, the, the proud one IX 205
m(o)ebles, moveable goods III 269, IX 84
moeve(n), adduce XV 70; upset XIX 288
moiste (v), moisten XVIII 369
molde, earth Prol. 67, I 44
molde, pattern XI 349
moled, spotted XIII 274; moles, spots
XIII 314
mone, prayer XV 26, 504
mone, moon VI 327
moné, money VI 224; moneilees VII 142
moniales, nuns X 316, XX 264
mood, feelings, anger X 261
moore (a), greater V 282
mooste, greatest Prol. 67
moot, moat V 586, XIX 368
moot-halle, council-chamber, court IV 135
moot (v), must XX 238 (= mote)

more, root XV 98, XIX 340
mornede, sulked XIII 59, III 170
morthereth, murders XVII 281
mortrews, stews XIII 41
morwenynge, morning Prol. 6
moste, must V 387; must go V 412;
might IV 112 (p.t. of moten)
mote, must I 138; moten, might V 512
mote, litigate I 176; motyng, action at law,
legal services VII 58
moton, a gold coin III 24
motyves, motions, ideas X 115
moustre, show XIII 361
mow(en), can Prol. 170 et passim
muche, tall VIII 71
muchel (a), much Prol. 202; great V 470
muchel (n), size XVI 182
muk, dung VI 142
muliere (a), legitimate II 119; n.
legitimate offspring XVI 219
murie, pleasant II 154; merry (euphem.)
XIII 351
murthe, entertainment Prol. 33, III 11;
joy XVIII 127
murthe(n) (v), gratify XI 398; cheer
XVII 243
musons, measures X 174
must (n), new wine XVIII 371
myd, with Prol. 147, I 116, IV 77
myddel, waist III 10
myghtful, powerful I 173
mynistren, have the use of XII 52
mynne, reflect XII 4; remember XV 460
mynours, miners Prol. 222
mynstralcie, music(al entertainment) III
11
mynut while, a minute's time XVII 231
myrthes, delights XI 20
mysbede, injure VI 45
mysdo, maltreat XVIII 97; mysdide
(p.t.), IV 99
mysfeet, misdeed XI 374
mysferde, went wrong III 344
myshappe (v), come to grief III 329
mysproud, arrogant XIII 435
mysruleth, abuses IX 60
mysse, be without Prol. 192, XII 99
mysseide, rebuked XVI 127; p.p. spoken
against V 68
mysshapen, deformed VII 94
mysstandeth, is wrong XI 380
mystloker, mistier X 183
myswonne, wrongfully obtained XIII 42
mytes, mites, pennies XIII 196; sg. mite
XIV 23

na, no I 183, II 109
nale, atte, at the ale(-house) VI 115
namely, especially II 146; in particular V
258
nappe, fall asleep V 387
n'aroos, did not arise XIX 52
nat, not Prol. 38; naught, I 101

381

neddres, adder's V 86
nede, need, necessity XX 4
nede (av), necessarily III 226; nedes V 253
nedé, the needy XX 37
nedfulle, necessary I 21
nedlere, needle-seller V 311
neet, animal XIX 268
neghen, approach XVII 60; p.t. XX 4
neigh, (a), near XI 212; av. nearly III 145
neighe, closely related XII 93
nelle, do not wish Prol. 109; nel he, if he does not wish XIX 467; neltow, if you do not wish VI 156 (= ne + wil)
nempne,(v), name I 21; nempnynge, IX 79
ner, nearly VI 178; nearer X 60
nere, should not be V 331; were not X 186
nerhande, almost XIII 1
nevelynge, running V 134
next(e), nearest XIII 372, XVII 289
noble, gold coin worth £⅓ III 45
noght, not Prol. 29 et passim
nolde, would not V 558, XI 64
nome, took XX 9 (p.t. of nyme)
nones, midday V 372
nonne, nun V 150, VII 29
noon, none VIII 114
norisseth, fosters XVI 33
no(u)mbre, number XX 255, 259; v. p.t. 256
nounpere, umpire V 331
nounpower, powerlessness XVII 313
nouthe, now III 290, VI 205
noy (n), trouble X 60
noyen, harm, vex II 127; p.t. II 20
nyce, foolish XVI 33
nyghtcomeris, comers by night XIX 144
nyght-olde, a night old, stale VI 308
nyppe, cold region, dark XVIII 163
nyste, did not know XIII 25 (= ne wiste)

o(o), one II 30; one and the same XVI 58; first XIX 86
ocupien, be active XVI 196
of, through Prol. 118; from III 88; for VI 127; by XVI 152
ofgon, obtain IX 107
ofraughte, reached to XVIII 9
ofsente, sent for III 102
ofter, oftener XI 50, XVIII 381
oke (v), ached XVII 196
olofte (av), above Prol. 157; up V 353
on cros wise, by crucifixion XIX 142
ondynge, smelling XIV 55
one, alone XI 297; self XVI 183
ones, once Prol. 146; at one time III 145
oonliche, only IX 141
oost, host III 266, XIX 338
or, before X 415 (= ar, er)
ordeigne, prepare XIX 320; p.t. established Prol. 119, VIII 100
ordre, order I 104; rank VI 166

organye, organ XVIII 8
orientals, oriental sapphires II 14
othergates, otherwise IX 193
othes, oaths II 93, V 307
oughte, owned III 68 (p.t. of owen)
outher, or III 306, V 53
outher (a. as n.), others IV 136
outherwhile, at (other, some) times Prol. 164, V 404, VIII 26
oute (av), in existence XII 144, 267
outwit (n), (physical) sense(s) XIII 288
over al, especially XIII 290
overcarke, over-burden III 316
overgilte, gilt over XV 124
overhoveth, hovers over III 208, XVIII 170
overhuppen, skip over XIII 68, XV 384
overlepe, spring on Prol. 200; p.t. 150
overmaistreth, overcomes IV 176
over-plentee, superfluity XIV 73
overreche, encroach XIII 373
overse(n), oversee VI 116; look at, study X 325; overseyen, forgotten V 372
overskipped, omitted XI 305
overspradde, covered XIX 207
overtilte, upturned XX 54, 135

paas, pass XIV 300
paast, pastry XIII 250, XIV 29
pak-nedle, packing-needle V 208
paie (v), satisfy VI 309
paiere, paymaster V 551
palle, strike XVI 30
palmere, (Jerusalem) pilgrim V 535
paltok, jacket XVIII 25
panel, panel of jurors III 317
paniers, baskets XV 290
panne, brain-pan, skull IV 78
parcell, portion X 63; pl. XI 305
parcelmele, by retail III 81; by portions XV 246
parceyved, comprehended Prol. 100; perceived V 152
parchemyn, parchment IX 38; deed XIV 193
parentrelynarie, with interlineations XI 305
parfit, perfect XI 271; parfitnesse, perfect virtue X 200
parformen, establish XIII 174; parfourneth, acts XIII 78; fulfils XV 325
parisshens, parishioners V 420
parled, spoken XVIII 270
parroked, enclosed XV 286
parten (v), share Prol. 81, V 42
partie, part I 7; party XVII 305
Pask wyke, Easter week XI 232
passed, past, ago XX 344; passeth, exceeds VII 173
passhed, dashed XX 100
passion, suffering XIII 90; XV 270
pastours, herdsmen X 457, XII 149

patente, deed XIV 191; document of authority XVIII 185
Paternoster-while, time taken to say an 'Our Father' V 342
patrymoyne, patrimony XX 234
paviloun, cloak III 296
pawme, palm (of hand) XVII 142
paye, to, satisfactorily V 549
payn, bread VII 122 et passim
paynym, pagan, heathen V 516, XI 162
pece, piece XIV 49; pl. cups III 89
peel, accusation XVII 305
peeren, appear Prol. 173; are equal to XV 516
pees, peace I 152; pays, XVI 159
peire, pair IX 167, XII 19, XIII 196
peired (p.p.), damaged III 128
peis, weight V 237; peised, weighed V 213
pelet, stone ball V 77
pelour, accuser XVIII 40
pelure, fur II 9, III 296
penaunce, suffering X 34, XI 279
penauncelees, without punishment X 460
penaunt (n), penitent IV 133, XIII 92
pencif, pensive, thoughtful VII 145
penitauncer, confessor XX 320
pennes, feathers XII 247
pens, pence II 223; penyes, XIX 379
penyworthes, bargains V 327
pepir, pepper XV 203
peraunter, perhaps XI 11
percen, pierce, penetrate X 459
percile, parsley VI 286
permutacion, exchange III 258; permute (v), XIII 110
perree, jewellery X 12
persaunt, piercing I 157
persone, form, character XVIII 336; pl. parsons III 150
pertliche, manifestly V 15; forthrightly V 23
pese, pea VI 169; pesen (pl.), 195; pescoddes, pea-pods VI 292
petit, little VII 57, XIV 242
peyne, pain I 169; peynen, take pains VII 42
phisike (v), treat medically XX 324
picche, cut VI 103
p(i)ere, equal III 205, IX 14; pl. VII 16
pik, pike-staff V 475; pikstaf, VI 103
piken (v), hoe XVI 17; p.t. VI 111
pil, pile, prop XVI 30
pileth, robs XIX 445; pilour, robber III 195; pl. XIX 418, XX 263
pioné, peony (-seed) V 305
pisseris, pissers' XX 219 (see note) .
pistle, epistle XII 29
pitaunce, portion, allowance V 266, XIII 55
pité, pity X 421; pitousliche (a), pitiable XVIII 58; av. forgivingly IV 98
plastred, treated with a plaster XVII 97

platte, threw (herself) flat V 62
plaunte coles, greens VI 286
playte (v), folded V 208
plede, plead (at law) VII 42; pledours, barristers VII 42; pledynge III 296
pleide(n), amused themselves Prol. 20; played 151
plener (a), full XVI 103; av. fully XI 108
plentevouse, bountiful X 82
plesynge, pleasure III 252
pletede(n), pleaded at law Prol. 213, VII 39
pleye, be active with III 309
pleyn, full, complete VII 102
pleyne, plead XIV 225; utter(s) XVII 295; p.t. complained Prol. 83
pleynt, complaint XI 248
plot, patch XIII 275
plowpote, plough-pusher VI 103
po, peacock's XII 257
Pocalips, Apocalypse (see note)
point, reason V 15; quality XIV 279; pl. respects XVIII 44; in p., ready XIII 110
poke, bag XIII 216; pokeful, VII 192
poketh, thrusts V 611; p.t. urged V 634
pokkes, plague-sores XX 98
pol, head XI 58; pl. XIII 246, XX 86
polshe, polish X 475
pondfold, pound, pinfold XVI 264
poole, pole XVIII 52
pope holy, hypocritically holy XIII 283
poret, cabbage VI 298; pl. leeks VI 286
portatif, portable I 157
porte, demeanour XIII 277
porthors, breviary XV 120
portreye, draw III 62, XV 181, XVII 171
pose, put it, suppose XVII 296
possed, pushed, dashed Prol. 151
possession, property XIV 270
possessioners, beneficed clergy V 143
posternes, side-doors V 619
postles, wandering preachers VI 149
potage, soup VI 150; potagere, stew-maker V 155
potel, pottle, ½ gal. measure V 342
potente, staff VIII 98
pouke, devil XIII 161, XIV 188
pounded, expounded Prol. 213
poundemele, (by) pounds at a time II 223
pous, pulse XVII 68
poustee, power V 36; pl. violent onsets XII 11
praktisour, practitioner XVI 107
prayed, preyed upon XX 86
preide, requested II 71
preiere, request VII 107
preise (v), value V 324; praise V 611
prentices, students XIX 232
prentishode, apprenticeship V 252
prest, prompt VI 196, XIII 250, XIV 220
presumpcion, supposition X 55
preve, practise V 42; experience IX 77

preien, pray XI 58; *p.t.* asked for XI 245
preynte, winked XIII 85, XVIII 21
pried, peered XVI 168
priked, spurred II 190, XVII 352
prik(i)ere, rider IX 8, XVIII 25
prikye, riding XVIII 11
prime, heigh, 9 a.m. VI 112
pris (*n*), value II 13; *a.* chief XIX 268
prison, prisoner XVIII 58; *pl.* XV 183
procuratour, agent XIX 260
propre, fine VII 148; distinct X 237;
  excellent XIII 51; **propreliche,** really
  XIV 283
provendreth, provides prebends for III
  150
provisours, provisors II 171 (*see note*)
prowor, purveyor XIX 262
pryvee, private X 99; intimate III 146
pryveliche, secretly III 82; quietly XIII
  55
publice (*v*), make public XI 105
pulte, thrust VIII 98
punfolde, pen, pinfold V 624; *see* XVI 264
purchaced, obtained VII 38
pure (*a*), sheer X 461; very VII 104; *av.*
  very XI 194; **purely,** integrally XVII
  143; entirely XIII 259
purfil, furred trimming V 26; **purfiled** II
  9
purpos, line of argument VIII 123
purveie, provide XIV 29; *p.t.* V 165
put, pit X 367, XIV 173; *pl.* dungeons V
  406
pye, magpie XI 346; **pies,** magpie's XII
  227
pyk, pike-staff V 535
pyked, peaked XX 219
pykeharneys, plunderers of armour XX
  263
pykoise, pick-axe III 309
pyl, fort XIX 366
pylours, pillagers XX 263
pynched, encroached XIII 370
pyne, pain, punishment II 104
pyned, tortured V 209; **pynynge,**
  punishment III 78
pynne (*v*), fasten bolt XX 299
pyries, pear-trees V 16

quartron, quarter (pound) V 213
quaved, quaked XVIII 61
queed, evil one XIV 189
quelt, dead (*p.p.* of **quelle**) XVI 114
queste, inquest, jury XX 162
queynt, destroyed XVIII 347
queyntely, ingeniously XIX 349
queyntise, cunning XVIII 274, XIX 354
quod, said Prol. 160 et passim
quyk (*a*), living XVI 114
quyk, as, as quickly as possible XIV 189
quyke (*v*), give life to XVIII 347; **quykne**
  XV 23

quyte, requite XI 192; pay XIII 10;
  release XVI 262; *p.p.* paid in full VI
  98, XVIII 358

radde, advised IV 110, V 45 (*p.t.* of **reden**)
radde, read III 338 (*p.t.* of **reden,** read)
radegundes, running sores XX 83
rageman, bull with seals Prol. 75; coward
  XVI 89
raik, way, desire Prol. 201
rakiere, scavenger V 315
rape (*n*), haste V 326; *v.* hasten IV 7; *p.t.*
  XVII 81; **rapeliche** (*av.*), quickly XVI
  273
rappen (doun), strike down, suppress I 95
rathe (*av*), early III 73, IX 13; **rather**
  (*comp.*), earlier, sooner IV 5, VIII 76
raton, rat Prol. 158; *pl.* 146; **ratonere,**
  rat-catcher V 315
raughte, obtained Prol. 75; stretched IV
  185; grasped VIII 35; moved XI 438
  (*p.t.* of **rechen**)
raunsoun, ransom XVIII 353; *v. p.t.*
  saved XVII 304
ravysshede, carried off IV 49, XI 7;
  seduced X 454
raxed, stretched V 392
rayes, striped cloths V 207
reaume, realm, kingdom Prol. 177; *pl.* I 96
reautee, royalty X 332, XIV 209
recche (*v*), care IV 33
recchelees, reckless XVIII 2; **-ly** (*av*), XI
  130
rechen, reach XI 361; suffice XIV 230
reconforted, comforted again V 280
record (*n*), witness XV 87; *v.* declare XV
  610; *p.t.* IV 172
recoverede, came to life XIX 161
recoverer, means of treatment XVII 69
recrayed, recreant III 259
recreaunt, defeated XVIII 100
redels, riddle(s) XIII 167; *pl.* 184
rede(n), advise I 175; declare XI 102;
  interpret XIII 184; **redde** (*p.t.*),
  instructed V 478
reed (*n*), advice XIII 374
redyngkyng, lackey, retainer V 316
reed, red II 15; **rede** XV 537, XIX 11
refuse, reject XVII 179; *p.t.* XIX 371
registre, list XX 271; **registrer,** registrar
  XIX 261
regne, reign III 285; *p.t.* became king
  XIX 52
regrater, retailer V 222; **regratrie,**
  retail-trade III 83
reherce, declare V 160; *p.t.* Prol. 184
rekene, give an account of I 22; number
  II 62; make settlement V 270
rekketh, cares XV 177 (=**reccheth**)
relees (*n*), release; **-ed** (*v. p.p.*), III 58
releve, support VII 32; restore XV 601
religion, (the) religious order(s) V 45, VI
  151

384

religious, member of religious order IV 125; *pl.* X 289; religiouses, X 314
relyede, rallied XX 148
remenaunt, rest XI 114, XVII 241
remes, realms VII 10
renable, eloquent Prol. 158
rende, tear Prol. 199
rendred, memorised V 207; expounded VIII 91; rendren, construe XV 610
reneye, abjure XI 125; reneyed, forsworn 160
renk, man Prol. 197, V 393; *pl.* XX 293
rennen, run II 183; renneres, runners IV 128; rennyng, (while) running (his course) XVIII 100
rental, record of rent due VI 90
renten, provide with incomes VII 32
rentes, income X 15, XIV 230
repented, had regrets V 335
repentedestow, did you repent? V 228
repreve, refute X 341; *p.t.* condemned XII 137
rerages, arrears V 242
resembled, likened XII 265
reson, argument XIV 308
resonable, proper, rational XIII 285
rest, rests Prol. 171; reste (*p.t.*), rested XVIII 6
retenaunce, retinue II 54
retorik, rhetoric, poetry XI 102
reve, reeve, bailiff II 111, XIX 260
reve (*v*), take away XIV 131, XVI 89
revel, revelry XX 181; *pl.* festivities XIII 441
reveris, thieves XIV 181
reward (*n*), heed XVII 268; *v,* recompense III 318; watch over XI 369; care for XIV 167
rewe, take pity V 468; rue XVI 142; it will grieve XVIII 396
rewful, compassionate XIV 147; -liche (*av.*), XIV 151; pitiably XII 47
rewmes, colds, rheums XX 83
reyn (*n*), rain III 208; *v.* X 310
ribanes, ornamental bands II 16
ribaudes, sinners V 505; evil ones XIV 203; *sg.* villain XVI 151
ribaudie, obscenities Prol. 44
ribibour, fiddler V 315
riche (*n*), kingdom VII 177
riche (*a*), rich; richesse, richness II 17; riches III 90; *pl.* III 23; richen (*v*), grow rich III 83
richels, incense XIX 90
riflede, rifled, ransacked V 230
right(e) (*a*), direct, very XVI 273; *av.* directly XII 295; straight XVI 151; exactly X 295; fully XVIII 371
rightful(le), just Prol. 127, III 342; -ly, justly VII 10
rightwisnesse, justice XVII 301, XVIII 164

ripe (*a*), ready V 390; matured XVIII 371; *v.* ripen XIX 319
risshe, rush IV 170, XI 429
robeth, clothe XV 339
roche, rock XVII 10
rody, red XIII 99
rogged, shook XVI 78
roileth, strays about X 295
rolle (*v*), record V 271
rometh, go forth Prol. 171; *p.t.* wandered VIII 1
romere, wanderer X 303; *pl.* IV 20
rongen, rang XVIII 428, XX 59
ronges, rungs XVI 44
ronne, run VIII 91
roon, rained XIV 66 (*p.t.* of reynen)
roos, arose X 230
ropen, reaped XIII 373
ropere, rope-maker V 316
rored, roared V 392
roten (*v*), rot X 114; *p.p.* XV 101
rotes, roots VI 103
rotey-time, rutting-time XI 337
roughte (ye), you would care XI 73
rouneth, whispers IV 14; *p.t.* V 326
route, throng Prol. 146, II 62
routhe, care X 310; pity XV 506
rowed, dawned XVIII 123
roynouse, unwholesome XX 83
ruddede, flushed XIII 99
rude, untrained XV 459
rufully, sorrowfully XVI 78, XVII 238
rugge, back XIV 212; ruggebone V 343
rusty, foul, obscene VI 73
ruthe, pity I 175 et passim
rutte, snored V 392, XII 152, XVIII 6
ruwet, trumpet V 343
ryde, copulated XI 337
rymes, rhymes, ballads V 396
ryt, rides, goes about Prol. 171 (= rydeth)

saaf, safe VIII 34; saved X 343
sacrificed, offered sacrifice XII 116
sad(de) (*a*), upright VIII 28; grave VIII 120; sadder, firmer X 456; sadnesse, seriousness VII 151; *v.* confirm X 242
sage (*a*), wise III 93, X 376
saille, dance XIII 233
salve (*n*), remedy XI 121; ointment XVII 77; *v.* heal X 268, XI 217
samplarie, exemplar XII 102
sandel, sendal, a thin rich silk VI 11
Sapience, the Book of Wisdom III 333
Sarsynes, Mahometans III 328; heathens XI 120
saufté, safety VII 36
saughtne, be reconciled IV 2
saulee, food XVI 11
saunz, without XIII 285
saut, assault XX 301
sauter, Psalter, Book of Psalms II 38
sautrie (*v*), play the psaltery XIII 233
save, protect Prol. 115; preserve XV 427

385

savore (v), make tasty VI 262; savoreth,
  meet (one's) taste VIII 110
sawes, sayings VII 138, IX 94
scalles, scabs XX 83
scape, escape III 57
scarlet, fine fabric, usually red II 15
scathe, harm, injury III 57, IV 79
science, knowledge XV 62; wisdom XVII
  173
scismatikes, schismatics XI 120
sclaundre, ill-repute III 57
scleyre, veil VI 7
scole, university X 298, XX 273; school,
  VII 31
scolers, schoolboys VII 31
scorne (v), jeer, speak scornfully X 329,
  XI 1
scryppe, bag VI 61
scryveynes, scribes, writers X 329
seche, search III 348; seek VII 164
see, sea IV 129, XI 326, XVIII 246
secret, private VII 23
secte, class, division V 491; garb XIV 258
seculer, layman IX 179
seel, seal Prol. 79, III 146, XIII 248
seem, horse-load (8 bushels) III 40
seet, sat XX 199
sege, abode, ? siege XX 311, 314
segge, man III 63, V 608; pl. Prol. 160
seigh, saw V 535, XI 363, XV 158
seint, holy I 84; saint Prol. 27 et passim
seise, take possession XIII 374; iseised,
  put in possession XVIII 283
seketh, penetrates XIV 6
selde, seldom Prol. 20 et passim
seles, seals Prol. 69; seleth, seal III 148
selkouthes, wonders XI 363; selkouthe (a),
  strange XV 587
selleris, merchants III 88
self, himself XI 249; selve (a), very XX 43
semblable (a), resembling X 363, XVIII 10
semblaunt, appearance VIII 120
semen, seem XV 206; semynge,
  resembling XV 391
semyvif, half-alive XVII 57
sene, visible XX 185
sense, incense XIX 75
serelepes, separately XVII 166
sergeant, serjeant-at-law III 295, XV 5
serk, shift, shirt V 65
sermon, discourse III 93, X 452
sestow, do you see? I 5
seten (p.t. pl.), sat V 339, VI 115, XIII 36
sette, plant V 541; settynge, planting
  Prol. 21; proceed XVI 36; p.t.
  esteemed VI 169; established XIII 153
sew(e), sowed XIII 374 (p.t. of sowen)
seweth, follows Prol. 45; sewe, XI 22
seye(thow), did you see? VIII 76
seyned, crossed V 449
shaar, ploughshare III 308
shadde (v. p.t.), shed XIX 58; shedde,
  XVII 291

shadweth, throws a shadow XVIII 434
shaft(e), form XI 395; figure XIII 296
shame, modesty XIV 330; shamedest,
  brought disgrace on III 190
shape, prepare III 17; cause VII 65;
  dispose XI 424; shapte (p.t.), created
  XVII 219; engineered XX 139
shappere, creator XVII 169
sharp (a), causing smart XX 307; av.
  loudly XVIII 39
shedynge, dropping (through) VI 9
she(e)f, quiverful III 326, XX 225; pl.
  sheaves XIX 332
sheltrom, defence XIV 81
shenden, damage II 126; corrupt III 155;
  mortify XI 424; shent (p.p.), ruined III
  135
shenfulliche, ignominiously III 277
shene, bright, glorious XVIII 411
shepsteres, dressmaker's XIII 330
shere, scissors XIII 330
sherewe, villain, evil person Prol. 192 et
  passim; v. p.t. cursed XI 406, XIII 330
sherewednesse, wickedness III 44
sherreves, sheriffs II 59
sherte, shirt XIV 330
shete, sheet V 107; pl. XIV 233
shette, shut Prol. 105; p.t. V 602
sheweth, professes X 252; p.t. cited III
  351
shewer, mirror, revealer XII 153
shewynge, representation XVII 154
shides, planks IX 132, X 397
shifte, shifted XX 167
shilden, shield X 404
shonye, avoid V 167; shonyeth, shuns XI
  435
shoon, shoes XIV 330
shoop, got Prol. 2; created, IX 66; pl.
  Prol. 122; got ready XI 437, XX 307
  (p.t. of shapen)
shoures, storms XVIII 411
shrape, scrape V 123, XI 431
shrift(e), confession V 75, XIV 89
shrof, confessed III 44, X 413 (p.t. of
  shryven)
shroudes, garments Prol. 2
shryve, confess Prol. 64, 89, V 302, XX
  281
shynes, shins XI 431
shyngled, clinker-built IX 142
sib, related V 625, X 152
sidder, lower V 190
siggen, say, declare XIII 306 (= seggen)
signe, stamp IV 129; pl. badges V 521
sike, sick XX 303; siknessse, VI 257
siked(e), sighed XIV 326, XVIII 265
sikel, sickle III 308, XIII 374
siker, sure I 132; sikerer (av), more
  surely V 502
silynge, gliding XVIII 306
sire, father Prol. 193; V 157
sisour, juryman II 165; pl. II 59

386

sith, since   Prol. 64, X 224; XIII 254

sithe, scythe   III 308

sithes, times   V 425, XIV 187

sithen, thereupon   Prol. 128; then   I 146;
   siththe,   V 488; **siththen,** next   X 249;
   sithenes, afterwards   VI 63

skile, argument   XI 1; reason   XII 216, *pl.*
   X 298; reasonable state of mind   XIX
   286

skipte, rose up hurriedly   XI 107

sle(e), slay, kill   V 577, X 363

sleighte, trick, stratagem   XVIII 161; *pl.*
   XIII 364

slepe, slept   XIV 68; **slepyng** (*n*), sleep
   Prol. 10

sleyest, deftest   XIII 297

sliken, make sleek   II 99

slowe(e), slew   X 53, XX 150 (*p.t.* of **slee**)

smaughte, smelled   V 357

smerte (*v*), hurt   III 168; *av.* sharply   XI
   434

smolder (*n*), fumes   XVII 324

smyt, strikes   XI 434; **smyte,** smitten   III
   324

smythye, hammer   III 307; **smytheth,**
   forges   III 324

so (*av*), as   V 8; *c.* provided that   IV 193

sobreliche, gravely   XIII 203; **sobretee,**
   sobriety   XIV 315

socour, help, succour   XX 170

soden, cooked   XV 293 (*p.p.* of **sethen**)

sodenes, sub-deans   XV 132

softe (*a*), mild   Prol.1; *av.* carefully   XIV
   210

soghte, sought   III 130 (*p.t.* of **sechen**)

sojourned, delayed   XVII 85

sokene, soke, district   II 111

solas, comfort, encouragement   XII 151; *v.*
   comfort   V 499; amuse   XII 22

soleyn, solitary person   XII 205

solve, sing by note (*sol-fa*)   V 417

somdel, somewhat   III 92, V 431

somme, sum, total   XVII 31

somone, sompne, summon   II 159, III 316

somonours, summoners   II 59, XV 132

sond, sand, shore   XI 326, XIX 78

sonde, bidding   IX 127

songen, sang   V 508, VI 115

songewarie, dream-interpretation   VII 149

sonken, sank   XI 224

sonne, sun   Prol. 1, V 492, XI 326, XV 48

soone (so), as soon (as)   X 226; at once   III
   47; **sonner,** sooner   X 414; **sonnest,**
   soonest   III 283

soore (*av*), strongly   XI 224; painfully
   XVIII 49

sooth, truth   Prol. 52; **-fast,** true   X 234;
   -liche, truly   III 5; **-nesse, -fastnesse,**
   truth(fulness)   II 24, XVI 186

sop, morsel   XV 180; thing of small value
   XIII 124

sope, soap   XIV 6

soper, supper   V 372, XVI 141

sorcerie, witchcraft   X 210, XV 12

so (that), provided (that)   XIII 135, IV 102

sothe, truth   I 86; **sothest** (*a*), truest   X
   438; *av.* most truly   III 283

sotil (*a*), skilful   XIII 297; clever, cunning
   XV 398, XVIII 54; subtle   XV 48;
   fine-drawn   XV 12

sotile (*v*), argue subtly   X 185; *p.t.* subtly
   planned   X 214

sottes, fools, sots   X 8

soude, payment   III 353; **soudeth,** pays
   XIX 432

souke, suck   XI 121

soule, soul's   XVIII 368

soupen, sup   II 97, VI 217, XIV 159

soure (*av*), bitterly, harshly   II 141, X 357

souteresse, female shoemaker   V 308;
   souters, shoemakers   V 407

sovereyn (*a*), supreme   Prol. 159;
   efficacious   X 206; *n. pl.* superiors   VI
   80; princes   X 423; **-ly, -liche** (*av*),
   supremely   X 202

sowne, tend to   XIX 456

space, opportunity   III 171

spak, spoke   V 212, XVI 90

spakliche (*a*), lively   XVIII 12; *av.* nimbly
   XVII 83

sparen, save   XII 51; *p.t.*   XV 143

spechelees, without voice   XV 36

spede, prosper   III 171; succeed   XVII 83

speke, speak   X 40; said   XII 192; spoke
   XIX 130

spekes (*n*), hollows, caves   XV 275

spelle, make out   XV 609

spelonkes, caves   XV 275

spences, expenses   XIV 207

sperhauk, sparrow-hawk   VI 196

spie (*n*), scout   XVII 1; *v.* look over   II 227

spille, destroy   III 272; waste   IX 98; die
   XV 135; put to death   XIX 304

spire (*n*), sprout   IX 101; *v.* inquire   XVII
   1

spores, spurs   XVIII 12

spredeth, spread   XV 92

spryng, rod, switch   V 40

spuen, vomit   X 40

stable (*v*), cause to rest   I 123

stale, stole   XIII 366 (*p.t.* of **stelen**)

stalworthe, sturdy   XVII 98

stant, stands   XVIII 43; appears   XV 541

starynge, glaring   X 4

stede, place   Prol. 96; *pl.*   V 47

stede, horse   XIII 293

stekie, stick fast   I 122

stele, handle   XIX 281

stere, stir   XVII 56

sterres, stars   VII 161, XI 362

sterve, die   XI 430, X 295

stewed, established, ordered   V 47

stif, strong   XV 592; *av.* firmly   VIII 33

stille, constantly   XV 224

stiward, deputy   XIX 258; *pl.* stewards
   Prol. 96

387

stok, trunk XVI 5; *pl.* stumps V 576; stocks IV 108
stonden, cost III 48
Stories, History VII 73
stottes, plough-horses XIX 269
stounde, short time VIII 66
stoupe, stoop V 386, XI 36
streyte, strictly Prol. 26
streyves, strays Prol. 94 (*see note*)
strik, go V 577; strook (*p.t.*), Prol. 183
struyen, destroy XV 595; struyden (*p.t.*), ibid
studie, ponder VII 144, XII 223
stuwes, brothels VI 70, XIV 251, XIX 438
stynte, stop X 220
styvest, strongest, stiffest XIII 293
subtileth, devises XIX 460
suede, followed VIII 76, XX 126
suffraunce, long-suffering VI 144; patience XI 378
suffre, allow, tolerate I 146, II 175; *p.t.* V 483
suggestion, reason, motive VII 65
suppriour, sub-prior V 169
suren, give one's word V 540
surquidous, presumptuous XIX 341
sustene, support IX 109
suster, sister in religion III 63; sustren (*pl.*), V 618
sute, guise, attire V 488; retinue XIV 256
suwen, follow X 202; seek XI 422
swelte, die V 152; swelted (*p.t.*), XX 105
swerye, swear XIV 35
swete, sweat VI 25, 128
swete, sweet Prol. 86; swetter, XIV 313; *av.* VI 217
swevene, dream Prol. 11, VII 162
sweyed, sounded Prol. 10
swich, such IV 69 et passim
swithe, very V 463; quickly III 162; exceedingly V 449
swonken, toiled Prol. 21 (*p.t.* of swynken)
swowe, faint V 152; swowned, fainted V 442
swynk (*n*), toil VI 233; *v.* Prol. 55
swynkeres, workmen XVII 210
sykir, certain III 49
symonie, simony Prol. 86, II 63
sympletee, simplicity X 167
syn, since XX 323
synguler, alone, single IX 35; unique XIII 282; sole XVI 208
sysour, juror XX 161
sythenes, since X 257
sythes, times Prol. 231

tabard, short coat V 193
taboure (*v*), play the tabour XIII 230
tacches, faults IX 148
tache, touchwood XVII 248
tail, number, train II 186; end III 351; sex(ual organs) III 131, XV 105; roots V 19

tailende, tail-end V 389; reckoning VIII 83
taillage, taxation XIX 37
taille, tally-stick IV 58; tale V 248
take, give I 56, IV 58
tale, account, estimation I 9, XIX 457
tales, speeches Prol. 48; gossip V 404
talewis, garrulous, tale-bearing III 131
tapur, taper XVII 280
Tarse, silken material XV 168
taseles, teazles XV 452
tastes, experiences, contact with XII 130
taverners, inn-keepers Prol. 228
taxeth, impose I 162; taxour, assessor VI 39
teche, direct I 84
te(e)me, plough-team VI 134, VII 2, XIX 263
tellen, keep account of Prol. 92; speak III 104
tellynge, tilling VI 248
teme, theme III 95, V 60, VI 22 (*pun* on teeme); proposition X 118
temporaltees, temporalities XX 128
tempred, tuned Prol. 51; tunes XIV 309
tendeden, kindled XVIII 239
tene (*n*), anger VI 116; pain VI 133; *v.* grieve III 322; vex V 425, VI 38; *p.t.* became angry II 115; teneful, painful III 349
teris, tears XIII 45
termes, expressions XII 237
thanne, then VI 33, VIII 69; XVI 69, 70
that, that which Prol. 38, III 84
thecche (*v*), thatch XIX 239
thee, prosper V 224
thef, thief XII 192; thefliche, like a thief XVIII 339
theigh, though Prol. 192, I 144
thenke, think XI 158
thennes, thence I 73, II 230
ther, where Prol. 194, IV 35; whereas III 197
therafter, accordingly VI 114, X 395; afterwards XI 25
therfore, for it IV 54, V 232
therfro, from there XI 353
thermyd(e), therewith VI 69, 158
therto, for that purpose XV 127
therunder, under (the form of) it XIX 388
thesternesse, darkness XVI 160
thider, thither, there II 162
thikke, thickly III 157
thilke, those same X 28
thirled, pierced I 174
thise, these Prol. 62, II 171
tho (*av*), when Prol. 176; then V 466
tho (*prn.*), those I 21; they V 326
tholie, suffer, endure IV 84; *p.t.* XVIII 71
thonked, thanked VIII 109; thonkyng, II 149
thorugh, through, by II 41 et passim

388

thoughte, intended (to go) XVI 175
thresshfold, threshold V 351
thretynge, threat XVIII 281
threve, number XVI 55
threw, fell V 351
thridde, third Prol. 121 et passim
throwe, time XVIII 76
thrumbled, bumped against V 351
thrungen, thronged V 510
thurst (n), thirst XVIII 369; v. thursteth, XVIII 368
thynke, think, intend I 21, X 209
tid, as, at once XVI 61
tidy, upright III 222, IX 105; useful III 346
tikel, loose, wanton III 131
tikes, villeins, serfs XIX 37
til, to V 601, XI 35, XVIII 223
tilde, dwelt XII 210
tilie, cultivate Prol. 120; tilieris, ploughmen, XV 362
tilthe, crops XIX 435
titeleris, tattlers XX 300
tixte, text XVII 13
to, after VI 29; for VII 136; on V 171; as, in the office of V 151, I 82
to (av), too VI 263, XIII 71
to-bollen, swollen up V 83
tobroke, broken down VII 28; destroyed VIII 88
tocleve, cleave asunder XII 146
todrowe, mutilated X 35
tofore, in the presence of V 450
toforn, before XII 131
toft, hillock Prol. 14, I 12
togideres, together I 197, II 84
toke (thei on), if they took III 85
tokene, sign, password V 597, X 158
tokenynge, in, as a sign, portent V 19, XVI 204
told, counted V 248
tolled out, stretched out to V 210
tollers, toll-collectors Prol. 221
tolugged, pulled about II 217
tome, leisure II 186
tonder, tinder XVII 248
tonne, tun, barrel XV 337
took, gave III 45, XI 169, XVII 2
top, top of the head III 140
torende, be torn apart X 114
torne, subvert III 42; be converted III 327; be overturned XV 545; convert XIII 210; p.t. converted XV 436
toshullen, peeled, flayed XVII 193
to synneward, as if tempting to sin XIII 345
toten, gaze XVI 22
to trutheward, towards truth XIV 309
touchen, deal with XV 74
travaille, work VII 43; effort XI 194, XIV 152; v. work VI 139; travel XVI 10
travaillours, labourers XIII 239

traversed, transgressed XII 285
treson, treachery XVIII 289, 293
tresorere, paymaster XX 260
tresour, treasure I 45
trespased, sinned, did wrong XII 285
tretour, traitor XVIII 381; criminal XIX 441
trewe, upright III 304; honest VII 54
trewe (n), truce VI 330; trewes XVIII 418
treweliche, justly, honestly VII 61
triacle, healing remedy I 148, V 49
trie, choice XV 168, XVI 4; -liche (av), Prol. 14
triennals, triennial masses VII 171, 180
trieste, choicest I 137
troden, copulated with XI 355
trolled, wandered XVIII 298
trompe, play the trumpet XIII 230; p.t. XVIII 424
troneth, enthrones I 133
trowe, believe I 145; trowestow, do you think XII 165
trowes, trees XV 96
trufle, trifle XII 139; nonsense XVIII 147
trusse, pack up II 219
truthe, honesty VII 96; righteousness (= a just man) XII 285; troth XX 118
tulieden, tilled XIV 67; tulying, XIV 63
tunycle, jacket XVI 168
tutour, overseer I 56
twey(n)e, two, twain V 32, 199
twyned, twisted XVII 206
tyd, as, quickly, at once XIII 318
tymbre, build XI 360; tymbred, would have built III 85
tyme, opportunity V 85; in tyme, at the right time X 184
tyne, lose I 113, IX 172; tynt, lost XVIII 140; tynynge, IX 99

umwhile, at times V 339
unblessed, vicious, accursed XIX 407
unbuxom(e), disobedient, rebellious II 83, XIII 275
unchargeth, unburdens XV 344
unkonnynge, unskilled, ignorant XII 184, XIII 13
uncoupled, unleashed Prol. 162, 207
uncristene, non-Christian, pagan X 346, XI 143
underfeng, received I 76, XI 118 (p.t. of underfonge); -fongen (p.p.), V 626, VII 172
undernome, criticised XIII 281; rebuked XX 51; p.t. of undernymen, V 114, XI 214
underpight, supported, propped XVI 23
undertake, affirm X 154, XIII 131; undertoke (p.t.), rebuked XI 91
undignely, unworthily XV 243
unesiliche, uncomfortably XIV 232

389

ungracious, lacking grace IX 195; unpleasing X 388; **-liche** (*av*), disgracefully XV 133
ungrave, unstamped IV 130
unhardy, lacking courage Prol. 180, XIII 122
unheled, uncovered XIV 232, XVII 322
unhende (*n*), discourtesy XX 186
unjoynen, dissolve XVIII 256
unkouthe, strange, alien VII 156
unkynde, ungenerous I 192, XIII 378; unnatural V 269
unlose, unloose, open Prol. 214
unlovelich, disagreeable XII 244
unmesurable, unfathomable XV 71
unmoebles, immoveable possessions III 269
unnethe, scarcely IV 60, XX 190
unpynned, unlocked XI 113; **-eth,** undo XVIII 263
unresonable, irrational XV 355
unrosted, uncooked V 603
unsavory, tasteless XV 431
unsavourly, ill-tastingly XIII 43
unseled, unsealed, unauthorised XIV 291
unskilful, unreasonable XIII 276
unspered, unbarred XVIII 86
untempred, untuned IX 103
unthende, small V 175
untidy, improper, indecent XX 119
untrewe, dishonest XV 107
untyled, untiled XIV 252
untyme, the wrong time IX 186
unwittily, foolishly III 106
up gesse, by guesswork, thoughtlessly V 415
upholderes, old-clothes men V 318
up-so-doun, upside-down XX 54
us selve, ourselves VII 128
usage, practice, custom VII 85
used, customary XVIII 380; **usen,** practise III 313, XVIII 106; **usedestow** (*p.t.*), V 236
usuré, usury XIX 353; **usurie** V 236

vauntwarde, vanguard XX 95
veille, watcher V 443
vendage, wine-harvest XVIII 370
venymousté, poison(ousness) XVIII 156
vernicle, image of Christ's face V 523
verred, instanced XV 268
verrey, true XVII 292
verset, short text XII 189
vertues, power(s) XIV 38
vertuous, potent, powerful Prol. 103
vesture, clothing I 23
vicory, vicar XIX 412
vigilies, vigils V 410
vileynye, base action XVIII 94
vitaillers, victuallers II 61
vitailles, foodstuffs V 437, XIII 216
voideth, removes XIV 94
vokettes, advocates II 61

wade, go XII 186
wafrer, wafer-seller XIII 226; **wafrestre,** V 632
wage, guarantee (by payment) IV 97; *p.p.* IV 100
waggeth, shakes XVI 41; *p.t.* XVIII 61
waggyng, rocking VIII 31
waiten, look (to do); *p.t.* VII 140; **waitynges,** lookings II 90
waken, wake, watch XVII 221
walkne, sky XV 361; **wolkne,** XVIII 237
walnote, walnut XI 258
Walshe, Welshman V 317
waltrot, absurdity XVIII 142 (*see note*)
walweth, toss VIII 41
wan, obtained V 457; earned XV 291; went IV 67
wangteeth, molars XX 191
wanhope, despair II 100, V 279, 445, XII 179
wanteth (hem), they lack XIV 172; **wantynge,** 176
wantounnesse, unchastity III 125; recklessness XII 6
wanye, wane VII 55; *p.t.* XV 3
war, aware II 8; **warv** XIII 70, XX 163
warde, guardian XVIII 323
wardemotes, ward-meetings Prol. 94
wardeyn, guardian I 55, XVI 187
ware (*v*), guard V 445, IX 180
wareyne, warren Prol. 163
warie, curse V 313
warisshen, cure XVI 105
warner, warren-keeper V 309
warp, threw out (= uttered) V 86, IX 32
warroke, fasten with girth IV 21
wastel, cake of fine flour V 286
wasten, destroy; **wastours,** destroyers Prol. 22; **wastyng,** expenditure V 25
watlede, wattled XIX 328
wawes, waves VIII 40
wayte, look after V 198
wayven, open V 602; *p.t.* drove XX 168
web, piece of woven cloth V 110; **webbe,** weaver V 211; **webbesters,** weavers Prol. 220
wed(de), pledge IV 146, V 240
weder, weather XVIII 412; *pl.* storms VIII 41, XV 481
wedes, clothes II 91, XI 234; *sg.* XX 211; weeds VI 111
wedlok, wedlock XVI 203; *pl.* marriages IX 154
weend (*imper.*), go III 266
weer, perplexity XI 116; doubt XVI 3
weet (*a*), wet XIV 42; *n.* V 530
weetshoed, wet-shod, with wet feet XIV 160, XVIII 1
weex, became III 331; fell V 279, XI 5; arose XIV 76; increased XV 3 (*p.t.* of **wexen**)
wehee, horse's neigh IV 23, VII 90
weke, wick XVII 206, 208

390

wel, good III 70; very III 162; much V 113; nearly XV 187

welawo, misery XIV 235

Welche, Welsh (flannel) V 195

welden, possess, control X 24, XI 72

wele, happiness XVIII 203

welfare, luxurious living XIX 356

welhope, good hope XIII 453

welle, spring, source XIV 307, XV 30; *v. p.t.* XIX 380

wel-libbynge, upright X 428

wem, stain XVIII 131

wenche, woman Prol. 54; servant-girl V 358; maiden XVI 100, XVIII 113

wenden, go Prol. 162; turn XVIII 203

wene, think, suppose III 302; **wende** (*p.t.*), V 234, **wendest,** III 192; expect V 469

wenynge (*n*), (mere) supposition XX 33

wepe, weep V 61; **wepte** (*p.t.*), XI 4; **wepten,** VII 37

wepene, weapon III 306, IX 182, XIX 219

werchen, do, practise IV 146; *imper.* work II 134

wer(i)e(n), wear III 295, XIV 329

werk, deed IV 146; **-manshipe,** (sexual) performance II 92; action IX 45, X 287

wernard, deceiver III 180; *pl.* II 129

werneth, refuse XX 12

werre, war XI 331, XIV 282, XX 163

werse, the, less III 175

wery, weary Prol. 7, XIII 204, XV 186

wesshen, washed II 221, XIII 28 (*p.t.* of **wasshen**)

wete (*n*), wet weather XVII 325

weve, weave V 548; **wevyng,** XV 450

wex, wax XVII 206; **wexed,** wax-polished V 345

wexen, grow III 302; become XIV 323; increase VIII 39; spring up XV 458

wey, way, road Prol. 48 et passim

weye, wey (portion of 3cwt) V 92

weye (*v*), weigh V 200; **weyen** (*p.p.*), I 178

weylawey, alas! XVIII 228

weyled, bewailed XIV 324

weyves, lost property Prol. 94

what, what sort of II 18; partly XIII 316

what so, what(so)ever IV 155, X 130

wheither, which XVI 96; do . . .? XV 197

whennes, whence V 525

wher, whether Prol. 171 (*contr.* of **wheither**)

wherof, to what end XI 91; means XIV 41

whi, why IX 87; **whyes,** reasons X 124, XII 218

whider, whither XV 13; **-out,** from whence XVI 12; **-ward,** which way V 300

whilom, formerly XV 359

whitlymed, lime-washed XV 113

who, whose, whoever IV 131, Prol. 144

wicche, witch XIII 337; sorcerer XVIII 46

widder, wider XVIII 363

wideweres, widowers IX 176

widewher, far and wide VIII 63

wight (*n*), thing X 272; person III 227; *a.* powerful IX 21; **-liche, -ly** (*av.*), vigorously VI 20, briskly X 219; **-nesse** (*n*), strength XIX 247

wightes, weights XIV 292

wike, week VI 256, X 96; **wyke** XI 232

wikkede, bad, difficult VI 1, VII 27; **-ly,** dishonestly V 200; **-lokest,** most evilly X 424

wilfulliche, voluntarily XX 49

wille (*n*), desire XIII 80

wilne (*v*), desire V 185; **wilnyng,** XIII 279

wisloker, more carefully XIII 342

wispe, wisp, handful V 345

wisse, instruct V 146; direct V 555; guide VII 128; *p.t.* I 74; **wissynge,** instruction XV 478

wiste, knew Prol. 12; **wisten,** recognised XI 236

wit, understanding XI 322; wisdom V 587; judgment V 364; *pl.* senses XIX 217; wits X 6

wite, know III 74; learn VI 210

witen, preserve VII 35; protect XVI 25

with, by means of III 2; **-alle,** moreover Prol. 123; **-oute,** on the outside XI 258

withdraweth, removes IX 97

withhalt, withholds (from) V 552; *p.t.* **withhelden,** kept II 229

with that, on condition that V 73, X 148

withwynde, woodbine V 518

witlees, out of my mind XIII 1

witte, laid the blame on I 31

witterly, certainly, to be sure I 74, III 176

wittily, ingeniously IX 4; **witty,** wise II 138; **witynge,** knowingly XIX 373

wo (*n*), trouble V 358; misery XIV 176; *a.* wretched, sorrowful III 153, V 3

wodewe, widow IX 164, 176

woke (*v*), moisten XV 338

wol(e), will V 246; desire VIII 49; *p.t.* **wolde,** wished I 169; **woldestow,** if you would III 49; **wol he, nel he,** willing or not XIX 467

wolle, wool VI 13; **-ward,** shirtless XVIII 1; **wollen webbesters,** wool-weavers I 220

wolt, wish XI 41 (= **wilt**)

wolveliche, wolveskynnes, wolf-like XV 116, VI 161

wombe, belly Prol. 59; womb XV 454, XVI 100; **-cloutes,** tripes XIII 62

wonder, (a cause for) w. III 183; *pl.* marvels, strange events Prol. 4, XV 481; *av.* wondrously XIV 6, XV 1; **-wise,** in wonderful manner I 124

wone, custom XV 245; **woned,** accustomed XV 182

wones, dwellings III 235; won(i)eth,
  dwell(s) II 75, 233
woon, plenty XX 171
woot, knows II 78, XVIII 205
wordeden, spoke, exchanged words IV
  46, X 425; wordynge, speaking XVII
  49 (pres. p. of worden)
worm, serpent X 107; worm XIV 42
worship, honour I 8; v. p.t. paid reverence
  to X 222
worstow, will you be V 613, XIX 409
wortes, vegetables V 160, VI 308
worthe, become I 26; be Prol. 187; shall
  be II 40; became (= fell) XIII 406; w.
  upon, redound upon XVI 157; w. up,
  mount VII 90
worthi, honourable XIX 24; -li, nobly II
  19
wouke, week V 92; pl. XVI 100
wowede, solicited IV 74; woweris, suitors
  XI 71
wowes, walls III 61
woxen, grown XIX 124
wrastle, wrestle XIV 224
wrathe (v.t.), anger, enrage II 117, X
  286; v.i. become angry III 183; p.t. IX
  129
wrecche (a), miserable; n.pl. wretches X
  80
wreke, avenge V 84; relieve, vent IX 183
wrighte, craftsman XI 348; pl. X 401
writhen, clenched XVII 176
wroghte, worked VI 113; made IX 154;
  caused X 34; acted X 424; p.p.
  created VI 313, VII 97
wroken, avenged II 195, XVIII 391 (p.p.
  of wreken)
wrong, wrung (sc. hands) III 237; twisted
  VI 175
wroth, angry III 331
wrotherhele, misfortune XIV 120
wryngynge, twisting V 84
wye, person V 533; man IX 113, XVII
  100
wyghtliche, speedily II 209
wyn, wine Prol. 229, V 176, XIII 60.
wynkyng, sleep V 3; drowse XI 5
wynne, earn IX 109; wynnynge, profit
  XIX 287
wyved, married IX 184
wyvene, of women, women's V 29
wyvyng, marrying IX 193

yaf, gave I 15, 107 (p.t. of yyve)
yald, submitted XII 193 (p.t. of yelden)
yarketh, prepares VII 78
yarn, ran V 440, XI 60 (p.t. of yernen)
yates, gates Prol. 104
ybaken, baked VI 182
ybarred, barred XIX 167
ybe, been XIV 95
ybedded, provided with a bed XV 534
ybet, beaten IV 93

yblessed, holy Prol. 78
yblowe, blown XVII 215
yborwed, borrowed XV 312
ycalled, capped XV 229
ycarped, spoken XV 301
ychose, chosen V 324
yclouted, patched VI 59
ycoped, dressed in a cope XX 345
ycorouned, crowned II 10
ycouped, slashed XVIII 14
ycoupled, married IX 125
ycrymyled, anointed XV 229
ydel, idle XII 1; idle people XIII 225
ydo, done XVIII 101; ydone, ended
  XVIII 53
yede, went I 73; walked XVII 101
yeep, lusty XI 18
yeer, year(s) Prol. 193; yeres, VII 18
yelde, yield V 368; give back V 456; pay
  back V 289; give up XIX 394
yeldynge, yielding II 105
yeme (n), heed X 195; note XVII 13
yeme, (v), govern VIII 53; care for IX
  202
yemere, guardian XIII 170
yepeliche, eagerly XV 188
yerdes, yards V 210; sg. rod XII 14
yeresyyve, New Year's gift VIII 53; pl.
  annual gifts III 100
yerne (av), eagerly IV 74; quickly V 424
yerne, run III 214, XV 188
yernen, long, desire XIII 184
yet, over and above VII 81; yit, XVII 245
yeven, given II 32 (p.p. of yyven)
yfounde, found X 253
yfruyted, in fruit XVI 39
yfryed, fried XIII 62
yglubbed, gulped down V 340
ygo, gone V 203
ygraced, thanked VI 124
ygrave, engraved XV 543
yheer, hear XVII 139; yherd, heard X
  103
yherberwed, lodged V 229
yholden, considered I 84
yholpe, helped XVII 62
yhonted, hounded down II 219
yhote, called I 63; ordered II 219
yhudde, hidden X 428
yif, if V 424
yiftes, gifts in payment VII 48
yilt, yields XVIII 100 (= yildeth)
yis, yes indeed V 124
yknowe(n), learnt XI 405; met XI 231;
  well known XV 20
ylakked, disparaged II 21
yleye(n), lain V 81, X 416
ylered, instructed XIII 213
yliche, alike V 487; ylik, XVIII 338
ylike, likewise I 50
ymaked, made II 73
ymaymed, injured XVII 191
ymped, grafted V 137

392

ynempned, named IX 54; XVI 203
ynome, taken XX 46 (*p.p.* of nyme)
ynowe, enough II 163
youre, yours XIII 110
ypassed, past, ago Prol. 193
ypersshed, pierced XVII 191
yplight, contracted V 198
yseighen, seen V 4; yseyen Prol. 160
ysekeles, icicles XVII 230
yserved, satisfied V 334, 413
yset, considered XV 224
yshewed, made manifest II 135
ysoden, boiled XV 431
yspilt, wasted V 436
yspoused, married IX 126
ytailed, recorded V 423

ytake, taken XI 261
ytermyned, decided I 97
yteynted, stretched XV 453
ytilied, gained in farming XV 107
ytouked, tucked XV 453
yvel (*a*), bad V 120; hard VI 48
yvele (*av*), badly V 166; wickedly X 322; poorly XII 98
yveles, diseases XX 85
ywasshen, washed IX 135
ywis, certainly XI 409
ywonne, won XVIII 354
yworthe, be (left alone) VI 84
ywroght, created IX 117
ywrye, twisted XIV 232
yyve, give V 106; give away X 309

Glossary of Latin and French Words

Amor, love XV 34
Anima, the Soul IX 8, XV 23
Animus, Will XV 24
apostata, apostate I 104
Archa Dei, the Ark of God X 280
Ave's, Hail Mary's XV 181
Beau fitz, fair son VII 163
Benedicite, bless me V 391
caristia, dearth XIV 72
Caro, the flesh, body IX 49
chaud, plus chaud, hot, very hot VI 311
Contra, 'I deny that' VIII 20, X 341
culorum, conclusion III 280, X 406
episcopus, bishop XV 43
ergo, therefore VIII 25, XVIII 341
extremis, in, in extreme circumstances X 344
fornicatores, fornicators II 181
gazophilacium, treasury XIII 197
genere, in, in the nature XIV 180
infamis, of ill repute V 166
ingratus, unkind XVII 256; ingrati, ungrateful XIV 168
licitum, allowed XI 96
Magi, Magi, Wise Men XIX 85
Metropolitanus, metropolitan XV 42

modicum, a little XVIII 215
multi, many XI 112
paroles, bele, fine words XV 113
pauci, few XI 114
parce, the command 'Spare' VIII 393
pecuniosus, moneyed XI 58
Penetrans-domos, Piercer of Homes XX 341
Placebo, psalm XV 125
pontifex, pontiff XV 42
presul, prelate XV 42
pur charitee, for the love of God VIII 11
quatriduanus, for four days XVI 114
quodlibet, general intellectual problem XV 380
Ramis Palmarum, Palm Sunday XVIII 6
Recordare, the offertory 'Remember' IV 120
Redemptor, redeemer XI 206
Regum, the Book of Kings III 259
sapienter, correctly XI 312
transgressores, lawbreakers I 96
turpiloquio, foul speech XIII 456
Vigilate, Keep Watch V 443
vie, douce, luxurious living XIV 122